1,001 LOW·FAT RECIPES

Edited by Sue Spitler

with Linda R. Yoakam, M.S., R.D.

Surrey Books

CHICAGO

1,001 LOW-FAT RECIPES is published by Surrey Books, Inc., 230 E. Ohio St., Suite 120, Chicago, IL 60611.

First edition: 5 6 7 8 9

This book is manufactured in the United States of America.

Library of Congress Cataloging-in-Publication data:
Spitler, Sue
     1,001 low-fat recipes / edited by Sue Spitler,
     with Linda R. Yoakam. — 1st ed.
     672p.   cm.
     Includes index.
     ISBN 0-940625-89-X (paper): $18.95
     1. Cookery. 2. Low-fat diet—Recipes. 3. Low-
     calorie diet—Recipes. 4. Salt-free diet—Recipes.
     I. Yoakam, Linda R. II. Title. III. Title: One
     thousand one low-fat recipes.
TX714.B867 1995   94-32175
641.5'638—dc20   CIP

Editorial and production: *Bookcrafters, Inc., Chicago*
Art direction: *Hughes & Co., Chicago*
Nutritional analyses: *Linda R. Yoakam, M.S., R.D.*
Cover and interior illustrations: *Laurel DiGangi*

For prices on quantity purchases or for free book catalog, contact Surrey Books at the above address.

This title is distributed to the trade by Publishers Group West.

Contents

Acknowledgments

The publisher, editors, and staff of Surrey Books wish to thank the eleven master chefs and recipe creators who contributed to this volume (arranged alphabetically):

Nancy Baggett   Carole Kruppa
Marlys Bielunski   Phyllis Magida
Ruth Glick   Betty Marks
Barbara Grunes   Susan Lamb Parenti
Erica Klein   Sue Spitler
                       Irene Yeh

Thanks and appreciation also go to Managing Editor Gene DeRoin, Art Director Sally Hughes, and Copyeditor Beth Iogha.

About This Cookbook

Can great taste and good health go hand-in-hand? Emphatically, yes! as these 1,001 recipes prove. How was it done? Mainly by using fresh, wholesome ingredients, substituting new "light" products for old fat-laden ones, and streamlining preparation techniques.

A key objective was to keep fat content low—at or below 35 percent of total calories per serving. This objective originated with the American Heart Association's dietary guideline that calls for total daily fat intake to be less than 30 percent of total daily calories. Since data in a recipe book is compiled for each dish separately—and since you'll probably add side dishes such as vegetables, potatoes, and bread to your daily menu—the total percentage of calories from fat for the entire day will likely be much lower than the figures for isolated items. The important point is that almost all of these recipes, in the context of responsible daily intake, help in meeting the AHA low-fat guideline.

Nutritional Data

The nutritional analyses for the recipes were derived using software highly regarded by nutritionists and dietitians. In particular, the percentages of calories from fat are based on actual lab values of ingredients rather than the general 4-4-9 rule; thus, they may vary slightly from the results of traditional formulas used for such calculations.

Although nutritional data is provided for each recipe in

this book, it should be remembered that such data are dependent on many variable factors, such as:

1. the variable sizes of vegetables and fruits;
2. a plus or minus 20 percent error factor on the nutritional labels of packaged foods;
3. differences among brands of processed foods;
4. cooking techniques and appliances;
5. exactness in following the recipe.

In the development of the nutritional data, ingredients listed as "optional" or "garnish" were not figured in; nor were ingredients followed by the words "to taste." Where alternative ingredients or amounts are listed, the first ingredient or amount was used in our calculations.

If you or someone for whom you're cooking has any health problem that mandates strict dietary requirements, it is important that you consult a physician, or registered dietitian before proceeding with any recipe in this book. Also, if you are a diabetic or require a diet that restricts calories, fat, or sodium, remember that the nutritional analysis may be accurate for the recipe we tested but, due to variables, not for the food you prepared.

In summary, we recommend that you use the nutritional data only as a starting point for healthier eating and for comparing recipes, allowing you to estimate intake of calories, fat, cholesterol, sodium, protein, and carbohydrates. We hope that these guidelines will be a valuable help in planning both delicious—and healthful—meals.

Healthful Ingredients

In order to achieve good taste with optimal nutritional value and low fat percentages, we emphasize fresh rather than processed ingredients throughout. We also call for many of the excellent new reduced-fat, fat-free, reduced-sodium, sodium-free, and "light" products now available. To the same end, whipped toppings substitute for whipped cream; egg substitute, for whole eggs; cocoa, for baker's chocolate; and so on.

Vegetable nonstick cooking spray is a boon to today's cook. It contains no fat, cholesterol, sodium, or calories, and it can be used regularly in place of oil, butter, or lard. We call for "vegetable cooking spray" consistently.

Natural herbs and spices further enhance flavors and create new taste combinations without loading dishes with fat, sodium, and cholesterol. In a few recipes we list *"bouquet garni"* as an ingredient. This traditional French combination of herbs consists of a few sprigs of parsley, thyme, and basil or tarragon—plus a bay leaf—all in a cheesecloth bag that is discarded before serving.

Substitutions

On occasion you might wish or need to substitute "regular" ingredients for the reduced-fat or "light" products listed. These will work just as well, but, of course, the nutritional data will be affected. Again, we might list a sauce or soup stock and refer you to this book's recipe for that item; a canned or reconstituted substitute may be used, though this will change the nutritional data, probably increasing the recipe's fat and sodium content.

Where herbs and spices are called for, dried products are intended unless the context obviously indicates a fresh item or the recipe specifically lists the ingredient as "fresh." Even then a dried version of the herb may be substituted, but you should use only half as much for equivalent flavor. Reversing the situation, if you substitute fresh for dried herbs, use about twice as much. Fresh parsley is always intended unless specifically stated otherwise.

Three Special Ingredients

In this cookbook, we frequently call for three ingredients that you may not ordinarily use. We ask you to try them because they add flavor or sweetening without adding fat or sodium, and they are readily available in most supermarkets:

Spike This seasoning is a blend of many natural herbs and spices. It is used to bring out the food's natural flavors and add piquancy. Spike comes in "regular" and "no-salt" blends; we have used the no-salt type in calculating nutritional data.

Equal® This well-known sugar substitute is called for in the many "no-sugar-added" recipes (see symbol on next page). One packet contains only 4 calories, as opposed to the 32 in the equivalent two teaspoons of sugar. It contains no sodium or saccharin. Equal® may be substituted for sugar even in recipes that do not call for it, but be advised that heating Equal® will diminish its sweetness. Recipes in this cookbook add Equal® only after cooking has been completed. One word of warning: Equal® contains aspartame and should not be used by phenylketonurics. Table sugar may be substituted for Equal®, using 2 teaspoons as equivalent to 1 packet; this will alter the nutritional data.

Fructose Sweeter than regular table sugar, this natural fruit sugar can be used in smaller quantities, thus reducing the number of calories in a dish. It contains no fat. Fructose is usually available in the baking or diet section. You can substitute regular table sugar for fructose in any recipe, but you will need to increase—by taste— the quantity called for. Conversely, you can substitute fructose for table sugar in any recipe, following package instructions for equivalencies.

Symbols for Cooking Techniques

To tell at a glance the cooking style called for in certain recipes, we have used six little symbols, which appear just to the left of the recipe title. Recipes not showing one or another of these symbols are prepared in usual ways such as baking, sautéing, simmering, and so on, as directed by the instructions.

Microwave   These recipes have been developed especially for the microwave oven. They are super-quick to make and super good to eat.

Stir-Fry   In wok or large skillet, stir-fries require only brief cooking at high heat. Usually having an oriental twist, many are widely popular for their high flavor and low fat content.

Crockpot   Slow cooking in a stoneware crock results in maximum flavor for one-pot meals, stews, and soups. Combine ingredients in the morning—enjoy a treat for dinner.

Barbecue   For outdoor cooking nothing beats a barbecue! You might be surprised to find recipes for pizza, fish, and appetizers made over the coals.

Make-Ahead Dishes   We have identified recipes that work well for quick meals out of the freezer. Your homemade frozen foods will almost always be lower in fat, sodium, and *price* than store-bought items. Many other recipes can also be frozen unless the instructions state otherwise.

No Sugar Added   These recipes may be suitable for people on sugar-restricted diets. In place of sugar as a listed ingredient, we have substituted Equal® brand sweetener made by The NutraSweet Company. Equal® contains no sugar, saccharin, or sodium and depends on aspartame for its sweetness. For more information about Equal® see preceding page.

Linda R. Yoakam, M.S., R.D.

Introduction

If your goal—for your family as well as yourself—is to eat less fat without sacrificing flavor or menu variety, this cookbook is for you. *1,001 Low-Fat Recipes* is probably the most extensive low-fat cookbook ever published. In it, we have tried to cover every major recipe category: appetizers, soups, salads, seafood, poultry, meats, vegetables, grains, pasta, breads, sauces, desserts, and beverages—and to bring every single recipe into line with the overwhelming consensus of diet and health professionals: *eat less fat*.

That was no easy task when it came to such old favorites as Chicken Vesuvio, Austrian Pork Loin, and Taco Salad or scrumptious desserts like Trifle, Cheesecake, and Banana Cream Pie. But the job of transforming these traditionally high-fat dishes into healthful, low-fat recipes—without losing their great tastes and textures—was a challenge greeted with enthusiasm by the battery of talented, nutrition-minded chefs who contributed to this collection. I believe they successfully met that challenge.

The Importance of Low-Fat Eating

The jury is in on high-fat consumption. To put it simply, medical research has linked high-fat foods with such diseases as heart attack, stroke, high blood pressure, diabetes, and even cancer. Yet, sadly, fat makes up nearly half of the average number of calories most of us consume daily—empty calories with little or no nutritional value. The low-fat recipes in this cookbook are designed to help you significantly reduce that percentage.

The American Heart Association, the National Academy of Sciences, the National Cancer Institute, and the American Diabetes Association all recommend that one's daily intake consist of no more than 30 percent of calories from fat. The great majority of our recipes meet or exceed that guideline. Our top limit per recipe was set at 35 percent of calories from fat, with the consideration that one's daily intake will include other low-fat or non-fat foods such as fruits, vegetables, and cereals, which will keep the daily count within the 30 percent guideline.

Each of these 1,001 recipes includes data on percentage of calories from fat, calorie count, both sodium and cholesterol content, diabetic exchanges, and other valuable nutritional figures to help you plan healthful and delicious meals. To ascertain daily nutritional goals, consult the chart below. These figures also fit the new food labeling standards, which are a good summarization of all the various guidelines.

DAILY NUTRITIONAL GOALS		
Nutrient	**Uppermost Daily Limit**	**Percent of 2,000-Calorie Daily Diet**
Calories	(Figures based on 2,000 calories daily)	100
% Calories from fat	—	30
Total fat	65 grams	—
Saturated fat	20 grams	—
Cholesterol	300 milligrams	—
Sodium	2,400 milligrams	—
Protein	—	10
Carbohydrate	—	60

Source: Nutrition Labeling and Education Act.

Maintaining a balanced, low-fat eating plan should be much easier when you cook with this collection of tried and tested recipes, covering virtually every menu category.

Another important key to healthful eating is not to overindulge. Thus, we have set the number of servings per recipe (which is the basis for the nutritional data) at moderate levels, yet not so low as to skimp on portions or reduce dining satisfaction.

A Low-Fat Eating Plan

The Food Guide Pyramid, designed by the United States Department of Agriculture, presents a simple plan for healthful daily eating. At the base of the Pyramid are breads, cereals, rice, pasta, and grains, with the recommendation that one eat 6–11 servings of these per day (½ cup of cooked cereal, pasta, or rice counts as a serving). At the next level come vegetables (3–5 half-cup servings) and fruits (2–4 medium pieces).

Higher on the Pyramid are foods that should be consumed in smaller quantities: 2–3 servings (1 cup each) of milk or yogurt or ½ oz. servings of cheese; and 2–3 servings from the group that includes meat, poultry, fish (2–3 ozs. per serving), beans (½ cup, cooked, per serving), and eggs (1 per serving). Finally, fats, oils, and sweets—at the narrowing tip of the Pyramid—should be used *sparingly*. The wide variety of recipes in this cookbook will help you follow the USDA's guide with tasty dishes in every one of the categories.

Lastly we have tried to simplify the recipes for easy, fuss-free cooking in minimum time. Actually, the reduced-fat versions of many old stand-bys are often much easier to make than the complicated, high-fat prototypes. For additional convenience, virtually all of the ingredients called for can readily be found at your local supermarket.

We hope *1,001 Low-Fat Recipes* will become your guide to making delicious, low-fat meals for your family each day and your friends who come to visit. We believe this collection is long overdue, and we trust that it will contribute to your good health and satisfy your good taste.

Sue Spitler

Chapter One

APPETIZERS & STARTERS

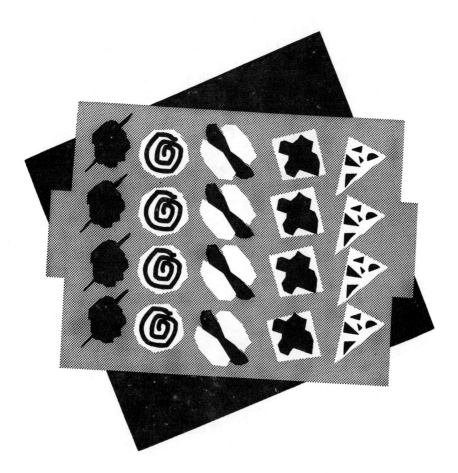

Baked Asparagus with Ham

Serves 4

Vegetable cooking spray
1½ lbs. asparagus
  8 thin slices boiled ham
  ¼ cup Parmesan cheese, freshly grated
  2 tablespoons white wine

Nutritional Data

PER SERVING:

Calories	114
% calories from fat	29
Fat (gm)	3.9
Sat. Fat (gm)	1.8
Cholesterol (mg)	19.9
Sodium (mg)	464
Protein (gm)	12.6
Carbohydrate (gm)	7.7

EXCHANGES:

Milk	0.0	Bread	0.0
Veg.	1.5	Meat	1.5
Fruit	0.0	Fat	0.0

Preheat oven to 350 degrees. Coat an 11" x 7" baking dish with vegetable cooking spray. Cut off tough asparagus ends. Tie asparagus together in 1 or 2 bunches with string. Pour cold salted water 2 to 3 inches deep in an asparagus cooker or tall stockpot. Place asparagus upright in water and boil.

Cover and cook over high heat 6 to 8 minutes, depending on size. Drain on paper towels; remove string.

Divide asparagus into 4 bundles. Wrap 2 ham slices around each bundle. Arrange wrapped asparagus bundles in a single layer in baking dish. Sprinkle with Parmesan cheese and pour white wine around asparagus. Bake 8 to 10 minutes or until cheese is melted.

Asparagus Provençal

Serves 4

2¼ lbs. asparagus
  1 cup diced tomatoes
     Vegetable cooking spray
  1 yellow bell pepper, chopped
  1 onion, chopped
  1 clove garlic, minced
  1 teaspoon *herbes de Provence*
  1 recipe Italian Vinaigrette (see p. 129)
  2 tablespoons fresh parsley, chopped

Nutritional Data

PER SERVING:

Calories	113
% calories from fat	8
Fat (gm)	1.2
Sat. Fat (gm)	0.2
Cholesterol (mg)	0
Sodium (mg)	18
Protein (gm)	7.6
Carbohydrate (gm)	21.1

EXCHANGES:

Milk	0.0	Bread	0.0
Veg.	4.0	Meat	0.0
Fruit	0.0	Fat	0.0

Trim and dry asparagus. Place asparagus in a steam basket, over boiling water. Steam 6 to 10 minutes. Freshly cut young asparagus cooks quickly, but the fatter spears may take longer. Drain asparagus well, and divide among four hot individual gratin dishes.

Add tomatoes and set aside.

Coat a small skillet with vegetable cooking spray and combine yellow pepper, onion, garlic, and herbs. Cook about 5 minutes. Add to vinaigrette, and pour over asparagus. Top with parsley.

Artichoke Dip

Serves 10

2	14-oz. cans artichokes, drained and chopped
½	cup Mock Sour Cream (see p. 497)
2	cups nonfat plain yogurt
1	tablespoon Parmesan cheese, grated
3	tablespoons scallions, chopped
2	tablespoons fresh chives, chopped
4	tablespoons Marsala wine

Nutritional Data

PER SERVING:

Calories	71
% calories from fat	30
Fat (gm)	2.5
Sat. Fat (gm)	2.2
Cholesterol (mg)	1.3
Sodium (mg)	105
Protein (gm)	4.7
Carbohydrate (gm)	7.5

EXCHANGES:

Milk	0.0	Bread	0.0
Veg.	2.0	Meat	0.0
Fruit	0.0	Fat	0.5

Preheat oven to 375 degrees. In a small bowl, combine all ingredients. Mix well. Spoon mixture into a greased casserole. Bake for 30 minutes or until golden brown. Serve immediately with crackers, vegetables, or black bread.

Artichokes with Green Sauce

Serves 4

1	8½-oz. can artichoke hearts
4	tablespoons white wine
2	tablespoons lemon juice
1	tablespoon parsley, finely chopped
½	teaspoon marjoram
¼	teaspoon tarragon

Drain artichoke hearts. Combine wine, lemon juice, and herbs. Pour mixture over artichoke hearts.

Nutritional Data

PER SERVING:

Calories	43
% calories from fat	4
Fat (gm)	0.2
Sat. fat (gm)	0
Cholesterol (mg)	0
Sodium (mg)	58.8
Protein (gm)	2.2
Carbohydrate (gm)	7.7

EXCHANGES:

Milk	0.0	Bread	0.0
Veg.	1.5	Meat	0.0
Fruit	0.0	Fat	0.0

Marinated Artichoke Hearts and Peppers

Serves 12

- ¾ cup water
- ¼ cup balsamic vinegar
- 3 teaspoons capers
- 2 teaspoons Dijon mustard
- ½ teaspoon dried basil
- 1 tablespoon fresh parsley, chopped
- 2 cloves garlic, minced
- 1 20-oz. can artichoke hearts
- 1 lb. red and yellow bell peppers, cut into strips (about 2 large peppers)
- 4 large black olives, sliced
- ¼ cup pimiento, diced
- ½ cup parsley, chopped
- Boston lettuce leaves

Nutritional Data

PER SERVING:

Calories	52
% calories from fat	9
Fat (gm)	0.6
Sat. Fat (gm)	0.1
Cholesterol (mg)	0
Sodium (mg)	79
Protein (gm)	2.5
Carbohydrate (gm)	11.4

EXCHANGES:

Milk	0.0	Bread	0.0
Veg.	2.0	Meat	0.0
Fruit	0.0	Fat	0.0

Combine water, vinegar, capers, mustard, basil, parsley, and garlic in a large bottle with tight-fitting lid. Shake well.

Put artichoke hearts, peppers, olives, pimiento, and parsley into a bowl. Pour dressing over vegetables and mix well.

Arrange lettuce leaves on a platter, and spoon marinated vegetables onto them. Place in refrigerator 2 hours before serving. When ready to serve, place toothpicks alongside platter.

Marinated Broccoli

Serves 8

- 2 lbs. broccoli, broken into bite-size pieces
- 3 tablespoons fresh lemon juice
- ½ cup low-calorie Italian dressing
- ½ cup red onion, sliced
- 1 teaspoon capers
- 1 tablespoon lemon peel, grated

Nutritional Data

PER SERVING:

Calories	54
% calories from fat	27
Fat (gm)	1.9
Sat. Fat (gm)	0.3
Cholesterol (mg)	1
Sodium (mg)	154
Protein (gm)	3.5
Carbohydrate (gm)	8.3

EXCHANGES:

Milk	0.0	Bread	0.0
Veg.	2.0	Meat	0.0
Fruit	0.0	Fat	0.0

In large saucepan, blanch broccoli in lightly salted water 3 to 5 minutes until just tender but firm. Rinse in cold water.

Drain broccoli and place on paper towel. Put broccoli in glass mixing bowl. Toss with lemon juice and Italian dressing. Add onion, capers, and lemon peel. Cover and chill 24 hours, stirring occasionally. Drain broccoli and serve with toothpicks.

Stuffed Celery

Serves 6 (6 appetizers each)

1 cup low-fat cottage cheese
¼ cup scallions, chopped
2 teaspoons fresh lemon juice
½ teaspoon Tamari soy sauce
1 teaspoon mustard
¼ cup pimiento, chopped
¼ cup fresh chives, chopped
1 clove garlic, minced
6 celery stalks, washed with leaves removed

Nutritional Data

PER SERVING:

Calories	52
% calories from fat	10
Fat (gm)	0.6
Sat. Fat (gm)	0.3
Cholesterol (mg)	1.7
Sodium (mg)	233
Protein (gm)	5.9
Carbohydrate (gm)	6.5

EXCHANGES:

Milk	0.0	Bread	0.0
Veg.	1.0	Meat	0.5
Fruit	0.0	Fat	0.0

Place cottage cheese and all ingredients except celery in a blender. Mix till smooth. Stuff celery with cheese mixture. Cut each stalk into 6 individual pieces. Serve each with a toothpick.

Endive Leaves with Ratatouille

Serves 20 (2 appetizers each)

Vegetable cooking spray
1 eggplant, cut into ½-inch cubes
1 zucchini, diced
2 tomatoes, diced
1 onion, diced
¼ cup fresh thyme, chopped
3 cloves garlic, minced
Pepper to taste
40 large leaves endive, preferably Belgian

Nutritional Data

PER SERVING:

Calories	14
% calories from fat	8
Fat (gm)	0.1
Sat. Fat (gm)	0
Cholesterol (mg)	0
Sodium (mg)	3.4
Protein (gm)	0.5
Carbohydrate (gm)	3.2

EXCHANGES:

Milk	0.0	Bread	0.0
Veg.	0.5	Meat	0.0
Fruit	0.0	Fat	0.0

In a large saucepan coated with vegetable cooking spray, sauté eggplant, zucchini, tomatoes, and onion for 5 minutes. Add thyme, garlic, and pepper. Cover and cook over low heat for 10 minutes.

When cool, spoon vegetable mixture into endive leaves. Arrange filled endive leaves in a fan pattern on a large platter.

Tabouleh

Serves 10

- 1   cup bulgur wheat
- 2   cups boiling water
- ½   cup scallions, chopped
- 5   tablespoons fresh mint, chopped
- 2   medium-size tomatoes, peeled, seeded, and chopped
- 1   cup parsley, chopped
- 1   tablespoon olive oil
- 6   tablespoons fresh lemon juice
- 10   large lettuce leaves

Nutritional Data

PER SERVING:

Calories	73
% calories from fat	19
Fat (gm)	1.7
Sat. Fat (gm)	0.2
Cholesterol (mg)	0
Sodium (mg)	10
Protein (gm)	2.4
Carbohydrate (gm)	13.6

EXCHANGES:

Milk	0.0	Bread	1.0
Veg.	0.0	Meat	0.0
Fruit	0.0	Fat	0.0

Put bulgur into a bowl and add boiling water. Stir, cover bowl, and let stand 35 minutes. Drain, squeezing out any remaining water between the palms of your hands. Put into a serving bowl. Add scallions, mint, tomatoes, and parsley. Toss gently. Add olive oil. Stir until well mixed. Add lemon juice and stir again until well mixed.

You can put the tabouleh in a serving bowl or on individual plates. Use lettuce leaves as scoops to eat the tabouleh.

Eggplant Salad

Serves 8

- 2   medium eggplants
-      Spike (see "About This Cookbook")
-      Vegetable cooking spray
- 4   cloves garlic, minced
- 1   tablespoon sharp paprika
- 1   teaspoon cumin, ground
- 1½   teaspoons olive oil
- 2   tablespoons vinegar, or lemon juice

Nutritional Data

PER SERVING:

Calories	39
% calories from fat	25
Fat (gm)	1.2
Sat. Fat (gm)	0.2
Cholesterol (mg)	0
Sodium (mg)	3.7
Protein (gm)	1
Carbohydrate (gm)	7.3

EXCHANGES:

Milk	0.0	Bread	0.0
Veg.	1.5	Meat	0.0
Fruit	0.0	Fat	0.0

Remove 3 vertical strips of skin from each eggplant, leaving it striped, then cut eggplant into ½-inch-thick slices. Sprinkle with Spike and leave to drain in colander 30 minutes. Rinse well, squeeze gently, and pat dry with paper towels.

Place a skillet on medium-high heat, and coat with vegetable cooking spray. Sauté eggplant slices a few at a time over high heat until golden brown on both sides. Drain.

Mash eggplant with garlic and spices. Over low heat, cook puree in cooking-spray-coated skillet until all liquid evaporates. Stir puree often to avoid scorching. Season with vinegar or lemon juice to taste.

Serve at room temperature with pita bread or crackers.

Eggplant Spread

Serves 8

1	eggplant
1	cup onion, minced
2	cloves garlic, minced
4	stalks celery, chopped
½	cup mushrooms, chopped
1	tomato, peeled and chopped
2	tablespoons fresh lemon juice
6	tablespoons canned tomato juice
½	teaspoon salt
½	teaspoon pepper
1	teaspoon fresh basil, crushed
½	teaspoon ground oregano
8	slices dark rye bread

Nutritional Data

PER SERVING:

Calories	115.6
% calories from fat	10
Fat (gm)	1.4
Sat. Fat (gm)	0.2
Cholesterol (mg)	0
Sodium (mg)	407
Protein (gm)	3.9
Carbohydrate (gm)	23.1

EXCHANGES:

Milk	0.0	Bread	1.0
Veg.	1.5	Meat	0.0
Fruit	0.0	Fat	0.0

Preheat oven to 400 degrees. Pierce eggplant with fork. Place eggplant on aluminum foil. Bake about 30 minutes or until tender.

Cool eggplant and peel. Mince eggplant and place it in large mixing bowl. Add remaining ingredients; mix well.

Check to adjust seasonings. Cover and chill. Stir before serving with slices of dark rye bread.

Caponata

Serves 10

1	medium eggplant, peeled and cut into ½-inch cubes (about 1 lb.)
¾	cup onion, chopped
⅓	cup celery, chopped
1	14½-oz. can chunky tomatoes
3	tablespoons wine vinegar
2	tablespoons tomato paste
1	teaspoon sugar
½	teaspoon Spike (see "About This Cookbook")
	Dash ground red pepper
1	tablespoon parsley, snipped
1	tablespoon basil
1	teaspoon oregano
1	teaspoon lemon juice

Nutritional Data

PER SERVING:

Calories	30
% calories from fat	7
Fat (gm)	0.3
Sat. Fat (gm)	0.04
Cholesterol (mg)	0
Sodium (mg)	74
Protein (gm)	1.1
Carbohydrate (gm)	7.1

EXCHANGES:

Milk	0.0	Bread	0.0
Veg.	1.5	Meat	0.0
Fruit	0.0	Fat	0.0

In a sprayed large skillet, cook eggplant, onion, and celery, covered, over medium heat for 5 to 8 minutes or till just tender.

Stir in tomatoes, wine vinegar, tomato paste, sugar, Spike, and red pepper. Cook, uncovered, over low heat for 5 minutes, stirring occasionally. Remove from heat.

Stir in parsley, basil, oregano, and lemon juice. Cool. Cover and refrigerate. Let stand at room temperature for 30 minutes before serving.

Hummus

Serves 10

2	15½-oz. cans garbanzo beans
1	tablespoon lemon juice
6-8	cloves garlic
1	tablespoon olive oil
½	cup parsley, chopped

In a food processor or blender, mix 1 can garbanzo beans with liquid and 1 can drained with lemon juice and garlic. Blend until smooth. Place mixture in bowl and pour olive oil over top. Sprinkle with parsley. Serve with pita bread triangles for dipping.

Nutritional Data

PER SERVING:

Calories	102
% calories from fat	25
Fat (gm)	3
Sat. Fat (gm)	0.4
Cholesterol (mg)	0
Sodium (mg)	352
Protein (gm)	4.3
Carbohydrate (gm)	15.3

EXCHANGES:

Milk	0.0	Bread	1.0
Veg.	0.0	Meat	0.0
Fruit	0.0	Fat	0.5

Low-Fat Chickpea Spread

Serves 8

1	15½-oz. can garbanzo beans (chickpeas), drained
2	tablespoons fresh lemon juice
2	cloves garlic, minced
1½	tablespoons tahini (available in health food stores or large supermarkets)

In large mixing bowl or food processor, combine garbanzo beans, lemon juice, garlic, and tahini; blend to smooth paste. Mound spread onto serving dish. Serve at room temperature with warm pita bread triangles.

Nutritional Data

PER SERVING:

Calories	76
% calories from fat	32
Fat (gm)	2.8
Sat. Fat (gm)	0.4
Cholesterol (mg)	0
Sodium (mg)	220
Protein (gm)	3.2
Carbohydrate (gm)	10.3

EXCHANGES:

Milk	0.0	Bread	0.5
Veg.	0.5	Meat	0.0
Fruit	0.0	Fat	0.5

Hot Bean Dip

Serves 4 (2-tablespoon servings)

1 8-oz. can of kidney, or pinto beans, rinsed and drained
2 cloves garlic, minced
¼ cup shallots, chopped
½ cup tofu (bean curd)
1 medium stalk celery, chopped
2 tablespoons mild salsa
2 tablespoons part-skim mozzarella cheese, grated
Parsley, chopped, for garnish

Nutritional Data

PER SERVING:

Calories	113
% calories from fat	2ʳ
Fat (gm)	3.5
Sat. Fat (gm)	0.8
Cholesterol (mg)	2
Sodium (mg)	291
Protein (gm)	9.3
Carbohydrate (gm)	12.7

EXCHANGES:

Milk	0.0	Bread	1.0
Veg.	0.0	Meat	0.0
Fruit	0.0	Fat	0.5

Mix all ingredients except last two in blender or food processor and puree. Place in 16-oz. microwave glass bowl, and microwave on High for 1 minute. Remove, stir to mix, sprinkle with cheese, and return to microwave on High for another 40 seconds, just until cheese melts. Garnish with chopped parsley. Serve as dip with vegetable crudités.

Sesame Chickpea Dip

Serves 8 (2-tablespoon servings)

1 cup canned chickpeas (garbanzos), rinsed and drained
2 tablespoons fresh lemon juice
1 tablespoon tahini (sesame paste), or peanut butter
⅛ teaspoon cayenne pepper
3 tablespoons water (or more to thin)
1 teaspoon toasted sesame seeds
1 teaspoon parsley, chopped

Nutritional Data

PER SERVING:

Calories	41
% calories from fat	34
Fat (gm)	1.6
Sat. Fat (gm)	0.2
Cholesterol (mg)	0
Sodium (mg)	114
Protein (gm)	1.7
Carbohydrate (gm)	5.4

EXCHANGES:

Milk	0.0	Bread	0.5
Veg.	0.0	Meat	0.0
Fruit	0.0	Fat	0.0

In a food processor fitted with a steel blade, blend together all ingredients but the last two. Turn into a 12-oz. glass dish and microwave on High for 1½ minutes, stirring midcycle. Remove, stir again to mix, and sprinkle with garnish of sesame seeds and parsley. Serve as dip with pita crisps or vegetable crudités.

Taco Dip

Serves 3 (½-cup servings)

1 lb. ripe Italian plum tomatoes, peeled, seeded, and chopped
¼ cup chopped green bell pepper
¼ cup sliced green onions (white and green parts)
1 large clove garlic, minced
1 tablespoon tarragon vinegar
1 tablespoon chopped basil
¼ teaspoon salt
¼ teaspoon black pepper
  Few drops hot sauce
  Chili powder to taste
1 packet Equal® (see "About This Cookbook")

Nutritional Data

PER SERVING:

Calories	46
% calories from fat	10
Fat (gm)	0.6
Sat. Fat (gm)	0.1
Cholesterol (mg)	0
Sodium (mg)	193
Protein (gm)	1.9
Carbohydrate (gm)	10.5

EXCHANGES:

Milk	0.0	Bread	0.0
Veg.	2.0	Meat	0.0
Fruit	0.0	Fat	0.0

Combine all ingredients except Equal® and pork rinds in saucepan. Bring to a boil, lower heat, and simmer for 20 minutes. Remove from heat and add Equal®. Adjust seasonings for taste. Chill before serving. Serve dip with low-calorie crunchy pork rinds and vegetable relishes.

❄ Marinated Mushrooms

Serves 8

¼ cup balsamic vinegar
2 tablespoons olive oil
2 tablespoons granulated sugar
1 teaspoon dried basil
1 teaspoon dried thyme
1 teaspoon dried oregano
1 tablespoon water
  Freshly ground pepper
1 medium red onion, sliced
1 lb. medium mushrooms
¼ cup chives, minced

Nutritional Data

PER SERVING:

Calories	37
% calories from fat	31
Fat (gm)	1.4
Sat. Fat (gm)	0.2
Cholesterol (mg)	0
Sodium (mg)	3
Protein (gm)	1.4
Carbohydrate (gm)	5.7

EXCHANGES:

Milk	0.0	Bread	0.0
Veg.	1.0	Meat	0.0
Fruit	0.0	Fat	0.5

In a large bowl, combine vinegar, oil, sugar, basil, thyme, oregano, water, and pepper. Stir until well mixed.

Separate onion into rings. Rinse mushrooms and trim stems. Add mushrooms and onion to vinegar mixture; mix lightly. Cover and refrigerate for at least 8 hours, stirring occasionally. Drain before serving. Place on platter with toothpicks; garnish with chives.

Variation: Add artichoke hearts, hearts of palm, or asparagus to the mushrooms for a different salad.

Note: This can be used as a first course by serving on a bed of interesting greens such as romaine, Boston lettuce, or arugula.

To Freeze: Place in vacuum-sealed bags; label and freeze for up to 2 months.

To Serve: Thaw in refrigerator and serve cold.

Herb-Marinated Mushrooms

Serves 12

1	tablespoon vegetable oil
⅔	cup tarragon wine vinegar
2	cloves garlic, minced
3	tablespoons sugar
½	teaspoon salt
2	tablespoons water
3	tablespoons crushed fresh basil, chopped
2	teaspoons ground tarragon
3	green onions, minced
1½	lbs. mushrooms, trimmed
1	tablespoon parsley, chopped
1	cup bread crumbs, toasted

Nutritional Data

PER SERVING:

Calories	49
% calories from fat	26
Fat (gm)	1.6
Sat. Fat (gm)	0.1
Cholesterol (mg)	0
Sodium (mg)	111
Protein (gm)	1.6
Carbohydrate (gm)	8.4

EXCHANGES:

Milk	0.0	Bread	0.0
Veg.	1.0	Meat	0.0
Fruit	0.0	Fat	0.5

In large glass bowl, combine all ingredients except bread crumbs; toss gently to mix. Cover with plastic wrap and refrigerate 3 to 4 hours. Toss marinated mushrooms and drain before serving. Sprinkle with bread crumbs. This makes a fine addition to a summer picnic.

Mushroom Pâté

Serves 10

Vegetable cooking spray
1 tablespoon margarine
2 lbs. mushrooms, finely chopped
¾ teaspoon Spike (see "About This Cookbook")
   Pepper, freshly ground to taste
   Egg substitute to equal 3 eggs
2 tablespoons skim milk

Nutritional Data

PER SERVING:

Calories	42
% calories from fat	29
Fat (gm)	1.5
Sat. Fat (gm)	0.3
Cholesterol (mg)	0.1
Sodium (mg)	43
Protein (gm)	3.6
Carbohydrate (gm)	4.7

EXCHANGES:

Milk	0.0	Bread	0.0
Veg.	1.0	Meat	0.0
Fruit	0.0	Fat	0.5

Coat 3-cup mold with vegetable cooking spray.

In heavy skillet, melt margarine. Add mushrooms. Cook over low heat, stirring frequently until liquid evaporates and mushrooms brown, about 35 minutes. Season with Spike and pepper. Remove from heat.

In separate bowl mix egg substitute with skim milk. To this, add 3 tablespoons mushroom mixture. Mix well. Combine egg mixture with mushrooms in skillet. Cook over low heat 2 to 3 minutes, stirring constantly.

Pour into mold. Chill until firm. Unmold and serve at room temperature with crackers.

Stuffed Mushrooms

Serves 10

20 large mushrooms
1   small onion, finely chopped
¼   cup parsley, chopped
2   tablespoons white wine
2   tablespoons pimiento, chopped
½   cup dry bread crumbs
¼   cup Parmesan cheese, grated
¼   teaspoon Spike (see "About This Cookbook")
¼   teaspoon pepper

Nutritional Data

PER SERVING:

Calories	80
% calories from fat	18
Fat (gm)	1.6
Sat. Fat (gm)	0.6
Cholesterol (mg)	2
Sodium (mg)	158
Protein (gm)	3.4
Carbohydrate (gm)	12.7

EXCHANGES:

Milk	0.0	Bread	1.0
Veg.	0.5	Meat	0.0
Fruit	0.0	Fat	0.0

Clean mushrooms. Remove and chop stems.

Preheat oven to 350 degrees. In a large skillet coated with vegetable cooking spray, cook mushrooms, stems, onion, and parsley till onion is tender. Stir in wine, pimiento, bread crumbs, Parmesan cheese, Spike, and pepper.

Arrange mushrooms in a shallow baking pan. Spoon cheese mixture into mushroom caps. Bake for 15 minutes or till mushrooms are tender and cheese mixture is heated through.

Mushroom Rolls

Serves 12

12	slices thin, nonfat white bread, crusts removed
	Butter-flavored vegetable cooking spray
1	lb. mushrooms, minced
3	tablespoons all-purpose flour
½	teaspoon salt
¾	cup evaporated skim milk
3	green onions, minced

Nutritional Data

PER SERVING:

Calories	77
% calories from fat	9
Fat (gm)	0.8
Sat. Fat (gm)	0.2
Cholesterol (mg)	0.5
Sodium (mg)	213
Protein (gm)	4.2
Carbohydrate (gm)	15.3

EXCHANGES:

Milk	0.0	Bread	1.0
Veg.	0.0	Meat	0.0
Fruit	0.0	Fat	0.0

Preheat oven to 400 degrees.

With rolling pin, roll each slice of bread until very thin; set aside.

Coat 12-inch, heavy, nonstick skillet with cooking spray. Add mushrooms. Sauté 4 to 6 minutes or until soft. Partially cover if necessary. Blend in flour, salt, and milk. Continue stirring over heat until mixture begins to thicken. Mix in green onions. Spread mixture evenly on each slice of bread. Roll up jelly-roll style. Arrange seam side down on cookie sheet. Bake 10 minutes or until beginning to brown. Slice rolls in thirds and serve.

Mushrooms in Vermouth

Serves 6

1   lb. fresh button mushrooms
½   cup dry vermouth
1   tablespoon olive oil
5   tablespoons red wine vinegar
2   tablespoons lemon juice
1   clove garlic, minced
2   tablespoons shallots, chopped
1   tablespoon fresh basil leaves, chopped
1   teaspoon Spike (see "About This Cookbook")
½   teaspoon pepper
1   teaspoon sugar
½   teaspoon dry mustard

Nutritional Data

PER SERVING:

Calories	69
% calories from fat	31
Fat (gm)	2.7
Sat. Fat (gm)	0.3
Cholesterol (mg)	0
Sodium (mg)	5
Protein (gm)	1.8
Carbohydrate (gm)	6.4

EXCHANGES:

Milk	0.0	Bread	0.0
Veg.	1.5	Meat	0.0
Fruit	0.0	Fat	0.5

Place mushrooms into jar with a tight-fitting lid. Combine remaining ingredients in blender and process until smooth. Pour mixture over mushrooms. Seal jar and store in refrigerator for up to 2 months.

Serve alone or as a garnish for meats or vegetables.

Onion Tart

Serves 6

4   tablespoons margarine
¼   cup white wine
½   teaspoon dried dill
2   garlic cloves, quartered
6   large onions, coarsely chopped
¼   cup fresh chives, minced
3   tablespoons sugar
1½   cups bread crumbs
1   cup matzoh, crumbled
1   cup part-skim mozzarella, shredded

Nutritional Data

PER SERVING:

Calories	323
% calories from fat	16
Fat (gm)	5.7
Sat. Fat (gm)	2.5
Cholesterol (mg)	16
Sodium (mg)	356
Protein (gm)	12.3
Carbohydrate (gm)	55.3

EXCHANGES:

Milk	0.0	Bread	3.0
Veg.	2.0	Meat	0.0
Fruit	0.0	Fat	1.0

Preheat oven to 375 degrees. Melt 3 tablespoons margarine in a large saucepan and add wine, dill, and garlic. Reduce heat to low and add onions, chives, and sugar. Stir gently until sugar has completely dissolved. Simmer another 5 minutes. Remove saucepan from heat.

Grease 9-inch pie pan with remaining margarine. Spoon thin layer of onion mixture into pan. Cover with thin layer of bread crumbs and crumbled matzoh. Repeat process until onion, bread crumbs, and matzoh are used up.

Top tart with mozzarella cheese, and bake 15 minutes or until cheese is melted and lightly browned. Remove tart from oven, cut into squares or wedges, and serve hot.

Potato Pancakes with Ginger Yogurt

Serves 8

Pancake Batter

- 4 large baking potatoes, about 2 lbs., peeled
- 3/4 cup onions, grated
- 2 egg whites, slightly beaten
- 1/4 teaspoon baking soda
- 1/2 teaspoon ground basil

  Canola oil, or vegetable cooking spray

Ginger Yogurt

- 2 cups plain nonfat yogurt
- 2 teaspoons candied ginger, minced
- 1/2 cup fresh chives, minced

Nutritional Data

PER SERVING:

Calories	116
% calories from fat	2
Fat (gm)	0.2
Sat. Fat (gm)	0.1
Cholesterol (mg)	1
Sodium (mg)	101
Protein (gm)	5.9
Carbohydrate (gm)	23.1

EXCHANGES:

Milk	0.0	Bread	1.5
Veg.	0.0	Meat	0.0
Fruit	0.0	Fat	0.0

Pancake Batter: Grate potatoes into deep mixing bowl, working quickly as potatoes brown fast. Mix in remaining batter ingredients except the oil. Cover bowl with plastic wrap and let stand in refrigerator 20 minutes. Stir before using.

Ginger Yogurt: In separate bowl mix together yogurt, ginger, and chives. Cover and refrigerate; stir before serving.

Coat a large nonstick skillet with cooking spray, or use canola oil. Pour batter onto hot pan by the tablespoon, making silver-dollar-size pancakes, about 1½ to 2 inches in diameter. Fry pancakes on both sides until cooked and golden brown. Turn once.

Place bowl of Ginger Yogurt on serving plate and surround with hot pancakes. Serve with toothpicks and cocktail napkins.

Potato Spinach Balls

Serves 8

		Nutritional Data	

1 10-oz. package frozen chopped spinach, defrosted, drained
3 cups cooked white mashed potatoes
2 egg whites, slightly beaten
4 cloves garlic, minced
½ cup parsley, minced
½ teaspoon each ingredient: ground mace, marjoram
   Olive oil, or vegetable cooking spray
2 tablespoons, or to taste, Parmesan cheese, grated
   Toothpicks

Nutritional Data

PER SERVING:

Calories:	86
% calories from fat:	10
Fat (gm):	1.1
Sat. Fat (gm):	0.6
Cholesterol (mg):	2.7
Sodium (mg):	314
Protein (gm):	4.4
Carbohydrate (gm):	16.7

EXCHANGES:

Milk	0.0	Bread	0.9
Veg.	0.6	Meat	0.2
Fruit	0.0	Fat	0.0

To prepare potato balls, squeeze spinach dry and place in deep mixing bowl. Mix in mashed potatoes, egg whites, garlic, parsley, mace, and marjoram. Using wet hands, shape mixture into 1½-inch balls; place on tray or plate.

Coat a nonstick skillet with olive oil or cooking spray and fry potato balls until cooked crisp and golden brown. Remove to serving plate, sprinkle with Parmesan cheese, and surround with cut vegetables. Serve hot and provide toothpicks.

Potato Cheese Chips

Serves 4 (4 slices per serving)

2 medium Idaho potatoes, about 1 lb.
2 ozs. low-fat shredded cheese such as Alpine Lace, part-skim mozzarella, etc.
¼ teaspoon each ingredient: garlic powder, chili powder, and dried basil
   Dash of pepper to taste

Nutritional Data

PER SERVING:

Calories	143
% calories from fat	10
Fat (gm)	1.6
Sat. Fat (gm)	0
Cholesterol (mg)	5
Sodium (mg)	84
Protein (gm)	6.4
Carbohydrate (gm)	27.0

EXCHANGES:

Milk	0.0	Bread	2.0
Veg.	0.0	Meat	0.0
Fruit	0.0	Fat	0.0

Wash potatoes and prick each with a fork. Wrap each potato in microwave-safe paper towel and place end-to-end in oven. Microwave on High for 4 to 5 minutes. Turn potatoes over and microwave on High another 4 to 5 minutes. Unwrap, let cool, and refrigerate.

When chilled, cut into ¼-inch slices and top with sprinkling of cheese, a dusting of combined spices, and dash of pepper.

Line oven with paper towels and arrange potato slices on them. Microwave for 30 to 40 seconds, just until cheese melts. Makes 16 slices.

Corn Crisps

Serves 4 (4 per serving)

16 nonfat corn tortilla chips
¼ cup low-fat mozzarella, or cheese substitute, shredded
2 tablespoons mild salsa

Line platter with wax paper and arrange tortilla chips over it. Sprinkle grated cheese over each chip and top with a dab of salsa. Microwave on High just until cheese melts, about 1 minute. Serve while warm.

Nutritional Data

PER SERVING:

Calories	75
% calories from fat	22
Fat (gm)	1.8
Sat. Fat (gm)	0.7
Cholesterol (mg)	4
Sodium (mg)	156
Protein (gm)	3.3
Carbohydrate (gm)	11.3

EXCHANGES:

Milk	0.0	Bread	1.0
Veg.	0.0	Meat	0.0
Fruit	0.0	Fat	0.0

Spicy Popcorn

Serves 8 (½-cup servings)

⅓ cup popping corn (use best available)
   Vegetable cooking spray
1 teaspoon each ingredient: paprika, chili powder
½ teaspoon garlic powder

Put corn into microwave popper. Microwave on High 3½ to 4 minutes. Transfer popcorn to serving bowl. Coat popcorn lightly with vegetable cooking spray. Sprinkle flavorings over hot popcorn, mixing well to coat.

Nutritional Data

PER SERVING:

Calories	15
% calories from fat	5
Fat (gm)	0.1
Sat. Fat (gm)	0
Cholesterol (mg)	0
Sodium (mg)	3
Protein (gm)	0.6
Carbohydrate (gm)	39

EXCHANGES:

Milk	0.0	Bread	0.0
Veg.	0.0	Meat	0.0
Fruit	0.0	Fat	0.0

Mexican Popcorn

Serves 8

7 cups air-popped popcorn
   Vegetable cooking spray
   Mexican seasoning

Coat popcorn with vegetable cooking spray. (This helps to keep seasoning on popcorn.) Sprinkle with Mexican seasoning to taste.

Nutritional Data

PER SERVING:

Calories	22
% calories from fat	0
Fat (gm)	0
Sat. Fat (gm)	0
Cholesterol (mg)	0
Sodium (mg)	0
Protein (gm)	0.9
Carbohydrate (gm)	4.4

EXCHANGES:

Milk	0.0	Bread	0.5
Veg.	0.0	Meat	0.0
Fruit	0.0	Fat	0.0

Roasted Peppers with Herbs

Serves 12

3	large red bell peppers (about 1½ lbs.)
3	large yellow bell peppers (about 1½ lbs.)
2	large green bell peppers (about 1 lb.)
1	clove garlic, halved
1	tablespoon olive oil
1	teaspoon Spike (see "About This Cookbook")
1	tablespoon *herbes de Provence*

Nutritional Data

PER SERVING:

Calories	51
% calories from fat	22
Fat (gm)	1.4
Sat. Fat (gm)	0.2
Cholesterol (mg)	0
Sodium (mg)	3.1
Protein (gm)	1.4
Carbohydrate (gm)	9.8

EXCHANGES:

Milk	0.0	Bread	0.0
Veg.	2.0	Meat	0.0
Fruit	0.0	Fat	0.0

Preheat oven to 400 degrees. Cut peppers in half lengthwise; discard seeds and membranes. Cut lengthwise into 1-inch strips; set aside.

Rub bottom of 13" x 9" x 2" baking dish with garlic halves; add peppers and oil, tossing well. Bake 35 to 40 minutes, or until peppers are tender and edges begin to blacken, stirring occasionally.

Combine Spike with *herbes de Provence;* sprinkle over peppers. Serve warm or cold.

Bruschetta

Serves 12

12	1-inch slices coarse bread, such as Italian country bread
2	cloves garlic, cut into 1-inch slices
2	tablespoons olive oil (optional)
2	tomatoes, sliced thin
12	fresh basil leaves, chopped

Nutritional Data

PER SERVING:

Calories	86
% calories from fat	12
Fat (gm)	1.2
Sat. Fat (gm)	0.3
Cholesterol (mg)	0
Sodium (mg)	177
Protein (gm)	2.8
Carbohydrate (gm)	16.1

EXCHANGES:

Milk	0.0	Bread	1.0
Veg.	0.5	Meat	0.0
Fruit	0.0	Fat	0.0

Grill bread over a fire or under broiler until just beginning to brown around edges. It should remain soft inside. Remove from heat and rub while still hot with a cut clove of garlic. Brush with olive oil and top with slice of tomato. Sprinkle with fresh basil.

Tomato Crostini

Serves 6

1½ cups fresh plum tomatoes (about 3 medium tomatoes), peeled, seeded, and chopped
12 slices Italian bread (from narrow baguette-type loaf)
2 large cloves garlic, peeled
2 tablespoons olive oil
12 tablespoons fresh basil, minced
1 tablespoon fresh oregano, minced
Spike, to taste (see "About This Cookbook")
Black pepper, freshly ground, to taste

Nutritional Data

PER SERVING:

Calories	140
% calories from fat	31
Fat (gm)	4.7
Sat. Fat (gm)	0.7
Cholesterol (mg)	0
Sodium (mg)	157
Protein (gm)	3.6
Carbohydrate (gm)	20.3

EXCHANGES:

Milk	0.0	Bread	1.0
Veg.	0.0	Meat	0.0
Fruit	0.0	Fat	1.0

Put tomatoes in colander and set aside to drain.

Grill or toast bread slices. Rub each slice with garlic, and drizzle each one with olive oil.

Place tomatoes in a bowl and top with remaining ingredients. Stir to mix well. Divide mixture evenly among bread slices and serve immediately.

Tomatoes with Mozzarella and Basil

Serves 4

4 tomatoes
Lettuce leaves, red leaves preferable
3 tablespoons low-fat chicken bouillon
1 teaspoon dry white wine
½ teaspoon oregano
1 teaspoon fresh basil
4 ozs. fat-free mozzarella cheese, shredded
Fresh basil leaves (optional)

Nutritional Data

PER SERVING:

Calories	72
% calories from fat	6
Fat (gm)	0.5
Sat. Fat (gm)	0.1
Cholesterol (mg)	5.1
Sodium (mg)	231
Protein (gm)	10.6
Carbohydrate (gm)	7.3

EXCHANGES:

Milk	0.0	Bread	0.0
Veg.	1.0	Meat	1.0
Fruit	0.0	Fat	0.0

Cut tomatoes into slices. Divide tomato slices into 4 individual servings and place on salad plates with lettuce leaves. Blend bouillon, wine, and seasonings. Drizzle over tomatoes. Sprinkle cheese on top. You can add fresh basil leaves for garnish.

"Sun-Dried" Tomatoes in Herb Oil

Serves 12 (makes 3 pints, 4 servings per pint)	Nutritional Data
	PER SERVING:

6   lbs. ripe Italian plum tomatoes
2   tablespoons Spike (see "About This Cookbook")
3   3-inch fresh rosemary sprigs
3   garlic cloves, unpeeled
1   teaspoon ground oregano
8   black peppercorns
1   teaspoon ground thyme
2½-3 cups olive oil

Nutritional Data

PER SERVING:

Calories	59
% calories from fat	25
Fat (gm)	1.9
Sat. Fat (gm)	0.3
Cholesterol (mg)	0
Sodium (mg)	21
Protein (gm)	2
Carbohydrate (gm)	10.9

EXCHANGES:

Milk	0.0	Bread	0.0
Veg.	2.0	Meat	0.0
Fruit	0.0	Fat	0.0

Preheat oven to 200 degrees. Line baking sheets with racks. Slice open tomatoes lengthwise but not completely in half. Arrange on racks, cut-side up. Sprinkle with Spike.

Bake 12 hours or until tomatoes reduce to about one-fourth their size and appear shriveled and deep red. Remove tomatoes from oven. Cool 1 hour.

Pack into sterilized pint jars (about 14 per pint). Add herbs and cover completely with olive oil. *Seal jar tightly.* Store in refrigerator 4 to 8 weeks before draining and using. Rinse the prepared tomatoes in warm water and drain before using.

Marinated Tortellini Vegetable Kabobs

Serves 12 (2 appetizers each)	Nutritional Data

⅔   cup water
½   cup wine or cider vinegar
1   teaspoon dried basil
1   teaspoon oregano
½   teaspoon dry mustard
½   teaspoon thyme
1   teaspoon Spike (see "About This Cookbook")
¼   teaspoon pepper, freshly ground
½   teaspoon dill
¼   teaspoon onion powder
¼   teaspoon garlic powder

Nutritional Data

PER SERVING:

Calories	74
% calories from fat	18
Fat (gm)	1.5
Sat. Fat (gm)	0.7
Cholesterol (mg)	7.9
Sodium (mg)	64
Protein (gm)	3.6
Carbohydrate (gm)	11.7

EXCHANGES:

Milk	0.0	Bread	0.5
Veg.	1.5	Meat	0.0
Fruit	0.0	Fat	0.0

24 cooked small fresh spinach tortellini
    with cheese; or 24 cheese tortellini; or
    48 tricolored tortellini
 1 cup button mushrooms (about 12)
 6 artichoke hearts, cut into quarters
12 cherry tomatoes, halved
24 (6-inch) skewers

Combine first 11 ingredients in a saucepan; gradually bring to a boil. Cook 30 seconds, stirring with a wire whisk. Remove from heat and let cool.

Alternate tortellini, mushrooms, artichokes, and tomatoes on skewers; place in a 13" x 9" x 2" baking dish. Pour dressing over kabobs, turning to coat. Cover and marinate in refrigerator 4 hours, turning occasionally. Drain and place on a serving platter.

Note: Only the tortellini and dressing should be frozen as follows.

To Freeze: Vacuum seal tortellini and dressing; label, and freeze up to 2 months.

To Serve: Thaw, add remaining vegetables to marinate, and complete the kabobs.

Vegetable Platter with Vinaigrette

Serves 8

 2 small ripe fresh tomatoes, sliced
 1 small cucumber, thinly sliced
 1 small carrot
 2 small zucchini, thinly sliced
 2 cloves garlic, minced
1/4 teaspoon Dijon-style mustard
1/4 cup Vinaigrette (see p. 128)

Nutritional Data

PER SERVING:

Calories	30
% calories from fat	8
Fat (gm)	0.3
Sat. Fat (gm)	0.1
Cholesterol (mg)	0
Sodium (mg)	76
Protein (gm)	1.3
Carbohydrate (gm)	6.3

EXCHANGES:

Milk	0.0	Bread	0.0
Veg.	1.0	Meat	0.0
Fruit	0.0	Fat	0.0

Arrange tomatoes around the edge of a serving plate. Arrange cucumber slices and then zucchini slices on plate, overlapping rows. Using a vegetable peeler, cut carrot into long strips. Place carrot strips in center of plate. Just before serving, drizzle Vinaigrette over vegetables.

Vegetable Caviar

Serves 10

1 small eggplant, peeled
1 small acorn squash, halved and seeded
3 large green bell peppers
1 medium head cauliflower, leaves removed
1 bunch broccoli, leaves removed and stems sliced
1 tablespoon garlic, finely chopped
3 tablespoons lemon juice
¼ cup white wine
1 tablespoon olive oil
4 tablespoons parsley, finely chopped

Nutritional Data

PER SERVING:

Calories	65
% calories from fat	22
Fat (gm)	1.8
Sat. Fat (gm)	0.2
Cholesterol (mg)	0
Sodium (mg)	41
Protein (gm)	3.4
Carbohydrate (gm)	10.4

EXCHANGES:

Milk	0.0	Bread	0.0
Veg.	2.0	Meat	0.0
Fruit	0.0	Fat	0.5

Preheat oven to 475 degrees. Place vegetables in baking dish. Bake 30 minutes and remove all vegetables except acorn squash and eggplant. Bake squash and eggplant 15 minutes longer.

After cooking, chop the green peppers. Cut eggplant into cubes. Scoop pulp from squash. Chop cauliflower and broccoli. Combine all vegetables in a medium-size bowl. Chop and mix thoroughly until mixture is well combined. Add garlic, lemon juice, wine, olive oil, and parsley. Blend thoroughly. Chill at least 2 hours before serving. Serve this with slices of black bread.

Vegetarian Antipasto

Serves 8

Dressing

4 teaspoons olive oil
2 tablespoons onion, diced
1 tablespoon red wine vinegar
1 tablespoon lemon juice
1 tablespoon fresh chives, minced
1 garlic clove, minced
¼ teaspoon basil
¼ teaspoon oregano

Vegetables

2 cups cauliflower florets, blanched or raw
24 asparagus spears, cooked
1 15½-oz. can artichoke hearts
1 large red onion, sliced and separated into rings

Nutritional Data

PER SERVING:

Calories	124
% calories from fat	30
Fat (gm)	4.6
Sat. Fat (gm)	0.6
Cholesterol (mg)	1.3
Sodium (mg)	339
Protein (gm)	7.6
Carbohydrate (gm)	16.5

EXCHANGES:

Milk	0.0	Bread	0.0
Veg.	3.0	Meat	0.0
Fruit	0.0	Fat	1.0

6   ozs. drained chickpeas
8   cherry tomatoes, cut in half
    Several large lettuce leaves for platter
½   cup fat-free mozzarella cheese,
    shredded
¼   cup black olives, sliced

Dressing: In small bowl, combine all ingredients for dressing; set aside.

Marinated Vegetable Mixture: In large bowl, combine cauliflower, asparagus, artichoke hearts, onion, chickpeas, and tomatoes. Pour dressing over vegetable mixture and toss to coat. Cover and refrigerate for at least 1 hour, tossing several times.

To Serve: Line large serving platter with lettuce. Spoon vegetable mixture into center of platter. Top with vegetables. Sprinkle with mozzarella cheese and olives.

Note: It is not recommended that you freeze this dish. Serve it fresh.

 # *Broiled Grapefruit*

Serves 4

2   medium grapefruits, cut in half
2   tablespoons dry sherry
2   packets Equal® (see "About This Cookbook")

Using a grapefruit knife, separate the flesh of the grapefruits from the shell and separate into sections, making sure they are loosened from the peel. Sprinkle with sherry and broil until the grapefruits are slightly brown and the tops glazed. Remove from the oven and sprinkle with Equal®. The alcohol in the sherry evaporates during broiling so no calories are added.

Nutritional Data

PER SERVING:

Calories	49
% calories from fat	2
Fat (gm)	0.1
Sat. Fat (gm)	0
Cholesterol (mg)	0
Sodium (mg)	0
Protein (gm)	0.7
Carbohydrate (gm)	10.3

EXCHANGES:

Milk	0.0	Bread	0.0
Veg.	0.0	Meat	0.0
Fruit	1.0	Fat	0.0

Citrus Supreme with Zesty Ginger Dressing

Serves 4

12   grapefruit sections
12   orange sections
4   crisp lettuce cups
    Zesty Ginger Dressing (recipe follows)

Place 3 grapefruit sections and 3 orange sections in each lettuce cup. Prepare Ginger Dressing. Spoon 1 tablespoon dressing over citrus.

Nutritional Data

PER SERVING:

Calories	112
% calories from fat	10
Fat (gm)	1.2
Sat. Fat (gm)	0.7
Cholesterol (mg)	4.9
Sodium (mg)	244
Protein (gm)	9.9
Carbohydrate (gm)	16.2

EXCHANGES:

Milk	0.0	Bread	0.0
Veg.	0.0	Meat	1.0
Fruit	1.0	Fat	0.0

Zesty Ginger Dressing

Serves 8

1   cup low-fat cottage cheese
2   tablespoons skim milk
3   packets Equal® (see "About This Cookbook")
¼   cup fat-free sour cream
1   tablespoon orange juice
6   teaspoons grated orange peel
2   teaspoons minced candied ginger

Place cottage cheese, milk, and Equal® in blender. Process till smooth. Add sour cream and remaining ingredients except candied ginger. Blend till smooth. Stir in candied ginger.

Nutritional Data

PER SERVING:

Calories	38
% calories from fat	13
Fat (gm)	0.6
Sat. Fat (gm)	0.4
Cholesterol (mg)	2.4
Sodium (mg)	122
Protein (gm)	4.5
Carbohydrate (gm)	3.7

EXCHANGES:

Milk	0.0	Bread	0.0
Veg.	0.0	Meat	0.5
Fruit	0.0	Fat	0.0

Melon Balls in Lambrusco

Serves 8

4   cantaloupes
2   cups Lambrusco (sparkling red wine)
½   cup maraschino cherries
2   seedless oranges, quartered and
     sliced thin
8   thin slices lemon
8   fresh mint leaves

Nutritional Data

PER SERVING:

Calories	132
% calories from fat	4
Fat (gm)	0.6
Sat. Fat (gm)	0
Cholesterol (mg)	0
Sodium (mg)	54
Protein (gm)	2.4
Carbohydrate (gm)	23

EXCHANGES:

Milk	0.0	Bread	0.0
Veg.	0.0	Meat	0.0
Fruit	1.5	Fat	1.0

Cut melons into halves; discard seeds. With a melon-ball cutter, make melon balls and place in large bowl. Reserve melon shells for refilling. Pour Lambrusco over melon balls and allow to marinate at room temperature 20 minutes. Stir, cover bowl, and place in refrigerator to chill 2 hours.

Remove from refrigerator and blend in maraschino cherries. Then put melon-ball mixture back into shells. Garnish with orange, lemon, and mint.

Heart-Healthy Deviled Eggs

Serves 8 (2 deviled eggs each)

8   eggs, hard boiled, cut in half, yolks
     discarded
½   cup low-fat cottage cheese
¼   cup fat-free mayonnaise
¼   cup green onion, finely minced
¼   cup celery, finely minced
¼   teaspoon celery seed
¼   teaspoon Spike (see "About This
     Cookbook")
1   teaspoon Dijon mustard
2   tablespoons parsley, minced

Nutritional Data

PER SERVING:

Calories	36
% calories from fat	6
Fat (gm)	0.2
Sat. Fat (gm)	0.1
Cholesterol (mg)	0.6
Sodium (mg)	220
Protein (gm)	5.4
Carbohydrate (gm)	2.6

EXCHANGES:

Milk	0.0	Bread	0.0
Veg.	0.0	Meat	1.0
Fruit	0.0	Fat	0.0

In medium bowl, beat cottage cheese and mayonnaise until fluffy. Add remaining ingredients and beat well. Stuff hard-boiled egg shells with the mixture and refrigerate. Before serving, dust with minced parsley.

Small Cocktail Quiche

Serves 30 (2 quiches each)

⅓ cup egg substitute
1 lb. low-fat cottage cheese
3 tablespoons fat-free yogurt
4 ozs. low-fat Swiss cheese, chopped well
½ cup Bisquick
Pepper to taste
1 tablespoon margarine, melted
Vegetable cooking spray

Nutritional Data

PER SERVING:

Calories	34
% calories from fat	34
Fat (gm)	1.2
Sat. Fat (gm)	0.6
Cholesterol (mg)	3.7
Sodium (mg)	141
Protein (gm)	3.1
Carbohydrate (gm)	2.1

EXCHANGES:

Milk	0.0	Bread	0.0
Veg.	0.0	Meat	0.5
Fruit	0.0	Fat	0.0

Preheat oven to 375 degrees. In large bowl, combine all ingredients. Blend until just mixed. Coat miniature muffin cups liberally with vegetable spray. Fill each cup ⅔ full. Bake for 25 to 30 minutes. Cool in cups before removing. Reheat 10 minutes before serving. Makes 5 dozen.

Goat's Cheese Vegetable Spread

Serves 16 (1-tablespoon servings)

2 tablespoons plain goat's cheese, softened
1 cup nonfat ricotta cheese
2 tablespoons parsley, minced
2 tablespoons scallions, chopped
2 tablespoons radishes, chopped
1 teaspoon fresh tarragon, or ½ teaspoon dried

Nutritional Data

PER SERVING:

Calories	13
% calories from fat	12
Fat (gm)	0.2
Sat. Fat (gm)	0.1
Cholesterol (mg)	1.9
Sodium (mg)	11
Protein (gm)	2.2
Carbohydrate (gm)	1.1

EXCHANGES:

Milk	0.0	Bread	0.0
Veg.	0.0	Meat	0.0
Fruit	0.0	Fat	0.0

In small bowl, mix all ingredients well. Refrigerate overnight to blend flavors. Use as spread on crackers, French bread, or bagel chips, or use vegetables to dip.

Yogurt Cheese

Serves 16

4 cups plain low-fat yogurt
1 clove garlic, finely minced
2 tablespoons parsley, minced
1 teaspoon each ingredient: minced thyme, oregano, and tarragon
½ teaspoon Spike, or to taste (see "About This Cookbook")

Nutritional Data

PER SERVING:

Calories	28
% calories from fat	22
Fat (gm)	0.7
Sat. Fat (gm)	0.4
Cholesterol (mg)	2.6
Sodium (mg)	30
Protein (gm)	2.3
Carbohydrate (gm)	3.3

EXCHANGES.

Milk	0.5	Bread	0.0
Veg.	0.0	Meat	0.0
Fruit	0.0	Fat	0.0

Rinse a long length of cheesecloth (about 1 foot) in cold water and wring out. Place yogurt in center, wrap cloth around it, and set in strainer or colander in a bowl. Refrigerate until thick, 8 to 14 hours or up to 24 hours. Discard whey (the separated liquid), and unwrap yogurt cheese. Place in mixing bowl and mix thoroughly with garlic, parsley, herbs, and Spike. Serve with crackers or fresh vegetables.

Chicken Salad Spread

Serves 7 (⅓-cup servings)

1½ cups skinless chicken breast, chopped
1 cup apples, chopped
½ cup nonfat sour cream
¼ cup green onions, chopped

Nutritional Data

PER SERVING:

Calories	55
% calories from fat	15
Fat (gm)	0.9
Sat. Fat (gm)	0.3
Cholesterol (mg)	20.6
Sodium (mg)	24
Protein (gm)	8.2
Carbohydrate (gm)	3.4

EXCHANGES:

Milk	0.0	Bread	0.0
Veg.	0.0	Meat	1.0
Fruit	0.0	Fat	0.0

In small bowl, mix all ingredients. Serve with warm pita chips.

Chestnut and Chicken Canapés

Serves 12 (4-tablespoon servings)	Nutritional Data	
	PER SERVING:	
12 chestnuts, fresh or dried		
2 cups cooked chicken breast meat, ground or finely minced	Calories	74
	% calories from fat	14
¼ cup celery, finely chopped	Fat (gm)	1.3
¼ cup pimiento, chopped	Sat. Fat (gm)	0.4
½ cup Mock Sour Cream (see p. 497)	Cholesterol (mg)	19.9
1 teaspoon Spike (see "About This Cookbook")	Sodium (mg)	42
	Protein (gm)	8.4
	Carbohydrate (gm)	6.7
1 teaspoon white pepper		
Assorted breads, plain or toasted	EXCHANGES:	

EXCHANGES:			
Milk	0.0	Bread	0.0
Veg.	1.0	Meat	1.0
Fruit	0.0	Fat	0.0

Cut an "X" in flat side of each chestnut shell with small, sharp knife. Cover nuts with boiling water, bring to boil, and simmer 45 minutes to 1 hour, covered. Drain, and while still hot, peel chestnuts. (If you use the dried, shelled chestnuts available at ethnic grocery stores, soak them in warm water 1 to 2 days; then simmer, drain, and use.)

In a blender, mix chestnuts, chicken, celery, pimiento, Mock Sour Cream, Spike, and white pepper. Process until smooth. Refrigerate until cold. (If you do not want a pureed spread, combine in a bowl instead of using blender.)

Using a sharp knife, cut crust off breads. With cookie cutters, cut bread in various shapes. Wrap tightly in plastic wrap and refrigerate. Before serving, spread bread with cold chestnut and chicken mixture.

Saucy Franks

Serves 8 (3 franks each)	Nutritional Data	
1 lb. cocktail franks	PER SERVING:	
2 tablespoons apple juice	Calories	159
2 tablespoons cornstarch	% calories from fat	35
⅔ cup low-fat chicken broth	Fat (gm)	6.8
⅔ cup red wine vinegar	Sat. Fat (gm)	0
4 tablespoons frozen concentrated pineapple juice	Cholesterol (mg)	0
	Sodium (mg)	498
4 tablespoons chopped pimiento	Protein (gm)	13.1
2 tablespoons soy sauce	Carbohydrate (gm)	11
½ teaspoon garlic powder		
½ teaspoon ground ginger	EXCHANGES:	

EXCHANGES:			
Milk	0.0	Bread	0.0
Veg.	0.0	Meat	2.0
Fruit	0.5	Fat	0.0

4 packets Equal® (see "About This Cookbook")

Sauté franks in apple juice about 5 minutes. Set aside. Combine cornstarch and chicken broth in small saucepan. Stir in remaining ingredients except Equal®. Cook over medium heat, stirring until thickened and bubbly. Remove from heat and stir in Equal®. Place franks in sauce and let stand for about 2 minutes. Place in serving dish surrounded by toothpicks.

Sweet & Sour Chicken Chunks

Serves 20

2½ lbs. cooked chicken breast, boneless, skinless, cut into ¾-in. pcs.
1 recipe Sweet-and-Sour Sauce (p. 513)
   Vegetable cooking spray
2 medium onions, thinly sliced
2 medium green bell peppers, seeded and cut into thin strips
1 clove garlic, finely chopped

Make Sweet-and-Sour Sauce.

In sprayed skillet, cook onions, green peppers, and garlic until tender. Add chicken and cook 1 to 2 minutes. Add Sweet-and-Sour Sauce; cook 2 minutes or until bubbly.

Nutritional Data

PER SERVING:

Calories	99
% calories from fat	16
Fat (gm)	1.8
Sat. Fat (gm)	0.5
Cholesterol (mg)	43.6
Sodium (mg)	100
Protein (gm)	16.8
Carbohydrate (gm)	3

EXCHANGES:

Milk	0.0	Bread	0.0
Veg.	0.0	Meat	2.0
Fruit	0.0	Fat	0.0

Clam Dip

Serves 8 (2-tablespoon servings)

¼ cup low-fat cottage cheese
¼ cup Mock Sour Cream (see p. 497)
1 6½-oz. can minced clams, drained
1 tablespoon shallots, minced
1 teaspoon horseradish
  Dash tabasco sauce or cayenne pepper

Whip cottage cheese and Mock Sour Cream in blender until smooth. Add remaining ingredients, blend, and place in 2-cup microwave-safe measure. Microwave on Medium (50%) 1 minute, stirring once. Serve warm or chilled with blue corn chips or crudités.

Nutritional Data

PER SERVING:

Calories	46
% calories from fat	12
Fat (gm)	0.6
Sat. Fat (gm)	0.1
Cholesterol (mg)	16.1
Sodium (mg)	92.2
Protein (gm)	7.7
Carbohydrate (gm)	1.9

EXCHANGES:

Milk	0.0	Bread	0.0
Veg.	0.0	Meat	1.0
Fruit	0.0	Fat	0.0

Clam Dip with Tarragon

Serves 8

8   ozs. 1% low-fat cottage cheese
1   8-oz. can minced clams, undrained
2   tablespoons plain nonfat yogurt
½   teaspoon garlic salt
1   teaspoon Worcestershire sauce
1   teaspoon fresh tarragon, minced, or ½
    teaspoon dried

Mix all ingredients, adding clam juice for consistency desired. Refrigerate. Stir before using. Serve with carrot and celery sticks for dipping.

Nutritional Data

PER SERVING:

Calories	65
% calories from fat	12
Fat (gm)	0.9
Sat. Fat (gm)	0.2
Cholesterol (mg)	20.3
Sodium (mg)	284
Protein (gm)	11
Carbohydrate (gm)	2.7

EXCHANGES:

Milk	0.0	Bread	0.0
Veg.	0.0	Meat	1.5
Fruit	0.0	Fat	0.0

Baked Clams

Serves 6

12 clams in shells
¾   cup dry bread crumbs
6   tablespoons white wine
¼   cup parsley, chopped
3   cloves garlic, finely chopped
½   teaspoon Spike (see "About This
    Cookbook")
½   teaspoon pepper

Nutritional Data

PER SERVING:

Calories	145
% calories from fat	11
Fat (gm)	1.7
Sat. Fat (gm)	0.2
Cholesterol (mg)	37.2
Sodium (mg)	157
Protein (gm)	16.1
Carbohydrate (gm)	12.9

EXCHANGES:

Milk	0.0	Bread	0.5
Veg.	0.0	Meat	2.0
Fruit	0.0	Fat	0.0

Preheat oven to 375 degrees. Open clams above bowl; remove clam muscle. Reserve clam juice and shells. Scrub shells under cold running water and place in a single layer in a shallow baking dish.

In a mixing bowl, stir together bread crumbs, wine, parsley, garlic, Spike, and pepper. Place 1 clam in each shell in baking dish. Spoon bread crumb mixture over clams. Bake uncovered for 15 to 20 minutes or until brown.

Warm Crabmeat Spread

Serves 8

8 ozs. 1% cottage cheese
1 tablespoon skim milk
6½ ozs. crabmeat, shell removed
2 tablespoons instant chopped onion
½ teaspoon cream-style horseradish
½ teaspoon salt
½ teaspoon pepper
Butter-flavored vegetable cooking spray

Nutritional Data

PER SERVING:

Calories	51
% calories from fat	11
Fat (gm)	0.6
Sat. Fat (gm)	0.2
Cholesterol (mg)	21.8
Sodium (mg)	333
Protein (gm)	8.5
Carbohydrate (gm)	2.4

EXCHANGES:

Milk	0.0	Bread	0.0
Veg.	0.0	Meat	1.0
Fruit	0.0	Fat	0.0

Preheat oven to 375 degrees.

Using food processor fitted with steel blade, or wooden spoon and bowl, beat cheese with milk until smooth. Add remaining ingredients. Coat baking dish with cooking spray. Bake 15 minutes. Serve hot on crackers.

Potato Crab Cakes

Serves 8

2 cups cooked white mashed potatoes
1 cup crabmeat, or surimi (imitation crabmeat)
2 egg whites, slightly beaten
½ teaspoon Worcestershire sauce
¼ teaspoon red pepper flakes
¼ cup parsley, minced
Olive oil, or vegetable cooking spray
2 teaspoons margarine

Nutritional Data

PER SERVING:

Calories	72
% calories from fat	19
Fat (gm)	1.6
Sat. Fat (gm)	0.4
Cholesterol (mg)	17.9
Sodium (mg)	235
Protein (gm)	5.4
Carbohydrate (gm)	9.5

EXCHANGES:

Milk	0.0	Bread	0.5
Veg.	0.0	Meat	0.5
Fruit	0.0	Fat	0.0

Peel, cook, mash, and cool potatoes. Spoon potatoes into a mixing bowl. Mix in crabmeat, egg whites, Worcestershire sauce, red pepper flakes, and parsley.

Shape batter into patties and set on a plate. Coat a non-stick skillet with oil or cooking spray and add margarine. Melt margarine over medium heat. Fry Potato Crab Cakes about 2 minutes on each side or until cakes have browned and are cooked. Remove to individual plates and serve hot.

Escargots Florentine

Serves 2

1 teaspoon unsalted butter
12 canned snails, washed
2 cups (firmly packed) fresh spinach, well rinsed and stemmed
Black pepper, freshly grated
1 oz. blue cheese, crumbled
2 tablespoons yogurt
2 tablespoons Parmesan, or Romano cheese, freshly grated
Lemon wedges

Nutritional Data

PER SERVING:

Calories	215
% calories from fat	32
Fat (gm)	7.5
Sat. Fat (gm)	4.5
Cholesterol (mg)	73.5
Sodium (mg)	466
Protein (gm)	26.5
Carbohydrate (gm)	10

EXCHANGES:

Milk	0.0	Bread	0.0
Veg.	2.0	Meat	3.0
Fruit	0.0	Fat	0.0

Melt butter in a sauté pan over medium heat. Add snails and spinach. Add black pepper to taste. Sauté over medium heat for about 3 to 4 minutes until spinach begins to wilt. Add blue cheese.

Reduce heat and simmer for 4 to 6 minutes until cheese is melted. Add yogurt and mix well.

Transfer mixture to 2 individual gratin dishes or ramekins. Sprinkle grated Parmesan or Romano cheese on top and place under broiler for 2 to 3 minutes until cheese is lightly browned.

Garnish with lemon wedges. Serve immediately.

Mussels in Spicy Sauce

Serves 6

3 cups canned mussels, drained
6 tablespoons fat-free mayonnaise
6 teaspoons mustard
3 teaspoons sherry
1½ teaspoons lemon juice
3 2½-oz. jars pimiento, chopped

Nutritional Data

PER SERVING:

Calories	161
% calories from fat	22
Fat (gm)	3.9
Sat. Fat (gm)	0.7
Cholesterol (mg)	42.9
Sodium (mg)	548
Protein (gm)	18.7
Carbohydrate (gm)	11.3

Place mussels on platter. Combine remaining ingredients. Spoon sauce over mussels.

EXCHANGES:

Milk	0.0	Bread	0.0
Veg.	0.0	Meat	3.0
Fruit	0.0	Fat	0.0

Salmon-Filled Mushroom Caps

Serves 6 (3 mushrooms each)

1	7½-oz. can salmon without bones
2	tablespoons fine dry bread crumbs
2	tablespoons green onion, finely chopped
2	tablespoons parsley, snipped
18	1½- to 2-inch fresh mushroom caps, washed and well drained
2	tablespoons canned pimiento, diced
3	tablespoons low-fat chicken bouillon

Nutritional Data

PER SERVING:

Calories	71
% calories from fat	25
Fat (gm)	2.3
Sat. Fat (gm)	0.6
Cholesterol (mg)	13.8
Sodium (mg)	205
Protein (gm)	8.9
Carbohydrate (gm)	3.9

EXCHANGES:

Milk	0.0	Bread	0.0
Veg.	0.5	Meat	1.0
Fruit	0.0	Fat	0.0

Preheat oven to 350 degrees. In a small mixing bowl, combine salmon, bread crumbs, green onion, and snipped parsley.

Remove mushroom stems from caps; reserve stems for another recipe. Place mushroom caps in a 15" x 10" x 1" baking pan, crown side down. Mound salmon mixture into caps. Place a little pimiento on top of each cap. Cover and chill 3 to 24 hours.

To serve, uncover, drizzle with bouillon, and bake for 15 to 20 minutes or until tender.

Salmon Fish Mold

Serves 6

1	package (3 ozs.) fat-free cream cheese
1	can (10½ ozs.) cream of mushroom soup
2	envelopes unflavored gelatin
¼	cup water
1	can (7.5 ozs.) salmon, drained and flaked
½	cup celery
½	cup chopped green onions
1	cup fat-free mayonaise
½	cup plain nonfat yogurt
1	green olive, cut in half

Garnishes (optional)

Cucumber slices
Pimiento strips
Chopped parsley
Cherry tomatoes

Nutritional Data

PER SERVING:

Calories	155
% calories from fat	34
Fat (gm)	5.8
Sat. Fat (gm)	1.6
Cholesterol (mg)	16.2
Sodium (mg)	968
Protein (gm)	14.2
Carbohydrate (gm)	10.9

EXCHANGES:

Milk	0.0	Bread	0.0
Veg.	0.0	Meat	1.5
Fruit	0.0	Fat	5.0

Combine cream cheese and soup in double boiler. Heat and stir until smooth. Dissolve gelatin in water according to package directions. Then add gelatin to soup mixture. Fold in remaining ingredients. Blend well and fold into a 5-quart mold. Chill till firm, 4 to 6 hours.

Unmold and garnish as follows: Place half of olive on the eye of the fish. Overlap the cucumber slices to resemble scales along the side of the fish. Decorate the mouth and tail with pimiento strips. Sprinkle parsley along the outer rim of cucumber slices. Decorate platter with cucumber slices and cherry tomatoes.

If serving mold as an appetizer, add zucchini slices or crackers for spreading.

Smoked Salmon Cream Cheese Rolls

Serves 4

¼ lb. smoked salmon (lox), sliced thin (about 4 1-oz. slices)
1 package (4 ozs.) fat-free cream cheese
2 tablespoons capers, chopped
4 large romaine lettuce leaves
  Lemon wedges
8 mini bagels

Nutritional Data

PER SERVING:

Calories	270
% calories from fat	8
Fat (gm)	2.4
Sat. Fat (gm)	0.4
Cholesterol (mg)	9.6
Sodium (mg)	866
Protein (gm)	18
Carbohydrate (gm)	42.9

EXCHANGES:

Milk	0.0	Bread	3.0
Veg.	0.0	Meat	1.0
Fruit	0.0	Fat	0.0

Spread very thin slices of smoked salmon with caper-studded cream cheese; roll up jelly-roll fashion. Cut rolls into 16, ½-inch slices. Place a romaine leaf on a plate. Place 4 salmon rounds in a row down the center of the leaf. Garnish with a lemon wedge. Serve with bagels.

Salmon Ball

Serves 10	Nutritional Data	
	Nutritional Data	
1 15½-oz. can salmon	PER SERVING:	
1 tablespoon lemon juice	Calories	84
1 tablespoon horseradish	% calories from fat	35
1 8-oz. container plain fat-free yogurt	Fat (gm)	3.3
1 tablespoon dried dill weed	Sat. Fat (gm)	0.8
4 green onions, chopped	Cholesterol (mg)	19.6
½ cup parsley, chopped	Sodium (mg)	273
Cucumber slices and celery sticks	Protein (gm)	10.5
	Carbohydrate (gm)	2.5

EXCHANGES:

Milk	0.0	Bread	0.0
Veg.	0.0	Meat	1.5
Fruit	0.0	Fat	0.0

Drain salmon and flake with fork into bowl. Mix in all other ingredients except parsley, cucumber slices, and celery. Shape into ball and roll in parsley flakes. Place on plate surrounded by cucumber slices and celery. *Do not freeze this dish.*

 # Shrimp Cocktail

Serves 8	Nutritional Data	
	Nutritional Data	
8 cups water	PER SERVING:	
¼ cup onion, sliced	Calories	124
1 clove garlic	% calories from fat	8
1 bay leaf	Fat (gm)	1.1
2 celery ribs with leaves	Sat. Fat (gm)	0.3
2 lbs. medium shrimp	Cholesterol (mg)	174
½ lemon, sliced	Sodium (mg)	264
1 recipe Zesty Cocktail Sauce (see p. 514)	Protein (gm)	19.4
	Carbohydrate (gm)	9.7

EXCHANGES:

Milk	0.0	Bread	0.0
Veg.	1.0	Meat	2.0
Fruit	0.0	Fat	0.0

Combine first 5 ingredients in stockpot. Wash, drain, and add shrimp; add lemon. Simmer shrimp about 5 minutes or until pink but not tightly curled. Drain immediately and chill.

Before serving, remove shells, but leave tails intact. Serve with Cocktail Sauce.

To Freeze: Vacuum seal each portion; label and freeze for up to 2 months.

To Serve: Put bags in boiling water, and bring water to a boil again. Boil 10 to 12 minutes.

Oriental Skewered Shrimp

Serves 6	Nutritional Data	
³/₄ cup medium-dry sherry	PER SERVING:	
¹/₄ cup soy sauce	Calories	131
¹/₂ teaspoon ground ginger	% calories from fat	7
36 raw medium shrimp, shelled and	Fat (gm)	0.9
deveined (about 1¹/₄ lbs.)	Sat. Fat (gm)	0.2
Wooden or bamboo skewers, about	Cholesterol (mg)	145.1
9 inches long	Sodium (mg)	523
Cherry tomatoes	Protein (gm)	17
Yellow pickled peppers	Carbohydrate (gm)	5.6
1 teaspoon sugar		

EXCHANGES:			
Milk	0.0	Bread	0.0
Veg.	1.0	Meat	2.0
Fruit	0.0	Fat	0.0

Combine sherry, soy sauce, and ginger. Heat just to boiling. Remove from heat. Cool to room temperature.

Wash shrimp. Thread 3 shrimp lenthwise, through the center, heads doubled up against the tails of each skewer. Thread cherry tomato or yellow pickled pepper at the of each skewer. Place on a platter and brush with sauce on all sides. Refrigerate for 1 hour.

Grill over medium coals for 6 to 10 minutes (can also be placed under the broiler), turning once. Heat remaining sauce to boiling. Remove from heat. Stir in sugar. Brush sauce over shrimp just before serving. Serve piping hot.

Shrimp Remoulade

Serves 12	Nutritional Data	
1¹/₂ lbs. shrimp	PER SERVING:	
¹/₄ cup reduced-fat mayonnaise	Calories	61
1 teaspoon fresh crushed tarragon, or	% calories from fat	29
¹/₂ teaspoon dried tarragon	Fat (gm)	1.9
2 cloves garlic, minced	Sat. Fat (gm)	0.3
1 teaspoon dry mustard	Cholesterol (mg)	88.7
2 teaspoons capers	Sodium (mg)	217
3 small sour pickles, minced	Protein (gm)	9.5
	Carbohydrate (gm)	1.1

EXCHANGES:			
Milk	0.0	Bread	0.0
Veg.	0.0	Meat	1.0
Fruit	0.0	Fat	0.0

Shell, devein, and rinse shrimp. Bring to boil, water in two-thirds-full saucepan. Carefully lower shrimp into water. Reduce heat to simmer.

Continue cooking only until shrimp turn pinkish white (no longer than 5 minutes). Drain.

Place shrimp in glass bowl. Combine remaining ingredients in small mixing bowl. Add dressing to shrimp. Chill overnight, tossing occasionally. Serve cold.

Pickled Scallops

Serves 12

Vegetable cooking spray (olive-oil flavored)
1   tablespoon olive oil, or canola oil
2   lbs. scallops
1   cup onion, sliced into rings
2   cloves garlic, minced
3/4 cup fresh orange juice
1/2 cup fresh lime juice
1/4 teaspoon hot pepper sauce, or to taste
1   orange, sliced thin, seeds removed
1   lime, sliced thin, seeds removed

Nutritional Data

PER SERVING:

Calories	100
% calories from fat	18
Fat (gm)	2.1
Sat. Fat (gm)	0.2
Cholesterol (mg)	32.2
Sodium (mg)	151
Protein (gm)	14.5
Carbohydrate (gm)	6.8

EXCHANGES:

Milk	0.0	Bread	0.0
Veg.	0.0	Meat	2.0
Fruit	0.0	Fat	0.0

Coat large nonstick skillet and heat olive oil. Sauté scallops lightly until opaque and tender. Place scallops in deep glass mixing bowl. Layer onion rings and garlic over scallops.

In small mixing bowl, combine orange juice, lime juice, hot pepper sauce, and orange and lime slices. Pour over scallops. Cover and chill up to 24 hours. Toss occasionally. Serve chilled.

Chapter Two

Soups, Bisques & Gumbos

Beef Stock

Serves 20 (about 3½ quarts)

½ cup dried mushrooms
2 lbs. short ribs of beef
2 lbs. beef marrow bones, cut into pieces
1 lb. ground beef chuck
1 large onion, coarsely chopped
1 clove garlic
4 medium carrots, cut into quarters
2 tablespoons Spike (see "About This Cookbook")
10 peppercorns
1 bay leaf
1 teaspoon basil
1 teaspoon thyme
3 sprigs parsley
3 stalks celery
1 cup dry red wine
1 tablespoon soy sauce
Water

Nutritional Data

PER SERVING:

Calories	24
% calories from fat	19
Fat (gm)	0.5
Sat. Fat (gm)	0.2
Cholesterol (mg)	3.2
Sodium (mg)	64
Protein (gm)	2.3
Carbohydrate (gm)	0.5

EXCHANGES:

Milk	0.0	Bread	0.0
Veg.	0.0	Meat	0.0
Fruit	0.0	Fat	0.0

Soak dried mushrooms in 1 cup of warm water for 15 minutes. Put all ingredients, including water in which mushrooms were soaked, into a 6- or 8-quart stockpot. Cover with cold water, 2 inches over ingredients. Place a loose-fitting lid on top and bring to a boil. Immediately adjust heat to a simmer, and cook for 3 to 4 hours. Turn off heat and cool.

When cool, strain stock into container and refrigerate. When cold, remove and discard all fat congealed on surface. Refrigerate stock for immediate use; or freeze for future use.

To Freeze: Divide into 3 or 4 portions and place in microwave-safe containers; label and freeze for up to 2 months.

To Serve: Thaw. Cover with microwave-safe plastic wrap, and cook on High for 3 to 5 minutes.

Chicken Stock

Serves 16 (about 4 quarts)

1 4-lb. chicken or 5-lb. fowl
2½ lbs. chicken necks and wings
1 veal knuckle, cracked (optional)
2 medium onions, stuck with several cloves
6 medium carrots, cut into quarters
2 medium leeks, cut into 1-inch pieces
3 stalks celery, including leaves
½ teaspoon basil

Nutritional Data

PER SERVING:

Calories	35
% calories from fat	25
Fat (gm)	0.9
Sat. Fat (gm)	0.3
Cholesterol (mg)	10
Sodium (mg)	11
Protein (gm)	3.3
Carbohydrate (gm)	0.8

½	teaspoon thyme	EXCHANGES:			
½	teaspoon tarragon	Milk	0.0	Bread	0.0
1	clove garlic	Veg.	0.0	Meat	0.5
2	tablespoons Spike (see "About This Cookbook")	Fruit	0.0	Fat	0.0
10	peppercorns				
6	sprigs parsley				
1	cup dry white wine				
	Cold water				

Place all ingredients into large 10-quart stockpot. Cover with cold water, 2 inches over ingredients. Place loose-fitting lid on top and bring to boil. Immediately adjust heat to simmer, and cook 3 to 4 hours. Turn off heat and cool.

When cool, strain stock into container and refrigerate. When cold, remove and discard all fat congealed on surface. Refrigerate stock for immediate use, or freeze for future use.

To Freeze: Divide into 3 or 4 portions and place in microwave-safe containers; label and freeze for up to 2 months.

To Serve: Thaw. Cover with microwave-safe plastic wrap, and cook on High for 3 to 5 minutes.

Fish Stock

	Serves 4 (about 4 cups)	***Nutritional Data***	
1½	lbs. fresh or frozen fish	PER SERVING:	
1	medium onion, finely chopped	Calories	47
3	stalks celery with leaves, cut in half	% calories from fat	2
1	medium carrot, finely diced	Fat (gm)	0.1
3	sprigs parsley	Sat. Fat (gm)	0
3	slices lemon	Cholesterol (mg)	6.7
8	peppercorns	Sodium (mg)	15
2	teaspoons Spike (see "About This Cookbook")	Protein (gm)	2.9
		Carbohydrate (gm)	1.3
¾	cup white wine		
3	cups cold water	EXCHANGES:	

EXCHANGES:			
Milk	0.0	Bread	0.0
Veg.	0.0	Meat	0.5
Fruit	0.0	Fat	0.0

Put all ingredients into stockpot. Bring to boil. Cover with loose-fitting lid, and immediately adjust heat to simmer. Cook for 30 minutes. Turn off heat and cool.

When cool, strain into container. Refrigerate stock if you are planning to use it within a day or two. Otherwise, store in freezer for future use.

To Freeze: Place in microwave-safe container; label and freeze for up to 2 months.

To Serve: Thaw and use as desired, or microwave on High 3 to 4 minutes.

Low-Salt Vegetable Stock

Serves 12 (about 9 cups)

Canola oil, or vegetable cooking spray
4   cloves garlic, crushed
2   cups onions, roughly chopped
3   ribs celery, sliced
3   cups carrots, peeled and sliced
1   cup turnip, sliced
1   cup raw potato, peeled and cubed
½   cup parsley, chopped
2   bay leaves
½   teaspoon each ingredient: thyme, pepper

Nutritional Data

PER SERVING:

Calories	4
% calories from fat	3
Fat (gm)	0
Sat. Fat (gm)	0
Cholesterol (mg)	0
Sodium (mg)	3
Protein (gm)	0.1
Carbohydrate (gm)	1.1

EXCHANGES:

Milk	0.0	Bread	0.0
Veg.	0.0	Meat	0.0
Fruit	0.0	Fat	0.0

Coat stockpot with canola oil or cooking spray. Sauté garlic, onions, and celery 5 minutes, covered, over medium heat, stirring occasionally. Add remaining ingredients and continue cooking 5 minutes. Add 3 quarts water. Bring stock to boil; reduce heat to simmer. Continue cooking 1¾ hours or until done. Stir stock occasionally.

When soup is cool, strain through double layer of cheesecloth. Use remaining vegetables as side dish or in stew. Store cooked stock in refrigerator or freezer.

Spicy Beef and Cabbage Soup

Serves 8

¾   lb. ground beef round
1   large onion, finely chopped
1   large clove garlic, minced
4   cups beef bouillon, reconstituted
     from cubes
3   cups water
2   celery stalks, including leaves,
     thinly sliced
2   large carrots, thinly sliced
3   bay leaves
1   15-oz. can reduced-sodium tomato
     sauce, or regular tomato sauce

Nutritional Data

PER SERVING:

Calories	172
% calories from fat	30
Fat (gm)	5.8
Sat. Fat (gm)	2.1
Cholesterol (mg)	26
Sodium (mg)	523
Protein (gm)	10.8
Carbohydrate (gm)	20.1

EXCHANGES:

Milk	0.0	Bread	0.5
Veg.	2.0	Meat	1.0
Fruit	0.0	Fat	0.5

3 cups cabbage, grated or very
   finely shredded
½ teaspoon dry mustard
2 tablespoons apple cider vinegar
2 tablespoons sugar
½ teaspoon dried thyme leaves
½ teaspoon dried marjoram leaves
¼ teaspoon ground cinnamon
⅛ teaspoon ground cloves
½ teaspoon black pepper
⅓ cup uncooked white rice
   Salt to taste

In large heavy soup pot, combine ground round, onion, and garlic. Cook over medium heat, stirring frequently, until meat is browned. Remove pot from heat. Turn meat and onion mixture out onto large plate covered with paper towels. When paper towels have absorbed the fat, return meat mixture to pot.

Add all remaining ingredients except rice. Bring to boil over high heat and simmer, covered, 15 minutes. Add rice. Lower heat, cover and simmer about 25 minutes or until cabbage and rice are cooked and flavors are well blended. Add salt if desired. Skim off and discard remaining fat from top of soup.

Keeps 4 to 5 days in refrigerator.

Cabbage Soup

Serves 6

1 medium cabbage head
2 large onions
2 carrots
1 large potato, peeled
3 cups skim milk
2 tablespoons low-fat yogurt
1 bay leaf
½ teaspoon dill weed
½ teaspoon rosemary
   Pepper, freshly ground to taste

Nutritional Data

PER SERVING:

Calories	135
% calories from fat	5
Fat (gm)	0.8
Sat. Fat (gm)	0.2
Cholesterol (mg)	2.3
Sodium (mg)	112
Protein (gm)	8.7
Carbohydrate (gm)	25.9

EXCHANGES:

Milk	0.5	Bread	0.5
Veg.	4.0	Meat	0.0
Fruit	0.0	Fat	0.0

Shred cabbage. Thinly slice onions, carrots, and potato. Place vegetables in heavy saucepan with small amount of water. Cover and cook slowly until tender.

Add milk, yogurt, bay leaf, dill weed, rosemary, and pepper. Continue to cook about 15 minutes longer.

Borscht

Serves 14 (1-cup servings)

4	lbs. beef shank
1	large marrow bone
1	tablespoon salt
1	can (1 lb.) tomatoes, undrained
1	medium onion, quartered
1	stalk celery, cut up
3	parsley sprigs
10	whole black peppercorns
2	bay leaves
3	cups coarsely shredded cabbage (1 lb.)
1½	cups thickly sliced, peeled carrot (4 medium)
1	cup onion, chopped
2	tablespoons fresh dill, or 3 teaspoons dried dill
⅓	cup cider vinegar
1	can (1 lb.) julienne beets, undrained
1½	teaspoons salt
2	packets Equal® (see "About This Cookbook")
	Dairy sour cream
	Snipped fresh dill or dried basil

Nutritional Data

PER SERVING:

Calories	215
% calories from fat	25
Fat (gm)	5.9
Sat. Fat (gm)	2.1
Cholesterol (mg)	69.3
Sodium (mg)	891
Protein (gm)	31.3
Carbohydrate (gm)	8.3

EXCHANGES:

Milk	0.0	Bread	0.0
Veg.	1.0	Meat	3.5
Fruit	0.0	Fat	0.0

Place beef, marrow bone, 1 tablespoon salt, and 2 quarts of water in 8-quart kettle. Bring to boiling. Reduce heat; simmer covered, 1 hour.

Add tomatoes, quartered onion, celery, parsley, black pepper, and bay leaves; simmer covered 2 hours.

Remove from heat. Lift out beef. Discard marrow bone. Strain soup into colander. (There should be 9 or 10 cups.) Return soup and beef to kettle.

Add cabbage, carrot, chopped onion, 2 tablespoons dill, vinegar, beets, and 1½ teaspoons salt. Bring to boiling. Reduce heat; simmer covered 30 minutes, or until beef and vegetables are tender. Remove from heat and stir in Equal®.

Refrigerate overnight. Next day, trim off fat. To serve, heat and garnish with dollops of sour cream and dill.

🗑 *Easy Goulash Soup*

Serves 8

1 large onion, finely chopped
1 large carrot, thinly sliced
1 large celery stalk, diced
2 large cloves garlic, minced
2 cups potatoes, peeled and diced
1 cup ³/₄-inch-long fresh green bean pieces,
   or 1 cup French-style frozen green beans
2 tablespoons pearl barley
1 lb. beef round, trimmed and cut into
   ³/₄-inch cubes
5 cups water
4 beef bouillon cubes
1 bay leaf
2 teaspoons sugar
1¹/₂ teaspoons paprika
¹/₂ teaspoon dry mustard
¹/₂ teaspoon dried thyme
¹/₄ teaspoon black pepper
1 15-oz. can reduced-sodium tomato sauce,
   or regular tomato sauce
2 tablespoons tomato paste
   Salt to taste

Nutritional Data

PER SERVING:

Calories	181
% calories from fat	14
Fat (gm)	2.8
Sat. Fat (gm)	0.8
Cholesterol (mg)	30.3
Sodium (mg)	551
Protein (gm)	14.9
Carbohydrate (gm)	25.3

EXCHANGES:

Milk	0.0	Bread	1.0
Veg.	2.0	Meat	1.0
Fruit	0.0	Fat	0.0

Combine onion, carrot, celery, garlic, potatoes, green beans, barley, beef, water, bouillon cubes, bay leaf, sugar, paprika, mustard, thyme, and pepper in crockpot. Cook on high setting 1 hour. Change setting to low and cook an additional 7 or 8 hours.

In medium-size bowl, stir together tomato sauce and tomato paste until well combined. Add to mixture. Cook an additional 1 to 1¹/₂ hours on high setting. Taste soup. Add salt if desired. Stir before serving.

This soup keeps 4 to 5 days in refrigerator.

🗑 *Chicken Gumbo*

Serves 6

1 10-oz. package frozen black-eyed peas,
   rinsed under hot water and thoroughly
   drained
2 large onions, finely chopped
1 medium pork hock (about ³/₄ lb.)
1 lb. chicken breasts, boneless, skinless,
   and all visible fat removed
2 large celery stalks, chopped

Nutritional Data

PER SERVING:

Calories	263
% calories from fat	12
Fat (gm)	3.6
Sat. Fat (gm)	0.8
Cholesterol (mg)	36.2
Sodium (mg)	789
Protein (gm)	21.6
Carbohydrate (gm)	39.5

		EXCHANGES:			
½	cup diced red bell pepper (if unavailable, substitute green bell pepper)	Milk	0.0	Bread	2.0
3	tablespoons uncooked long-grain white rice	Veg.	2.0	Meat	1.5
		Fruit	0.0	Fat	0.0
1	large bay leaf				
1	10-oz. package frozen succotash, rinsed under hot water and thoroughly drained				
1	cup frozen sliced okra, rinsed under cool water and thoroughly drained				
4	cups chicken bouillon reconstituted from chicken bouillon cubes and hot water				
1	15-oz. can tomatoes, undrained				
2	tablespoons parsley leaves, finely chopped (optional)				
¼	teaspoon dried thyme leaves				
¼	teaspoon black pepper				

In order listed, put peas, onions, pork hock, chicken, celery, red pepper, rice, bay leaf, succotash, okra, and bouillon into crockpot. Cover pot and turn to high setting. Cook 30 minutes. Then continue cooking on high 3 hours longer, or reduce heat to low and continue cooking 7 hours longer.

Using slotted spoon, remove chicken pieces from pot and set aside to cool. Discard pork hock and bay leaf. Stir juice from tomatoes into pot. Chop tomatoes and stir them into pot, along with parsley, thyme, and pepper. Continue cooking on low about 15 minutes longer until soup is thoroughly heated.

When chicken is cool enough to handle, cut it into bite-size pieces. Stir chicken into gumbo and cook several minutes longer until very hot. If gumbo is too thick, thin with a little hot water before serving.

Keeps up to 2 days in refrigerator.

Chinese Hot Pot

Serves 8

4	13¾-oz. cans low-sodium condensed chicken broth		
1	cup white wine		
¼	cup Tamari soy sauce		
2	3½-oz. packages Oriental-style noodles (without flavor packets)		
8	ozs. Oriental-style vegetables, such as mushrooms, carrots, broccoli		
1	jar baby corn		
1	cup fresh pea pods		
1	lb. chicken breasts, boneless, skinless, and cut into bite-size pieces		
1-2	teaspoons sugar, to taste		

Nutritional Data

PER SERVING:

Calories	200
% calories from fat	6
Fat (gm)	1.4
Sat. Fat (gm)	0.3
Cholesterol (mg)	22.9
Sodium (mg)	574
Protein (gm)	11.6
Carbohydrate (gm)	30.3

EXCHANGES:

Milk	0.0	Bread	2.0
Veg.	0.0	Meat	1.0
Fruit	0.0	Fat	0.0

1   bunch watercress, trimmed
4   green onions, cut into 1-inch lengths

Combine broth, wine, soy, and sugar in 5-quart skillet or stovetop casserole. Break noodles in half; add to skillet with vegetables, corn, pea pods, and chicken. Bring to boil. Reduce heat to medium-low; cook 3 minutes. Remove pan from heat. Stir in sugar, watercress and onions. Serve immediately.

Egg Drop Soup

Serves 8

2   scallions
2   egg whites
2   tablespoons cornstarch
2   tablespoons water
6   cups Chicken Stock (see p. 40)
   White pepper to taste

Nutritional Data	
PER SERVING:	
Calories	39
% calories from fat	17
Fat (gm)	0.7
Sat. Fat (gm)	0.2
Cholesterol (mg)	7.6
Sodium (mg)	22
Protein (gm)	3.4
Carbohydrate (gm)	2.6

EXCHANGES:			
Milk	0.0	Bread	0.0
Veg.	0.5	Meat	0.5
Fruit	0.0	Fat	0.0

Wash and cut scallions into 1-inch pieces. Set aside. Beat egg whites thoroughly. Set aside.

Dissolve 1 tablespoon cornstarch in 2 tablespoons cold water. Heat Chicken Stock in saucepan until it boils. Add cornstarch slowly until stock thickens gradually. Add scallions, and stir a few times. Remove from heat. Stir in egg whites with a fork. Serve, letting each person add pepper to taste.

To Freeze: Place in microwave-safe container; label and freeze for up to 2 months.

To Serve: Thaw. Cover with microwave-safe plastic wrap and cook on High for 3 to 5 minutes.

Chicken-in-the-Pot

Serves 8

1   5-lb. chicken, whole
   Water to cover
3½   quarts water
1   large onion, studded with 1 whole clove
8   medium carrots, peeled
6   leeks, washed and trimmed
8   stalks celery
8   sprigs parsley
½   cup mushrooms, sliced
½   lb. small white onions
   Rice, cooked (4 cups)

Nutritional Data	
PER SERVING:	
Calories	362
% calories from fat	18
Fat (gm)	7.1
Sat. Fat (gm)	1.9
Cholesterol (mg)	80.4
Sodium (mg)	133
Protein (gm)	30.7
Carbohydrate (gm)	42.8

EXCHANGES:			
Milk	0.0	Bread	2.0
Veg.	3.0	Meat	2.5
Fruit	0.0	Fat	0.0

Clean chicken and truss legs and wings. Place in large soup kettle, add water to cover, and bring to boil. Cook for a few minutes. Remove chicken and discard water. Wash kettle and return chicken. Cover chicken with 3½ quarts water, and skim scum that rises to surface as chicken cooks. When no more scum appears, simmer chicken, covered, 1 hour.

Peel onion, stud with clove, and add to chicken together with 1 carrot, 2 leeks, 2 celery stalks, and ½ the parsley. Continue to simmer soup for 1 more hour. Correct seasonings. Remove chicken and set aside to keep warm.

Using a fine sieve, strain soup into a clean kettle, discarding vegetables. Add remaining carrots, leeks, celery, and parsley to kettle, and simmer until vegetables are tender. Add mushrooms and white onions and simmer another 20 minutes or until vegetables are tender.

Cut chicken into serving pieces and place in wide, deep bowls. Arrange some vegetables and ½ cup rice in each bowl; ladle hot soup over all. Serve immediately.

Matzoh Ball and Vegetable Soup

Serves 6

Matzoh Balls

1 large egg plus 2 large egg whites
1 tablespoon canola, safflower, or corn oil
½ cup plus 1 tablespoon matzoh meal
¼ teaspoon (generous) salt
2½ tablespoons Chicken Stock (see p. 40), or broth (defatted)

Soup

6-8 cups Chicken Stock (see p. 40), or broth (defatted)
1 stalk celery, diced
1 large carrot, diced
1 cup frozen lima beans
1½ cups small cauliflower pieces
⅛ teaspoon black pepper

Nutritional Data

PER SERVING:

Calories	164
% calories from fat	24
Fat (gm)	4.4
Sat. Fat (gm)	0.8
Cholesterol (mg)	45.9
Sodium (mg)	180
Protein (gm)	9.3
Carbohydrate (gm)	19.4

EXCHANGES:

Milk	0.0	Bread	1.0
Veg.	1.0	Meat	0.5
Fruit	0.0	Fat	1.0

To prepare matzoh balls, in small bowl, lightly beat egg, egg whites, and oil together, using a fork. Add matzoh meal, salt, and 2½ tablespoons Chicken Stock. Stir with medium-size spoon to combine well, making sure matzoh meal is completely moistened. Cover mixture and refrigerate at least 1 hour or up to 6 hours.

When matzoh ball mixture is thoroughly chilled, bring 3 quarts of water to boil in large pot. To form matzoh balls, scoop up about 2 teaspoons of matzoh ball mixture and shape into a 1¼-inch ball with moistened fingers. Make sure ball is fairly round and smooth, but do not press it together too tightly. Drop matzoh ball into boiling water. Repeat with remaining mixture, making 12 balls. Cover pot, reduce heat, and gently boil matzoh balls 30 to 35 minutes.

After matzoh balls begin to cook, combine remaining soup stock, celery, carrot, lima beans, cauliflower, and black pepper in Dutch oven or soup pot. Bring it to a boil over medium-high heat. Cover, reduce heat, and cook about 20 to 25 minutes.

When matzoh balls are done, remove them from cooking water with slotted spoon and gently place them in Chicken Stock. Cover and simmer 4 to 5 minutes.

Greek Lemon Soup

Serves 4

- 1 quart low-sodium chicken broth
- 1 tablespoon cornstarch
- ¼ cup uncooked rice
- 4 tablespoons fresh lemon juice
- Egg substitute equivalent to 3 eggs

Nutritional Data

PER SERVING:

Calories	102
% calories from fat	7
Fat (gm)	0.8
Sat. Fat (gm)	0
Cholesterol (mg)	0
Sodium (mg)	148
Protein (gm)	8.3
Carbohydrate (gm)	15

EXCHANGES:

Milk	0.0	Bread	1.0
Veg.	0.0	Meat	0.5
Fruit	0.0	Fat	0.0

Take 1 cup chicken broth and stir in cornstarch. After cornstarch has dissolved, pour into saucepan and add rest of chicken broth. Heat broth on medium heat, add rice, and cook until tender. Remove from heat.

Bring egg substitute to room temperature. Beat lemon juice into egg substitute. Whisk half the broth, a little at a time, into egg substitute mixture. Pour egg substitute mixture back into remaining broth, mixing well. Return to low heat and cook, stirring constantly, just until soup is thickened.

Malaysian-Style Chicken and Scallion Soup

Serves 6

5½ cups Chicken Stock (see p. 40), or broth, defatted, divided
2 tablespoons fresh ginger root, peeled and coarsely chopped
1 large clove garlic, minced
1 lemon slice, ¼-inch thick
½ teaspoon (generous) anise seeds
½ teaspoon coriander seeds
¼ teaspoon cumin seeds
¼ teaspoon whole black peppercorns
2 medium chicken breast halves, skinless, boneless, and cut into 1-inch-long by ⅛-inch-thick strips
1 cup green onions (scallions), including tops, coarsely shredded
  Chopped fresh cilantro for garnish (optional)

Nutritional Data

PER SERVING:

Calories	87
% calories from fat	21
Fat (gm)	2
Sat. Fat (gm)	0.5
Cholesterol (mg)	33.6
Sodium (mg)	32.6
Protein (gm)	12.4
Carbohydrate (gm)	2.4

EXCHANGES:

Milk	0.0	Bread	0.0
Veg.	0.5	Meat	1.5
Fruit	0.0	Fat	0.0

In large pot over high heat, combine 5 cups stock, ginger root, garlic, lemon slice, anise, coriander, cumin, and peppercorns. Bring mixture to boil; lower heat and simmer, covered, for 30 minutes.

Meanwhile, in small saucepan, combine remaining ½ cup stock and chicken pieces. Bring to simmer over medium-high heat. Lower heat and gently poach chicken covered, 2 to 3 minutes or until pieces are just cooked through. Turn out chicken into a colander, discarding stock. Thoroughly rinse chicken to remove any scum. Set aside to drain.

Strain simmered broth-herb mixture through very fine sieve, discarding seasoning ingredients. Rinse out large pot previously used and return strained broth and green onions to it. Simmer 2 minutes. Add chicken and simmer 1 minute longer.

Serve in small bowls or cups. Garnish servings with chopped cilantro leaves if desired.

Mulligatawny

Serves 6

2 teaspoons canola, safflower, or corn oil
2 large onions, coarsely chopped
2 large celery stalks, coarsely chopped
1 large clove garlic, minced
4 cups Chicken Stock (see p. 40), or broth, defatted
2 large Winesap or other tart, flavorful apples, peeled and coarsely chopped
2 medium carrots, coarsely chopped
1/4 cup parsley leaves, coarsely chopped
2 tablespoons sweet red bell pepper (if unavailable, substitute sweet green bell pepper), coarsely chopped
1 cup water
1/2 cup all-purpose potatoes, peeled and diced
2 1/2 teaspoons curry powder
1 teaspoon chili powder
1/2 teaspoon ground allspice
1/4 teaspoon dried thyme leaves
1/4 teaspoon black pepper, preferably freshly ground
1 1/2 lbs. bony chicken pieces (wings, backs, etc.)
1 lb. (2 medium) chicken breast halves, skinless
1 1/4 cups canned tomatoes, chopped
Salt to taste
Finely chopped parsley leaves for garnish (optional)

Nutritional Data

PER SERVING:

Calories	200
% calories from fat	22
Fat (gm)	5
Sat. Fat (gm)	1
Cholesterol (mg)	40.8
Sodium (mg)	148
Protein (gm)	16.7
Carbohydrate (gm)	22

EXCHANGES:

Milk	0.0	Bread	0.5
Veg.	3.0	Meat	1.5
Fruit	0.0	Fat	0.0

Combine oil, onions, celery, and garlic in large pot. Cook over medium heat, stirring, 4 to 5 minutes until onions are limp. Add 1 tablespoon Chicken Stock if needed to prevent vegetables from burning. Add apples, carrots, parsley, and sweet peppers and cook, stirring, 3 to 4 minutes longer. Stir in remaining stock, water, potatoes, curry powder, chili powder, allspice, thyme, and pepper. Add chicken. Bring mixture to boil; then lower heat and simmer, covered, 1 hour and 10 minutes.

Remove pot from heat. Remove chicken from pot; discard bony pieces and set breasts aside to cool. Skim off and discard fat on soup surface, using large, shallow spoon. Stir in tomatoes.

Using a measuring cup, scoop about 2 cups vegetables and liquid from pot and transfer to blender or food processor.

Blend or process until mixture is completely pureed. Return puree to pot.

When chicken breasts are cool enough to handle, remove meat from bones and cut into bite-size pieces. Return it to pot, and add salt if desired. Reheat mixture until piping hot. Garnish with parsley.

Keeps 3 days in refrigerator.

Spicy North African-Style Chicken Soup

Serves 7

2	teaspoons olive oil
3	cups red onion (if unavailable, substitute yellow onion), coarsely chopped
2	large cloves garlic, minced
5	cups Chicken Stock (see p. 40), or broth, defatted and divided
1	cup water
2	chicken breast halves, skins removed (about 1 lb.)
2	large celery stalks, thinly sliced
1/2	cup parsley leaves, finely chopped
1	14 1/2-16-oz. can tomatoes, undrained
1	cinnamon stick, 3 inches long
2	large bay leaves
3/4	teaspoon dried marjoram leaves
1	teaspoon dried thyme leaves
1/8	teaspoon ground cloves
	Dash (generous) cayenne pepper
1/4	teaspoon black pepper
1/2	cup (scant) dry bulgur wheat, or brown rice

Nutritional Data

PER SERVING:

Calories	166
% calories from fat	19
Fat (gm)	3.6
Sat. Fat (gm)	0.7
Cholesterol (mg)	33.4
Sodium (mg)	143
Protein (gm)	14.8
Carbohydrate (gm)	17.9

EXCHANGES:

Milk	0.0	Bread	0.5
Veg.	2.0	Meat	1.5
Fruit	0.0	Fat	0.0

In large pot, combine olive oil, onion, garlic, and 3 tablespoons of Chicken Stock. Cook over medium heat, stirring frequently, about 5 or 6 minutes or until onion is tender. Add remaining stock, water, chicken, celery, and parsley; then add tomatoes, breaking them up with large spoon. Add cinnamon stick, bay leaves, marjoram, thyme, ground cloves, cayenne, and black pepper. Stir to mix well.

Bring mixture to boil. Lower heat, cover, and simmer about 35 to 40 minutes or until mixture is tender. With a slotted spoon, remove chicken and reserve it in medium-size bowl. Remove cinnamon stick and bay leaves and discard. With a large, shallow spoon, skim fat from top of soup and discard.

Bring soup to boil. Stir in bulgur wheat. Lower heat and simmer an additional 40 to 45 minutes until bulgur is tender. Meanwhile, remove chicken meat from bones, and cut it into bite-size pieces. When bulgur is tender, return chicken to pot and simmer an additional 2 to 3 minutes.

Keeps 3 to 4 days in refrigerator.

Lamb and White Bean Soup

Serves 8

1½	cups dry Great Northern or navy beans, sorted and washed
2	lamb shanks (about 1¾ lbs. total), cracked
6	cups beef bouillon reconstituted from cubes
2	cups water
2	large carrots, sliced
2	large celery stalks, sliced
1	large onion, very finely chopped
2	large cloves garlic, minced
3	bay leaves
1½	teaspoons dried thyme leaves
1¼	teaspoons dried marjoram leaves
½	teaspoon (scant) ground celery seed
½	teaspoon dry mustard
¼	teaspoon black pepper
3	cups cabbage, thinly sliced
	Salt to taste

Nutritional Data

PER SERVING:

Calories	193
% calories from fat	20
Fat (gm)	4.4
Sat. Fat (gm)	1.3
Cholesterol (mg)	59.4
Sodium (mg)	763
Protein (gm)	22.9
Carbohydrate (gm)	16.6

EXCHANGES:

Milk	0.0	Bread	0.5
Veg.	2.0	Meat	2.0
Fruit	0.0	Fat	0.0

Put beans in large heavy pot and cover with about 2 inches of cold water. Bring to a boil over high heat. Cover, lower heat, and simmer 2 minutes. Remove pot from heat and let stand at room temperature for 1 hour. Drain beans in colander and discard soaking water.

Return beans to pot in which they were cooked. Add all remaining ingredients except cabbage and salt. Bring to boil, lower heat, and simmer 1 hour. Add cabbage and simmer an additional 30 to 40 minutes until beans are very tender.

Remove and discard bay leaves. With slotted spoon, remove bones and meat to a medium-size bowl. When shanks are cool enough to handle, cut lean meat into bite-size pieces and return them to pot.

Refrigerate soup overnight. Before serving, use a large, shallow spoon to remove solidified fat from top of pot. A few shreds of cabbage will come away with the fat and can be discarded, too. Reheat soup carefully over medium heat, stirring constantly to prevent burning. Add salt if desired.

Keeps 4 to 5 days in refrigerator.

Chinese Pork and Watercress Soup

Serves 6

2½ ozs. fresh pork loin, well trimmed and cut into very thin 1-inch-long strips

1 small clove garlic, halved

1 ¼-inch-thick slice fresh ginger root, peeled

5½ cups Chicken Stock (see p. 40), or broth, defatted and divided

4-5 scallions, including 1 inch of green top, quartered lengthwise and cut into 1-inch lengths

1 tablespoon dry sherry

1 teaspoon reduced-salt soy sauce

⅔ cup cooked white rice

1½ cups (lightly packed) fresh, tender watercress sprigs

Nutritional Data

PER SERVING:

Calories	72
% calories from fat	21
Fat (gm)	1.6
Sat. Fat (gm)	0.5
Cholesterol (mg)	13.7
Sodium (mg)	46.7
Protein (gm)	5.3
Carbohydrate (gm)	6.1

EXCHANGES:

Milk	0.0	Bread	0.5
Veg.	0.0	Meat	0.5
Fruit	0.0	Fat	0.0

Combine pork strips, garlic clove halves, and ginger root in small saucepan. Add ½ cup of stock and bring mixture to simmer over medium-high heat. Simmer, covered, 6 to 7 minutes or until pork is cooked through. Remove pan from heat.

Using slotted spoon, transfer pork strips to colander. Rinse pork thoroughly under cool water to remove any froth; set aside to drain. Strain broth used to cook pork through a very fine sieve into 2- to 3-quart saucepan; discard garlic and ginger root.

Add remaining 5 cups of stock, scallions, sherry, soy sauce, and rice to sieved broth. Bring mixture to a boil. Then lower heat and simmer, covered, for 2 minutes.

Stir in watercress. Remove pan from heat and let stand 30 seconds or until watercress is wilted but not cooked. Serve immediately.

Caldo de Peixe
(Fish Soup)

Serves 8

1   teaspoon Spike (see "About This Cookbook")
2-3 green (unripe) bananas, sliced in rounds
1   yellow onion, sliced
2   tablespoons olive oil
2   cloves garlic, minced
1   bay leaf
1   chili pepper, or ½ teaspoon cayenne pepper
1   bunch parsley, finely chopped
2   large tomatoes, chopped
4   cups hot water
¼   cup tapioca flour, or "minute" tapioca
¼   cup dry bread crumbs
½   small cabbage, chopped
4-6 large potatoes, chopped in chunks
4-6 sweet potatoes, chopped in chunks
2   lbs. fish, without bones: flounder, salmon, orange roughy, halibut

Nutritional Data

PER SERVING:

Calories	348
% calories from fat	17
Fat (gm)	6.6
Sat. Fat (gm)	1
Cholesterol (mg)	36.4
Sodium (mg)	105
Protein (gm)	27.7
Carbohydrate (gm)	45.5

EXCHANGES:

Milk	0.0	Bread	2.0
Veg.	1.0	Meat	2.5
Fruit	0.5	Fat	0.0

Place Spike in mixing bowl and add bananas. Pour in enough water to cover banana pieces. Soak 10 to 15 minutes to draw out "pucker" quality of unripe fruit.

In deep skillet, brown onion in oil over moderate heat. Add garlic, bay leaf, chili pepper, parsley, and tomatoes, and sauté for several minutes, stirring frequently. Stir in 4 cups hot water.

In separate bowl, use some of hot broth to whisk tapioca flour into a thin, smooth paste. Bring soup in skillet almost to boil, and add paste and bread crumbs, stirring vigorously. Immediately reduce heat to simmer.

Drain bananas and add them to skillet along with cabbage and potatoes. Gently lay in fish, cover with water, and simmer 20 to 30 minutes or until everything is cooked.

Cioppino Mediterranean

Serves 6

- ¼ cup chopped green bell pepper
- 2 tablespoons finely chopped onion
- 1 clove garlic, minced
- 1 tablespoon oil
- 1 16-oz. can tomatoes, undrained, cut up
- 1 16-oz. can tomato sauce
- ½ cup dry red wine
- 3 tablespoons snipped parsley
- ½ teaspoon salt
- ¼ teaspoon oregano
- ¼ teaspoon basil
  Dash pepper
- 1 lb. frozen or fresh flounder fillets (thawed if frozen)
- 1 4½-oz. can shrimp, drained
- 1 7½-oz. can minced clams, undrained
- 2 packets Equal® (see "About This Cookbook")

Nutritional Data

PER SERVING:

Calories	218
% calories from fat	19
Fat (gm)	4.5
Sat. Fat (gm)	0.7
Cholesterol (mg)	96.1
Sodium (mg)	903
Protein (gm)	28.6
Carbohydrate (gm)	12.6

EXCHANGES:

Milk	0.0	Bread	0.0
Veg.	2.0	Meat	3.5
Fruit	0.0	Fat	0.0

In large saucepan, cook green pepper, onion, and garlic in oil until tender, but not brown. Add undrained tomatoes, tomato sauce, wine, parsley, salt, oregano, basil, and pepper. Bring to boiling. Reduce heat; cover and simmer 20 minutes.

Cut fillets into pieces. Add flounder to broth; simmer 5 minutes. Add shrimp and undrained clams; continue simmering covered about 3 minutes more. Remove from heat and stir in Equal®.

*Hearty Fish Soup or Red Clam Chowder**

Serves 8

- Vegetable cooking spray
- 2 celery stalks, chopped
- 2 carrots, sliced
- 1 green bell pepper, chopped
- 1⅓ qts. canned low-sodium tomatoes
- 1 6-oz. bottle clam juice
- 3 medium potatoes, peeled and diced
- ½ teaspoon black pepper, freshly ground
- 1 teaspoon oregano
- 6 fresh basil leaves, torn up
- ½ lb. fillet of sole, cut into bite-size pieces
- ½ lb. flounder, cut into bite-size pieces

Nutritional Data

PER SERVING:

Calories	138
% calories from fat	6
Fat (gm)	0.9
Sat. Fat (gm)	0.2
Cholesterol (mg)	15.4
Sodium (mg)	94
Protein (gm)	8.8
Carbohydrate (gm)	20.3

EXCHANGES:

Milk	0.0	Bread	0.5
Veg.	2.0	Meat	1.0
Fruit	0.0	Fat	0.0

½ lb. orange roughy, cut into
  bite-size pieces
1 cup dry white wine
6 tablespoons parsley, chopped
6 basil leaves, chopped, for garnish

Coat large stockpot with vegetable cooking spray. Add onion, celery, carrots, and green pepper. Cook until just *al dente*. Add tomatoes, clam juice, and potatoes. Cook over medium heat 5 minutes. Add pepper, oregano, and basil. Cover and simmer 20 minutes or until potatoes are done.

Add fish and wine, cover, and continue simmering 10 minutes. Sprinkle with chopped parsley and add additional basil before serving.

Note: To make clam chowder, substitute 6 10-oz. cans minced clams or 4 lbs. fresh clams for the fish. Add clams just before serving.

15-Minute Soup

Serves 6

Vegetable cooking spray
½ medium onion, finely chopped
2 cloves garlic, chopped
4 thin slices day-old bread
2 medium tomatoes, peeled, seeded, and finely chopped
3 cups low-sodium fish stock, or clam juice
3 cups water
Pepper, freshly ground
1 teaspoon paprika
½ cup dry sherry
24 clams or mussels in the shell, cleaned
2 tablespoons parsley, finely chopped, for garnish

Nutritional Data

PER SERVING:

Calories	143
% calories from fat	9
Fat (gm)	1.5
Sat. Fat (gm)	0.3
Cholesterol (mg)	21.9
Sodium (mg)	121
Protein (gm)	10.5
Carbohydrate (gm)	14.1

EXCHANGES:

Milk	0.0	Bread	0.5
Veg.	1.0	Meat	1.5
Fruit	0.0	Fat	0.0

Coat large saucepan with vegetable cooking spray, and sauté onion until soft. Add garlic and bread and sauté for a few minutes longer. Add tomatoes and sauté briefly, stirring. Stir in fish stock or clam juice and water, and season to taste with pepper. Add paprika, sherry, and clams or mussels.

Cook, covered, just until clams or mussels open, about 5 minutes. Total cooking time should add up to 15 minutes. Garnish soup with parsley. Serve with crusty bread and dry white wine.

Variations: Use rice, about 3 tablespoons, instead of bread. Vegetables such as green peas can also be added. You may also substitute ½ lb. medium prawns (shrimp), peeled and halved, for clams or mussels if you like.

Kakavia
(Greek-style Bouillabaisse)

Serves 12

4-6	lbs. whole cleaned fish: striped bass, sea bass, or red snapper
	Vegetable cooking spray
4	cups onion, chopped
2	stalks celery, cubed
1	tablespoon garlic, minced
2	leeks, sliced
3	large carrots, peeled and cubed
1	tablespoon Spike (see "About This Cookbook")
1	tablespoon pepper
3	tablespoons fresh lemon juice
1	1-lb. can plum tomatoes, undrained
4	cups water
12	clams, scrubbed
12	shrimps, shelled and deveined
12	mussels, scrubbed and cleaned
1	cup white wine
3	bay leaves
½	teaspoon dried thyme
1	tablespoon parsley, minced

Nutritional Data

PER SERVING:

Calories	237
% calories from fat	14
Fat (gm)	3.8
Sat. Fat (gm)	0.9
Cholesterol (mg)	82
Sodium (mg)	223
Protein (gm)	33.9
Carbohydrate (gm)	13

EXCHANGES:

Milk	0.0	Bread	0.0
Veg.	2.0	Meat	3.5
Fruit	0.0	Fat	0.0

Cut fish into small pieces. Coat large stockpot with vegetable cooking spray. Sauté onion, celery, garlic, and leeks over medium heat for 5 minutes. Add carrots, Spike, pepper, lemon juice, tomatoes, and water.

Add seafood and remaining ingredients. Simmer 15 minutes or until clams and mussels open. Serve in deep bowls with crusty garlic bread.

Gumbo

Serves 8

	Canola oil, or vegetable cooking spray
1	cup onions, sliced
2	cups okra, sliced
3	cups tomatoes, peeled, seeded, chopped
4	cups Fish Stock, or Chicken Stock (see pp. 41, 40)
1	green bell pepper, seeded, sliced
¼	teaspoon red pepper flakes

Nutritional Data

PER SERVING:

Calories	195
% calories from fat	8
Fat (gm)	1.8
Sat. Fat (gm)	0.4
Cholesterol (mg)	84.2
Sodium (mg)	118
Protein (gm)	20
Carbohydrate (gm)	21.2

¾	lb. red snapper fillets, remove bones	EXCHANGES:			
¾	lb. extra-large shrimp, peeled and	Milk	0.0	Bread	1.0
	deveined	Veg.	1.0	Meat	2.0
1	teaspoon gumbo file powder	Fruit	0.0	Fat	0.0
2	bay leaves				
2	cups hot, cooked rice				

In pan coated with canola oil or cooking spray, sauté onions and okra over medium heat until onions are tender, about 5 minutes, stirring occasionally. Stir in tomatoes and stock. Simmer 5 minutes. Stir in remaining ingredients except rice and gumbo file powder.

Simmer 10 minutes or until shrimp and fish are cooked and turn opaque. Discard bay leaves. Remove gumbo from heat and stir in gumbo file powder.

Scoop rice into soup bowls. Ladle hot soup over rice. Serve hot.

Sherried Crab and Mushroom Bisque

Serves 6

		Nutritional Data	
1	tablespoon nondiet, tub-style margarine, divided	PER SERVING:	
1⅓	lbs. fresh mushrooms, trimmed and sliced, divided	Calories	168
		% calories from fat	26
		Fat (gm)	5.1
⅔	cup onions, chopped	Sat. Fat (gm)	1.7
2	tablespoons celery with leaves, chopped	Cholesterol (mg)	38.5
2	tablespoons carrot, chopped	Sodium (mg)	203
1½	tablespoons all-purpose white flour	Protein (gm)	12
2½	cups Chicken Stock (see p. 40), or broth, defatted and divided	Carbohydrate (gm)	17.8
¾	cup all-purpose potatoes, peeled and diced	EXCHANGES:	

		EXCHANGES:			
⅛	teaspoon dried thyme leaves	Milk	0.0	Bread	0.5
⅛	teaspoon white pepper	Veg.	2.0	Meat	1.0
1	tablespoon tomato paste	Fruit	0.0	Fat	0.5
1½	teaspoons reduced-salt soy sauce				
1⅓	cups whole milk				
6	ozs. fresh lump crabmeat, cartilage and shell removed				
1	tablespoon fresh chives, finely chopped (optional)				
2	tablespoons dry or medium-dry sherry				

In large pot, combine half the margarine and a generous half of the mushrooms over medium-low heat. Cook, stirring until mushrooms begin to release their juices. Increase heat to medium-high and continue cooking 4 to 5 minutes longer or until most juice evaporates from pot.

Turn out cooked mushrooms into bowl and reserve. Add remaining margarine and mushrooms, onions, celery, and carrots to pot. Return to heat, medium-low, and cook about 6 minutes longer until onions and mushrooms are limp. Stir in flour until smoothly incorporated. Continue cooking, stirring, 1 minute longer.

Add 1½ cups Chicken Stock, potato, thyme, and pepper. Bring mixture to boil over medium-high heat. Lower heat, cover, and simmer, stirring frequently to prevent potatoes from sticking, until potatoes are tender, about 10 minutes.

Transfer contents of pot to a blender. Add tomato paste and blend until mixture is completely pureed and smooth. Return puree to pot along with remaining chicken stock, soy sauce, milk, reserved cooked mushrooms, crabmeat, chives, and sherry. Bring mixture just to a simmer and serve immediately in small bowls.

Keeps 24 hours in refrigerator.

White Fish Chowder

Serves 6

2	teaspoons margarine
1	large onion, finely chopped
1	large clove garlic, chopped
1	large stalk celery, diced
2	cups Fish Stock (see p. 41), or 2 cups vegetable bouillon reconstituted from packets or cubes, or 2 cups chicken bouillon reconstituted from cubes or packets, divided
2	cups 2% milk, divided
2½	cups potatoes, peeled and cut into ¾-inch cubes (about 1 large potato)
1	cup frozen lima beans
1	large carrot, diced
1½	teaspoons dried basil leaves
½	teaspoon dried marjoram leaves
¼	teaspoon dried thyme leaves
¼	teaspoon dry mustard
¼	teaspoon ground celery seed
¼	teaspoon white pepper
1	tablespoon plus 1 teaspoon cornstarch
1	lb. (fresh or frozen and thawed) skinless flounder fillets, or halibut, or orange roughy
1	cup frozen corn kernels
	Salt to taste

Nutritional Data

PER SERVING:

Calories	291
% calories from fat	13
Fat (gm)	4.3
Sat. Fat (gm)	1.6
Cholesterol (mg)	43.7
Sodium (mg)	152
Protein (gm)	21.1
Carbohydrate (gm)	40.9

EXCHANGES:

Milk	0.3	Bread	2.0
Veg.	2.0	Meat	2.0
Fruit	0.0	Fat	0.0

In large saucepan or small Dutch oven, combine margarine, onion, garlic, celery, and 2 tablespoons of stock. Cook 5 or 6 minutes at medium heat, stirring frequently, until onion is tender. If liquid begins to evaporate, add a bit more stock.

Add remaining stock, 1 cup milk, potatoes, lima beans, carrot, basil, marjoram, thyme, dry mustard, celery seed, and pepper. Bring to boil over medium-high heat, stirring occasionally. Cover pan. Lower heat and simmer about 15 minutes or until potatoes are tender. While soup is cooking, cut flounder fillets into 1-inch pieces and set aside.

In small cup, mix together cornstarch and remaining 1 cup of milk. Add to soup. Raise heat to medium-high. Cook soup, stirring frequently, until it boils and thickens, about 3 or 4 minutes. Lower heat to medium-low.

Add flounder and corn to soup. Stir to mix well. Cook soup an additional 5 or 6 minutes or until flounder flakes easily with edge of large spoon. Add salt if desired.

Keeps 2 to 3 days in refrigerator.

Maine Clam Chowder

Serves 8

32 Littleneck clams, or other fresh small clams, washed

Canola oil, or vegetable cooking spray

1 cup onions, chopped

½ cup celery, sliced

1 carrot, sliced thin

4 all-purpose potatoes, about 2 lbs., scrubbed, peeled, and cubed

2 cups skim milk

½ cup clam juice

¼ cup all-purpose flour

¼ teaspoon white pepper

Nutritional Data

PER SERVING:

Calories	148
% calories from fat	5
Fat (gm)	0.8
Sat. Fat (gm)	0.2
Cholesterol (mg)	19.6
Sodium (mg)	95
Protein (gm)	11.3
Carbohydrate (gm)	23.8

EXCHANGES:

Milk	0.0	Bread	1.0
Veg.	0.5	Meat	1.0
Fruit	0.0	Fat	0.0

Wash clams and discard any that are open. Put closed clams in large saucepan; add 6 cups hot water. Cover and cook over medium heat 5 to 10 minutes or until clams open. Discard any clams that do not open. Remove clams from shell. Discard shells. Chop clams; reserve. Strain liquid through double layer of cheesecloth; set liquid aside.

Lightly coat bottom of large pan or soup pot with canola oil or cooking spray. Sauté onions, celery, carrot, and potatoes, covered, 5 minutes over medium heat. Stir occasionally. Add skim milk, reserve clam liquid, and clam juice. Cover and simmer 25 to 30 minutes or until all vegetables are tender.

Remove ½ cup of soup to small bowl. Whisk in flour and pepper. Stir flour mixture into chowder. Add chopped clams. Continue cooking until chowder thickens slightly.

Ladle chowder into bowls. Serve with chowder crackers if desired.

New York City Clam Chowder

Serves 8

32	Littleneck clams, or other fresh small clams, washed well		
	Olive oil, or vegetable cooking spray		
4	all-purpose potatoes, about 2 lbs., scrubbed, peeled, cubed, or sliced		
1	cup onions, sliced		
2	carrots		
1	28-oz. can crushed tomatoes, undrained		
½	cup clam juice		
⅓	cup parsley, chopped		
½	teaspoon thyme		
¼	teaspoon pepper		
2	bay leaves		
¼	teaspoon hot red sauce (optional)		

Nutritional Data

PER SERVING:

Calories	137
% calories from fat	6
Fat (gm)	1
Sat. Fat (gm)	0.1
Cholesterol (mg)	18.6
Sodium (mg)	223
Protein (gm)	10
Carbohydrate (gm)	23.1

EXCHANGES:

Milk	0.0	Bread	1.0
Veg.	1.5	Meat	0.5
Fruit	0.0	Fat	0.0

Wash clams and discard any that are open. Put clams in large saucepan; add 3 cups water. Cover and cook over medium-high heat 5 minutes or until clams open. Discard any clams that do not open. Leave clams in shells. Strain liquid through double layer of cheesecloth and reserve for chowder.

Coat large pot with olive oil or cooking spray. Sauté potatoes, onions, and carrots about 5 minutes, covered, over medium heat, stirring occasionally. Mix in crushed tomatoes, clam juice, parsley, thyme, pepper, bay leaves, and hot red sauce. Add strained clam juice.

Bring chowder to boil. Reduce heat to simmer; cover. Cook 45 minutes or until all vegetables are tender. Add clams in shells. Cook another 3 minutes. Discard bay leaves.

Ladle chowder into deep bowls. Put bowl for discarded clam shells on table. Serve chowder hot.

White Clam Chowder with Corn

Serves 5

1 tablespoon margarine
1 medium onion, chopped
1 large celery stalk, chopped
1 tablespoon all-purpose white flour
1 cup bottled clam juice, or substitute chicken broth, defatted
1 10½-oz. can minced clams, undrained
1 large bay leaf
¼ teaspoon dried marjoram leaves
⅛ teaspoon (generous) black pepper, or to taste
2 cups all-purpose potatoes, peeled and cubed (¼-inch cubes)
2 cups frozen yellow corn kernels, rinsed under warm water and thoroughly drained
1 cup 2% milk
  Salt to taste

Nutritional Data

PER SERVING:

Calories	224
% calories from fat	15
Fat (gm)	4.1
Sat. Fat (gm)	1.2
Cholesterol (mg)	40.7
Sodium (mg)	157
Protein (gm)	11.1
Carbohydrate (gm)	39.6

EXCHANGES:

Milk	0.0	Bread	2.0
Veg.	1.0	Meat	1.0
Fruit	0.0	Fat	0.0

In large pot, melt margarine over medium-high heat. Add onions and celery and cook, stirring, until onions are limp, about 5 minutes. Stir in flour until incorporated. Cook, stirring, 30 seconds. Stir in bottled clam juice, continuing to stir until mixture is well blended.

Add juice drained from canned clams (reserve minced clams for adding later), bay leaf, marjoram, pepper, and potatoes. Bring mixture to boil. Reduce heat and simmer mixture, covered and stirring occasionally, 10 minutes. Add corn and continue simmering 5 minutes longer. Discard bay leaf.

Using measuring cup, scoop up 1 cup vegetables and liquid from pot and transfer to blender or food processor. Mix until thoroughly pureed. Return puree to soup, along with milk and minced clams. Bring chowder to simmer and stir in salt if desired. Serve immediately.

Chowder may also be refrigerated up to 48 hours and reheated.

Seafood Pasta Soup

Serves 8

½ lb. small pasta shells
2 tablespoons olive oil
½ cup onion, diced
½ cup green bell pepper, diced
½ cup red or yellow bell pepper, diced
½ teaspoon garlic, minced
½ lb. mushrooms, sliced
1 14-oz. can Italian plum tomatoes, chopped
2 cups chicken broth
½ cup white wine
1 lb. sea scallops, halved if large
¼ cup parsley, chopped
   Pepper, freshly ground to taste
½ cup Parmesan cheese, freshly grated

Nutritional Data

PER SERVING:

Calories	256
% calories from fat	25
Fat (gm)	7.3
Sat. Fat (gm)	1.9
Cholesterol (mg)	29.3
Sodium (mg)	520
Protein (gm)	19.7
Carbohydrate (gm)	26.2

EXCHANGES:

Milk	0.0	Bread	1.5
Veg.	1.0	Meat	2.0
Fruit	0.0	Fat	0.0

Cook pasta according to package directions. Drain, toss with 1 tablespoon olive oil. Reserve.

Heat remaining oil over medium heat in large Dutch oven. Add onion, peppers, garlic, and mushrooms. Cook until peppers are just crisp-tender and mushrooms are soft, about 5 minutes.

Add tomatoes, broth, and wine. Heat to boil. Add scallops, parsley, pepper, and reserved pasta. Cover and return to boil.

Remove from heat. Let stand 5 minutes. To serve, ladle soup into bowls and sprinkle with Parmesan cheese.

Easy Spinach-Pasta Soup with Basil

Serves 5

1 10-oz. package frozen and thawed leaf spinach
2 teaspoons extra-virgin olive oil
1 small onion, finely chopped
1 small clove garlic, minced
6 cups chicken broth (defatted), or chicken bouillon reconstituted from cubes or granules
1 cup water
¾ cup 2-inch-long pieces of uncooked vermicelli or other extra-fine spaghetti
¼ cup fresh basil leaves, chopped, or 1½ tablespoons dried basil leaves

Nutritional Data

PER SERVING:

Calories	207
% calories from fat	21
Fat (gm)	5
Sat. Fat (gm)	1.2
Cholesterol (mg)	14.1
Sodium (mg)	354
Protein (gm)	11.3
Carbohydrate (gm)	27.6

EXCHANGES:

Milk	0.0	Bread	1.5
Veg.	1.5	Meat	0.5
Fruit	0.0	Fat	0.5

1/4 teaspoon black pepper
1 cup Italian-style (plum) tomatoes,
   drained and chopped
1 cup cooked garbanzo beans, or canned
   garbanzo beans, well drained
2 tablespoons Parmesan cheese, freshly
   grated, for garnish (optional)

Let spinach drain in colander. Press down to remove as much excess water as possible. Transfer spinach to cutting board. Trim away coarse stems and discard. Finely chop spinach and return it to colander to drain further.

In very large pot over medium heat, combine oil, onion, and garlic and cook, stirring frequently, until onion is tender. Add broth and water and bring mixture to rolling boil over high heat. Stir in vermicelli and continue cooking 2 minutes.

Stir spinach, basil, pepper, tomatoes, and beans into pot. Continue cooking 6 to 7 minutes longer or until spinach and pasta are tender. Serve immediately, sprinkled with a little grated Parmesan if desired.

Italian Bean Soup

Serves 14 (1-cup servings)

1 cup dried navy beans
2 quarts water
1 cup onion, chopped
1 cup green bell pepper, chopped
1 cup carrots, chopped
1/2 cup celery, chopped
1 teaspoon dried basil
1 teaspoon oregano
1 teaspoon vegetable-flavored bouillon
   granules
1/4 teapoon dry mustard
2 cloves garlic, minced
3 8-oz. cans tomato sauce
1/2 cup whole wheat elbow macaroni,
   uncooked
1 15-oz. can garbanzo beans, drained

Nutritional Data

PER SERVING:

Calories	125
% calories from fat	7
Fat (gm)	1
Sat. Fat (gm)	0.2
Cholesterol (mg)	0
Sodium (mg)	489
Protein (gm)	6.3
Carbohydrate (gm)	24.4

EXCHANGES:

Milk	0.0	Bread	1.5
Veg.	0.5	Meat	0.0
Fruit	0.0	Fat	0.0

Sort and wash beans; place in Dutch oven. Cover with water 2 inches above beans; bring to a boil and cook over high heat 3 minutes. Remove from heat; cover and let stand 1 hour.

Drain beans; add 2 quarts water and next 10 ingredients. Cover and simmer 1 1/2 hours or until beans are tender, stirring occasionally.

Add macaroni and garbanzo beans and cook about 15 minutes or until macaroni is tender.

Pasta Fagioli

Serves 8

1	cup dried pinto beans
3	cups Chicken Stock (see p. 40)
1¼	cups onion, chopped
½	cup celery, chopped
1¼	cups carrots, sliced
2½	cups tomatoes, diced
1	cup green bell pepper, diced
1	clove garlic, minced
1	teaspoon oregano
1	teaspoon basil
½	teaspoon rosemary
¼	teaspoon cayenne pepper, ground
½	cup cooked macaroni

Nutritional Data

PER SERVING:

Calories	156
% calories from fat	6
Fat (gm)	1.2
Sat. Fat (gm)	0.2
Cholesterol (mg)	3.8
Sodium (mg)	26
Protein (gm)	8.5
Carbohydrate (gm)	28.8

EXCHANGES:

Milk	0.0	Bread	1.0
Veg.	2.0	Meat	0.5
Fruit	0.0	Fat	0.0

Soak beans overnight in water to cover; drain. Put beans in stockpot and cover with water. Cook, covered, until almost tender, a little over 1 hour. Drain; return to stockpot.

Add Chicken Stock and onion and cook, covered, 20 minutes. Add remaining vegetables and seasonings. Cook, covered, 20 to 30 minutes or longer. Add macaroni and more broth if necessary; heat through and serve or freeze.

To Freeze: Place in microwave-safe container; label and freeze for up to 2 months.

To Serve: Thaw. Cover with microwave-safe plastic wrap, and cook on High for 3 to 5 minutes.

White Bean Soup Provençale

Serves 10

2	tablespoons light olive oil
1	cup celery, chopped
1	cup onion, chopped
3	cloves garlic
2	teaspoons dried sage
6	cups Chicken Stock (see p. 40), divided
2	cups water
1	lb. dried navy beans, soaked overnight, drained
2	teaspoons fresh lemon juice
	Spike (see "About This Cookbook")
	Pepper, freshly ground

Nutritional Data

PER SERVING:

Calories	202
% calories from fat	17
Fat (gm)	3.9
Sat. Fat (gm)	0.7
Cholesterol (mg)	6.1
Sodium (mg)	19
Protein (gm)	11.4
Carbohydrate (gm)	30

EXCHANGES:

Milk	0.0	Bread	2.0
Veg.	1.0	Meat	0.5
Fruit	0.0	Fat	0.0

Garnish

3   large plum tomatoes, chopped
¼   cup fresh basil leaves, cut julienne

Heat oil in 4-quart saucepan or stockpot. When hot, add celery, onion, garlic, and sage. Cook until onion is softened, about 5 minutes. Add 5 cups stock and water. Heat to boil. Add beans. Heat to boil again. Reduce heat; simmer covered until beans are tender, about 1½ hours, stirring occasionally.

Remove 2 cups bean mixture and puree with 1 cup reserved stock in food processor or blender until smooth. Return pureed mixture to pot. Stir well to combine. Add lemon juice and seasonings to taste.

This soup can be made ahead and frozen or refrigerated as long as 3 days. Reheat gently, thinning with water as needed. Adjust seasonings and lemon juice. To serve, garnish with tomato and basil.

Easy Beef Sausage and Black Bean Soup

Serves 6 (1-cup servings)

½   lb. reduced-fat fully cooked smoked beef sausage links
1   cup carrots, thinly sliced
1   cup celery, thinly sliced
¾   cup water
2   19-oz. cans low-sodium black bean soup
     Nonfat plain yogurt
     Parsley, chopped

Nutritional Data

PER SERVING:

Calories	195
% calories from fat	24
Fat (gm)	5.3
Sat. Fat (gm)	1
Cholesterol (mg)	24
Sodium (mg)	359
Protein (gm)	12.9
Carbohydrate (gm)	24.2

EXCHANGES:

Milk	0.0	Bread	1.5
Veg.	0.5	Meat	1.0
Fruit	0.0	Fat	0.5

In 3-quart saucepan, combine carrots, celery, and water. Bring to a boil; reduce heat to low. Cover and simmer 5 minutes or until vegetables are crisp-tender.

Meanwhile, cut beef sausages lengthwise in half and then crosswise into ½-inch-thick slices. Add sausage and soup to vegetables, stirring to blend. Bring to boil; reduce heat to low. Simmer, uncovered, 10 minutes, stirring occasionally.

Serve with yogurt and parsley.

Hearty Split Pea, Bean, and Barley Soup

Serves 14

15   cups water
1   meaty ham bone, or 2 large pork hocks (about 2 lbs. total)
2   cups (1 lb.) dry green split peas, soaked overnight, drained
½   cup pearl barley
½   cup dry black-eyed peas, soaked overnight, drained
½   cup dry navy beans, soaked overnight, drained
3   bay leaves
2   beef bouillon cubes (or up to 5, as needed)
2   large onions, coarsely chopped
2   large carrots, thinly sliced
2   large celery stalks, including leaves, thinly sliced
2   cloves garlic, minced
½   teaspoon (generous) dried thyme leaves
½   teaspoon ground celery seed
½   teaspoon black pepper
   Salt to taste

Nutritional Data

PER SERVING:

Calories	189
% calories from fat	7
Fat (gm)	1.6
Sat. Fat (gm)	0.4
Cholesterol (mg)	6.5
Sodium (mg)	150
Protein (gm)	12
Carbohydrate (gm)	33.3

EXCHANGES:

Milk	0.0	Bread	2.0
Veg.	0.5	Meat	0.5
Fruit	0.0	Fat	0.0

In large, heavy soup pot, combine water, ham bone or pork hocks, split peas, barley, black-eyed peas, and beans. Bring to boil over high heat. Add bay leaves, 2 bouillon cubes, onions, carrots, celery, garlic, thyme, celery seed, and pepper. Cover and lower heat. Simmer, stirring occasionally, until beans are tender and split peas have thickened the soup, about 2 to 2½ hours.

As soup thickens, lower heat and stir more frequently to prevent split peas from sticking to bottom of pot. Taste soup. If more bouillon cubes are needed, add them, along with salt if desired. When beans are tender, remove ham bone or pork hocks. If pork hocks have been used, discard them. If ham bone has been used, reserve and cool slightly.

Meanwhile, remove soup from heat and skim fat off top with large, shallow spoon, and discard. Then, if a ham bone has been used, cut meat into bite-size pieces and return it to soup. Bring soup to a boil again. Stir well before serving.

This soup tastes wonderful reheated. However, it must be stirred carefully to prevent split peas from sticking. If it thickens too much in refrigerator, thin with a bit more water during reheating.

Keeps 4 to 5 days in refrigerator.

Lentil Soup

Serves 8

3 cups dried lentils
3 quarts cold water
½ lb. beef brisket, flank or stew meat
1 medium leek, finely chopped
3 large carrots, finely chopped
½ cup celery, chopped
1 cup onion, finely chopped
2 tablespoons flour
¼ cup white wine

Nutritional Data

PER SERVING:

Calories	179
% calories from fat	9
Fat (gm)	1.9
Sat. Fat (gm)	0.5
Cholesterol (mg)	16.7
Sodium (mg)	42.6
Protein (gm)	14.7
Carbohydrate (gm)	25.6

EXCHANGES:

Milk	0.0	Bread	1.0
Veg.	2.0	Meat	1.0
Fruit	0.0	Fat	0.0

Rinse and sort lentils under cold water. In large stockpot, bring water to boil. Add lentils, beef, leek, carrots, and celery. Return mixture to boil, reduce heat, cover, and simmer for 40 minutes.

Remove beef and brown in skillet over low heat. When it is very hot, add onions. Cook 15 minutes, stirring frequently. Sprinkle flour over onions. Stir until flour browns. Pour 1 cup of lentil mixture over onions and stir vigorously.

Add white wine and cook 1 minute longer. Add contents of skillet to lentils. Simmer 30 minutes.

Broccoli Bisque

Serves 6

1 cup onion, minced
3 stalks celery
½ cup leek, thinly sliced
2 cloves garlic, minced
2 tablespoons margarine
1½ lbs. broccoli, trimmed
3 cups chicken broth
1 12-oz. can evaporated skim milk
¼ teaspoon dry mustard
1 teaspoon Spike (see "About This Cookbook")
Pepper, to taste

Nutritional Data

PER SERVING:

Calories	169
% calories from fat	26
Fat (gm)	5.2
Sat. Fat (gm)	1.1
Cholesterol (mg)	2.5
Sodium (mg)	594
Protein (gm)	11.9
Carbohydrate (gm)	21.5

EXCHANGES:

Milk	0.5	Bread	0.0
Veg.	3.0	Meat	0.0
Fruit	0.0	Fat	1.0

In large covered kettle, sauté onion, celery, leek, and garlic in margarine until tender. Remove florets from broccoli and reserve. Slice stalks. Add slices and chicken broth to kettle; simmer 15 minutes; remove from heat.

Puree mixture in food processor or blender. Return to kettle and stir in evaporated skim milk and broccoli florets. Add seasonings. Simmer 10 minutes. Serve hot or cold.

❄ *Carrot Soup with Dill*

Serves 4

2	cups raw carrots, sliced
1/4	cup green onions with tops, chopped
3	tablespoons parsley, chopped
1	tablespoon diet margarine
1	tablespoon arrowroot
1½	cups Chicken Stock (see p. 40)
½	cup evaporated skim milk
⅛	cup fresh dill, chopped

Nutritional Data

PER SERVING:

Calories	84
% calories from fat	21
Fat (gm)	2
Sat. Fat (gm)	0.4
Cholesterol (mg)	4.8
Sodium (mg)	95
Protein (gm)	4.4
Carbohydrate (gm)	11.8

EXCHANGES:

Milk	0.5	Bread	0.0
Veg.	1.0	Meat	0.0
Fruit	0.0	Fat	0.5

Steam carrots about 20 minutes. Put aside. In stockpot cook onions and parsley in margarine until onions are softened. Sprinkle with arrowroot and cook, stirring occasionally, 2 minutes. Remove pot from heat and gradually blend in Chicken Stock. Return to heat; cook and stir until smooth and slightly thickened.

Place carrots in blender, and pour in 1 cup of stock mixture. Blend until smooth. Place carrot mixture in pot with stock and add skim milk. Heat gently (do not boil) and cook 2 minutes more. Ladle into soup cups and sprinkle with dill.

To Freeze: Place in microwave-safe container; label and freeze for up to 2 months.

To Serve: Thaw. Cover with microwave-safe plastic wrap, and cook on High for 3 to 5 minutes.

Cauliflower Soup

Serves 4

1	lb. cauliflower, trimmed, cut into florets
1	medium carrot, peeled and diced
1	stalk celery with leaves, sliced
½	onion, sliced
1	teaspoon chicken bouillon granules mixed with ½ cup water
2	cups water
1/4	cup nonfat dry milk
1	teaspoon curry powder

Nutritional Data

PER SERVING:

Calories	71
% calories from fat	8
Fat (gm)	0.7
Sat. Fat (gm)	0.1
Cholesterol (mg)	0.8
Sodium (mg)	73
Protein (gm)	4.8
Carbohydrate (gm)	13.4

		EXCHANGES:			
1	teaspoon caraway seeds	Milk	0.0	Bread	0.0
½	teaspoon red pepper flakes	Veg.	2.5	Meat	0.0
	Salt and pepper, to taste	Fruit	0.0	Fat	0.0
	Juice of ½ lemon				
	Parsley for garnish				
	Dash paprika				

Place cauliflower, carrot, celery, onion, bouillon granules, and water in 2-quart measure. Microwave on High for 8 minutes, stirring once, until cauliflower stems are soft. Let cool a few minutes, and place in blender or food processor with 2 cups of water (as needed to thin) and puree. Add milk and curry powder and process for a few seconds.

Return to measure, stir in caraway seeds, red pepper flakes, and salt and pepper to taste. Microwave about 2 to 3 minutes to warm. Stir in lemon juice, and garnish with parsley and dash of paprika.

Iowa Corn Soup

Serves 8

Butter-flavored vegetable cooking spray
1	tablespoon canola oil
1	cup onion, sliced
2	tablespoons all-purpose flour
3	cups frozen corn niblets, thawed and drained
3	cups skim milk
2	cups evaporated skim milk
½	teaspoon each ingredient: salt, pepper
2	tablespoons cornstarch
¼	cup parsley, minced

Nutritional Data

PER SERVING:
Calories	170
% calories from fat	11
Fat (gm)	2.1
Sat. Fat (gm)	0.3
Cholesterol (mg)	3.5
Sodium (mg)	258
Protein (gm)	10.3
Carbohydrate (gm)	29.5

EXCHANGES:
Milk	1.0	Bread	1.0
Veg.	0.5	Meat	0.0
Fruit	0.0	Fat	0.0

Coat large nonstick pot. Heat oil and sauté onion over medium heat until soft, about 5 minutes. Add remaining ingredients, except cornstarch and parsley, and cook until warm.

Remove ½ cup soup and whisk with cornstarch. Stir mixture back into soup. Continue cooking over medium heat until soup thickens slightly. Add parsley. Serve hot.

Mexican Corn Soup

Serves 4

1	carrot, shredded (about ½ cup)
1	medium green bell pepper, chopped (½ cup)
¼	cup shallots, chopped
1	teaspoon vegetable oil
1	cup corn niblets (fresh, canned, or frozen—thawed)
2	cups chicken broth
½	cup nonfat dry milk mixed with enough water to make 1 cup
⅛	teaspoon red pepper flakes
¼	teaspoon celery seed

Nutritional Data

PER SERVING:

Calories	115
% calories from fat	15
Fat (gm)	2.1
Sat. Fat (gm)	0.4
Cholesterol (mg)	2.1
Sodium (mg)	443
Protein (gm)	7.4
Carbohydrate (gm)	18.3

EXCHANGES:

Milk	0.5	Bread	0.5
Veg.	1.0	Meat	0.0
Fruit	0.0	Fat	0.5

Place carrot, green pepper, and shallots in 2-quart casserole or measure with vegetable oil, and microwave on High for 3 minutes. Add remaining ingredients, and transfer and mix in food processor or blender, a little at a time. Return to original container and microwave on High 2 to 3 minutes until warm, stirring once.

Leek and Carrot Yogurt Soup

Serves 8

1	tablespoon canola oil
	Canola oil, or vegetable cooking spray
2	large leeks, washed and thinly sliced
2	cups carrots, sliced, cooked, and drained
½	teaspoon ground cinnamon
½	teaspoon freshly ground nutmeg
½	teaspoon salt
¼	teaspoon white pepper
1¼	quarts low-salt chicken broth
1½	cups plain nonfat yogurt

Nutritional Data

PER SERVING:

Calories	85
% calories from fat	25
Fat (gm)	2.5
Sat. Fat (gm)	0.2
Cholesterol (mg)	0.8
Sodium (mg)	222
Protein (gm)	4.6
Carbohydrate (gm)	11.7

EXCHANGES:

Milk	0.0	Bread	0.0
Veg.	2.5	Meat	0.0
Fruit	0.0	Fat	0.5

Heat oil in heavy pot coated with canola oil or cooking spray. Add leeks and sauté until soft, stirring occasionally. Mix in carrots. Add remaining ingredients, except yogurt. Simmer, covered, until carrots are tender.

Remove carrots and leeks and puree in blender or food processor fitted with steel blade. Return vegetables to soup in pot. Slowly add yogurt, stirring constantly. Heat through but do not boil.

Leek and Pumpkin Soup

Serves 8

Butter-flavored vegetable cooking spray
1 tablespoon canola oil
3 leeks, washed and sliced thin
1 large potato, peeled and cubed
1 16-oz. can pumpkin
3 cups low-salt chicken broth
½ teaspoon ground cinnamon
¼ teaspoon ground allspice
¼ teaspoon ground nutmeg
1 12-oz. can evaporated skim milk

Nutritional Data

PER SERVING:

Calories	120
% calories from fat	17
Fat (gm)	2.4
Sat. Fat (gm)	0.3
Cholesterol (mg)	1.3
Sodium (mg)	87
Protein (gm)	5.7
Carbohydrate (gm)	20.1

EXCHANGES:

Milk	0.5	Bread	0.5
Veg.	1.0	Meat	0.0
Fruit	0.0	Fat	0.5

Coat nonstick saucepan with cooking spray. Heat oil and sauté leeks and potatoes until soft, stirring constantly, about 5 minutes. Mix in pumpkin and chicken broth. Simmer 15 minutes, covered, stirring occasionally. Blend in cinnamon, allspice, nutmeg, and skim milk. Simmer until soup is warm and vegetables are tender. Serve hot.

Mushroom Barley Soup with Herbs

Serves 8

2 tablespoons vegetable oil
2 cups onions, finely chopped
1 cup carrots, diced
½ cup celery, finely chopped
1 lb. mushrooms, sliced
1 teaspoon garlic, minced
½ teaspoon celery seed
1 teaspoon thyme
1 teaspoon basil
1 teaspoon tarragon
2 cups Beef Stock (see p. 40)
2 cups Chicken Stock (see p. 40)
2 cups water
½ cup pearl barley
3 tablespoons fresh parsley, chopped

Nutritional Data

PER SERVING:

Calories	131
% calories from fat	29
Fat (gm)	4.5
Sat. Fat (gm)	0.6
Cholesterol (mg)	5.1
Sodium (mg)	23
Protein (gm)	4.9
Carbohydrate (gm)	18.4

EXCHANGES:

Milk	0.0	Bread	0.5
Veg.	2.0	Meat	0.0
Fruit	0.0	Fat	1.0

Heat oil in stockpot and add onions, carrots, and celery. Cover and cook, stirring occasionally, until tender, about 5 minutes. Stir in mushrooms, garlic, and herbs; cook covered 3 minutes more.

Add Beef Stock, Chicken Stock, and 2 cups water to pot. Add barley. Bring to boil, reduce heat, and simmer covered 1½ hours. Freeze or sprinkle parsley on soup and serve.

To Freeze: Place in microwave-safe container; label and freeze for up to 2 months.

To Serve: Thaw. Cover with microwave-safe plastic wrap, and cook on High for 3 to 5 minutes.

Italian Mushroom Soup

Serves 4

Vegetable cooking spray
2 medium onions, chopped
1 lb. fresh mushrooms, thinly sliced
6 tablespoons rich tomato puree, or 3 tablespoons tomato paste
4 cups Chicken Stock (see p. 40), or broth (homemade or low-sodium canned)
6 tablespoons sweet vermouth Spike, to taste (see "About This Cookbook")
1 tablespoon fresh basil, minced
¼ cup fresh chives, minced
   Parmesan cheese, freshly grated (optional)

Nutritional Data

PER SERVING:

Calories	132
% calories from fat	10
Fat (gm)	1.6
Sat. Fat (gm)	0.3
Cholesterol (mg)	10.1
Sodium (mg)	113
Protein (gm)	6.9
Carbohydrate (gm)	16.3

EXCHANGES:

Milk	0.0	Bread	0.0
Veg.	3.0	Meat	0.0
Fruit	0.0	Fat	1.0

Coat heavy saucepan with vegetable cooking spray and add onions. Cook until onions are translucent. Add mushrooms and cook until they are softened. Stir in tomato puree and Chicken Stock. Heat to boiling, then reduce heat and stir in vermouth. Season to taste with Spike. Simmer a few minutes.

Serve hot, sprinkled with basil and chives. You can also top with dash of Parmesan cheese if you like.

Jellied Mushroom Soup

Serves 8

1 lb. mushrooms, trimmed and minced
   Butter-flavored vegetable cooking spray
1 quart chicken consommé
2 envelopes unflavored gelatin
½ teaspoon salt
¼ teaspoon pepper
1 teaspoon fresh crushed tarragon, or ½ teaspoon dried tarragon
¼ cup sherry
   Watercress leaves

Nutritional Data

PER SERVING:

Calories	41
% calories from fat	6
Fat (gm)	0.2
Sat. Fat (gm)	0
Cholesterol (mg)	0
Sodium (mg)	605
Protein (gm)	3.4
Carbohydrate (gm)	4

EXCHANGES:

Milk	0.0	Bread	0.0
Veg.	1.5	Meat	0.0
Fruit	0.0	Fat	0.0

Heat pot coated with cooking spray. Sauté mushrooms until tender, stirring often. Cover if necessary to cook mushrooms. Add consommé and simmer 5 minutes. Place gelatin in ½ cup water and allow to stand 5 minutes to dissolve; stir it into hot soup. Stir in salt, pepper, tarragon, and sherry. Pour soup into individual small bowls and refrigerate until set. Garnish with watercress leaves before serving.

Japanese Mushroom Soup with Noodles

Serves 6

1	oz. dried mushrooms
½	small onion
1	clove garlic
1½	lbs. fresh mushrooms, minced
2	tablespoons margarine
¼	teaspoon thyme
4	cups chicken broth
1	cup dry white wine
¼	lb. no-yolk noodles
½	lb. snow peas
½	cup radishes, sliced
1	tablespoon red wine vinegar
	Pepper, freshly ground, to taste
2	teaspoons parsley, chopped

Nutritional Data

PER SERVING:

Calories	214
% calories from fat	24
Fat (gm)	5.9
Sat. Fat (gm)	1.2
Cholesterol (mg)	0.7
Sodium (mg)	575
Protein (gm)	10.3
Carbohydrate (gm)	24.9

EXCHANGES:

Milk	0.0	Bread	1.0
Veg.	3.0	Meat	0.0
Fruit	0.0	Fat	1.0

Pour 3 cups boiling water over dried mushrooms and let stand at least 2 hours. Take softened mushrooms from liquid and reserve liquid. In food processor, mince dried mushrooms, onions, garlic, and about ¾ of the fresh mushrooms.

Melt 1 tablespoon margarine in soup pot, add minced mushroom mixture, and cook over medium-high heat about 1 minute. Add second tablespoon margarine and continue cooking about 2 minutes. Add thyme, chicken broth, wine, and mushroom liquid to pot and bring to boil. Lower heat and simmer 30 minutes.

Strain mushroom broth and discard vegetables. Bring broth back to simmer. Add noodles and cook about 12 minutes or until tender. Add remainder of mushrooms, snow peas, and radishes to broth and cook about 2 minutes. Stir in vinegar and cook 1 more minute. Remove from heat and stir in pepper and parsley.

French Onion Soup

Serves 6

1 lb. onions, finely sliced
Vegetable cooking spray
Pepper
½ teaspoon mustard
2 teaspoons plain flour
4 cups Beef Stock (see p. 40), or low-sodium canned
1 cup white wine
4-6 slices French bread, lightly toasted
1 oz. (¼ cup) Parmesan cheese, freshly grated

Nutritional Data

PER SERVING:

Calories	147.6
% calories from fat	16
Fat (gm)	2.6
Sat. Fat (gm)	1.1
Cholesterol (mg)	10
Sodium (mg)	196.3
Protein (gm)	6.5
Carbohydrate (gm)	16.9

EXCHANGES:

Milk	0.0	Bread	0.5
Veg.	2.0	Meat	0.0
Fruit	0.0	Fat	1.0

Coat large skillet with vegetable cooking spray, then add onion rings, pepper, and mustard. Cook over very gentle heat, stirring occasionally until onion is browned (20 to 30 minutes).

Add flour and stir until smooth. Add stock and white wine, stirring constantly, then bring to boil and simmer 30 minutes. Taste and adjust seasoning.

Place slices of toasted bread on bottom of soup tureen or in individual soup bowls, sprinkling with cheese. Pour hot soup carefully onto bread. Place under broiler until cheese begins to brown. Serve immediately.

Red Onion and Apple Soup with Curry

Serves 6

1 tablespoon margarine
1¼ lbs. red onions (about 4 medium), thinly sliced
5½ cups Chicken Stock (see p. 40), or broth (defatted)
1 cup water
2 cups peeled and cored tart cooking apples, coarsely grated or shredded, divided
½ cup carrots, finely shredded
1 large bay leaf
1 teaspoon mild curry powder
¼ teaspoon chili powder
⅛ teaspoon dried thyme leaves

Nutritional Data

PER SERVING:

Calories	113
% calories from fat	24
Fat (gm)	3.1
Sat. Fat (gm)	0.7
Cholesterol (mg)	9.3
Sodium (mg)	40
Protein (gm)	4.4
Carbohydrate (gm)	15.9

EXCHANGES:

Milk	0.0	Bread	0.0
Veg.	2.0	Meat	0.0
Fruit	0.5	Fat	0.5

⅛ teaspoon ground allspice
¼ teaspoon (generous) black pepper
Salt to taste
Chutney for garnish (optional)

In large pot, melt margarine over medium heat. Add onions and cook over medium heat, stirring frequently, until soft and slightly translucent. Add tablespoon or two of stock if necessary to prevent onions from burning. Add remainder of stock, water, 1 cup of apples, and all remaining ingredients except salt and chutney. Bring mixture to boil over medium-high heat. Cover, lower heat, and simmer about 25 minutes.

Stir in reserved 1 cup of apples and simmer 5 minutes longer. Discard bay leaf. Stir in salt if desired. Garnish each serving with teaspoon or two of chutney.

Keeps 3 or 4 days in refrigerator.

Parsley Soup

Serves 4

2 potatoes, peeled and cut up
2 onions, chopped
1 tablespoon margarine
1 10¾-oz. can condensed chicken broth
1 cup parsley, fresh snipped
½ teaspoon Spike (see "About This Cookbook")
Worcestershire sauce, dash
White pepper to taste
2 12-oz. cans evaporated skim milk

Nutritional Data

PER SERVING:

Calories	293
% calories from fat	13
Fat (gm)	4.3
Sat. Fat (gm)	1.1
Cholesterol (mg)	6.9
Sodium (mg)	746
Protein (gm)	20.4
Carbohydrate (gm)	43.7

EXCHANGES:

Milk	2.0	Bread	1.0
Veg.	1.0	Meat	0.0
Fruit	0.0	Fat	1.0

Cook potatoes, onions, and margarine in medium saucepan until tender. Add broth, parsley, Spike, and Worcestershire; season with white pepper if desired. Transfer to blender; mix until smooth. Return to saucepan and add milk; heat through.

 # Vichyssoise

Serves 4

1 cup Chicken Stock (see p. 40)
1 cup potatoes, peeled and cubed
1½ cups leeks, well washed, chopped
2 cups skim milk
Few dashes celery seed
¼ teaspoon salt
Dash pepper, freshly ground

Nutritional Data

PER SERVING:

Calories	136
% calories from fat	6
Fat (gm)	1
Sat. Fat (gm)	0.4
Cholesterol (mg)	5.7
Sodium (mg)	216
Protein (gm)	7.1
Carbohydrate (gm)	24.6

	EXCHANGES:			
1 tablespoon part-skim ricotta cheese	Milk	0.5	Bread	1.0
Few dashes cayenne pepper	Veg.	1.0	Meat	0.0
	Fruit	0.0	Fat	0.0

Place broth, potatoes, and leeks in food processor and blend to liquefy. Turn into 2-quart measure, and microwave 3 to 5 minutes until vegetables are tender. Place remaining ingredients in food processor, add cooked vegetables, and blend again until smooth. Pour into bowl and chill before serving. Top with dusting of cayenne.

As a variation, this may also be made with sweet potatoes.

Potato Barley Soup

Serves 8

Olive oil, or vegetable cooking spray
1   cup onions, chopped
3   cloves garlic, minced
3   cups all-purpose potatoes, peeled, diced
2   large carrots, sliced
3   ribs celery, sliced
1   parsnip, sliced
2   bay leaves
1   cup tomato juice
3/4 cup barley
4   cups low-salt Vegetable Stock
    (see p. 42)
1/2 teaspoon each ingredient: salt, pepper, thyme, marjoram

Nutritional Data

PER SERVING:

Calories	169
% calories from fat	3
Fat (gm)	0.6
Sat. Fat (gm)	0.1
Cholesterol (mg)	0
Sodium (mg)	271
Protein (gm)	4.6
Carbohydrate (gm)	37.8

EXCHANGES:

Milk	0.0	Bread	2.0
Veg.	2.0	Meat	0.0
Fruit	0.0	Fat	0.0

Coat soup pot lightly with olive oil or cooking spray. Sauté onions, garlic, and potatoes 5 minutes, covered, stirring occasionally, over medium heat. Add remaining ingredients. Simmer, partially covered, 25 minutes or until vegetables and barley are tender, stirring occasionally. Discard bay leaves; taste to adjust seasonings. For smoother taste, you can puree soup, reheat, and serve.

Potato Pistou

Serves 6

2 cups onions, chopped
4 all-purpose potatoes, peeled, diced
4 tomatoes, peeled, seeded, chopped
3/4 cup green beans, trimmed, cut into 1½-inch pieces
2 medium zucchini, sliced
1 cup tomatoes, crushed
1/4 teaspoon each ingredient: pepper, marjoram, saffron threads
1½ cups firmly packed fresh basil leaves
5 cloves garlic
1/4 cup Parmesan cheese, freshly grated

Nutritional Data

PER SERVING:

Calories	159
% calories from fat	11
Fat (gm)	2
Sat. Fat (gm)	0.9
Cholesterol (mg)	3.3
Sodium (mg)	97
Protein (gm)	6.1
Carbohydrate (gm)	32.1

EXCHANGES:

Milk	0.0	Bread	1.0
Veg.	3.0	Meat	0.0
Fruit	0.0	Fat	0.5

Pour 2 quarts water into soup pot; simmer onions and potatoes 35 minutes. Add tomatoes, green beans, zucchini, crushed tomatoes, pepper, and marjoram. Soak saffron in 1 tablespoon hot water for 5 minutes; drain and spoon flavored liquid into soup. Simmer 20 minutes.

Puree vegetables in food processor, then return them to clean pot. Bring soup to boil; reduce heat to simmer.

While soup is simmering, puree basil, garlic, and cheese in food processor fitted with steel blade. Blend the paste into soup. Ladle soup into individual bowls and serve hot.

Southwest-Style Potato-Corn Chowder con Queso

Serves 5

2 teaspoons margarine
2/3 cup green onions, chopped, including tops
1 tablespoon all-purpose white flour
3 cups Vegetable Stock (see p. 42), or vegetable bouillon reconstituted from cubes or granules
3½ cups all-purpose potatoes, peeled and cubed (½-inch cubes)
1 large bay leaf
1/2 teaspoon dry mustard
1/4 teaspoon dried marjoram leaves
1/4 teaspoon white pepper, or to taste
1 10-oz. package frozen yellow corn kernels

Nutritional Data

PER SERVING:

Calories	319
% calories from fat	18
Fat (gm)	6.7
Sat. Fat (gm)	3
Cholesterol (mg)	18.1
Sodium (mg)	587
Protein (gm)	12.9
Carbohydrate (gm)	54.6

EXCHANGES:

Milk	0.5	Bread	3.0
Veg.	1.0	Meat	0.0
Fruit	0.0	Fat	1.0

3   ozs. reduced-fat sharp Cheddar cheese,
    cut into chunks
2½ cups 2% milk
1   4-oz. can chopped mild green chilies, well
    drained
    Finely chopped fresh chives for garnish
    (optional)

In large pot over medium-high heat, melt margarine. Add green onions and cook, stirring, until soft, about 5 minutes. Stir in flour and cook, stirring until smoothly incorporated and lightly browned, about 30 seconds. Gradually add stock, stirring until mixture is smooth and well blended.

Add potatoes, bay leaf, mustard, marjoram, and pepper. Bring mixture to boil. Lower heat and simmer, covered, 15 minutes; stir frequently to prevent potatoes from sticking to bottom of pot. Add corn and continue simmering about 5 minutes longer, until it is cooked through.

Discard bay leaf. Using measuring cup, scoop up 1 cup of vegetables and liquid from pot and transfer to blender or food processor. Sprinkle cheese over top. If blender is used, add ½ cup milk. Mix until thoroughly pureed, about 1 minute. Return puree to pot, along with remaining milk and green chilies. Heat, stirring, about 5 minutes longer or until soup just comes to simmer. Serve immediately, garnished with chopped fresh chives if desired.

Keeps for 2 or 3 days in refrigerator.

 # *Squash Soup*

Serves 6 (1-cup servings)

	Nutritional Data
2 acorn or butternut squash, about 1 lb. each	**PER SERVING:**
½ cup onion, chopped	Calories 97
2 cups Chicken Stock (see p. 40)	% calories from fat 7
½ teaspoon cinnamon, ground	Fat (gm) 0.9
¼ teaspoon coriander, ground	Sat. Fat (gm) 0.4
¼ teaspoon cumin, ground	Cholesterol (mg) 5.4
⅛ teaspoon turmeric	Sodium (mg) 156
Black pepper, freshly ground, to taste	Protein (gm) 5
1 tablespoon apple cider vinegar	Carbohydrate (gm) 18.8

Nutritional Data

PER SERVING:

Calories			97
% calories from fat			7
Fat (gm)			0.9
Sat. Fat (gm)			0.4
Cholesterol (mg)			5.4
Sodium (mg)			156
Protein (gm)			5
Carbohydrate (gm)			18.8

EXCHANGES:

Milk	0.0	Bread	1.0
Veg.	0.5	Meat	0.0
Fruit	0.0	Fat	0.0

2   acorn or butternut squash, about
    1 lb. each
½   cup onion, chopped
2   cups Chicken Stock (see p. 40)
½   teaspoon cinnamon, ground
¼   teaspoon coriander, ground
¼   teaspoon cumin, ground
⅛   teaspoon turmeric
    Black pepper, freshly ground, to taste
1   tablespoon apple cider vinegar
1   cup buttermilk
4   tablespoons nonfat dry milk
1   tablespoon low-sodium soy sauce
1   tablespoon parsley, chopped

Place whole squash in oven and microwave on High for 2 minutes. Pierce deeply several times with fork. Microwave on

High for 6 to 8 minutes more until soft, turning squash over and rotating twice. Let stand 5 minutes or until cool enough to handle. Slice squash in half, discard seeds, and scrape out pulp. There should be about 3 cups of pulp.

Let squash cool for 10 minutes; then turn into blender or food processor with onion and Chicken Stock and puree. Transfer to an 8-cup measuring bowl and add spices, vinegar, milks, and soy sauce. Microwave for 2 to 3 minutes until soup simmers. Adjust seasoning and serve with garnish of parsley.

 # Snow Pea Soup

Serves 4

4	cups Chicken Stock (see p. 40)
1/4	cup scallions, minced
1/4	cup carrots, finely chopped
1	clove garlic, minced
1	teaspoon fresh ginger root, peeled and grated
1	teaspoon low-sodium soy sauce
1/4	cup mushrooms, sliced
1	cup snow peas (about 1/4 lb.), washed and trimmed
4	ozs. firm tofu (bean curd) cut into 1/2-inch cubes
	Scallions, additional, for garnish

Nutritional Data

PER SERVING:

Calories	71
% calories from fat	23
Fat (gm)	1.8
Sat. Fat (gm)	0.4
Cholesterol (mg)	10.1
Sodium (mg)	69
Protein (gm)	6.5
Carbohydrate (gm)	5

EXCHANGES:

Milk	0.0	Bread	0.0
Veg.	1.0	Meat	1.0
Fruit	0.0	Fat	0.0

Place stock, scallions, carrots, garlic, ginger root, and soy sauce in 8-cup measure. Microwave on High for 8 to 10 minutes. Add mushrooms and cook 5 minutes more on High. Add snow peas and microwave for 1 minute more on High. Stir in tofu and garnish with scallions.

Sorrel Soup

Serves 10

1	lb. fresh sorrel, or spinach, chopped
6	green onions, chopped
2	quarts water
1/2	teaspoon salt
1/4	cup fresh lemon juice
1	egg white, slightly beaten
1	cup plain nonfat yogurt

Nutritional Data

PER SERVING:

Calories	25
% calories from fat	4
Fat (gm)	0.1
Sat. Fat (gm)	0
Cholesterol (mg)	0.4
Sodium (mg)	154
Protein (gm)	2.8
Carbohydrate (gm)	3.8

EXCHANGES:

Milk	0.0	Bread	0.0
Veg.	1.0	Meat	0.0
Fruit	0.0	Fat	0.0

Wash and chop sorrel, and place in saucepan with 1 cup water. Simmer 10 minutes. Transfer sorrel to large saucepan. Add green onions, 2 quarts water, salt, and juice; bring mixture to boil. Reduce heat to simmer, partially cover, and continue cooking 15 minutes.

Taste; soup should be tart. Simmer 10 minutes more. Remove 1 cup soup and combine it with egg white. Return to pot and stir to blend. Cover soup and chill. Stir in yogurt.

Spinach Soup

Serves 12

1	cup water
1	large leek
1	carrot, peeled and sliced
1	celery stalk, sliced
6	cups chicken broth
6	large bunches fresh spinach, stems removed
3	tablespoons Parmesan cheese, freshly grated
	Croutons (optional)

Nutritional Data

PER SERVING:

Calories	61
% calories from fat	24
Fat (gm)	1.8
Sat. Fat (gm)	0.5
Cholesterol (mg)	2.4
Sodium (mg)	125
Protein (gm)	6.4
Carbohydrate (gm)	6.8

EXCHANGES:

Milk	0.0	Bread	0.0
Veg.	2.0	Meat	0.0
Fruit	0.0	Fat	0.0

In large saucepan, bring to boil water, leek, carrot, and celery. Reduce heat and simmer until vegetables are tender. Add chicken broth and bring to boil. Add spinach. Cook 2 minutes uncovered until spinach wilts. Transfer to food processor in small batches. Puree until very smooth. Transfer to large bowl. Serve garnished with grated cheese and (optional) croutons.

This soup is best used immediately as the color will change if left standing.

Fresh Tomato Soup

Serves 6

2¼	lbs. fresh tomatoes
1	tablespoon vegetable oil
4	scallions, chopped
4	cloves garlic, minced
2½	cups chicken broth
4	tablespoons fresh basil, minced
1	bay leaf
2	teaspoons sugar
½	cup white wine
2	cups fresh tomatoes, chopped
1	tablespoon parsley, minced

Nutritional Data

PER SERVING:

Calories	111
% calories from fat	28
Fat (gm)	3.7
Sat. Fat (gm)	0.6
Cholesterol (mg)	0.4
Sodium (mg)	347
Protein (gm)	4.4
Carbohydrate (gm)	14.3

EXCHANGES:

Milk	0.0	Bread	0.0
Veg.	3.0	Meat	0.0
Fruit	0.0	Fat	0.5

Place tomatoes (a few at a time) in large pot of boiling water. Leave in about 30 seconds. Remove and slip off skins. Quarter tomatoes and remove seeds. Put tomatoes in blender and mix 1 minute.

Heat oil in large saucepan and sauté chopped scallions until transparent. Add garlic and tomatoes. Lower heat and simmer 5 minutes. Stir in chicken broth, herbs, and sugar. Cover pan and simmer 30 minutes. Add wine and chopped tomatoes and cook another 15 minutes. Remove from heat and stir in parsley.

NO SUGAR ADDED *Tomato-Orange Soup*

Serves 6

3   medium tomatoes, peeled, seeded, and chopped
2   small oranges
3/4   cup chopped onion
2   packets instant chicken broth mix dissolved in 1½ cups hot water
1   cup tomato juice, chilled, mixed with 1 packet Equal® (see "About This Cookbook")
½   cup dry white wine
1   tablespoon red wine vinegar
¼   teaspoon salt
¼   teaspoon pepper

Nutritional Data

PER SERVING:

Calories	65
% calories from fat	7
Fat (gm)	0.5
Sat. Fat (gm)	0
Cholesterol (mg)	0
Sodium (mg)	553
Protein (gm)	1.7
Carbohydrate (gm)	12.3

EXCHANGES:

Milk	0.0	Bread	0.0
Veg.	1.0	Meat	0.0
Fruit	0.5	Fat	0.0

Place chopped tomatoes in large bowl. Remove zest of 1 orange and set aside. Remove and discard peel from both oranges. Cut oranges into cubes and add to tomatoes.

Add remaining ingredients, except orange zest, and stir to combine. Cover and chill for at least 1 hour to allow flavors to develop. Garnish with orange zest.

▣ Tomato Vegetable Soup

Serves 4

3 cups canned Italian plum tomatoes
1 tablespoon frozen apple juice concentrate
1 tablespoon scallions, minced (reserve green tops for garnish)
2 whole cloves
1 bay leaf
½ cup frozen peas, thawed
½ cup corn kernels (canned or, if frozen, thawed)
   Dash pepper

Nutritional Data

PER SERVING:

Calories	76
% calories from fat	8
Fat (gm)	0.7
Sat. Fat (gm)	0.1
Cholesterol (mg)	0
Sodium (mg)	378
Protein (gm)	3.3
Carbohydrate (gm)	16.4

EXCHANGES:

Milk	0.0	Bread	1.0
Veg.	0.0	Meat	0.0
Fruit	0.0	Fat	0.0

Puree tomatoes in blender or food processor, and turn into a 9-inch-deep glass bowl or soup tureen. Add apple juice, scallions, cloves, and bay leaf and cover with vented plastic wrap. Microwave on High for 2 minutes.

Remove plastic, stir, and add peas and corn. Cover and microwave on High for 3 to 4 minutes more until heated through. Remove bay leaf and cloves, stir, and garnish with remaining green scallions and dashes of pepper.

▣ Crunchy Vegetable Soup

Serves 4

1½ cups asparagus, about 6 spears
1 medium carrot, chopped fine
1 stalk celery, chopped fine
2 tablespoons onion, chopped
2 medium mushrooms, sliced
1 cup Chicken Stock (see p. 40)
1 cup nonfat plain yogurt
   Dash tarragon
   Dash cayenne pepper
   Pepper, to taste
   Diced pimientos for garnish

Nutritional Data

PER SERVING:

Calories	64
% calories from fat	7
Fat (gm)	0.5
Sat. Fat (gm)	0.2
Cholesterol (mg)	3.5
Sodium (mg)	63
Protein (gm)	5.6
Carbohydrate (gm)	9.6

EXCHANGES:

Milk	0.0	Bread	0.0
Veg.	2.0	Meat	0.0
Fruit	0.0	Fat	0.0

Place asparagus spears on dish with a little water and cover with wax paper. Microwave on High for 5 to 6 minutes. Cut into 1-inch pieces and place in food processor with vegetables and Chicken Stock. Process until finely chopped.

Turn into 8-cup measure and microwave on High for 6 to 8 minutes until soup simmers. Stir in yogurt. Serve with dusting of tarragon, cayenne, and pepper and garnish of diced pimientos.

May be served warm or chilled. Any combination of vegetables may be used for this potage—broccoli, cauliflower, cucumbers, radishes—just as long as they are crunchable.

Garlic Vegetable Soup

Serves 8

2	tablespoons olive oil
1	cup leeks, finely chopped
5	cloves garlic
2½	quarts water
½	cup white beans, cooked
1	lb. fresh tomatoes, peeled, seeded, and coarsely chopped
1	cup new potatoes, diced
1	cup carrots, coarsely chopped
½	cup celery, chopped
1	cup fresh green beans, cut up
4	tablespoons dried basil
1	tablespoon tarragon
2	tablespoons tomato paste
	Pepper, freshly ground

Nutritional Data

PER SERVING:

Calories	125
% calories from fat	27
Fat (gm)	4
Sat. Fat (gm)	0.5
Cholesterol (mg)	0
Sodium (mg)	57
Protein (gm)	3.7
Carbohydrate (gm)	20.7

EXCHANGES:

Milk	0.0	Bread	0.5
Veg.	2.0	Meat	0.0
Fruit	0.0	Fat	0.5

Heat olive oil in large saucepan. Add leeks and garlic and sauté over low heat for 5 minutes. Add remaining ingredients, and simmer over medium heat 30 minutes, stirring occasionally. Serve hot.

Confetti Soup

Serves 8

2	carrots, sliced
1	cup leek, or green onions, sliced
1	10-oz. package frozen broccoli, chopped
1	10-oz. package frozen cauliflower
1½	cups chicken broth
3	cups skim milk
1	tablespoon cornstarch
1	teaspoon Spike (see "About This Cookbook")
	Pepper, freshly ground, to taste

Nutritional Data

PER SERVING:

Calories	79
% calories from fat	7
Fat (gm)	0.6
Sat. Fat (gm)	0.2
Cholesterol (mg)	1.7
Sodium (mg)	217
Protein (gm)	6
Carbohydrate (gm)	13.3

EXCHANGES:

Milk	0.5	Bread	0.0
Veg.	1.5	Meat	0.0
Fruit	0.0	Fat	0.0

In large saucepan, cook carrots and leek or onions until almost tender. Add broccoli, cauliflower, and chicken broth. Continue to cook until vegetables are tender.

In blender, mix half the vegetables until smooth and return to saucepan. Combine 1/2 cup skim milk with cornstarch; add to vegetable mixture in saucepan. Boil, stirring constantly, until thickened.

Stir in remaining milk and Spike. Cook and stir 1 to 2 minutes more. Remove from heat and add pepper.

Garden Green Soup

Serves 4

1 teaspoon canola oil
4 shallots, sliced
3 cloves garlic, minced
4 cups mixed greens, rinsed well and shredded (use combination of romaine and red leaf or Boston lettuce, spinach, escarole, and sorrel)
2 cups skim milk
1 cup Chicken Stock (see p. 40)
1 tablespoon oat bran
1/4 cup fresh basil, chopped, or 1 teaspoon dried
Rind of 1 lemon, grated
Pepper, to taste

Nutritional Data

PER SERVING:

Calories	87
% calories from fat	18
Fat (gm)	1.9
Sat. Fat (gm)	0.3
Cholesterol (mg)	4.5
Sodium (mg)	84
Protein (gm)	6.7
Carbohydrate (gm)	11.6

EXCHANGES:

Milk	0.5	Bread	0.0
Veg.	1.0	Meat	0.0
Fruit	0.0	Fat	0.5

Place oil, shallots, and garlic in 2-quart measure, and microwave on High for 2 minutes. Add greens and stir to combine. Microwave on High for 2 to 3 minutes, stirring, until greens are wilted.

Add remaining ingredients and transfer to food processor, 2 cups at a time, to blend. Return to original container and microwave until hot, 5 to 8 minutes. Serve warm or chilled.

Vegetarian Minestrone

Serves 10

3 tablespoons olive oil
2 cloves garlic
1/2 cup onion, chopped
3 large carrots, cut into 1/2-inch slices
2 medium potatoes, diced
1 medium leek, thinly sliced
3 stalks celery
1 cup parsley, tightly packed
2/3 cup cannellini beans, or Great Northern, picked over and rinsed, soaked in water overnight, drained
1 14-oz. can Italian plum tomatoes, undrained

Nutritional Data

PER SERVING:

Calories	200
% calories from fat	25
Fat (gm)	5.9
Sat. Fat (gm)	1
Cholesterol (mg)	1.3
Sodium (mg)	344
Protein (gm)	6.9
Carbohydrate (gm)	29.3

EXCHANGES:

Milk	0.0	Bread	1.5
Veg.	2.0	Meat	0.0
Fruit	0.0	Fat	1.0

```
6   cups water
1   15-oz. can chickpeas
½   cup small elbow macaroni
2   zucchini, cut into ½-inch slices
2   cups shredded cabbage, loosely packed
1   tablespoon oregano
1   tablespoon basil
1   cup red wine
8   teaspoons Parmesan cheese,
    freshly grated
```

In large soup pot, heat olive oil. Sauté garlic and onion until onion becomes limp, about 3 minutes. Add carrots, potatoes, leek, celery, ½ the parsley, cannellini beans, and plum tomatoes with juice plus 6 cups of water. Bring to boil, cover, and reduce heat. Simmer until cannellini beans are soft, about 1 hour.

Add chickpeas, macaroni, and zucchini. Cook uncovered over medium heat 5 minutes, adding water if soup becomes too thick. Add cabbage, oregano, basil, and red wine. Cook about 5 additional minutes. Ladle soup into bowls and top with 1 teaspoon Parmesan cheese and remaining parsley.

Spicy Oatmeal Soup

Serves 8

```
1   tablespoon margarine
1   tablespoon peanut oil
2   large leeks, or green onions, cleaned and
    thinly sliced (about 2½ cups)
4   carrots, peeled and cut into ½-inch slices
2   medium potatoes, diced
2   medium zucchini, sliced
2   stalks celery, thinly sliced
6   cups chicken broth
1   tablespoon dried chives
1   tablespoon dried shallots
½   tablespoon tarragon
½   teaspoon basil
1   tablespoon sodium-free Spike
    (see "About This Cookbook")
2   drops hot sauce, or to taste
½   cup quick-cooking oatmeal
1   cup white wine
```

Nutritional Data

PER SERVING:

Calories	168
% calories from fat	25
Fat (gm)	4.8
Sat. Fat (gm)	1
Cholesterol (mg)	0.8
Sodium (mg)	631
Protein (gm)	6.5
Carbohydrate (gm)	20.8

EXCHANGES:

Milk	0.0	Bread	1.0
Veg.	2.0	Meat	0.0
Fruit	0.0	Fat	1.0

Heat margarine and peanut oil in large saucepan and add leeks. Cook 2 to 3 minutes over medium to high heat. Add carrots, potatoes, zucchini, celery, and chicken broth. Bring to a boil.

Add chives, shallots, tarragon, basil, Spike, and hot sauce. Boil gently 20 minutes. Add oatmeal and cook another 5 minutes. Add wine and cook another 15 minutes.

Tangy Zucchini Soup

Serves 5

1	medium onion, finely chopped
1	small clove garlic, minced
2	cups zucchini, diced
½	cup potato, peeled and diced
3	cups chicken bouillon reconstituted from cubes or granules
2	tablespoons parsley leaves, chopped
¼	teaspoon dry mustard
⅛	teaspoon white pepper
	Dash (generous) cayenne pepper
½	cup buttermilk
½	cup whole milk
	Salt, to taste
	Zucchini slices, thin, for garnish (optional)

Nutritional Data

PER SERVING:

Calories	67
% calories from fat	20
Fat (gm)	1.7
Sat. Fat (gm)	0.7
Cholesterol (mg)	4.2
Sodium (mg)	600
Protein (gm)	3.4
Carbohydrate (gm)	11.5

EXCHANGES:

Milk	0.0	Bread	0.5
Veg.	1.0	Meat	0.0
Fruit	0.0	Fat	0.0

In medium-size saucepan, combine onion, garlic, zucchini, potato, bouillon, parsley, mustard, white pepper, and cayenne. Bring to boil over high heat. Cover, lower heat, and simmer 12 to 15 minutes until potato is very tender. Remove pan from heat. Cool mixture slightly.

In batches, mix in blender on low speed for 10 seconds. Then raise speed to high and puree until almost completely smooth but some parsley flecks remain. Transfer puree to medium-size glass or ceramic bowl. Stir in buttermilk and milk.

Cover and chill 4 to 5 hours. Taste soup; add salt if desired. Serve in cups or small bowls. If desired, garnish each serving with thin zucchini slice.

Keeps 2 to 3 days in refrigerator.

Andalusian Gazpacho

Serves 8

4	large tomatoes, peeled and quartered
2	cucumbers, peeled and sliced
½	green bell pepper, seeded and sliced
1	small onion, peeled and quartered
3	cloves garlic
1	tablespoon olive oil
2	tablespoons white vinegar
3	slices white bread, trimmed and cubed
½	teaspoon pepper
½	cup green onion, chopped, for garnish
½	green bell pepper, minced, for garnish
1	large tomato, chopped, for garnish

Nutritional Data

PER SERVING:

Calories	70
% calories from fat	28
Fat (gm)	2.4
Sat. Fat (gm)	0.4
Cholesterol (mg)	0
Sodium (mg)	58
Protein (gm)	2.1
Carbohydrate (gm)	11.4

EXCHANGES:

Milk:	0.0	Bread:	0.0
Veg.:	2.0	Meat:	0.0
Fruit:	0.0	Fat	0.5

Puree until smooth first 9 ingredients in food processor with steel blade or in blender with 1 cup water. Place soup in deep bowl. Cover and chill. Soup will be thick but not solid. Serve in cups and sprinkle with garnishes.

Gazpacho

Serves 4

3	cups tomatoes, peeled, seeded, and chopped
1½	cups tomato juice
¾	cup cucumber, peeled, seeded, and chopped
⅓	cup onion, chopped
⅓	cup green bell pepper, chopped
2	tablespoons balsamic vinegar
¼	teaspoon hot sauce
1	clove garlic, minced
4	cucumber slices and 4 teaspoons minced green bell pepper (optional, for garnish)

Nutritional Data

PER SERVING:

Calories	71
% calories from fat	8
Fat (gm)	0.7
Sat. Fat (gm)	0.1
Cholesterol (mg)	0
Sodium (mg)	339
Protein (gm)	2.6
Carbohydrate (gm)	16.3

EXCHANGES:

Milk	0.0	Bread	0.0
Veg.	3.0	Meat	0.0
Fruit	0.0	Fat	0.0

Combine first 5 ingredients in blender; process until almost smooth. Pour into large bowl. Stir in vinegar and next two ingredients; cover and chill at least 2 hours. Garnish with cucumber slices and minced bell pepper, if desired. Serve chilled.

To Freeze: Place in microwave-safe container; label and freeze for up to 2 months.

To Serve: Thaw. Cover with microwave-safe plastic wrap, and cook on High for 3 to 5 minutes. Garnish with cucumber slices and minced bell pepper.

Cantaloupe-Lime Cooler

Serves 5

¼ cup sugar
1 tablespoon cornstarch
Dash (generous) salt
¾ cup cold water
½ large cantaloupe, peeled, seeded, and cut into 1-inch chunks (about 4 cups)
Zest, grated, from 1 lime
1 tablespoon (generous) fresh lime juice
Thin lime slices for garnish (optional)

Nutritional Data

PER SERVING:

Calories	90
% calories from fat	3
Fat (gm)	0.4
Sat. Fat (gm)	0
Cholesterol (mg)	0
Sodium (mg)	12
Protein (gm)	1.1
Carbohydrate (gm)	22.5

EXCHANGES:

Milk	0.0	Bread	0.0
Veg.	0.0	Meat	0.0
Fruit	1.5	Fat	0.0

Stir together sugar, cornstarch, and salt in small saucepan. Gradually stir in water until mixture is smooth. Bring to a boil over medium heat and cook, stirring about 1 minute or until mixture thickens. Set aside to cool slightly.

In blender, combine sugar-water mixture with cantaloupe. Mix on low speed until all pieces are partially pureed. Then raise speed to high, and mix until desired consistency is reached. Transfer to medium-size bowl. Stir in lime zest and lime juice. Cover and chill 4 to 5 hours or overnight. Stir before serving. If desired, garnish individual portions with small slice of lime.

Keeps 1 or 2 days in refrigerator.

Iced Strawberry-Buttermilk Soup

Serves 5

3 cups loose-packed frozen cut rhubarb, partially thawed
¾ cup granulated sugar (or more, to taste)
½ cup cranberry juice cocktail, divided
1 tablespoon fresh lemon juice
1½ tablespoons cornstarch
3 tablespoons Grand Marnier, or kirsch (cherry liqueur), or orange juice
2⅔ cups ripe strawberries, hulled, or frozen (partially thawed) loose-packed whole strawberries
1½ cups buttermilk (approximately), divided
1 teaspoon vanilla extract
Fresh or frozen strawberry slices for garnish

Nutritional Data

PER SERVING:

Calories	241
% calories from fat	4
Fat (gm)	1.1
Sat. Fat (gm)	0.4
Cholesterol (mg)	2.7
Sodium (mg)	83
Protein (gm)	3.6
Carbohydrate (gm)	52.3

EXCHANGES:

Milk	0.0	Bread	0.0
Veg.	0.0	Meat	0.0
Fruit	4.0	Fat	0.0

In medium-size saucepan, stir together rhubarb, sugar, and 1/4 cup cranberry juice over medium heat. Bring mixture to simmer, stirring. Simmer, stirring occasionally, 7 to 9 minutes or until rhubarb is very tender.

Meanwhile, stir together remaining 1/4 cup cranberry juice, lemon juice, cornstarch, and Grand Marnier in cup until well blended and smooth. Stir cornstarch mixture into rhubarb mixture until smoothly incorporated. Cook, stirring, about 2 minutes longer or until mixture thickens and becomes clear.

In batches, transfer mixture to blender. Mix until completely pureed and smooth, about 2 minutes, for each batch. If mixture looks and tastes smooth at this point, transfer it to storage container. If bits of rhubarb remain, strain mixture through fine sieve into storage container.

Combine strawberries, 1 1/4 cups buttermilk, and vanilla in blender. Process until very smooth. Strain puree through very fine sieve into bowl, pressing down on solids with large spoon to force through as much juice and pulp as possible; discard seeds. Stir strained strawberries into rhubarb mixture. Add sugar to taste if soup is too tart; stir until sugar dissolves. Place soup in freezer for 1 1/2 to 2 1/2 hours or until very cold and a few ice crystals have formed around edges but mixture is not frozen.

Stir soup to break up any ice crystals. Divide soup among small, chilled bowls. Pour about 2 teaspoons of buttermilk into center of each bowl. Using small spoon, stir once through soup and buttermilk to produce a swirled effect. Garnish each serving with several strawberry slices and serve immediately.

Keeps up to 24 hours in refrigerator.

Summer Fruit Soup

Serves 6

- 3 cups watermelon cubes, divided into 2 portions
- 2 cups whole fresh strawberries, divided into 2 portions
- ½ cup fresh orange juice
- 1½ teaspoons fresh lemon juice
- 1 tablespoon cornstarch
- ½ teaspoon allspice
- ¼ teaspoon cinnamon
- ⅛ teaspoon ginger
- ⅛ teaspoon mace
- 2 packets Equal® (see "About This Cookbook")
- ¾ cup skim milk
  Lemon peel for garnish

Nutritional Data

PER SERVING:

Calories	68
% calories from fat	8
Fat (gm)	0.7
Sat. Fat (gm)	0.1
Cholesterol (mg)	0.5
Sodium (mg)	18
Protein (gm)	2
Carbohydrate (gm)	14.8

EXCHANGES:

Milk	0.0	Bread	0.0
Veg.	0.0	Meat	0.0
Fruit	1.0	Fat	0.0

Place half of melon in blender or food processor and puree. Add half of strawberries and process again. Repeat with the other half. Strain fruit mixture into medium saucepan.

In small cup, combine orange and lemon juices with cornstarch. Stir into fruit mixture. Add spices. Heat, stirring until mixture comes to a boil.

Remove from heat, stir in Equal® and milk. Cover and chill before serving. Garnish with lemon peel.

Tropical Melon Soup

Serves 4

½   small cantaloupe, peeled, seeded, and cut into 1-inch chunks
1½   cups honeydew melon chunks
¼   cup fresh lemon juice
¼   cup fresh orange juice
¼   cup dry white wine
2   packets Equal® (see "About This Cookbook")
Lime zest, mixed with 2 tablespoons coconut

Nutritional Data

PER SERVING:

Calories	110
% calories from fat	10
Fat (gm)	1.4
Sat. Fat (gm)	0.7
Cholesterol (mg)	0
Sodium (mg)	22
Protein (gm)	2
Carbohydrate (gm)	23.1

EXCHANGES:

Milk	0.0	Bread	0.0
Veg.	0.0	Meat	0.0
Fruit	1.5	Fat	0.5

Place melon chunks in blender or food processor and mix until pureed (do this in 2 batches). Add juices and wine; continue processing. Stir in Equal®. Garnish with lime zest and coconut. Chill before serving.

Cucumber Yogurt Soup

Serves 4

3   cups yogurt
1½   cups cucumber, peeled, seeded, and grated
1   teaspoon Spike (see "About This Cookbook")
¾   cup cold water
1   teaspoon white pepper
1   tablespoon dill, minced
3   tablespoons fresh chives, minced
1   tablespoon garlic, minced
4   thin slices cucumber

Nutritional Data

PER SERVING:

Calories	120
% calories from fat	21
Fat (gm)	2.8
Sat. Fat (gm)	1.7
Cholesterol (mg)	10.5
Sodium (mg)	122
Protein (gm)	9.6
Carbohydrate (gm)	14.5

EXCHANGES:

Milk	1.0	Bread	0.0
Veg.	0.5	Meat	0.0
Fruit	0.0	Fat	0.5

Put all ingredients, except cucumber slices, in mixing bowl. Stir until blended. Chill well. Serve in chilled bowls and top each with cucumber slice. Serve with garlic bread.

Chapter Three

SALADS &
SALAD
DRESSINGS

Caesar Salad

Serves 6

1	recipe Caesar Dressing, omitting Parmesan cheese (see p. 132)
1	large head romaine
6	anchovy fillets, drained and chopped
1	clove garlic
1½	tablespoons crumbled blue cheese
1½	tablespoons Parmesan cheese, freshly grated
¾	cup croutons
	Juice of ½ lemon

Nutritional Data

PER SERVING:

Calories	55
% calories from fat	30
Fat (gm)	1.9
Sat. Fat (gm)	0.8
Cholesterol (mg)	6
Sodium (mg)	650
Protein (gm)	4.4
Carbohydrate (gm)	5.5

EXCHANGES:

Milk	0.0	Bread	0.0
Veg.	1.0	Meat	0.0
Fruit	0.0	Fat	0.5

Prepare dressing; refrigerate 1 hour.

Trim core from romaine. Separate into leaves, discarding wilted or discolored ones. Place in salad basket. Rinse under cold, running water; shake well to remove excess moisture. (Or wash under cold running water; drain and dry on paper towels.) Place romaine in a plastic bag; store in refrigerator until crisp and cold, several hours or overnight.

Add chopped anchovies to dressing. Keep refrigerated. Rub garlic clove into surface of large wooden salad bowl and then discard.

Cut coarse ribs from large leaves of romaine. Tear in bite-size pieces into salad bowl. Shake dressing well, and pour ½ cup over romaine. Sprinkle with both kinds of cheese and croutons. Toss until all romaine is coated with salad dressing.

Pour lemon juice directly over salad; toss well. Add remaining dressing, toss well, and serve immediately.

West Coast Salad

Serves 4

¼	cup plus 3 tablespoons raspberry-flavored vinegar, divided
1	tablespoon vegetable oil
1½	teaspoons water
1	tablespoon honey
2½	cups water
4	4-oz. chicken breast halves, boneless and skinless

Nutritional Data

PER SERVING:

Calories	171
% calories from fat	30
Fat (gm)	5.8
Sat. Fat (gm)	1
Cholesterol (mg)	45.7
Sodium (mg)	86
Protein (gm)	19.1
Carbohydrate (gm)	11.8

½ lb. fresh spinach
1 cup fresh raspberries
½ cup mushrooms, sliced
1 cup alfalfa sprouts

EXCHANGES:			
Milk	0.0	Bread	0.0
Veg.	2.0	Meat	2.0
Fruit	0.0	Fat	0.0

Combine 3 tablespoons vinegar, oil, water, and honey in jar. Cover tightly and shake vigorously. Chill.

Bring 2½ cups water and remaining ¼ cup vinegar to boil in large, nonaluminum skillet. Add chicken; cover; reduce heat, and simmer 10 minutes or until chicken is done. Drain. Cut chicken into cubes.

Remove stems from spinach; wash leaves thoroughly and pat dry on paper towels. Gently rinse raspberries; drain. Arrange chicken and raspberries evenly among 4 spinach-lined plates. Carefully ring plate with mushrooms and place 1 or 2 slices among raspberries. Drizzle with dressing. Top salad with alfalfa sprouts.

Confetti Chicken Salad

Serves 4

3 medium bell peppers (if possible: 1 yellow, 1 green, 1 red), seeded, cut into strips
2 cups cooked chicken breast, boneless, skinless, and cubed
1½ cups corn, fresh or frozen, cooked, drained, cooled
1 green onion, sliced
2 tablespoons cider vinegar
1 tablespoon olive oil
1 tablespoon parsley, chopped
1 clove garlic, minced
½ teaspoon oregano
   Salt, or salt substitute
   Black pepper, freshly ground, to taste

Nutritional Data

PER SERVING:

Calories	221
% calories from fat	33
Fat (gm)	8.3
Sat. Fat (gm)	1.8
Cholesterol (mg)	58
Sodium (mg)	54
Protein (gm)	21.6
Carbohydrate (gm)	17

EXCHANGES:			
Milk	0.0	Bread	1.0
Veg.	0.0	Meat	3.0
Fruit	0.0	Fat	0.0

Combine peppers, chicken, corn, and green onions in large bowl. In separate bowl, whisk together remaining ingredients. Pour over chicken mixture. Chill and serve.

Creole Chicken Salad

Serves 4

- 2 small heads Boston lettuce, torn into pieces
- 6 plum tomatoes, sliced
- 2 small onions, sliced
- 4 teaspoons cayenne pepper
- 3 teaspoons paprika
- 2 teaspoons ground black pepper
- 1 teaspoon chili powder
- 1 teaspoon garlic powder
- 1 teaspoon salt substitute
- 4 chicken breast halves, boneless and skinless (about 1 lb.)
  Louisiana Dressing (recipe follows)

Nutritional Data

PER SERVING:

Calories	242
% calories from fat	27
Fat (gm)	7.8
Sat. Fat (gm)	1.4
Cholesterol (mg)	45.7
Sodium (mg)	271
Protein (gm)	21.5
Carbohydrate (gm)	24

EXCHANGES:

Milk	0.0	Bread	1.0
Veg.	2.0	Meat	2.0
Fruit	0.0	Fat	0.0

Toss together lettuce, tomatoes, and onions in large bowl and set aside. Combine spices in small bowl, mixing well. Season both sides of chicken breasts well with spice mixture.

Broil or grill chicken 5 to 6 minutes per side until cooked through. Allow to cool. Cut into 1-inch pieces and add to vegetables. Pour Louisiana Dressing over all and toss well.

Louisiana Dressing

- ¼ cup Dijon mustard
- 1 tablespoon olive oil
- 2 tablespoons dry white wine
- 1 tablespoon honey
- 1½ teaspoons sugar
  Salt, or salt substitute
  Black pepper, freshly ground, to taste

Whisk together all ingredients, pour over Creole Chicken Salad, and coat well.

Greek Smoked Chicken Salad

Serves 4

- 10 ozs. fresh spinach leaves
- 1 bunch bok choy, stems trimmed, leaves sliced
- 6 ozs. smoked chicken breast, boneless, skinless, and cut into thin strips
- 2 turkey, or vegetarian, bacon slices, cut into ½-inch pieces
- 6 tablespoons Dijon mustard

Nutritional Data

PER SERVING:

Calories	131
% calories from fat	33
Fat (gm)	5.1
Sat. Fat (gm)	1.9
Cholesterol (mg)	46.2
Sodium (mg)	986
Protein (gm)	16.2
Carbohydrate (gm)	7

		EXCHANGES:			
2	tablespoons red wine vinegar	Milk	0.0	Bread	0.0
2	tablespoons water	Veg.	1.0	Meat	2.0
1	oz. feta cheese, crumbled	Fruit	0.0	Fat	0.0

Combine spinach, bok choy, and chicken in large bowl and set aside. Cook bacon in large skillet until crisp; remove, drain, and discard skillet drippings.

Using very low heat, add mustard and vinegar to skillet, and whisk together until smooth. Whisk in water. Increase heat slightly, and add bacon and feta, stirring until heated through, but do not boil.

Add enough dressing to greens and chicken to coat salad well. Serve remaining dressing on the side.

Oriental Chicken Salad

Serves 6

3½	tablespoons Tamari soy sauce		
1	tablespoon vegetable oil		
2	tablespoons balsamic vinegar		
1	tablespoon sugar		
1	clove garlic, minced		
2	tablespoons fresh chives, chopped		
3	cups lettuce, torn		
1½	cups cooked chicken breast, chopped		
1	8-oz. can sliced water chestnuts, drained		
¼	cup green onions, diagonally sliced		
1	package pea pods, thawed		
1	cup red cabbage, chopped		
	Chow mein noodles (optional)		

Nutritional Data

PER SERVING:

Calories	146
% calories from fat	30
Fat (gm)	4.9
Sat. Fat (gm)	1
Cholesterol (mg)	29
Sodium (mg)	620
Protein (gm)	12.7
Carbohydrate (gm)	13.5

EXCHANGES:			
Milk	0.0	Bread	0.0
Veg.	3.0	Meat	1.5
Fruit	0.0	Fat	0.0

In small bowl, whisk together first 6 dressing ingredients. Set aside. In large bowl, combine remaining salad ingredients except chow mein noodles. Just before serving, toss salad with dressing and top with chow mein noodles.

Chicken with Spinach and Bean Salad

Serves 4

Bean Salad

1	15-oz. can Great Northern beans, drained, rinsed, and patted dry
½	cup celery, chopped
½	cup tomato, chopped
¼	cup red onion, chopped
3	tablespoons white wine
1	teaspoon balsamic vinegar
½	teaspoon dried oregano
½	teaspoon dried tarragon
	Spike, to taste (see "About This Cookbook")
	Black pepper, freshly ground, to taste

Chicken with Spinach

	Vegetable cooking spray
1	10-oz. package fresh spinach, washed and stems removed
2	cloves garlic, minced
2	tablespoons pine nuts
	Black pepper, freshly ground, to taste
2	10-oz. whole chicken breasts, boneless, skinless, split, and pounded to flatten

Nutritional Data

PER SERVING:

Calories	298
% calories from fat	17
Fat (gm)	5.8
Sat. Fat (gm)	0.8
Cholesterol (mg)	57.2
Sodium (mg)	127
Protein (gm)	32.6
Carbohydrate (gm)	29.3

EXCHANGES:

Milk	0.0	Bread	1.5
Veg.	1.0	Meat	2.8
Fruit	0.0	Fat	0.0

Bean Salad: In small bowl, combine beans, celery, tomato, and red onion. In separate bowl, whisk together wine, vinegar, oregano, and tarragon. Season with Spike and pepper. Add dressing to bean mixture and toss gently.

Chicken with Spinach: In large skillet coated with vegetable cooking spray, over medium heat, cook spinach with water clinging to its leaves until wilted and soft, 4 to 5 minutes. Drain excess water. Add garlic and pine nuts. Cook and stir 3 minutes. Season with pepper and set aside.

Place chicken breasts on broiler pan and set pan about 5 inches from heat. Broil breasts, turning once, until they are cooked through, 3 to 4 minutes on each side.

Reheat spinach if necessary. Distribute spinach evenly among four heated serving plates. Place chicken breast on top of each spinach portion. Place bean salad on each plate. Serve at once.

Chicken and Raspberry Salad

Serves 8

Dressing

¼ cup raspberry vinegar
1 tablespoon olive oil
1 tablespoon honey mustard
¼ teaspoon salt
¼ teaspoon black pepper, freshly ground

Salad

2 large pears, peeled, cored, and julienned
2 tablespoons fresh lime juice
3 cups radicchio, or other lettuce, washed, dried, and torn into bite-size pieces
1 red onion, sliced paper-thin and separated into rings
2½ cups cooked chicken, boneless and skinless, julienned
1 cup fresh raspberries, rinsed and dried on paper towels

Nutritional Data

PER SERVING:

Calories	134
% calories from fat	27
Fat (gm)	4.1
Sat. Fat (gm)	0.8
Cholesterol (mg)	36.9
Sodium (mg)	130
Protein (gm)	14.4
Carbohydrate (gm)	10.4

EXCHANGES:

Milk	0.0	Bread	0.0
Veg.	0.0	Meat	2.0
Fruit	0.5	Fat	0.0

Dressing: Combine raspberry vinegar, olive oil, honey mustard, salt, and pepper in small bowl and reserve.

Salad: Toss pears in 2 tablespoons lime juice. Arrange pears with radicchio, onion rings, and chicken in attractive glass serving bowl. Add dressing and toss well to combine. Sprinkle with fresh raspberries.

Chicken and Wild Rice Salad

Serves 6

1¼ cups wild rice, rinsed
3¼ cups water
¼ teaspoon salt, or salt substitute
½ tablespoon white wine vinegar
1 tablespoon olive oil
    Salt, or salt substitute
    Black pepper, freshly ground, to taste
2 whole smoked chicken breasts, boneless, skinless, and cut into 1-inch pieces
½ bunch green onions, chopped
¼ cup golden raisins

Nutritional Data

PER SERVING:

Calories	290
% calories from fat	26
Fat (gm)	8.5
Sat. Fat (gm)	1.3
Cholesterol (mg)	30
Sodium (mg)	751
Protein (gm)	17.9
Carbohydrate (gm)	36.2

EXCHANGES:

Milk	0.0	Bread	1.5
Veg.	0.0	Meat	2.0
Fruit	1.0	Fat	0.5

Curried Chutney Dressing
(recipe follows)
6   large (or 12 small) lettuce leaves

In large saucepan, combine wild rice with water and 1/4 teaspoon salt (or salt substitute). Bring to boil and reduce to simmer. Cover and cook 45 to 50 minutes.

Transfer to large bowl, and toss well with vinegar, oil, salt (or salt substitute), and pepper. Allow to cool.

Add chicken, green onions, raisins, and Curried Chutney Dressing; mix well to coat. Serve on lettuce leaves.

Curried Chutney Dressing

1   clove garlic, minced
1   tablespoon white wine vinegar
2   tablespoons fresh lemon juice
3/4   tablespoon curry powder
1 1/2 tablespoons bottled mango chutney
2   tablespoons olive oil
1/4   cup nonfat sour cream
1-2   tablespoons water
1/4   cup fresh coriander, minced

In blender or food processor, combine garlic, vinegar, lemon juice, curry powder, and chutney; blend until smooth. With motor running, add oil in a stream; then add sour cream and water. Blend until smooth. Stir in coriander before pouring over chicken and rice mixture.

Curried Rice, Chicken, and Fruit Salad

Serves 7

Dressing

1/4   cup reduced-fat mayonnaise
1/2   cup nonfat buttermilk
3   tablespoons nonfat dry milk powder
2   teaspoons mild curry powder, or to taste
1/2   teaspoon salt, or to taste (optional)
1/4   teaspoon white pepper

Salad

1   lb. chicken breast, boneless, skinless, and trimmed of all fat
1   15 1/4-oz. can juice-packed pineapple tidbits, well drained
2 1/4 cups cooked long-grain white rice

Nutritional Data

PER SERVING:

Calories	210
% calories from fat	17
Fat (gm)	3.9
Sat. Fat (gm)	0.7
Cholesterol (mg)	30
Sodium (mg)	62
Protein (gm)	12.9
Carbohydrate (gm)	31.3

EXCHANGES:

Milk	0.0	Bread	1.0
Veg.	0.0	Meat	1.5
Fruit	1.0	Fat	0.0

    1   large red bell pepper, seeded and cubed (if
        unavailable, substitute green bell pepper)
    1½ cups green seedless grapes
    2   tablespoons sliced green onion tops

Dressing: Place mayonnaise in large serving bowl.
Gradually whisk in buttermilk. With large spoon, stir in nonfat
milk powder, curry powder, salt, if desired, and pepper.

Salad: Cut or tear each breast into 2 or 3 large pieces.
Place chicken pieces in medium-size pot. Cover with 1 inch of
water, and bring to a boil. Cover pot, reduce heat, and simmer
10 to 13 minutes or until chicken is cooked through. Cool
chicken in colander under cold running water. Dry with paper
towels, cut into bite-size pieces, and reserve.

Drain pineapple in colander. Stir pineapple into dressing
mixture. Add rice, reserved chicken, red pepper, grapes, and
scallions to bowl with salad dressing. Toss to coat well. Cover
and refrigerate several hours, stirring occasionally. Garnish
with additional chopped green onions, if desired.

Brown Rice and Chicken Salad

Serves 8

2	cups uncooked brown rice
2	cups water
2	cups chicken breast, cooked and diced
12	scallions, thinly sliced
2	celery ribs, chopped
2	medium green bell peppers, chopped
½	cup pitted black olives, sliced
¼	cup pimiento, minced
½	pint cherry tomatoes
½	cup parsley, chopped
½	cup radishes, sliced
¼	cup olive oil
¼	cup white wine vinegar

Nutritional Data

PER SERVING:

Calories	340
% calories from fat	34
Fat (gm)	13.7
Sat. Fat (gm)	2.2
Cholesterol (mg)	29
Sodium (mg)	321
Protein (gm)	14.2
Carbohydrate (gm)	40.8

EXCHANGES:

Milk	0.0	Bread	2.0
Veg.	2.0	Meat	1.5
Fruit	0.0	Fat	1.5

In a covered saucepan, cook rice in water until liquid is
absorbed and rice is fluffy, approximately 45 minutes. Remove
from heat and cool. Add remaining ingredients and toss.

Imitation crabmeat or tuna can be added instead of chicken.

Rice Salad

Serves 6

1½ cups uncooked long-grain rice
⅓ cup Italian Vinaigrette (see p. 129)
3 scallions, chopped
1 tablespoon parsley, chopped
1 tablespoon basil, chopped
⅓ cup red or green bell pepper, diced
⅓ cup celery, diced
⅓ cup cucumber, peeled and diced
2 large firm tomatoes, peeled, seeded, and diced
¼ cup chopped Italian hot marinated peppers
2 tablespoons capers
¼ cup pitted Italian black olives, chopped
Spike, to taste (see "About This Cookbook")
Pepper, freshly ground, to taste
1 large firm tomato, seeded and cut into wedges
Black or green olives
Parsley sprigs

Nutritional Data

PER SERVING:

Calories	273
% calories from fat	28
Fat (gm)	8.7
Sat. Fat (gm)	1.9
Cholesterol (mg)	3.5
Sodium (mg)	335
Protein (gm)	5.2
Carbohydrate (gm)	41.8

EXCHANGES:

Milk	0.0	Bread	2.5
Veg.	1.0	Meat	0.0
Fruit	0.0	Fat	1.5

Bring 4 cups of water to boil, add rice, reduce heat, and simmer for 15 minutes, until rice is cooked *al dente*. Drain, and place rice in mixing bowl. Add Vinaigrette and scallions. Combine well. Set aside to cool.

When cooled, add remaining salad ingredients, toss to mix thoroughly, and adjust for taste with Spike and pepper. Mound salad on serving platter, and garnish with tomato wedges, olives, and parsley.

Sombreros

(Taco Salad)

Serves 8

Vegetable cooking spray
1 lb. chicken breast, ground
8 ozs. mild taco sauce
1 head iceberg lettuce, shredded
10 scallions, chopped
1 pint cherry tomatoes, halved
6 ozs. light taco cheese, shredded
8 flour tortillas
Parsley sprigs (optional)

Nutritional Data

PER SERVING:

Calories	251
% calories from fat	27
Fat (gm)	7.5
Sat. Fat (gm)	0.7
Cholesterol (mg)	34.1
Sodium (mg)	491
Protein (gm)	19
Carbohydrate (gm)	26.8

EXCHANGES:

Milk	0.0	Bread	1.5
Veg.	1.0	Meat	2.0
Fruit	0.0	Fat	0.0

Spray large saucepan and brown chicken. Drain well. Mix with taco sauce. In large salad bowl, arrange lettuce. Layer scallions, tomatoes, and cheese on top of lettuce. Add chicken mixture. Spray tortillas lightly and bake at 300 degrees until crisp, about 5 minutes. Place 1 tortilla on each plate and mound the meat mixture on top. Garnish with sprig of parsley, if desired.

Thai Pork Salad

Serves 6

3½ ozs. uncooked rice sticks, or angel hair pasta

Dressing

1½ tablespoons reduced-sodium soy sauce
3 tablespoons dry sherry
2 tablespoons defatted chicken broth
1 teaspoon apple cider vinegar
2 tablespoons sesame oil
2 teaspoons granulated sugar
¾ teaspoon ground ginger
2-3 drops hot oil, or hot pepper sauce

Pork

¾ lb. pork loin chops, trimmed of all fat and cut into thin strips
1½ tablespoons reduced-sodium soy sauce
2 teaspoons apple cider vinegar
¼ teaspoon black pepper

Salad

3 cups shredded lettuce
1½ cups cooked black beans, or 1 15-oz. can black beans, rinsed and well drained
1 large tomato, diced
1 large cucumber, peeled, seeded, and sliced
1 large red bell pepper, seeded and diced
¾ cup fresh cilantro, coarsely chopped
2 tablespoons green onion tops, chopped

Nutritional Data

PER SERVING:

Calories	263
% calories from fat	30
Fat (gm)	8.8
Sat. Fat (gm)	2
Cholesterol (mg)	25.5
Sodium (mg)	300
Protein (gm)	13.8
Carbohydrate (gm)	31.2

EXCHANGES:

Milk	0.0	Bread	1.5
Veg.	0.5	Meat	2.0
Fruit	0.0	Fat	0.5

Cook rice sticks according to package directions. Rinse and cool in colander under cold running water, breaking up long noodles with fingers. Set aside to drain.

Dressing: In large salad bowl, combine soy sauce with sherry, chicken broth, vinegar, sesame oil, sugar, ginger, and hot oil. Stir to mix well. Set aside.

Pork: Place chops in nonstick spray-coated skillet. Sprinkle with soy sauce, vinegar, and black pepper. Toss to coat. Cook over medium-high heat, turning several times, until cooked through. Transfer pork and any pan juices to bowl with dressing mixture. Stir to coat.

Salad: Add lettuce, black beans, tomato, cucumber, red pepper, cilantro, and green onion to bowl containing other ingredients. Stir to mix well. Stir in rice noodles. Refrigerate 1 or 2 hours, stirring occasionally, or up to 6 hours before serving. Garnish with additional cilantro sprigs, if desired.

California Crab Salad

Serves 4

8	ozs. crabmeat, fresh or frozen (defrost if frozen)
½	cup water chestnuts, sliced
½	cup celery, thinly sliced
¼	cup green onion, sliced
	Lettuce leaves
4	stalks cooked or canned asparagus
4	artichoke hearts, canned or fresh cooked
2	tablespoons chopped pimiento
2	tablespoons chopped parsley
1	cup fresh bean sprouts
	Capri Dressing (see p. 130)

Nutritional Data

PER SERVING:

Calories	147
% calories from fat	14
Fat (gm)	2.7
Sat. Fat (gm)	0.5
Cholesterol (mg)	59.2
Sodium (mg)	412
Protein (gm)	18.6
Carbohydrate (gm)	13.6

EXCHANGES:

Milk	0.0	Bread	0.0
Veg.	1.5	Meat	2.0
Fruit	0.0	Fat	0.0

Place crab, water chestnuts, celery, and onion in a bowl. Mix well. Place lettuce leaves on each of 4 plates. Top with scoop of crab salad. Place 1 asparagus stalk and 1 artichoke heart on each plate. Garnish with pimiento and parsley. Top with sprouts. Serve with Capri Dressing.

Crab Salad Louis

Serves 4

⅓	cup fat-free mayonnaise
⅔	cup low-fat plain yogurt
2	tablespoons skim milk
¼	cup low-sodium chili sauce
¼	cup green bell pepper, chopped
¼	cup green onions, chopped
2	tablespoons green olives, chopped
	Juice of ½ lemon
	Lettuce
2	cups imitation crabmeat chunks
¼	cup fresh chives, minced

Nutritional Data

PER SERVING:

Calories	124
% calories from fat	14
Fat (gm)	2
Sat. Fat (gm)	0.6
Cholesterol (mg)	13.9
Sodium (mg)	887
Protein (gm)	9.8
Carbohydrate (gm)	17.4

EXCHANGES:

Milk	0.0	Bread	1.0
Veg.	0.0	Meat	1.0
Fruit	0.0	Fat	0.0

For the dressing, mix first 8 ingredients in small bowl. Line 4 individual bowls with lettuce. Toss crabmeat with salad dressing. Spoon crabmeat salad into individual serving bowls and garnish with chives.

Mock Lobster Salad with Avocado Sauce

Serves 6

Light Avocado Sauce

¼ medium avocado, peeled
¼ cup plain nonfat yogurt
2 teaspoons red wine vinegar
¼ teaspoon each ingredient: hot pepper sauce, salt, tarragon
¼ cup cholesterol- and fat-free mayonnaise

Salad

Canola oil, or vegetable cooking spray
1¼ lbs. mahimahi, or monk fish, fillets
1 tablespoon orange peel, grated
4 cups assorted lettuce (Boston, head, romaine, or oak leaf), washed, dried well, and torn into bite-size pieces
1 large tomato, sliced thin
1 orange, sliced thin
1½ cups red onions, sliced thin

Nutritional Data

PER SERVING:

Calories	143
% calories from fat	14
Fat (gm)	2.2
Sat. Fat (gm)	0.4
Cholesterol (mg)	69.2
Sodium (mg)	314
Protein (gm)	19.5
Carbohydrate (gm)	11.4

EXCHANGES:

Milk	0.0	Bread	0.0
Veg.	2.0	Meat	2.0
Fruit	0.0	Fat	0.0

Light Avocado Sauce: In small bowl, mash avocado, discarding stone. Mix in yogurt, vinegar, hot pepper sauce to taste, salt, and tarragon. Add mayonnaise and blend well. Taste to adjust seasonings. Cover and refrigerate until needed.

Salad: Coat skillet with canola oil or cooking spray and cook fish 6 to 8 minutes, turning once or twice. Fish is done when it turns opaque and is slightly firm to the touch. Sprinkle fish with orange peel as it cooks. The fish slices better when chilled, so you may cook it the day before and refrigerate covered. Cut fish into thin slices, or into chunks, and put in deep bowl. Toss fish with Avocado Sauce.

Divide and arrange lettuce among 6 salad plates. Spoon mahimahi salad in center of each plate. Arrange tomato and orange slices around salad. Sprinkle salads with thin slices of red onion. Serve chilled.

Baked Seafood Salad

Serves 6

1   small green bell pepper, chopped
1   small onion, chopped
1   cup celery, chopped
½   lb. imitation crabmeat (surimi)
½   lb. shrimp, boiled
1   lb. small scallops, cooked
1   cup Mock Sour Cream (see p. 497)
1   teaspoon Spike (see "About This Cookbook")
1   teaspoon Worcestershire sauce
1   cup bread crumbs
2   tablespoons margarine

Nutritional Data

PER SERVING:

Calories	241
% calories from fat	23
Fat (gm)	6.1
Sat. Fat (gm)	1.3
Cholesterol (mg)	54.6
Sodium (mg)	738
Protein (gm)	24.6
Carbohydrate (gm)	21.5

EXCHANGES:

Milk	0.0	Bread	1.0
Veg.	0.0	Meat	3.0
Fruit	0.0	Fat	0.0

Preheat oven to 350 degrees. Mix all ingredients except bread crumbs and margarine in casserole. Sprinkle bread crumbs on top; dot with margarine. Bake 30 minutes. Do not overbake.

Seafood Pasta Salad with Divine Cream Dressing

Serves 10

Pasta

1   lb. pasta shells
⅓   cup olive oil
¼   cup white wine vinegar
1   tablespoon sherry wine vinegar
    Pepper, freshly ground, to taste

Nutritional Data

PER SERVING:

Calories	518
% calories from fat	31
Fat (gm)	18.3
Sat. Fat (gm)	2.4
Cholesterol (mg)	56.7
Sodium (mg)	977
Protein (gm)	38.2
Carbohydrate (gm)	52.2

EXCHANGES:

Milk	0.0	Bread	3.0
Veg.	1.0	Meat	4.0
Fruit	0.0	Fat	1.0

Cook pasta *al dente*. Drain, rinse in cold water, and place in large bowl. Mix with oil and vinegars. Season to taste with pepper. Cover and refrigerate.

Keeps 2 days in refrigerator.

Vegetables

12   thin asparagus spears (fresh if possible), trimmed and cut into 1½-inch lengths
2½   cups broccoli florets, cut into bite-size pieces
2½   cups peas, fresh or frozen
10   scallions
1   pint cherry tomatoes
2   large heads romaine lettuce, torn into bite-size pieces

Separately boil or steam asparagus and broccoli until crisp-tender, about 15 minutes. Steam fresh peas briefly or use defrosted, uncooked frozen peas. Mince scallions; combine with tomatoes. If you are not making salad to be served now, store vegetables in separate plastic bags in refrigerator. These can be prepared up to 2 days in advance.

Seafood

2	lbs. bay scallops, or halved sea scallops
2	lbs. imitation crabmeat, cut into 2-inch lengths
1/3	cup olive oil
3	tablespoons white wine vinegar
3	tablespoons red wine vinegar
1	clove garlic, minced
2	scallions, minced
	Pepper, freshly ground, to taste
1	teaspoon Spike (see "About This Cookbook")

Poach scallops in simmering water until opaque, about 2 minutes. Drain. Combine scallops and crabmeat in bowl. Add oil, vinegars, and garlic; mix well. Reserve minced scallions, Spike, and pepper for salad assembly.

Divine Cream Dressing

1/3	cup white wine vinegar
2	tablespoons Dijon mustard
1/2	cup packed fresh basil leaves; or 4 tablespoons dried basil, crushed
2	cloves garlic
1/3	cup vegetable oil
1	cup Mock Sour Cream (see p. 497)
1/2	cup skim milk
3	tablespoons parsley, minced
1/4	cup chives, snipped

In food processor or blender, combine vinegar, mustard, basil, and garlic. Add oil slowly and mix until smooth. Add Mock Sour Cream, skim milk, parsley, and chives. Process until smooth.

To Assemble: Arrange romaine as a border on large platter. Toss pasta with vegetables and tomato-scallion mixture. Place in center of platter and make a well in center of pasta. Drain seafood; toss with minced scallions, pepper, and Spike. Mound in center of pasta. Serve with Divine Cream Dressing.

Easy Cold Pasta Salad

Serves 8

2   green bell peppers, seeded and chopped
1   cup Spanish onion, chopped
1   cup artichoke hearts, drained and
    quartered
1   cup tomatoes, chopped
1   lb. small no-egg pasta, cooked *al dente*
    and cooled
1   cup plain nonfat yogurt
3   tablespoons red wine vinegar
½   teaspoon salt
¼   teaspoon white pepper
½   teaspoon powdered garlic
1   teaspoon Worcestershire sauce

Nutritional Data

PER SERVING:

Calories	241
% calories from fat	7
Fat (gm)	1.8
Sat. Fat (gm)	0.3
Cholesterol (mg)	0.5
Sodium (mg)	193
Protein (gm)	10.7
Carbohydrate (gm)	46.1

EXCHANGES:

Milk	0.0	Bread	2.5
Veg.	2.0	Meat	0.0
Fruit	0.0	Fat	0.0

In deep mixing bowl, toss vegetables with cooked, drained pasta. In small bowl, combine yogurt, wine vinegar, and seasonings. Drizzle dressing over salad and toss well. Chill until ready to serve.

Rotini Salad with Tuna

Serves 6

1   recipe Italian Dressing (see p. 131)
8   ozs. rotini
2   6½-oz. cans white tuna, water packed
2   medium tomatoes, chopped
1   cup mushrooms, sliced
1   4-oz. jar marinated artichoke hearts
¼   cup green bell pepper, sliced
¼   cup radishes, sliced
¼   cup fat-free mozzarella
    cheese, shredded
¼   cup pitted black olives, sliced (optional)

Nutritional Data

PER SERVING:

Calories	291
% calories from fat	20
Fat (gm)	6.4
Sat. Fat (gm)	1.4
Cholesterol (mg)	28
Sodium (mg)	624
Protein (gm)	24.6
Carbohydrate (gm)	34.7

EXCHANGES:

Milk	0.0	Bread	2.0
Veg.	1.0	Meat	2.0
Fruit	0.0	Fat	0.0

Cook rotini, drain. Combine with remaining ingredients. Pour dressing over salad. Chill. May be made without tuna.

Salade Niçoise
with Dressing

Serves 10

Salad

2	lbs. green beans, cut in 1½-inch lengths
2	green bell peppers, cut in thin rounds
2	cups celery, sliced
1	pint cherry tomatoes
5	medium red potatoes, cooked and sliced, with skins
21	ozs. canned tuna, water packed, drained
10	large pitted black olives
1	large red onion, thinly sliced
2	tablespoons fresh basil, chopped, or 1 tablespoon dried basil
⅓	cup parsley, finely chopped
¼	cup scallions, finely chopped

Dressing Niçoise

2	teaspoons Dijon mustard
2	tablespoons wine vinegar
6	tablespoons olive oil
2	cloves garlic, minced
1	teaspoon fresh thyme, or ½ teaspoon dried thyme
	Pepper, freshly ground, to taste

Nutritional Data

PER SERVING:

Calories	423
% calories from fat	34
Fat (gm)	17.2
Sat. Fat (gm)	2.3
Cholesterol (mg)	17.9
Sodium (mg)	184
Protein (gm)	30.6
Carbohydrate (gm)	43.7

EXCHANGES:

Milk	0.0	Bread	2.0
Veg.	2.0	Meat	4.0
Fruit	0.0	Fat	1.0

Salad: Steam beans until crisp-tender, about 15 minutes. Drain and rinse under cold water. Place beans, green peppers, celery, tomatoes, and potatoes or large platter, arranging in symmetrical pattern. Flake tuna over vegetables. Scatter olives and red onions over all. Sprinkle with basil, parsley, and scallions. Drizzle with dressing after bowl has been presented.

Dressing: Shake all dressing ingredients in tightly covered jar and refrigerate 1 hour.

Asparagus with Fresh Fruit Dressing

Serves 4

12 large stalks asparagus, cooked and chilled
   Shredded dark green lettuce
4 tablespoons chopped melon (cantaloupe or honeydew)
4 large fresh strawberries, sliced
1 small apple, finely chopped
1 teaspoon fresh lemon juice
1 packet Equal® (see "About This Cookbook)

Nutritional Data

PER SERVING:

Calories	35
% calories from fat	6
Fat (gm)	0.3
Sat. Fat (gm)	0
Cholesterol (mg)	0
Sodium (mg)	3
Protein (gm)	1.5
Carbohydrate (gm)	7.9

EXCHANGES:

Milk	0.0	Bread	0.0
Veg.	0.5	Meat	0.0
Fruit	0.5	Fat	0.0

Arrange asparagus on a bed of lettuce. Combine fruits, lemon juice, and Equal®. Top each salad with a fourth of the fruit mixture.

Mandarin Beets with Citrus Dressing

Serves 6

Beets

1 recipe Citrus Dressing (recipe follows)
2 bunches beets, cooked, cooled, and thinly sliced
2 red onions, thinly sliced
1 11-oz. can mandarin orange segments, drained

Citrus Dressing

1 tablespoon vegetable oil
2 tablespoons fruit-only orange marmalade
2 tablespoons fresh lemon juice
3/4 teaspoon salt
   Dash pepper

Nutritional Data

PER SERVING:

Calories	104
% calories from fat	20
Fat (gm)	2.4
Sat. Fat (gm)	0.3
Cholesterol (mg)	0
Sodium (mg)	312
Protein (gm)	1.9
Carbohydrate (gm)	20.2

EXCHANGES:

Milk	0.0	Bread	0.0
Veg.	2.0	Meat	0.0
Fruit	0.5	Fat	0.5

Beets: Place beets, onions, and mandarin orange segments in bowl. Pour dressing over salad and toss well.

Dressing: Shake all ingredients in tightly covered jar. Makes about 1/2 cup of dressing.

Pickled Beet Salad

Serves 4

- 2 cups canned beets (no salt or sugar added), undrained
- 1 tablespoon red wine vinegar
- 1 bay leaf
- 1 whole clove
- 1 packet Equal® (see "About This Cookbook")
  Shredded lettuce
- ½ small onion, sliced and separated into rings

Nutritional Data

PER SERVING:

Calories	41
% calories from fat	2
Fat (gm)	0.1
Sat. Fat (gm)	0
Cholesterol (mg)	0
Sodium (mg)	324
Protein (gm)	1.2
Carbohydrate (gm)	9.7

EXCHANGES:

Milk	0.0	Bread	0.0
Veg.	2.0	Meat	0.0
Fruit	0.0	Fat	0.0

Drain beet juice into small skillet. Add vinegar, bay leaf, and clove. Bring to boil and simmer for 1 minute. Remove from heat and add Equal®.

Let mixture cool. Pour cooled juice over beets and allow to marinate overnight in refrigerator. Lift beets with slotted spoon from juice and serve on bed of shredded lettuce. Garnish with onion rings.

Crunchy Broccoli Salad

Serves 4

- 2 lbs. fresh broccoli
- ½ lb. fresh mushrooms, sliced
- ¼ cup Mock Sour Cream (see p. 497)
- ½ cup fat-free mayonnaise
- 1 teaspoon sugar
- ⅛ teaspoon pepper
- 1 teaspoon onion, grated
- 1 clove garlic, crushed
- 1 8-oz. can water chestnuts, drained and sliced

Nutritional Data

PER SERVING:

Calories	142
% calories from fat	7
Fat (gm)	1.2
Sat. Fat (gm)	0.2
Cholesterol (mg)	0.4
Sodium (mg)	477
Protein (gm)	9.4
Carbohydrate (gm)	28.9

EXCHANGES:

Milk	0.0	Bread	0.0
Veg.	5.0	Meat	0.0
Fruit	0.0	Fat	0.0

Cut off and discard tough ends of broccoli stalks. Break florets into small clusters. Reserve stems for another use. Steam broccoli for about 10 minutes or until crisp-tender.

In small bowl, combine mushrooms, Mock Sour Cream, mayonnaise, sugar, pepper, onion, and garlic. In large salad bowl, combine cooked broccoli and water chestnuts. Add creamed mixture; toss lightly. Cover and refrigerate 2 hours or more to blend flavors.

Moroccan Carrot Salad

Serves 8

- 8 medium carrots
- 2 teaspoons paprika
- ½ teaspoon cinnamon
- 1 teaspoon ground cumin
- 1 tablespoon fresh lemon juice
- 1 tablespoon sugar
- 2 tablespoons white wine
- ½ teaspoon black pepper, freshly ground
  Spike (see "About This Cookbook")
- 2 onions, chopped and sautéed, kept warm

Nutritional Data

PER SERVING:

Calories	58
% calories from fat	5
Fat (gm)	0.3
Sat. Fat (gm)	0
Cholesterol (mg)	0
Sodium (mg)	27
Protein (gm)	1.4
Carbohydrate (gm)	13.1

EXCHANGES:

Milk	0.0	Bread	0.0
Veg.	2.0	Meat	0.0
Fruit	0.0	Fat	0.0

Peel carrots and thinly slice or cut into julienne strips. You should have about 2 cups.

Place spices, lemon juice, and sugar in mortar and grind with pestle to emulsify. Gradually work in wine. Season to taste with pepper and Spike.

Heat medium pot of water to boiling. Drop in carrots and cook until tender, about 20 minutes. Drain carrots and put them in bowl.

Toss immediately with vinaigrette from mortar. If carrots seem gritty, add a tablespoon of cold water to smooth out dressing. Add onions and toss again.

Slaw Polonaise

Serves 5

- ½ cup low-fat yogurt
- ¼ cup buttermilk
- 1 packet Equal® (see "About This Cookbook")
  Garlic powder to taste
- 2 tablespoons dill pickle, minced
- 1 teaspoon poppy seed
  Dash salt
  Dash pepper
- 1 lb. cabbage, shredded
  Paprika

Nutritional Data

PER SERVING:

Calories	44
% calories from fat	11
Fat (gm)	0.6
Sat. Fat (gm)	0.1
Cholesterol (mg)	0.9
Sodium (mg)	96
Protein (gm)	2.9
Carbohydrate (gm)	7.7

EXCHANGES:

Milk	0.0	Bread	0.0
Veg.	1.5	Meat	0.0
Fruit	0.0	Fat	0.0

Combine all ingredients except cabbage and paprika in blender. Mix for 1 minute. Refrigerate until needed. At serving time, toss dressing with cabbage and sprinkle with paprika.

Chinese Coleslaw

Serves 4

1	small head cabbage, shredded
1	tablespoon olive oil
½	cup white vinegar
⅓	cup sugar
1	teaspoon coarse salt
¼	teaspoon pepper, freshly ground
½	cup radishes, sliced
2	teaspoons dried shallots

Put cabbage into bowl. In jar with tight-fitting lid, combine oil, vinegar, sugar, salt, pepper, radishes, and shallots. Shake well to blend. Pour dressing over cabbage and mix well. Refrigerate.

Nutritional Data

PER SERVING:

Calories	158
% calories from fat	20
Fat (gm)	3.9
Sat. Fat (gm)	0.5
Cholesterol (mg)	0
Sodium (mg)	588
Protein (gm)	4.6
Carbohydrate (gm)	30.8

EXCHANGES:

Milk	0.0	Bread	1.0
Veg.	2.0	Meat	0.0
Fruit	0.0	Fat	1.0

Favorite Coleslaw

Serves 6

¼	cup Dijon mustard
¼	cup fat-free mayonnaise
2	teaspoons sugar
1	teaspoon fresh lemon juice
½	teaspoon salt
1	medium cabbage, shredded

Mix mustard, mayonnaise, sugar, lemon juice, and salt. Add cabbage and toss well.

Nutritional Data

PER SERVING:

Calories	34
% calories from fat	18
Fat (gm)	0.7
Sat. Fat (gm)	0.1
Cholesterol (mg)	0
Sodium (mg)	624
Protein (gm)	1.2
Carbohydrate (gm)	6.4

EXCHANGES:

Milk	0.0	Bread	0.0
Veg.	1.5	Meat	0.0
Fruit	0.0	Fat	0.0

Court Salad with Raspberry Vinaigrette

Serves 10

Salad

1	bunch watercress, washed and torn into bite-size pieces
2	heads Bibb lettuce, torn into bite-size pieces
1	lb. mushrooms, sliced
1	15-oz. can artichoke hearts, drained

Nutritional Data

PER SERVING:

Calories	222
% calories from fat	31
Fat (gm)	8
Sat. Fat (gm)	1.2
Cholesterol (mg)	0
Sodium (mg)	398
Protein (gm)	7.6
Carbohydrate (gm.)	32.3

1   bunch white radishes, sliced
½   cup Raspberry Vinaigrette (see below)
1   cup raspberries
    10 French rolls

EXCHANGES:			
Milk	0.0	Bread	1.5
Veg.	2.0	Meat	0.0
Fruit	0.0	Fat	1.5

Raspberry Vinaigrette

1   tablespoon raspberry vinegar
⅛   teaspoon salt
4   tablespoons olive oil
¼   teaspoon Dijon mustard
¼   teaspoon pepper, freshly ground
1-2 tablespoons water

Place greens, mushrooms, artichoke hearts, and radishes in large bowl. Shake vinaigrette ingredients together and drizzle over salad, then toss. Serve with berries on top of each mound of greens.

Cucumber Dill Salad

Serves 4

½   cup cottage cheese
2   tablespoons skim milk
½   teaspoon dried dill
½   teaspoon salt
¼   teaspoon pepper
1   tablespoon dill pickle, finely chopped
1   medium cucumber, thinly sliced
½   red onion, thinly sliced and separated
    into rings

Nutritional Data

PER SERVING:

Calories	41
% calories from fat	9
Fat (gm)	0.4
Sat. Fat (gm)	0.2
Cholesterol (mg)	1.4
Sodium (mg)	419
Protein (gm)	4.6
Carbohydrate (gm)	5.2

EXCHANGES:			
Milk	0.0	Bread	0.0
Veg.	1.0	Meat	0.5
Fruit	0.0	Fat	0.0

Place cottage cheese and milk in blender. Process until whipped and creamy. Add dill, salt, pepper, and dill pickle and mix well. Refrigerate until ready to use. Before serving, combine cucumber and onion slices in bowl. Pour dressing over.

Divine Cucumber Salad

Serves 6

6	medium or 3 large cucumbers, peeled and thinly sliced
1	large red onion, sliced and separated into rings
½	cup white vinegar
3	tablespoons sugar
1	teaspoon coarse salt
¼	teaspoon pepper, freshly ground
¼	teaspoon ginger, ground
1	tablespoon chives, fresh or freeze-dried
	Dash oregano

Nutritional Data

PER SERVING:

Calories	75
% calories from fat	5
Fat (gm)	0.4
Sat. Fat (gm)	0.1
Cholesterol (mg)	0
Sodium (mg)	363
Protein (gm)	2.4
Carbohydrate (gm)	18

EXCHANGES:

Milk	0.0	Bread	1.0
Veg.	0.0	Meat	0.0
Fruit	0.0	Fat	0.0

Layer cucumbers in bowl. Add onions. In jar with tight-fitting lid, combine vinegar, sugar, salt, pepper, ginger, chives, and oregano. Shake well. Pour dressing over cucumbers and refrigerate.

Classic Greek Salad

Serves 6

4	plump tomatoes, cored and quartered
1	cucumber, peeled and cut into ¼-inch slices
1	green bell pepper, seeded and cut into thin, round slices
1	yellow bell pepper, seeded and cut into thin, round slices
1	red bell pepper, seeded and cut into thin, round slices
2-3	anchovies (optional)
12	black olives (optional)
1	large red onion, peeled and cut into thin slices
2	tablespoons feta cheese, crumbled
¾	cup prepared fat-free Italian dressing

Nutritional Data

PER SERVING:

Calories	70
% calories from fat	20
Fat (gm)	1.6
Sat. Fat (gm)	0.9
Cholesterol (mg)	4.7
Sodium (mg)	489
Protein (gm)	2.4
Carbohydrate (gm)	12.1

EXCHANGES:

Milk	0.0	Bread	0.0
Veg.	2.5	Meat	0.0
Fruit	0.0	Fat	0.0

Combine tomatoes, cucumber, peppers, anchovies, olives, onions, and feta cheese in medium-size bowl. Pour on dressing.

Spring Salad

Serves 4	**Nutritional Data**	
4 small carrots	PER SERVING:	
12 radishes	Calories	297
2 heads romaine lettuce	% calories from fat	11
1 bunch arugula	Fat (gm)	3.7
¼ cup prepared fat-free Italian dressing	Sat. Fat (gm)	0.8
12 slices Italian bread	Cholesterol (mg)	0
2 tablespoons Parmesan cheese,	Sodium (mg)	772
coarsely grated (optional)	Protein (gm)	10.1
	Carbohydrate (gm)	56

EXCHANGES:			
Milk	0.0	Bread	3.0
Veg.	2.0	Meat	0.0
Fruit	0.0	Fat	0.5

Scrub carrots and radishes. Grate them coarsely by hand or in food processor. Wash and dry romaine; remove outer leaves and reserve for another use. Wrap hearts in damp paper towels and refrigerate until ready to use. Wash and dry arugula; wrap in damp towels and refrigerate.

Add carrots and radishes to bowl and toss to coat with dressing. Marinate at room temperature for about 20 minutes.

To serve, arrange romaine hearts, bread, and arugula on individual plates. Top with vegetables, spooning some of vegetables and dressing over bread rounds. Garnish with Parmesan.

Italian Mixed Salad

Serves 6	**Nutritional Data**	
6 cups greens (combine endive, butter	PER SERVING:	
lettuce, dandelion, purple kale, arugula,	Calories	48
and romaine)	% calories from fat	17
1 cup chive blossoms	Fat (gm)	1.1
1 red onion, sliced thinly	Sat. Fat (gm)	0.5
1 recipe Italian Vinaigrette (see p. 129)	Cholesterol (mg)	1.6
2 tablespoons Parmesan cheese,	Sodium (mg)	60
freshly grated	Protein (gm)	2.5
	Carbohydrate (gm)	7.5

EXCHANGES:			
Milk	0.0	Bread	0.0
Veg.	2.0	Meat	0.0
Fruit	0.0	Fat	0.0

Place greens, chive blossoms, and onion in bowl. Toss lightly. Pour dressing over greens, and toss again. Sprinkle on Parmesan cheese.

Harlequin Salad

Serves 6	Nutritional Data	
3 medium firm tomatoes, sliced and seeded	**PER SERVING:**	
½ cup Dijonaise Sauce (see p. 496)	Calories	92
4 oz. part-skim mozzarella cheese, sliced	% calories from fat	32
1 small cucumber, peeled and sliced	Fat (gm)	3.6
¼ cup white wine	Sat. Fat (gm)	2
2 tablespoons fresh lemon juice	Cholesterol (mg)	10.7
¼ teaspoon mustard	Sodium (mg)	315
¼ teaspoon Spike (see "About This	Protein (gm)	5.7
Cookbook")	Carbohydrate (gm)	10
2 tablespoons capers		
6 fresh basil leaves, chopped	**EXCHANGES:**	
Oregano sprigs, fresh	Milk 0.0 **Bread** 0.0	
	Veg. 2.5 **Meat** 0.0	
	Fruit 0.0 Fat 0.5	

On one end of an oval or round serving dish, place 1 slice of tomato. Spread 1 teaspoon of the Dijonaise Sauce on it. On top of that, overlapping tomato but not covering it completely, place a slice of mozzarella. On top of mozzarella, without covering completely, place 1 cucumber slice. Repeat in an attractive pattern, starting with tomato slice until all ingredients are used.

Make dressing by combining in mixing bowl wine, lemon juice, mustard, and Spike. Add capers and basil, and combine. When ready to serve, garnish plate with oregano, placing some in center if you are using a round serving platter. Drizzle dressing over salad and serve.

Basque Tomatoes

Serves 8	Nutritional Data	
8 firm tomatoes	PER SERVING:	
½ cup parsley, chopped	Calories	41
1 clove garlic, minced	% calories from fat	31
1 teaspoon salt	Fat (gm)	1.6
1 teaspoon sugar	Sat. Fat (gm)	0.2
¼ teaspoon pepper	Cholesterol (mg)	0
½ cup black olives (optional)	Sodium (mg)	288
2 teaspoons olive oil	Protein (gm)	1.2
2 tablespoons tarragon vinegar	Carbohydrate (gm)	6.9
1 teaspoon Dijon mustard		
	EXCHANGES:	
	Milk 0.0 Bread 0.0	
	Veg. 1.5 Meat 0.0	
	Fruit 0.0 Fat 0.0	

Slice tomatoes and spread them in shallow dish. Sprinkle with parsley. Combine remaining ingredients, mix well, and pour over tomatoes. Drain before serving. Cover and refrigerate. Drain before serving. May be made 2 days ahead.

 # Tomato-Basil Aspic

Serves 6

1	envelope unflavored gelatin
1/4	cup cold water
1 1/4	cups boiling water
3	tablespoons sweet basil vinegar
1/8	teaspoon black pepper
	Dash salt
2	tablespoons onion juice
4	ozs. tomato paste
1	packet Equal® (see "About This Cookbook")
	Lettuce leaves
	Parsley sprigs

Nutritional Data

PER SERVING:

Calories	22
% calories from fat	6
Fat (gm)	0.2
Sat. Fat (gm)	0
Cholesterol (mg)	0
Sodium (mg)	151
Protein (gm)	1.7
Carbohydrate (gm)	4.1

EXCHANGES:

Milk	0.0	Bread	0.0
Veg.	1.0	Meat	0.0
Fruit	0.0	Fat	0.0

Soften gelatin in cold water. Add boiling water and stir until gelatin is dissolved. Add vinegar, pepper, salt, onion juice, and tomato paste; blend. Add Equal® and stir again. Pour into 6 individual molds and chill. Unmold on lettuce and garnish with parsley.

Italian Tomato and Green Bean Salad

Serves 4

6	Italian plum tomatoes, sliced
1/2	cup scallions, chopped
1	lb. green beans, cooked crisp-tender
1/2	cup mushrooms, chopped
1/3	cup prepared fat-free French dressing
	Parsley sprigs

Nutritional Data

PER SERVING:

Calories	99
% calories from fat	7
Fat (gm)	0.8
Sat. Fat (gm)	0.1
Cholesterol (mg)	0
Sodium (mg)	192
Protein (gm)	3.4
Carbohydrate (gm)	21.7

EXCHANGES:

Milk	0.0	Bread	1.0
Veg.	1.5	Meat	0.0
Fruit	0.0	Fat	0.0

Arrange vegetables on plates. Drizzle with dressing and garnish with parsley.

South-of-the-Border Bean Salad

Serves 8

- ½ cup prepared fat-free French dressing
- 1 16-oz. can whole green beans, drained
- 1 15-oz. can garbanzo beans, drained
- 1 15-oz. can kidney beans, drained
- 1 12-oz. can whole kernel corn with sweet peppers, drained
- 1 medium onion, thinly sliced and separated into rings
- ½ cup low-fat taco cheese, shredded
- 8 lettuce cups

Nutritional Data

PER SERVING:

Calories	175
% calories from fat	12
Fat (gm)	2.4
Sat. Fat (gm)	0.2
Cholesterol (mg)	3.7
Sodium (mg)	721
Protein (gm)	8.6
Carbohydrate (gm)	30.3

EXCHANGES:

Milk	0.0	Bread	2.0
Veg.	0.0	Meat	0.5
Fruit	0.0	Fat	0.0

Toss beans, corn, and onion with dressing. Refrigerate at least 1 hour. Before serving, toss with cheese and spoon into lettuce cups.

Parsley and Garbanzo Bean Salad

Serves 12

- 4 cups parsley, chopped
- 2 15½-oz. cans garbanzo beans, drained
- 1 large green bell pepper, chopped
- ½ cup green onions, chopped
- 1 large tomato, seeded and diced
- ¼ cup fresh lemon juice
- 1 clove garlic, minced
- Salt and pepper, to taste
- 2 tablespoons olive oil

Nutritional Data

PER SERVING:

Calories	105
% calories from fat	31
Fat (gm)	3.8
Sat. Fat (gm)	0.5
Cholesterol (mg)	0
Sodium (mg)	304
Protein (gm)	4.2
Carbohydrate (gm)	14.9

EXCHANGES:

Milk	0.0	Bread	1.0
Veg.	0.5	Meat	0.0
Fruit	0.0	Fat	0.5

In large bowl, combine parsley, beans, green pepper, onions, and tomatoes. In another bowl, blend lemon juice, garlic, salt, and pepper and whisk in olive oil in a thin stream. Toss well with salad.

Award-Winning Macaroni Salad

Serves 6

8	ozs. uncooked small elbow macaroni
1	cup whipped low-fat cottage cheese
1/4	cup low-fat yogurt
2	tablespoons vinegar
2	tablespoons mustard
1	teaspoon sugar
1	tablespoon fresh lemon juice
1/4	teaspoon celery seed
1/4	teaspoon oregano
	Pepper, freshly ground, to taste
1	package frozen peas, thawed
1/2	cup celery, diced
1/4	cup green onions, chopped

Nutritional Data

PER SERVING:

Calories	219
% calories from fat	6
Fat (gm)	1.3
Sat. Fat (gm)	0.5
Cholesterol (mg)	2.3
Sodium (mg)	234
Protein (gm)	12.6
Carbohydrate (gm)	38.5

EXCHANGES:

Milk	0.0	Bread	2.5
Veg.	0.0	Meat	0.5
Fruit	0.0	Fat	0.0

Cook macaroni according to package directions; drain. Pour cold water over macaroni; let stand while preparing salad.

In small bowl, combine cottage cheese, yogurt, vinegar, mustard, sugar, lemon juice, celery seed, oregano, and pepper.

In large salad bowl, combine cooked macaroni, peas, celery, and onion. Pour dressing over macaroni; toss to blend. Serve immediately or cover and refrigerate until ready to serve.

Country Potato Salad with Mustard Dressing

Serves 8

24	boiled new potatoes, about 1¼ lbs., with skin
4	hard-boiled egg whites, chopped
1	cup celery, diced
1	cup sweet marinated peppers, chopped, drained (optional)
1/4	cup plain nonfat yogurt
3	tablespoons cholesterol-free, reduced-calorie mayonnaise
2	teaspoons stone-ground mustard
1/2	teaspoon each ingredient: white pepper, garlic powder

Nutritional Data

PER SERVING:

Calories	92
% calories from fat	16
Fat (gm)	1.7
Sat. Fat (gm)	0.4
Cholesterol (mg)	0.1
Sodium (mg)	108
Protein (gm)	3.6
Carbohydrate (gm)	16

EXCHANGES:

Milk	0.0	Bread	1.0
Veg.	0.0	Meat	0.0
Fruit	0.0	Fat	0.5

Scrub potatoes. Put potatoes in saucepan and cover with water; bring to boil over medium-high heat. Reduce heat to medium and continue cooking until potatoes are fork-tender, 15 to 20 minutes. Drain; pat dry and cool.

Slice or dice potatoes. Put potatoes into salad bowl and toss with egg whites, celery, and peppers.

In small bowl, mix yogurt, mayonnaise, mustard, pepper, and garlic powder. Toss salad with dressing. Refrigerate salad before serving, or serve at room temperature.

Smoked Turkey Potato Salad

Serves 8

2½	cups boiled red or new potatoes, unpeeled or peeled
	Olive oil, or vegetable cooking spray
1	tablespoon noncholesterol margarine
1½	cups smoked skinless white turkey meat, cubed or shredded
2	cups celery, chopped
¼	cup dried onion flakes
½	cup parsley, chopped
3	hard-boiled egg whites, chopped
½	teaspoon each ingredient: basil, paprika
¼	teaspoon each ingredient: salt, pepper
3	tablespoons fat-free mayonnaise
¼	cup plain nonfat yogurt

Nutritional Data

PER SERVING:

Calories	144
% Calories from fat	16
Fat (gm)	2.6
Sat. Fat (gm)	0.6
Cholesterol (mg)	17.8
Sodium (mg)	193
Protein (gm)	10.2
Carbohydrate (gm)	20.6

EXCHANGES:

Milk	0.0	Bread	1.0
Veg.	1.0	Meat	1.0
Fruit	0.0	Fat	0.0

Slice potatoes. Coat nonstick skillet lightly with oil or cooking spray. Melt margarine over medium heat. Fry potatoes, stirring as they turn a golden brown, 3 to 5 minutes. Potatoes will break up into pieces. Set aside.

In large serving bowl, toss turkey, potatoes, and remaining ingredients, except mayonnaise and yogurt. In small bowl, mix mayonnaise and yogurt for dressing. Toss salad with dressing.

Serve cold or at room temperature on a bed of lettuce.

German Potato Salad

Serves 8

1²/₃	lbs. small new or red potatoes, with skin	
	Olive oil, or vegetable cooking spray	
½	cup onions, chopped	
⅓	cup low-salt Chicken or Vegetable Stock (see pp. 40, 42)	
⅓	cup cider vinegar	
2	tablespoons sugar	
¾	teaspoon each ingredient: marjoram, celery seeds	
¼	teaspoon each ingredient: salt, white pepper	
2	tablespoons imitation bacon bits	

Nutritional Data

PER SERVING:

Calories	97
% calories from fat	5
Fat (gm)	0.6
Sat. Fat (gm)	0.1
Cholesterol (mg)	0.4
Sodium (mg)	114
Protein (gm)	2.4
Carbohydrate (gm)	21.9

EXCHANGES:

Milk	0.0	Bread	1.5
Veg.	0.0	Meat	0.0
Fruit	0.0	Fat	0.0

Place scrubbed new potatoes in saucepan and cover with water. Bring to boil over medium-high heat. Cook 15 to 20 minutes or until potatoes are just fork-tender. Drain, pat dry, and cool.

Coat nonstick skillet with oil or cooking spray. Sauté onions, partially covered, over medium heat until tender. Stir occasionally. Stir in stock, vinegar, sugar, marjoram, seeds, salt, and pepper. Bring mixture to boil; cook 1 minute and remove from heat.

Cut potatoes in halves or slices; put in salad bowl. Toss with bacon bits. Add hot dressing and toss again. Serve hot or at room temperature.

 # Mock Potato Salad

Serves 8

1	medium rutabaga	
	Pot of boiling water	
1	packet Equal® (see "About This Cookbook")	
1	tablespoon fresh lemon juice	
1	cup minced celery with leaves	
½	cup scallions, finely chopped	
1	medium dill pickle, chopped	
1½	teaspoons salt	
	Dash paprika	
½	cup plain nonfat yogurt	

Nutritional Data

PER SERVING:

Calories	18
% calories from fat	4
Fat (gm)	0.1
Sat. Fat (gm)	0
Cholesterol (mg)	0.3
Sodium (mg)	264
Protein (gm)	1.2
Carbohydrate (gm)	3.6

EXCHANGES:

Milk	0.0	Bread	0.0
Veg.	0.5	Meat	0.0
Fruit	0.0	Fat	0.0

Peel rutabaga and cut into 4 pieces. Drop into boiling water. Continue to boil until tender, about 30 minutes.

Drain well. After rutabaga has cooled, dice (should be about 2 cups), and place in salad bowl. Sprinkle with Equal® and lemon juice. Add celery, scallions, pickle, salt, paprika, and yogurt to rutabaga. Toss well. Chill before serving.

Spinach Salad with Poppy Seed Dressing

NO SUGAR ADDED

Serves 8

4	packets Equal®	
⅓	cup white vinegar	
½	cup white wine	
½	cup water	
1	teaspoon dry mustard	
1	teaspoon dried shallots	
2	tablespoons poppy seeds	
1	lb. fresh spinach, stems removed, cut into bite-size pieces	
½	lb. fresh mushrooms, sliced thin	

Nutritional Data

PER SERVING:

Calories	46
% calories from fat	24
Fat (gm)	1.4
Sat. Fat (gm)	0.2
Cholesterol (mg)	0
Sodium (mg)	47
Protein (gm)	2.7
Carbohydrate (gm)	5

EXCHANGES:

Milk	0.0	Bread	0.0
Veg.	1.5	Meat	0.0
Fruit	0.0	Fat	0.0

Combine the first 7 ingredients in tight-fitting jar. Shake to blend. Refrigerate. Makes ½ cup dressing.

When ready to serve, place spinach and mushrooms in bowl. Stir dressing and pour over salad. Toss well.

Wilted Spinach Salad

Serves 4

3	quarts spinach leaves, rinsed and drained
1	cup mushrooms, sliced
2	teaspoons vegetable oil
1	tablespoon plus 1 teaspoon fresh lemon juice
1	tablespoon plus 1 teaspoon hoisin sauce
1	teaspoon sesame oil
1	teaspoon sugar
1	teaspoon sesame seeds
8	small breadsticks

Nutritional Data

PER SERVING:

Calories	137
% calories from fat	34
Fat (gm)	5.7
Sat. Fat (gm)	0.8
Cholesterol (mg)	0
Sodium (mg)	279
Protein (gm)	6.8
Carbohydrate (gm)	18

EXCHANGES:

Milk	0.0	Bread	0.5
Veg.	2.0	Meat	0.0
Fruit	0.0	Fat	1.0

Tear spinach into bite-size pieces; combine with mushrooms. Heat vegetable oil, lemon juice, hoisin sauce, and sesame oil in large, deep skillet over medium heat, stirring constantly, until bubbly.

Remove skillet from heat; stir in sugar. Stir spinach and mushrooms into skillet; toss until greens are slightly wilted and well coated. Sprinkle with sesame seeds. Serve with breadsticks.

Waldorf Salad

Serves 6

2	medium Delicious apples, chopped
2	stalks celery, chopped
1/3	cup walnuts, coarsely chopped
1/2	cup golden raisins
1/2	cup Mock Sour Cream (see p. 497)
1	tablespoon honey
4-6	lettuce cups
	Apple slices

Nutritional Data

PER SERVING:

Calories	118
% calories from fat	20
Fat (gm)	2.9
Sat. Fat (gm)	0.3
Cholesterol (mg)	0.5
Sodium (mg)	56
Protein (gm)	3.1
Carbohydrate (gm)	22.5

EXCHANGES:

Milk	0.0	Bread	0.0
Veg.	0.0	Meat	0.0
Fruit	1.5	Fat	0.5

Mix chopped apples, celery, walnuts, and raisins with Mock Sour Cream. Add honey and stir to blend. Spoon salad into lettuce cups. Garnish with apple slices.

Tropical Fruit Boats with Banana Dressing

Serves 4

2	pineapples, cut in half
1	cup strawberries
1	medium banana, sliced
1	cup blueberries
1	cup watermelon balls
1	cup cantaloupe balls
2	kiwi fruits, peeled and sliced
1/2	cup low-fat cottage cheese
1	medium banana, cut up
2-3	tablespoons pineapple juice
1	tablespoon honey
2	tablespoons orange peel, grated

Nutritional Data

PER SERVING:

Calories	254
% calories from fat	6
Fat (gm)	2
Sat. Fat (gm)	0.4
Cholesterol (mg)	1.3
Sodium (mg)	126
Protein (gm)	6.2
Carbohydrate (gm)	59

EXCHANGES:

Milk	0.0	Bread	0.0
Veg.	0.0	Meat	0.5
Fruit	4.0	Fat	0.0

Run a serrated knife around perimeter of each pineapple half and remove pineapple meat, leaving ¼-inch shell. Place pineapple meat in bowl. Add strawberries, banana, blueberries, watermelon, cantaloupe, and kiwi fruit; toss well to mix.

To make dressing, place cottage cheese, banana, pineapple juice, and honey in blender and process until smooth. Spoon fruit into pineapple halves. Top with 2 tablespoons dressing. Sprinkle grated orange peel on top.

Blueberry Bavarian Salad

Serves 8

Salad

1½	cups hot water
1	package black raspberry gelatin
½	package lemon gelatin
1	can blueberry pie filling
	Grated rind of 1 lemon
2	teaspoons fresh lemon juice
2	tablespoons sugar

Topping

1	cup Mock Sour Cream (seep. 497)
2	tablespoons sugar
2	teaspoons lemon rind, grated

Nutritional Data

PER SERVING:

Calories	175
% calories from fat	2
Fat (gm)	0.3
Sat. Fat (gm)	0.1
Cholesterol (mg)	0.8
Sodium (mg)	110
Protein (gm)	3.6
Carbohydrate (gm)	41.6

EXCHANGES:

Milk	0.0	Bread	2.0
Veg.	0.0	Meat	0.0
Fruit	0.5	Fat	0.0

Salad: Mix hot water and gelatins; stir until dissolved Cool until syrupy; add pie filling, grated lemon rind, lemon juice, and sugar. Pour into mold or individual molds; chill until firm.

Topping: Combine all ingredients; mix well. Serve over salad.

Cranberry Cream Salad

Serves 6

1	3-oz. package cherry gelatin
1	cup hot water
1	1-lb. can whole cranberry sauce
½	cup celery, diced
¼	cup golden raisins
1	cup Mock Sour Cream (see p. 497)

Dissolve gelatin in hot water. Chill until slightly thickened. Fold cranberry sauce into gelatin with celery and raisins. Fold in Mock Sour Cream. Pour mixture into 1-quart mold. Chill until firm.

Nutritional Data

PER SERVING:

Calories	200
% calories from fat	2
Fat (gm)	0.4
Sat. Fat (gm)	0.2
Cholesterol (mg)	1
Sodium (mg)	150
Protein (gm)	4.2
Carbohydrate (gm)	47.3

EXCHANGES:

Milk	0.0	Bread	0.0
Veg.	0.0	Meat	0.5
Fruit	3.0	Fat	0.0

Cottage Cheese Lime Mold

Serves 6

1 envelope diet lime gelatin
½ cup plain nonfat yogurt
½ cup nonfat mayonnaise
1 teaspoon fresh lemon juice
3 packets Equal® (see "About This Cookbook")
1 lb. cottage cheese (2 cups)
½ cantaloupe, finely diced

Nutritional Data

PER SERVING:

Calories	135
% calories from fat	11
Fat (gm)	1.6
Sat. Fat (gm)	0.9
Cholesterol (mg)	6.7
Sodium (mg)	597
Protein (gm)	13.7
Carbohydrate (gm)	16.9

EXCHANGES:

Milk	0.0	Bread	0.0
Veg.	0.0	Meat	1.5
Fruit	1.0	Fat	0.0

Prepare gelatin according to package directions, but do not add cold water. Add yogurt, mayonnaise, and lemon juice to gelatin. Beat with hand electric beater or rotary beater. Add Equal® to cottage cheese and cantaloupe. Fold cottage cheese mixture into yogurt mixture.

Rinse 1-quart mold with cold water; shake out excess. Pour salad mixture into mold. Refrigerate until set, 3 to 4 hours, before serving.

*Vinaigrette Dressing

Serves 10 (1-tablespoon servings)

½ cup olive oil
2 tablespoons red wine vinegar
1 teaspoon celery salt
1 teaspoon dry mustard
1 clove garlic, finely chopped
   Dash salt
   Dash pepper

Nutritional Data

PER SERVING:

Calories	98
% calories from fat	49
Fat (gm)	11
Sat. Fat (gm)	1.4
Cholesterol (mg)	0
Sodium (mg)	205.1
Protein (gm)	0.1
Carbohydrate (gm)	0.4

EXCHANGES:

Milk	0.0	Bread	0.0
Veg.	0.0	Meat	0.0
Fruit	0.0	Fat	2.0

Shake all ingredients in tightly covered jar. Makes about ⅔ cup dressing, or 10 tablespoons.

*Note: Although this basic salad dressing, alone, contains more than an acceptable percentage of calories from fat, the *total* salad in which it's used should meet our guideline of 35% or fewer calories of fat per serving.

Italian Vinaigrette

Serves 12 (1-tablespoon servings)

¼	cup fresh lemon juice
¼	cup red wine vinegar
¼	cup white wine
1	teaspoon oregano
1	teaspoon basil
½	teaspoon dry mustard
½	teaspoon onion powder
1	clove garlic, minced
1	tablespoon chives, chopped
1	teaspoon thyme
½	teaspoon rosemary

Nutritional Data

PER SERVING:

Calories	7.4
% calories from fat	5
Fat (gm)	0.1
Sat. Fat (gm)	0
Cholesterol (mg)	0
Sodium (mg)	3
Protein (gm)	0.1
Carbohydrate (gm)	1.2

EXCHANGES:

Milk	0.0	Bread	0.0
Veg.	0.0	Meat	0.0
Fruit	0.0	Fat	0.0

Combine all ingredients. Chill for 1 or 2 hours to allow herbs to blend. Makes ¾ cup.

Balsamic Dressing

Serves 16 (1-tablespoon servings)

¾	cup water
¼	cup balsamic vinegar*
3	teaspoons capers
2	teaspoons Dijon mustard
1	teaspoon tarragon
1	teaspoon thyme
1	teaspoon fresh basil
1	tablespoon parsley, chopped

Nutritional Data

PER SERVING:

Calories	6
% calories from fat	9
Fat (gm)	0.1
Sat. Fat (gm)	0
Cholesterol (mg)	0
Sodium (mg)	17
Protein (gm)	0.1
Carbohydrate (gm)	1.4

EXCHANGES:

Milk	0.0	Bread	0.0
Veg.	0.0	Meat	0.0
Fruit	0.0	Fat	0.0

Combine all ingredients. Adjust vinegar to taste; you may feel that it has a strong flavor. Store in covered container. Makes about 1 cup.

*Note: If you don't have balsamic vinegar, substitute another kind; but if you choose another vinegar, combine water in equal proportions.

Capri Dressing

Serves 5 (½-cup servings)

½ cup cottage cheese, whipped in blender
2 tablespoons horseradish
1 tablespoon low-calorie mayonnaise
1 tablespoon fresh lemon juice
1 teaspoon Worcestershire sauce
½ teaspoon dry mustard
2 packets Equal® (see "About This Cookbook")
2 tablespoons parsley

Nutritional Data

PER SERVING:

Calories	32
% calories from fat	32
Fat (gm)	1.1
Sat. Fat (gm)	0.2
Cholesterol (mg)	2
Sodium (mg)	172
Protein (gm)	3
Carbohydrate (gm)	2.4

EXCHANGES:

Milk	0.0	Bread	0.0
Veg.	0.0	Meat	0.5
Fruit	0.0	Fat	0.0

Place all ingredients except parsley in blender and whirl for 1 minute. Mix in parsley and refrigerate until ready to use. For fish salads, or use as a fish sauce. Makes 2½ cups of dressing.

Cumberland Dressing

Serves 16 (2-tablespoon servings)

1 bottle (12 ozs.) low-calorie ketchup (no sugar or salt added)
1 cup pure apple juice
½ cup red wine vinegar
Juice of 1 lemon, strained
1 teaspoon dry mustard
Black pepper, coarsely ground
1 packet Equal® (see "About This Cookbook")
2 stalks celery, finely chopped
1 cucumber, peeled
1 green or red sweet bell pepper, chopped
Tops of 2 green onions

Nutritional Data

PER SERVING:

Calories	36
% calories from fat	4
Fat (gm)	0.2
Sat. Fat (gm)	0
Cholesterol (mg)	0
Sodium (mg)	9.6
Protein (gm)	0.6
Carbohydrate (gm)	9.2

EXCHANGES:

Milk	0.0	Bread	0.0
Veg.	1.5	Meat	0.0
Fruit	0.0	Fat	0.0

Blend all ingredients except vegetables, being careful to dissolve mustard so there will be no lumps. Fold vegetables in just before serving to preserve freshness. Makes 2 cups of dressing.

French Dressing

Serves 4 (2-tablespoon servings)

- ¼ cup lemon juice
- ¼ cup low-sodium ketchup
- ¼ cup red wine vinegar
- 2 tablespoons sugar
- 1 tablespoon fresh chives, minced
- 1 tablespoon fresh parsley, minced
- 1 tablespoon onion, minced
- 1 clove garlic, crushed
- ½ teaspoon dry mustard
- ¼ teaspoon paprika
- Dash salt
- Dash pepper

Nutritional Data

PER SERVING:

Calories	52
% calories from fat	4
Fat (gm)	0.2
Sat. Fat (gm)	0
Cholesterol (mg)	0
Sodium (mg)	5
Protein (gm)	0.6
Carbohydrate (gm)	13.7

EXCHANGES:

Milk	0.0	Bread	0.5
Veg.	0.0	Meat	0.0
Fruit	0.0	Fat	0.0

Shake all ingredients in tightly covered jar. Refrigerate at least 3 hours. Makes ½ cup of dressing.

Italian Dressing

Serves 4 (2-tablespoon servings)

- 1 cup tomato juice
- 1 teaspoon olive oil
- ¼ cup fresh lemon juice
- ¼ cup tarragon vinegar
- 1 teaspoon sugar
- ¼ teaspoon dry mustard
- ¼ teaspoon paprika
- ⅛ teaspoon thyme, ground
- 2 cloves garlic, crushed

Shake all ingredients in tightly covered jar. Refrigerate at least 2 hours. Makes 1½ cups of dressing.

Nutritional Data

PER SERVING:

Calories	34
% calories from fat	29
Fat (gm)	1.3
Sat. Fat (gm)	0.2
Cholesterol (mg)	0
Sodium (mg)	221
Protein (gm)	0.7
Carbohydrate (gm)	6.3

EXCHANGES:

Milk	0.0	Bread	0.5
Veg.	0.0	Meat	0.0
Fruit	0.0	Fat	0.0

Russian Dressing

Serves 8 (2-tablespoon servings)

⅓ cup low-calorie mayonnaise
1⅓ cups cottage cheese, whipped in
    blender with 2 tablespoons skim milk
⅓ cup tomato juice
1 tablespoon fresh lemon juice
2 tablespoons onion flakes
1 tablespoon chopped parsley
   Drop of hot sauce

Place all ingredients in blender and whirl for 1 minute. Cover and refrigerate until ready to use. Makes 1 cup of dressing.

Nutritional Data

PER SERVING:

Calories	37
% calories from fat	14
Fat (gm)	0.6
Sat. Fat (gm)	0.3
Cholesterol (mg)	1.7
Sodium (mg)	197
Protein (gm)	5
Carbohydrate (gm)	2.9

EXCHANGES:

Milk	0.0	Bread	0.0
Veg.	0.0	Meat	0.5
Fruit	0.0	Fat	0.0

Caesar-Style Dressing

Serves 4 (2-tablespoon servings)

4 tablespoons tarragon vinegar
7 tablespoons fat-free chicken broth
1 teaspoon fresh lemon juice
2 teaspoons Dijon mustard
1 tablespoon Parmesan cheese,
   freshly grated
1 teaspoon seasoned salt
¼ teaspoon dry mustard
1 egg white

Nutritional Data

PER SERVING:

Calories	19
% calories from fat	34
Fat (gm)	0.8
Sat. Fat (gm)	0.3
Cholesterol (mg)	1.2
Sodium (mg)	646
Protein (gm)	2.2
Carbohydrate (gm)	1.3

EXCHANGES:

Milk	0.0	Bread	0.0
Veg.	0.0	Meat	0.0
Fruit	0.0	Fat	0.0

Place all ingredients in blender. Process for 30 seconds. Refrigerate. Dressing is best when used immediately. Makes ½ cup of dressing.

Spring Garden Dill Dressing

Serves 8 (2-tablespoon servings)

- ½ cup low-fat cottage cheese
- ½ cup low-fat yogurt
- 2 tablespoons fresh dill, minced, or 1 tablespoon dried dill
- 1 tablespoon parsley, minced
- ½ teaspoon Dijon mustard
- 1 tablespoon fresh lemon juice

Combine all ingredients in food processor or blender and mix on medium speed for 30 seconds. Chill before serving. Keeps 1 week in refrigerator. Stir before serving. Makes 1 cup.

Nutritional Data

PER SERVING:

Calories	21
% calories from fat	17
Fat (gm)	0.4
Sat. Fat (gm)	0.2
Cholesterol (mg)	1.5
Sodium (mg)	73
Protein (gm)	2.6
Carbohydrate (gm)	1.8

EXCHANGES:

Milk	0.0	Bread	0.0
Veg.	0.0	Meat	0.5
Fruit	0.0	Fat	0.0

Strawberry Dressing

Serves 8 (2-tablespoon servings)

- ½ cup low-fat yogurt
- ⅓ cup red onions, chopped
- ¼ cup strawberries, sliced
- 3 tablespoons fresh lemon juice
- 2 teaspoons tarragon vinegar
- 1 teaspoon honey
- 1 teaspoon paprika
- ½ teaspoon lemon rind, grated
- Dash dry mustard

Nutritional Data

PER SERVING:

Calories	18
% calories from fat	13
Fat (gm)	0.3
Sat. Fat (gm)	0.2
Cholesterol (mg)	0.9
Sodium (mg)	10
Protein (gm)	0.9
Carbohydrate (gm)	3.4

EXCHANGES:

Milk	0.0	Bread	0.0
Veg.	0.5	Meat	0.0
Fruit	0.0	Fat	0.0

Place all ingredients in blender. Process on medium speed until smooth. Store tightly covered in refrigerator. Keeps 3 to 5 days. Stir before serving. Makes 1 cup.

Thousand Island Dressing

Serves 8 (3-tablespoon servings)

³/₄	cup cottage cheese, whipped in blender with 2 tablespoons skim milk
½	cup tomato juice
1	tablespoon dill pickle, chopped
2	teaspoons onion flakes
2	teaspoons green bell pepper, minced
2	packets Equal® (see "About This Cookbook")

Nutritional Data

PER SERVING:

Calories	22
% calories from fat	10
Fat (gm)	0.2
Sat. Fat (gm)	0.1
Cholesterol (mg)	1
Sodium (mg)	159
Protein (gm)	2.9
Carbohydrate (gm)	2.1

EXCHANGES:

Milk	0.0	Bread	0.0
Veg.	0.0	Meat	0.5
Fruit	0.0	Fat	0.0

Place all ingredients in blender and whirl for 1 minute. Cover and refrigerate until ready to use. Makes 1½ cups.

Creamy Yogurt Dressing

Serves 10 (2-tablespoon servings)

1	cup (8 ozs.) plain yogurt
¼	cup green onion, chopped
2	tablespoons Parmesan cheese, freshly grated
½	packet Equal® (see "About This Cookbook")
½	teaspoon salt
¼	teaspoon dried dill

Nutritional Data

PER SERVING:

Calories	21
% calories from fat	32
Fat (gm)	0.7
Sat. Fat (gm)	0.5
Cholesterol (mg)	2.4
Sodium (mg)	146
Protein (gm)	1.8
Carbohydrate (gm)	1.8

EXCHANGES:

Milk	0.0	Bread	0.0
Veg.	0.0	Meat	0.0
Fruit	0.0	Fat	0.5

Combine all ingredients in blender and process at medium speed until smooth. Store in refrigerator. Dressing is best when used within 1 week. Makes 1¼ cups of dressing.

Note: Dressing may be used as a dip for celery, carrot sticks, and other fresh vegetables, or for coleslaw or cucumber salad.

Chapter Four

SEAFOOD: FISH & SHELLFISH

Bluefish Florentine

Serves 4

- 1 medium onion, sliced
- 1 teaspoon olive oil
- 4 cups spinach leaves, rinsed well, stems trimmed, or 10 ozs. frozen spinach, thawed
- 1 tablespoon frozen orange juice concentrate
- 1 teaspoon olive oil
- 1 teaspoon reduced-sodium soy sauce
- 1 lb. bluefish fillets
  Dash paprika
  Dash pepper
- 4 thin slices lemon
  Parsley, chopped, for garnish

Nutritional Data

PER SERVING:

Calories	196
% calories from fat	34
Fat (gm)	7.4
Sat. Fat (gm)	1.4
Cholesterol (mg)	68.2
Sodium (mg)	159
Protein (gm)	25.5
Carbohydrate (gm)	6.3

EXCHANGES:

Milk	0.0	Bread	0.0
Veg.	1.0	Meat	3.0
Fruit	0.0	Fat	0.0

Arrange sliced onion and olive oil on microwave-safe platter. Cover with plastic wrap and microwave on High for 2 minutes until onion is tender. Add spinach, cover, and microwave another 2 minutes on High. Let rest covered.

Meanwhile, mix together orange juice, oil, and soy sauce and drizzle over spinach. Set aside and keep warm.

Rinse fish and place in 8" x 10" microwave-safe baking dish. Season with paprika and pepper and cover with wax paper. Microwave on High for 3 to 4 minutes, turning once, and rotating dish.

Fish is done when it flakes easily with fork. Remove fish and place over spinach. Top each fillet with lemon slice and parsley garnish.

Teriyaki Bass

Serves 6

Bass

- 1½ lbs. sea bass fillets

Teriyaki Marinade

- ¼ cup light soy sauce
- 1 teaspoon sugar
- 2 tablespoons sake, or dry white wine
- 2 cloves garlic, minced
- ½ teaspoon fresh ginger, peeled and grated
- ¼ teaspoon red pepper flakes
  Canola oil, or vegetable cooking spray

Nutritional Data

PER SERVING:

Calories	115
% calories from fat	19
Fat (gm)	2.3
Sat. Fat (gm)	0.6
Cholesterol (mg)	47
Sodium (mg)	195
Protein (gm)	21.4
Carbohydrate (gm)	0.6

EXCHANGES:

Milk	0.0	Bread	0.0
Veg.	0.0	Meat	2.5
Fruit	0.0	Fat	0.0

Bass: Cut fish into 1-inch pieces and place on a plate.

Teriyaki Marinade: Combine all ingredients in small bowl. Brush fish with marinade on both sides. Let stand for 20 minutes.

Arrange fish pieces on broiling pan coated with canola oil or cooking spray. Broil fish about 6 inches from heat for 7 to 8 minutes or until it flakes easily when tested with fork.

Transfer fish to warm serving platter and serve immediately.

Cajun Catfish on the Grill

Serves 4

Cajun Spice Rub (makes about ⅓ cup)

4	teaspoons paprika
1	tablespoon cayenne pepper
2	teaspoons garlic powder
1	teaspoon each ingredient: oregano, onion powder
½	cup whole wheat bread crumbs

Catfish

1¼	lbs. catfish fillets
	Canola oil, or vegetable cooking spray

Nutritional Data

PER SERVING:

Calories	210
% calories from fat	22
Fat (gm)	5.1
Sat. Fat (gm)	1.2
Cholesterol (mg)	98
Sodium (mg)	161
Protein (gm)	27.6
Carbohydrate (gm)	12.8

EXCHANGES:

Milk	0.0	Bread	0.5
Veg.	0.0	Meat	3.0
Fruit	0.0	Fat	0.0

Cajun Spice Rub: Mix together paprika, cayenne, garlic powder, oregano, onion powder, and bread crumbs. Let spices stand 30 minutes to allow flavors to meld together.

Catfish: Wash fish and pat dry. Sprinkle and rub about 1 teaspoon of Cajun flavoring onto each side of fillets.

Arrange catfish fillets on grill rack coated with canola oil or cooking spray. Over hot coals, grill fish 4 to 5 minutes, turn once, and grill until fish is done to taste. Fish will become opaque and flake easily when prodded with fork. Using long-handled spatula, transfer fish to serving platter. Good served with corn bread.

Cajun Fish

Serves 6

Rice and Vegetables

1	cup uncooked long-grain white rice
2	teaspoons nondiet, tub-style canola margarine, or corn oil margarine
1	cup onion, chopped
1	clove garlic, minced
1	16-oz. can tomatoes, undrained, coarsely chopped
1	large green bell pepper, seeded and chopped
2	cups mixed zucchini and yellow squash cubes, or 2 cups of either
1/2	teaspoon dried basil leaves
1/2	teaspoon dried thyme leaves
1/4	teaspoon dried marjoram leaves
1/8	teaspoon black pepper
2-3	drops hot pepper sauce (optional)
1/4	teaspoon salt, or to taste (optional)

Fish

1	lb. fresh or frozen (thawed) skinless fish fillets, such as flounder, sole, halibut, turbot, or other lean white fish
1/2	teaspoon dried basil leaves
1/4	teaspoon salt (optional)
1/8	teaspoon black pepper

Nutritional Data

PER SERVING:

Calories	221
% calories from fat	10
Fat (gm)	2.6
Sat. Fat (gm)	0.4
Cholesterol (mg)	35.5
Sodium (mg)	193
Protein (gm)	16.5
Carbohydrate (gm)	32.7

EXCHANGES:

Milk	0.0	Bread	1.0
Veg.	2.0	Meat	2.0
Fruit	0.0	Fat	0.0

Preheat oven to 200 degrees.

Rice and Vegetables: Cook rice according to package directions. Set aside.

In large, nonstick skillet, combine margarine, onion, and garlic. Cook over medium heat 6 to 7 minutes or until onion is tender, stirring frequently. Add tomatoes, green pepper, and squash. Add basil, thyme, marjoram, black pepper, and hot pepper sauce, if desired. Stir to combine well. Bring to boil. Cover, reduce heat, and cook 10 to 15 minutes or until vegetables are tender, stirring occasionally. Add salt, if desired. Remove vegetables to serving platter, and keep warm in oven until fish is cooked.

Fish: Rinse out and dry skillet in which vegetables were cooked. Coat with cooking spray. Sprinkle basil, salt, if desired, and black pepper evenly over fish.

In batches, if necessary, transfer fish to skillet, and cook over medium heat until cooked through, 2 to 5 minutes per side.

To serve, arrange rice on large serving platter or on individual plates. Top with vegetable mixture, then fish fillets.

Cod with Green Sauce

Serves 4

1½ lbs. fresh asparagus
2 tablespoons olive oil
2 cloves garlic, crushed
1 tablespoon parsley, chopped
2 lbs. cod, cut into 4 slices
1 tablespoon fresh lemon juice
½ teaspoon Spike (see "About This Cookbook")
Black pepper, freshly ground

Nutritional Data

PER SERVING:

Calories	274
% calories from fat	28
Fat (gm)	8.7
Sat. Fat (gm)	1.3
Cholesterol (mg)	89.9
Sodium (mg)	135
Protein (gm)	41.5
Carbohydrate (gm)	7.9

EXCHANGES:

Milk	0.0	Bread	0.0
Veg.	1.0	Meat	4.5
Fruit	0.0	Fat	0.0

Cut off woody ends of asparagus. In large saucepan, simmer, uncovered, 8 to 10 minutes until almost tender. Drain asparagus and reserve cooking water.

Heat oil in heavy casserole. Add garlic and parsley, and sauté 2 minutes. Add fish slices and 1 cup reserved asparagus cooking water. Add lemon juice, Spike, and pepper. Cover and simmer 10 minutes.

Arrange asparagus tips over fish. Cover and continue cooking 10 minutes until cod and asparagus are tender. Serve from casserole.

Baked Cod Provençal

Serves 4

4 cod fillets, about 1¼ lbs.
Vegetable cooking spray
1 medium onion, chopped
2 cloves garlic, finely chopped
1½ lbs. tomatoes, seeded, drained, and chopped
1 tablespoon capers
¼ cup chopped fresh basil, or 1 teaspoon dried and crumbled basil
4 pitted black olives, sliced
1 tablespoon fresh lemon juice
1 teaspoon oregano, crumbled
½ teaspoon Spike (see "About This Cookbook")
¼ teaspoon pepper, freshly ground

Nutritional Data

PER SERVING:

Calories	169
% calories from fat	12
Fat (gm)	2.2
Sat. Fat (gm)	0.3
Cholesterol (mg)	56.2
Sodium (mg)	157
Protein (gm)	25.5
Carbohydrate (gm)	13.2

EXCHANGES:

Milk	0.0	Bread	0.0
Veg.	1.0	Meat	3.0
Fruit	0.0	Fat	0.0

Preheat oven to 450 degrees. Arrange fillets in 8" x 8" x 2" square baking dish. Bake 10 minutes or until cooked through.

Coat a medium-size skillet with cooking spray, and add onion and garlic. Sauté over medium heat 3 to 5 minutes or until onions are translucent. Add tomatoes, capers, basil, olives, lemon juice, oregano, Spike, and pepper. Simmer, stirring occasionally, 8 to 10 minutes. Spoon sauce over fish.

Microwave Flounder with Mint Dressing

Serves 4

Mint Dressing

- ½ cup nonfat plain yogurt
- ¼ cup nonfat ricotta cheese
- 2 teaspoons stone-ground mustard
- 3 tablespoons fresh mint leaves, minced

Flounder

- 1¼ lbs. flounder fillets, 4 serving pieces
- 2 tablespoons fresh mint leaves, minced

Nutritional Data

PER SERVING:

Calories	154
% calories from fat	10
Fat (gm)	1.7
Sat. Fat (gm)	0.4
Cholesterol (mg)	70
Sodium (mg)	174
Protein (gm)	29.5
Carbohydrate (gm)	4.5

EXCHANGES:

Milk	0.0	Bread	0.0
Veg.	0.0	Meat	3.0
Fruit	0.0	Fat	0.0

Mint Dressing: Mix together yogurt, ricotta cheese, mustard, and mint leaves in small glass bowl. Cover and refrigerate until ready to serve. Mix before serving, and taste to adjust seasonings.

Flounder: Using microwave-safe glass dish, arrange fish evenly. Sprinkle fish with mint leaves. Cover dish securely with plastic wrap for microwave. Place in microwave and cook 2 to 4 minutes on High. If fish is not cooked, continue cooking until fish is opaque and flakes easily when prodded with fork.

Remove from microwave and cut slits into plastic wrap to expel steam before discarding. Spoon Mint Dressing onto individual dishes and set fish over it.

Baked Flounder with Orange Sauce

Serves 6

Butter-flavored vegetable cooking spray
1 medium onion, minced
1 clove garlic, minced
1 large orange, peeled
½ cup seasoned bread crumbs
6 5-oz. flounder fillets
1½ cups fresh orange juice
1½ tablespoons orange zest, grated
1 teaspoon sugar
¼ teaspoon ground ginger
¼ teaspoon dry mustard
1 tablespoon cornstarch, dissolved in two tablespoons water

Nutritional Data

PER SERVING:

Calories	208
% calories from fat	9
Fat (gm)	2
Sat. Fat (gm)	0.5
Cholesterol (mg)	66.5
Sodium (mg)	369
Protein (gm)	26
Carbohydrate (gm)	20.3

EXCHANGES:

Milk	0.0	Bread	0.0
Veg.	0.0	Meat	3.0
Fruit	1.0	Fat	0.0

Preheat oven to 375 degrees. Heat nonstick skillet coated with cooking spray over medium heat. Add onion and garlic and sauté until tender, about 5 minutes, stirring often. Remove from heat.

Chop orange and discard seeds. Mix orange and bread crumbs into onion and garlic mixture.

Spoon filling evenly over thick end of each fillet. Roll up fillets, jelly-roll style. Place rolls, seam side down, in oven-proof dish such as pie plate.

In small saucepan, mix together orange juice, zest, sugar, ginger, and mustard. Bring to boil over medium heat. Stir cornstarch mixture into orange juice mixture and continue cooking, stirring often, until sauce thickens slightly. Pour sauce over flounder rolls.

Place baking dish on middle rack and bake 6 to 8 minutes or until fish flakes easily when tested and has become slightly opaque.

Place rolled fillet on each plate and drizzle with sauce. Serve hot.

Flounder with Pesto

Serves 4

4	4-oz. fresh or frozen sole or flounder fillets (about ½-inch thick)
2	tablespoons fresh lemon juice
2	tablespoons shallots, finely chopped
1	clove garlic, minced
½	teaspoon black pepper, freshly ground
¼	cup Pesto Sauce (see p. 503)

Nutritional Data

PER SERVING:

Calories	112
% calories from fat	16
Fat (gm)	2
Sat. Fat (gm)	0.7
Cholesterol (mg)	55.3
Sodium (mg)	124
Protein (gm)	20.2
Carbohydrate (gm)	2.6

EXCHANGES:

Milk	0.0	Bread	0.0
Veg.	0.5	Meat	2.0
Fruit	0.0	Fat	0.0

Preheat oven to 400 degrees. Thaw fish, if frozen. Place each fillet on a 9" x 9" piece of heavy foil or parchment paper. Fold each fillet crosswise in half.

In small bowl, stir together lemon juice, shallots, garlic, and pepper. Spoon evenly over fish. Spoon pesto evenly over fish.

Seal each square of foil or paper by folding edges together. Place in 15" x 10" x 1" baking pan. Bake about 15 minutes or until fish puffs slightly and flakes easily with fork (carefully open to check doneness).

Sweet-and-Sour Grouper

Serves 4

	Olive oil, or vegetable cooking spray
1¼	lbs. grouper, cut into serving-size portions
1	cup onions, sliced
⅓	cup red wine vinegar
1½	teaspoons each ingredient: minced parsley, sugar
1	teaspoon basil
½	teaspoon mint, chopped
¼	teaspoon white pepper

Nutritional Data

PER SERVING:

Calories	156
% calories from fat	9
Fat (gm)	1.5
Sat. Fat (gm)	0.3
Cholesterol (mg)	52
Sodium (mg)	60
Protein (gm)	28
Carbohydrate (gm)	6.4

EXCHANGES:

Milk	0.0	Bread	0.0
Veg.	1.0	Meat	2.5
Fruit	0.0	Fat	0.0

Coat skillet with olive oil or cooking spray and pan fry grouper until done. Turn once, using spatula. Fish will be opaque and flake easily when prodded with fork. Remove fish and set aside.

Coat pan again and fry onions until tender, 4 to 5 minutes, over medium heat, stirring occasionally. Stir in vinegar, parsley, sugar, basil, mint, and white pepper. Cover pan and simmer 4 to 5 minutes.

Place fish in sauce and cover. Simmer 2 minutes or until fish is hot. Place fish in individual dishes and serve with pasta salad.

If serving fish cold, put fish in shallow bowl and drizzle sauce over it. Cover and refrigerate overnight.

 # Lemon Halibut

Serves 4	**Nutritional Data**	
1¼ lbs. halibut or haddock fillets	PER SERVING:	
Juice of 2 lemons	Calories	160
Dash dill weed	% calories from fat	19
Paprika	Fat (gm)	3.2
Pepper	Sat. Fat (gm)	0.5
Parsley sprigs for garnish	Cholesterol (mg)	45.5
	Sodium (mg)	77
	Protein (gm)	29.6
	Carbohydrate (gm)	2

Rinse and pat dry fish, and arrange in 2-quart oblong glass baking dish. Spoon lemon juice over fish and dust fillets with dill weed, paprika, and pepper. Cover with vented plastic wrap, and microwave on High for 2 minutes.

EXCHANGES:

Milk	0.0	Bread	0.0
Veg.	0.0	Meat	3.0
Fruit	0.0	Fat	0.0

Fish is done if it flakes easily when pierced with fork. Garnish with parsley sprigs.

Note: Any fish fillets will taste good cooked this simple way. Try it with sole, cod, snapper, or flounder.

Halibut Steaks Marengo

Serves 4	**Nutritional Data**	
1¼ lbs. halibut steaks	PER SERVING:	
Dash salt and pepper	Calories	214
1 medium tomato, diced	% calories from fat	29
¼ cup mushrooms, sliced	Fat (gm)	6.9
1¼ cups onion, sliced	Sat. Fat (gm)	0.7
¼ cup celery, diced	Cholesterol (mg)	45.5
1 tablespoon fresh lemon juice	Sodium (mg)	88
1 tablespoon canola oil	Protein (gm)	30.5
¼ teaspoon dried thyme	Carbohydrate (gm)	6.6
Parsley, chopped, for garnish		

EXCHANGES:

Milk	0.0	Bread	0.0
Veg.	1.0	Meat	3.5
Fruit	0.0	Fat	0.0

Place fish in shallow baking dish and sprinkle with salt and pepper. Top with diced tomato and set aside.

In 2-cup measure, mix mushrooms, onion, celery, lemon juice, oil, and thyme. Cover with vented plastic wrap, and microwave on High for 2 to 3 minutes. Spoon over fish.

Microwave fish, covered with wax paper, 6 minutes on High. Halibut is cooked if it flakes easily when pierced with fork. Garnish with fresh parsley.

Broiled Mahimahi with Mint

Serves 4

½ cup dry bread crumbs
2 cloves garlic, minced
2 tablespoons fresh parsley, minced
2 tablespoons fresh mint, minced
¼ teaspoon white pepper
1¼ lbs. mahimahi fillets

Nutritional Data

PER SERVING:

Calories	177
% calories from fat	9
Fat (gm)	1.7
Sat. Fat (gm)	0.4
Cholesterol (mg)	106.3
Sodium (mg)	221
Protein (gm)	28.7
Carbohydrate (gm)	9.9

EXCHANGES:

Milk	0.0	Bread	0.5
Veg.	0.0	Meat	2.5
Fruit	0.0	Fat	0.0

Preheat oven to 375 degrees. Mix together bread crumbs, garlic, parsley, mint, and pepper. Set aside.

Wash and pat dry mahimahi fillets. Set fish on nonstick cookie sheet. Sprinkle flavored bread crumbs over fish.

Bake fish 15 to 20 minutes. Turn fish if necessary, using spatula. Cook fish until opaque and just firm to touch. Remove to serving plate and serve hot.

Monkfish Florentine Sauté

Serves 4

1 tablespoon margarine, melted
1 tablespoon shallots, minced
Flour for dusting
1½ lbs. monkfish, cut into large chunks
1 large yellow bell pepper, cut into thin strips
1 large red bell pepper, cut into thin strips
½ lb. fresh spinach, washed and torn
½ cup mushrooms, sliced
2 fresh lemons, juiced
Salt and pepper, to taste

Nutritional Data

PER SERVING:

Calories	188
% calories from fat	27
Fat (gm)	5.8
Sat. Fat (gm)	0.6
Cholesterol (mg)	43.1
Sodium (mg)	111
Protein (gm)	27.5
Carbohydrate (gm)	7.2

EXCHANGES:

Milk	0.0	Bread	0.0
Veg.	1.0	Meat	3.5
Fruit	0.0	Fat	0.0

Put margarine into skillet and add shallots; cook until lightly browned. Turn heat up until few drops of water thrown on surface will sizzle. Meanwhile, put flour into plastic bag, add fish, and shake until lightly coated.

Add monkfish and peppers to hot skillet and sauté 4 minutes, shaking skillet vigorously. Add spinach, mushrooms, and lemon juice and stir until spinach wilts and sauce thickens. Season to taste. Serve immediately.

Perch or Butterfish with Pineapple-Ginger Topping

Serves 6

Marinade

2 tablespoons light soy sauce
2 tablespoons dry white wine
2 cloves garlic, minced

Fish

1¼ lbs. perch, or butterfish, fillets, cut into serving-size pieces
Canola oil, or vegetable cooking spray
3 egg whites, slightly beaten
1 tablespoon cornstarch

Pineapple-Ginger Topping

1 cup bean sprouts, blanched in hot water, drained
½ teaspoon ginger root, peeled and freshly grated
1 can (8 ozs.) pineapple chunks, no sugar added, drained
¼ cup pineapple juice

Nutritional Data

PER SERVING:

Calories	132
% calories from fat	7
Fat (gm)	1
Sat. Fat (gm)	0.2
Cholesterol (mg)	83.5
Sodium (mg)	146
Protein (gm)	21.3
Carbohydrate (gm)	9.1

EXCHANGES:

Milk	0.0	Bread	0.0
Veg.	0.0	Meat	2.0
Fruit	0.5	Fat	0.0

Marinade: Combine soy sauce, wine, and garlic. Put fish in shallow glass dish and sprinkle with marinade. Let fish stand 30 minutes. Drain.

Fish: Coat nonstick skillet with canola oil or cooking spray. Dip fish in beaten egg whites mixed with cornstarch. (Reserve remaining dip.) Sauté fish until cooked on both sides. Fish will turn opaque when cooked.

Pineapple-Ginger Topping: In saucepan, heat remaining egg whites with ginger and bean sprouts. Add pineapple chunks and juice.

Put cooked fish on serving platter and drizzle Pineapple-Ginger Topping over fish. Serve hot. Good with whole wheat noodles or cooked rice.

Snapper en Papillote

Serves 6

Parchment or foil wrap
2   tablespoons margarine, softened
2   tablespoons fresh parsley, chopped
2   tablespoons white wine
3   tablespoons garlic, minced
    Dash white pepper
6   red snapper fillets, or pampano, about 7 ozs. each
4   medium tomatoes, sliced
2   large zucchini, julienned
2   leeks, julienned
    Thyme leaves
    Oregano leaves

Nutritional Data

PER SERVING:

Calories	285
% calories from fat	22
Fat (gm)	6.9
Sat. Fat (gm)	1.4
Cholesterol (mg)	72.8
Sodium (mg)	149
Protein (gm)	42.7
Carbohydrate (gm)	11.2

EXCHANGES:

Milk	0.0	Bread	0.0
Veg.	2.0	Meat	4.0
Fruit	0.0	Fat	0.0

Preheat oven to 425 degrees. Cut 6 pieces of parchment or foil, each about 18" x 12". Fold each sheet in half and, using pinking shears, round off unfolded edges. Unfold each sheet and set aside.

Place margarine in mixing bowl. Add parsley, wine, and garlic and mix until blended. Season with white pepper. Cover and store in refrigerator until ready to use.

Spread portion of garlic margarine in center of 1 sheet. Place fish fillet on butter, and top with tomato slice. Place 2 tablespoons of zucchini and leek on top of tomato, and sprinkle with herbs. Repeat this procedure with remaining sheets.

Fold paper over fish and pinch edges at close intervals to seal them. Place packages on cookie sheet. Cook fish for 10 minutes. Transfer packages to dinner plate. Slice each open with sharp knife, and fold back paper to let aroma escape.

Microwave Orange Roughy with Port Sauce

Serves 4

Port Sauce

Olive oil, or vegetable cooking spray
3	green onions, minced
1½	cups nonfat lemon yogurt
1	tablespoon lemon rind
3	tablespoons port
⅛	teaspoon each ingredient: white pepper, tarragon

Orange Roughy

1¼	lbs. orange roughy fillets, cut into 4 serving pieces
2	tablespoons port
2	tablespoons fresh chives, minced

Nutritional Data

PER SERVING:

Calories	184
% calories from fat	4
Fat (gm)	0.8
Sat. Fat (gm)	0
Cholesterol (mg)	25.1
Sodium (mg)	132
Protein (gm)	20.3
Carbohydrate (gm)	18.6

EXCHANGES:

Milk	0.5	Bread	0.0
Veg.	0.0	Meat	3.0
Fruit	0.0	Fat	0.0

Port Sauce: Coat a small nonstick skillet with olive oil or cooking spray and sauté green onions, until tender, over medium heat, stirring occasionally. Remove from heat and transfer to small bowl. Spoon in yogurt, lemon rind, and port. Stir in pepper and tarragon. Cover and refrigerate until serving time.

Orange Roughy: Coat a microwave-safe dish with olive oil or cooking spray, and arrange fish with thin ends, if necessary, tucked under thicker ends to make fish even. Sprinkle fish with port and chives. Cover securely with plastic wrap for microwave.

Microwave 3 to 4 minutes on High. If fish is not cooked, continue cooking until it is opaque and flakes easily when prodded with fork. Remove from microwave; uncover plastic wrap away from you to avoid escaping steam.

Serve fish with dollop of Port Sauce. Good with linguine.

Orange Roughy in Parchment

Serves 6

Parchment for cooking
Butter-flavored vegetable cooking spray
1½ lbs. orange roughy fillets, cut into
     6 serving pieces
6   red bell pepper rings
6   large mushrooms, sliced thinly
3   tablespoons parsley, chopped
¼   teaspoon nutmeg, freshly grated
1   teaspoon dried tarragon
½   teaspoon salt

Nutritional Data

PER SERVING:

Calories	85
% calories from fat	10
Fat (gm)	0.9
Sat. Fat (gm)	0.1
Cholesterol (mg)	22.6
Sodium (mg)	263
Protein (gm)	17
Carbohydrate (gm)	1.4

EXCHANGES:

Milk	0.0	Bread	0.0
Veg.	0.0	Meat	2.0
Fruit	0.0	Fat	0.0

Preheat oven to 425 degrees. Cut 6 pieces of cooking parchment (or aluminum foil) into rectangles 3 inches longer than orange roughy fillets. Coat paper with cooking spray. Arrange fillet of orange roughy on coated side of each paper and top with red pepper ring. Arrange sliced mushroom on each piece of fish. Sprinkle with parsley, nutmeg, and tarragon. Sprinkle with salt.

Fold sides, then ends of paper, envelope style, around each fillet. Arrange packages on nonstick cookie sheet. Bake packages 6 to 8 minutes or until fish is cooked; paper will brown lightly.

Place each package on plate and serve hot. Allow guests to open their own package.

 # Salmon Tarragon

Serves 4

1   lb. salmon fillet, cut into 4 pieces
¼   cup fresh lemon juice
½   teaspoon dried tarragon
     Pepper
1   tablespoon pimientos, drained, chopped

Nutritional Data

PER SERVING:

Calories	109
% calories from fat	30
Fat (gm)	3.8
Sat. Fat (gm)	0.8
Cholesterol (mg)	20.3
Sodium (mg)	69
Protein (gm)	16.3
Carbohydrate (gm)	1.6

EXCHANGES:

Milk	0.0	Bread	0.0
Veg.	0.0	Meat	2.0
Fruit	0.0	Fat	0.0

Wash and pat dry fillets. Mix lemon juice, tarragon, and a few dashes of pepper. Arrange fish in glass baking dish, thick sides outward, and spoon marinade over fillets. Let rest a few minutes to absorb flavor.

Cover with wax paper and microwave on Medium High (70%) for 5 to 6 minutes, until fish flakes easily when pierced with fork. Turn pieces midcycle for even cooking. Garnish with pimientos.

Balsamic-Glazed Salmon Fillets

Serves 6

Vegetable cooking spray
4 cloves garlic, minced
1 tablespoon white wine
1 tablespoon honey
⅓ cup balsamic vinegar
4 teaspoons Dijon mustard
¼ teaspoon Spike (see "About This Cookbook")
Pepper, freshly ground, to taste
6 salmon fillets, each about 5 oz., rinsed and patted dry
1 tablespoon fresh oregano, chopped
12 fresh basil leaves, julienned

Nutritional Data

PER SERVING:

Calories	163
% calories from fat	29
Fat (gm)	5
Sat. Fat (gm)	1
Cholesterol (mg)	25.4
Sodium (mg)	914
Protein (gm)	20.6
Carbohydrate (gm)	7.2

EXCHANGES:

Milk	0.0	Bread	0.0
Veg.	0.0	Meat	3.0
Fruit	0.0	Fat	0.0

Preheat oven to 475 degrees. Cook garlic in small skillet coated with vegetable cooking spray over medium heat until garlic is soft, about 3 minutes. Do not brown.

Add wine, honey, vinegar, mustard, Spike, and pepper. Stir well to combine. Simmer, uncovered, until slightly thickened, about 3 minutes. If not using right away, refrigerate. Gently reheat before using.

Arrange fillets in single layer on baking pan lined with foil and coated with vegetable cooking spray. Brush with warm glaze. Sprinkle on oregano. Bake on upper rack until fish is tender and flakes with a fork, 10 to 14 minutes, depending on thickness of fillets. Do not overcook. Brush with remaining glaze. Sprinkle very lightly with Spike and pepper.

Use spatula to transfer to warm serving platter. Garnish fillets with julienne basil.

Poached Salmon

Serves 4

2   lb. (or larger) piece of salmon
½   cup dry white wine
½   cup water
1   teaspoon celery salt
1   teaspoon Spike (see "About This Cookbook")
2   green onions, sliced
1   tablespoon fresh lemon juice
½   lemon, thinly sliced

Nutritional Data

PER SERVING:

Calories	209
% calories from fat	34
Fat (gm)	7.6
Sat. Fat (gm)	1.6
Cholesterol (mg)	40.7
Sodium (mg)	187
Protein (gm)	32.4
Carbohydrate (gm)	0.2

EXCHANGES:

Milk	0.0	Bread	0.0
Veg.	0.0	Meat	4.0
Fruit	0.0	Fat	0.0

Place salmon in crockpot. Pour in wine and water. Add celery salt, Spike, onions, and lemon juice. Place lemon slices across salmon. Cover and cook on Low 2 to 3 hours or until salmon flakes when tested with a fork.

Remove salmon from crockpot. Strain poaching juices into plastic container and refrigerate for soup. Remove skin and bones from salmon. Cut half of salmon into 4 serving-size pieces. Place on platter with 4 dollops of mustard on top of each piece.

Sweet-and-Sour Salmon

Serves 5

1   cup water
¼   cup red wine vinegar
1   shallot, chopped
1   tablespoon pickling spice
1   teaspoon cracked peppercorn
5   salmon steaks (3 ozs. each)
1   packet Equal® (see "About This Cookbook")

Nutritional Data

PER SERVING:

Calories	82
% calories from fat	31
Fat (gm)	2.9
Sat. Fat (gm)	0.6
Cholesterol (mg)	15.3
Sodium (mg)	51
Protein (gm)	12.2
Carbohydrate (gm)	1.4

EXCHANGES:

Milk	0.0	Bread	0.0
Veg.	0.0	Meat	1.5
Fruit	0.0	Fat	0.0

Mix all ingredients except salmon and Equal®. Marinate salmon for 2 to 3 hours in mixture. Drain marinade into small shallow pan or skillet; heat marinade to a simmer.

Use spatula to place salmon steaks into hot liquid. Cover lightly with foil. Cook salmon until it is opaque and flakes. Remove salmon to platter. Add Equal® to sauce and garnish each steak with 1 tablespoon of poaching liquid.

Salmon Flan

Serves 4

Vegetable cooking spray
2 small onions, diced
6 egg whites
1 egg yolk
1 6¼-oz. can pink salmon, boneless and skinless, drained
½ cup skim milk
2 tablespoons nonfat yogurt
1 teaspoon dried dill
¼ teaspoon Spike (see "About This Cookbook")

Nutritional Data

PER SERVING:

Calories	136
% calories from fat	27
Fat (gm)	4
Sat. Fat (gm)	1.1
Cholesterol (mg)	71.8
Sodium (mg)	332
Protein (gm)	17.8
Carbohydrate (gm)	6.2

EXCHANGES:

Milk	0.0	Bread	0.0
Veg.	0.0	Meat	2.5
Fruit	0.0	Fat	0.0

Preheat oven to 250 degrees. Coat 4, 1-cup soufflé dishes or custard cups with vegetable cooking spray. Also coat small skillet and cook onion until soft, about 5 minutes. Whisk egg whites and yolk in medium-size bowl. Add onions, salmon, skim milk, yogurt, and seasonings. Divide among soufflé dishes.

Bake for 20 minutes. Stir gently, then continue baking until soufflés are set in center, about 40 minutes longer, for a total of 60 minutes. Soufflés may be garnished with dollop of yogurt and topped with dill.

Salmon Mousse

Serves 4 (reduce portions if not main course)

Vegetable cooking spray
1 cup nonfat yogurt
1 10½-oz. can low-fat cream of mushroom soup
2 envelopes unflavored gelatin
¼ cup water
2 7¾-oz. cans salt-free salmon, boneless and skinless, drained
½ cup celery, chopped
½ cup green onion, chopped
1 cup low-fat cottage cheese

Nutritional Data

PER SERVING:

Calories	284
% calories from fat	35
Fat (gm)	10.8
Sat. Fat (gm)	2.8
Cholesterol (mg)	29.6
Sodium (mg)	944
Protein (gm)	32.6
Carbohydrate (gm)	12.6

EXCHANGES:

Milk	1.0	Bread	0.0
Veg.	0.0	Meat	3.5
Fruit	0.0	Fat	0.0

½   teaspoon Spike (see "About This
    Cookbook")
    Cucumber, green olives, pimiento
    (optional)

Coat 2-quart fish mold with vegetable cooking spray and
set aside.

Combine yogurt and soup in double boiler. Heat over
medium heat until smooth.

Dissolve gelatin in water according to package directions,
then add to soup mixture. Fold in remaining ingredients. Blend
well and turn into 2-quart mold. Refrigerate until firm. Garnish
with thinly sliced cucumber, overlapping to form scales.

You can use sliced green olives for eyes and pimiento strips
for tail. Serve with crackers, bagel chips, or party breads.

Salmon Cakes with Dill Sauce

Serves 6

1   lb. potatoes, peeled and quartered
1   15½-oz. can salmon, drained
¼   cup nonfat yogurt
¼   cup green onions, sliced
3   tablespoons parsley, chopped
2   tablespoons fresh lemon juice
¼   teaspoon cracked pepper
1   cup fresh bread crumbs
2   tablespoons olive oil
1   teaspoon diet margarine
1   recipe Dill Sauce (see p. 499)

Nutritional Data

PER SERVING:

Calories	316
% calories from fat	35
Fat (gm)	11.2
Sat. Fat (gm)	2.1
Cholesterol (mg)	32.8
Sodium (mg)	567
Protein (gm)	21.5
Carbohydrate (gm)	32.1

EXCHANGES:

Milk	0.0	Bread	2.0
Veg.	0.0	Meat	2.0
Fruit	0.0	Fat	1.0

Place potatoes, with water to cover, in stockpot and cook
until fork-tender, about 20 minutes. Drain and mash. Add to
potatoes remaining ingredients except olive oil, margarine,
and Dill Sauce.

Mix well and shape into 6 large patties. Heat olive oil and
margarine in stockpot and cook 3 patties until browned,
about 5 minutes per side. Transfer to plate. Repeat with
remaining patties. Serve with Dill Sauce.

To Freeze: Place in microwave-safe container; label and
freeze for up to 2 months.

To Serve: Thaw. Cover with microwave-safe plastic wrap,
and cook on High 3 to 5 minutes.

Salmon Loaf
with Two Sauces

Serves 6

1 recipe White Sauce (see p. 498)
1 recipe Dill Sauce (see p. 499)
1 16-oz. can salmon, undrained
2 egg whites, lightly beaten
2 tablespoons onion, minced
½ cup celery, chopped
2 tablespoons green bell pepper, minced
2 tablespoons chives, minced
1 teaspoon fresh dill
1 cup dried bread crumbs
1 tablespoon fresh lemon juice
  Vegetable cooking spray

Nutritional Data

PER SERVING:

Calories	354.7
% calories from fat	35
Fat (gm)	12.6
Sat. Fat (gm)	2.8
Cholesterol (mg)	36.3
Sodium (mg)	745.8
Protein (gm)	28.7
Carbohydrate (gm)	31.1

EXCHANGES:

Milk	1.0	Bread	1.0
Veg.	0.0	Meat	2.5
Fruit	0.0	Fat	1.5

Preheat oven to 350 degrees. Drain salmon over bowl, reserving juice. Add water to salmon juice to make ½ cup. Put salmon, ½ cup liquid, and remaining ingredients into bowl. Mix to blend. Turn into mold, coated with vegetable cooking spray, or a 9" x 5" loaf pan. Bake until golden, 30 to 40 minutes.

Unmold and cool 5 minutes. To serve, cut into 1-inch slices. Pass both sauces so guests can select the one they want or some of both.

Note: This loaf is good enough to serve without a sauce.

Marinated Salmon
with Pasta

Serves 4

1 lb. cooked salmon
2 medium tomatoes, chopped
  (about 1½ cups)
1 onion, thinly sliced and separated
  into rings
½ cup pitted black olives, sliced
2 cloves garlic, crushed
2 tablespoons olive oil
2 tablespoons parsley, minced

Nutritional Data

PER SERVING:

Calories	506
% calories from fat	34
Fat (gm)	18.9
Sat. Fat (gm)	2.9
Cholesterol (mg)	62.9
Sodium (mg)	634
Protein (gm)	35.1
Carbohydrate (gm)	49

½ teaspoon dried basil leaves
1 teaspoon dried oregano leaves
¼ teaspoon pepper, freshly ground
2 cups uncooked pasta bows
Lettuce leaves
¼ cup carrots, shredded (optional)

EXCHANGES:
Milk	0.0	Bread	2.5
Veg.	2.0	Meat	4.0
Fruit	0.0	Fat	2.0

Mix all ingredients except pasta, lettuce, and carrots. Cover and refrigerate while pasta cooks. Cook pasta as directed on package; drain. Toss with salmon mixture. Refrigerate until ready to serve. Arrange on lettuce leaves and garnish with carrots.

Spectacular Salmon Burgers

Serves 4

1 12½-oz. can salt-free boneless, skinless pink salmon, or 1½ cups cooked salmon
1 egg white, beaten
½ cup seasoned bread crumbs
¼ cup onions, chopped
½ teaspoon dried thyme
½ teaspoon cracked pepper
1 teaspoon Spike (see "About This Cookbook")
1 tablespoon corn oil
Lettuce leaves
Tomato slices
2 small pita bread rounds, halved crosswise
Dill Sauce (see p. 499)

Nutritional Data

PER SERVING:
Calories	388
% calories from fat	32
Fat (gm)	13.4
Sat. Fat (gm)	2.8
Cholesterol (mg)	24.2
Sodium (mg)	716
Protein (gm)	27.5
Carbohydrate (gm)	37.8

EXCHANGES:
Milk	0.5	Bread	2.0
Veg.	0.0	Meat	3.0
Fruit	0.0	Fat	1.0

Drain canned salmon, reserving 2 tablespoons of liquid. Or use 2 tablespoons of water if using fresh-cooked salmon.

In mixing bowl, stir together reserved liquid, egg white, bread crumbs, onion, thyme, pepper, and Spike. Add drained salmon; mix well. Shape into 4, ½-inch-thick patties.

In skillet, cook patties in hot oil over medium heat 2 to 3 minutes or until first side is brown. Turn and cook 2 minutes more until remaining side is brown. Serve each patty with lettuce and tomato in a pita half. Top with Dill Sauce.

Salmon Steak Tartare

Serves 6

1½	lbs. center-cut salmon fillets (must be fresh)
	Juice of 4 limes
2	red onions, minced and divided
1¼	cups fresh cilantro, minced
¼	teaspoon each ingredient: Tabasco sauce, Dijon mustard, freshly ground pepper
½	teaspoon salt
2	tablespoons large capers, drained
4	hard-boiled eggs, whites only, chopped

Nutritional Data

PER SERVING:

Calories	179
% calories from fat	21
Fat (gm)	4.1
Sat. Fat (gm)	0.7
Cholesterol (mg)	58.7
Sodium (mg)	319
Protein (gm)	26.1
Carbohydrate (gm)	8.7

EXCHANGES:

Milk	0.0	Bread	0.0
Veg.	1.0	Meat	3.0
Fruit	0.0	Fat	0.0

Hand chop or grind salmon with lime juice and 1 onion in food processor until medium fine. Mix in cilantro, Tabasco, mustard, pepper, and salt. Shape into mound in center of serving plate.

Garnish salmon mound with capers, chopped egg whites, and remaining minced onion. Serve chilled with thin slices of rye bread or crackers (not included in nutritional data).

Grilled Red Snapper with Jalapeño Mayonnaise

Serves 4

Jalapeño Mayonnaise

½	cup fat-free mayonnaise
½	cup plain nonfat yogurt
2	jalapeño peppers, seeded, chopped (use caution; wear rubber gloves and do not rub your eyes)
¼	cup fresh cilantro, minced
¼	teaspoon cumin

Red Snapper

3	lbs. whole red snapper, cleaned, scaled, with head and tail intact
	Canola oil, or vegetable cooking spray
1	hinged fish rack for grill
1	lemon, sliced
2	tablespoons tarragon wine vinegar
1	tablespoon fresh tarragon, or 1 teaspoon dried tarragon

Nutritional Data

PER SERVING:

Calories	395
% calories from fat	11
Fat (gm)	4.8
Sat. Fat (gm)	1
Cholesterol (mg)	125.3
Sodium (mg)	762
Protein (gm)	72.3
Carbohydrate (gm)	12.6

EXCHANGES:

Milk	0.0	Bread	0.5
Veg.	0.0	Meat	7.0
Fruit	0.0	Fat	0.0

Jalapeño Mayonnaise: In small bowl, combine mayonnaise, yogurt, peppers, cilantro, and cumin. Taste to adjust seasonings. Cover and refrigerate until needed. Stir before serving.

Red Snapper: Set fish on grill rack coated with canola oil or cooking spray. Put lemon slices in fish cavity. Sprinkle fish with tarragon vinegar and tarragon.

Close fish rack. Arrange charcoal for indirect grilling, and place fish in center of grill. Cover grill and cook about 20 minutes, turning once or twice, until fish turns opaque and flakes easily with fork. Remove fish to serving platter, and serve with Jalapeño Mayonnaise.

Chili Snapper with Salsa

Serves 4

Snapper

1 lb. red snapper fillets
   Juice of ½ lemon or 1 lime
   Saucy Salsa (recipe follows)

Rinse fish with cold water and arrange, skin-down, on serving platter or in baking dish. Drizzle on lemon or lime juice. Spread salsa over fish and cover with wax paper. Microwave on High 3 minutes. Remove paper, turn dish, and microwave another 3 minutes until fish flakes easily with fork.

Nutritional Data

PER SERVING:

Calories	146
% calories from fat	11
Fat (gm)	1.8
Sat. Fat (gm)	0.4
Cholesterol (mg)	41.6
Sodium (mg)	60
Protein (gm)	24.5
Carbohydrate (gm)	7

EXCHANGES:

Milk	0.0	Bread	0.0
Veg.	1.0	Meat	2.5
Fruit	0.0	Fat	0.0

Saucy Salsa

3   cloves garlic, minced
½   cup onion, chopped
4   ozs. tomato puree
4   ozs. fresh ripe tomatoes, chopped,
    or canned Italian plum tomatoes,
    drained and crushed
1   fresh green chili, chopped
½   teaspoon ground cumin
½   teaspoon dried oregano

Place garlic and onion in 1-quart glass measure, and microwave on High 1½ to 2 minutes. Add remaining ingredients and cover with plastic wrap. Microwave on High 2 to 3 minutes and stir to blend.

▧ *Fillet of Sole Dijonnaise*

Serves 4

1¼	lbs. fillet of sole
6	medium stalks asparagus, cut diagonally into 2-inch pieces
1	tablespoon low-fat mayonnaise
1½	tablespoons Dijon mustard
	Juice of 1 lemon
1	tablespoon chopped chives (dried or frozen fresh)
	Dash pepper
	Few dashes paprika
	Parsley, chopped, for garnish

Nutritional Data

PER SERVING:

Calories	137
% calories from fat	20
Fat (gm)	2.9
Sat. Fat (gm)	0.5
Cholesterol (mg)	67.8
Sodium (mg)	183
Protein (gm)	24.7
Carbohydrate (gm)	2.2

EXCHANGES:

Milk	0.0	Bread	0.0
Veg.	0.0	Meat	2.5
Fruit	0.0	Fat	0.0

Arrange fillets in 2-quart baking dish, tucking under thin edges, with thick parts to outside of dish. Arrange asparagus around outside of dish, with 1 or 2 stalks in-between fillets.

Mix mayonnaise, mustard, lemon, and chives and spread over fish. Sprinkle with dashes of pepper and paprika.

Microwave on High 3 to 4 minutes, rotating and moving fillets to cook them evenly. Cover and microwave another minute, until fish flakes easily with fork. Let stand covered for another minute or two. Top fish with dusting of parsley.

Gingered Sole

Serves 4

2	teaspoons low-sodium soy sauce
1	tablespoon frozen orange juice concentrate
1	clove garlic, minced
1	tablespoon sesame oil
2	teaspoons fresh ginger, peeled and minced
1¼	lbs. fillet of sole or flounder
	Dash pepper
1	teaspoon sesame seeds, toasted
	Parsley, chopped, for garnish

Nutritional Data

PER SERVING:

Calories	159
% calories from fat	31
Fat (gm)	5.3
Sat. Fat (gm)	0.9
Cholesterol (mg)	66.5
Sodium (mg)	191
Protein (gm)	24.2
Carbohydrate (gm)	2.3

EXCHANGES:

Milk	0.0	Bread	0.0
Veg.	0.0	Meat	2.5
Fruit	0.0	Fat	0.5

In small jar, mix together soy sauce, orange juice, garlic, sesame oil, and ginger. Shake to blend and let rest at least 15 minutes to develop taste.

In 8" x 10" microwave-safe dish arrange fish, tucking under any thin edges. Spoon sauce over fish and cover with wax paper. Microwave on High 1½ to 2 minutes. Rotate dish and turn fish. Microwave on High another 1½ to 2 minutes. Let stand a minute before uncovering, then top fish with dash of pepper, sprinkling of toasted sesame seeds, and chopped parsley.

Microwave Sole
with Cucumber Sauce

Serves 4

Cucumber Sauce

1 cup cucumber, peeled, seeded, and chopped
1 cup nonfat ricotta cheese
¼ cup nonfat plain yogurt
2 tablespoons dried dill weed, chopped
½ teaspoon rosemary
3 cloves garlic, minced

Sole

Olive oil, or vegetable cooking spray
½ cup onion, minced
1¼ lbs. Dover sole fillets, 4 portions
1 cucumber, scored with fork, cut in thin slices

Nutritional Data

PER SERVING:

Calories	197
% calories from fat	8
Fat (gm)	1.8
Sat. Fat (gm)	0.4
Cholesterol (mg)	72.8
Sodium (mg)	151
Protein (gm)	34.2
Carbohydrate (gm)	12.7

EXCHANGES:

Milk	0.5	Bread	0.0
Veg.	1.0	Meat	2.5
Fruit	0.0	Fat	0.0

Cucumber Sauce: Using food processor fitted with steel blade, mix together cucumbers, ricotta cheese, yogurt, dill weed, rosemary, and garlic. Spoon sauce into glass bowl, cover, and refrigerate until serving.

Sole: Use microwave-safe glass dish or glass pie plate coated with olive oil or cooking spray and sprinkled with onions. Arrange fish tucked under so that it is even in thickness, and place evenly on plate. Cover securely with plastic wrap for microwave. Put plate in microwave and cook 2 minutes on High. If fish is not cooked, continue until done. Fish is done when it is opaque and flakes easily with fork.

Remove from microwave and place sole on individual plates. Arrange cucumbers in overlapping pattern on fish to resemble scales.

Spoon Cucumber Sauce on the side. Serve hot.

Sole with Rosemary Potatoes

Serves 6

- 4 baking potatoes
- Canola oil, or vegetable cooking spray
- 2 tablespoons rosemary
- ½ teaspoon garlic powder
- ¼ teaspoon pepper
- 1¼ lbs. sole fillets
- 4 shallots, minced
- 1 small red onion, chopped
- 1 large clove garlic, minced

Nutritional Data

PER SERVING:

Calories	238
% calories from fat	5
Fat (gm)	1.3
Sat. Fat (gm)	0.3
Cholesterol (mg)	44.3
Sodium (mg)	81
Protein (gm)	19.3
Carbohydrate (gm)	37.4

EXCHANGES:

Milk	0.0	Bread	1.0
Veg.	1.0	Meat	2.5
Fruit	0.0	Fat	0.0

Preheat oven to 400 degrees. Scrub potatoes and cut each into 6 or 8 wedges. Set wedges on nonstick cookie sheet coated with canola oil or cooking spray. Sprinkle potatoes with rosemary, garlic powder, and pepper.

Bake potatoes about 45 minutes or until they are golden brown, crisp, and done to taste. Turn potatoes 3 to 4 times while baking.

About 15 minutes before potatoes are done, wash fish and pat dry. Sauté shallots, onion, and garlic in nonstick skillet coated with canola oil or cooking spray until soft, stirring occasionally over medium heat. Fold each fillet of fish in half and add to skillet. Cook fish over medium-high heat 2 to 4 minutes. Turn fish once, carefully with spatula, picking up pieces of shallots, onions, and garlic as you do so. Continue cooking only a few minutes, until done to taste. Fish will be opaque and flake easily with fork.

Serve fish with garlic, onion, and shallots over and around it and hot rosemary potatoes on the side.

Fillet of Sole Veronique

Serves 4

1½ lbs. fillet of sole (4 fillets)
    Spike (see "About This Cookbook")
¾ cup dry white wine
    Vegetable cooking spray
1 tablespoon flour
⅓ cup evaporated skim milk
1 8-oz. can seedless green grapes, drained,
    or ¾ cup fresh seedless grapes

Nutritional Data

PER SERVING:

Calories	214
% calories from fat	8
Fat (gm)	1.9
Sat. Fat (gm)	0.5
Cholesterol (mg)	80.5
Sodium (mg)	154
Protein (gm)	30.5
Carbohydrate (gm)	10.1

EXCHANGES:

Milk	0.0	Bread	0.0
Veg.	0.0	Meat	3.5
Fruit	0.5	Fat	0.0

Sprinkle cold fillets with Spike and place in skillet. Pour wine over fish.

In piece of wax paper exactly the size of skillet, cut small hole in center. Coat wax paper with vegetable cooking spray and place it, coated side down, on top of fish.

Bring liquid in skillet to boil. Simmer over low heat 10 to 12 minutes until fish flakes easily with fork. Using large, broad spatula, remove fish to serving platter. Place in warm oven.

Place cooking liquid in saucepan. Slowly add flour and continue stirring with whisk while mixture cooks. Continue cooking until sauce is thickened and smooth. There should be about 1 cup of sauce.

Add evaporated skim milk to sauce, along with grapes. Heat to just below boiling. Remove from heat, and pour over fillets.

Fillet of Sole Veracruzana

Serves 2

1 tablespoon olive oil, divided
¼ cup onion, diced
1 clove garlic, minced
½ cup green bell pepper, diced
¼ cup chilies, diced
1 15½-oz. can chunky tomatoes
1 cup fresh tomato, cubed
2 tablespoons white wine
4 pitted black olives, sliced

Nutritional Data

PER SERVING:

Calories	296
% calories from fat	31
Fat (gm)	10.7
Sat. Fat (gm)	1.5
Cholesterol (mg)	66.5
Sodium (mg)	516
Protein (gm)	28.2
Carbohydrate (gm)	22.7

10	ozs. sole fillets	EXCHANGES:			
2	tablespoons fresh cilantro, chopped	Milk	0.0	Bread	0.0
2	tablespoons fresh parsley, chopped	Veg.	4.0	Meat	3.0
		Fruit	0.0	Fat	0.0

In 1-quart casserole, place 1 teaspoon oil, onion, and garlic
and cover. Microwave on High 2 minutes. Remove from oven
and place remaining ingredients in casserole. Cover.
Microwave on High 10 to 12 minutes, giving dish half-turn
after 5 minutes. Remove from oven and let stand, covered,
about 2 minutes before serving.

To Freeze: Label casserole and freeze up to 2 months.

To Serve: Thaw. Cover with microwave-safe plastic wrap,
and cook on High 3 to 5 minutes.

Grilled Swordfish with Chili-Lime Sauce

Serves 6

Swordfish

		Nutritional Data

PER SERVING:

Calories	153
% calories from fat	29
Fat (gm)	4.8
Sat. Fat (gm)	1.2
Cholesterol (mg)	37.2
Sodium (mg)	365
Protein (gm)	19.7
Carbohydrate (gm)	7.3

1¼ lbs. swordfish, cut into
serving-size pieces

3 small pieces apple wood, hickory, plum
wood, or aromatic chips of your choice,
soaked, drained
Vegetable cooking spray

Brushing Sauce

1 teaspoon olive oil
2 tablespoons fresh lime juice
¼ teaspoon pepper
2 tablespoons parsley, minced

EXCHANGES:			
Milk	0.0	Bread	0.0
Veg.	1.0	Meat	2.5
Fruit	0.0	Fat	0.0

Chili-Lime Sauce

¼ cup chili sauce
2 cups tomatoes, chopped
2 jalapeño peppers, seeded and chopped
(use caution; wear rubber gloves and
do not rub your eyes)
Juice of ½ lime

Swordfish: Cut into serving-size pieces and place on a plate.

Brushing Sauce: Mix together olive oil, juice, pepper, and
parsley. Brush swordfish with sauce. Let stand 1 hour.

Chili-Lime Sauce: In small bowl, mix together chili sauce,
tomatoes, peppers, and juice. Set aside.

When coals are hot, sprinkle aromatic chips on coals. Grill
fish on rack coated with cooking spray. Cook 4 to 6 minutes,
then turn fish with long-handled spatula and continue cook-

ing until done. Time will depend on thickness of fish and heat of coals. Do not overcook fish.

Remove fish to individual dishes, and spoon Chili-Lime Sauce over it. Serve hot.

Tuna Almondine

Serves 6

Vegetable cooking spray
2 envelopes unflavored gelatin
½ cup cold water
1 cup boiling water
1 lb. low-fat cottage cheese, whipped
2 tablespoons fresh lemon juice
¼ teaspoon garlic powder
¼ teaspoon Spike (see "About This Cookbook")
⅓ cup green onions, finely chopped
2 tablespoons pimientos, chopped
2 7-oz. cans tuna, water packed, drained
¼ cup almonds, sliced and lightly toasted

Nutritional Data

PER SERVING:

Calories	172
% calories from fat	19
Fat (gm)	3.8
Sat. Fat (gm)	0.9
Cholesterol (mg)	22.8
Sodium (mg)	534
Protein (gm)	29.3
Carbohydrate (gm)	4

EXCHANGES:

Milk	0.0	Bread	0.0
Veg.	0.0	Meat	4.0
Fruit	0.0	Fat	0.5

Coat 5½-cup fish mold with vegetable cooking spray and set aside.

In large bowl, sprinkle unflavored gelatin over cold water; let stand 1 minute. Add boiling water and stir until gelatin is completely dissolved. With rotary beater, blend in cottage cheese until smooth. Stir in lemon juice, garlic powder, and Spike. Fold in green onions, pimiento, and tuna.

Pour into coated mold; chill until firm. Before serving, unmold onto platter and garnish with almonds, overlapping to form scales. Serve with crackers, bagel chips, or party breads.

Tuna and Noodles

Serves 4

1 5¼-oz. can low-sodium chicken broth
1 12-oz. can evaporated skim milk
1 clove garlic, minced
¼ teaspoon white pepper
1 cup Parmesan cheese, freshly grated
8 ozs. no-yolk noodles
1 6½-oz. can tuna in spring water
¼ cup pimiento, chopped
½ cup parsley, chopped

Nutritional Data

PER SERVING:

Calories	448
% calories from fat	19
Fat (gm)	9.9
Sat. Fat (gm)	5.2
Cholesterol (mg)	36.3
Sodium (mg)	758
Protein (gm)	37.8
Carbohydrate (gm)	50.5

EXCHANGES:

Milk	1.0	Bread	2.5
Veg.	0.0	Meat	4.0
Fruit	0.0	Fat	0.0

Bring chicken broth and evaporated skim milk to a boil. Add garlic and white pepper. Cook and stir for 30 seconds. Remove from heat. Add Parmesan cheese; cover and set aside for 5 minutes.

Cook noodles according to package directions. Drain and keep warm.

Transfer sauce to blender; mix until smooth. Drain and flake tuna and stir into sauce. Heat in medium saucepan until warm. To assemble, place egg noodles on warm platter, top with sauce and tuna. Sprinkle with pimiento and parsley.

Marinated Trout

Serves 4

4 8-oz. fresh or frozen pan-dressed rainbow trout, or lake perch
Spike, to taste (see "About This Cookbook"
Pepper, to taste
½ cup white wine
1 tablespoon fresh lemon juice
½ teaspoon dried thyme, crushed
½ teaspoon dried oregano, crushed
1 cup mushrooms, sliced
1 medium carrot, chopped (½ cup)
1 small onion, chopped (⅓ cup)
1 clove garlic, minced
¼ cup chicken broth
Vegetable cooking spray

Nutritional Data

PER SERVING:

Calories	311
% calories from fat	24
Fat (gm)	7.9
Sat. Fat (gm)	1.5
Cholesterol (mg)	129.8
Sodium (mg)	117
Protein (gm)	47.9
Carbohydrate (gm)	4.5

EXCHANGES:

Milk	0.0	Bread	0.0
Veg.	1.0	Meat	5.5
Fruit	0.0	Fat	0.0

Thaw fish, if frozen. Place fish in shallow baking dish. Sprinkle with Spike and pepper.

For marinade, stir together wine, lemon juice, thyme, and oregano; pour over fish. Cover, and marinate in refrigerator for 2 hours. Drain fish, reserving marinade. Pat fish dry.

In 12-inch skillet coated with vegetable cooking spray, cook mushrooms, carrot, onion, and garlic until tender but not brown. Push to edges of skillet. Add fish, and cook 4 minutes on each side. Add marinade and broth.

Cover and simmer about 4 minutes or until fish flakes easily with fork. Transfer fish and vegetables to platter; cover. Simmer marinade mixture until reduced to ¼ cup; spoon over fish.

Pan-Fried Trout

Serves 4

1¼   lbs. trout fillets
⅓   cup white cornmeal
¼   teaspoon each ingredient: freshly ground black pepper, anise seeds
½   cup fresh cilantro or parsley, minced
     Canola oil, or vegetable cooking spray

Nutritional Data

PER SERVING:

Calories	207
% calories from fat	23
Fat (gm)	5.2
Sat. Fat (gm)	1
Cholesterol (mg)	81.1
Sodium (mg)	42
Protein (gm)	30.2
Carbohydrate (gm)	8

EXCHANGES:

Milk	0.0	Bread	0.5
Veg.	0.0	Meat	3.0
Fruit	0.0	Fat	0.0

Run fingers over fish to check if there are any remaining bones. If so, remove them with kitchen tweezers. Wash fish and pat dry.

Mix together cornmeal, spices, and cilantro. Roll fillets in mixture, pressing it gently into fish.

Fry fish in nonstick skillet coated with canola oil or cooking spray over medium heat until cooked, about 5 minutes each side. Turn once. Fish will be browned and crisp on outside, firm to the touch, and flake easily with fork.

Using a spatula, transfer trout to individual plates. Serve hot.

Baked Whitefish with Sun-Dried Tomato Stuffing

Serves 8

Sun-Dried Tomato Stuffing

     Olive oil, or vegetable cooking spray
1   cup onions, chopped
¼   cup shallots, minced
1   cup celery, sliced
¾   cup sun-dried tomatoes, reconstituted in hot water, shredded
2   cups tomatoes, chopped
½   cup dry bread crumbs
¼   teaspoon each ingredient: chervil, white pepper

Nutritional Data

PER SERVING:

Calories	230
% calories from fat	33
Fat (gm)	8.5
Sat. Fat (gm)	1.3
Cholesterol (mg)	69.6
Sodium (mg)	231
Protein (gm)	25.1
Carbohydrate (gm)	13.5

EXCHANGES:

Milk	0.0	Bread	0.5
Veg.	1.0	Meat	3.0
Fruit	0.0	Fat	0.0

Fish

2 lbs. whitefish, red snapper, or sea
bass, whole, with trimmed off belly
flap, or filleted

2 tablespoons sliced almonds

Sun-Dried Tomato Stuffing: Coat nonstick skillet with
olive oil or cooking spray and sauté onions, shallots, and celery over medium heat until tender, stirring occasionally. Add
sun-dried and chopped tomatoes and continue cooking 5 minutes. Mix in bread crumbs, chervil, and white pepper. Mix all
ingredients together.

Fish: Place fish in coated baking dish, and spoon stuffing
over it. Sprinkle with almonds.

Preheat oven to 375 degrees and bake fish and stuffing 15
to 20 minutes or until fish is cooked. Fish will turn opaque
and flake easily with a fork. Serve hot.

Fish Fillets
with Picante Sauce

Serves 4

1½ lbs. fresh or frozen fish fillets
    Paprika
1 cup yogurt
½ teaspoon mustard
½ teaspoon dried dill
½ teaspoon dried thyme
1 tablespoon fresh lemon juice
1 teaspoon Spike (see "About This
    Cookbook")
½ teaspoon pepper, freshly ground
2 tablespoons parsley, minced
    Vegetable cooking spray

Nutritional Data

PER SERVING:

Calories	177
% calories from fat	15
Fat (gm)	2.7
Sat. Fat (gm)	1
Cholesterol (mg)	83.3
Sodium (mg)	173
Protein (gm)	31.5
Carbohydrate (gm)	4.9

EXCHANGES:

Milk	0.5	Bread	0.0
Veg.	0.0	Meat	3.5
Fruit	0.0	Fat	0.0

Preheat oven to 350 degrees. If using frozen fish, thaw.
Dust fillets with paprika. Coat small baking dish with vegetable cooking spray, and place fish in it.

Combine yogurt, mustard, dill, thyme, lemon juice, Spike,
and pepper. Blend well, and spread over fish. Bake 20 minutes or until fish flakes easily with fork. Sprinkle with parsley,
and serve.

Broiled Fish Steaks with Garlic-Lemon Sauce

Serves 4

4	fish steaks (any fish), about 1½ lbs.
2	tablespoons bread crumbs
2	cloves garlic, minced
2	tablespoons fresh lemon juice
1	teaspoon Spike (see "About This Cookbook")
½	teaspoon paprika
2	tablespoons white wine

Nutritional Data

PER SERVING:

Calories	159
% calories from fat	12
Fat (gm)	2
Sat. Fat (gm)	0.5
Cholesterol (mg)	79.8
Sodium (mg)	147
Protein (gm)	28.9
Carbohydrate (gm)	3.6

EXCHANGES:

Milk	0.0	Bread	0.0
Veg.	0.0	Meat	3.0
Fruit	0.0	Fat	0.0

Broil steaks about 5 minutes on each side. Meanwhile, make sauce by combining bread crumbs, garlic, lemon juice, Spike, and paprika and mix well. Add wine gradually while stirring to make thick creamy mixture. Serve fish topped with sauce.

Fish Basque

Serves 4

	Vegetable cooking spray
1	lb. fish fillets (or steaks): sole, grouper, orange roughy, cod, swordfish, salmon, or flounder
¼	cup bottled clam juice
½	cup dry white wine
½	cup canned tomatoes, drained and mashed
2	tablespoons parsley, chopped
½	teaspoon Spike (see "About This Cookbook")
3	tablespoons scallions, chopped
1	teaspoon thyme
1	bay leaf
	Black pepper, freshly ground

Nutritional Data

PER SERVING:

Calories	121
% calories from fat	10
Fat (gm)	1.3
Sat. Fat (gm)	0.3
Cholesterol (mg)	53.2
Sodium (mg)	153
Protein (gm)	19.5
Carbohydrate (gm)	2.2

EXCHANGES:

Milk	0.0	Bread	0.0
Veg.	0.5	Meat	2.0
Fruit	0.0	Fat	0.0

Coat 10-inch skillet with vegetable cooking spray. Lay fish in skillet. Add clam juice, wine, tomatoes, parsley, Spike, scallions, thyme, and bay leaf. Cover. Cook over medium heat 15 minutes. Discard bay leaf.

Remove fish to heated serving dish and keep warm. Raise heat under skillet and cook, without allowing to boil, until liquid is reduced to approximately 3 tablespoons. Add pepper and pour sauce over fish. Serve hot.

Baked Fish with Tomato Basil Sauce

Serves 4

Tomato Basil Sauce

Vegetable cooking spray
½ cup green onions, chopped
1   clove garlic, minced
2   9½-oz. cans whole tomatoes, drained and chopped
½ cup green bell pepper, minced
½ cup mushrooms, sliced
1   tablespoon basil
1   teaspoon cayenne pepper
1   teaspoon Spike (see "About This Cookbook")
1   tablespoon fresh lemon juice

Fish

1½ lbs. whitefish fillets, or any similar fish such as turbot, monkfish, or snapper
    Juice of 1 lemon
½ cup dry white wine
2   tablespoons parsley, chopped

Nutritional Data

PER SERVING:

Calories	301
% calories from fat	32
Fat (gm)	10.8
Sat. Fat (gm)	1.7
Cholesterol (mg)	104.3
Sodium (mg)	314
Protein (gm)	35.5
Carbohydrate (gm)	10.4

EXCHANGES:

Milk	0.0	Bread	0.0
Veg.	2.0	Meat	4.5
Fruit	0.0	Fat	0.0

Tomato Basil Sauce: In skillet coated with vegetable cooking spray, sauté onions and garlic until soft, about 5 minutes. Add tomatoes, green pepper, and mushrooms. Cook about 5 minutes. Add basil, pepper, and Spike. Cook, stirring, until mixture thickens slightly, about 8 minutes. Remove from heat. Stir in lemon juice.

Fish: Preheat oven to 375 degrees. Rinse fish with cold water. Pat dry on paper towel. Place fish in shallow baking dish. Sprinkle with lemon juice. Pour wine over fish. Bake until fish flakes easily with fork, about 10 minutes. Remove fish to warm serving platter and spoon Tomato Basil Sauce on top of fish. Sprinkle with parsley.

Hawaiian Baked Fish

Serves 4

1½	cups packaged precooked rice
1	lb. fresh (or thawed frozen) flounder fillets, or other mild-flavored fish such as turbot or monkfish
2	tablespoons diet margarine
1	tablespoon instant minced onion
1	tablespoon pimiento, diced
1	teaspoon salt
1	teaspoon parsley flakes
½	teaspoon curry powder (optional)
1¼	cups pineapple juice
2	tablespoons fresh lemon juice
3	packets Equal® (see "About This Cookbook")

Nutritional Data

PER SERVING:

Calories	245
% calories from fat	16
Fat (gm)	4.4
Sat. Fat (gm)	0.9
Cholesterol (mg)	61.4
Sodium (mg)	697
Protein (gm)	23.6
Carbohydrate (gm)	26.6

EXCHANGES:

Milk	0.0	Bread	1.0
Veg.	0.0	Meat	2.0
Fruit	1.0	Fat	0.0

Preheat oven to 325 degrees. Cook rice according to package directions and place in ovenproof serving dish. Place fish in baking dish; dot with margarine. Bake 25 minutes; remove fish with spatula and place over rice. Keep warm in low oven while preparing sauce.

Combine minced onion, pimiento, salt, parsley, curry powder, pineapple juice, and lemon juice in saucepan; cover and heat to boiling. Remove from heat; stir in Equal®. Spoon sauce over fish and rice.

Fish Stew with Vegetables and Garlic

Serves 6

2	tablespoons olive oil
1	large red onion, peeled, halved, and sliced
2-3	lbs. small white potatoes, peeled and cut into ½-inch slices
2	large carrots, peeled and cut into 1-inch slices
1-2	celery ribs, cut into ½-inch pieces
	Black pepper, freshly ground, to taste
1	teaspoon basil
4-6	cloves garlic, chopped
	Spike, to taste (see "About This Cookbook")
2½	lbs. fresh fish fillets, cut into 2-inch squares
¼	cup fresh lemon juice, strained

Nutritional Data

PER SERVING:

Calories	348
% calories from fat	18
Fat (gm)	6.8
Sat. Fat (gm)	1.1
Cholesterol (mg)	88.7
Sodium (mg)	160
Protein (gm)	34.8
Carbohydrate (gm)	36.6

EXCHANGES:

Milk	0.0	Bread	1.5
Veg.	1.0	Meat	4.0
Fruit	0.0	Fat	0.0

In large heavy pot, heat olive oil and sauté onions until translucent. Add potatoes, carrots, celery, and pepper and sauté 3 to 4 minutes, stirring constantly with wooden spoon. Add basil and garlic and enough water to almost cover vegetables. Bring to boil, reduce heat, season with Spike, cover, and simmer 10 to 15 minutes until vegetables are about half cooked.

Add fish and stir gently so fish doesn't fall apart. Simmer, covered, another 10 to 15 minutes, adding a little water if necessary to keep pot moist, until fish is tender, vegetables are cooked, and most of liquid is absorbed.

Remove lid and pour in lemon juice. Continue to cook 3 to 5 minutes before taking pot off heat. Season with freshly ground pepper and serve hot.

Asparagus- and Mushroom-Stuffed Fish Rolls

Serves 4

- 4 fresh or frozen fish fillets, such as flounder, turbot, or monkfish
- 1 10-oz. package frozen asparagus
- 4 green onions, halved lengthwise
- 1/2 cup mushrooms, chopped
- 2 teaspoons margarine
- 3 tablespoons dry white wine
- 1/4 teaspoon Spike (see "About This Cookbook")
- 1/4 teaspoon garlic powder
- 2 tablespoons water
- 1 cup celery, chopped
- 1 1/2 teaspoons cornstarch
- 1 tablespoon cold water
- 1 tomato, sliced
- 1/4 cup parsley, chopped

Nutritional Data

PER SERVING:

Calories	250
% calories from fat	14
Fat (gm)	3.9
Sat. Fat (gm)	0.8
Cholesterol (mg)	99
Sodium (mg)	197
Protein (gm)	43.7
Carbohydrate (gm)	7.4

EXCHANGES:

Milk	0.0	Bread	0.0
Veg.	1.0	Meat	4.0
Fruit	0.0	Fat	0.0

Preheat oven to 400 degrees. Thaw fish if frozen. Cook asparagus and onions, covered, in small amount of boiling water for about 3 minutes. Drain. Place in dish and add chopped mushrooms. Set aside.

Dot each fish fillet with 1/2 teaspoon of margarine. Place one-fourth of the asparagus-mushroom mixture across center of each fillet; roll up fish and fasten with wooden picks. Place rolls in baking dish, about 8 inches square.

Combine wine, Spike, and garlic powder with water and sprinkle over fish. Cover; bake 30 to 35 minutes. Remove fish to serving platter; keep warm.

Measure pan juices, adding enough water to equal 3/4-cup liquid. Cook celery in liquid for 5 minutes. Combine cornstarch and 1 tablespoon cold water; stir into celery mixture. Cook and stir until bubbly. Cook 2 minutes more. Pour sauce over fish and garnish with tomato slices and parsley.

Finnan Haddie

Serves 6

1½	lbs. finnan haddie (smoked haddock), defrosted if necessary
2	cups skim milk
1	teaspoon cholesterol-free margarine
2	cups white mushrooms, sliced
1	onion, sliced thin
1	teaspoon stone-ground mustard
3	hard-boiled egg whites, chopped
¼	cup fresh chives, chopped

Nutritional Data

PER SERVING:

Calories	192
% calories from fat	10
Fat (gm)	2.1
Sat. Fat (gm)	0.4
Cholesterol (mg)	88.1
Sodium (mg)	956
Protein (gm)	34
Carbohydrate (gm)	7.7

EXCHANGES:

Milk	0.0	Bread	0.0
Veg.	1.0	Meat	4.0
Fruit	0.0	Fat	0.0

Cover fish with water and let stand in bowl 1 hour. Drain. Cut fish in quarters and put in saucepan. Cover finnan haddie with milk. Simmer 15 to 20 minutes, covered. Drain and flake fish with fork. Discard milk.

Heat margarine in nonstick skillet. Sauté onion and mushrooms until tender, about 5 minutes, over medium heat, stirring occasionally. Stir in mustard and flaked fish.

Spoon fish onto individual dishes, sprinkle with egg whites and chives, and serve hot. You might want to serve finnan haddie with toast points or cooked white rice.

Paella Valenciana

Serves 6

12	clams
12	mussels
2	tablespoons olive oil
1	cup onion, chopped
2	green bell peppers, chopped
1	clove garlic, minced
1	lb. chicken breast, boneless and skinless, cut into small pieces

Nutritional Data

PER SERVING:

Calories	474
% calories from fat	15
Fat (gm)	8.3
Sat. Fat (gm)	1.5
Cholesterol (mg)	164
Sodium (mg)	342
Protein (gm)	39.9
Carbohydrate (gm)	61.6

		EXCHANGES:		
2	large tomatoes, seeded and chopped	Milk	0.0	Bread	3.0
1½	cups uncooked long-grain rice	Veg.	3.0	Meat	3.5
	Large pinch saffron threads, soaked in	Fruit	0.0	Fat	0.0

2 large tomatoes, seeded and chopped
1½ cups uncooked long-grain rice
Large pinch saffron threads, soaked in
1 tablespoon water
1 teaspoon Spike (see "About This Cookbook")
2 cups liquid from steaming clams and mussels
1 lb. jumbo shrimp, cleaned and deveined
1 package frozen green peas, thawed
1 can artichoke hearts
½ cup roasted peppers, sliced
2 ozs. pimiento, chopped
½ cup parsley, chopped
1 large lemon, cut into slices

Scrub clams and mussels thoroughly. Place about 1 inch of water in deep pot. Bring to boil. Add clams and mussels. Cover and steam 7 to 8 minutes or until shells open. Remove shellfish from broth and set aside. Strain liquid into 2-cup measure and reserve. Add chicken broth if necessary to make 2 cups.

Add oil to paella pot with chopped onion, green peppers, garlic, and chicken. Sauté about 5 minutes, stirring often. When chicken is opaque, add tomatoes, rice, and saffron with its soaking water. Add Spike and pour in reserved 2 cups of broth. Bring to boil, stir once, and reduce heat so liquid simmers very slowly.

After 10 minutes, add shrimp, pushing them down among other ingredients. After 5 minutes, add peas, artichoke hearts, roasted peppers, and pimiento. Cook about 5 more minutes.

Before adding mussels and clams, cover pot and let sit 5 minutes. Sprinkle with parsley and arrange lemon slices on top.

Bouillabaisse

Serves 10

1 cup onions, chopped
½ cup celery, chopped
1 clove garlic, minced
¼ cup olive oil
2 packets Butter Buds
1 cup water
1 cup white wine
2 14½-oz. cans whole tomatoes, undrained and chopped
3 leeks (white portion), cleaned and finely sliced into matchsticks

Nutritional Data

PER SERVING:

Calories	294
% calories from fat	35
Fat (gm)	11.3
Sat. Fat (gm)	1.9
Cholesterol (mg)	43.4
Sodium (mg)	513
Protein (gm)	30.1
Carbohydrate (gm)	14.3

EXCHANGES:

Milk	0.0	Bread	0.0
Veg.	2.0	Meat	4.0
Fruit	0.0	Fat	0.5

1   bay leaf
1   teaspoon dried thyme
1   teaspoon orange peel, grated
3   lbs. fresh or frozen and thawed salmon,
    boneless, skinless, and cubed
½   lb. imitation crabmeat
½   lb. bay scallops
12 mussels
¼   cup parsley, chopped

In Dutch oven over medium-high heat, sauté onion, celery, and garlic in olive oil until tender, about 7 minutes. Add Butter Buds, water, and wine. Stir in tomatoes, leeks, herbs, and grated orange peel and bring to boil. Reduce heat to low and simmer 10 minutes. Stir in salmon, crab, scallops, and mussels. Over high heat, return to boil. Reduce heat to low and simmer 10 minutes more. Stir in parsley.

Creole Jambalaya

Serves 4

2   tablespoons diet margarine
1   cup cooked ham, diced
½   cup green bell pepper, chopped
½   cup onion, chopped
1   clove garlic, minced
1   10¾-oz. can condensed, low-salt
    tomato soup
⅓   cup water
1   medium bay leaf, crushed
¼   teaspoon ground oregano
¼   teaspoon salt
    Dash pepper
1   6¾-oz. can shrimp, drained
2   packets Equal® (see "About This
    Cookbook")
1½ cups cooked rice

Nutritional Data

PER SERVING:

Calories	285
% calories from fat	23
Fat (gm)	7.1
Sat. Fat (gm)	1.4
Cholesterol (mg)	93.5
Sodium (mg)	828
Protein (gm)	21.3
Carbohydrate (gm)	33

EXCHANGES:

Milk	0.0	Bread	2.0
Veg.	0.5	Meat	2.5
Fruit	0.0	Fat	0.0

Melt margarine in large skillet. Stir in ham, green pepper, onion, and garlic. Add soup, water, bay leaf, oregano, salt, and pepper. Cook over medium-high heat 20 minutes. Add shrimp; cook until heated through, 2 to 3 minutes. Remove from heat; stir in Equal®. Serve over rice.

Creole Shrimp

Serves 4

1 16-oz. can Italian plum tomatoes
1 medium onion, chopped
1 medium green bell pepper, diced
½ teaspoon chili powder
   Few hot red pepper flakes
1 bay leaf
1 lb. medium shrimp, peeled, deveined, and rinsed

Nutritional Data

PER SERVING:

Calories	129
% calories from fat	10
Fat (gm)	1.4
Sat. Fat (gm)	0.3
Cholesterol (mg)	174.2
Sodium (mg)	389
Protein (gm)	20.3
Carbohydrate (gm)	8.9

EXCHANGES:

Milk	0.0	Bread	0.0
Veg.	1.5	Meat	2.0
Fruit	0.0	Fat	0.0

In 2-quart measure or casserole, mix together all ingredients except shrimp, breaking up tomatoes with fork. Cover with vented plastic wrap, and microwave on High for 5 to 8 minutes, until green pepper is soft and sauce is bubbling, stirring once.

Add shrimp, stir to mix, cover, and microwave on High for 2 to 3 minutes until shrimp are pink. Do not overcook. Remove bay leaf, let stand for 3 minutes, and serve over rice if desired.

Shrimp Louisiana

Serves 4

1 15-oz. can tomato puree
½ cup water
3 tablespoons white vinegar
3 tablespoons Worcestershire sauce
2 tablespoons orange juice concentrate, thawed
1 tablespoon mustard
¼ teaspoon hot sauce
½ teaspoon garlic powder
¼ teaspoon salt
3 packets Equal® (see "About This Cookbook")
12 ozs. cooked shrimp

Nutritional Data

PER SERVING:

Calories	172
% calories from fat	8
Fat (gm)	1.4
Sat. Fat (gm)	0.3
Cholesterol (mg)	166.1
Sodium (mg)	509
Protein (gm)	20.6
Carbohydrate (gm)	18.3

EXCHANGES:

Milk	0.0	Bread	0.0
Veg.	2.0	Meat	2.0
Fruit	0.5	Fat	0.0

In saucepan combine all sauce ingredients except Equal®. Slowly bring to boil, stirring constantly. Remove from heat. Stir in Equal®. Add shrimp to sauce and serve. Makes 2½ cups.

Baked Shrimp with Asparagus

Serves 8

- 2 lbs. asparagus
- 2 lbs. medium shrimp, in shells
- 1/2 lb. potatoes
- Vegetable cooking spray
- 2/3 cup onion, chopped
- 1/4 cup evaporated skim milk
- 1/4 cup Parmesan cheese, freshly grated
- 1 teaspoon basil
- 1/4 cup seasoned bread crumbs

Nutritional Data

PER SERVING:

Calories	178
% calories from fat	12
Fat (gm)	2.4
Sat. Fat (gm)	1
Cholesterol (mg)	176.9
Sodium (mg)	372
Protein (gm)	24.5
Carbohydrate (gm)	15.2

EXCHANGES:

Milk	0.0	Bread	0.5
Veg.	1.0	Meat	2.0
Fruit	0.0	Fat	0.0

Trim asparagus, cutting off 1 inch of hard root from lower half of stalk. Wash thoroughly in 1 or 2 changes of cold water. Place asparagus in steamer basket over boiling water and steam until barely tender, about 8 minutes. Drain and set aside to cool. When asparagus has cooled, cut into pieces 1½ inches long.

Shell shrimp and devein. Wash in cold water. Pat thoroughly dry with paper towels. Set aside.

Wash potatoes and boil them, unpeeled, in large pot of water. When done, drain, peel, and pass potatoes through food mill or potato ricer into bowl large enough to accommodate all other ingredients.

Coat medium saucepan with vegetable cooking spray and add onion. Over medium heat, sauté onion until it becomes translucent. Add asparagus, turn up heat to high, and sauté asparagus, turning it constantly, 3 to 4 minutes.

Transfer asparagus with all pan juices to bowl containing potatoes. Add milk and cheese. Mix well. Add basil and shrimp and toss to mix well.

Preheat oven to 450 degrees. Choose large oven-to-table baking dish. Coat bottom with vegetable spray. Pour into it entire contents of bowl, leveling with large spoon, and sprinkle on bread crumbs. Bake on top shelf 15 to 20 minutes.

Shrimp Diane

Serves 4

¼	cup white wine
1	tablespoon margarine
2	tablespoons shallots, finely minced
½	cup mushrooms, thinly sliced
8	artichoke hearts
¼	cup fresh chives, snipped
4	tablespoons pimiento, chopped
1	lb. medium shrimp, shelled and deveined
1	lemon, sliced
	Parsley sprigs for garnish

Nutritional Data

PER SERVING:

Calories	158
% calories from fat	18
Fat (gm)	4.1
Sat. Fat (gm)	0.9
Cholesterol (mg)	174.2
Sodium (mg)	277
Protein (gm)	21
Carbohydrate (gm)	9.7

EXCHANGES:

Milk	0.0	Bread	0.0
Veg.	2.0	Meat	2.0
Fruit	0.0	Fat	0.0

Prepare sauce first by combining wine, margarine, and shallots in saucepan. Place over medium-high heat, cover, and bring to boil. Lower heat and add mushrooms, artichoke hearts, chives, and pimiento. Simmer 2 minutes. Keep warm.

Use steamer large enough so shrimp can be steamed directly on rack in single layer. Steam over water to which 1 sliced lemon has been added. Steam shrimp about 2 minutes or until they turn pink. Watch carefully; do not overcook.

Once shrimp are steamed, add to saucepan containing wine sauce. With two spoons, mix shrimp with sauce and remove from heat. Spoon shrimp over rice or couscous.

To Freeze: Vacuum seal each portion; label and freeze for up to 2 months.

To Serve: Put bags in boiling water, and bring water to boil again. Boil 10 to 12 minutes.

Shrimp with Feta Cheese

Serves 4

	Vegetable cooking spray
4	scallions, finely chopped, including green part
2	green bell peppers, finely chopped
1	small red chili pepper, finely chopped
1	bunch parsley, finely chopped
1	teaspoon oregano
	Black pepper, freshly ground, to taste
½	lb. medium shrimp, washed, peeled, and deveined
4	medium tomatoes, peeled and chopped

Nutritional Data

PER SERVING:

Calories	136
% calories from fat	28
Fat (gm)	4.4
Sat. Fat (gm)	2.6
Cholesterol (mg)	101.4
Sodium (mg)	300
Protein (gm)	13.8
Carbohydrate (gm)	11.5

EXCHANGES:

Milk	0.0	Bread	0.0
Veg.	1.0	Meat	2.0
Fruit	0.0	Fat	0.0

1   teaspoon sugar
¼   cup feta cheese, crumbled
3   tablespoons skim milk

Coat large skillet with vegetable cooking spray and add scallions. Sauté until translucent. Add green peppers, chili pepper, parsley, oregano, and black pepper. Continuing sautéing another 5 minutes.

Reduce heat, add shrimp, and cook, uncovered, at least 4 minutes, stirring occasionally with wooden spoon. Add tomatoes and sugar, and simmer another 5 minutes. Add cheese and milk and simmer, uncovered, over low heat for additional 20 minutes.

Garlic, Shrimp, and Vegetable Stir-Fry

Serves 5

1¼ cups uncooked long-grain white rice
2   tablespoons dry sherry
2   tablespoons defatted chicken broth
2   tablespoons reduced-sodium soy sauce
2   teaspoons sesame oil
2   large cloves garlic, minced
2   drops hot oil
½   lb. snow peas, stem ends removed
1   red bell pepper, seeded and cut into cubes
¼   cup thinly sliced green onion
1   lb. medium shrimp, uncooked, peeled, and deveined
¼   cup water
2   teaspoons cornstarch
2   tablespoons hoisin sauce
½   teaspoon fresh lemon juice

Nutritional Data

PER SERVING:

Calories	303
% calories from fat	9
Fat (gm)	3.1
Sat. Fat (gm)	0.6
Cholesterol (mg)	139.3
Sodium (mg)	455
Protein (gm)	20.7
Carbohydrate (gm)	45.1

EXCHANGES:

Milk	0.0	Bread	2.5
Veg.	1.5	Meat	1.5
Fruit	0.0	Fat	0.0

Cook rice according to package directions.

In large nonstick skillet, stir together sherry, broth, soy sauce, sesame oil, garlic, and hot oil.

Add snow peas, red pepper, and onion and cook quickly over medium-high heat, stirring, 2 minutes. Add shrimp and simmer, stirring, 4 or 5 minutes longer or until shrimp curls.

In cup, stir together water and cornstarch. Add to pan and cook, stirring, 1 or 2 minutes or until sauce thickens. Stir in hoisin sauce and lemon juice.

Serve shrimp and vegetables over rice.

Hot Garlic Shrimp

Serves 4

1 lb. large shrimp
1 tablespoon olive oil
4 cloves garlic, smashed or minced
½-1 teaspoon red pepper flakes
Dash cumin
3 tablespoons fresh lemon juice
Parsley, chopped, for garnish

Nutritional Data	
PER SERVING:	
Calories	126
% calories from fat	32
Fat (gm)	4.4
Sat. Fat (gm)	0.7
Cholesterol (mg)	174.2
Sodium (mg)	200
Protein (gm)	18.9
Carbohydrate (gm)	2.1

EXCHANGES:			
Milk	0.0	Bread	0.0
Veg.	0.0	Meat	2.5
Fruit	0.0	Fat	0.0

Peel and devein shrimp, and rinse in cold water. Mix olive oil and garlic in glass measuring cup, and microwave on High 1 minute.

In 2-quart round casserole, mix shrimp with oil and garlic, and sprinkle with red pepper, a few dashes of cumin, and lemon juice. Stir to mix, and arrange shrimp in circular fashion, thick ends to outside of bowl.

Cover with vented plastic wrap, and microwave on High 3 to 4 minutes turning shrimp once. Remove when shrimp are pink. Let stand another minute to complete cooking. Dust with parsley.

 # Peking Shrimp

Serves 4

6 dried black mushrooms
4 green onions, with tops
16 pea pods (fresh, preferred, or frozen)
Vegetable cooking spray
¾ lb. raw medium shrimp, in shells
1 teaspoon arrowroot
1 teaspoon water
2 teaspoons garlic, finely chopped
¼ cup Chicken Stock (see p. 40)

Nutritional Data	
PER SERVING:	
Calories	98
% calories from fat	8
Fat (gm)	0.9
Sat. Fat (gm)	0.2
Cholesterol (mg)	131.2
Sodium (mg)	151
Protein (gm)	15.4
Carbohydrate (gm)	6.9

EXCHANGES:			
Milk	0.0	Bread	0.0
Veg.	1.0	Meat	1.5
Fruit	0.0	Fat	0.0

Soak mushrooms in hot water 20 minutes or until soft; drain. Squeeze out excess moisture. Remove and discard stems; cut caps into thin strips.

Cut green onions diagonally into 1-inch pieces. Cut pea pods into 1-inch pieces. Peel shrimp, wash, and devein. Pat dry with paper towels. Mix arrowroot and water.

Heat sprayed wok until very hot. Add shrimp and garlic; stir-fry until shrimp are pink. Remove shrimp from wok.

Add mushrooms, green onions, and pea pods to wok and stir-fry 2 minutes. Add Chicken Stock and bring to boil. Cover and cook 1 minute. Stir in arrowroot mixture and return shrimp to wok. Cook and stir 30 seconds or until shrimp are hot.

To Freeze: Vacuum seal each portion; label and freeze for up to 2 months.

To Serve: Put bags in boiling water, and bring water to boil again. Boil 10 to 12 minutes.

Steamed Maine Lobster with Shrimp Sauce

Serves 4

Shrimp Sauce

¼   cup shallots, chopped
½   cup cooked shrimp, chopped
     Canola oil, or vegetable cooking spray
1   tablespoon margarine
1   tablespoon all-purpose flour
½   cup fish stock
2   tablespoons skim or 2% milk
¼   teaspoon ground cardamom

Lobster

2   whole lobsters, 1¼-1½ lbs.
     Seaweed or lime wedges for garnish

Nutritional Data

PER SERVING:

Calories	182
% calories from fat	16
Fat (gm)	4.7
Sat. Fat (gm)	0.9
Cholesterol (mg)	105.2
Sodium (mg)	263
Protein (gm)	26
Carbohydrate (gm)	6.5

EXCHANGES:

Milk	0.0	Bread	0.0
Veg.	0.0	Meat	3.5
Fruit	0.0	Fat	0.0

Shrimp Sauce: Sauté shallots in small saucepan coated with canola oil or cooking spray until soft. Stir in shrimp and cook 1 minute. Set aside.

In another small saucepan, melt margarine. Whisk in flour and continue cooking and stirring until flour is absorbed. Add fish stock, milk, cardamom, and shrimp. Stir until sauce thickens slightly. Serve hot.

Lobster: Heat water to boil in steamer or kettle. If using a rack on a pan, the pan must rise at least 1 inch above water level. Put lobsters on rack and cover pot. Reduce heat to simmer and steam lobsters 12 to 15 minutes; the rule of thumb is 10 minutes per pound.

Carefully remove lobsters and cut in half for 4 servings. Pass Shrimp Sauce at table. Lobsters are sweet and moist, and although they are classically served with drawn butter, this recipe works just great without it.

Cajun Grilled Soft-Shell Crabs

Serves 4

Vegetables

1 medium zucchini
3/4 lb. white mushrooms

Crabs

8 soft-shell crabs
1 tablespoon Cajun Spice Rub (recipe follows)
4 bamboo skewers, presoaked
Vegetable cooking spray
1 lemon, sliced

Cajun Spice Rub (makes about 2 1/2 tablespoons)

2 teaspoons cayenne pepper
1 teaspoon bell pepper, ground
2 teaspoons dried onion, minced
1/2 teaspoon garlic powder
1/4 teaspoon dried thyme
1/4 teaspoon salt
1/8 teaspoon white pepper

Nutritional Data

PER SERVING:

Calories	174
% calories from fat	11
Fat (gm)	2.1
Sat. Fat (gm)	0.3
Cholesterol (mg)	96
Sodium (mg)	539
Protein (gm)	31
Carbohydrate (gm)	9.7

EXCHANGES:

Milk	0.0	Bread	0.0
Veg.	1.0	Meat	3.0
Fruit	0.0	Fat	0.0

Vegetables: Cut zucchini into 1 1/2-inch pieces. Trim mushrooms. Set vegetables aside.

Crabs: On cutting surface, cut off face portion of each crab. Lifting shell gently on both sides of back, scrape off gills. Lift shell and remove sand receptacle from under mouth area. Discard all portions removed from crabs. Wash crabs and pat dry with paper towels.

Cajun Spice Rub: Mix ingredients together and brush crabs.

Thread vegetables and crabs onto skewers, threading crabs through their top edge. Arrange skewers on grill rack coated with cooking spray and grill 3 minutes. Continue grilling until crabs are reddish color, 3 to 4 minutes longer. Serve hot garnished with lemon slices.

Soft-Shell Crabs with Herb Breading

Serves 4

Vegetable cooking spray
2   teaspoons margarine
4   cloves garlic, minced
¼   cups shallots, minced
¼   cup seasoned bread crumbs
8   soft-shell crabs, cleaned, washed, and patted dry
¼   teaspoon each ingredient: pepper, chervil, thyme
¼   cup fresh chives, minced

Nutritional Data

PER SERVING:

Calories	197
% calories from fat	17
Fat (gm)	3.7
Sat. Fat (gm)	0.6
Cholesterol (mg)	96
Sodium (mg)	703
Protein (gm)	30.1
Carbohydrate (gm)	9.5

EXCHANGES:

Milk	0.0	Bread	0.5
Veg.	0.0	Meat	3.0
Fruit	0.0	Fat	0.0

Prepare crabs and set aside.

Coat nonstick skillet with cooking spray and add margarine. Sauté garlic and shallots until just beginning to brown, over medium heat, stirring occasionally. Mix in bread crumbs and cook until browned, 2 to 3 minutes. Add crabs and sauté over medium heat, turning once until cooked. Crabs will brown when cooked. Sprinkle crabs with pepper, chervil, and thyme.

Place 2 crabs on each plate. Sprinkle with bread crumbs and chives. Serve only 1 crab as an appetizer course.

King Crab Legs Japanese Style

Serves 4

Wasabi

2   teaspoons cold water
2   tablespoons wasabi powder (Japanese green horseradish powder)
2   cups pickled ginger

Crab Legs

4   lbs. frozen split crab legs, defrosted in refrigerator
Vegetable cooking spray

Nutritional Data

PER SERVING:

Calories	177
% calories from fat	11
Fat (gm)	2
Sat. Fat (gm)	0.2
Cholesterol (mg)	60.1
Sodium (mg)	1264
Protein (gm)	23.8
Carbohydrate (gm)	14.2

EXCHANGES:

Milk	0.0	Bread	1.0
Veg.	0.0	Meat	3.0
Fruit	0.0	Fat	0.0

Wasabi: Stir water with wasabi powder in shallow dish until thick paste is formed. If necessary, add more water, 1/2 teaspoon at a time. Allow wasabi to stand 15 minutes; then stir.

Remove pickled ginger from packet, divide, and mound on 4 individual dinner plates. Dollop wasabi next to ginger and set aside.

Crab Legs: Place cut side down on barbecue grill coated with cooking spray over ashen coals. Cover grill and smoke 2 to 4 minutes or until crabmeat is done to taste. It will have light brownish, smoked appearance. Arrange crab legs on dinner plates, and provide bowl for crab shells.

Coquilles Saint Jacques
(Scallops Baked in Shells)

Serves 6

2 cups dry white wine
Vegetable cooking spray
Bouquet garni (see p. 369)
2 lbs. (1 quart) scallops
1 teaspoon Spike (see "About This Cookbook")
1/2 lb. mushrooms
6 shallots
1 tablespoon parsley, minced
1/2 cup Butter Buds, divided
1 teaspoon fresh lemon juice
1/4 cup flour
1/4 cup evaporated skim milk
1/3 cup bread crumbs

Nutritional Data

PER SERVING:

Calories	209
% calories from fat	6
Fat (gm)	1.3
Sat. Fat (gm)	0.2
Cholesterol (mg)	30
Sodium (mg)	452
Protein (gm)	18.3
Carbohydrate (gm)	16.5

EXCHANGES:

Milk	0.0	Bread	0.5
Veg.	1.0	Meat	2.5
Fruit	0.0	Fat	0.0

Preheat oven to 450 degrees.

Coat 6 baking shells or ramekins with vegetable cooking spray.

Heat in saucepan, wine and bouquet garni.

Wash scallops in cold water and drain. Add scallops, with Spike, to wine. Cover and simmer about 10 minutes or until tender. Remove bouquet garni, drain scallops, and reserve liquid. Cut scallops into bite-size pieces and set aside.

Clean and chop mushrooms and add to saucepan with shallots, parsley, and 1/4 cup Butter Buds. Add lemon juice and simmer 5 to 10 minutes. Strain liquid into seasoned wine. Add vegetable mixture to scallops. Set aside.

Make a roux by combining 1/4 cup Butter Buds and flour in saucepan. Cook over low heat until mixture bubbles. Remove

from heat and gradually stir in wine-vegetable liquid. Return to
heat and bring rapidly to boil, stirring constantly; cook 1 to 2
minutes longer.

Remove sauce from heat and gradually add skim milk,
stirring vigorously. Add to scallop mixture.

Fill shells or ramekins, piling high in center. Sprinkle with
bread crumbs. Place in oven for 8 to 10 minutes to brown
and serve.

Scallops with Linguine and Peppers

Serves 6		Nutritional Data	
1	cup onions, chopped	**PER SERVING:**	
½	cup parsley, or cilantro, minced	Calories	304
¾	cup carrots, grated	% calories from fat	15
1	cup roasted green chilies, peeled	Fat (gm)	5.2
	and chopped	Sat. Fat (gm)	1.2
1	teaspoon Worcestershire sauce	Cholesterol (mg)	21.2
	Salt and black pepper, freshly ground,	Sodium (mg)	239
	to taste	Protein (gm)	18.1
1	lb. linguine pasta	Carbohydrate (gm)	48.4
½	lb. scallops		

EXCHANGES:			
Milk	0.0	Bread	3.0
Veg.	1.0	Meat	1.0
Fruit	0.0	Fat	0.0

In medium saucepan, add water to cover onion, parsley,
carrots, green chilies, Worcestershire sauce, salt, and pepper.
Simmer 5 minutes. While sauce is simmering, cook linguine in
6 cups boiling water. Drain well.

To cook scallops, bring 1 quart water to boil. Add scallops,
reduce heat, and simmer 3 to 4 minutes or until scallops
become opaque. Drain and serve over linguine. Top with sauce.

Scallops with Apples and Pea Pods

Serves 4

12 ozs. fresh or frozen scallops
¼ cup apple cider or juice
2 teaspoons cornstarch
1 tablespoon soy sauce
2 tablespoons cooking oil
3 small apples, cored and sliced
1 medium onion, chopped
1 medium red bell pepper, chopped
1 6-oz. package frozen pea pods, or 1 cup fresh peas with pods

Nutritional Data

PER SERVING:

Calories	243
% calories from fat	29
Fat (gm)	8
Sat. Fat (gm)	1
Cholesterol (mg)	28.4
Sodium (mg)	397
Protein (gm)	16.7
Carbohydrate (gm)	27.6

EXCHANGES:

Milk	0.0	Bread	0.0
Veg.	1.0	Meat	2.0
Fruit	1.0	Fat	1.0

Thaw scallops, if frozen. Cup up any large scallops. Stir apple juice into cornstarch; stir in soy sauce. Set aside.

Heat wok over high heat; add 1 tablespoon oil. Stir-fry apples, onion, and pepper 3 minutes or until just tender; remove from wok.

Add remaining oil to wok. Stir-fry scallops 4 to 5 minutes or until done. Stir soy mixture and add it to scallops. Cook and stir until thickened and bubbly; cook and stir 2 minutes more. Stir pea pods into scallop mixture; stir in apples, onion, and pepper mixture. Cover and cook 1 to 2 minutes until pea pods are done.

To Freeze: Vacuum seal each portion; label and freeze for up to 2 months.

To Serve: Put bags in boiling water, and bring water to boil again. Boil 10 to 12 minutes.

Marinated Scallop Burritos

Serves 6

Hot Tomato Salsa

3 large tomatoes, peeled, seeded, and chopped
3 jalapeño peppers, seeded and chopped (use caution; wear rubber gloves and do not rub your eyes)

Nutritional Data

PER SERVING:

Calories	171
% calories from fat	20
Fat (gm)	3.8
Sat. Fat (gm)	0.5
Cholesterol (mg)	15.1
Sodium (mg)	295
Protein (gm)	10.5
Carbohydrate (gm)	24.1

3	cloves garlic, minced
½	cup fresh cilantro, minced
¼	teaspoon pepper

Scallops

| 24 | scallops, wash and pat dry |

Marinade

¼	cup tarragon vinegar
2	tablespoons olive oil
2	tablespoons fresh cilantro
½	teaspoon each ingredient: cumin powder, chili powder

EXCHANGES:

Milk	0.0	Bread	1.5
Veg.	0.0	Meat	1.0
Fruit	0.0	Fat	0.0

Accompaniments

| 6 | small flour tortillas |
| 1 | red bell pepper, seeded and chopped, for garnish |

Hot Tomato Salsa: Chop tomatoes and put them in small glass bowl. Mix in peppers, garlic, cilantro, and pepper. Cover lightly and refrigerate until serving time.

Scallops: Bring about 1 quart of water to boil over medium-high heat. Add scallops and simmer 3 to 4 minutes or until scallops turn opaque. Drain well; pat dry. Transfer to plastic bag.

Marinade: Combine ingredients and pour into plastic bag with scallops. Seal securely and turn bag several times so that marinade touches all surfaces of the scallops. Place in shallow dish and refrigerate overnight.

At serving time, separate marinade and scallops. Show your guests how to assemble a burrito: put 4 scallops on warm tortilla, spoon Hot Tomato Salsa over scallops, and sprinkle with peppers. Roll up tortilla, making a burrito. Fold in one end and begin eating at open end. You might want to serve refried beans and rice and/or a salad.

Grilled Scallop Kebobs

Serves 4

⅝	lb. fresh or frozen scallops
¼	cup white wine
2	tablespoons fresh lime or lemon juice
1	tablespoon parsley, snipped
1	clove garlic, minced
½	teaspoon dried basil, crushed
½	teaspoon dried oregano, crushed
½	teaspoon Spike (see "About This Cookbook")
	Dash pepper
1	medium zucchini, cut into ½-inch slices
1	medium green or red bell pepper, cut into 1-inch squares
8	fresh mushrooms
8	cherry tomatoes

Nutritional Data

PER SERVING:

Calories	94
% calories from fat	9
Fat (gm)	0.9
Sat. Fat (gm)	0.1
Cholesterol (mg)	22.5
Sodium (mg)	117
Protein (gm)	13.1
Carbohydrate (gm)	2.3

EXCHANGES:

Milk	0.0	Bread	0.0
Veg.	1.0	Meat	1.5
Fruit	0.0	Fat	0.0

Thaw scallops if frozen. Halve any large ones. Place in plastic bag, and refrigerate.

For marinade, in small bowl stir together wine, lime or lemon juice, parsley, garlic, basil, oregano, Spike, and pepper. Pour marinade over scallops. Seal bag. Marinate in refrigerator for 3 to 4 hours, turning bag occasionally.

Meanwhile, cook zucchini, pepper, and mushrooms, covered, in small amount of boiling water for 2 minutes. Drain.

Drain scallops, reserving marinade. Alternately thread scallops, zucchini, pepper, and mushrooms onto 8 12-inch skewers.

Place skewers on greased grill rack. Grill uncovered directly over medium-hot coals for 10 to 12 minutes or until scallops are opaque, brushing with marinade and turning occasionally. Add tomatoes to ends of skewers the last minute of cooking.

Note: If rain dampens your barbecue, broil the scallop and vegetable kebabs 4 to 5 inches from heat for times given.

Scallops with Mushrooms in Wine Sauce

Serves 4

1 lb. scallops
1 cup dry white wine
2 tablespoons unsalted margarine
2 scallions, chopped
1 cup mushrooms, sliced
5 tablespoons unsalted margarine
3 tablespoons flour
1/2 cup evaporated skim milk
1/4 cup fresh chives, snipped
1 cup soft bread crumbs
   Parsley for garnish

Nutritional Data

PER SERVING:

Calories	307
% calories from fat	35
Fat (gm)	12
Sat. Fat (gm)	2.4
Cholesterol (mg)	38.8
Sodium (mg)	280
Protein (gm)	23.5
Carbohydrate (gm)	17.8

EXCHANGES:

Milk	0.5	Bread	1.0
Veg.	0.0	Meat	2.5
Fruit	0.0	Fat	1.0

Place scallops in bottom of casserole dish and add wine. Microwave, covered, on Medium-High 4 to 6 minutes until scallops are tender. Do not overcook. Strain and reserve liquid.

Place 2 tablespoons margarine in 2-cup glass measure and add scallions and mushrooms. Microwave on High 3 to 5 minutes.

Wine Sauce: In microwave on High, melt 3 tablespoons margarine in 4-cup glass, about 45 to 50 seconds. Add reserved wine liquid and flour to margarine and whisk together. Microwave on High 2 minutes; add milk and chives, whisking well. Microwave on High 2 to 4 minutes more until thick enough to coat a spoon, whisking every 2 minutes.

Add scallions, mushrooms, and scallops to sauce and heat 2 minutes on Medium-High until hot.

Melt remaining 2 tablespoons of margarine in small bowl, on High 45 to 55 seconds, and add bread crumbs until combined. Sprinkle over scallop mixture and garnish with parsley.

To Freeze: Vacuum seal each portion; label and freeze for up to 2 months.

To Serve: Put bags in boiling water, and bring water to boil again. Boil 10 to 12 minutes.

Nutty Sea Scallops

Serves 4

1¼	lbs. sea scallops, halved horizontally
½	cup dry white wine
1	small jalapeño pepper, chopped (use caution; wear rubber gloves and do not rub your eyes)
1	teaspoon olive oil
2	cloves garlic, smashed or minced
¼	cup shallots, chopped
	Juice of ½ lemon
½	cup green peas (if frozen, thawed)
¼	cup red bell pepper, chopped
1	cup mushrooms, sliced
½	teaspoon dried dill weed
2	tablespoons peanuts, chopped
	Parsley, chopped, for garnish

Nutritional Data

PER SERVING:

Calories	218
% calories from fat	19
Fat (gm)	4.6
Sat. Fat (gm)	0.6
Cholesterol (mg)	47.3
Sodium (mg)	373
Protein (gm)	26.8
Carbohydrate (gm)	12.6

EXCHANGES:

Milk	0.0	Bread	0.5
Veg.	1.0	Meat	3.0
Fruit	0.0	Fat	0.0

Marinate scallops in wine with jalapeño pepper for a few hours before cooking.

In 8" x 12" microwave-safe dish, combine oil, garlic, and shallots, and microwave on High 2 minutes. Add lemon juice, peas, bell pepper, mushrooms, and dill and mix well. Microwave on High 2 minutes and stir.

Arrange scallops over cooked ingredients, and microwave on High 2 to 3 minutes, rotating dish once, until scallops are opaque. Let stand a minute before sprinkling on chopped peanuts and dusting of parsley.

♨Scallops in Ginger Sauce

Serves 4

- 1 1-inch piece ginger root, peeled and quartered
- 4 large cloves garlic, quartered
- 2 green onions, cut into pieces
  Vegetable cooking spray
- ½ teaspoon crushed red pepper
- 3 tablespoons sugar
- 2 teaspoons low-salt soy sauce
- 3 tablespoons ketchup
- ¼ cup dry white wine
- 1 teaspoon white vinegar
- 2 lbs. sea scallops
- 8 10-inch wooden skewers, soaked in water 15 minutes, drained

Nutritional Data

PER SERVING:

Calories	272
% calories from fat	9
Fat (gm)	2.7
Sat. Fat (gm)	0
Cholesterol (mg)	96.5
Sodium (mg)	722
Protein (gm)	42.9
Carbohydrate (gm)	18.2

EXCHANGES:

Milk	0.0	Bread	0.0
Veg.	0.5	Meat	5.0
Fruit	0.0	Fat	0.0

Combine ginger, garlic, and green onion in food processor and mince. Coat nonstick skillet with cooking spray and heat. Sauté ginger, garlic, and green onion about 1 minute. Set aside.

Combine red pepper, sugar, soy sauce, ketchup, wine, and vinegar. Stir this into onion mixture. Simmer 1 minute more.

Thread drained scallops onto skewers. Place scallops on grill rack coated with cooking spray, and over hot coals cook 2 to 3 minutes on each side or until scallops have lost their translucency.

Remove from heat and transfer to serving platter. Drizzle sauce over scallops.

🔲 Teriyaki Sea Scallops

Serves 4

- 2 tablespoons dry sherry
- 1 tablespoon low-sodium soy sauce
- 2 tablespoons water
- 1 tablespoon sesame oil
- 2 teaspoons ginger root, peeled and grated
- 1 teaspoon frozen orange juice concentrate
- 2 cloves garlic, minced
- 1 lb. sea scallops
- 1 tablespoon fresh lemon juice
  Paprika
  Parsley, chopped, for garnish

Nutritional Data

PER SERVING:

Calories	147
% calories from fat	27
Fat (gm)	4.3
Sat. Fat (gm)	0.6
Cholesterol (mg)	37.8
Sodium (mg)	314
Protein (gm)	19.6
Carbohydrate (gm)	5

EXCHANGES:

Milk	0.0	Bread	0.0
Veg.	0.0	Meat	2.5
Fruit	0.0	Fat	0.0

Combine sherry, soy sauce, water, oil, ginger, orange juice, and garlic in 8" x 10" glass baking dish. Add scallops and marinate in refrigerator up to 4 hours, turning to coat, or at room temperature for 1/2 hour.

When ready to cook, cover with vented plastic wrap, and microwave on High 2 to 3 minutes. Turn scallops over and rotate dish; then microwave on High another 2 to 3 minutes. Scallops are cooked when they turn opaque. Let sit, covered, for 3 minutes. Spoon lemon juice over scallops, dust with paprika, and sprinkle on fresh parsley.

🔥 *Scallops in White Wine*

Serves 4

1/4	cup diet margarine
1/4	cup dry white wine
3	tablespoons parsley, minced
1	tablespoon shallots, or green onions, chopped
2	tablespoons light, dry sherry
1	teaspoon tarragon
1	teaspoon thyme
1	lb. scallops
1/2	lb. mushrooms, sliced

Nutritional Data

PER SERVING:

Calories	188
% calories from fat	33
Fat (gm)	6.9
Sat. Fat (gm)	1.1
Cholesterol (mg)	37.8
Sodium (mg)	317
Protein (gm)	20.5
Carbohydrate (gm)	7

EXCHANGES:

Milk	0.0	Bread	0.0
Veg.	1.0	Meat	2.5
Fruit	0.0	Fat	0.5

Combine margarine, wine, parsley, shallots or onions, sherry, and herbs in crockpot. Cook, uncovered, on High until sauce bubbles and is reduced slightly. Add scallops and mushrooms. Cover. Cook 10 to 15 minutes or until cooked through.

To Freeze: Vacuum seal each portion; label and freeze for up to 2 months.

To Serve: Put bags in boiling water, and bring water to boil again. Boil 10 to 12 minutes.

Grilled Mussels

Serves 4

	Heavy-duty aluminum foil
24	mussels, cleaned
1	7-oz. can baby corn ears, drained
4	green onions, chopped
8	broccoli pieces
4	tablespoons white wine

Nutritional Data

PER SERVING:

Calories	130
% calories from fat	15
Fat (gm)	2.2
Sat. Fat (gm)	0.4
Cholesterol (mg)	24
Sodium (mg)	299
Protein (gm)	12.1
Carbohydrate (gm)	14.3

Cut 4 double sheets of aluminum foil large enough to hold 6 mussels and equal portions of vegetables.

Arrange mussels, corn ears, and onion in center of each foil sheet. Add broccoli and sprinkle with wine.

Fold packages tightly. On barbecue, place directly over hot coals. Cook 3 to 4 minutes, turn packages, and grill 2 to 3 minutes longer. Test one package to see if it is done. Discard any unopened mussels. Serve hot.

EXCHANGES:			
Milk	0.0	Bread	1.0
Veg.	0.0	Meat	1.5
Fruit	0.0	Fat	0.0

Microwave Thai Mussels

Serves 2

Thai Flavoring

Olive oil, or vegetable cooking spray
3 cloves garlic, minced
½ cup bread crumbs
¼ teaspoon pepper
1 teaspoon Thailand commercially bottled fish sauce
⅓ cup fresh cilantro, minced

Mussels

16 mussels, well scrubbed

Nutritional Data

PER SERVING:

Calories	256
% calories from fat	19
Fat (gm)	5.2
Sat. Fat (gm)	1
Cholesterol (mg)	48.8
Sodium (mg)	593
Protein (gm)	24.1
Carbohydrate (gm)	26.6

EXCHANGES:			
Milk	0.0	Bread	1.5
Veg.	0.0	Meat	3.0
Fruit	0.0	Fat	0.0

Thai Flavoring: Coat nonstick skillet with olive oil or cooking spray and sauté garlic 1 minute, or until cooked, stirring occasionally, over medium heat. Add bread crumbs, pepper, fish sauce, and cilantro. Cook over low heat until bread crumbs are just toasted. Remove from heat and reserve.

*Mussels: Using microwave-safe glass dish, pie plate, or deep dish, arrange mussels on sides, keeping them in single layer. Cover dish securely with plastic wrap for microwave. Microwave 1½ to 2 minutes or until mussels are open.

Remove dish from microwave and take off plastic wrap, allowing steam to escape away from you. Remove mussels, with liquid, to deep dish. Sprinkle with Thai Flavoring.

*Note: Wash mussels well and discard any that are open before cooking; discard any mussels that are closed after cooking.

Steamed Clams Over Spaghetti

Serves 4

24	fresh clams, scrubbed; remember, if clams are open before cooking, do not use them; if they are not open after cooking, discard them
	Vegetable cooking spray
4	cloves garlic, minced
1	cup onions, minced
¼	cup parsley, minced
½	teaspoon oregano
¼	teaspoon white pepper
1	cup water
3	cups hot, cooked spaghetti
4	teaspoons Parmesan cheese, freshly grated

Nutritional Data

PER SERVING:

Calories	263
% calories from fat	9
Fat (gm)	2.6
Sat. Fat (gm)	0.6
Cholesterol (mg)	39.7
Sodium (mg)	107
Protein (gm)	21.2
Carbohydrate (gm)	37.7

EXCHANGES:

Milk	0.0	Bread	2.0
Veg.	0.0	Meat	2.0
Fruit	0.0	Fat	0.0

Scrub clams and rinse well under cold running water.

Coat skillet with cooking spray, and sauté garlic and onions for about 4 minutes, stirring occasionally, over medium heat. Add parsley, oregano, and white pepper. Add clams and water. Cover tightly; steam over medium heat 5 minutes or until clams open. Discard any unopened clams.

Spoon spaghetti into soup bowls. Arrange clams over spaghetti; pour broth into bowls. Sprinkle with Parmesan cheese, and serve hot.

Chapter Five

POULTRY: CHICKEN, TURKEY & CORNISH HENS

Chicken Marengo

Serves 4

4 chicken breast halves, boneless, skinless
¼ cup flour
Dash salt and pepper
1 tablespoon olive oil
1 clove garlic, crushed
3 tablespoons onion, chopped
4 tomatoes, quartered
1 cup white wine
Herb bouquet (sprig of parsley and 1 teaspoon each thyme, rosemary, tarragon in
cheesecloth bag)
1 cup mushrooms, sliced
½ cup pitted black olives, sliced (optional)
½ cup chicken broth
2 tablespoons cornstarch

Nutritional Data

PER SERVING:

Calories	246
% calories from fat	22
Fat (gm)	6.1
Sat. Fat (gm)	1.1
Cholesterol (mg)	48.3
Sodium (mg)	57.9
Protein (gm)	20
Carbohydrate (gm)	17.7

EXCHANGES:

Milk	0.0	Bread	1.0
Veg.	1.0	Meat	2.5
Fruit	0.0	Fat	0.0

Rinse and pat chicken dry. Shake chicken in bag containing flour and dash of salt and pepper. Heat oil in skillet, add chicken and brown. Add garlic and onions. Continue to cook on medium heat. Add tomatoes, wine, herb bouquet, mushrooms, and olives (if used). Cover and simmer over low heat about ½ hour.

To thicken, put chicken broth and cornstarch into screw-top jar. Shake well. Remove chicken from skillet and discard herb bouquet. Gradually add broth-cornstarch liquid to mixture in skillet, stirring constantly. Boil 3 to 5 minutes until mixture thickens. Arrange chicken on hot platter. Cover with sauce.

Chicken Cacciatore

Serves 4

Chicken and Vegetables

1 lb. chicken breast, boneless, skinless, and
cut into 6 or 7 large pieces
¼ teaspoon salt (optional)
¼ teaspoon black pepper
1 tablespoon olive oil
1 large onion, chopped
8 ozs. fresh mushrooms, cleaned and sliced
2 cloves garlic, minced
½ cup defatted chicken broth, divided
1 tablespoon white flour
½ cup dry sherry, or white wine
1 cup canned tomatoes (preferably
Italian style), drained and chopped

Nutritional Data

PER SERVING:

Calories	463
% calories from fat	16
Fat (gm)	8.3
Sat. Fat (gm)	2
Cholesterol (mg)	49
Sodium (mg)	264
Protein (gm)	29.5
Carbohydrate (gm)	60.2

EXCHANGES:

Milk	0.0	Bread	3.0
Veg.	3.0	Meat	3.0
Fruit	0.0	Fat	0.0

1 large green bell pepper, seeded and cut
   into strips
½ teaspoon dried oregano leaves
½ teaspoon dried basil leaves
½ teaspoon dried thyme leaves
   Salt and pepper, to taste (optional)
   Vegetable cooking spray

To Serve

1 8-oz. package thin spaghetti, cooked
   according to package directions
2 teaspoons Parmesan cheese, freshly
   grated, per serving

Sprinkle chicken with salt, if desired, and pepper. Coat Dutch oven or large, heavy pot with cooking spray, and cook chicken pieces over medium heat, turning frequently until they begin to brown. With slotted spoon, remove chicken to medium-size bowl and set aside.

Add oil, onion, mushrooms, garlic, and 3 tablespoons broth to pot. Stir up any browned bits from pot bottom. Cook over medium heat, stirring frequently, 5 or 6 minutes or until onion is tender. If liquid begins to evaporate, add more broth.

Add flour and stir into smooth paste. Stir in remaining chicken broth and sherry, and continue to stir until mixture thickens slightly. Add tomatoes, green pepper, oregano, basil, and thyme.

Return chicken to pot. Cover and simmer 30 minutes. Taste sauce and add additional salt and pepper if desired.

Serve individual portions of chicken and sauce over pasta. Top with Parmesan cheese.

Arroz con Pollo

Serves 7

1   lb. chicken breast, boneless, skinless,
    trimmed of all fat, and cut into bite-
    size pieces
2   teaspoons olive oil
1   large onion, chopped
2   cloves garlic, minced
2½ cups defatted chicken broth, divided
½   cup dry sherry
1   large green bell pepper, seeded and diced
1   large red bell pepper, seeded and diced
    (if unavailable, substitute yellow or green
    bell pepper)
¼   teaspoon saffron threads
¼   teaspoon black pepper

Nutritional Data

PER SERVING:

Calories	246
% calories from fat	12
Fat (gm)	3.2
Sat. Fat (gm)	0.6
Cholesterol (mg)	26.1
Sodium (mg)	147
Protein (gm)	15.8
Carbohydrate (gm)	34.5

EXCHANGES:

Milk	0.0	Bread	2.0
Veg.	1.0	Meat	1.5
Fruit	0.0	Fat	0.0

Dash cayenne pepper
1⅛ cups uncooked long-grain white rice
1½ cups green peas (fresh or frozen)
     Vegetable cooking spray

Coat Dutch oven or large pot with cooking spray, and cook chicken pieces over medium heat, turning frequently, 6 or 8 minutes, until they begin to brown and are cooked through. Remove and set aside in medium bowl.

In same pot, combine oil, onion, garlic, and 3 tablespoons broth. Stir up any brown bits from pan bottom. Cook over medium heat, stirring frequently, 6 or 7 minutes, or until onion is tender. If liquid begins to evaporate, add a bit more broth.

Add remaining broth along with sherry, green and red peppers, and reserved chicken. Stir in saffron, black pepper, cayenne pepper, rice, and peas. Bring to boil. Reduce heat and simmer 20 minutes or until rice is tender. Stir before serving.

Chicken-Fried Rice

Serves 6

3   cups water
3   tablespoons reduced-sodium soy sauce
1   teaspoon five-spice powder
¼   teaspoon salt (optional)
⅛   teaspoon red pepper flakes
1½   cups uncooked long-grain white rice
3   tablespoons defatted chicken broth
2   teaspoons sesame oil
4   cups thinly sliced bok choy leaves
     and stems
1   red bell pepper, seeded and diced
¼   cup thinly sliced green onion
1   cooked chicken breast, boneless, skinless
     (8 to 9 ozs.), and cut into small cubes
1   8-oz. can sliced water chestnuts,
     well drained
2   teaspoons brown sauce
2   teaspoons rice vinegar

Nutritional Data

PER SERVING:

Calories	275
% calories from fat	11
Fat (gm)	3.3
Sat. Fat (gm)	0.7
Cholesterol (mg)	32.1
Sodium (mg)	310
Protein (gm)	16.6
Carbohydrate (gm)	43.5

EXCHANGES:

Milk	0.0	Bread	2.5
Veg.	1.0	Meat	1.5
Fruit	0.0	Fat	0.0

In medium saucepan, stir together water, soy sauce, five-spice powder, salt, if desired, and red pepper flakes. Add rice. Cover and bring to boil. Reduce heat and cook 20 minutes or until water is absorbed and rice is tender.

When rice is done, combine broth and oil in large, nonstick skillet. Add bok choy, red pepper, and green onion and cook over medium-high heat, stirring, 2 to 3 minutes. Add cooked rice, cooked chicken, water chestnuts, brown sauce, and vinegar and cook additional 3 to 4 minutes or until flavors are well blended.

❄ Award-Winning Chicken

Serves 4

- 1 tablespoon olive oil
- 4 chicken breast halves, boneless and skinless
  Pepper, freshly ground
- ½ cup onion, chopped
- ¼ cup green bell pepper, chopped
  Sauce of your choice (recipes follow)

Nutritional Data

(Does not include sauce)

PER SERVING:

Calories	183
% calories from fat	33
Fat (gm)	6.5
Sat. Fat (gm)	1.3
Cholesterol (mg)	73
Sodium (mg)	64
Protein (gm)	27.1
Carbohydrate (gm)	2.6

EXCHANGES:

Milk	0.0	Bread	0.0
Veg.	0.5	Meat	3.0
Fruit	0.0	Fat	0.0

Heat olive oil in stockpot over medium-high heat. Add chicken breast halves, and sprinkle with freshly ground pepper. Cook until golden, about 4 to 5 minutes per side.

Add chopped onion and green bell pepper and cook until tender, about 3 to 4 minutes.

Add your choice of sauce to pot (recipes follow) and cook about 3 to 5 minutes. Serve sauce over chicken breasts and top with garnish.

To Freeze: Vacuum seal individual portions; label and freeze for up to 2 months.

To Serve: Put bags in boiling water, and bring water to boil again. Boil 10 to 12 minutes.

SAUCES FOR AWARD WINNING CHICKEN (all serve 4)*

Greek Style

- ¾ cup Chicken Stock (see p. 40)
- 2 tablespoons fresh lemon juice
- 1 tablespoon grated lemon peel
- 1 teaspoon oregano
- 8 sliced olives for garnish (optional)

Nutritional Data

PER SERVING:

Calories	11
% calories from fat	17
Fat (gm)	0.2
Sat. Fat (gm)	0.1
Cholesterol (mg)	1.9
Sodium (mg)	2
Protein (gm)	0.7
Carbohydrate (gm)	1.3

EXCHANGES:

Milk	0.0	Bread	0.0
Veg.	0.0	Meat	0.0
Fruit	0.0	Fat	0.0

Place all ingredients (except garnish) in small saucepan and heat until hot; do not boil.

To Freeze: Vacuum seal individual portions; label and freeze for up to 2 months.

To Serve: Put bags in boiling water, and bring water to boil again. Boil 10 to 12 minutes.

Note: Preparation, Freezing, and Serving instructions are the same as above for all four variations that follow.

French Style

⅓ cup Chicken Stock (see p. 40)
⅓ cup red wine
½ lb. mushrooms
1 jar pearl onions
1 teaspoon thyme
4 tablespoons parsley, minced, for garnish (optional)

Nutritional Data

PER SERVING:

Calories	34
% calories from fat	8
Fat (gm)	0.3
Sat. Fat (gm)	0.1
Cholesterol (mg)	0.8
Sodium (mg)	198
Protein (gm)	1.6
Carbohydrate (gm)	3.8

EXCHANGES:

Milk	0.0	Bread	0.0
Veg.	1.0	Meat	0.0
Fruit	0.0	Fat	0.0

Italian Style

½ cup low-fat yogurt
1 tablespoon basil
1 small chopped tomato
1 tablespoon oregano
Dash freshly ground pepper
4 anchovies or fresh parsley for garnish (optional)

Nutritional Data

PER SERVING:

Calories	31
% calories from fat	19
Fat (gm)	0.7
Sat. Fat (gm)	0.3
Cholesterol (mg)	1.8
Sodium (mg)	23
Protein (gm)	2
Carbohydrate (gm)	4.8

EXCHANGES:

Milk	0.5	Bread	0.0
Veg.	0.0	Meat	0.0
Fruit	0.0	Fat	0.0

Mexican Style

¾ cup Chicken Stock (see p. 40)
1 jalapeño pepper, minced (use caution; wear rubber gloves and do not rub your eyes)
1 teaspoon chili powder
⅓ cup low-fat yogurt
1 small diced tomato
2 tablespoons cilantro, chopped, for garnish (optional)

Nutritional Data

PER SERVING:

Calories	29
% calories from fat	21
Fat (gm)	0.7
Sat. Fat (gm)	0.3
Cholesterol (mg)	3.1
Sodium (mg)	128
Protein (gm)	2
Carbohydrate (gm)	3.5

EXCHANGES:

Milk	0.0	Bread	0.0
Veg.	1.0	Meat	0.0
Fruit	0.0	Fat	0.0

Chinese Style

⅓ cup Chicken Stock (see p. 40)
½ lb. mushrooms
½ cup water chestnuts, sliced
4 scallions, sliced
3 tablespoons sesame seeds for garnish (optional)

Nutritional Data

PER SERVING:

Calories	28
% calories from fat	10
Fat (gm)	0.3
Sat. Fat (gm)	0.1
Cholesterol (mg)	0.8
Sodium (mg)	5
Protein (gm)	1.7
Carbohydrate (gm)	5.3

EXCHANGES:

Milk	0.0	Bread	0.0
Veg.	1.0	Meat	0.0
Fruit	0.0	Fat	0.0

Chicken with Apples and Cider

Serves 4

1 3½-lb. chicken, skinned
  Vegetable cooking spray (olive-oil flavored)
6 firm apples
  Pepper, freshly ground
3 tablespoons all-purpose flour
2 cups hard cider, divided
  Bouquet garni (see p. 369)
¾ cup evaporated skim milk
2 tablespoons parsley, chopped

Nutritional Data

PER SERVING:

Calories	598
% calories from fat	24
Fat (gm)	15.6
Sat. Fat (gm)	4.3
Cholesterol (mg)	180.7
Sodium (mg)	230
Protein (gm)	62.8
Carbohydrate (gm)	39.7

EXCHANGES:

Milk	0.5	Bread	0.0
Veg.	0.0	Meat	8.0
Fruit	2.0	Fat	0.0

Preheat oven to 375 degrees. Cut chicken into 4 portions. Coat flameproof casserole with vegetable cooking spray and add chicken. Brown on all sides. Remove and drain.

Peel, core, and slice 2 of the apples, sprinkle with pepper, and sauté until beginning to brown. Sprinkle in flour and cook gently, stirring occasionally, until flour is light brown. Add 1¼ cups cider and bring to boil, stirring constantly.

Replace chicken pieces and add bouquet garni. Cover with tight-fitting lid. Bake for 1 hour.

Meanwhile, peel, core, and cut into quarters remaining 4 apples. Coat small skillet with vegetable cooking spray and add apples. Sauté until browned lightly. Place in ovenproof dish with 3 tablespoons water. Cover and place in oven, under casserole, until needed.

When chicken is cooked, remove it from casserole and place it on heated serving dish. Bring sauce to boil, add remaining cider, and boil rapidly 10 minutes. Strain and return to rinsed saucepan.

Add apples and milk. Reheat very gently without boiling. Adjust seasoning. Pour over chicken. Garnish with parsley.

✳ Chicken with Herbs

Serves 8

1	3-lb. chicken, skinless, cut into serving parts (use all white meat if you prefer)
¼	cup dry white wine
3	cloves garlic, minced
1	tablespoon tarragon
1	tablespoon basil
1	teaspoon thyme
1	teaspoon oregano
1	teaspoon black pepper, freshly ground
3	green onions with tops
	Parsley sprigs, fresh

Nutritional Data

PER SERVING:

Calories	176
% calories from fat	34
Fat (gm)	6.5
Sat. Fat (gm)	1.8
Cholesterol (mg)	76.8
Sodium (mg)	76
Protein (gm)	25.3
Carbohydrate (gm)	1.6

EXCHANGES:

Milk	0.0	Bread	0.0
Veg.	0.0	Meat	3.0
Fruit	0.0	Fat	0.0

Place chicken parts in shallow bowl. Pour wine over and sprinkle with garlic, herbs, and pepper. Place green onions and some parsley on top of chicken, and set bowl on rack over boiling water in steamer. Cover pot and steam 45 minutes or until juices run clear when pierced with fork. The more crowded the pieces, the longer it will take to cook.

To Freeze: Place in microwave-safe container; label and freeze for up to 2 months.

To Serve: Thaw. Cover with microwave-safe plastic wrap, and cook on High 3 to 5 minutes.

Braised Chicken with Tomatoes

Serves 6

6	chicken breast halves, boneless, skinless (about 3 lbs.)
	Black pepper, freshly ground, to taste
3	cloves garlic, minced
½	cup dry white wine
¼	cup balsamic vinegar
5	plum tomatoes, seeded and chopped
2	tablespoons black olives, sliced (optional)
1	tablespoon dried rosemary
2	tablespoons fresh oregano, or 1 tablespoon dried oregano
	Vegetable cooking spray

Nutritional Data

PER SERVING:

Calories	149
% calories from fat	21
Fat (gm)	3.4
Sat. Fat (gm)	0.7
Cholesterol (mg)	45.7
Sodium (mg)	145
Protein (gm)	17.9
Carbohydrate (gm)	8.7

EXCHANGES:

Milk	0.0	Bread	0.0
Veg.	2.0	Meat	2.0
Fruit	0.0	Fat	0.0

Grind some pepper over chicken. Heat large skillet coated with vegetable cooking spray over medium-high heat. Add chicken, and sear on all sides, turning occasionally, for about 10 minutes. Transfer chicken to platter; cover with aluminum foil to keep warm.

Drain off all but about 3 tablespoons of pan drippings. Over medium heat, sauté garlic in pan drippings for about 1 minute. Turn up heat to medium-high, add wine, and simmer vigorously until wine is reduced by half. Add vinegar, chopped tomatoes, olives, and rosemary.

Return chicken to pan, cover, and simmer gently for 10 to 12 minutes or until juices run clear when chicken thigh is pierced with tip of paring knife. Serve immediately.

Breast of Chicken in Mushroom Sauce

Serves 4

- ¼ oz. dried porcini or shiitake mushrooms
- ¼ cup onion, chopped
- ¼ lb. fresh mushrooms, cleaned and sliced
- ⅓ cup dry white wine
- ½ lb. plum tomatoes (4-5), peeled, seeded, and chopped
- Spike, to taste (see "About This Cookbook")
- Black pepper, freshly ground, to taste
- 1 tablespoon fresh basil, chopped, or 1 teaspoon dried basil
- 1 tablespoon fresh oregano, chopped, or 1 teaspoon dried oregano
- 4 chicken breast halves (about 1½ lbs.), boneless and skinless
- ½ cup chicken broth, or salt-free canned chicken broth
- Vegetable cooking spray

Nutritional Data

PER SERVING:

Calories	181
% calories from fat	18
Fat (gm)	3.6
Sat. Fat (gm)	1.3
Cholesterol (mg)	70.9
Sodium (mg)	191
Protein (gm)	26.9
Carbohydrate (gm)	6.7

EXCHANGES:

Milk	0.0	Bread	0.0
Veg.	1.0	Meat	3.0
Fruit	0.0	Fat	0.0

Soak dried porcini in about ½ cup hot water until soft, about 10 minutes.

In small skillet coated with vegetable cooking spray, over medium heat, add onions and sliced mushrooms, and sauté for about 2 minutes, until onions are soft and mushrooms give off their moisture. Add wine, and cook until alcohol evaporates, about 1 minute. Add tomatoes, and crush with back of spoon.

Add reserved porcini, including strained soaking liquid. Simmer sauce over medium-high heat to reduce slightly, about 3 minutes. Season with Spike, pepper, basil, and oregano.

In large skillet coated with vegetable cooking spray, over medium-high heat, cook chicken breasts for 5 minutes, turning once, until nicely browned on both sides. Drain off excess pan drippings. Add chicken broth, and cook 2 to 3 minutes longer or until chicken is cooked through.

Add mushroom sauce to chicken. Stir well, and cook for 1 minute. Serve immediately.

Sautéed Chicken Breasts with Sage

Serves 4

4	chicken breast halves (6 oz. each), boneless and skinless
3	tablespoons fresh lemon juice
28	fresh whole sage leaves
1	teaspoon Spike (see "About This Cookbook")
	Black pepper, freshly ground, to taste
4	slices lemon
	Vegetable cooking spray

Nutritional Data

PER SERVING:

Calories	147
% calories from fat	21
Fat (gm)	3.4
Sat. Fat (gm)	1
Cholesterol (mg)	68.6
Sodium (mg)	60
Protein (gm)	25.5
Carbohydrate (gm)	3.2

EXCHANGES:

Milk	0.0	Bread	0.0
Veg.	0.0	Meat	3.0
Fruit	0.0	Fat	0.0

Place chicken in 8-inch-square glass baking dish coated with vegetable cooking spray. Add lemon juice, and sage leaves. Cover, and set aside at room temperature for 30 minutes. Remove chicken from marinade, and pat dry. Strain marinade into small bowl; reserve sage leaves separately.

In skillet coated with vegetable cooking spray, place chicken breasts, smooth side down, and cook until nicely browned on bottom, about 5 minutes. Turn breasts and season them with Spike and pepper. Tuck reserved sage leaves around chicken, and cook until chicken is browned on bottom and just white throughout, about 5 minutes longer.

Remove skillet from heat. Transfer chicken to cutting board. Slice chicken breasts diagonally, 1/2-inch thick, and arrange on warm platter. Place sage leaves over chicken. Cover loosely with foil.

Pour off grease, then heat skillet over moderately high heat until hot. Pour in reserved marinade, and stir with wooden spoon, scraping up brown bits from bottom of pan. Sauce will boil almost immediately. As soon as it becomes brown glaze (in less than 1 minute), pour sauce over chicken, and garnish with lemon halves.

Stuffed Chicken Breasts

Serves 6

Stuffing

1 tablespoon canola oil margarine, or corn oil margarine
2 cups onions, chopped
2 large celery stalks, diced
1 cup cabbage, finely chopped
1 small carrot, diced
2 tablespoons parsley leaves, chopped
1 cup defatted chicken broth, divided
½ teaspoon dried basil leaves
⅛ teaspoon black pepper
3½ cups seasoned commercial, cube-style stuffing

Chicken

6 large chicken breast halves (2½-3 lbs.), skin removed and trimmed of all fat
1 teaspoon nondiet, tub-style canola oil margarine, or corn oil margarine
¼ teaspoon dried basil leaves
¼ teaspoon dried thyme leaves
¼ teaspoon salt (optional)
⅛ teaspoon black pepper

Garnish

Parsley sprigs (optional)

Nutritional Data	
PER SERVING:	
Calories	272
% calories from fat	22
Fat (gm)	6.7
Sat. Fat (gm)	1.2
Cholesterol (mg)	76.2
Sodium (mg)	396
Protein (gm)	32
Carbohydrate (gm)	20.2

EXCHANGES:			
Milk	0.0	Bread	1.0
Veg.	1.0	Meat	3.0
Fruit	0.0	Fat	0.0

Preheat oven to 350 degrees.

Stuffing: In large, nonstick skillet, combine margarine, onion, celery, cabbage, carrot, parsley, and 3 tablespoons broth. Cook over medium heat, stirring frequently, until onion is tender, about 6 or 7 minutes. If liquid begins to evaporate, add a bit more broth. Stir in basil and black pepper. Add stuffing and remaining broth. Stir to mix well. Transfer to 9½" x 13" baking pan.

Chicken: Place breasts over stuffing, bone side down. Spread margarine over chicken. Sprinkle evenly with basil, thyme, salt, if desired, and black pepper. Bake 20 minutes. Move chicken to side of pan, and stir stuffing. Rearrange chicken over stuffing, and bake an additional 30 to 35 minutes or until chicken is cooked through.

Transfer stuffing to serving platter, and arrange chicken on top. Or serve individual portions of chicken over stuffing.

Garnish: Sprinkle with parsley sprigs, if desired.

Grilled Chicken Breasts with Sauerkraut

Serves 6

3   chicken breasts, halved, boneless
    and skinless
1/4 cup canola oil
1/3 cup red wine marinade
1   clove garlic, minced
1/2 teaspoon paprika
1/4 cup parsley, chopped
1/4 teaspoon pepper
    Butter-flavored vegetable cooking spray
3   cups prepared sauerkraut
1   teaspoon caraway seeds

Nutritional Data

PER SERVING:

Calories	220
% calories from fat	27
Fat (gm)	6.5
Sat. Fat (gm)	1.2
Cholesterol (mg)	73
Sodium (mg)	813
Protein (gm)	29.1
Carbohydrate (gm)	10.7

EXCHANGES:

Milk	0.0	Bread	0.0
Veg.	2.0	Meat	3.0
Fruit	0.0	Fat	0.0

Rinse and pat dry chicken breasts. Place in large plastic bag. Combine next 6 ingredients, and add marinade to bag. Seal bag and turn chicken a few times to coat. Place bag on cookie sheet. Marinate 1 hour at room temperature (or 2 hours in refrigerator), turning occasionally.

Meanwhile, coat skillet with cooking spray and heat. Add sauerkraut and caraway seeds. Simmer, uncovered, until all visible liquid has evaporated. Sauerkraut should be very dry.

When briquets become ashen, remove chicken from plastic bag. Place breasts on grill rack coated with cooking spray and cook, uncovered, over direct heat 3 to 4 minutes on each side.

When chicken is done, transfer sauerkraut to serving platter. Arrange chicken attractively on top of sauerkraut. Serve immediately.

Grilled Chicken Breasts with Fennel

Serves 6

    Butter-flavored nonstick cooking spray
3   chicken breasts, halved, boneless
    and skinless
1/2 cup fennel seeds for aromatic (optional)
1/4 teaspoon black pepper, freshly ground
1   tablespoon virgin olive oil
1   large bulb fennel, sliced and
    partially cooked
1   tangerine, peeled and divided into
    sections

Nutritional Data

PER SERVING:

Calories	173
% calories from fat	29
Fat (gm)	5.4
Sat. Fat (gm)	1.2
Cholesterol (mg)	73
Sodium (mg)	71
Protein (gm)	27
Carbohydrate (gm)	2.7

When barbecue coals are ashen, place chicken breasts on grill rack coated with cooking spray. Grill 3 to 4 minutes on each side. Do not overcook chicken.

Sprinkle fennel seeds on hot coals. Brush fennel bulb with olive oil and sprinkle with pepper. Grill fennel 1 to 2 minutes on each side. Serve chicken and grilled fennel together with tangerine sections as garnish.

EXCHANGES:			
Milk	0.0	Bread	0.0
Veg.	0.0	Meat	3.0
Fruit	0.0	Fat	0.0

Grilled Pomegranate Chicken with Pasta

Serves 6

- 1 large pomegranate
- 1½ cups plain nonfat yogurt
- 1 chicken, about 3 lbs., skinless
- 3 cups egg noodles
- 3 oranges, peeled and sliced

Nutritional Data

PER SERVING:

Calories	366
% calories from fat	24
Fat (gm)	9.6
Sat. Fat (gm)	2.4
Cholesterol (mg)	127.7
Sodium (mg)	115
Protein (gm)	38.5
Carbohydrate (gm)	29.1

EXCHANGES:			
Milk	0.0	Bread	1.5
Veg.	0.0	Meat	4.0
Fruit	0.5	Fat	0.0

Cut pomegranate in half. Use manual or electric juicer to extract juice. Strain but reserve 6 tablespoons of seeds for garnish. Combine juice with yogurt.

Arrange chicken in glass dish and brush it completely with yogurt mixture. Cover with plastic wrap and marinate at room temperature 1 hour (or 2 hours in refrigerator), turning occasionally.

Grill chicken, indirect method, on grill rack, covered, 1 hour or until done. Check occasionally to see if more coals are needed. Turn chicken over if necessary. Juices will run clear when done. Remove cover last 5 minutes of cooking time. (Or you can bake chicken at 375 degrees 1 hour until done.)

While chicken cooks, prepare pasta according to package directions. Transfer noodles to serving platter with raised sides.

Carve chicken and arrange pieces over noodles. Sprinkle with pomegranate seeds and orange slices. You can grill oranges slices on grill rack until warm, if desired.

♨ *Chicken on the Grill*

Serves 6

1 whole fresh chicken, about 3 lbs.
1 cup bread crumbs
1 teaspoon tarragon
4 cloves garlic, minced
1 orange, cut into wedges
2 cups hickory chips

Nutritional Data

PER SERVING:

Calories	297
% calories from fat	29
Fat (gm)	9.4
Sat. Fat (gm)	2.5
Cholesterol (mg)	102.4
Sodium (mg)	222
Protein (gm)	35.8
Carbohydrate (gm)	15.5

EXCHANGES:

Milk	0.0	Bread	1.0
Veg.	0.0	Meat	4.0
Fruit	0.0	Fat	0.0

Rinse chicken inside and out and pat dry. Pat bread crumbs onto moist chicken, and sprinkle with tarragon and garlic. Place orange wedges in cavity of chicken.

Soak hickory chips in water 30 minutes. Prepare barbecue grill for indirect grilling method. When briquets are ashen, drain hickory chips and scatter them over hot coals.

Place chicken, breast side up, on ungreased grid over dripping pan. Grill, covered, over indirect heat 1 hour, checking after 30 minutes to see if coals need replenishing. To test for doneness, insert fork into deepest part of thigh. If juices run clear and joints move easily, chicken is done. If juices run pink, chicken needs more grilling.

Remove chicken from grill and let rest 15 minutes at room temperature before serving. Discard skin.

Roast Stuffed Capon

Serves 8

4   cups day-old bread, shredded
3   tablespoons skim milk
1/4 cup onion, finely chopped
1/2 cup parsley, chopped
1   oz. Romano cheese, grated
1   large egg, beaten
2/3 cup dry white wine
     Spike, to taste (see "About This
     Cookbook")
     Black pepper, freshly ground, to taste
1   5-lb. capon
2   tablespoons fresh rosemary
1/2 cup dry white wine
     Vegetable cooking spray

Nutritional Data

PER SERVING:

Calories	242
% calories from fat	37
Fat (gm)	9.8
Sat. Fat (gm)	3
Cholesterol (mg)	86.3
Sodium (mg)	166
Protein (gm)	22.4
Carbohydrate (gm)	9

EXCHANGES:

Milk	0.0	Bread	0.5
Veg.	0.0	Meat	3.0
Fruit	0.0	Fat	0.5

Preheat oven to 350 degrees. To make stuffing, put bread in small bowl, and add milk. Crumble bread in milk, and set aside.

In large skillet coated with vegetable cooking spray, brown onion, and sauté for about 5 minutes or until browned. Transfer to large bowl, add soaked bread, parsley, cheese, egg, 2/3 cup wine, Spike, and pepper. Mix well.

Wash and dry capon inside and out. Stuff filling loosely into body cavity. Sew or skewer opening closed and truss capon. Put capon on rack in roasting pan, coat capon with vegetable cooking spray, and rub breast with Spike, if desired. Sprinkle rosemary over capon.

Roast capon 2½ hours, or until meat is tender and internal temperature registers 180 degrees, basting occasionally with wine. Carve capon into serving pieces, and serve with stuffing.

Chicken with Laurel

Serves 4

1 5-lb. roasting chicken
4 large oranges
1 medium onion, sliced
6 fresh bay leaves, or 3 or 4 dry bay leaves
¼ cup orange juice
2 cups peas, cooked and drained
   Small cluster fresh bay leaves
   Vegetable cooking spray (olive-oil flavored)

Nutritional Data

PER SERVING:

Calories	432
% calories from fat	33
Fat (gm)	15.6
Sat. Fat (gm)	4.3
Cholesterol (mg)	112
Sodium (mg)	68
Protein (gm)	43.4
Carbohydrate (gm)	28.9

EXCHANGES:

Milk	0.0	Bread	1.0
Veg.	0.0	Meat	5.5
Fruit	1.0	Fat	0.0

Preheat oven to 350 degrees.

Reserve chicken neck and giblets for other uses. Pull off and discard lumps of fat from chicken. Rinse chicken inside and out; pat dry. Cut one unpeeled orange into chunks; fill neck and body cavities of chicken with orange chunks, onion, and bay leaves. Tie chicken legs together with piece of kitchen string; also tie length of string around breast portion of chicken to secure wings.

Place chicken, breast down, on rack in large roasting pan. Roast, uncovered, 30 minutes. Turn chicken breast up. Coat skin with olive oil-flavored cooking spray, and roast 30 more minutes. Continue to roast until meat near thighbone is no longer pink (about 30 more minutes); cut to test.

Meanwhile, grate 1 teaspoon peel (colored part only) from one of remaining oranges. Squeeze enough juice from same orange to make ¼ cup; set peel and juice aside. Cut off and discard peel and white membrane from remaining 2 oranges. Slice fruit crosswise, and set aside. Reserve small strip of peel for garnish.

When chicken is done, discard orange chunks, onion, and bay leaves from cavities. Tip chicken to drain juices from body into roasting pan; transfer chicken to platter, and cover with foil to keep warm.

Skim and discard fat from pan drippings. Add grated orange peel and orange juice; bring to boil over high heat, stirring to incorporate browned bits. Reduce heat to medium. Pour mixture into small pan. Warm over medium heat until bubbly, then carefully ignite with a match; stir into sauce. Pour sauce into serving bowl.

Arrange peas on platter around chicken; garnish with strip of orange peel. Surround chicken with orange slices, and garnish with cluster of bay leaves. Offer sauce to spoon over meat.

Note: Lemon balm may be used instead of bay leaves in this recipe.

Moroccan Chicken and Chickpeas

Serves 8

2	cups (1 lb.) dried chickpeas
2	quarts cold water
3½	teaspoons Spike, divided (see "About This Cookbook")
1	onion, peeled and quartered
1	bay leaf
1	4-lb. roasting chicken, skinned
2	cloves garlic, crushed
1	teaspoon ground ginger
¼	teaspoon pepper, freshly ground
1	tablespoon water
½	cup onion, chopped
1	teaspoon turmeric
2	tablespoons parsley, chopped
1	(2-inch) cinnamon stick
1	10¾-oz. can condensed chicken broth, undiluted
1	cup onion, sliced
½	cup raisins

Nutritional Data

PER SERVING:

Calories	460
% calories from fat	22
Fat (gm)	11.5
Sat. Fat (gm)	2.5
Cholesterol (mg)	102.9
Sodium (mg)	354
Protein (gm)	46.2
Carbohydrate (gm)	43

EXCHANGES:

Milk	0.0	Bread	2.0
Veg.	0.0	Meat	5.0
Fruit	0.5	Fat	0.0

The day before you plan to make this meal, pick over chickpeas and place them in large bowl; cover with cold water; refrigerate, covered, overnight.

The next day, drain chickpeas; turn into large pot. Add 2 quarts cold water, 2 teaspoons Spike, quartered onion, and bay leaf. Bring to boil; reduce heat and simmer, covered, 1½ hours or until tender. Drain and set aside. Remove and discard onion and bay leaf.

Meanwhile, rinse chicken well; dry with paper towels. Sprinkle inside with 1 teaspoon Spike. Tuck wings under body; then tie legs together at ends with twine.

In small bowl, combine garlic, ginger, ½ teaspoon Spike, pepper, and 1 tablespoon water; mix well. Brush mixture over entire surface of chicken. Refrigerate chicken in large bowl, covered with plastic wrap or foil, 1 hour.

In 6-quart Dutch oven, combine chopped onion, turmeric, chopped parsley, cinnamon stick, and chicken broth. Over medium heat, bring to boil, stirring constantly. Lower heat, then add chicken, breast side down, and any juices left in bottom of bowl. Simmer, covered, 1 hour or until chicken is tender. Turn chicken frequently, using wooden spoons. Remove cooked chicken to serving platter. Discard cinnamon stick.

To sauce left in Dutch oven, add sliced onion, raisins, and drained chickpeas. Bring to boil; cook, stirring frequently, until onion is soft and flavors have blended, about 15 minutes.

Before serving, remove twine. Reheat chicken in chickpea mixture 5 minutes. Serve chicken and chickpeas together.

Moroccan-Style Cornish Hens Stuffed with Couscous

Serves 8

Stuffing

- ¾ cup raisins
- 3 tablespoons dry white wine
- ½ teaspoon saffron threads, chopped
- 1 cup instant couscous
- 1½ cups water
- 2 tablespoons olive oil
- 2 medium onions, chopped
- 2 teaspoons cinnamon
- 1 tablespoon honey
  Spike, to taste (see "About This Cookbook")
  Pepper, freshly ground

Basting Mixture

- ¼ cup dark honey
- ¾ teaspoon cinnamon
- ¼ teaspoon turmeric, or ground cumin
  Pepper, freshly ground

Cornish Hens

- 4 Rock Cornish game hens, about 1½ lbs. each, skinned

Nutritional Data

PER SERVING:

Calories	555
% calories from fat	27
Fat (gm)	16.4
Sat. Fat (gm)	4
Cholesterol (mg)	153.6
Sodium (mg)	509
Protein (gm)	53.6
Carbohydrate (gm)	43.5

EXCHANGES:

Milk	0.0	Bread	2.0
Veg.	0.0	Meat	6.5
Fruit	1.0	Fat	0.0

Stuffing: Soak raisins in hot water for 30 minutes; drain and set aside.

Heat wine in small saucepan over medium heat until warm. Remove from heat, add saffron, and let steep 15 minutes.

Put couscous in shallow baking dish (9-inch square will do nicely). In saucepan, heat water until boiling, then pour over couscous and stir well. Cover with foil and let stand 15 minutes. Fluff couscous with fork.

Add olive oil to medium sauté pan over medium heat. Add chopped onions, and cook until tender and translucent, 8 to 10 minutes. Add cinnamon and cook 2 minutes. Add saffron-infused wine and cook 1 minute.

Stir onion mixture, raisins, and honey into couscous. Season to taste with Spike and pepper. Let cool.

Basting Mixture: Combine honey, cinnamon, and turmeric. Season to taste with pepper; set aside.

Cornish Hens: Preheat oven to 450 degrees. Spoon cooled stuffing into cavities of hens. Place hens on rack in shallow roasting or sheet pan. Baste occasionally with the Basting Mixture. Hen is done when juices run clear when thigh is pierced with skewer, about 45 minutes.

Chicken Catalan Style

Serves 4

- 1 3-lb. chicken, skinned and cut into serving pieces
  Vegetable cooking spray (olive-oil flavored)
- ½ teaspoon Spike (see "About This Cookbook")
  Black pepper, freshly ground
- 2 onions, finely chopped
- 1 clove garlic, minced
- 2 tomatoes, peeled, seeded, and chopped
- 1 bay leaf
- ½ cup dry white wine
- 1 small eggplant
- 1 teaspoon Spike (see "About This Cookbook")
- ½ cup water
- 2 zucchini, sliced
- 2 green or red bell peppers
- ½ cup tomato sauce
- 1 teaspoon fresh cilantro
- 1 teaspoon basil
- 2 tablespoons parsley, chopped

Nutritional Data

PER SERVING:

Calories	427
% calories from fat	28
Fat (gm)	13.4
Sat. Fat (gm)	3.6
Cholesterol (mg)	153.6
Sodium (mg)	348
Protein (gm)	53.1
Carbohydrate (gm)	18.3

EXCHANGES:

Milk	0.0	Bread	0.0
Veg.	3.0	Meat	6.5
Fruit	0.0	Fat	0.0

Preheat oven to 350 degrees.

Brown chicken in skillet coated with vegetable cooking spray. Remove chicken and season with Spike and pepper. Place chicken in casserole.

Sauté onions and garlic in same skillet 3 minutes. Add tomatoes, bay leaf, and white wine. Simmer mixture 5 minutes. Transfer to casserole. Cover and bake 30 minutes.

Meantime, cut eggplant into small cubes and sprinkle with Spike. Allow eggplant to stand 10 minutes to drain bitter juices. Add ½ cup water to skillet and add eggplant and zucchini. Sauté over moderate heat 5 minutes until lightly browned.

Remove membranes and seeds from peppers and chop. Add peppers to skillet and sauté 5 minutes.

Add eggplant, zucchini, and peppers to casserole. Add tomato sauce, cilantro, and basil. Continue cooking 30 minutes until chicken is tender. Sauce should be thick. Remove bay leaf.

Arrange chicken pieces and sauce on hot serving dish. Top with parsley.

Cantonese Chicken

Serves 6

- 6 chicken breast halves, boneless and skinless (about 2 lbs.)
- 6 dried Chinese or Japanese shiitake mushrooms soaked in hot water 20-30 minutes, squeezed dry, cut into strips
- 3 tablespoons low-sodium soy sauce
- 2 tablespoons oyster sauce
- 2 tablespoons dry cooking sherry
- 2 teaspoons garlic, minced
- 2 teaspoons ginger root, peeled, minced
- 1½ tablespoons arrowroot
- 1 teaspoon sesame oil
- ½ teaspoon sugar
- Salt, or salt substitute, to taste
- Vegetable cooking spray
- 4 scallions, green part only, cut into 2-inch lengths

Nutritional Data

PER SERVING:

Calories	163
% calories from fat	19
Fat (gm)	3.4
Sat. Fat (gm)	0.9
Cholesterol (mg)	62.6
Sodium (mg)	503
Protein (gm)	23.7
Carbohydrate (gm)	7.1

EXCHANGES:

Milk	0.0	Bread	0.0
Veg.	1.5	Meat	2.5
Fruit	0.0	Fat	0.0

Place chicken and mushrooms in large mixing bowl. In separate dish, combine all remaining ingredients except scallions. Pour sauce mixture over chicken and mushrooms, toss well, cover, and marinate at room temperature 30 to 40 minutes.

In large skillet coated with vegetable cooking spray, over high heat, stir-fry scallions 1 minute. Add chicken and mari-

nade. Heat to boiling. Cover, reduce heat, and cook about 20
minutes, stirring occasionally.

Chicken China Moon

Serves 4

1	tablespoon sesame seeds, toasted
2	teaspoons ginger root, peeled and grated
	Sweetener equivalent to 2 tablespoons sugar
2	tablespoons low-sodium soy sauce
	Vegetable cooking spray
4	chicken breast halves, boneless, skinless, and pounded thin
2	tablespoons green onion, chopped

Nutritional Data

PER SERVING:

Calories	166
% calories from fat	24
Fat (gm)	4.2
Sat. Fat (gm)	1
Cholesterol (mg)	73
Sodium (mg)	328
Protein (gm)	28
Carbohydrate (gm)	2.5

EXCHANGES:

Milk	0.0	Bread	0.0
Veg.	0.0	Meat	3.0
Fruit	0.0	Fat	0.0

Combine sesame seeds, ginger, sweetener, and soy sauce
and stir well. Apply nonstick spray to grill or broiling pan.
Using sesame-soy mixture for basting, grill chicken over medium hot coals—or broil—4 minutes on each side until cooked
through. Garnish with green onion and serve.

Stir-Fry Chicken with Broccoli & Rice

Serves 6

1/4	cup light soy sauce
1½	tablespoons dry sherry
3/4	teaspoon ground ginger
1½	lbs. chicken breast, boneless, skinless, and cut into 1-inch pieces
1	lb. broccoli, peeled
	Vegetable cooking spray
1/2	cup mushrooms
1/4	cup pimiento, minced
1/2	cup celery
1/2	cup scallions, sliced
1	large clove garlic, crushed
3	cups cooked rice

Nutritional Data

PER SERVING:

Calories	232
% calories from fat	9
Fat (gm)	2.5
Sat. Fat (gm)	0.7
Cholesterol (mg)	45.7
Sodium (mg)	423
Protein (gm)	22.5
Carbohydrate (gm)	28.9

EXCHANGES:

Milk	0.0	Bread	1.5
Veg.	1.0	Meat	2.0
Fruit	0.0	Fat	0.0

In small bowl, combine soy sauce, sherry, ginger, and chick-
en. Let stand 10 minutes. Trim florets from broccoli and
reserve. Cut tough ends from stalks and discard. Slice stalks
diagonally into 1/4-inch pieces. Steam florets and stalk slices 4 to
5 minutes until crisp-tender. Drain and rinse under cold water.

Heat sprayed wok or large skillet. Add mushrooms, pimiento, celery, scallions, and garlic. Cook 4 minutes, stirring constantly. Transfer mixture to bowl. Add chicken mixture and cook until chicken is done. Add mushroom mixture and broccoli; cook 1 to 2 minutes. Serve with rice.

♨ Canton Chicken & Rice

Serves 4

3/4 lb. chicken breast, boneless, skinless
Vegetable cooking spray
4 tablespoons low-sodium soy sauce
3 tablespoons sherry wine
1 teaspoon vinegar
2 tablespoons honey
2 scallions (green and white parts), minced
1 large clove garlic, minced
1 teaspoon ginger root, peeled and grated
1/4 teaspoon cayenne pepper, or to taste
1 tablespoon sugar
4 cups cooked rice

Nutritional Data

PER SERVING:

Calories	344
% calories from fat	5
Fat (gm)	1.9
Sat. Fat (gm)	0.5
Cholesterol (mg)	34.3
Sodium (mg)	560
Protein (gm)	18.4
Carbohydrate (gm)	58.6

EXCHANGES:

Milk	0.0	Bread	3.5
Veg.	0.0	Meat	1.5
Fruit	0.0	Fat	0.0

Spray wok or skillet and sauté chicken pieces until nicely browned on both sides, about 4 to 5 minutes. Blend soy sauce, sherry, vinegar, and honey; add soy sauce mixture and all other ingredients to wok.

Cover tightly and simmer gently for about half an hour or until chicken is tender. Stir a few times while cooking. Remove from heat and place chicken pieces on platter with rice. Spoon sauce over chicken.

Chicken Chow Mein

Serves 4

1 cup celery, sliced on diagonal
1 medium green bell pepper, seeded, cut into thin strips
1 medium onion, cut into thin wedges
1 teaspoon canola oil
1 cup mushrooms, sliced
12 ozs. fresh bean sprouts, rinsed and drained
8 ozs. water chestnuts, rinsed and drained
2 ozs. pimientos, drained and chopped
2 tablespoons reduced-sodium soy sauce
1/2 cup Chicken Stock (see p. 40)
1 tablespoon oat bran
3/4 lb. cooked chicken (or turkey) breasts, sliced thinly against grain

Nutritional Data

PER SERVING:

Calories	311
% calories from fat	12
Fat (gm)	5.2
Sat. Fat (gm)	1.1
Cholesterol (mg)	73.5
Sodium (mg)	372
Protein (gm)	37.2
Carbohydrate (gm)	33.9

EXCHANGES:

Milk	0.0	Bread	0.0
Veg.	5.0	Meat	3.5
Fruit	0.0	Fat	0.0

In 2-quart glass measure or casserole, combine celery, green pepper, onions, and oil. Microwave on High until tender, about 3 to 4 minutes, stirring once.

Microwave mushrooms for 2 minutes in separate dish and drain when tender. Combine with vegetables, along with bean sprouts, water chestnuts, and pimientos.

Mix soy sauce, Chicken Stock, and oat bran and add to vegetables. Cover with wax paper and microwave on High 5 to 6 minutes, stirring twice.

Add chicken or turkey pieces, mix, and let stand, covered, for 6 or 7 minutes until warmed through. Microwave on High for another minute to heat if necessary. Serve with brown rice and a few chow mein noodles.

 # Chicken Crunch

Serves 6

1	2½-3 lb. frying chicken
1	cup buttermilk
½	teaspoon garlic powder
½	teaspoon paprika (hot or mild)
¼	teaspoon thyme
¼	teaspoon salt
2	cups cornflakes, finely crushed

Nutritional Data

PER SERVING:

Calories	217
% calories from fat	31
Fat (gm)	7.2
Sat. Fat (gm)	2
Cholesterol (mg)	85.7
Sodium (mg)	276
Protein (gm)	28.7
Carbohydrate (gm)	7.3

EXCHANGES:

Milk	0.0	Bread	0.5
Veg.	0.0	Meat	3.5
Fruit	0.0	Fat	0.0

Cut chicken into pieces and remove skin with help of paper towel. Rinse and pat dry. Dip chicken pieces into buttermilk.

Combine all spices and crushed cornflakes in paper bag. Shake chicken pieces in bag until coated, and place in 12-inch glass baking dish with thicker pieces toward outside.

Cover with wax paper. Microwave on High 7 to 8 minutes, then turn chicken pieces and rotate dish. Microwave on High another 6 to 8 minutes.

Chicken Dijon

Serves 4

1 lb. chicken breast, boneless, skinless, and cut into 4 pieces
2 tablespoons Dijon mustard
2 tablespoons fat-free mayonnaise
   Pepper
   Paprika
   Chives, chopped, for garnish

Nutritional Data

PER SERVING:

Calories	102
% calories from fat	22
Fat (gm)	2.4
Sat. Fat (gm)	0.6
Cholesterol (mg)	45.7
Sodium (mg)	235
Protein (gm)	17.2
Carbohydrate (gm)	1.9

EXCHANGES:

Milk	0.0	Bread	0.0
Veg.	0.0	Meat	2.0
Fruit	0.0	Fat	0.0

Place chicken between two pieces of wax paper and pound to thickness of ½ inch. Mix together mustard, mayonnaise, and dashes of pepper and paprika. Coat one side of chicken with half of mustard mixture and place in 8-inch glass baking dish.

Cover with microwave-safe paper towel. Microwave on High 3 minutes. Turn chicken and coat with remaining mustard sauce. Cover again and microwave on High another 3 minutes, until chicken is cooked. Garnish with dash of paprika and sprinkling of chopped chives.

 # Coq au Vin

Serves 6

1 2½-lb. broiler-fryer, cut up and skinned (or 3 skinned chicken breasts, halved, or 3 drumsticks and 3 thighs)
⅔ cup green onions, chopped
8 small white onions, peeled
½ lb. whole mushrooms
1 clove garlic, crushed
1 teaspoon Spike (see "About This Cookbook")
¼ teaspoon pepper
½ teaspoon thyme
8 small new potatoes, scrubbed
1 cup Chicken Stock (see p. 40)
   Parsley, chopped
1 cup Burgundy wine

Nutritional Data

PER SERVING:

Calories	379
% calories from fat	18
Fat (gm)	7.6
Sat. Fat (gm)	2.1
Cholesterol (mg)	87
Sodium (mg)	119
Protein (gm)	32.6
Carbohydrate (gm)	38

EXCHANGES:

Milk	0.0	Bread	2.0
Veg.	1.0	Meat	4.0
Fruit	0.0	Fat	0.0

In stockpot, sauté green onions and chicken until chicken is browned on all sides. Add chicken and onions to crockpot with small white onions, mushrooms, garlic, Spike, pepper, thyme, potatoes, Chicken Stock, and parsley. Cook on Low 8 to 10 hours. During last hour, add Burgundy.

To Freeze: Place in microwave-safe container; label and freeze for up to 2 months.

To Serve: Thaw in refrigerator. Reheat and garnish with parsley before serving.

Chicken Veronique

Serves 4

- 2 whole, large chicken breasts
- 2 tablespoons vegetable oil
- 1 cup mushrooms, sliced
- 3 tablespoons green onions, sliced
- 1 cup Chicken Stock (see p. 40)
- 1 tablespoon all-purpose flour
- 1 cup seedless green grapes, halved
- ¼ cup dry white wine
- 1 tablespoon capers
- 2 cups cooked rice

Nutritional Data

PER SERVING:

Calories	355
% calories from fat	27
Fat (gm)	10.5
Sat. Fat (gm)	1.9
Cholesterol (mg)	75.5
Sodium (mg)	99
Protein (gm)	30.5
Carbohydrate (gm)	30.4

EXCHANGES:

Milk	0.0	Bread	1.5
Veg.	0.0	Meat	4.0
Fruit	0.5	Fat	0.0

Bone chicken breasts, and cut meat into 1-inch pieces; set aside.

In wok, heat vegetable oil and stir-fry mushrooms and onions about 2 minutes or until soft. Add chicken pieces and stir-fry about 5 minutes or until chicken is white.

Blend Chicken Stock and flour; add to chicken mixture. Cook and stir until thickened and bubbly. Stir in grapes, wine, and capers; cook 1 minute longer. Spoon chicken over rice in bowl.

To Freeze: Vacuum seal individual portions; label and freeze for up to 2 months.

To Serve: Put bags in boiling water, and bring to boil again. Boil 10 to 12 minutes.

Middle-Eastern Chicken

Serves 6

Nonstick cooking spray
- 1 lb. chicken breast, boneless, skinless, trimmed of all fat, and cut into 6 or 7 large pieces
- 1 large onion, chopped
- 2 cloves garlic, minced
- 2 teaspoons olive oil
- 1¾ cups defatted chicken broth
- 1 green bell pepper, seeded and diced
- 2 cups fresh tomato, chopped
- 2 cups cooked garbanzo beans, or 1 15-oz. can garbanzo beans, well drained

Nutritional Data

PER SERVING:

Calories	334
% calories from fat	13
Fat (gm)	5.1
Sat. Fat (gm)	0.9
Cholesterol (mg)	30.5
Sodium (mg)	419
Protein (gm)	21.3
Carbohydrate (gm)	52.6

EXCHANGES:

Milk	0.0	Bread	2.5
Veg.	1.0	Meat	1.5
Fruit	0.5	Fat	0.0

½ cup raisins
1 large bay leaf
1½ teaspoons dried thyme leaves
1 teaspoon ground cumin
¼ teaspoon ground allspice
⅛ teaspoon ground cloves
⅛ teaspoon black pepper
1 cup uncooked couscous
Salt, to taste (optional)
Chopped parsley for garnish (optional)

Coat Dutch oven or large, heavy pot with cooking spray. Cook chicken pieces over medium heat, turning frequently, until they begin to brown. With slotted spoon, remove chicken to medium bowl and set aside.

To same pot, add onion, garlic, oil, and 2 tablespoons broth. Stir up any browned bits from bottom of pot. Cook over medium heat, stirring frequently, 5 or 6 minutes or until onion is tender. If liquid begins to evaporate, add more broth.

Return chicken to pot. Add remaining broth, green pepper, tomato, garbanzos, raisins, bay leaf, thyme, cumin, allspice, cloves, and black pepper. Bring to boil, reduce heat, and simmer, covered, 20 to 25 minutes or until chicken is tender. Remove bay leaf and discard.

Add couscous and stir to mix well. Boil 2 minutes, covered. Remove pot from heat; stir up any couscous sticking to bottom. Allow mixture to stand 10 to 15 minutes, covered. Add salt to taste, if desired.

Arrange couscous on serving platter and top with chicken and sauce. Garnish with chopped parsley, if desired.

Grecian Chicken

Serves 4

1 frying chicken (about 2 lbs.), cut up
3 tablespoons oregano
1 teaspoon garlic powder
¼ teaspoon salt
¼ teaspoon pepper
1 tablespoon diet margarine
1 cup fresh lemon juice
1 cup white table wine
1 teaspoon Worcestershire sauce
¼ teaspoon garlic powder
2 tablespoons cornstarch
¼ cup water

Nutritional Data

PER SERVING:

Calories	346
% calories from fat	31
Fat (gm)	12.4
Sat. Fat (gm)	3.7
Cholesterol (mg)	145.1
Sodium (mg)	370
Protein (gm)	37.9
Carbohydrate (gm)	13.3

EXCHANGES:

Milk	0.0	Bread	0.0
Veg.	0.0	Meat	5.0
Fruit	1.0	Fat	0.0

Preheat oven to 375 degrees. Sprinkle chicken pieces with oregano, 1 teaspoon garlic powder, salt, and pepper. Place chicken skin side up in nonstick shallow casserole. Melt margarine; brush chicken pieces. Bake for 40 minutes.

Combine lemon juice, wine, Worcestershire sauce, and 1/4 teaspoon garlic powder; pour over chicken. Cover and bake 20 minutes or until tender. Remove chicken.

Combine cornstarch and water; add to pan juices. Cook over medium heat, stirring constantly until thickened. Serve sauce over chicken.

 # Sesame Chicken

Serves 4

1/4 cup reduced-sodium soy sauce
1 scallion, sliced
1 tablespoon Dijon mustard
1 teaspoon sesame oil
1 tablespoon ginger root, peeled and chopped
1 tablespoon frozen orange juice concentrate
1 lb. chicken breast, boneless, skinless, and cut into 1-inch cubes
1 tablespoon toasted sesame seeds
1 tablespoon parsley, chopped

Nutritional Data

PER SERVING:

Calories	133
% calories from fat	31
Fat (gm)	4.4
Sat. Fat (gm)	0.9
Cholesterol (mg)	45.7
Sodium (mg)	620
Protein (gm)	19.1
Carbohydrate (gm)	3.4

EXCHANGES:

Milk	0.0	Bread	0.0
Veg.	0.0	Meat	2.5
Fruit	0.0	Fat	0.0

Mix together first 6 ingredients in 1-quart measure. Add chicken and marinate for at least 1 hour, turning a few times. When ready to cook, remove chicken and arrange it in 9-inch baking dish.

Cover with wax paper and microwave on High for 3 to 4 minutes. Turn chicken pieces, cover again, and microwave on High for another 3 to 4 minutes. Chicken is done when it is white. Sprinkle with sesame seeds and parsley.

Chicken Limone

Serves 4

2 lbs. boneless and skinless chicken breasts*
Dash salt
White pepper, to taste
½ cup all-purpose flour
2 tablespoons olive oil
Juice of 1 lemon
1 tablespoon Italian parsley, chopped
½ cup dry white wine
Sliced lemon for garnish

Nutritional Data

PER SERVING:

Calories	318
% calories from fat	31
Fat (gm)	10.8
Sat. Fat (gm)	2
Cholesterol (mg)	91.5
Sodium (mg)	81
Protein (gm)	35.2
Carbohydrate (gm)	13.2

EXCHANGES:

Milk	0.0	Bread	1.0
Veg.	0.0	Meat	4.5
Fruit	0.0	Fat	0.0

Pound chicken until it is flat, then season with salt and pepper to taste. Flour chicken on one side only. Sauté on floured side in batches, portioning olive oil for each batch, until chicken is cooked, about 20 to 25 minutes.

Return chicken to skillet, add lemon juice, and sprinkle with parsley. Pour wine over chicken, turn heat up to high, and let wine bubble about 2 minutes.

Arrange chicken on individual, heated plates. Pour pan juices over chicken and garnish with slice of lemon.

Note: Veal is excellent in this recipe for a change.

Chicken Vesuvio

Serves 8

8 chicken breast halves, boneless and skinless (about 3 lbs.)
4 large red potatoes
1 tablespoon olive oil
¼ cup fresh lemon juice
1 tablespoon fresh rosemary leaves
2 teaspoons garlic, minced
1 teaspoon Spike (see "About This Cookbook")
¼ cup green onions, chopped
¼ cup pitted black olives, sliced (optional)
1 cup mushrooms, sliced

Nutritional Data

PER SERVING:

Calories	183
% calories from fat	19
Fat (gm)	3.8
Sat. Fat (gm)	0.8
Cholesterol (mg)	45.7
Sodium (mg)	44.2
Protein (gm)	18.6
Carbohydrate (gm)	18.4

EXCHANGES:

Milk	0.0	Bread	1.0
Veg.	0.0	Meat	2.0
Fruit	0.0	Fat	0.0

Rinse chicken pieces well and dry thoroughly. Scrub and quarter each potato without peeling. Place chicken and potatoes in casserole. Season by drizzling olive oil and lemon juice over chicken and potatoes. Sprinkle on rosemary, garlic, and Spike. Marinate in refrigerator for at least 30 minutes, turning occasionally.

Preheat oven to 425 degrees. Remove chicken from refrigerator and add onion. Bake chicken for 30 minutes. Lower oven temperature to 400 degrees and add olives and mushrooms. Cook another 30 minutes. Place chicken on platter and pour pan juices over all.

Chicken and Leeks with Basil Sauce

Serves 6

2	lbs. chicken breasts, boneless, skinless
3	tablespoons margarine
1	lb. leeks, cleaned and julienned
2	tablespoons shallots, chopped
½	cup cognac
1	cup dry white wine
3	cups Chicken Stock (see p. 40)
2	cups evaporated skim milk
1	tomato, peeled, seeded, and diced
10	fresh basil leaves, chopped
	Dash salt
	Black pepper, freshly ground

Nutritional Data

PER SERVING:

Calories	423
% calories from fat	28
Fat (gm)	13
Sat. Fat (gm)	3.2
Cholesterol (mg)	77.1
Sodium (mg)	248
Protein (gm)	34.1
Carbohydrate (gm)	22.9

EXCHANGES:

Milk	0.8	Bread	0.0
Veg.	2.0	Meat	4.0
Fruit	1.0	Fat	2.0

Preheat oven to 400 degrees. Melt margarine in skillet over medium-high heat. Briefly sauté chicken in batches only until browned. Transfer chicken to casserole, leaving margarine and pan juices in skillet.

Bake chicken 15 minutes or until juices run clear. Remove chicken from oven and set aside.

Sauté julienne of leek in pan juices for 5 minutes and remove. Sauté shallots until transparent. Remove and set aside. Add cognac to pan, flame, and reduce to syrup. Add white wine and reduce to glaze.

Add Chicken Stock and reduce to ¼ cup, about 20 minutes. Add evaporated skim milk and boil for 2 minutes. Add diced tomato, basil, leeks, and shallots. Season to taste with salt and pepper. Add chicken to sauce and cook until hot, 3 to 4 minutes. Pour sauce over chicken and serve.

Chicken Risotto

Serves 8

Butter-flavored vegetable cooking spray
1 tablespoon canola oil
2 cloves garlic, minced
1 large onion, thinly sliced
1 large red bell pepper, seeded and chopped
2½ cups leftover grilled or broiled chicken, boneless, skinless, and cut into cubes
1 tablespoon unsalted butter
1½ cups uncooked arborio rice
3 cups low-salt chicken broth, divided
¼ teaspoon salt
¼ teaspoon black pepper, freshly ground
1 tablespoon Parmesan cheese, freshly grated

Nutritional Data

PER SERVING:

Calories	349
% calories from fat	21
Fat (gm)	8
Sat. Fat (gm)	2.4
Cholesterol (mg)	55.5
Sodium (mg)	188
Protein (gm)	23.4
Carbohydrate (gm)	43.8

EXCHANGES:

Milk	0.0	Bread	2.5
Veg.	1.0	Meat	3.0
Fruit	0.0	Fat	0.0

Coat large nonstick skillet with cooking spray. Heat oil. Add garlic, onion, and bell pepper and cook over medium heat about 5 minutes. Add chicken and combine well. Transfer chicken and vegetables to bowl and reserve.

Coat a clean nonstick skillet with cooking spray. Heat butter. Add rice and stir. Add 1½ cups of chicken broth, cover, and simmer over medium heat about 15 minutes or until liquid is absorbed. Add salt, pepper, and remaining chicken broth. Cover and continue cooking until rice is tender, about 10 minutes.

Stir chicken and vegetables into rice mixture and heat until warm. Spoon risotto onto serving platter with raised sides and bring it to table. Sprinkle with cheese.

Malabar Chicken with Yellow Rice

Serves 4

½ teaspoon canola oil
1 small onion, sliced
½ cup carrots, chopped
½ teaspoon ginger root, peeled and minced
½ tablespoon garlic, minced
¾ lb. chicken pieces, boneless, skinless, and cut into strips
½ tablespoon curry powder
½ cup plain nonfat yogurt, room temperature
¼ cup almonds, sliced and toasted
¼ cup fresh cilantro
Yellow Rice (recipe follows)

Nutritional Data

PER SERVING:

Calories	339
% calories from fat	20
Fat (gm)	7.4
Sat. Fat (gm)	1
Cholesterol (mg)	34.8
Sodium (mg)	490
Protein (gm)	19.5
Carbohydrate (gm)	47.3

EXCHANGES:

Milk	0.0	Bread	2.5
Veg.	1.0	Meat	1.5
Fruit	0.0	Fat	1.0

Prepare Yellow Rice. Preheat oven to 350 degrees.

Heat oil in large skillet. Sauté onion over medium heat until brown, about 5 minutes. Increase heat and add carrots, ginger, and garlic; cook 1 minute. Add chicken and stir in curry powder.

Reduce heat, cover, and cook 5 to 6 minutes, stirring occasionally, until chicken is cooked through. Uncover and remove from heat. Stir in yogurt.

Pour half of Yellow Rice into baking dish. Spread chicken mixture over rice. Top with remaining rice, cover, and bake 25 minutes until heated through. Sprinkle with almonds and cilantro and serve.

Yellow Rice

1	teaspoon canola oil
1	teaspoon ginger root, peeled and minced
1	cup white basmati rice
1	tablespoon dried currants
1	tablespoon jalapeño pepper, chopped (use caution; wear rubber gloves and do not rub your eyes)
½	teaspoon turmeric
3	whole cardamon pods
2	whole cloves
1	small cinnamon stick
	Pinch saffron threads
1¾	cups water
¾	teaspoon salt, or salt substitute

Heat oil in saucepan over high heat, and sauté ginger for 30 seconds. Stir in rice, currants, jalapeño, turmeric, cardamon, cloves, cinnamon, and saffron and cook 1 minute. Add water and salt and bring to boil. Reduce heat, cover, and simmer 10 to 15 minutes until water is absorbed.

South Indian Chicken Curry

Serves 4

2	stalks celery, chopped (about 1 cup)
½	cup green bell pepper, chopped
¾	cup fresh mushrooms, chopped
3	cloves garlic, minced
1	small onion, chopped
1	tablespoon fresh ginger root, peeled and minced
1	tablespoon olive oil
⅛	teaspoon turmeric
¼	teaspoon ground cumin
1	tablespoon mild curry powder

Nutritional Data

PER SERVING:

Calories	166
% calories from fat	31
Fat (gm)	5.8
Sat. Fat (gm)	1.1
Cholesterol (mg)	46.2
Sodium (mg)	81.9
Protein (gm)	19.7
Carbohydrate (gm)	9

EXCHANGES:

Milk	0.0	Bread	0.0
Veg.	2.0	Meat	2.0
Fruit	0.0	Fat	0.0

½   cup nonfat plain yogurt
1   lb. chicken breast, boneless, skinless, and
    sliced thinly on diagonal

Place first 6 ingredients and oil in 1-quart glass measure and microwave on High for 3 minutes, stirring once. Mix spices with yogurt. Turn all ingredients, including chicken, into a casserole and let marinate in refrigerator for several hours.

Before cooking, bring to room temperature. Cover with lid or paper towels, and microwave on High for 3 to 4 minutes. Stir and return to microwave; cook on High another 3 to 4 minutes. Serve with basmati rice, noodles, or on top of baked potato halves.

Napa Valley Braised Chicken

Serves 4

4   chicken breast halves, boneless and
    skinless
1   tablespoon canola oil
1   clove garlic, minced
2   tablespoons onion, chopped
2   tablespoons flour
2   tablespoons parsley, chopped
    Salt, or salt substitute, to taste
    Pepper, freshly ground, to taste
1   bay leaf
1   cup white wine
1   cup dry cooking sherry
1   cup white seedless grapes, halved

Nutritional Data

PER SERVING:

Calories	325
% calories from fat	19
Fat (gm)	6.6
Sat. Fat (gm)	1.2
Cholesterol (mg)	73
Sodium (mg)	70
Protein (gm)	27.7
Carbohydrate (gm)	12.9

EXCHANGES:

Milk	0.0	Bread	0.0
Veg.	0.0	Meat	3.5
Fruit	1.0	Fat	1.5

In large skillet, brown chicken in oil over medium heat, along with garlic and onion. Stir in flour, parsley, salt, pepper, and bay leaf. Add wine and sherry, bring to low boil, and reduce heat to simmer. Cover and cook 50 minutes. Add grapes and simmer another 10 minutes.

Simmered Chicken

Serves 8

1 chicken, quartered (about 4½ lbs.)
2 large stalks celery, with tops, cut in half
1 large carrot, halved
1 medium onion, halved
1 teaspoon Spike (see "About This Cookbook")
5 peppercorns
1 teaspoon thyme
1 tablespoon parsley, minced
4 cups water

Nutritional Data

PER SERVING:

Calories	232
% calories from fat	34
Fat (gm)	8.4
Sat. Fat (gm)	2.3
Cholesterol (mg)	103.4
Sodium (mg)	99.8
Protein (gm)	34.3
Carbohydrate (gm)	2.8

EXCHANGES:

Milk	0.0	Bread	0.0
Veg.	1.0	Meat	4.0
Fruit	0.0	Fat	0.0

Place all ingredients in stockpot and bring to boil. Lower heat; cover and simmer 30 to 40 minutes until chicken is tender. Remove chicken; cool. Skim broth if necessary. Strain into container; cool to room temperature. Cover and refrigerate until cold. Remove fat from surface before using.

Skin chicken. Remove meat from breast in one piece, and cut remaining portions into bite-size pieces. Refrigerate in covered containers separately from broth.

You should have 1½ lbs. boneless chicken meat and 5 cups broth. Serve over noodles, with boiled potatoes, etc.

To Freeze: Place in microwave-safe container; label and freeze for up to 2 months.

To Serve: Thaw. Cover with microwave-safe plastic wrap, and cook on High 3 to 5 minutes.

Chicken Stew and Dumplings

Serves 6

6 chicken breast halves, boneless and skinless (about 2½ lbs.)
Salt and pepper, to taste
Vegetable cooking spray
½ cup water
1 cup onion, sliced
1 teaspoon Spike (see "About This Cookbook")
1 can cream of chicken soup
1 soup can skim milk
1 10-oz. package frozen mixed vegetables
1 cup biscuit mix (no cholesterol)
⅓ cup skim milk

Nutritional Data

PER SERVING:

Calories	276
% calories from fat	26
Fat (gm)	7.8
Sat. Fat (gm)	1.5
Cholesterol (mg)	50.8
Sodium (mg)	722
Protein (gm)	23.3
Carbohydrate (gm)	27.8

EXCHANGES:

Milk	0.0	Bread	1.0
Veg.	1.5	Meat	3.0
Fruit	0.0	Fat	0.0

Sprinkle chicken with salt and pepper; brown in large, heavy pan coated with vegetable cooking spray. Add water, onion, and Spike; cover. Simmer for 30 minutes. Stir in soup mixed with 1 soup-can-quantity of skim milk; add mixed vegetables. Cover and bring to boil. Simmer for 10 minutes, stirring occasionally.

Combine biscuit mix and 1/3 cup skim milk; spoon onto stew. Cook for 10 minutes. Cover; cook 10 minutes longer.

Chicken and Pasta

Serves 6

Vegetable cooking spray
1 cup red bell pepper, chopped
1/2 cup scallions, chopped
1 cup snow peas, cut in halves
3 cups leftover grilled or broiled chicken (or other poultry), boneless, skinless, and cut into cubes
3/4 cup nonfat plain yogurt
1/2 teaspoon salt
1/4 teaspoon black pepper, freshly ground
12 ozs. whole wheat pasta, cooked

Nutritional Data

PER SERVING:

Calories	329
% calories from fat	11
Fat (gm)	4.3
Sat. Fat (gm)	1.6
Cholesterol (mg)	59.5
Sodium (mg)	265
Protein (gm)	33.4
Carbohydrate (gm)	46.8

EXCHANGES:

Milk	0.0	Bread	2.0
Veg.	0.5	Meat	3.0
Fruit	0.0	Fat	0.0

In a large, sprayed skillet, sauté pepper, scallions, and snow peas until tender. Add chicken; cook until hot, 2 to 3 minutes. Stir in yogurt, salt, and pepper; cook 1 to 2 minutes more. Spoon over warm pasta on platter and toss.

Chicken Parmesan

Serves 4

4 split chicken breasts, skinless
3/4 cup Parmesan cheese, freshly grated
6 tablespoons olive oil
1 clove garlic, minced
3 tablespoons flour
1 1/2 cups Chicken Stock (see p. 40)
1/2 cup sherry
1 cup mushroom caps
1 teaspoon each ingredient: thyme, tarragon
2 tablespoons parsley, chopped
1 lb. cooked spaghetti

Nutritional Data

PER SERVING:

Calories	939
% calories from fat	31
Fat (gm)	31.7
Sat. Fat (gm)	7.6
Cholesterol (mg)	91.6
Sodium (mg)	423
Protein (gm)	52.3
Carbohydrate (gm)	100

EXCHANGES:

Milk	0.0	Bread	6.0
Veg.	1.0	Meat	4.5
Fruit	0.0	Fat	5.0

Preheat oven to 350 degrees.

Dip chicken in cheese. Heat olive oil in heavy skillet; brown chicken until golden turning to brown evenly. Remove from skillet; place in casserole.

Drain all but 3 tablespoons of oil from skillet. Add garlic; cook until soft. Stir in flour until smooth. Add Chicken Stock, sherry, mushrooms, and spices. Cook, stirring until smooth and slightly thickened.

Pour over chicken. Bake 30 to 40 minutes. Sprinkle with parsley; serve with spaghetti.

Chicken Paillards

Serves 4

- 1 lb. chicken breasts, boneless, skinless, and halved
- Salt, to taste
- ½ teaspoon black pepper
- 1 teaspoon whipped butter
- 1 teaspoon canola oil
- ¼ cup Chicken Stock (see p. 40)
- 2 cloves garlic, minced
- 2 tablespoons fresh lemon juice
- 4 slices lemon
- Paprika
- 2 tablespoons parsley, chopped, for garnish

Nutritional Data

PER SERVING:

Calories	115
% calories from fat	30
Fat (gm)	3.8
Sat. Fat (gm)	1
Cholesterol (mg)	48
Sodium (mg)	48
Protein (gm)	17.3
Carbohydrate (gm)	2.9

EXCHANGES:

Milk	0.0	Bread	0.0
Veg.	0.0	Meat	2.0
Fruit	0.0	Fat	0.0

Place chicken between 2 sheets of wax paper and pound to ½-inch-thick *paillards*. Season each side of chicken with salt and pepper, and set aside in baking dish.

Place butter and oil in 1-cup glass measure, and microwave on 50% for 1 minute, until butter melts. Combine with Chicken Stock, garlic, and lemon juice. Spoon juice over chicken, cover with wax paper, and microwave on High for 5 to 6 minutes, turning once and rotating dish.

Chicken is done when it is no longer pink. Top each *paillard* with lemon slice, dash of paprika, and parsley garnish, and spoon sauce over each piece.

Chicken Paprikash

Serves 4

1	lb. chicken breast, boneless and skinless
1	teaspoon canola oil
2	medium onions, chopped fine
2	cloves garlic, minced
1	medium green bell pepper, chopped
1	cup mushrooms, sliced
1	cup stewed tomatoes, crushed
2½	teaspoons sweet Hungarian paprika
1	teaspoon poppy seeds
¼	cup Mock Sour Cream (see p. 497)
	Salt and pepper, to taste

Nutritional Data

PER SERVING:

Calories	173
% calories from fat	24
Fat (gm)	4.6
Sat. Fat (gm)	1
Cholesterol (mg)	46.5
Sodium (mg)	220
Protein (gm)	20.7
Carbohydrate (gm)	12.5

EXCHANGES:

Milk	0.0	Bread	0.0
Veg.	2.5	Meat	2.0
Fruit	0.0	Fat	0.0

Cut chicken (against the grain) into thin slices. Heat browning dish on High for 5 minutes, or follow manufacturer's directions. Brown chicken slices a few at a time and set aside.

Place oil, onions, garlic, and green pepper in 1-quart measure or casserole and microwave on High for 3 minutes, stirring. Add mushrooms and microwave on High another 2 minutes. Mix in tomatoes and paprika, stir to combine, and then add chicken and poppy seeds.

Cover with wax paper and microwave on High for 4 to 5 minutes, stirring once. Remove, let rest a few minutes, then add Mock Sour Cream and adjust seasoning. Serve over noodles or rice.

Chicken Piccata

Serves 6

1½	lbs. chicken breasts, boneless, skinless, and split
	Vegetable cooking spray (olive-oil flavored)
½	teaspoon Spike (see "About This Cookbook")
½	teaspoon tarragon
¼	teaspoon pepper, freshly ground
¼	cup fresh lemon juice
¼	cup Butter Buds
1	tablespoon capers

Nutritional Data

PER SERVING:

Calories	99
% calories from fat	19
Fat (gm)	2
Sat. Fat (gm)	0.5
Cholesterol (mg)	45.7
Sodium (mg)	185
Protein (gm)	16.8
Carbohydrate (gm)	2.2

EXCHANGES:

Milk	0.0	Bread	0.0
Veg.	0.0	Meat	2.0
Fruit	0.0	Fat	0.0

On board, place chicken breasts smooth side down and cover with plastic wrap. Pound each to ¼-inch thickness with mallet. Dry meat with paper towels.

Coat medium-size skillet with vegetable cooking spray and add a few pieces of chicken. Cook about 4 minutes on each side until golden. Remove to platter and keep warm while cooking remaining chicken. Sprinkle cooked chicken with Spike, tarragon, and pepper.

Add lemon juice, Butter Buds, and capers to skillet and cook over moderate heat, stirring to incorporate brown particles from pan. When sauce has reduced, about 5 minutes, return chicken to skillet and continue cooking 5 more minutes.

 # Chicken Tarragon

Serves 4	Nutritional Data	
1 lb. chicken breast, boneless and skinless	PER SERVING:	
2 tablespoons low-sodium soy sauce mixed	Calories	111
with 2 tablespoons water	% calories from fat	26
Juice of 1 lemon	Fat (gm)	3.1
2 cloves garlic, minced	Sat. Fat (gm)	0.7
1 teaspoon sesame oil	Cholesterol (mg)	45.7
2 teaspoons dried tarragon	Sodium (mg)	304
Pepper	Protein (gm)	17.8
	Carbohydrate (gm)	2.4

EXCHANGES:			
Milk	0.0	Bread	0.0
Veg.	0.0	Meat	2.0
Fruit	0.0	Fat	0.0

Trim chicken of any fat and cut into cubes or thin slices. Combine with soy sauce and lemon juice and let marinate 15 minutes.

Place garlic and sesame oil in 1-cup measure and microwave 1 minute on High. In 1-quart casserole, combine oil and garlic with chicken marinade, add tarragon and pepper, and cover with vented plastic wrap. Microwave on Medium (50%) 4 to 6 minutes, stirring, until chicken is cooked through.

Ploughman's Chicken

Serves 6	Nutritional Data
2 teaspoons olive oil	PER SERVING:
1 large onion, thinly sliced	Calories 306
2 stalks celery, cut into 1-inch pieces	% calories from fat 17
3 lbs. chicken pieces, skin removed	Fat (gm) 5.7
½ cup vermouth	Sat. Fat (gm) 1.3
¾ cup defatted Chicken Stock (see p. 40)	Cholesterol (mg) 91.5
1 teaspoon garlic, minced	Sodium (mg) 138
½ teaspoon dried thyme	Protein (gm) 36.2
	Carbohydrate (gm) 21.6

Salt, or salt substitute and ground pepper, to taste
4   new potatoes, cut into 1½-inch cubes
Parsley

EXCHANGES:			
Milk	0.0	Bread	1.5
Veg.	0.0	Meat	4.0
Fruit	0.0	Fat	0.0

Heat oil in large skillet and sauté onion and celery over medium heat 3 to 4 minutes. Add chicken, increase heat, and cook 1 minute. Add vermouth and bring to boil for 1 minute.

Add remaining ingredients, except potatoes and parsley, bring to boil, and lower to simmer 10 minutes. Add potatoes and simmer, covered, another 30 to 35 minutes. Garnish with parsley and serve.

Chicken Romanov

Serves 4

4   chicken breast halves, boneless, skinless, and cut into strips
2   tablespoons canola oil
1   cup onion, chopped
4   tablespoons flour
1¾   cups defatted Chicken Stock (see p. 40)
½   cup nonfat sour cream

Nutritional Data

PER SERVING:

Calories	273
% calories from fat	35
Fat (gm)	10.5
Sat. Fat (gm)	1.4
Cholesterol (mg)	73
Sodium (mg)	230
Protein (gm)	31.9
Carbohydrate (gm)	12.8

EXCHANGES:			
Milk	0.0	Bread	0.5
Veg.	0.5	Meat	4.0
Fruit	0.0	Fat	0.0

Heat oil in large skillet. Add onion and cook over medium heat 2 to 3 minutes until tender. Remove onion and set aside.

Add chicken strips and sauté 4 to 5 minutes until tender. Sprinkle with flour and stir well in skillet. Gradually add stock, stirring until smooth. Add onion and cook until thickened, stirring occasionally.

Reduce heat, add sour cream, and heat through. Do not bring to boil. Serve immediately.

Chicken Saltimbocca

Serves 6

3   large chicken breasts, boneless, skinless, and halved lengthwise
6   thin slices boiled ham
3   tablespoons part-skim mozzarella cheese, shredded
1   medium tomato, seeded and chopped
1   teaspoon oregano
⅓   cup dry bread crumbs
2   tablespoons parsley, snipped

Nutritional Data

PER SERVING:

Calories	199
% calories from fat	23
Fat (gm)	4.8
Sat. Fat (gm)	1.6
Cholesterol (mg)	82.5
Sodium (mg)	293
Protein (gm)	31.5
Carbohydrate (gm)	5.6

EXCHANGES:			
Milk	0.0	Bread	0.0
Veg.	0.5	Meat	3.5
Fruit	0.0	Fat	0.0

Preheat oven to 350 degrees.

Place chicken, boned side up, on cutting board. Place clear plastic wrap over it. Working from center out, pound lightly with meat mallet to about 5" x 5". Remove wrap.

Place ham slice and ½ tablespoon mozzarella cheese on each cutlet. Top with some tomato and dash of oregano. Sprinkle with mixture of bread crumbs and parsley. Bake 40 to 45 minutes.

Paella

Serves 5

½ lb. chicken breast, boneless, skinless, trimmed of fat, and cut into bite-size pieces
2 teaspoons olive oil
1 large onion, chopped
2 cloves garlic, minced
2¾ cups reduced-sodium, defatted chicken broth, or regular defatted chicken broth, divided
¼ teaspoon crushed saffron threads
1 14¾-oz. can Italian-style tomatoes, undrained
1 14¾-oz. jar water-packed artichoke hearts, drained
1 large red bell pepper, seeded and diced (if unavailable substitute green or yellow bell pepper)
1 large green bell pepper, seeded and diced
1 teaspoon dried thyme leaves
½ teaspoon dried basil leaves
⅛ teaspoon cayenne pepper
⅛ teaspoon black pepper
¼ lb. Canadian bacon, cut into thin strips
1¼ cups uncooked long-grain white rice
½ lb. medium shrimp, peeled and deveined
¼ teaspoon salt, or to taste (optional)
Vegetable cooking spray

Nutritional Data

PER SERVING:

Calories	376
% calories from fat	13
Fat (gm)	5.7
Sat. Fat (gm)	1.1
Cholesterol (mg)	96.2
Sodium (mg)	719
Protein (gm)	27.9
Carbohydrate (gm)	56.1

EXCHANGES:

Milk	0.0	Bread	3.0
Veg.	2.0	Meat	2.0
Fruit	0.0	Fat	0.0

In Dutch oven or large pot coated with cooking spray, cook chicken pieces over medium heat, turning frequently, 6 to 8 minutes or until they begin to brown. Remove and set aside in medium bowl.

In same pot, combine oil, onion, garlic, and 3 tablespoons broth. Stir up any brown bits from pan bottom. Cook over medium heat, stirring frequently, 6 to 7 minutes or until onion is tender. If liquid begins to evaporate, add more broth.

Add saffron and remaining broth. Add tomatoes, breaking them up with large spoon, artichoke hearts, red pepper, green pepper, thyme, basil, cayenne pepper, black pepper, reserved chicken, and bacon.

Add rice. Bring to boil. Cover, reduce heat, and simmer 15 minutes or until rice is almost tender. Add shrimp and cook an additional 5 to 6 minutes or until shrimp is curled and rice is tender. Add salt, if desired.

Stir before serving.

 # Chicken Creole

Serves 5

1	cup defatted chicken broth
1	6-oz. can tomato paste
1	large onion, chopped
2	cups chopped cabbage
1	large green bell pepper, seeded and diced
2	large cloves garlic, minced
1	bay leaf
1	tablespoon fresh lemon juice
1	tablespoon Worcestershire sauce
1	tablespoon granulated sugar
2	teaspoons dried basil leaves
2	teaspoons Dijon mustard
1/4	teaspoon black pepper
3-4	drops hot pepper sauce
2 1/2	lbs. large chicken breast halves, skin and fat removed
1 1/4	cups uncooked long-grain white rice

Nutritional Data

PER SERVING:

Calories	423
% calories from fat	11
Fat (gm)	5
Sat. Fat (gm)	1.3
Cholesterol (mg)	91.5
Sodium (mg)	482
Protein (gm)	40.3
Carbohydrate (gm)	53.6

EXCHANGES:

Milk	0.0	Bread	2.5
Veg.	2.5	Meat	3.5
Fruit	0.0	Fat	0.0

In bottom of large crockpot, whisk together chicken broth and tomato paste until smooth. Add onion, cabbage, green pepper, garlic, bay leaf, lemon juice, Worcestershire sauce, sugar, basil, mustard, black pepper, and hot pepper sauce. Stir to mix well. Add chicken.

Cover and cook on High 1 hour. Stir chicken into sauce. Reduce heat to low, and cook an additional 5 to 6 hours. Remove and discard bay leaf.

A half hour before serving, cook rice according to package directions. Remove chicken. When cool enough to handle, cut into slices and discard bones. Serve individual portions of chicken and vegetables over rice.

Chicken Thighs Picante

Serves 6

Picante Sauce

1½ cups tomatoes, peeled and finely diced
½   cup onion, chopped
¼   cup fresh cilantro, chopped
2   jalapeño peppers, minced (use caution; wear rubber gloves and do not rub your eyes)
¼   cup tomato juice

Chicken

6   chicken thighs, skinless
1   teaspoon garlic powder
2   cups cooked brown or white rice

Nutritional Data

PER SERVING:

Calories	160
% calories from fat	23
Fat (gm)	3.9
Sat. Fat (gm)	1.1
Cholesterol (mg)	30.9
Sodium (mg)	210
Protein (gm)	10.8
Carbohydrate (gm)	19.6

EXCHANGES:

Milk	0.0	Bread	1.0
Veg.	1.0	Meat	1.0
Fruit	0.0	Fat	0.0

Picante Sauce: Combine ingredients.

Chicken: Preheat oven to 375 degrees. Sprinkle thighs with picante sauce and garlic powder. Arrange thighs on foil-lined cookie sheet. Bake 50 to 60 minutes or until done. Thighs are done if juices run clear when meat is pricked with fork.

Arrange thighs over hot rice on serving platter. Top with remaining Picante Sauce.

Chicken Tostadas with Salsa

Serves 6

Hot Green Salsa

1   12-oz. can tomatillos, drained
½   cup onion, chopped
2   jalapeño peppers, split lengthwise and seeded (use caution; wear rubber gloves and do not rub your eyes)
3   cloves garlic, halved
¼   teaspoon salt
¼   cup fresh cilantro

Tostadas

6   corn tortillas
1   cup lettuce, shredded
1   cup tomatoes, chopped
2   cups leftover grilled or broiled chicken, boneless, skinless, and shredded
    Vegetable cooking spray

Nutritional Data

PER SERVING:

Calories	174
% calories from fat	18
Fat (gm)	3.5
Sat. Fat (gm)	0.7
Cholesterol (mg)	39.3
Sodium (mg)	309
Protein (gm)	17.1
Carbohydrate (gm)	18.8

EXCHANGES:

Milk	0.0	Bread	1.0
Veg.	0.5	Meat	2.0
Fruit	0.0	Fat	0.0

Hot Green Salsa: Place tomatillos, onion, peppers, garlic, salt, and cilantro in food processor fitted with steel blade and pulse several times until finely chopped. Transfer salsa to serving bowl.

Tostadas: Heat skillet coated with cooking spray. This will take less than 1 minute. Cook each tortilla, turning with tongs until both sides are golden brown.

Immediately arrange fried tortillas on serving platter and bring to table hot. Diners should sprinkle each tortilla with layers of lettuce, chicken, and tomatoes. Top everything with the Hot Green Salsa.

Santa Fe Chicken Olé

Serves 6

6	chicken breast halves, boneless and skinless
2	teaspoons ground cumin, divided
1	teaspoon garlic salt
1	tablespoon canola oil
1	cup cooked, or canned, black beans, rinsed and drained
1	cup frozen corn
2/3	cup picante sauce
1/2	cup red bell pepper, diced
2	tablespoons fresh cilantro, chopped

Nutritional Data

PER SERVING:

Calories	239
% calories from fat	23
Fat (gm)	6.2
Sat. Fat (gm)	1.1
Cholesterol (mg)	73
Sodium (mg)	602
Protein (gm)	30.6
Carbohydrate (gm)	15.8

EXCHANGES:

Milk	0.0	Bread	1.0
Veg.	0.0	Meat	3.0
Fruit	0.0	Fat	0.0

Season chicken with 1 teaspoon cumin and garlic salt. Heat oil in skillet, add chicken, and cook over medium heat, 3 to 4 minutes.

In separate bowl, combine beans, corn, picante sauce, bell pepper, and remaining cumin. Spoon mixture over chicken and cook, uncovered, 6 to 7 more minutes at reduced heat.

Remove chicken to platter, but leave bean mixture in skillet. Cook beans on high heat another 2 to 3 minutes, stirring frequently. Spread bean mixture over chicken, top with cilantro, and serve with extra picante sauce on the side.

Chicken or Turkey Chili

Serves 8

Nonstick cooking spray
1 cup onion, chopped
3 cloves garlic, minced
3 tablespoons chili powder
1 teaspoon ground cumin
1 14½-oz. can crushed tomatoes, undrained
3 cups leftover grilled or broiled chicken or turkey, boneless, skinless, and diced
1 16-oz. can red kidney beans, drained

Nutritional Data

PER SERVING:

Calories	172
% calories from fat	17
Fat (gm)	3.3
Sat. Fat (gm)	0.7
Cholesterol (mg)	44.3
Sodium (mg)	377
Protein (gm)	20.8
Carbohydrate (gm)	15.5

EXCHANGES:

Milk	0.0	Bread	0.5
Veg.	1.0	Meat	2.0
Fruit	0.0	Fat	0.0

Heat large skillet coated with cooking spray and sauté onion and garlic about 5 minutes, stirring occasionally. Add chili powder, cumin, and tomatoes. Simmer 5 minutes more.

Stir in chicken or turkey and beans, and cook another 5 minutes. Serve immediately. You may wish to serve corn chips or corn bread with this dish.

 # Chili con Chicken

Serves 4

12 ozs. chicken breasts, boneless and skinless
3 tablespoons fresh lemon juice
1 teaspoon virgin olive oil
2 cloves garlic, minced
2 medium onions, sliced
2 red and green bell peppers, julienned
1 teaspoon ground cumin
1½ teaspoons dried oregano
2 teaspoons fresh chili pepper, finely chopped, or 1 teaspoon dried hot pepper flakes
½ teaspoon pepper
2 tablespoons parsley, chopped, for garnish

Nutritional Data

PER SERVING:

Calories	120
% calories from fat	22
Fat (gm)	2.9
Sat. Fat (gm)	0.6
Cholesterol (mg)	34.3
Sodium (mg)	34.8
Protein (gm)	14
Carbohydrate (gm)	10.1

EXCHANGES:

Milk	0.0	Bread	0.0
Veg.	1.5	Meat	1.5
Fruit	0.0	Fat	0.0

Slice chicken into ½-inch strips and sprinkle with lemon juice. Set aside. Place oil, garlic, and onion in 2-quart casserole, and microwave on High, uncovered, for 2 minutes. Add pepper strips, cumin, oregano, and chili. Mix, cover with wax paper, and microwave on High for another 2 minutes, stirring once. Transfer to serving platter.

Top vegetables with chicken strips. Cover with wax paper and microwave on High for 2 to 3 minutes; then turn chicken pieces. Microwave on High for another 1 to 2 minutes, until chicken is no longer pink. Season with pepper and garnish with parsley.

Chicken Fajitas in Pitas

Serves 4

6	chicken breast halves, boneless, skinless, and cut into thin strips
1	tablespoon canola oil
	Dash paprika
2	whole pitas, warmed, cut into halves
4	tablespoons salsa
4	tablespoons nonfat sour cream

Nutritional Data

PER SERVING:

Calories	339
% calories from fat	28
Fat (gm)	8.9
Sat. Fat (gm)	1.7
Cholesterol (mg)	110
Sodium (mg)	386
Protein (gm)	44.3
Carbohydrate (gm)	19.5

EXCHANGES:

Milk	0.0	Bread	1.0
Veg.	0.0	Meat	5.0
Fruit	0.0	Fat	0.0

Heat oil in large skillet. Add chicken strips, sprinkle with paprika, and sauté over medium heat, stirring frequently, 4 to 5 minutes or until chicken is no longer pink inside.

Remove from heat and place 1/4 of chicken in each pita pocket. Top with tablespoon of salsa and sour cream and serve.

Chicken Burritos with a Bite

Serves 8

1	tablespoon canola oil
1	lb. chicken, ground
1/8	teaspoon ground cumin
1/8	teaspoon garlic powder
1/8	teaspoon dried basil, crushed
1	cup onion, chopped
1	16-oz. can pinto beans, drained and rinsed
4	tablespoons canned green chili peppers, chopped
8	flour tortillas
	Vegetable cooking spray
1/2	cup low-fat Cheddar cheese, shredded
	Taco sauce

Nutritional Data

PER SERVING:

Calories	290
% calories from fat	24
Fat (gm)	7.7
Sat. Fat (gm)	1.7
Cholesterol (mg)	47.1
Sodium (mg)	586
Protein (gm)	23.8
Carbohydrate (gm)	30.3

EXCHANGES:

Milk	0.0	Bread	2.0
Veg.	0.0	Meat	2.5
Fruit	0.0	Fat	0.0

Preheat oven to 325 degrees. Heat oil in large skillet over medium heat. Add chicken, cumin, garlic, basil, and onion. Brown chicken, stirring often. Add beans and chili peppers.

Wrap tortillas together in aluminum foil, heat in oven 10 to 12 minutes, and remove. Increase oven temperature to 350 degrees. Place portion of chicken mixture on top of each tortilla, roll up, and tuck in edges.

Place tortillas in baking dish coated with cooking spray, sprinkle with cheese, and bake 15 minutes. Serve with taco sauce.

Cancun Chicken Loaf

Serves 4

- 1 lb. extra-lean chicken, ground
- 1/4 cup uncooked rolled oats
- 1/2 cup onion, minced
- Dash garlic powder
- 1/8 teaspoon ground coriander
- 1/8 teaspoon dried thyme, crushed
- 4 tablespoons low-sodium tomato sauce
- 1 egg, beaten
- 1 tablespoon toasted sunflower seeds
- 3 tablespoons canned green chili peppers, diced
- Vegetable cooking spray

Nutritional Data

PER SERVING:

Calories	247
% calories from fat	27
Fat (gm)	7.2
Sat. Fat (gm)	1.8
Cholesterol (mg)	140
Sodium (mg)	169
Protein (gm)	36.2
Carbohydrate (gm)	7.2

EXCHANGES:

Milk	0.0	Bread	0.0
Veg.	1.0	Meat	4.0
Fruit	0.0	Fat	0.0

Preheat oven to 350 degrees. Mix together all ingredients and shape into loaf. Place in glass baking dish that has been coated with cooking spray. Bake 1 hour.

Chicken Mini Pies

Serves 4

- 2 tablespoons diet margarine
- 4 tablespoons onion, chopped
- 4 tablespoons flour
- 2 teaspoons instant chicken bouillon granules
- 1/4 teaspoon ground sage
- Dash ground pepper
- 1 1/2 cups skim milk
- 1 cup water
- 1 cup cooked chicken, ground
- 1 cup frozen mixed vegetables
- 2 tablespoons parsley, chopped
- 1 package (6) refrigerated biscuits

Nutritional Data

PER SERVING:

Calories	256
% calories from fat	24
Fat (gm)	6.9
Sat. Fat (gm)	1
Cholesterol (mg)	28.1
Sodium (mg)	882
Protein (gm)	17.2
Carbohydrate (gm)	32.4

EXCHANGES:

Milk	0.0	Bread	1.5
Veg.	1.5	Meat	1.5
Fruit	0.0	Fat	0.5

Preheat oven to 400 degrees. Heat diet margarine in large skillet. Cook onion 3 to 4 minutes over medium heat until tender. Add flour, bouillon, sage, and pepper, stirring constantly. Gradually add milk and water. Cook, stirring constantly, until thickened.

Add chicken, vegetables, and parsley and heat until mixture is consistency of stew. Remove from heat and pour into 4 individual casseroles.

Top each casserole with 1 biscuit. (Reserve and refrigerate remaining 2 biscuits for other use.) Place casseroles on baking sheet, and bake 10 to 12 minutes until biscuits are lightly browned.

Chicken Mousse

Serves 6

2	envelopes unflavored gelatin
2	cups Chicken Stock (see p. 40)
1	lb. cooked chicken meat, shredded
5	tablespoons dry sherry
1	teaspoon dried leaf tarragon
½	cup green onions, chopped
	Pepper, freshly ground, to taste
½	cup fat-free mayonnaise
½	cup Mock Sour Cream (see p. 497)
2	teaspoons tomato paste
	To garnish: Watercress, black olives, and cherry tomatoes
	Vegetable cooking spray

Nutritional Data

PER SERVING:

Calories	185
% calories from fat	18
Fat (gm)	3.5
Sat. Fat (gm)	1
Cholesterol (mg)	61.7
Sodium (mg)	365
Protein (gm)	26.5
Carbohydrate (gm)	6.4

EXCHANGES:

Milk	0.0	Bread	0.0
Veg.	1.0	Meat	3.0
Fruit	0.0	Fat	0.0

Lightly coat 5- to 6-cup mold with vegetable cooking spray. In small saucepan, combine gelatin and ½ cup stock. Stir well; let stand 3 minutes. Stir over low heat until gelatin dissolves; cool slightly.

Combine remaining stock, gelatin mixture, and rest of ingredients in blender or food processor fitted with steel blade. Mix until smooth. Pour into coated mold. Cover and refrigerate until set.

Run tip of knife around edge of mold to loosen. Place serving plate over mousse; invert mousse onto plate. Garnish with watercress, olives, and cherry tomatoes.

Chicken and Vegetable Terrine

Serves 6

1	small green bell pepper
1	small red bell pepper
2	small carrots
1	zucchini
1	yellow squash
1½	lbs. chicken breasts, boneless, skinless, and diced
1	clove garlic, crushed
½	teaspoon ground nutmeg
2	tablespoons fresh lemon juice
	Egg substitute equal to 3 eggs
1½	cups evaporated skim milk
½	cup mixed fresh herbs, such as basil, tarragon, dill, and parsley
	Vegetable cooking spray

Nutritional Data

PER SERVING:

Calories	182
% calories from fat	12
Fat (gm)	2.4
Sat. Fat (gm)	0.7
Cholesterol (mg)	47.7
Sodium (mg)	166
Protein (gm)	25.3
Carbohydrate (gm)	14.6

EXCHANGES:

Milk	0.5	Bread	0.0
Veg.	1.0	Meat	2.0
Fruit	0.0	Fat	0.0

Preheat oven to 325 degrees.

Wash peppers, carrots, zucchini, and yellow squash. Remove pepper seeds and peel vegetables as needed. Dice all vegetables and blanch lightly in boiling water. Drain and reserve.

In food processor, puree chicken. Add garlic, nutmeg, and lemon juice. Process; then add egg substitute. Process again and add evaporated skim milk and chopped herbs. Mix well.

Pour chicken mixture into bowl and chill slightly. Fold in blanched vegetables, then spoon mixture into a 4" x 8" loaf pan coated with vegetable cooking spray. Bake 1 to 1½ hours or until terrine pulls away from sides of pan and is firm to touch. Cool terrine, then chill overnight in refrigerator.

To serve, cut into ½-inch slices. You can garnish each slice with marinated artichoke heart.

Around the World Drumsticks

Serves 9 (2 drumsticks each)

1½	teaspoons ground ginger
1½	teaspoons ground coriander
1½	teaspoons ground allspice
1	teaspoon ground cinnamon
1	teaspoon red pepper flakes
½	teaspoon salt
¼	cup rice wine, or sake
3	tablespoons low-sodium soy sauce
2	teaspoons sesame oil
1	tablespoon sugar
1	tablespoon fresh ginger, minced
1	tablespoon garlic, minced
18	chicken drumsticks, skin and fat removed
	Vegetable cooking spray

Nutritional Data

PER SERVING:

Calories	175
% calories from fat	32
Fat (gm)	6.1
Sat. Fat (gm)	1.5
Cholesterol (mg)	82
Sodium (mg)	379
Protein (gm)	25.6
Carbohydrate (gm)	3.1

EXCHANGES:

Milk	0.0	Bread	0.0
Veg.	0.0	Meat	3.0
Fruit	0.0	Fat	0.0

In dry skillet or wok, stir-fry ground ginger, coriander, all-spice, cinnamon, red pepper flakes, and salt over moderate heat 2 minutes. Remove from heat and add wine, soy sauce, sesame oil, sugar, ginger, and garlic; allow to cool.

Place chicken in large plastic bag, add marinade to coat chicken, seal bag, and chill overnight. Discard marinade and grill drumsticks on rack coated with cooking spray, turning frequently, 10 to 12 minutes cooked through.

Apricot Turkey Breast

Serves 4

1	lb. turkey breast, boneless
1	teaspoon paprika
	Pinch cayenne pepper
1½	tablespoons sugar-free apricot preserves*
2	teaspoons Dijon mustard
2	tablespoons parsley, chopped, for garnish

Nutritional Data

PER SERVING:

Calories	137
% calories from fat	17
Fat (gm)	2.6
Sat. Fat (gm)	0.8
Cholesterol (mg)	49.6
Sodium (mg)	81.1
Protein (gm)	21.7
Carbohydrate (gm)	5.8

EXCHANGES:

Milk	0.0	Bread	0.0
Veg.	0.0	Meat	2.5
Fruit	0.5	Fat	0.0

Place turkey breast between 2 sheets of wax paper and pound with mallet until flattened. Mix paprika and cayenne, and dust one side of turkey with half of mixture. Place, coated side up, on 10" x 12" baking dish.

Cover with wax paper and microwave on Medium (50%) for 3 to 4 minutes. Turn, dust with remaining paprika-cayenne mixture, cover, and microwave on Medium another 1 minute until turkey is no longer pink.

Mix apricot preserves with mustard, and coat turkey. Roll up coated turkey and secure with toothpicks. Return to microwave and cook on High another 1 minute. Slice into rounds and serve with garnish of parsley.

Note: Sugar-free marmalade may be substituted for apricot preserves.

 # Turkey Marsala

Serves 4

12 ozs. turkey breast cutlets, sliced thin on diagonal
1 teaspoon dried rosemary, crushed
2 tablespoons Marsala wine (or sherry)
¼ cup dry white wine
   Pepper
   Parsley sprigs for garnish

Nutritional Data

PER SERVING:

Calories	100
% calories from fat	17
Fat (gm)	1.8
Sat. Fat (gm)	0.6
Cholesterol (mg)	37.2
Sodium (mg)	39.7
Protein (gm)	16.1
Carbohydrate (gm)	0.4

EXCHANGES:

Milk	0.0	Bread	0.0
Veg.	0.0	Meat	2.0
Fruit	0.0	Fat	0.0

Heat a browning dish on High 5 minutes in microwave. Place half of turkey slices on dish, and microwave on High 1 to 2 minutes. Repeat with remaining turkey slices. Combine turkey slices and microwave on High until no longer pink, about 1 minute.

Mix rosemary and wine and let steep a few minutes. When turkey is white, add wine mixture and microwave another 1 to 2 minutes on High. Season with fresh pepper and serve with parsley garnish. Let stand a few minutes before serving.

 # Turkey Peppercorn

Serves 4

1 lb. turkey breast cutlets, pounded to ¼-inch thickness
1 tablespoon black (or green) peppercorns, crushed in blender
½ cup dry white wine
1 tablespoon brandy
1 tablespoon parsley, chopped, for garnish

Nutritional Data

PER SERVING:

Calories	145
% calories from fat	15
Fat (gm)	2.4
Sat. Fat (gm)	0.8
Cholesterol (mg)	49.6
Sodium (mg)	48
Protein (gm)	21.6
Carbohydrate (gm)	1.3

EXCHANGES:

Milk	0.0	Bread	0.0
Veg.	0.0	Meat	2.5
Fruit	0.0	Fat	0.0

Rinse turkey cutlets and pat dry. Press crushed peppercorns firmly into both sides of turkey cutlets. Smack cutlets with side of cleaver or sauté pan to make peppercorns adhere.

Place cutlets in 12-inch glass casserole, and add wine and brandy. Microwave on High for 2 to 3 minutes. Stir. Serve with garnish of parsley.

Poached Turkey Breast with Herbs and Wine

Serves 4

- 1 cup parsley, chopped
- 1 tablespoon garlic, minced
- 2 tablespoons fresh lemon juice
- 1 tablespoon olive oil
- 1 lb. turkey breast, boneless and skinless
- 1 sprig sorrel leaves
- 3 thin slices carrot
- 1 cup Chicken Stock (see p. 40)
- 1 cup white wine
- 4 medium red-skinned potatoes
- 4 large carrots, peeled and cut into 2-inch pieces
- 1 cup green beans, cut in half
- 1 cup zucchini, sliced
- 6 cherry tomatoes and fresh basil leaves, for garnish

Nutritional Data

PER SERVING:

Calories	369
% calories from fat	16
Fat (gm)	6.5
Sat. Fat (gm)	1.4
Cholesterol (mg)	50.6
Sodium (mg)	95
Protein (gm)	26.8
Carbohydrate (gm)	42.6

EXCHANGES:

Milk	0.0	Bread	1.5
Veg.	3.0	Meat	3.0
Fruit	0.0	Fat	0.0

Put parsley, garlic, lemon juice, and olive oil in blender and mix until smooth.

Gently run spoon under turkey skin to separate from flesh, leaving skin attached at one end. Spread parsley mixture over breast, and arrange sorrel leaves and carrot slices in decorative pattern. Replace skin and secure with skewers to hold herbs against turkey.

Place turkey, skin side up, in large stockpot. Add Chicken Stock and wine. Bring to boil over medium-high heat. Reduce heat to low, cover, and simmer 1 hour. Scatter potatoes and carrots around turkey and cover. Simmer 15 minutes. Add green beans and zucchini and simmer 10 minutes more or until potatoes and carrots are tender and meat juices run clear when breast is pierced.

Place turkey on cutting board and let stand 10 minutes, loosely covered with foil. Remove vegetables from broth and place around edge of serving platter.

Remove skewers from turkey and discard skin. Carve 1/2 of breast and add to platter with vegetables. Cut 1/2 more breast into slices and freeze in bag for another meal.

Pour 1/2 of broth over turkey to moisten, and garnish with tomatoes and basil leaves.

To Freeze: Place in microwave-safe container; label and freeze for up to 2 months.

To Serve: Thaw. Cover with microwave-safe plastic wrap, and cook on High 3 to 5 minutes.

Turkey Teriyaki

Serves 4

1	lb. turkey breast, or boneless, skinless chicken breasts
2	tablespoons low-sodium soy sauce mixed with 2 tablespoons water
1	tablespoon Dijon mustard
2	tablespoons ginger root, peeled and grated
2	cloves garlic, minced
1	tablespoon orange rind, grated
1	teaspoon sesame oil
1/4	cup dry sherry
2	cups mushrooms, sliced
1	cup green peas (if frozen, thawed)

Nutritional Data

PER SERVING:

Calories	198
% calories from fat	18
Fat (gm)	3.9
Sat. Fat (gm)	1
Cholesterol (mg)	49.6
Sodium (mg)	364
Protein (gm)	25.4
Carbohydrate (gm)	11

EXCHANGES:

Milk	0.0	Bread	0.5
Veg.	0.5	Meat	2.5
Fruit	0.0	Fat	0.0

Wash turkey or chicken and pat dry. Cut into 1/2-inch cubes. Blend remaining ingredients, except mushrooms and peas, and pour over turkey. Let turkey marinate for at least 1 hour or, preferably, overnight in refrigerator. Turn several times.

Place mushrooms in 1-quart measure, and microwave on High 2 minutes until soft. Drain and reserve.

Place turkey with some of marinade in 8-inch-square baking dish and cover with wax paper. Microwave on High 2 to 3 minutes. Turn poultry pieces and rotate dish. Microwave on High another 2 to 3 minutes.

Add mushrooms and peas, and microwave on High another 1 to 2 minutes until warmed through. Serve with rice or noodles.

Turkey-Stuffed Peppers

Serves 6

6	medium green bell peppers
1	lb. turkey, ground
1	cup cooked rice
2	tablespoons onion, minced
1	tablespoon Worcestershire sauce
1	clove garlic, minced
1/4	teaspoon pepper
1	cup (8 oz.) low-sodium tomato sauce
1/2	cup water
1	oz. skim mozzarella cheese, shredded

Nutritional Data

PER SERVING:

Calories	179
% calories from fat	33
Fat (gm)	6.6
Sat. Fat (gm)	2.1
Cholesterol (mg)	30.8
Sodium (mg)	93
Protein (gm)	13.3
Carbohydrate (gm)	16.3

EXCHANGES:

Milk	0.0	Bread	0.5
Veg.	1.5	Meat	1.5
Fruit	0.0	Fat	0.5

Cut off tops of green peppers; remove seeds and membrane.

Mix turkey with rice, onion, Worcestershire sauce, garlic, and pepper. Mix half of tomato sauce with turkey mixture, then spoon mixture into peppers; cover.

Place in microwave and cook 18 to 22 minutes, giving dish quarter-turn every 5 minutes. Add water and remaining tomato sauce. Sprinkle cheese over each pepper. Recover and return to microwave. Cook 1 to 2 minutes until cheese melts.

To Freeze: Place in microwave-safe container; label and freeze for up to 2 months.

To Serve: Thaw. Cover with microwave-safe plastic wrap, and cook on High 3 to 5 minutes.

Turkey Enchiladas Casserole

Serves 6

- 1 lb. lean turkey, ground
- 1/4 cup onion, chopped
- 2 cloves garlic, minced
- 6 ozs. tomato sauce
- 1 teaspoon bottled chilies, chopped
- 2 teaspoons chili powder
- 1 teaspoon fresh lemon juice
- 1/2 teaspoon pepper
- 1/4 cup green peas (if frozen, thawed)
- 4 corn tortillas
- 2 ozs. fat-free mozzarella, shredded
  Dash cayenne pepper

Nutritional Data

PER SERVING:

Calories	166
% calories from fat	34
Fat (gm)	6.3
Sat. Fat (gm)	1.6
Cholesterol (mg)	29.8
Sodium (mg)	314
Protein (gm)	14.9
Carbohydrate (gm)	12.7

EXCHANGES:

Milk	0.0	Bread	1.0
Veg.	0.0	Meat	2.0
Fruit	0.0	Fat	0.0

Mix ground turkey, onion, and garlic and place in 2-quart casserole. Microwave on High 4 to 6 minutes, stirring, until turkey loses pink color. Drain.

Stir in tomato sauce, chilies, chili powder, lemon juice, and pepper, and microwave on High another 4 to 6 minutes, stirring midcycle. Stir in peas.

In 1 1/2-quart baking dish or casserole, layer tortillas, turkey mixture, and cheese alternately, topping with some of cheese and dash of cayenne. Microwave on High 2 to 3 minutes until cheese bubbles. Let stand a minute or so before serving.

Turkey Meatballs

Serves 4

1 lb. turkey, ground
3/4 cup Italian-seasoned bread crumbs
1 medium onion, chopped
2 egg whites
1/2 teaspoon dried leaf marjoram
1 teaspoon dried oregano
1 teaspoon dried basil
1 teaspoon Spike (see "About This Cookbook")
1/4 teaspoon black pepper, freshly ground
1/2 cup white wine or water
2 cups Basic Tomato-Basil Sauce (see p. 501), or purchased tomato sauce

Nutritional Data

PER SERVING:

Calories	318
% calories from fat	31
Fat (gm)	11.2
Sat. Fat (gm)	2.7
Cholesterol (mg)	42.2
Sodium (mg)	543
Protein (gm)	21.9
Carbohydrate (gm)	28.5

EXCHANGES:

Milk	0.0	Bread	1.0
Veg.	2.5	Meat	2.0
Fruit	0.0	Fat	1.5

Preheat oven to 350 degrees.

In large bowl, combine turkey, bread crumbs, onion, egg whites, marjoram, oregano, basil, Spike, and pepper. This is best mixed with your hands. Slowly pour wine into turkey mixture. Mix with hands 1 minute or until mixture forms large ball.

Shape into small uniform meatballs, and place in shallow, ungreased, nonstick baking pan. Place pan under broiler until meatballs are browned.

Cover meatballs with tomato sauce. Bake 30 to 35 minutes or until meatballs are firm and no longer pink in center and sauce is bubbly. Spoon meatballs and sauce over cooked pasta, rice, or polenta.

Italian Turkey Burgers

Serves 4

1/2 lb. turkey, ground
1/4 cup egg substitute, or 2 egg whites
3/4 cup Italian-flavored bread crumbs
1 cup white mushrooms, thinly sliced
1/2 cup red wine
1/2 cup plain nonfat yogurt
Vegetable cooking spray

Nutritional Data

PER SERVING:

Calories	200
% calories from fat	22
Fat (gm)	4.9
Sat. Fat (gm)	1.4
Cholesterol (mg)	21.6
Sodium (mg)	684
Protein (gm)	14.1
Carbohydrate (gm)	19.6

EXCHANGES:

Milk	0.0	Bread	1.0
Veg.	0.0	Meat	1.5
Fruit	0.0	Fat	1.0

With your hands, combine turkey with egg substitute. Separate mixture into 4 balls, then flatten into patties. Pour bread crumbs onto plate. Coat turkey burgers with bread crumbs.

Coat large nonstick skillet with cooking spray. Add turkey burgers, and cook over medium heat 3 to 5 minutes on each side or until golden brown and center is no longer pink. Remove from heat.

Transfer turkey burgers to shallow baking dish and place in 275-degree oven to keep warm.

In same pan, sauté mushrooms 5 minutes or until softened. Stir wine and yogurt into pan, and bring liquid to boil.

Remove turkey from oven and place on individual dinner plates or serving platter. Serve turkey burgers with sauce.

Deviled Dogs

Serves 4

- 4 turkey wieners, split lengthwise
- 4 hot dog buns
- 1 16-oz. can vegetarian beans
- 2 teaspoons mustard
- 2 ozs. low-fat taco cheese, shredded
- 1 cup tomato, chopped
- 1 cup scallions, chopped
- ¼ cup jalapeño peppers, chopped (use caution; wear rubber gloves and do not rub your eyes)

Nutritional Data

PER SERVING:

Calories	373
% calories from fat	30
Fat (gm)	13.1
Sat. Fat (gm)	3.4
Cholesterol (mg)	63.2
Sodium (mg)	1558
Protein (gm)	20.7
Carbohydrate (gm)	47.2

EXCHANGES:

Milk	0.0	Bread	2.0
Veg.	4.0	Meat	1.0
Fruit	0.0	Fat	2.0

Preheat oven to 350 degrees. Place wieners in buns. Mix remaining ingredients in bowl. Place hot dogs in square baking dish. Spoon bean mixture over wieners. Bake until warm, about 20 minutes.

Note: You can also grill hot dogs on barbecue grill and heat beans and vegetables before spooning over hot dogs.

Tex-Mex Pitas with Homemade Salsa

Serves 8

½ cup plain low-fat yogurt
¼ cup Salsa (recipe follows)
1 lb. turkey, ground
1 tablespoon garlic, minced
1 teaspoon pepper, cracked
1 tablespoon chili powder
1 cup onion, chopped
1 can zesty tomato soup
4 pita breads, cut in half
   Shredded lettuce
1 cup tomato, diced

Nutritional Data

PER SERVING:

Calories	219
% calories from fat	25
Fat (gm)	6.3
Sat. Fat (gm)	1.6
Cholesterol (mg)	22.7
Sodium (mg)	484
Protein (gm)	12.5
Carbohydrate (gm)	30.2

EXCHANGES:

Milk	0.0	Bread	1.5
Veg.	1.0	Meat	1.5
Fruit	0.0	Fat	0.0

Combine yogurt and Salsa and set aside. Cook turkey, garlic, pepper, chili powder, and onion in pot until meat loses its pink color. Drain off spices. Return meat to pot and add tomato soup.

Cook 15 minutes on medium heat. Adjust seasonings if needed. Spread some salsa mixture into each pita half, then spoon in turkey filling. Garnish with shredded lettuce and tomato.

Salsa

Serves 16

3 large vine-ripened tomatoes, seeded and chopped
¾ cup green onions, chopped
3 tablespoons green chilies, minced (use jalapeño if you want it hot; don't forget to wear gloves)
1 tablespoon cilantro, minced
½ teapoon celery seed
1 tablespoon red wine vinegar
   Black pepper, freshly ground

Place all ingredients in bowl and mix well. Chill before serving. Makes 2+ cups.

Grilled Cornish Hens with Fruit Sauce

Serves 6

3 Cornish hens, all visible fat and skin removed
1/4 cup whole cloves, soaked briefly in water, drained
1 large lemon, cut into 6 wedges, divided
1½ cups Fruit Sauce (recipe follows)
Nonstick cooking spray

Nutritional Data

PER SERVING:

Calories	353
% calories from fat	30
Fat (gm)	11.6
Sat. Fat (gm)	3.2
Cholesterol (mg)	137.7
Sodium (mg)	233
Protein (gm)	44.9
Carbohydrate (gm)	12.2

EXCHANGES:

Milk	0.0	Bread	0.0
Veg.	0.0	Meat	5.5
Fruit	1.0	Fat	0.0

Wash and pat dry hens. Prepare barbecue grill for indirect grilling method. When briquets become ashen, sprinkle drained cloves over them as an aromatic.

Place 1 lemon wedge in each hen cavity, and arrange hens on grill coated with cooking spray, breast side up, over drip pan. Grill, covered, over indirect heat 45 minutes or until joints move easily and juices run clear when hens are pierced in thigh with fork.

Cut hens in half and transfer to serving platter. Discard cooked lemon wedges and garnish with remaining wedges. Pass Fruit Sauce at table.

Fruit Sauce

½ cup port wine
½ cup cranberry juice
1/4 cup cherry all-fruit preserves
2 tablespoons fresh lemon juice
1/4 teaspoon nutmeg, freshly grated
1/4 teaspoon salt
1/4 teaspoon black pepper, freshly ground

Combine all ingredients in small saucepan, and bring to boil over medium heat. Reduce heat and simmer 5 minutes or until preserves are dissolved and sauce is hot. Serve warm with Grilled Cornish Hens. Makes 1½ cups.

Cornish Hens with Grilled Papaya

Serves 6

Papaya Basting Sauce

1 ripe papaya, peeled, seeded, and cut into
   ½-inch cubes (1½ cups)
½ cup fresh orange juice

Cornish Hens

3 Cornish hens (about 2 lbs.)
   Vegetable cooking spray

Grilled Papaya

3 tablespoons light brown sugar
2 teaspoons light rum
1 ripe papaya, sliced, seeds removed
   (1½ cups)

Nutritional Data

PER SERVING:

Calories	359
% calories from fat	30
Fat (gm)	11.6
Sat. Fat (gm)	3.2
Cholesterol (mg)	137.7
Sodium (mg)	137
Protein (gm)	45.2
Carbohydrate (gm)	15.7

EXCHANGES:

Milk	0.0	Bread	0.0
Veg.	0.0	Meat	5.5
Fruit	1.0	Fat	0.0

Papaya Basting Sauce: Place papaya cubes in food processor fitted with steel blade and puree. Add orange juice and pulse to combine.

Cornish Hens: Wash and dry hens. Butterfly hens by cutting down length of backbone with kitchen scissors or poultry shears. Remove skin. Open bird to flat position. Use heel of your hand to pound sharply on breastbone until it cracks and hens lie flat. Brush hens with Papaya Basting Sauce.

Prepare grill. When coals become ashen, place butterflied hens, skin side up, over coals on grid coated with cooking spray. Grill, covered, over direct heat about 20 minutes, turning every 4 minutes with long-handled tongs. Brush hens twice more with basting sauce as you turn them. Hens are done if juices run clear when pricked with fork. Pass extra basting sauce at table or pour over hens before serving.

Grilled Papaya: Five minutes before hens are done, mix sugar and rum together. Brush cut sides of papaya slices with sugar-rum mixture. Place papaya slices on grill screen 1 minute.

Arrange hens and papaya slices on serving platter and bring to table.

Chapter Six

MEATS:
BEEF, VEAL,
LAMB & PORK

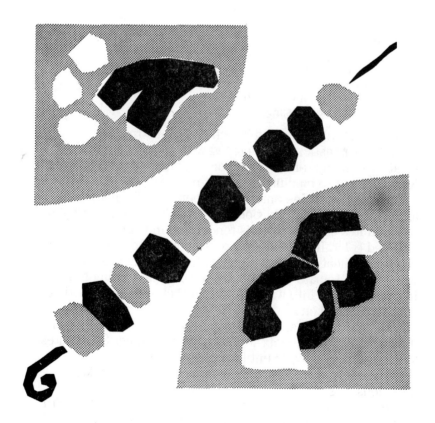

Beef Stroganoff

Serves 7

1 lb. beef top round, trimmed of all fat
1 large onion, finely chopped
½ lb. mushrooms, washed, trimmed, and sliced
2 large cloves garlic, minced
2 teaspoons canola margarine, or corn oil margarine
2 cups defatted beef broth, divided
¼ cup red Burgundy wine
3 tablespoons tomato paste
¼ cup water
1 tablespoon white flour
2 teaspoons granulated sugar
1 teaspoon dried thyme leaves
1 teaspoon prepared horseradish
1 large bay leaf
¼ teaspoon black pepper
¼ teaspoon salt, or to taste (optional)
¾ cup nonfat sour cream

To Serve

1½ cups uncooked long-grain white rice, or 10 to 12 ozs. uncooked medium non-fat noodles
Parsley sprigs for garnish (optional)
Vegetable cooking spray

Nutritional Data

PER SERVING:

Calories	301
% calories from fat	11
Fat (gm)	3.7
Sat. Fat (gm)	0.8
Cholesterol (mg)	39.9
Sodium (mg)	210
Protein (gm)	23.3
Carbohydrate (gm)	42.1

EXCHANGES:

Milk	0.0	Bread	2.0
Veg.	1.0	Meat	2.5
Fruit	0.0	Fat	0.0

Cut meat into very thin 2-inch diagonal strips.

In large nonstick skillet coated with cooking spray, cook meat over medium-high heat 6 or 7 minutes or until browned. Remove meat to medium bowl and reserve.

In skillet, combine onion, mushrooms, garlic, margarine, and 3 tablespoons broth. Cook over medium heat, stirring, 6 to 7 minutes or until onion is tender and mushrooms have changed color. If liquid begins to evaporate, add more broth.

Return meat to skillet, along with remaining broth and wine. Stir in tomato paste until well combined. Bring to boil. In cup, stir flour into water. Add to skillet and cook, stirring, until liquid thickens.

Add sugar, thyme, horseradish, bay leaf, pepper, and salt, if desired, and stir to mix well. Cover and simmer 30 minutes, stirring occasionally, or until meat is tender.

Meanwhile, cook rice or noodles according to package directions.

Reduce heat under skillet so that liquid does not boil. Stir sour cream into broth. Heat 2 or 3 minutes more.

Serve individual portions of Beef Stroganoff over rice or noodles, or arrange rice on serving platter and top with Beef Stroganoff. Garnish with parsly sprigs, if desired.

30-Minute Beef Paprikash

Serves 5

1 lb. boneless beef top sirloin steak, cut 1-inch thick
1 tablespoon vegetable oil
2 medium onions, sliced
1 16-oz. package sauerkraut, rinsed and drained
1 tablespoon paprika
¼ cup water
1 13¾ to 14¼-oz. can ready-to-serve beef broth
½ cup water
¼ cup tomato paste (half of 6-oz. can)
½ teaspoon caraway seed
⅛ teaspoon red pepper, ground
3½ cups uncooked medium noodles
   Parsley, chopped
¼ cup dairy sour half-and-half

Nutritional Data

PER SERVING:

Calories	389
% calories from fat	32
Fat (gm)	13.9
Sat. Fat (gm)	4.9
Cholesterol (mg)	110.7
Sodium (mg)	1060
Protein (gm)	34.8
Carbohydrate (gm)	31.5

EXCHANGES:

Milk	0.0	Bread	1.5
Veg.	2.0	Meat	4.0
Fruit	0.0	Fat	0.0

Trim fat from beef steak. Cut beef into 1-inch pieces and then cut each in half. In large skillet or Dutch oven, heat oil over medium-high heat until hot. Add beef (half at a time) and stir-fry 1½ to 2 minutes or until outside surface is no longer pink. Remove from skillet with slotted spoon; set aside.

In same skillet, add onions, sauerkraut, paprika, and ¼ cup water. Cook and stir until onions are tender, about 3 minutes. Stir in broth, ½ cup water, tomato paste, caraway seed, red pepper, and noodles, stirring to separate noodles. Bring to boil; reduce heat to medium. Cover tightly and simmer 10 minutes or until noodles are tender.

Remove from heat; return beef to skillet. Cover and let stand 1 minute. Sprinkle with parsley; serve with sour half-and-half.

Italian Beef
Stir-Fry with Pasta

Serves 4

1	lb. beef round tip steaks, cut ⅛- to ¼-inch thick
1½	cups uncooked medium shell or farfalle (bow tie) pasta
1	tablespoon olive oil
2	cloves garlic, crushed
¼	teaspoon salt
⅛	teaspoon pepper
3	cups (8 ozs.) mushrooms, sliced
1	cup cherry tomato halves
¼	cup prepared fat-free Italian dressing
1	tablespoon Parmesan cheese, freshly grated
1	tablespoon parsley, chopped

Nutritional Data

PER SERVING:

Calories	353
% calories from fat	24
Fat (gm)	9.5
Sat. Fat (gm)	2.5
Cholesterol (mg)	64.7
Sodium (mg)	434
Protein (gm)	29.8
Carbohydrate (gm)	36.1

EXCHANGES:

Milk	0.0	Bread	2.0
Veg.	1.0	Meat	3.5
Fruit	0.0	Fat	0.0

Cook pasta according to package directions. Keep warm.

Meanwhile, stack beef steaks; cut lengthwise in half and then crosswise into 1-inch-wide strips. In large nonstick skillet, heat oil over medium-high heat until hot. Add beef and garlic (half at a time) and stir-fry 1 minute or until outside surface is no longer pink. (Do not overcook.) Season with salt and pepper. Remove from skillet with slotted spoon; keep warm.

In same skillet, add mushrooms; stir-fry 3 minutes or until tender. Return beef to skillet and add tomatoes and dressing; heat through.

Spoon beef mixture over hot pasta; sprinkle with cheese and parsley.

Beef and Tomato
Stir-Fry

Serves 5

1	cup uncooked long-grain white rice
	Marinade and Beef
¾	lb. beef flank steak
3	tablespoons dry sherry
2	tablespoons reduced-sodium soy sauce
1	teaspoon five-spice powder
1½	teaspoons rice vinegar
¼	teaspoon ground ginger
	Dash black pepper
2-3	drops hot oil (optional)
1	tablespoon cornstarch

Nutritional Data

PER SERVING:

Calories	325
% calories from fat	23
Fat (gm)	8.1
Sat. Fat (gm)	2.5
Cholesterol (mg)	31.5
Sodium (mg)	311
Protein (gm)	17.8
Carbohydrate (gm)	42.7

Sauce and Vegetables

2 large tomatoes
1 tablespoon sesame oil
1 medium yellow or white onion, sliced into rings
3/4 cup defatted reduced-sodium chicken broth, or regular defatted chicken broth, divided
1 tablespoon brown sauce
2 teaspoons rice vinegar
1 8-oz. can sliced water chestnuts, drained
2 tablespoons green onion, chopped
1/4 teaspoon salt, or to taste (optional)
Additional sliced green onion tops for garnish (optional)

EXCHANGES:			
Milk	0.0	Bread	2.0
Veg.	2.0	Meat	2.0
Fruit	0.0	Fat	0.5

Cook rice according to package directions.

Marinade and Beef: With sharp knife, cut flank steak diagonally into thin strips, trimming away and discarding all visible fat.

In medium bowl, mix together sherry, soy sauce, five-spice powder, vinegar, ginger, pepper, and hot oil, if desired. Stir to mix well. Add cornstarch and stir to incorporate thoroughly. Add beef and stir to coat well. Set aside 15 to 20 minutes, stirring occasionally.

Sauce and Vegetables: While beef is marinating, remove skins from tomatoes easily by filling a Dutch oven or large saucepan with about 5 inches of water. Bring to boil over high heat. When water boils, add tomatoes and cook 1 minute, stirring. Remove tomatoes from boiling water, and place in colander under cold running water. When tomatoes are cool enough to handle, pull off skin and discard. Core and chop tomatoes, and set aside in medium bowl.

Combine sesame oil, onion, and 2 tablespoons broth in large, nonstick skillet. Cook over medium heat, stirring frequently, until onion is almost tender, 4 or 5 minutes. Remove beef from marinade with slotted spoon and add to skillet. Cook, stirring, until beef is browned, about 2 to 3 minutes. Add remaining marinade to skillet along with remaining broth. Raise heat and cook, stirring, until mixture has thickened slightly and boils.

Stir in brown sauce and vinegar. Add tomato pieces, water chestnuts, green onion, and salt, if desired. Bring to simmer. Lower heat and simmer 2 minutes or until tomato is slightly cooked. Serve beef mixture over rice. Garnish with additional chopped green onion tops, if desired.

Wok Steak with
☗ Sweet-and-Sour Sauce

Serves 6

1 recipe Sweet-and-Sour Sauce (recipe follows)
1 tablespoon vegetable oil
1 medium onion, sliced
1 large zucchini, cut into half-dollar slices
½ lb. pea pods
½ lb. mushrooms, sliced
½ 8-oz. can water chestnuts, sliced
1 lb. beef fillet, or London broil, thinly sliced
2 tablespoons sesame seeds

Nutritional Data

PER SERVING:

Calories	220
% calories from fat	34
Fat (gm)	8.9
Sat. Fat (gm)	2.4
Cholesterol (mg)	42.7
Sodium (mg)	256
Protein (gm)	18.3
Carbohydrate (gm)	17.8

EXCHANGES:

Milk	0.0	Bread	0.5
Veg.	2.0	Meat	2.0
Fruit	0.0	Fat	0.5

Prepare Sweet-and-Sour Sauce; set aside.

In wok or skillet, heat 2 tablespoons oil. Add vegetables in order of listing, allowing 1 minute cooking time between each addition. Move vegetables to one side of wok and place steak in oil.

Cook about 1 minute and turn; cook 1 minute more. Toss steak with vegetables. Add Sweet-and-Sour Sauce and sesame seeds. Heat 1 minute. Serve immediately.

Sweet-and-Sour Sauce

1 tablespoon cornstarch
⅓ cup chicken broth
⅓ cup red wine vinegar
2 tablespoons frozen concentrated pineapple juice
2 tablespoons chopped pimiento
1 tablespoon soy sauce
¼ teaspoon garlic powder
¼ teaspoon ground ginger
1 teaspoon sugar

Nutritional Data

PER SERVING:

Calories	10
% calories from fat	2
Fat (gm)	0
Sat. Fat (gm)	0
Cholesterol (mg)	0
Sodium (mg)	81
Protein (gm)	0.2
Carbohydrate (gm)	2.2

EXCHANGES:

Milk	0.0	Bread	0.0
Veg.	0.0	Meat	0.0
Fruit	0.0	Fat	0.0

Combine cornstarch and chicken broth in small saucepan. Stir in all remaining ingredients. Cook over medium heat, stirring, until thickened and bubbly. Serve warm. Makes 1 cup.

Pepper Steak

Serves 4

1⅓ lbs. sirloin steak
2 tablespoons ground black peppercorns
¼ cup Armagnac
2 tablespoons Dijon mustard
2 tablespoons evaporated skim milk
Vegetable cooking spray

Heat skillet coated with vegetable cooking spray. Sprinkle meat with pepper, and place into hot pan. Cook on both sides. Flambé with Armagnac.

Remove meat from skillet, and place on plate. Add mustard and evaporated skim milk to skillet, and stir well. Simmer to desired consistency. Taste, and add more pepper if desired. Pour sauce over meat, and serve.

Nutritional Data

PER SERVING:

Calories	294
% calories from fat	27
Fat (gm)	8.7
Sat. Fat (gm)	3.3
Cholesterol (mg)	108.2
Sodium (mg)	189
Protein (gm)	37.8
Carbohydrate (gm)	7.7

EXCHANGES:

Milk	0.0	Bread	0.0
Veg.	0.0	Meat	5.5
Fruit	0.0	Fat	0.0

Beef Kabobs

Serves 6

Balsamic Brushing Sauce

1 teaspoon canola oil
⅓ cup balsamic vinegar
½ teaspoon dry mustard
½ teaspoon dried basil
¼ cup fresh cilantro, or parsley, chopped

Kabobs

6 wooden skewers, soaked in cold water 20 minutes and drained
1 lb. lean beef tenderloin, or other lean beef, trimmed of all fat and cut into 1-inch pieces
½ lb. large fresh mushrooms, cleaned and trimmed
2 red bell peppers, seeded and cut into squares
6 small summer squash, cut into halves
Vegetable cooking spray

Nutritional Data

PER SERVING:

Calories	160
% calories from fat	34
Fat (gm)	6.1
Sat. Fat (gm)	2
Cholesterol (mg)	42.6
Sodium (mg)	38
Protein (gm)	16.3
Carbohydrate (gm)	10.5

EXCHANGES:

Milk	0.0	Bread	0.0
Veg.	2.0	Meat	2.0
Fruit	0.0	Fat	0.0

Prepare barbecue grill. You can impart additional flavor to meat by adding 3 to 4 cups hickory chips that have been soaked in cold water 15 minutes and drained.

Balsamic Brushing Sauce: Combine ingredients in small bowl, and place bowl near grill.

Kabobs: Thread each skewer alternatively with beef, mushrooms, peppers, and squash. Brush with sauce.

When coals are ashen, coat grill rack with cooking spray and place it on grill. Grill kabobs 9 to 12 minutes, rotating them every 3 to 4 minutes and brushing them with sauce when you turn. Meat should be done to just medium for best results. Serve on bed of rice (not included in nutritional data).

Steak on a Skewer

Serves 6

- 1²/₃ lbs. lean beef steaks, sirloin or fillet
- 2 tablespoons low-fat beef broth
- 2 tablespoons red wine
- 1 clove garlic, crushed
- 1 teaspoon Spike (see "About This Cookbook")
- ¼ teaspoon black pepper, freshly ground
- ¼ teaspoon sugar
- 1 teaspoon rosemary, crushed
- 1 large tomato, cut into eighths

Nutritional Data

PER SERVING:

Calories	168
% calories from fat	28
Fat (gm)	5.1
Sat. Fat (gm)	1.9
Cholesterol (mg)	63.5
Sodium (mg)	63
Protein (gm)	26.9
Carbohydrate (gm)	1.6

EXCHANGES:

Milk	0.0	Bread	0.0
Veg.	0.0	Meat	3.5
Fruit	0.0	Fat	0.0

Cut steak into ½-inch cubes. Combine other ingredients except tomato, and marinate steak 3 or 4 hours in mixture.

String on 6 long skewers, putting each tomato wedge after 2 or 3 steak cubes. Broil 3 minutes near heat, brush with marinade, turn, brush again, and broil 2 minutes more. Brush with marinade again before serving.

Barbecued Steak with Tarragon

Serves 4

Tarragon Drizzle

1 teaspoon canola oil
2 tablespoons red wine vinegar
1 tablespoon fresh tarragon, or ½ tablespoon dried tarragon

Tarragon Dressing

Vegetable cooking spray
1 teaspoon canola oil
3 medium shallots, minced
2 cloves garlic, minced
2 teaspoons sugar
2 tablespoons tarragon vinegar
¾ cup tomato puree
¼ teaspoon salt
½ teaspoon dried tarragon
⅛ teaspoon pepper, freshly ground

Steak

1 lb. eye of round steak, trimmed of all fat

Nutritional Data	
PER SERVING:	
Calories	232
% calories from fat	31
Fat (gm)	7.7
Sat. Fat (gm)	2
Cholesterol (mg)	72
Sodium (mg)	374
Protein (gm)	28.3
Carbohydrate (gm)	9.5

EXCHANGES:			
Milk	0.0	Bread	0.0
Veg.	1.0	Meat	4.0
Fruit	0.0	Fat	0.0

Tarragon Drizzle: Mix together all ingredients. Brush steak and let it stand 1 hour in refrigerator.

Tarragon Dressing: Coat nonstick saucepan with cooking spray. Heat oil. Add shallots and garlic, and sauté over medium heat 3 to 4 minutes or until tender, stirring often to make sure they don't brown. Add sugar, vinegar, and tomato puree. Simmer sauce a few minutes. Season with salt, tarragon, and pepper; set aside.

Steak: Prepare barbecue grill for direct method of cooking. Place steak on coated grate. Cook 2 minutes on each side, then continue grilling until steak is done to your taste. (If you prefer it slightly pink in the center, it will take 4 to 8 minutes more of grilling, depending on thickness of meat.)

Place meat on platter and let it rest 5 minutes. Meanwhile, reheat dressing. Slice steak into thin strips across grain, and drizzle with Tarragon Dressing. Serve hot.

Steak Da Vinci

Serves 4

1¼ lbs. lean, boneless beef round steak
    Vegetable cooking spray
1   cup onion, chopped
1   cup green bell pepper, chopped
1   clove garlic, minced
¼   cup dried shallots
1   14½-oz. can whole tomatoes, undrained
    and chopped
1   teaspoon beef-flavored bouillon granules
1   teaspoon oregano
½   teaspoon basil
1   teaspoon garlic powder
½   cup mushrooms, sliced
2   cups hot, cooked linguine
4   tablespoons parsley, chopped
¼   cup Parmesan cheese, freshly grated

Nutritional Data

PER SERVING:

Calories	359
% calories from fat	21
Fat (gm)	8.3
Sat. Fat (gm)	3.1
Cholesterol (mg)	80.8
Sodium (mg)	587
Protein (gm)	36.8
Carbohydrate (gm)	34.3

EXCHANGES:

Milk	0.0	Bread	1.5
Veg.	2.0	Meat	3.5
Fruit	0.0	Fat	0.0

Trim any fat from steak and cut steak into 1-inch cubes. Coat large nonstick skillet with cooking spray; place over medium-high heat until hot. Add steak and cook until browned. Remove from skillet; set aside.

Rinse skillet under hot water and dry. Coat again with cooking spray. Add onion, green pepper, garlic, and shallots to skillet and sauté about 3 minutes or until tender. Return steak to skillet; add tomatoes and next 4 ingredients, stirring well.

Cover meat mixture, reduce heat, and simmer about 30 minutes. Add mushrooms and simmer another 30 minutes. Uncover and cook mixture an additional 15 minutes or until meat is tender. Serve meat over linguine and sprinkle with parsley and cheese.

Swiss Steak

Serves 6

1½ lbs. round Steak, ½-inch thick
1   teaspoon instant meat tenderizer
¼   cup flour
1½ teaspoons Spike (see "About This
    Cookbook")
1   teaspoon garlic powder
1   medium onion, sliced thin
1   16-oz. can tomatoes
½   cup mushrooms, sliced

Nutritional Data

PER SERVING:

Calories	180
% calories from fat	23
Fat (gm)	4.5
Sat. Fat (gm)	1.4
Cholesterol (mg)	60.6
Sodium (mg)	469
Protein (gm)	24.2
Carbohydrate (gm)	9.8

EXCHANGES:

Milk	0.0	Bread	0.0
Veg.	1.0	Meat	3.0
Fruit	0.0	Fat	0.0

Pound steak with mallet until about ¼-inch thick. Cut meat into 6 pieces. Sprinkle with tenderizer, then coat with mixture of flour, Spike, and garlic powder. Place in 3-quart casserole. Cover with onion.

Break up tomatoes with fork and pour over top. Add mushrooms and stir. Cover dish and place in microwave. Cook 12 minutes on High. Rearrange meat so bottom pieces are on top. Cover and continue cooking 10 to 12 minutes or until tender.

To Freeze: Place in microwave-safe container; label and freeze for up to 2 months.

To Serve: Thaw. Cover with microwave-safe plastic wrap, and cook on High 3 to 5 minutes.

🔥 *Grilled Steak Salad*

Serves 4

Steak and Marinade

4 ozs. boneless, lean, choice sirloin, trimmed of all fat
2 tablespoons shallot, minced
1 teaspoon fresh thyme, minced
¼ cup diet French dressing
   Salt and pepper, freshly ground, to taste
   Olive-oil-flavored vegetable cooking spray

Salad Mixture

¾ cup spinach leaves, washed and trimmed
¾ cup curly endive, cut into 2-inch pieces
¾ cup mâche (lamb's lettuce), washed and left whole
1 head radicchio leaves, cut into 2-inch pieces
¾ cup Napa cabbage, cut into 2-inch pieces
1 cup carrots, julienned
1 cup pea pods
¼ cup diet French dressing

Nutritional Data

PER SERVING:

Calories	138
% calories from fat	29
Fat (gm)	4.6
Sat. Fat (gm)	1.3
Cholesterol (mg)	20.9
Sodium (mg)	299
Protein (gm)	8.8
Carbohydrate (gm)	16

EXCHANGES:

Milk	0.0	Bread	0.0
Veg.	3.0	Meat	1.0
Fruit	0.0	Fat	0.0

Steak and Marinade: Place meat in pan and add shallots, thyme, and salad dressing. Season lightly with salt and pepper. Place in refrigerator 1 hour.

Salad Mixture: Combine all ingredients, except French dressing, in large bowl, cover with damp towel, and refrigerate until needed.

While coals are heating, remove salad mixture from refrigerator and let stand at room temperature. When coals are ashen, toss salad mixture with salad dressing and divide among 4 serving plates.

Remove steaks from marinade and place on grill coated with cooking spray. Sear 2 minutes on each side. Continue grilling 8 to 10 minutes, turning once, until steak is pink in center or until done to your taste.

Transfer steak to cutting surface, let stand 10 minutes, and slice very thin on diagonal, across grain. Place slices on top of each salad. Drizzle with remaining dressing, or serve dressing on the side.

Steak 'n Salad with Yogurt Horseradish Sauce

Serves 6

Yogurt Horseradish Sauce

2	cups plain nonfat yogurt
2	tablespoons prepared white horseradish
¼	cup parsley, minced

Steak

1¼	lbs. boneless sirloin steak, trimmed of all fat
¼	tablespoon black pepper, freshly ground
2	cloves garlic, minced
	Olive-oil-flavored vegetable cooking spray

Salad

2	heads red leaf lettuce, washed and dried
2	tomatoes, sliced thinly
1	medium red onion, sliced thinly
½	teaspoon salt
¼	teaspoon black pepper, freshly ground

Nutritional Data

PER SERVING:

Calories	254
% calories from fat	32
Fat (gm)	9
Sat. Fat (gm)	3.4
Cholesterol (mg)	64.3
Sodium (mg)	309
Protein (gm)	28.4
Carbohydrate (gm)	14.3

EXCHANGES:

Milk	0.5	Bread	0.0
Veg.	1.5	Meat	3.0
Fruit	0.0	Fat	0.0

Yogurt Horseradish Sauce: Spoon yogurt into bowl and blend in horseradish and parsley. Cover and refrigerate until needed. Stir before serving.

Steak: When coals are ashen, sprinkle both sides of meat with pepper and garlic. Place steak on grate coated with cooking spray and sear 1 minute on each side. Continue grilling 5 minutes on each side or until steak is pink in center or done to your taste. Transfer meat to platter and let stand 10 minutes. Slice it thin, against grain.

Salad: Divide lettuce leaves evenly among 6 plates, add tomato and onion slices, and sprinkle with salt and pepper. Arrange meat slices over salad and top with large dollop of Yogurt Horseradish Sauce. Pass extra sauce at table.

⛭ Pot Roast of Beef

Serves 6

6 potatoes, peeled and sliced
6 carrots, peeled and sliced
2 onions, peeled and sliced
2 ribs of celery with tops, sliced
1 3-lb. beef chuck arm roast
   Pepper, to taste
½ cup Beef Stock (see p. 40)

Nutritional Data

PER SERVING:

Calories	425
% calories from fat	25
Fat (gm)	11.7
Sat. Fat (gm)	4.2
Cholesterol (mg)	161
Sodium (mg)	134
Protein (gm)	54.9
Carbohydrate (gm)	22.3

EXCHANGES:

Milk	0.0	Bread	1.0
Veg.	1.5	Meat	7.0
Fruit	0.0	Fat	0.0

Put vegetables in crockpot. Season meat with pepper and place in pot. Add Beef Stock. Cover and cook on Low 10 to 12 hours or on High 4 to 5 hours. Remove meat and vegetables.

To Freeze: Place in microwave-safe container; label and freeze for up to 2 months.

To Serve: Thaw, then microwave on High 7 to 9 minutes.

Note: Freezing and Serving instructions are the same for the six variations that follow.

POT ROAST OF BEEF VARIATIONS (all serve 6)

German Style: Add 3 or 4 medium dill pickles, 1 teaspoon dill weed, and 1 tablespoon wine vinegar.

Nutritional Data

PER SERVING:

Calories	428
% calories from fat	25
Fat (gm)	11.7
Sat. Fat (gm)	4.2
Cholesterol (mg)	161
Sodium (mg)	599
Protein (gm)	54.9
Carbohydrate (gm)	23

EXCHANGES:

Milk	0.0	Bread	1.0
Veg.	1.5	Meat	7.0
Fruit	0.0	Fat	0.0

Italian Style: Add 1 cup of tomato sauce, 1 teaspoon oregano, and 1 teaspoon basil.

Nutritional Data

PER SERVING:

Calories	439
% calories from fat	25
Fat (gm)	11.8
Sat. Fat (gm)	4.2
Cholesterol (mg)	161
Sodium (mg)	382
Protein (gm)	55.5
Carbohydrate (gm)	25.5

EXCHANGES:

Milk	0.0	Bread	1.0
Veg.	1.5	Meat	7.0
Fruit	0.0	Fat	0.0

Chinese Style: Add white part of 4 medium green onions, 2 tablespoons chopped ginger root, 1 tablespoon minced garlic, 1 cup water, 3 table-spoons low-sodium soy sauce. Garnish with peel of 1 orange.

Nutritional Data

PER SERVING:

Calories	433
% calories from fat	25
Fat (gm)	11.7
Sat. Fat (gm)	4.2
Cholesterol (mg)	161
Sodium (mg)	399
Protein (gm)	55.7
Carbohydrate (gm)	23.5

EXCHANGES:

Milk	0.0	Bread	1.0
Veg.	1.5	Meat	7.0
Fruit	0.0	Fat	0.0

Mexican Style: Add ½ cup chopped green onion, 1 tablespoon minced garlic, 1 cup beef broth mixed with 2 tablespoons tomato paste, and ¼ cup chili powder. Garnish with ¼ cup raisins.

Nutritional Data

PER SERVING:

Calories	451
% calories from fat	26
Fat (gm)	12.8
Sat. Fat (gm)	4.3
Cholesterol (mg)	161
Sodium (mg)	360
Protein (gm)	56.3
Carbohydrate (gm)	26.7

EXCHANGES:

Milk	0.0	Bread	1.0
Veg.	1.5	Meat	7.0
Fruit	0.0	Fat	0.0

Scandinavian Style: Add 1 cup thinly sliced onions, 12 oz. beef broth, or 1¼ cups beef stock, 2 tablespoons cider vinegar, and 2 tablespoons sugar. Garnish with fresh dill.

Nutritional Data

PER SERVING:

Calories	455
% calories from fat	24
Fat (gm)	11.9
Sat. Fat (gm)	4.3
Cholesterol (mg)	161
Sodium (mg)	298
Protein (gm)	55.7
Carbohydrate (gm)	29.1

EXCHANGES:

Milk	0.0	Bread	1.0
Veg.	2.0	Meat	7.0
Fruit	0.0	Fat	0.0

French Style: Add 1 cup fresh sliced mushrooms, 1 lb. small peeled onions, and 1 cup red wine.

Nutritional Data

PER SERVING:

Calories	484
% calories from fat	22
Fat (gm)	11.9
Sat. Fat (gm)	4.2
Cholesterol (mg)	161
Sodium (mg)	163
Protein (gm)	56.1
Carbohydrate (gm)	30

EXCHANGES:

Milk	0.0	Bread	1.0
Veg.	3.0	Meat	7.0
Fruit	0.0	Fat	0.0

Oriental Sliced Beef

Serves 4

- 2 tablespoons reduced-sodium soy sauce
- 2 tablespoons water
- 1 teaspoon sesame oil
- 1 clove garlic, minced
- 1 teaspoon Dijon mustard
- 1 teaspoon ginger root, peeled and grated
- 1 lb. beef eye of round steak, sliced thin across the grain (this is done more easily if steak is partially frozen)
- 1 red bell pepper, julienned
- 4 scallions, chopped
- 1 teaspoon toasted sesame seeds (optional)
  Parsley, chopped, for garnish

Nutritional Data

PER SERVING:

Calories	145
% calories from fat	26
Fat (gm)	4
Sat. Fat (gm)	1.2
Cholesterol (mg)	54.2
Sodium (mg)	330
Protein (gm)	23.7
Carbohydrate (gm)	2.4

EXCHANGES:

Milk	0.0	Bread	0.0
Veg.	0.0	Meat	3.0
Fruit	0.0	Fat	0.0

Blend first 6 ingredients and place in 2-quart casserole. Add sliced meat and stir to coat. Mix in peppers and scallions. Microwave on High 3 to 4 minutes, stirring once.

Remove from oven and check for doneness. Some pieces may be more rare than others, and your choice will dictate further cooking for another minute or so. Garnish with sesame seeds and chopped parsley.

Sukiyaki

Serves 6

- 4½ cups water, divided
- 5 ozs. transparent noodles (bean threads), uncooked
- ¼ cup sugar
- 2 tablespoons soy sauce
- ¼ cup sake (rice wine)
- ¼ teaspoon beef-flavored bouillon granules
- 1 lb. lean, boneless sirloin steak

Nutritional Data

PER SERVING:

Calories	300
% calories from fat	21
Fat (gm)	7
Sat. Fat (gm)	2.8
Cholesterol (mg)	50.4
Sodium (mg)	435
Protein (gm)	19.8
Carbohydrate (gm)	37.7

1	cup carrots, diagonally sliced
2	medium onions, cut into thin strips
6	green onions, cut into 1½-inch pieces
2	cups mushrooms, sliced
4	cups packed Chinese cabbage leaves
1	cup bamboo shoots

EXCHANGES:

Milk	0.0	Bread	2.0
Veg.	1.5	Meat	2.0
Fruit	0.0	Fat	0.0

Bring 4 cups water to boil in large stockpot; add noodles and cook 2 minutes. Drain. Cut noodles with kitchen shears into 3-inch pieces. Set aside.

Combine ¼ cup water, sugar, soy sauce, sake, and bouillon granules in bowl. Mix well and set aside.

Partially freeze steak about 20 minutes. Slice it diagonally, across.grain, into ¹⁄₁₆-inch strips. Set aside.

Heat remaining ¼ cup water in wok. Add beef; stir-fry 2 to 3 minutes. Add ¼ cup soy sauce mixture and carrots; stir-fry 1 minute, stirring frequently. Add onions; stir-fry 3 minutes. Add mushrooms; stir-fry 30 seconds. Add noodles and ¼ cup soy sauce mixture; stir-fry 2 minutes. Add Chinese cabbage, bamboo shoots, and remaining soy sauce mixture; toss well. Serve warm.

To Freeze: Place in microwave-safe container; label and freeze for up to 2 months.

To Serve: Thaw, then place in microwave on High 7 to 9 minutes.

Satay-Style Beef and Pasta

Serves 5

1	lb. boneless beef top sirloin, or top round steak, cut 1-inch thick, or flank steak
2	tablespoons teriyaki sauce
6	ozs. uncooked vermicelli, or thin spaghetti
	Vegetable cooking spray
½	cup cucumber, seeded and chopped

Peanut Butter Sauce

3	tablespoons teriyaki sauce
2	tablespoons creamy peanut butter
1	tablespoon water
⅛-¼	teaspoon ground ginger
⅛-¼	teaspoon crushed red pepper

Nutritional Data

PER SERVING:

Calories	332
% calories from fat	30
Fat (gm)	11.1
Sat. Fat (gm)	3.6
Cholesterol (mg)	55.9
Sodium (mg)	762
Protein (gm)	25.5
Carbohydrate (gm)	31.7

EXCHANGES:

Milk	0.0	Bread	2.0
Veg.	0.0	Meat	3.0
Fruit	0.0	Fat	0.5

Trim fat from beef steak. Cut steak lengthwise in half, then crosswise into ⅛-inch-thick strips. Add 2 tablespoons teriyaki sauce to beef; toss to coat.

Cook vermicelli according to package directions. Meanwhile, in medium bowl, combine sauce ingredients, mixing until well blended. Add hot vermicelli; toss to coat. Keep warm.

Coat large nonstick skillet with cooking spray. Heat over medium-high heat until hot. Add beef (half at a time) and stir-fry 1 to 2 minutes or until outside surface is no longer pink. (Do not overcook.) Add to vermicelli mixture; toss lightly. Sprinkle with cucumber; serve immediately.

Weeknight Beef Stew

Serves 4

- 2 cups cooked pot roast, beef cubed
- 2 medium red potatoes, cut into 1/4-inch-thick slices
- 2/3 cup water
- 1 teaspoon dried oregano leaves
- 1/2 teaspoon salt
- 1 cup frozen peas
- 2 teaspoons cornstarch, dissolved in 1 tablespoon fresh lemon juice

Nutritional Data

PER SERVING:

Calories	227
% calories from fat	24
Fat (gm)	5.9
Sat. Fat (gm)	2.2
Cholesterol (mg)	57.3
Sodium (mg)	342
Protein (gm)	22
Carbohydrate (gm)	20.7

EXCHANGES:

Milk	0.0	Bread	1.5
Veg.	0.0	Meat	2.5
Fruit	0.0	Fat	0.0

In medium saucepan, combine beef, potatoes, water, oregano, and salt. Bring to boil; reduce heat to low. Cover tightly and simmer 10 to 12 minutes or until potatoes are tender. Stir in peas; heat through. Add cornstarch mixture; cook and stir 1 minute or until sauce is thickened and bubbly.

Crockpot Beef Stew

Serves 6

- 1 large onion, finely chopped
- 2 cloves garlic, minced
- 1 lb. all-purpose potatoes, peeled or unpeeled, and cut into 3/4-inch cubes (about 3 1/2 cups)
- 1 1/2 cups coarsely shredded cabbage
- 1 large carrot, peeled and sliced
- 1/4 cup uncooked long-grain white rice
- 1 lb. beef round, trimmed of all fat and cut into small, bite-size pieces
- 1 1/2 cups defatted beef broth, or bouillon
- 3/4 cup red wine
- 1/4 cup ketchup
- 2 teaspoons packed light brown sugar
- 1/2 tablespoon apple cider vinegar
- 1 1/2 teaspoons dried thyme leaves
- 1 teaspoon chili powder
- 1/2 teaspoon dry mustard
- 1/4 teaspoon black pepper

Nutritional Data

PER SERVING:

Calories	304
% calories from fat	11
Fat (gm)	3.6
Sat. Fat (gm)	1
Cholesterol (mg)	40.5
Sodium (mg)	294
Protein (gm)	20.2
Carbohydrate (gm)	44.3

EXCHANGES:

Milk	0.0	Bread	2.5
Veg.	1.0	Meat	2.0
Fruit	0.0	Fat	0.0

In large crockpot, combine onion, garlic, potatoes, cabbage, carrot, and rice. Add meat. In 4-cup measure or similar bowl, stir together broth, wine, ketchup, brown sugar, vinegar, thyme, chili powder, mustard, and black pepper. Pour mixture over meat and vegetables. Cover crockpot and cook 1 hour on High. Stir meat and vegetables into sauce, and cook an additional 6½ to 8 hours on Low.

Beef Ragout

Serves 8

- 2 lbs. lean beef, cut into 1-inch cubes
- 3 cups beef broth
- 1 clove garlic, chopped
- ½ teaspoon pepper, freshly ground
- 1 teaspoon oregano
- 1 teaspoon thyme
- 2 cups carrots, sliced
- 2 cups celery, sliced
- ½ lb. small white onions
  Flour (optional)

Nutritional Data

PER SERVING:

Calories	215
% calories from fat	35
Fat (gm)	8.4
Sat. Fat (gm)	2.9
Cholesterol (mg)	77.2
Sodium (mg)	386
Protein (gm)	27.1
Carbohydrate (gm)	7.2

EXCHANGES:

Milk	0.0	Bread	0.0
Veg.	1.0	Meat	3.5
Fruit	0.0	Fat	0.0

Place beef on cookie sheet under broiler, turning to brown evenly. Put into pot with broth, garlic, pepper, oregano, and thyme. Cover, and simmer for 1 to 1½ hours until meat is almost tender.

Add carrots and celery and cook for 20 minutes. Add onions and cook for 15 minutes more. Remove garlic, taste for seasoning, and thicken, if you wish, with flour-and-water paste (not included in Nutritional Data).

⛯ Boeuf Bourguignon
(Beef Stew with Wine)

Serves 8

  Vegetable cooking spray
- 3 lbs. beef rump or chuck, cut into 1½-inch cubes
- 1 large carrot, peeled and sliced
- 1 medium onion, sliced
- 3 tablespoons flour
- 2 cups Beef Stock (see p. 40)
- 1 tablespoon tomato paste
- 2 cloves garlic, minced
- 1 tablespoon thyme
- 1 teaspoon tarragon
- 1 bay leaf

Nutritional Data

PER SERVING:

Calories	301
% calories from fat	24
Fat (gm)	8.1
Sat. Fat (gm)	2.8
Cholesterol (mg)	121.1
Sodium (mg)	113
Protein (gm)	41.9
Carbohydrate (gm)	11.1

EXCHANGES:

Milk	0.0	Bread	0.0
Veg.	2.0	Meat	5.0
Fruit	0.0	Fat	0.0

½   lb. white onions, peeled, or 1 jar
     white onions
1   lb. mushrooms, sliced
½   cup red or Burgundy wine

Heat skillet and coat with cooking spray. Brown beef, carrots, and onion well. Add flour and Beef Stock. Mix well. Transfer to crockpot. Add tomato paste, garlic, thyme, tarragon, bay leaf, and onions. Cover and cook on Low 8 to 10 hours. Add mushrooms and wine about 1 hour before serving.

To Freeze: Vacuum seal each portion; label and freeze for up to 2 months.

To Serve: Put bags in boiling water, and bring water to boil again. Boil 10 to 12 minutes.

Attila's Beef Goulash

Serves 4

1   lb. boneless, lean beef chuck, trimmed of all fat and cut into 1-inch cubes
3   medium onions, chopped
1   large green bell pepper, chopped (about 2 cups)
3   cloves garlic, minced
1   teaspoon olive oil
2   tablespoons Hungarian paprika
¼   teaspoon salt
¼   teaspoon black pepper
1   tablespoon balsamic vinegar
1   cup tomato sauce
1   cup mushrooms, sliced

Nutritional Data

PER SERVING:

Calories	268
% calories from fat	23
Fat (gm)	7
Sat. Fat (gm)	2.1
Cholesterol (mg)	79.1
Sodium (mg)	563
Protein (gm)	29.7
Carbohydrate (gm)	23.7

EXCHANGES:

Milk	0.0	Bread	0.0
Veg.	3.0	Meat	3.5
Fruit	0.0	Fat	0.0

Heat browning dish for 5 minutes on High. When ready, remove from oven and place beef cubes on dish, turning as they brown. Microwave on High 4 minutes, stirring once. Drain.

Place onions, green pepper, garlic, and oil in 2-quart measure and microwave on High 5 minutes, stirring once or twice. Meantime, combine paprika, salt, and pepper and stir into meat. Add vinegar and tomato sauce.

When vegetables are soft, turn meat mixture into measuring cup and stir to blend. Cover with vented plastic wrap, and microwave on High 5 minutes. Stir and return to oven. Microwave on Medium (50%) for 30 minutes, stirring a few times. During last 10 minutes, add mushrooms.

Let rest 5 to 10 minutes before serving with noodles, rice, or potatoes. (Goulash is even better if served the following day.)

For a variation, add ¼ cup nonfat plain yogurt, if desired.

Shepherd's Pie

Serves 7

Beef Filling

1   lb. beef round steak
1   large onion, finely chopped
1   clove garlic, minced
2   teaspoons olive oil
1¼   cups defatted beef broth, divided
1   8-oz. can tomato sauce
2   medium carrots, peeled and thinly sliced
2   celery stalks, thinly sliced
2   cups 2-inch-long green bean pieces, stem
     ends removed
2   large bay leaves
1   teaspoon dried thyme leaves
½   teaspoon dried marjoram leaves
¼   teaspoon dry mustard
¼   teaspoon black pepper
¼   teaspoon salt, or to taste (optional)
     Dash cayenne pepper
     Vegetable cooking spray

Potato Topping

4   cups all-purpose potatoes, peeled and cut
     into 1-inch cubes
¼   cup 1% fat milk (approximate)
⅓   cup nonfat yogurt
1   oz. (¼ cup) reduced-fat sharp Cheddar
     cheese, grated
1   tablespoon canola margarine, or corn oil
     margarine
½   teaspoon salt, scant, or to taste (optional)
⅛   teaspoon, generous, white pepper

Nutritional Data

PER SERVING:

Calories	282
% calories from fat	20
Fat (gm)	6.6
Sat. Fat (gm)	1.5
Cholesterol (mg)	37.4
Sodium (mg)	393
Protein (gm)	19.4
Carbohydrate (gm)	37.9

EXCHANGES:

Milk	0.0	Bread	2.0
Veg.	1.0	Meat	2.0
Fruit	0.0	Fat	0.0

Preheat oven to 350 degrees.

Beef Filling: Trim off and discard all fat from meat. Cut into very thin 2-inch-long diagonal strips.

In Dutch oven or large ovenproof pot coated with cooking spray, brown meat over medium-high heat, about 6 or 7 minutes. Remove meat to medium-size bowl and reserve.

In Dutch oven, combine onion, garlic, oil, and 3 tablespoons broth. Cook over medium heat, stirring, 6 to 7 minutes or until onion is tender. If liquid begins to evaporate, add more broth.

Return meat to pot with onion and garlic.

Stir in tomato sauce and remaining beef broth. Stir in carrots, celery, and green beans. Add bay leaves, thyme, marjoram, mustard, pepper, salt, if desired, and cayenne pepper. Stir to mix well. Bake, covered, 1 hour or until meat is tender.

Potato Topping: Meanwhile, in large saucepan, combine potatoes and enough water to cover. Cover and bring to boil over high heat. Lower heat and simmer 15 to 17 minutes or until potatoes are very tender. Drain potatoes well in colander.

Return potatoes to pot in which they were cooked, and add remaining topping ingredients. Mash with potato masher. If mixture seems too stiff to spread, add a bit more milk.

Remove stew from oven and uncover. Drop Potato Topping by large spoonfuls onto bubbling mixture. Carefully spread out topping with back of large spoon, making attractive peaks.

Return to oven and bake, uncovered, 17 to 20 minutes or until potatoes are heated through and begin to brown.

Grilled Stuffed Pepper Slices

Serves 8

- ½ lb. lean beef, ground
- ½ cup dry bread crumbs
- ½ teaspoon ground ginger
- 2 cloves garlic, minced
- ¼ teaspoon salt
- ¼ teaspoon black pepper, freshly ground
- ⅓ cup onion, chopped
- ¼ cup water chestnuts, minced
- 2 tablespoons dry white wine
- 2 teaspoons low-salt soy sauce
- 4 large red bell peppers, seeded and quartered along natural lines
  Olive-oil-flavored vegetable cooking spray

Nutritional Data

PER SERVING:

Calories	98
% calories from fat	35
Fat (gm)	3.8
Sat. Fat (gm)	1.4
Cholesterol (mg)	17.6
Sodium (mg)	173
Protein (gm)	6.8
Carbohydrate (gm)	8.5

EXCHANGES:

Milk	0.0	Bread	0.0
Veg.	1.5	Meat	1.0
Fruit	0.0	Fat	0.0

Combine ground beef and bread crumbs in deep bowl. Mix in ginger, garlic, salt, pepper, onion, water chestnuts, wine, and soy sauce. Stuff and mound mixture into pepper quarters.

When barbecue coals are hot, place stuffed peppers, meat side down, on grill rack coated with cooking spray, 4 to 6 inches from heat source. Cook stuffed peppers 3 minutes. Using long-handled spatula, turn each pepper over and continue grilling 2 to 4 minutes or until meat is cooked through. Peppers will be charred.

Transfer peppers to serving dish and serve hot. Try serving with whole scallions, lightly coated with cooking spray and grilled 1 to 2 minutes on each side.

Easy Beef Stuffed Peppers

Serves 4

4 medium green, red, or yellow bell peppers

Filling

3/4 lb. lean beef, ground
3/4 cup onions, chopped
1 cup cooked rice
1 tablespoon ketchup
1/2 teaspoon dried oregano leaves
1/2 teaspoon salt (optional)
1/4 teaspoon pepper

Topping

1 14 1/2-oz. can Italian-style tomatoes, diced and undrained
1 tablespoon ketchup
1/2 teaspoon dried oregano leaves

Nutritional Data

PER SERVING:

Calories	275
% calories from fat	35
Fat (gm)	10.9
Sat. Fat (gm)	4.2
Cholesterol (mg)	52.8
Sodium (mg)	315
Protein (gm)	19.2
Carbohydrate (gm)	25.5

EXCHANGES:

Milk	0.0	Bread	1.0
Veg.	2.0	Meat	2.0
Fruit	0.0	Fat	1.0

Preheat oven to 350 degrees. Cut bell peppers lengthwise in half; remove seeds. Place cut side down in microwave-safe oblong baking dish. Microwave, uncovered, at High 4 minutes. Turn cut side up.

Filling: In medium bowl, combine filling ingredients, mixing lightly but thoroughly. Spoon about 1/2 cup beef mixture into each bell pepper half.

Topping: In small bowl, combine topping ingredients; spoon over bell pepper halves. Cover dish tightly with foil. Bake 40 to 45 minutes or until beef mixture is cooked.

To serve, place peppers on serving platter. Spoon pan juices over top.

Dolmades
(Stuffed Grape Leaves)

Serves 12

2 lbs. ground turkey
2 egg whites
1/2 cup uncooked rice
1 medium onion, finely chopped
1 teaspoon Spike (see "About This Cookbook")
1/2 teaspoon pepper, freshly ground
1/2 teaspoon oregano
1/2 teaspoon garlic powder
1 1-lb. jar grape leaves in brine
1 46-oz. can low-sodium tomato juice

Nutritional Data

PER SERVING:

Calories	152
% calories from fat	34
Fat (gm)	5.8
Sat. Fat (gm)	1.6
Cholesterol (mg)	28.1
Sodium (mg)	58
Protein (gm)	12.5
Carbohydrate (gm)	12.7

EXCHANGES:

Milk	0.0	Bread	0.5
Veg.	1.0	Meat	1.5
Fruit	0.0	Fat	0.0

Mix first 8 ingredients well. Roll 1 rounded teaspoon of meat mixture in each grape leaf. Large leaves may be cut in half. Place veined, or underside, of leaf next to meat mixture. Fold leaves around meat; place in large flat pan or skillet. Cover with tomato juice. Simmer 1½ hours. Flavor is improved by reheating.

BBQ Beef and Potato Hash

Serves 4

- ¾ lb. cooked beef, cut into ½-inch pieces
- 2 tablespoons vegetable oil
- 3 cups frozen potatoes O'Brien
- 1 cup green, red, or yellow bell pepper, chopped
- ½ cup onion, chopped
- ¼ teaspoon pepper
- ¼ cup prepared barbecue sauce, or beef gravy

Nutritional Data

PER SERVING:

Calories	376
% calories from fat	34
Fat (gm)	14.1
Sat. Fat (gm)	4
Cholesterol (mg)	91.3
Sodium (mg)	567
Protein (gm)	32.3
Carbohydrate (gm)	29.7

EXCHANGES:

Milk	0.0	Bread	1.5
Veg.	1.0	Meat	4.0
Fruit	0.0	Fat	0.5

In large nonstick skillet, heat oil over medium-high heat until hot. Add potatoes, bell pepper, and onion; cook 10 to 15 minutes or until potatoes are browned and crisp, stirring occasionally.

Add beef and pepper; mix lightly. Stir in barbecue sauce and continue cooking 2 to 3 minutes or until heated through.

Confetti Sloppy Joes

Serves 4

- 1 lb. lean beef, ground
- 1 small onion, chopped
- ¾ cup prepared barbecue sauce
- ½ cup frozen corn, defrosted
- ¼ teaspoon salt (optional)
- ⅛ teaspoon pepper
- 4 hamburger buns, split
- ½ cup green bell pepper, chopped

Nutritional Data

PER SERVING:

Calories	422
% calories from fat	34
Fat (gm)	16.1
Sat. Fat (gm)	5.9
Cholesterol (mg)	70.4
Sodium (mg)	885
Protein (gm)	26.5
Carbohydrate (gm)	42.3

EXCHANGES:

Milk	0.0	Bread	2.0
Veg.	3.0	Meat	3.0
Fruit	0.0	Fat	1.0

In large nonstick skillet, brown ground beef and onion over medium heat 8 to 10 minutes or until beef is no longer pink, breaking up into 3/4-inch crumbles. Pour off drippings. Stir in barbecue sauce, corn, salt (optional), and pepper; heat through, stirring occasionally.

Spoon equal amount of beef mixture on bottom half of each bun; top with bell pepper. Close with top half of bun.

Beef and Bean Burritos

Serves 8

1   lb. lean beef, ground
1   medium onion, chopped
1   tablespoon Spicy Seasoning Mix
    (recipe follows)
½   teaspoon salt
1   8-oz. can tomato sauce
1   15-oz. can pinto beans, drained
    and mashed
8   flour tortillas (each about 8 inches),
    warmed
    Thinly sliced lettuce, chopped tomatoes,
    and sliced green onions (optional)

Nutritional Data

PER SERVING:

Calories	279
% calories from fat	31
Fat (gm)	9.7
Sat. Fat (gm)	3.1
Cholesterol (mg)	35.2
Sodium (mg)	728
Protein (gm)	16.8
Carbohydrate (gm)	31

EXCHANGES:

Milk	0.0	Bread	2.0
Veg.	0.0	Meat	2.0
Fruit	0.0	Fat	0.5

In large nonstick skillet, brown ground beef and onion over medium heat 8 to 10 minutes or until beef is no longer pink, breaking up into 3/4-inch crumbles. Pour off drippings.

Sprinkle Spicy Seasoning Mix and salt over beef. Stir in tomato sauce. Simmer 10 minutes, stirring occasionally. Stir in beans; heat through.

To assemble, spoon equal amount of beef mixture in center of each tortilla. Add lettuce, tomatoes, and green onions, if desired. Fold bottom edge up over filling. Fold right and left sides to center, overlapping edges.

Spicy Seasoning Mix

3   tablespoons chili powder
2   teaspoons ground cumin
1½   teaspoons garlic powder
¾   teaspoon dried oregano leaves
½   teaspoon ground red pepper

Combine all ingredients. Cover and store in airtight container. Shake before using to blend. Makes about 1/3 cup.

Tamale Pie

Serves 8

1 lb. beef round, ground
1 large onion, finely chopped
1 large green bell pepper, seeded and diced
1 clove garlic, minced
2 15-oz. cans tomato sauce
4 cups cooked kidney beans, or 2 16-oz. cans kidney beans, well drained
1½ cups frozen corn kernels
1 tablespoon chili powder, or to taste
1 teaspoon ground cumin
¼ teaspoon salt (optional)
¼ teaspoon black pepper
   Dash cayenne pepper (optional)
1 9-oz. package 6-inch-round corn tortillas

Nutritional Data

PER SERVING:

Calories	363
% calories from fat	20
Fat (gm)	8.5
Sat. Fat (gm)	2.9
Cholesterol (mg)	35.2
Sodium (mg)	738
Protein (gm)	23
Carbohydrate (gm)	52.1

EXCHANGES:

Milk	0.0	Bread	3.0
Veg.	1.5	Meat	2.0
Fruit	0.0	Fat	0.0

Conventional Method: Preheat oven to 350 degrees.

In 3-quart flameproof, ovenproof casserole, combine ground round, onion, green pepper, and garlic. Cook over medium heat, stirring frequently, until beef has changed color. Remove casserole from burner.

Turn out meat mixture onto large plate lined with paper towels to absorb any excess fat. Return to casserole. Add tomato sauce, kidney beans, corn, chili powder, cumin, salt, if desired, black pepper, and cayenne pepper, if desired. Stir to mix well. Scoop out 5 cups of mixture and reserve in medium-size bowl.

Lay half the tortillas over mixture remaining in casserole, overlapping and covering entire surface. Add 2½ cups of reserved meat and bean mixture over tortillas, spreading it out with back of large spoon. Lay remaining tortillas over mixture in casserole, overlapping and covering entire surface. Top with remaining meat and bean mixture, spreading it out evenly with tortillas.

Bake, uncovered, 45 to 50 minutes or until sauce begins to bubble and flavors are well blended.

Microwave Method: In 2½-quart microwave-safe casserole, stir together ground round, onion, green pepper, and garlic. Cover and microwave on High 6 to 8 minutes, stirring meat and breaking it up 1 or 2 times during microwaving, until meat is cooked through. With large soon, break up any remaining large pieces of meat.

Turn out meat mixture onto large plate lined with paper towels to absorb any excess fat. Return to casserole. Add tomato sauce, kidney beans, corn, chili powder, cumin, salt, if desired, black pepper, and cayenne pepper, if desired.

Stir to mix well. Layer casserole with tortillas as directed above under "conventional method."

Cover with casserole lid and microwave on High 15 to 17 minutes or until mixture is heated through and flavors are well blended. Allow casserole to rest on flat surface 5 minutes before serving.

 # Speedy Chili

Serves 8	Nutritional Data		
2 lbs. beef, ground	**PER SERVING:**		
Vegetable cooking spray	Calories		368
2 large onions, chopped	% calories from fat		36
3 cloves garlic, minced	Fat (gm)		14.8
½ teaspoon pepper, freshly ground	Sat. Fat (gm)		5.5
1 6-oz. can tomato paste	Cholesterol (mg)		70.4
2 10½-oz. cans zesty tomato sauce	Sodium (mg)		1079
2 15½-oz. cans kidney beans	Protein (gm)		29.7
2 tablespoons chili powder	Carbohydrate (gm)		30.9
1 teaspoon oregano			
2 tablespoons parsley, chopped	**EXCHANGES:**		
	Milk 0.0	Bread	1.0
	Veg. 3.0	Meat	3.0
	Fruit 0.0	Fat	1.0

Place ground beef in large saucepan coated with vegetable cooking spray. Add onions and garlic and sauté until meat is browned. Add remaining ingredients (except parsley) and bring to boil. Reduce heat to simmer, and simmer 15 minutes. Spoon into serving tureen and top with parsley.

To Freeze: Vacuum seal each portion; label and freeze for up to 2 months.

To Serve: Thaw in refrigerator or in bowl of water. Serve chilled.

20-Minute Beef Chili

Serves 4	Nutritional Data		
2 cups cooked pot roast, beef cubed	**PER SERVING:**		
1 8-oz. jar mild salsa	Calories		282
1 tablespoon chili powder	% calories from fat		29
1 15-oz. can low-sodium kidney beans,	Fat (gm)		9
drained and rinsed	Sat. Fat (gm)		4.3
½ cup Cheddar cheese, shredded	Cholesterol (mg)		72.2
¼ cup green onions, sliced	Sodium (mg)		651
	Protein (gm)		29.2
	Carbohydrate (gm)		21
	EXCHANGES:		
	Milk 0.0	Bread	1.5
	Veg. 0.0	Meat	3.0
	Fruit 0.0	Fat	0.0

In medium saucepan, combine beef, salsa, and chili powder. Bring to boil; reduce heat to low. Cover tightly and simmer 10 minutes. Stir in beans; heat through. Serve with cheese and green onions.

Meat Loaf Marvel

Serves 4

1	lb. ground beef top round steak	
1/4	cup green bell pepper, chopped	
1/4	cup red bell pepper, chopped	
3/4	cup onion, chopped	
3	cloves garlic, minced	
1/2	cup whole wheat bread crumbs	
1	tablespoon reduced-sodium soy sauce	
1	tablespoon mustard	
	Dash black pepper	
1	baby dill pickle, chopped	

Nutritional Data

PER SERVING:

Calories	242
% calories from fat	24
Fat (gm)	6.3
Sat. Fat (gm)	2
Cholesterol (mg)	72
Sodium (mg)	560
Protein (gm)	30
Carbohydrate (gm)	15

EXCHANGES:

Milk	0.0	Bread	0.5
Veg.	0.0	Meat	4.0
Fruit	0.0	Fat	0.0

Mix all ingredients together and mold into long, round loaf, about 2 inches deep. Arrange in circle on 9-inch pie plate or deep casserole. Microwave on High 3 to 4 minutes. Baste with sauce and drain off excess. After rotating plate, microwave on High another 3 to 4 minutes.

All-American Meat Loaf

Serves 8

Sauce

1/2	cup tomato sauce
1/2	cup barbecue sauce

Meat Loaf

1	lb. lean beef, ground
1	lb. turkey, ground
1	tablespoon garlic powder
1/4	teaspoon pepper, freshly ground
1/4	teaspoon allspice, ground
2	tablespoons Worcestershire sauce
1 1/2	cups quick rolled oats
1	can Campbell's zesty tomato soup
1/2	cup chili sauce
1/2	cup Mock Sour Cream (see p. 497)
2	tablespoons dried onions
2	egg whites
1/2	cup parsley, chopped
	Parsley sprigs

Nutritional Data

PER SERVING:

Calories	330
% calories from fat	35
Fat (gm)	12.9
Sat. Fat (gm)	4.2
Cholesterol (mg)	57.4
Sodium (mg)	882
Protein (gm)	24
Carbohydrate (gm)	29.2

EXCHANGES:

Milk	0.0	Bread	1.0
Veg.	3.0	Meat	3.0
Fruit	0.0	Fat	0.5

Sauce: In saucepan, combine sauce ingredients. Simmer, uncovered, about 15 minutes. Remove from heat and set aside.

Meat Loaf: Combine meat with all remaining ingredients except parsley sprigs. Form into 8" x 4" x 3" loaf. Place loaf in greased 9" x 13" glass baking dish. Cover with heavy foil. Chill 1 hour. Bring to room temperature.

Preheat oven to 350 degrees. Bake covered 1 hour. Drain meat and use paper towels to absorb any remaining juices. Spoon Sauce on top of meat loaf and bake uncovered 20 to 30 minutes or until loaf is glazed a dark brown. Turn off oven.

With door ajar, leave meat loaf in oven 10 minutes. Remove to platter and garnish with parsley.

Veal Marsala with Mushrooms

Serves 4

1	lb. veal, thinly sliced
	Vegetable cooking spray
½	teaspoon dried whole rosemary, crushed
¼	teaspoon Spike (see "About This Cookbook")
½	teaspoon pepper, freshly ground
1	teaspoon olive oil
2	cloves garlic, minced
2	cups mushrooms, sliced
1	teaspoon cornstarch
⅓	cup chicken broth
½	cup dry Marsala wine

Nutritional Data

PER SERVING:

Calories	159
% calories from fat	23
Fat (gm)	4.1
Sat. Fat (gm)	1.2
Cholesterol (mg)	80.5
Sodium (mg)	132
Protein (gm)	23.2
Carbohydrate (gm)	3.4

EXCHANGES:

Milk	0.0	Bread	0.0
Veg.	0.5	Meat	3.0
Fruit	0.0	Fat	0.0

Put veal between 2 pieces of wax paper and pound lightly. Coat skillet with cooking spray and add veal and seasonings. Sauté 2 minutes, then add olive oil and garlic. Sauté 2 more minutes, then add mushrooms.

While mushrooms are cooking, mix cornstarch in chicken broth and add to veal mixture along with wine. Cook on low heat about 10 more minutes.

Sautéed Veal with Peppers and Olives

Serves 4

1	lb. veal, thinly sliced and lightly pounded
¼	cup flour, for dusting
2	medium yellow bell peppers, cored and sliced
1	medium red bell pepper, cored and sliced
1	medium green bell pepper, cored and sliced
3	cloves garlic, minced
2	teaspoons fresh basil leaves

Nutritional Data

PER SERVING:

Calories	254
% calories from fat	15
Fat (gm)	4.5
Sat. Fat (gm)	1.1
Cholesterol (mg)	80.4
Sodium (mg)	224
Protein (gm)	25.8
Carbohydrate (gm)	17.6

1   teaspoon fresh rosemary leaves, lightly crushed (omit if only dried are available)
½   teaspoon fresh thyme leaves, or ¼ teaspoon dried thyme, crushed
Vegetable cooking spray (olive-oil flavored)
1½ cups ripe tomatoes, peeled, chopped, and seeded (canned chunky tomatoes may be used)
1   cup salt-free beef broth
1   cup dry red wine, such as zinfandel
¼   cup Marsala wine
6   pitted black olives, sliced
Juice of ½ lemon (1 tablespoon)
2   tablespoons fresh basil and parsley combined, chopped

EXCHANGES:

Milk	0.0	Bread	0.5
Veg.	2.0	Meat	3.0
Fruit	0.0	Fat	0.0

Cut veal into serving pieces and lightly dust with flour; set aside.

Coat skillet with vegetable cooking spray. Over high heat, sauté peppers, garlic, basil, rosemary, and thyme. Remove from skillet. In several batches, quickly sauté veal over high heat in same skillet until lightly browned. Remove from skillet and set aside with peppers.

Add tomatoes to skillet, along with broth, red wine, and Marsala, and boil to reduce in volume while you stir to blend brown bits left from sautéing. Cook to reduce to about 1 cup.

Return peppers and meat to sauce, toss in olives, and squeeze lemon juice over all. Serve immediately topped with basil and parsley.

Veal with Mushroom-Dijon Sauce

Serves 4

Sauce

3/₄ cup chicken broth
3/4 cup dry white wine
1   small onion, chopped
3   tablespoons fresh lemon juice
10 whole peppercorns
¼   cup chives, minced
2   tablespoons honey
2   teaspoons Dijon mustard
1½ cups mushrooms, sliced
2   tablespoons water
2   teaspoons all-purpose flour
¼   cup parsley, chopped
Lemon slices

Nutritional Data

PER SERVING:

Calories	526
% calories from fat	34
Fat (gm)	19.6
Sat. Fat (gm)	3.9
Cholesterol (mg)	161
Sodium (mg)	294
Protein (gm)	47.6
Carbohydrate (gm)	26.8

EXCHANGES:

Milk	0.0	Bread	1.0
Veg.	2.0	Meat	6.0
Fruit	0.0	Fat	1.5

Veal

2 lbs. veal scallops
   White pepper, to taste
½ cup all-purpose flour
¼ cup olive oil
   Juice of 1 lemon
½ cup dry white wine

Sauce: Combine chicken broth with next 5 ingredients in large pot. Bring mixture to boil over medium heat. Cover, reduce heat, and simmer 5 minutes. Strain cooking liquid; discard onion, peppercorns, and chives.

Add honey, mustard, and mushrooms to chicken broth; stir well. Bring to boil and cook 10 minutes.

Combine water and flour; stir well. Add to broth; cook 1 minute or until slightly thickened, stirring constantly. Remove from heat, add parsley and lemon slices, and prepare veal.

Veal: Pound veal scallops until they are flat, and season with pepper. Flour veal on one side only. Sauté on floured side in batches, using 2 tablespoons of olive oil for each batch, until veal turns white, about 45 to 60 seconds over medium-high heat.

Return all veal to skillet, add lemon juice and wine, and pour Sauce over veal; heat through. Arrange veal on serving platter and pour Sauce over. Sprinkle with parsley.

Veal Piccata

Serves 4

1   lb. veal, thinly sliced
3   tablespoons flour
      Vegetable cooking spray (olive-oil flavored)
1½   cups mushrooms, sliced
½   lemon
½   cup dry white wine
3   tablespoons parsley, chopped
8   lemon slices

Nutritional Data

PER SERVING:

Calories	171
% calories from fat	15
Fat (gm)	2.9
Sat. Fat (gm)	1
Cholesterol (mg)	80.4
Sodium (mg)	58
Protein (gm)	23.4
Carbohydrate (gm)	9

EXCHANGES:

Milk	0.0	Bread	0.5
Veg.	0.0	Meat	3.0
Fruit	0.0	Fat	0.0

Cut veal slices into serving pieces, then coat each piece with flour. Coat skillet with vegetable cooking spray and add veal. Cook over high heat until lightly browned on both sides. Add sliced mushrooms and sauté until lightly browned. Squeeze lemon over veal in pan; then add wine. Stir all ingredients, and cook 1 minute more. Arrange veal on serving platter, garnishing with parsley and lemon slices.

Veal Lady Sharon

Serves 4

Vegetable cooking spray
4 lean loin veal chops
Pepper, to taste
2 medium onions, chopped
1 lb. mushrooms, sliced
1 tablespoon flour
1 tablespoon tomato paste
3/4 cup Chicken Stock (see p. 40)
2/3 cup white wine
1 teaspoon Herbes de Provence
1 small bay leaf
1/2 cup pitted black olives, sliced (optional)
2 tablespoons parsley, minced

Nutritional Data

PER SERVING:

Calories	245
% calories from fat	24
Fat (gm)	6.7
Sat. Fat (gm)	2.3
Cholesterol (mg)	91.9
Sodium (mg)	126
Protein (gm)	26.6
Carbohydrate (gm)	13.4

EXCHANGES:

Milk	0.0	Bread	0.0
Veg.	2.0	Meat	3.0
Fruit	0.0	Fat	0.0

Preheat oven to 325 degrees.

In large saucepan coated with vegetable spray, quickly brown veal chops, seasoned with pepper. Transfer chops to shallow casserole.

In same stockpot, sauté onions. Add remaining ingredients except parsley. Cover and cook 5 minutes.

Pour mixture over chops and bake 1 hour. Sprinkle with parsley and serve.

Herbed Veal Chops

Serves 6

Vegetable cooking spray
6 small veal chops, trimmed
1 teaspoon Spike (see "About This Cookbook")
1/4 teaspoon pepper
2 tablespoons parsley, minced
1/2 teaspoon basil
1/2 teaspoon sage
1/3 cup white wine

Nutritional Data

PER SERVING:

Calories	176
% calories from fat	30
Fat (gm)	5.6
Sat. Fat (gm)	1.6
Cholesterol (mg)	100.1
Sodium (mg)	77
Protein (gm)	27.2
Carbohydrate (gm)	0.4

EXCHANGES:

Milk	0.0	Bread	0.0
Veg.	0.0	Meat	3.0
Fruit	0.0	Fat	0.0

Sauté veal chops in skillet coated with vegetable cooking spray over high heat, turning to brown evenly. Sprinkle with remaining ingredients except wine, and continue to cook over low heat for 10 minutes, turning several times. Add wine, and cook for 10 minutes more.

Remove chops to heated platter. Adjust seasoning of liquid. Stir, bring to boil, and pour over chops.

Veal Chops and Mushrooms

Serves 4

Vegetable cooking spray
4 lean loin veal chops
1 medium onion, chopped
1 lb. mushroom caps
1 8-oz. jar white onions
1 tablespoon flour
1 tablespoon tomato paste
3/4 cup chicken broth
2/3 cup dry white wine
1/4 cup dried shallots
1/4 cup chives, minced
1 teaspoon tarragon
1 teaspoon basil
1 small bay leaf

Nutritional Data

PER SERVING:

Calories	261
% calories from fat	23
Fat (gm)	6.9
Sat. Fat (gm)	2.4
Cholesterol (mg)	90.2
Sodium (mg)	270
Protein (gm)	27.5
Carbohydrate (gm)	16.9

EXCHANGES:

Milk	0.0	Bread	0.0
Veg.	3.0	Meat	3.5
Fruit	0.0	Fat	0.0

Preheat oven to 325 degrees.

Heat large heavy skillet coated with vegetable cooking spray. Brown veal chops quickly in skillet over high heat. Transfer chops to shallow casserole. In same skillet over medium heat, sauté onions. Add remaining ingredients except parsley.

Cover skillet and cook 5 minutes. Pour mixture over chops. Cover casserole. Bake 1 hour.

Veal Cutlets with Mushrooms

Serves 6

1/2 teaspoon salt
1/4 teaspoon pepper
1/4 teaspoon ground nutmeg
1 1/4 lbs. veal cutlets, thinly sliced
    Butter-flavored vegetable cooking spray
1 cup onion, sliced
2 cups mushrooms, sliced

Nutritional Data

PER SERVING:

Calories	104
% calories from fat	29
Fat (gm)	3.3
Sat. Fat (gm)	1.3
Cholesterol (mg)	59
Sodium (mg)	228
Protein (gm)	14.9
Carbohydrate (gm)	3.4

EXCHANGES:

Milk	0.0	Bread	0.0
Veg.	0.5	Meat	2.0
Fruit	0.0	Fat	0.0

Sprinkle salt, pepper, and nutmeg over veal cutlets and reserve. Coat non-stick skillet with cooking spray. Sauté onions and mushrooms until tender over medium heat, stirring occasionally. Partially cover if necessary. Add veal, brown quickly on both sides, but do not overcook. Remove veal to warm serving tray. Pour vegetables over veal. Serve with no-yolk noodles and nonfat sour cream (not included in nutritional data).

Veal Rolls with Mushrooms

Serves 8

Butter-flavored vegetable cooking spray
2 cloves garlic, minced
1 cup onion, sliced
1 lb. mushrooms, sliced
8 veal scallops (about 2 lbs.), pounded thin and trimmed of fat and membranes
¼ teaspoon salt
¼ teaspoon pepper
1 cup dry white wine
1 cup fat-free chicken broth

Nutritional Data

PER SERVING:

Calories	137
% calories from fat	27
Fat (gm)	4.1
Sat. Fat (gm)	1.5
Cholesterol (mg)	70.8
Sodium (mg)	143
Protein (gm)	18.6
Carbohydrate (gm)	4.8

EXCHANGES:

Milk	0.0	Bread	0.0
Veg.	1.0	Meat	2.0
Fruit	0.0	Fat	0.0

Coat large nonstick skillet with cooking spray. Sauté garlic and onion until tender over medium heat, stirring occasionally. Partially cover if necessary. Add mushrooms and sauté until tender; remove from heat.

Sprinkle veal with salt and pepper. Divide vegetables among veal scallops, and roll scallops up. Tie scallops with kitchen string.

Coat larger nonstick skillet with cooking spray, heat, and sauté veal rolls until golden brown on all sides; do not overcook. Pour wine and broth into skillet and cover. Simmer 10 to 15 minutes or until veal is tender. Place 1 veal roll on each plate; serve hot.

Veal Scallops with Lemon Sauce

Serves 6

Butter-flavored vegetable cooking spray
1½ lbs. veal scallops, flattened, fat and membranes removed
¼ cup all-purpose flour
2 tablespoons fresh lemon juice
1 tablespoon lemon zest
2 tablespoons cognac
2 large lemons, cut into wedges for garnish
½ cup parsley, chopped

Nutritional Data

PER SERVING:

Calories	130
% calories from fat	22
Fat (gm)	3.3
Sat. Fat (gm)	1.3
Cholesterol (mg)	59
Sodium (mg)	53
Protein (gm)	15.2
Carbohydrate (gm)	8.8

EXCHANGES:

Milk	0.0	Bread	0.0
Veg.	1.0	Meat	2.0
Fruit	0.0	Fat	0.0

Coat large skillet with cooking spray. Dust veal scallops with flour. Brown scallops lightly on both sides; do not overcook. Remove veal and place on heated serving dish. Add lemon juice, zest, and cognac to skillet and heat through. Drizzle over veal. Garnish with lemon wedges, and trim with parsley.

Veal Stew with Wine

Serves 6

Vegetable cooking spray
1 large onion, chopped
1 large clove garlic, minced
1½ lbs. lean veal, sliced
¼ cup water
½ cup tomato sauce
1 cup white wine
1 teaspoon Spike (see "About This Cookbook")
¼ teaspoon black pepper, freshly ground
Flour

Nutritional Data

PER SERVING:

Calories	256
% calories from fat	31
Fat (gm)	8.5
Sat. Fat (gm)	3.1
Cholesterol (mg)	128.1
Sodium (mg)	243
Protein (gm)	32.5
Carbohydrate (gm)	4.3

EXCHANGES:

Milk	0.0	Bread	0.0
Veg.	1.0	Meat	4.0
Fruit	0.0	Fat	0.0

In large saucepan coated with vegetable cooking spray, brown onion and garlic for 2 minutes. Add veal, and turn to brown evenly. Add remaining ingredients except flour, cover, and simmer until veal is tender, about 45 minutes. Add more wine or water if needed. Thicken juices with flour-and-water paste, and adjust seasoning.

Roast Leg of Lamb

Serves 8

Leg of lamb (about 4 lbs.)
3 cloves garlic, slivered
1 tablespoon rosemary
2 teaspoons Spike (see "About This Cookbook")
1/2 teaspoon black pepper, freshly ground
4 cups rice, cooked

Nutritional Data	
PER SERVING:	
Calories	353
% calories from fat	27
Fat (gm)	10.3
Sat. Fat (gm)	3.6
Cholesterol (mg)	114.7
Sodium (mg)	88.6
Protein (gm)	38.7
Carbohydrate (gm)	23

EXCHANGES:			
Milk	0.0	Bread	1.5
Veg.	0.0	Meat	4.5
Fruit	0.0	Fat	0.0

Preheat oven to 375 degrees. Wipe lamb, trim off fat, and make small slits in number of places with sharp knife. Insert garlic slivers, and rub with mixture of rosemary, Spike, and pepper.

Roast about 1 1/4 hours for rare lamb, 1 1/2 hours for pink, and up to 2 hours for well done. Do not cover. Serve with rice.

Oriental Lamb Chops

Serves 4

4 loin lamb chops
1/4 cup light, low-sodium soy sauce
4 cloves garlic, minced
2 cups rice, cooked

Nutritional Data	
PER SERVING:	
Calories	240
% calories from fat	20
Fat (gm)	5.2
Sat. Fat (gm)	1.8
Cholesterol (mg)	57.3
Sodium (mg)	573
Protein (gm)	22
Carbohydrate (gm)	24.2

EXCHANGES:			
Milk	0.0	Bread	1.5
Veg.	0.0	Meat	2.5
Fruit	0.0	Fat	0.0

Marinate lamb chops in soy sauce about 1/2 hour. Remove them from marinade and place on broiler pan. Pour marinade over chops, and spoon minced garlic onto chops. Broil chops 10 to 15 minutes on each side. Remove from broiler and serve with rice.

Savory Lamb Shanks

Serves 7

2 lbs. lamb shanks
1 tablespoon white flour
2 cups onion, chopped
2 cloves garlic, minced
2 teaspoons olive oil
2 cups defatted chicken broth, divided
1 14 1/2-oz. can tomatoes, undrained
2 large carrots, peeled and sliced
1/2 cup brown lentils

Nutritional Data	
PER SERVING:	
Calories	368
% calories from fat	20
Fat (gm)	8.1
Sat. Fat (gm)	2.3
Cholesterol (mg)	89.3
Sodium (mg)	268
Protein (gm)	33.6
Carbohydrate (gm)	40.1

1   medium green bell pepper, seeded
     and cubed
1/4 cup parsley leaves, chopped
2   bay leaves
2   teaspoons dried thyme leaves
1/4 teaspoon ground cinnamon
1/8 teaspoon ground cloves
1/8 teaspoon ground black pepper
1 1/4 cups uncooked brown rice
     Parsley sprigs for garnish (optional)

EXCHANGES:			
Milk	0.0	Bread	2.0
Veg.	2.0	Meat	3.0
Fruit	0.0	Fat	0.0

Preheat broiler. Adjust rack about 3 inches from heat.

In shallow baking pan, sprinkle flour over lamb shanks. Stir to coat with flour. Spread out pieces so they are separated from one another. Broil 10 to 14 minutes or until shanks are browned on all sides, turning once or twice. Remove from pan with slotted spoon.

Meanwhile, in Dutch oven or large heavy pot, combine onion, garlic, oil, and 3 tablespoons broth. Cook over medium heat, stirring, 6 or 7 minutes or until onion is tender. If liquid begins to evaporate, add a bit more broth.

Add lamb shanks to pot, along with remaining broth, tomatoes, carrots, lentils, green pepper, parsley, bay leaves, thyme, cinnamon, cloves, and black pepper. Stir to mix well, breaking up tomatoes with spoon. Bring to boil. Cover, reduce heat, and simmer 1 1/2 to 2 hours or until lamb shanks are tender, stirring occasionally.

After lamb has cooked about 1 hour, cook brown rice according to package directions.

Remove and discard bay leaves from lamb mixture. Remove and reserve lamb shanks. Carefully skim off and discard any fat from surface of liquid. When shanks are cool enough to handle, cut off lean meat and return it to pot. Discard bones and fat.

Arrange rice on serving platter. Top with lamb mixture.

Gingered Indian Lamb

Serves 4

1   lb. lean lamb
1/4 cup ginger root, peeled and chopped fine
1   medium onion, chopped rough
4   cloves garlic, smashed
8   ozs. canned Italian plum tomatoes, drained
     Juice of 1/2 lemon
1/4 teaspoon turmeric
1/4 teaspoon celery seed
1/2 teaspoon cumin

Nutritional Data

PER SERVING:

Calories	204
% calories from fat	25
Fat (gm)	5.8
Sat. Fat (gm)	1.9
Cholesterol (mg)	57.6
Sodium (mg)	204
Protein (gm)	22.6
Carbohydrate (gm)	15.7

1	tablespoon curry powder, mild or hot	EXCHANGES:			
1/4	cup nonfat plain yogurt	Milk	0.0	Bread	0.5
1	cup frozen peas	Veg.	1.0	Meat	2.5
1/2	cup mushrooms, sliced (optional)	Fruit	0.0	Fat	0.0

Trim all fat from lamb and cut, against grain, into 1-inch pieces. Place ginger root, onions, garlic, and tomatoes in 8" x 10" glass baking dish, and cover with vented plastic wrap. Microwave on High 2 minutes. Remove wrap and stir in all remaining ingredients except peas and mushrooms.

Cover and refrigerate a few hours or overnight. Stir from time to time. When ready to prepare for meal, remove from refrigerator and let rest at room temperature about 1/2 hour. Then cover with vented plastic wrap and microwave on High 5 minutes. Add peas and mushrooms, and microwave another 1 minute until warmed through.

Irish Stew

Serves 6

1 1/2	lbs. shoulder of lamb, cut into 1-inch cubes
6	white potatoes, thinly sliced
6	white onions
2 1/2	teaspoons Spike (see "About This Cookbook")
2	teaspoons rosemary
1/2	teaspoon thyme
6	carrots, sliced
1	bay leaf
2	cups water

Nutritional Data

PER SERVING:

Calories	318
% calories from fat	17
Fat (gm)	6
Sat. Fat (gm)	2
Cholesterol (mg)	67.6
Sodium (mg)	92
Protein (gm)	25
Carbohydrate (gm)	41.6

EXCHANGES:

Milk	0.0	Bread	2.0
Veg.	2.0	Meat	2.0
Fruit	0.0	Fat	0.0

Place lamb, potatoes, and onions in crockpot. Sprinkle with Spike, rosemary, and thyme. Place carrots in pot and mix well. Add bay leaf and water. Cover and cook on High 1 hour; turn to Low and cook additional 10 to 12 hours.

To Freeze: Vacuum seal individual portions; label and freeze for up to 2 months.

To Serve: Put bags in boiling water, and bring to boil again. Boil 10 to 12 minutes.

Grilled Minted Lamb Patties

Serves 8

1	lb. lean lamb, ground
1/2	cup onion, chopped
3	tablespoons parsley, minced
1/4	tablespoon salt
1/4	teaspoon pepper, freshly ground
2	tablespoons fresh lemon juice
1/4	cup cooked rice
1/4	teaspoon ground cinnamon
1/4	teaspoon ground allspice
3	teaspoons fresh or dried mint, chopped
	Olive-oil-flavored vegetable cooking spray

Nutritional Data

PER SERVING:

Calories	74
% calories from fat	32
Fat (gm)	2.5
Sat. Fat (gm)	0.9
Cholesterol (mg)	28.7
Sodium (mg)	89.8
Protein (gm)	9.4
Carbohydrate (gm)	2.8

EXCHANGES:

Milk	0.0	Bread	0.0
Veg.	0.0	Meat	1.5
Fruit	0.0	Fat	0.0

Combine ground lamb with all ingredients except cooking spray. Divide mixture into 8 equal portions. Form meat around bamboo skewers, which have been soaked in cold water for 15 minutes and drained. Refrigerate prepared skewers until barbecue grill is ready.

When coals are hot, place ground lamb skewers on grill rack coated with cooking spray 4 to 6 inches above heat source. Grill lamb about 6 minutes or until just cooked through, turning often.

Transfer meat to individual plates and serve with sliced cucumbers and tomatoes (not included in nutritional data).

Lamb Kabobs with Spicy Lemon Sauce

Serves 6

Sauce

1/2	cup boiling water
3	small, dried, hot red chilies, such as cayenne, tepin, or hontaka, crumbled
2	teaspoons cumin
2	teaspoons paprika
5	cloves garlic, minced
1/4	cup fresh lemon juice
2	tablespoons white wine
3	tablespoons fresh cilantro, chopped
1/2	lemon or lime, peel and all, finely chopped (you can do this in a food processor)

Nutritional Data

PER SERVING:

Calories	258
% calories from fat	34
Fat (gm)	9.6
Sat. Fat (gm)	3.3
Cholesterol (mg)	112.7
Sodium (mg)	102
Protein (gm)	36
Carbohydrate (gm)	5.8

EXCHANGES:

Milk	0.0	Bread	0.0
Veg.	1.0	Meat	4.5
Fruit	0.0	Fat	0.0

Lamb Kabobs

2½   lbs. lamb shoulder or leg, cut into
      ½-inch-thick slices
      Salt and pepper, to taste
1   teaspoon fresh thyme leaves, or ½ tea-
      spoon dried thyme
      Vegetable cooking spray
2-3   tomatoes, sliced

Sauce: Pour boiling water over crumbled chilies; let stand until it reaches room temperature. Puree mixture in blender or processor.

Combine cumin, paprika, and garlic with lemon juice. Stir in wine, cilantro, and lemon or lime. Add pureed chilies, and set sauce aside while you prepare meat.

Lamb Kabobs: Sprinkle meat with salt, pepper, and thyme. Either sauté in skillet coated with vegetable cooking spray, or thread meat onto skewers with tomatoes and grill until medium rare. When halfway cooked, spoon a little Sauce onto meat. Serve meat with remaining Sauce. Rice or potatoes and salad make good accompaniments.

Lamb-Stuffed Cabbage Rolls

Serves 6

1   red or white cabbage (about 2½-3 lbs.)
1   onion, minced
1   tablespoon safflower oil
1   teaspoon curry powder
1   lb. lean lamb, ground (beef may be
      substituted)
½   cup dry whole wheat bread crumbs
1   egg white
½   teaspoon black pepper, freshly ground
¼   teaspoon coriander, ground
1   8-oz. can tomato sauce

Nutritional Data

PER SERVING:

Calories	210
% calories from fat	26
Fat (gm)	6.3
Sat. Fat (gm)	1.4
Cholesterol (mg)	52.1
Sodium (mg)	372
Protein (gm)	19.7
Carbohydrate (gm)	20.1

EXCHANGES:

Milk	0.0	Bread	0.5
Veg.	2.0	Meat	2.5
Fruit	0.0	Fat	0.0

Remove and discard any discolored cabbage leaves and cut out core. Rinse cored cabbage and place on rack over boiling water. Cover and steam 5 minutes. Remove leaves with tongs until you have 12 leaves. Cut out thick part of rib along base of each leaf. Set aside.

Mix together remaining ingredients for filling (except tomato sauce) and place in microwave-safe bowl. Microwave on High 4 minutes.

Place 2 to 2½ tablespoons of filling on each leaf, roll one turn, tuck in sides, and continue to roll. Place rolls, seam side down, on plate. Set aside.

Shred remaining cabbage and place in shallow dish. Arrange cabbage rolls in circular pattern over cabbage. Place dish on rack over boiling water, cover pot, and steam 20 to 25 minutes. Serve with tomato sauce.

To Freeze: Place in microwave-safe container; label and freeze for up to 2 months.

To Serve: Thaw. Cover with microwave-safe plastic wrap, and cook on High 3 to 5 minutes.

Moussaka

Serves 10

3	medium eggplants, peeled
1	cup onion, finely chopped
1	tablespoon olive oil
1	lb. lean lamb, ground
1	lb. turkey, ground
1	cup drained canned or fresh tomatoes, or 3 tablespoons tomato paste
⅓	cup parsley, chopped
1	cup white wine
¼	teaspoon nutmeg
	Black pepper, freshly ground
3	egg whites
½	cup fine bread crumbs

Nutritional Data

PER SERVING:

Calories	195
% calories from fat	34
Fat (gm)	7.3
Sat. Fat (gm)	1.9
Cholesterol (mg)	39.8
Sodium (mg)	145
Protein (gm)	16.2
Carbohydrate (gm)	12.3

EXCHANGES:

Milk	0.0	Bread	0.0
Veg.	2.0	Meat	2.5
Fruit	0.0	Fat	0.0

Cut eggplants lengthwise into 1/4- to 1/2-inch-thick slices. Place in colander and set aside.

Meanwhile, sauté onion and ground meats in olive oil. Add tomatoes, parsley, and white wine and simmer gently about 45 minutes. Add nutmeg and black pepper.

Quickly sauté eggplant until lightly browned on all sides.

Beat 3 egg whites until stiff but not dry, and fold beaten whites with bread crumbs into cooked and cooled meat mixture.

Assemble ingredients in a 9" x 13" microwave-safe dish, layering eggplant, meat, and eggplant again. Microwave on High 25 minutes.

To Freeze: Place in microwave-safe container; label and freeze for up to 2 months.

To Serve: Thaw. Cover with microwave-safe plastic wrap, and cook on High 3 to 5 minutes.

Austrian Pork Loin with Apples and Cranberry Sauce

Serves 5

Pork and Fruit

- 1 lb. boneless pork loin, trimmed of all fat and cut into ¼-inch slices
- ½ teaspoon dried thyme leaves
- ¼ teaspoon black pepper
- ¼ teaspoon salt (optional)
- 1 cup onion, chopped
- 2 teaspoons nondiet, tub-style corn oil margarine, or canola margarine
- 2 large tart apples, peeled, cored, and thinly sliced
- 1 16-oz. can whole cranberry sauce
- 1 tablespoon Worcestershire sauce
- 1 tablespoon apple cider vinegar
- 2 tablespoons packed brown sugar

To Serve

- 8 ozs. reduced-fat egg noodles, cooked according to package directions

Nutritional Data

PER SERVING:

Calories	479
% calories from fat	17
Fat (gm)	9
Sat. Fat (gm)	2.6
Cholesterol (mg)	40.9
Sodium (mg)	115
Protein (gm)	19.7
Carbohydrate (gm)	81.6

EXCHANGES:

Milk	0.0	Bread	2.5
Veg.	0.0	Meat	2.0
Fruit	3.0	Fat	0.0

Sprinkle pork with thyme, pepper, and salt, if desired. In Dutch oven or large heavy pot, combine pork, onion, and margarine. Cook over medium heat, stirring frequently, until pork has changed color.

Add apples, cranberry sauce, Worcestershire sauce, vinegar, and brown sugar and stir to mix well. Bring to boil. Reduce heat, cover, and simmer 40 minutes, stirring occasionally, until pork is tender.

Serve over cooked noodles.

Pot-Roasted Pork

Serves 6

- 1 4-lb. boneless pork loin roast
- 1 tablespoon rosemary
- 1 teaspoon cracked pepper
- 1 clove garlic, sliced
- 2 medium onions, sliced
- 2 bay leaves
- 1 whole clove
- 1 cup hot water
- 2 tablespoons white wine

Nutritional Data

PER SERVING:

Calories	422
% calories from fat	34
Fat (gm)	15.5
Sat. Fat (gm)	5.3
Cholesterol (mg)	140.5
Sodium (mg)	161
Protein (gm)	62
Carbohydrate (gm)	4.4

Rub pork roast with rosemary and pepper. Make tiny slits in meat and insert slivers of garlic. Place roast in broiler pan and broil 15 minutes to remove excess fat.

EXCHANGES:
Milk	0.0	Bread	0.0
Veg.	1.0	Meat	7.5
Fruit	0.0	Fat	0.0

Put 1 sliced onion in bottom of crockpot. Add browned pork roast and remaining onion, along with other ingredients. Cover and cook on Low until done, about 10 hours.

Note: To thicken gravy, first remove roast to serving platter. Blend 2 tablespoons cornstarch with 2 tablespoons water to form smooth paste. Set crockpot on High and pour in paste. Stir well and let come to boil, about 15 minutes, until thickened.

To Freeze: Place in microwave-safe container; label and freeze for up to 2 months.

To Serve: Thaw. Microwave on High 12 to 14 minutes.

Pork with Hoisin Sauce

Serves 8

Pork and Marinade

- ½ cup dry white wine
- 2 cloves garlic, minced
- 2 tablespoons sugar
- 1 tablespoon low-salt soy sauce
- ⅓ cup hoisin sauce
- 1¾ lbs. lean pork tenderloin

Honey Brushing Sauce

- ¼ cup low-salt soy sauce
- 2 tablespoons honey

Nutritional Data

PER SERVING:

Calories	159
% calories from fat	21
Fat (gm)	3.7
Sat. Fat (gm)	1.3
Cholesterol (mg)	70.6
Sodium (mg)	383
Protein (gm)	22.8
Carbohydrate (gm)	7

EXCHANGES:

Milk	0.0	Bread	0.5
Veg.	0.0	Meat	2.5
Fruit	0.0	Fat	0.0

Pork and Marinade: Combine wine, garlic, sugar, soy sauce, and hoisin sauce. Put pork in large, self-sealing plastic bag and add marinade. Seal bag securely and turn several times so that all of pork is coated by marinade. Marinate pork in refrigerator 2 to 3 hours, turning occasionally.

Honey Brushing Sauce: Mix soy sauce and honey.

When barbecue coals are hot, remove pork from marinade. Place meat on grill rack 4 to 6 inches from heat source. Grill pork until done, turning and brushing with Honey Brushing Sauce every 2 to 3 minutes. Pork should be cooked through and golden brown on outside.

Transfer pork to platter and let stand 5 minutes. Cut pork into thin slices. This is good hot or cold.

🐷 Cantonese Pork Dinner

Serves 6

1½	lbs. pork steak, ½-inch thick, cut into strips
2	tablespoons vegetable oil
1	large onion, sliced
1	red bell pepper, cut into strips
1	cup fresh mushrooms
1	8-oz. can tomato sauce
3	tablespoons brown sugar
1½	tablespoons vinegar
2	teaspoons Worcestershire sauce
1	tablespoon sherry
3	cups cooked rice

Nutritional Data

PER SERVING:

Calories	354
% calories from fat	28
Fat (gm)	10.8
Sat. Fat (gm)	2.7
Cholesterol (mg)	53.5
Sodium (mg)	329
Protein (gm)	26.7
Carbohydrate (gm)	36.2

EXCHANGES:

Milk	0.0	Bread	2.0
Veg.	1.0	Meat	3.0
Fruit	0.0	Fat	1.0

Brown pork strips in oil to remove excess fat. Drain on paper towels. Place pork strips and remaining ingredients in crockpot and cover. Cook on Low 6 to 8 hours or High 4 hours. Serve over rice.

To Freeze: Vacuum seal each portion; label and freeze for up to 2 months.

To Serve: Put bags in boiling water, and bring water to boil again. Boil 10 to 12 minutes.

Pork and Vegetable Stir-Fry

Serves 4

1	lb. boneless pork loin, fat trimmed
4	teaspoons cornstarch
4	tablespoons sherry, or white wine
1	tablespoon vegetable oil
2	cloves garlic
3	teaspoons ginger root, peeled and minced
4	cups broccoli florets
2	zucchini, sliced ½-inch wide
¼	cup carrots, grated

Seasoning Sauce

4	tablespoons water
4	tablespoons sherry, or white wine
2	teaspoons cornstarch
2	teaspoons light soy sauce

Nutritional Data

PER SERVING:

Calories	276
% calories from fat	31
Fat (gm)	9.6
Sat. Fat (gm)	2.5
Cholesterol (mg)	52.7
Sodium (mg)	178
Protein (gm)	26.9
Carbohydrate (gm)	14

EXCHANGES:

Milk	0.0	Bread	0.5
Veg.	1.5	Meat	3.5
Fruit	0.0	Fat	0.0

Cut meat into thin strips, about 2 inches long.

In bowl, mix cornstarch and sherry, stir in meat, and let stand 10 minutes or longer until marinated (up to 2 hours).

In small bowl, combine Seasoning Sauce ingredients and mix well.

In wok, heat oil over high heat. Add garlic, ginger, and meat; stir-fry 1 minute. Add broccoli, zucchini, and carrot and stir-fry 2 minutes or until crisp-tender; add water if necessary to prevent scorching. Stir in Seasoning Sauce and stir-fry another minute.

To Freeze: Vacuum seal each portion; label and freeze for up to 2 months.

To Serve: Put bags in boiling water, and bring water to boil again. Boil 10 to 12 minutes.

Pork in Orange Sauce

Serves 4

1	tablespoon orange peel, finely shredded
½	cup orange juice
2	tablespoons soy sauce
2	teaspoons cornstarch
⅛	teaspoon ground ginger
2	large carrots, thinly sliced
2	stalks celery, chopped (1 cup)
	Vegetable cooking spray
1	lb. lean boneless pork loin, cut into ½-inch cubes
8	medium cashews (optional)
2	teaspoons sugar

Nutritional Data

PER SERVING:

Calories	202
% calories from fat	27
Fat (gm)	5.9
Sat. Fat (gm)	2
Cholesterol (mg)	52.7
Sodium (mg)	605
Protein (gm)	24.2
Carbohydrate (gm)	12.1

EXCHANGES:

Milk	0.0	Bread	0.0
Veg.	1.5	Meat	3.0
Fruit	0.0	Fat	0.0

Combine orange peel, orange juice, soy sauce, cornstarch, and ginger; set aside. Cook carrots and celery in skillet coated with vegetable cooking spray until tender. Remove. Add pork and cook 4 to 5 minutes or until browned. Add orange juice mixture, cashews, and sugar. Cook and stir until thickened and bubbly. Return vegetables to skillet. Cover and heat through 1 minute.

⬛ Sweet-and-Sour Pork

Serves 4

	Vegetable cooking spray
½	cup red bell pepper, cut in strips
¼	cup scallions, sliced
¼	cup carrots, shredded
2	cloves garlic, minced
1	lb. boneless pork loin, cut into cubes
½	cup Chicken Stock (see p. 40)

Nutritional Data

PER SERVING:

Calories	185
% calories from fat	29
Fat (gm)	5.8
Sat. Fat (gm)	2
Cholesterol (mg)	52.4
Sodium (mg)	235
Protein (gm)	23.5
Carbohydrate (gm)	8.7

2	teaspoons red wine vinegar
2	teaspoons soy sauce
1	teaspoon brown sugar, firmly packed
1	tablespoon water
2	teaspoons cornstarch
½	cup pineapple chunks (no sugar added)

EXCHANGES:

Milk	0.0	Bread	0.0
Veg.	1.5	Meat	3.0
Fruit	0.0	Fat	0.0

To sprayed, heated wok, add pepper, scallions, carrots, and garlic. Sauté until vegetables are crisp-tender, about 5 minutes. Stir in pork cubes, Chicken Stock, vinegar, soy sauce, and brown sugar. Bring to boil, and reduce heat, and let simmer 5 minutes.

In small bowl, combine water and cornstarch, stirring to dissolve cornstarch. Add to wok, along with pineapple, and cook, stirring constantly, until mixture is thickened. Serve over rice.

To Freeze: Vacuum seal each portion; label and freeze for up to 2 months.

To Serve: Put bags in boiling water, and bring water to boil again. Boil 10 to 12 minutes.

Pork Scaloppine

Serves 4

1⅓	lbs. pork tenderloin
1	clove garlic, crushed
1	teaspoon salt
¼	teaspoon black pepper, freshly ground
½	teaspoon rosemary
½	teaspoon sage
2	teaspoons fresh lemon juice
	Vegetable cooking spray

Nutritional Data

PER SERVING:

Calories	195
% calories from fat	27
Fat (gm)	5.6
Sat. Fat (gm)	1.9
Cholesterol (mg)	107.5
Sodium (mg)	611
Protein (gm)	33.5
Carbohydrate (gm)	0.7

EXCHANGES:

Milk	0.0	Bread	0.0
Veg.	0.0	Meat	4.0
Fruit	0.0	Fat	0.0

Trim off fat, and cut pork into ⅓-inch slices. Brown in skillet coated with vegetable cooking spray, turning once. Add remaining ingredients, reduce heat, and cook for about 10 minutes. If pork sticks, add 1 to 2 tablespoons of water.

Roast Pork Chops Calypso

Serves 4

- 4   center-cut pork chops
- ½   teaspoon pepper
- 1   teaspoon Spike (see "About This Cookbook")
- 1   teaspoon ginger, ground
- ½   teaspoon cloves, ground
- 2   cloves garlic, minced
- 2   bay leaves, crumbled
- 1   cup dark rum
- 2½   cups Chicken Stock (see p. 40)
- ½   cup brown sugar
- ⅓   cup fresh lime juice
- 2   teaspoons arrowroot
       Zest of 1 lime

Nutritional Data

PER SERVING:

Calories	439
% calories from fat	22
Fat (gm)	10.9
Sat. Fat (gm)	3.7
Cholesterol (mg)	69.3
Sodium (mg)	68.3
Protein (gm)	20.8
Carbohydrate (gm)	31.6

EXCHANGES:

Milk	0.0	Bread	2.0
Veg.	0.0	Meat	3.0
Fruit	0.0	Fat	3.0

Preheat oven to 325 degrees. Place chops in shallow baking dish. Add remaining ingredients and bake 50 to 60 minutes, basting frequently. Keep stirring until gravy has thickened.

To Freeze: Place in microwave-safe container; label and freeze for up to 2 months.

To Serve: Thaw, then microwave on High 7 to 9 minutes.

Pork Chop Delight

Serves 6

- 6   pork chops
       Black pepper
       Spike (see "About This Cookbook")
- 2   medium sweet potatoes, or substitute white potatoes
- 1   large onion, sliced
- 2   small apples, cubed
- 3   tablespoons brown sugar
- 1   large green bell pepper
- 1   teaspoon oregano
- 1   teaspoon thyme
- 2   cups apple cider

Nutritional Data

PER SERVING:

Calories	472
% calories from fat	29
Fat (gm)	15.7
Sat. Fat (gm)	5.3
Cholesterol (mg)	94.5
Sodium (mg)	89
Protein (gm)	29.5
Carbohydrate (gm)	55.6

EXCHANGES:

Milk	0.0	Bread	2.0
Veg.	0.0	Meat	4.0
Fruit	2.0	Fat	0.0

Trim fat from pork chops, season with pepper and Spike. Brown in skillet to remove excess fat, about 10 minutes. Drain and place in crockpot. Add remaining ingredients in order listed. Cover and cook on Low 8 to 10 hours or on High 3 to 4 hours.

To Freeze: Vacuum seal each portion; label and freeze for up to 2 months.

To Serve: Put bags in boiling water, and bring water to boil again. Boil 10 to 12 minutes.

Pork Chops Parmesan

Serves 4

3 tablespoons cornmeal, or whole wheat flour, or bread crumbs
1 tablespoon Parmesan cheese, freshly grated
½ teaspoon black pepper, freshly ground
½ teaspoon Spike (see "About This Cookbook")
½ teaspoon basil
4 pork loin chops, about ½-inch thick
  Vegetable cooking spray (olive-oil flavored)
3 green onions, chopped
1 clove garlic, minced
¼ teaspoon fennel seeds, crushed
3 tablespoons parsley, chopped
6 cups cooked no-yolk noodles

Nutritional Data

PER SERVING:

Calories	371
% calories from fat	29
Fat (gm)	11.6
Sat. Fat (gm)	3.9
Cholesterol (mg)	64.2
Sodium (mg)	83
Protein (gm)	25.5
Carbohydrate (gm)	39.5

EXCHANGES:

Milk	0.0	Bread	2.5
Veg.	0.0	Meat	3.0
Fruit	0.0	Fat	0.5

Combine cornmeal, Parmesan cheese, black pepper, Spike, and basil. Trim pork chops of all visible fat, pat dry, and dredge in cornmeal mixture.

Coat skillet with vegetable cooking spray and place over medium heat. Place chops in skillet and reduce heat to low. Sauté chops 10 minutes on each side. Then add onion, garlic, and fennel; continue sautéing another 10 minutes, stirring to keep from sticking. Place chops on platter and sprinkle with parsley. Serve with noodles

Hickory-Grilled Pork Chops with Seasoned Onions

Serves 4

Seasoned Onions

  Olive-oil-flavored vegetable cooking spray
1 teaspoon canola oil
3 cloves garlic, minced
2 cups onion, sliced
½ teaspoon salt
¼ teaspoon paprika
¼ teaspoon dried oregano

Nutritional Data

PER SERVING:

Calories	504
% calories from fat	20
Fat (gm)	11.3
Sat. Fat (gm)	3.2
Cholesterol (mg)	51.1
Sodium (mg)	322
Protein (gm)	24.7
Carbohydrate (gm)	75

Pork Chops

		EXCHANGES:			
4	butterflied loin pork chops, about 1 lb. total, trimmed of all fat	Milk	0.0	Bread	4.5
3	cups hickory chips, soaked in cold water 30 minutes and drained	Veg.	1.5	Meat	2.5
6	cups cooked brown rice	Fruit	0.0	Fat	0.5

Seasoned Onions: Coat nonstick skillet with cooking spray. Heat oil. Sauté garlic, onion, salt, paprika, and oregano. Partially cover and cook 5 minutes or until tender, stirring occasionally. Set aside. Reheat before serving.

Pork Chops: When barbecue coals are ashen, sprinkle hickory chips over them. Cook on grate or grill rack coated with cooking spray. Arrange pork chops, open side down, on grate. Sear chops 1 minute on each side. Continue grilling 4 to 6 minutes; turn and grill 5 to 6 minutes longer. Chops are done when opaque in center. Transfer to plates, and spoon Seasoned Onions over chops. Serve hot on bed of brown rice.

Barbecued Pork Chops with Herbed Tomato Sauce

Serves 6

Olive-oil-flavored vegetable cooking spray

3	cloves garlic, minced
1	cup onion, chopped
3/4	cup green bell pepper, seeded and chopped
1/2	cup bread crumbs
3/4	lb. mushrooms, cleaned, trimmed, and sliced (if mushrooms are small, leave whole)
3	cups tomatoes, peeled and chopped
1 1/2	teaspoons dried oregano, crumbled
1 1/2	teaspoons dried basil, crumbled
1	teaspoon dried marjoram, crumbled
1 1/2	teaspoons fennel seeds
1/4	teaspoon salt
1/3	cup water
6	1/2-inch-thick pork chops, about 1 1/2 lbs., trimmed of all fat

Nutritional Data

PER SERVING:

Calories	324
% calories from fat	32
Fat (gm)	12.7
Sat. Fat (gm)	4.1
Cholesterol (mg)	67.4
Sodium (mg)	222
Protein (gm)	42.6
Carbohydrate (gm)	18

EXCHANGES:

Milk	0.0	Bread	0.5
Veg.	2.0	Meat	4.5
Fruit	0.0	Fat	0.0

Coat nonstick skillet with cooking spray. Add garlic, onion, and peppers and sauté over medium heat 4 to 5 minutes, stirring occasionally. Add bread crumbs and mushrooms and cook 2 minutes. Stir in tomatoes, oregano, basil, marjoram, fennel seeds, salt, and water. Simmer sauce 5 to 10 minutes, covered, stirring occasionally. Set sauce aside.

Brush pork chops with sauce. When coals are ashen, place chops on grate coated with cooking spray and sear 1 minute on each side. Continue grilling 3 to 4 minutes on each side or until cooked to medium. Meanwhile, reheat sauce to drizzle on plated chops.

Creole Pork Chops

Serves 4	Nutritional Data	
4 loin pork chops, 1-inch thick (about 1 lb.)	PER SERVING:	
1 medium onion, chopped	Calories	524
1 small green bell pepper, cut into strips	% calories from fat	19
½ cup celery, sliced thin on diagonal	Fat (gm)	11
2 tablespoons parsley, chopped	Sat. Fat (gm)	3.7
1 teaspoon canned chopped green	Cholesterol (mg)	63
chili peppers	Sodium (mg)	318
Dash salt and pepper	Protein (gm)	26.5
2 cloves garlic, minced	Carbohydrate (gm)	78.2
1 14-oz. can stewed tomatoes, drained		
6 cups cooked rice	EXCHANGES:	

Milk	0.0	Bread	4.5	
Veg.	2.0	Meat	2.5	
Fruit	0.0	Fat	0.5	

Trim all fat off chops, rinse, and pat dry. Arrange in 12-inch-square glass baking dish, thick parts to outside. Add onions, pepper, celery, parsley, and chili peppers. Cover with vented plastic wrap, and microwave at Medium-high (70%) 5 minutes. Rotate dish, turn chops over, and microwave at 70% another 5 minutes.

Add remaining ingredients, cover with vented plastic wrap, and microwave on Medium-high (70%) another 15 minutes, until chops are cooked through. Let stand covered 5 to 10 minutes before serving over bed of rice.

Cuban Pork Sandwiches

Serves 4	Nutritional Data	
2 tablespoons olive oil	PER SERVING:	
2 large onions, sliced thin	Calories	383
⅓ cup fresh cilantro, chopped	% calories from fat	30
¼ teaspoon black pepper	Fat (gm)	12.6
1 cup gravy	Sat. Fat (gm)	2.5
1 lb. cooked pork, sliced	Cholesterol (mg)	24.9
4 soft hero rolls (6-inch long), cut length-	Sodium (mg)	760
wise in half	Protein (gm)	18.3
	Carbohydrate (gm)	48.8

4	slices tomato, cut in half	EXCHANGES:			
4	large pitted black olives, sliced	Milk	0.0	Bread	2.5
	Pimiento, diced, for garnish (optional)	Veg.	1.0	Meat	1.5
		Fruit	0.0	Fat	2.0

Heat oil in stockpot over medium heat. Add onions and cook 10 to 15 minutes, stirring several times until golden. Add cilantro and pepper. Stir well. Put onion mixture in small bowl and set aside.

In same pot, heat gravy over medium-low heat. When gravy is hot, add pork slices and heat through.

Place rolls, cut sides up, on individual plates. Arrange pork slices on rolls. Top with onion mixture. Pour gravy over sandwiches and garnish with tomato, olives, and pimiento.

Hoppin' John

Serves 6

		Nutritional Data	
2	10-oz. packages frozen black-eyed peas, thawed	PER SERVING:	
1	large onion, chopped	Calories	296
2	cloves garlic, minced	% calories from fat	13
1	green bell pepper, seeded and chopped	Fat (gm)	4.4
1	large carrot, peeled and chopped	Sat. Fat (gm)	1.1
1	16-oz. can reduced-sodium stewed tomatoes, or regular stewed tomatoes	Cholesterol (mg)	20.8
		Sodium (mg)	705
2½	cups defatted chicken broth	Protein (gm)	22.4
8	ozs. ham steak, trimmed of all fat and diced	Carbohydrate (gm)	43.9
2	teaspoons dried thyme leaves		
½	teaspoon dry mustard		
⅛	teaspoon celery salt		
2	bay leaves		
¼	teaspoon black pepper		
2-3	drops Tabasco sauce (optional)		
¾	cup uncooked long-grain brown rice		
	Salt, to taste (optional)		

EXCHANGES:

Milk	0.0	Bread	2.0
Veg.	2.0	Meat	2.0
Fruit	0.0	Fat	0.0

Combine all ingredients except rice and salt in large crockpot. Stir to mix well. Cover and cook on High 1 hour. Add rice and stir to mix well. Reduce heat and cook on Low 7 to 8 hours until rice is done and flavors are well blended. Remove and discard bay leaves. Stir. Add salt, if desired.

Rabbit, Farmer Style

Serves 6

- 1½ lbs. rabbit pieces, boneless and skinless
  Juice of 1 large lemon
- ½ cup all-purpose flour
  Spike (see "About This Cookbook")
  Black pepper, freshly ground
- 1½ cups onion, coarsely chopped
- 1 tablespoon fresh rosemary, or 1 teaspoon dried rosemary
- 1 cup dry white wine
- 1 cup shelled fresh peas, boiled, or frozen peas, thawed
  Vegetable cooking spray

Nutritional Data

PER SERVING:

Calories	266
% calories from fat	24
Fat (gm)	6.9
Sat. Fat (gm)	2
Cholesterol (mg)	67.7
Sodium (mg)	33
Protein (gm)	26.9
Carbohydrate (gm)	16.5

EXCHANGES:

Milk	0.0	Bread	1.0
Veg.	0.0	Meat	3.5
Fruit	0.0	Fat	0.0

Place rabbit pieces in bowl, and cover with cold water. Add lemon juice, cover, and refrigerate overnight.

Remove rabbit pieces from water, and dry well. Combine flour, 1 teaspoon Spike, and 1 teaspoon pepper, and lightly flour rabbit pieces.

Heat large skillet coated with vegetable cooking spray to medium-high heat. Add rabbit pieces, and brown them on all sides. Sprinkle with rosemary, and remove from heat.

Preheat oven to 375 degrees. Spread onion in bottom of baking dish. Top with rabbit pieces, wine, peas, Spike, and pepper to taste. Cover dish with foil, and bake 35 minutes or until rabbit pieces are tender. Serve in baking dish.

Chapter Seven

VEGETARIAN ENTREES

Ali Baba Casserole

Serves 8

4	medium sweet potatoes, peeled and cut into ½-inch dice (about 4 cups)
2	large onions, cut into ½-inch dice (about 2 cups)
3	cups cooked garbanzo beans (may be canned)
1	cup Chicken Stock (see p. 40)
½	cup red bell pepper, diced
½	cup mushrooms, sliced
3	cups zucchini, sliced
1	cup yellow squash, sliced
2	large tomatoes, seeded and cut into ½-inch dice

Sauce

1	tablespoon fresh lemon juice
½	teaspoon cayenne pepper, ground
½	teaspoon garlic powder
¼	teaspoon saffron
½	teaspoon coriander, ground
¾	teaspoon cinnamon, ground

Nutritional Data

PER SERVING:

Calories	193
% calories from fat	8
Fat (gm)	1.7
Sat. Fat (gm)	0.1
Cholesterol (mg)	1.3
Sodium (mg)	20
Protein (gm)	8.3
Carbohydrate (gm)	38.1

EXCHANGES:

Milk	0.0	Bread	2.0
Veg.	2.0	Meat	0.0
Fruit	0.0	Fat	0.0

Combine sweet potatoes, onions, garbanzos, and Chicken Stock in large stockpot. Bring to boil, reduce heat, and simmer, covered, 20 minutes or until onions and potatoes are almost tender. Add remaining vegetables and cook, covered, 10 minutes. Uncover and cook 10 minutes longer.

Sauce: Combine all ingredients in small saucepan and heat until spices dissolve. Mixture will resemble paste. Add to cooked vegetables, and cook, uncovered, 5 minutes. Serve over brown rice or freeze.

To Freeze: Place in microwave-safe container; label and freeze for up to 2 months.

To Serve: Thaw. Cover with microwave-safe plastic wrap, and cook on High for 3 to 5 minutes.

Mixed Grain and Bean Casserole con Queso

Serves 7

1 medium onion, chopped
1 clove garlic, minced
½ cup uncooked wild rice, rinsed and drained
2 large bay leaves
⅔ cup uncooked orzo
1 cup frozen corn kernels
⅓ cup uncooked couscous
2 cups cooked kidney beans, or 1 15-oz. can kidney beans, washed and drained
1 cup 1% cottage cheese
1 4-oz. can chopped green chilies, drained
1½ teaspoons chili powder
¼ teaspoon dry mustard
½ teaspoon salt, or to taste (optional)
⅛ teaspoon black pepper, or to taste
6 ozs. (1¼ cups) reduced-fat sharp Cheddar cheese, grated
Parsley sprigs, or chopped chives, for garnish (optional)

Nutritional Data

PER SERVING:

Calories	335
% calories from fat	13
Fat (gm)	4.8
Sat. Fat (gm)	2.1
Cholesterol (mg)	14.5
Sodium (mg)	663
Protein (gm)	20.4
Carbohydrate (gm)	53.5

EXCHANGES:

Milk	0.0	Bread	3.0
Veg.	2.0	Meat	1.0
Fruit	0.0	Fat	0.0

In large heavy pot, bring 3 quarts water to boil. Add onion, garlic, wild rice, and bay leaves. Cover, reduce heat slightly, and boil 30 minutes. Add orzo, cover, and boil additional 10 minutes. Add corn. Cover and cook an additional 3 minutes. Add couscous. Cover and cook additional 2 minutes. Remove pot from burner, and allow to stand 5 minutes.

Preheat oven to 375 degrees.

Drain grains in colander. Remove bay leaves and discard. Transfer to 3-quart, ovenproof casserole. Stir in kidney beans, cottage cheese, and chilies. Stir in chili powder, mustard, salt, if desired, and pepper. Gently stir in Cheddar cheese. Bake, covered, until heated through, 30 to 35 minutes.

Garnish with parsley, or chopped chives, if desired.

Cabbage Stuffed with Vegetables

Serves 4

- 1 medium to large round, green cabbage
  Vegetable cooking spray
- 1 medium onion, chopped
- 2 cloves garlic, minced
- 2 cups mushrooms, chopped
- 3 large fresh tomatoes
- 1 zucchini, chopped
- 1 15½-oz. can kidney beans
- 1 teaspoon thyme
- 1 tablespoon crushed red pepper
- 3 cups chicken broth (homemade or low-sodium)
- 1 teaspoon basil
- 1 teaspoon Spike (see "About This Cookbook")
  Pepper, freshly ground
- 1 bay leaf

Nutritional Data

PER SERVING:

Calories	216
% calories from fat	9
Fat (gm)	2.6
Sat. Fat (gm)	0.2
Cholesterol (mg)	0
Sodium (mg)	697
Protein (gm)	16.2
Carbohydrate (gm)	40.2

EXCHANGES:

Milk	0.0	Bread	1.0
Veg.	4.0	Meat	1.0
Fruit	0.0	Fat	0.0

Preheat oven to 300 degrees.

Discard any damaged outer leaves from cabbage. Wash cabbage under cold water, then steam or blanch in boiling water 5 to 7 minutes or until knife goes into center easily. Lift out cabbage and let cool.

Coat skillet with vegetable cooking spray, and sauté onion and garlic until onion is translucent. Add mushrooms, tomatoes, zucchini, kidney beans, thyme, and red pepper and cook about 5 minutes.

Place cabbage in large casserole and gently fold back outer leaves to reveal center. Using fruit knife, scoop out center of cabbage to make space for filling. Carefully fold leaves back over filling and tie cabbage together with string. Pour enough chicken broth or water to come halfway up cabbage. Add remaining ingredients and cover casserole. Place in oven 1 hour. Lift out cabbage, remove string, and cut into wedges for serving.

Stuffed Cabbage Rolls with Tomato Sauce

Serves 5

1 medium green cabbage
1 lb. mushrooms, chopped
¼ cup uncooked converted rice
1 cup canned tomatoes, drained
2 egg whites, slightly beaten
1 medium onion, peeled and grated
1 medium carrot, peeled and grated
1 teaspoon Spike (see "About This Cookbook")
¼ cup vinegar
½ cup light-brown sugar, firmly packed
1 cup canned tomato sauce

Nutritional Data

PER SERVING:

Calories	210
% calories from fat	4
Fat (gm)	0.9
Sat. Fat (gm)	0.1
Cholesterol (mg)	0
Sodium (mg)	436
Protein (gm)	7.2
Carbohydrate (gm)	47.7

EXCHANGES:

Milk	0.0	Bread	2.0
Veg.	3.0	Meat	0.0
Fruit	0.0	Fat	0.0

Drop cabbage into stockpot of boiling water and cook 4 to 8 minutes or until outer leaves come off easily. Drain and cool. Remove 10 large outer leaves and set aside. Discard tough inner core and chop up rest of cabbage. Spread chopped cabbage over bottom of crockpot.

In bowl, combine mushrooms, rice, and tomatoes. Add egg whites and mix well. Add onion, carrot, and Spike and mix again. Spread some of mixture in center of each large cabbage leaf, leaving a flap on either side. Roll up leaves and tuck in side flaps. Place rolls in crockpot.

In small bowl, combine vinegar, sugar, and tomato sauce and pour over rolls. Cover crockpot and cook on Low 8 to 10 hours.

To Freeze: Place in microwave-safe container; label and freeze for up to 2 months.

To Serve: Thaw in refrigerator and place in microwave. Microwave on High 7 to 9 minutes. Garnish before serving.

Carrot Patties

Serves 4

½ cup egg substitute
2 cups cooked carrots, pureed
½ teaspoon salt
¼ teaspoon white pepper
3 tablespoons parsley, chopped
½ cup all-purpose flour
Butter-flavored vegetable cooking spray
1 tablespoon canola oil
3 onions, sliced thinly

Nutritional Data

PER SERVING:

Calories	148
% calories from fat	23
Fat (gm)	3.9
Sat. Fat (gm)	0.3
Cholesterol (mg)	0
Sodium (mg)	352
Protein (gm)	5.6
Carbohydrate (gm)	24

In deep bowl, mix egg substitute with carrots, salt, pepper, and parsley. Sprinkle flour over batter. Set aside. In large nonstick skillet coated with cooking spray, heat oil. Sauté onions until tender, stirring occasionally. Remove onions to serving plate. Reheat pan, adding more oil only if necessary. Fry carrot patties until golden brown on both sides. Arrange over onions.

EXCHANGES:

Milk	0.0	Bread	0.5
Veg.	3.0	Meat	0.0
Fruit	0.0	Fat	0.5

Crepes Florentine with Spinach Filling

Serves 6 (1 crepe each)

Crepes

1⅓ cups all-purpose flour
¼ teaspoon salt
1½ cups skim milk
2 teaspoons vegetable oil
3 egg whites, beaten
1 egg yolk, beaten
   Vegetable cooking spray

Spinach Filling

3 tablespoons margarine
3 tablespoons all-purpose flour
1 cup skim milk
¾ cup water
¼ teaspoon nutmeg
3 tablespoons Parmesan cheese, freshly grated
1 10-oz. package frozen chopped spinach, cooked

Nutritional Data

PER SERVING:

Calories	261
% calories from fat	33
Fat (gm)	9.6
Sat. Fat (gm)	2.4
Cholesterol (mg)	39.6
Sodium (mg)	335
Protein (gm)	11.8
Carbohydrate (gm)	32.1

EXCHANGES:

Milk	0.5	Bread	1.5
Veg.	0.5	Meat	0.0
Fruit	0.0	Fat	2.0

Crepes: Combine flour and salt in small bowl; stir well. Gradually add milk, oil, and eggs. Beat, using wire whisk, until smooth. Cover and chill at least 1 hour and up to 24 hours.

Coat 10-inch crepe pan or nonstick skillet with cooking spray and place over medium-high heat until hot. Remove pan from heat and spoon 3 tablespoons batter into pan; quickly tilt pan in all directions so batter covers bottom with a thin film. Cook about 1 minute. Lift edge of crepe to test for doneness. Crepe is ready for turning when it can be shaken loose from pan. Turn crepe and cook 30 seconds on other side.

Place crepes on towel and allow to cool. Repeat procedure until all batter is used. Stack crepes between layers of wax paper to prevent sticking. Makes about 15, 8-inch crepes.

Crepes can be frozen easily. Stack between single layers of wax paper, and wrap in plastic wrap. Seal in an airtight container to freeze up to 1 month. Thaw frozen crepes in refrigerator before using.

Spinach Filling: Melt margarine and add flour, stirring constantly until flour is well mixed and slightly cooked, about 2 minutes. Add milk slowly, continuing to mix. When it starts to thicken slightly, add water, nutmeg, and cheese. Cook until sauce thickens again slightly, about 5 minutes. Add sauce to cooked and drained spinach. Makes filling for 6 large crepes.

To assemble crepes: Spoon ⅓ cup Spinach Filling down center of crepe, roll up, and place, seam side down, on serving plates. Top with dollop of filling.

Eggplant Parmesan

Serves 4

1 medium eggplant
1 6-oz. can low-sodium tomato paste
1 cup water
1 14½-oz. can low-sodium chunky tomatoes
1 tablespoon oregano
1 tablespoon basil
1 cup mozzarella cheese, shredded
3 tablespoons Parmesan cheese, freshly grated

Nutritional Data

PER SERVING:

Calories	182
% calories from fat	32
Fat (gm)	6.9
Sat. Fat (gm)	3.9
Cholesterol (mg)	19.7
Sodium (mg)	264
Protein (gm)	12.4
Carbohydrate (gm)	20.8

EXCHANGES:

Milk	0.0	Bread	0.5
Veg.	2.0	Meat	1.0
Fruit	0.0	Fat	1.0

Peel eggplant; cut into ⅛-inch slices.

In bowl, combine tomato paste, water, and tomatoes. Mix well. Add oregano and basil. Spread sauce on bottom of 2-quart casserole. Layer half of eggplant, more sauce, and half the mozzarella cheese. Repeat layers. Finish by sprinkling Parmesan cheese on top. Cover casserole.

Place in microwave and cook on High 14 to 16 minutes, giving dish a quarter-turn after 8 minutes. Continue to cook 1 to 2 minutes until all cheese has melted.

To Freeze: Label casserole and freeze for up to 2 months.

To Serve: Thaw and place in microwave on High for 7 to 9 minutes.

Stuffed Eggplant Rolls

Serves 6 (2 rolls each)

1	medium eggplant (about 1¼ lbs.)
1	egg
½	cup skim milk
2	tablespoons vegetable oil
1	cup dried bread crumbs

Filling

12	ozs. cottage cheese
½	cup parsley leaves
	Oregano leaves

Sauce

1	15-oz. can tomato sauce
1	cup water
2	tablespoons oregano
2	tablespoons parsley
1	teaspoon garlic powder
¼	teapoon black peper
2	packets Equal® (see "About This Cookbook")
2	tablespoons Parmesan cheese, freshly grated
	Vegetable cooking spray

Nutritional Data

PER SERVING:

Calories	229
% calories from fat	30
Fat (gm)	8
Sat. Fat (gm)	1.9
Cholesterol (mg)	40
Sodium (mg)	848
Protein (gm)	13.8
Carbohydrate (gm)	27.2

EXCHANGES:

Milk	0.0	Bread	1.0
Veg.	2.0	Meat	1.0
Fruit	0.0	Fat	1.0

About 40 minutes before serving, preheat broiler. Coat 15½ " x 10½" jelly-roll pan with vegetable cooking spray lightly in an up-and-down motion. Cut eggplant lengthwise into 12 ⅛-inch slices.

In pie plate with fork, mix egg, milk, and oil. Place bread crumbs on wax paper. Dip eggplant slices in egg mixture, then coat with bread crumbs. Arrange slices in jelly-roll pan in 1 layer; broil 5 to 7 minutes until tender and lightly browned.

Filling: Meanwhile, as eggplant is broiling, prepare filling. In medium bowl, mix cottage cheese, parsley, and oregano. Remove eggplant from oven and set aside. Adjust oven temperature to 400 degrees. Starting along narrow end of eggplant slice, evenly spoon about 2 rounded tablespoons of filling in ½-inch-wide strip; roll eggplant jelly-roll fashion. Repeat with remaining eggplant slices. Place eggplant rolls, seam side down, in 12" x 8" baking dish. Return to oven and bake 10 to 15 minutes or until heated through.

Sauce: While eggplant is baking, prepare sauce. In medium saucepan, add all sauce ingredients except Equal® and Parmesan cheese. Bring to boil. Remove from heat and stir in Equal®. Remove eggplant from oven and place rolls on platter. Cover with sauce and sprinkle with Parmesan cheese.

Stuffed Grape Leaves
(Dolmades)

Serves 8

- 1 16-oz. jar grape leaves (available at specialty food stores), drained
  Olive-oil-flavored vegetable cooking spray
- 1 cup onion, minced
- 2 cups uncooked rice
- 3/4 cup currants
- 2 teaspoons fresh mint leaves, or 1 teaspoon dried mint leaves, chopped
- 2 teaspoons fresh dill weed, minced
- 1/2 teaspoon ground cinnamon
- 1/4 teaspoon pepper
  Juice of 1 lemon

Nutritional Data

PER SERVING:

Calories	201
% calories from fat	3
Fat (gm)	0.8
Sat. Fat (gm)	0.1
Cholesterol (mg)	0
Sodium (mg)	10
Protein (gm)	4.9
Carbohydrate (gm)	42.9

EXCHANGES:

Milk	0.0	Bread	2.5
Veg.	1.0	Meat	0.0
Fruit	0.1	Fat	0.0

Carefully unfold grape leaves and rinse under cold water. Line large nonstick skillet with layer of any broken leaves and set aside.

Coat separate nonstick skillet with cooking spray and heat. Sauté onion until tender, stirring occasionally. Stir in rice and cook until coated. Stir in currants, mint, dill, cinnamon, and pepper. Remove from heat.

Arrange about 1 tablespoon of rice mixture on each grape leaf, and roll up loosely, jelly-roll style, tucking edges under. Continue until all stuffing is used. Arrange layer of stuffed grape leaves over bottom of prepared skillet; continue stacking until all stuffed grape leaves have been placed. Drizzle 2 cups hot water over all, and add lemon juice. Place heavy plate, to weigh down food, over stuffed grape leaves.

Bring mixture to boil, reduce heat to simmer, and continue simmering about 45 minutes until cooked. Remove to serving platter. Good warm or cold.

Mushrooms Ragout

Serves 8

- 1 oz. imported dried wild mushrooms, such as cepes, porcini, or chanterelle
  Boiling water to cover
  Vegetable cooking spray (olive-oil flavored)
- 2 large shallots, minced
- 1/2 lb. fresh wild mushrooms, stems trimmed, thickly sliced

Nutritional Data

PER SERVING:

Calories	52
% calories from fat	10
Fat (gm)	0.7
Sat. Fat (gm)	0.1
Cholesterol (mg)	0
Sodium (mg)	16
Protein (gm)	2.3
Carbohydrate (gm)	8.1

½   lb. fresh cultivated mushrooms (use
    1 lb. cultivated mushrooms if fresh
    wild mushrooms are unavailable),
    stems trimmed, thickly sliced
4   cloves garlic, minced
½   cup dry red wine
1   cup soaking liquid from dried
    mushrooms
1   teaspoon thyme
1   teaspoon tarragon
½   teaspoon rosemary
1   cup vegetable broth
    Salt and freshly ground pepper, to taste

EXCHANGES:			
Milk	0.0	Bread	0.0
Veg.	1.5	Meat	0.0
Fruit	0.0	Fat	0.0

Place dried mushrooms in bowl and pour on boiling water to cover. Let sit 30 minutes while you prepare remaining ingredients.

Coat large skillet with vegetable cooking spray and add shallots. Cook over low heat, stirring often, about 15 minutes or until golden brown. Add fresh wild and cultivated mushrooms or just cultivated mushrooms if wild are not available. Sauté 5 to 10 minutes. Drain dried mushrooms and retain liquid. Rinse mushrooms thoroughly to remove any debris, squeeze dry, and add to skillet along with garlic and wine. Stir together and sauté a few minutes.

Strain soaking liquid from dried mushrooms and measure about 1 cup; add to mushrooms along with thyme, tarragon, rosemary, and vegetable broth. Bring to simmer and simmer, covered, 20 minutes. Uncover and raise heat to high. Reduce liquid by half, and add salt and pepper to taste.

The ragout will keep a few days and can be frozen.

Garden Pesto Pie

Serves 6

Crust

3   cups unsifted all-purpose flour
2   packages fast-rising yeast
2   teaspoons sugar
1   teaspoon salt
1   cup very warm water (120-130 degrees)
½   teaspoon olive oil
    Vegetable cooking spray

Filling

½   teaspoon olive oil
1   cup onion, finely chopped
15 ozs. light ricotta cheese
8   ozs. egg substitute
⅛   teaspoon salt

Nutritional Data

PER SERVING:

Calories	409
% calories from fat	17
Fat (gm)	7.5
Sat. Fat (gm)	2.6
Cholesterol (mg)	21.3
Sodium (mg)	734
Protein (gm)	23.7
Carbohydrate (gm)	61.5

EXCHANGES:			
Milk	0.0	Bread	3.5
Veg.	1.0	Meat	2.0
Fruit	0.0	Fat	0.5

½   teaspoon white pepper
⅛   teaspoon nutmeg, grated
2   cups Pesto Sauce (see p. 503)

Crust: Combine 1½ cups flour, yeast, sugar, and salt in large bowl. With electric mixer at low speed, beat in water and olive oil until smooth. With hands, mix in enough additional flour to make stiff dough.

On lightly floured board, knead dough, adding flour as necessary, until smooth and elastic, 5 minutes. Place in greased bowl; cover with towel. Let rise in warm place (85 degrees), free from drafts, 30 minutes. Coat 12-inch tart pan with vegetable spray.

Filling: Place small skillet, coated with vegetable cooking spray on medium heat. Add oil. Add onion; sauté until soft. Whisk together ricotta cheese, egg substitute, salt, pepper, nutmeg, and Pesto Sauce in medium-size bowl. Add sautéed onion. Spoon into crust. Bake 25 to 30 minutes in 375-degree, preheated oven.

Asparagus Pie

Serves 2

¼   lb. fresh asparagus
1   cup low-fat cottage cheese
1   tablespoon fresh lemon juice
3   tablespoons onion, chopped
1   tablespoon fresh dill weed, minced
    Egg substitute equal to 1 egg, slightly beaten
2   sheets frozen phyllo pastry, thawed
    Vegetable cooking spray (butter-flavored)
½   cup parsley, snipped

Nutritional Data

PER SERVING:

Calories	178
% calories from fat	14
Fat (gm)	2.7
Sat. Fat (gm)	0.9
Cholesterol (mg)	5
Sodium (mg)	609
Protein (gm)	20.1
Carbohydrate (gm)	17.5

EXCHANGES:

Milk	0.0	Bread	1.0
Veg.	1.0	Meat	1.5
Fruit	0.0	Fat	0.0

Snap off tough ends of asparagus. Cook asparagus, covered, in small amount of boiling water 8 minutes or until crisp-tender. Drain well; set aside.

Combine next 5 ingredients in small bowl; stir until well blended and set aside.

You will need to work with 1 phyllo sheet at a time. Begin by lightly coating each sheet with cooking spray; fold in half crosswise, and lightly coat again with cooking spray. Set aside. Repeat procedure with remaining phyllo.

Place phyllo sheets, one on top of the other, on baking sheet coated with cooking spray. Spoon cottage cheese mixture over half of phyllo to within ½ inch of edges; top with asparagus. Using spatula, lift unfilled half of phyllo and fold over asparagus, tucking edges under to seal.

Preheat oven to 350 degrees. Lightly coat phyllo with cooking spray; bake 40 minutes or until golden. Remove from oven; let stand 5 minutes. Garnish with parsley. Serve warm, using sharp knife.

Stuffed Pepper Rolls

Serves 8

6	green, yellow, and red bell peppers
½	cup bread crumbs
2	tablespoons capers, chopped
1	tablespoon pine nuts
4	tablespoons currants, soaked in water for 30 minutes and drained
2	tablespoons fresh parsley, chopped
2	tablespoons fresh basil, chopped
¼	cup celery, chopped
¼	cup onion, chopped
¼	teaspoon hot pepper flakes
	Salt, to taste
	Pepper, to taste
3	tablespoons Basic Tomato-Basil Sauce (see p. 501), or canned tomato sauce

Nutritional Data

PER SERVING:

Calories	139
% calories from fat	8
Fat (gm)	9.2
Sat. Fat (gm)	1.2
Cholesterol (mg)	0
Sodium (mg)	77
Protein (gm)	3.4
Carbohydrate (gm)	15.6

EXCHANGES:

Milk	0.0	Bread	0.3
Veg.	0.9	Meat	0.0
Fruit	0.2	Fat	0.1

Preheat oven to 350 degrees.

Wash peppers, cut in half lengthwise, and remove seeds and inner membrane.

In mixing bowl, combine bread crumbs, capers, pine nuts, currants, parsley, basil, celery, onion, hot pepper flakes, and salt and pepper to taste. Mix well, and place 2 or 3 tablespoons of mixture into each pepper half. Place peppers in baking dish large enough to hold them tightly together in single layer.

Mix tomato sauce with 1 cup water, and pour evenly over peppers. Bake for 30 minutes or until peppers are cooked but still firm. Transfer to serving platter, and serve hot.

Grilled Sweet
Pepper Sandwiches

Serves 6

6 slices Italian bread
Butter-flavored vegetable cooking spray
1 large Vidalia onion, sliced
2 red bell peppers, seeded and sliced
2 yellow bell peppers, seeded and sliced
¼ cup capers, undrained

Nutritional Data	
PER SERVING:	
Calories	117
% calories from fat	10
Fat (gm)	1.3
Sat. Fat (gm)	0.3
Cholesterol (mg)	0
Sodium (mg)	286
Protein (gm)	3.4
Carbohydrate (gm)	23.9

EXCHANGES:			
Milk	0.0	Bread	1.5
Veg.	1.0	Meat	0.0
Fruit	0.0	Fat	0.0

Prepare barbecue grill, and when coals are hot, toast bread on grill rack coated with cooking spray, 4 to 6 inches from heat source, 2 minutes on each side or until lightly browned. Transfer to serving plate.

Remove rack to recoat with cooking spray. Grill onions and peppers on rack about 5 minutes, turning once or twice. Vegetables will begin to char and be tender. Spoon vegetables into bowl and toss with capers. Mound vegetable mixture on warm toast and serve hot.

Green and Gold Stir-Fry

Serves 6

2 tablespoons vegetable oil
1 cup leeks, thinly sliced
1 cup green bell pepper, chopped
1 cup yellow bell pepper, chopped
2 cups broccoli florets
2 cups yellow summer squash, cut in wedges
1 tablespoon dried garlic, minced
1 tablespoon oregano
2 tablespoons basil
2 tablespoons fresh chives, minced

Nutritional Data	
PER SERVING:	
Calories	130
% calories from fat	33
Fat (gm)	5.3
Sat. Fat (gm)	0.7
Cholesterol (mg)	0
Sodium (mg)	23
Protein (gm)	3.6
Carbohydrate (gm)	20.2

EXCHANGES:			
Milk	0.0	Bread	0.5
Veg.	2.0	Meat	0.0
Fruit	0.0	Fat	1.0

Heat wok and add vegetable oil and leeks. Stir-fry 2 minutes. Add green and yellow peppers, and stir-fry 1 more minute. Add broccoli and yellow squash with dried garlic, and stir-fry about 3 minutes or until crisp-tender. Add herbs and chives, and stir-fry 1 more minute.

To Freeze: Vacuum seal individual portions; label and freeze for up to 2 months.

To Reheat: Put bags in boiling water, and bring to boil again. Boil 10 to 12 minutes.

Potatoes, Fiesole Style

Serves 8

2	lbs. potatoes, peeled or unpeeled, washed and sliced in pieces 1/4-inch thick
1	medium onion, thinly sliced
6	tablespoons Classic Spaghetti Sauce (see p. 500), or canned tomato sauce
1	tablespoon fresh oregano, chopped
1	tablespoon fresh basil, chopped
1	teaspoon Spike (see "About This Cookbook")
1/2	teaspoon pepper, freshly ground
1/2	lb. mozzarella cheese, shredded
3	tablespoons bread crumbs
	Vegetable cooking spray

Nutritional Data

PER SERVING:

Calories	222
% calories from fat	23
Fat (gm)	5.7
Sat. Fat (gm)	3.2
Cholesterol (mg)	20
Sodium (mg)	232
Protein (gm)	11.6
Carbohydrate (gm)	31.8

EXCHANGES:

Milk	0.0	Bread	2.0
Veg.	0.0	Meat	1.0
Fruit	0.0	Fat	0.5

Preheat oven to 400 degrees.

Coat 10-inch-square baking dish with vegetable cooking spray. Place layer of potatoes in bottom of dish and upright along sides. Place layer of onions over potatoes in bottom of dish, cover with thin layer of sauce, sprinkle with oregano, basil, Spike, and pepper, and top with layer of cheese.

Repeat process until all ingredients are used, finishing with layer of cheese. Sprinkle with bread crumbs, cover dish with aluminum foil, and bake 30 minutes. Remove foil, and bake another 15 minutes. Serve potatoes hot from baking dish.

Potato Masala with Spinach

Serves 6

	Olive oil, or vegetable cooking spray
1	tablespoon canola oil
3/4	teaspoon ground cumin
4	cloves garlic, minced
1/2	teaspoon ginger root, peeled and grated
6	all-purpose potatoes, 5 to 6 ozs. each, unpeeled, diced
1	teaspoon curry powder
1/4	teaspoon each ingredient: red chili flakes, salt, pepper, turmeric
12	ozs. fresh spinach, washed, trimmed
1	cup canned chickpeas, drained

Nutritional Data

PER SERVING:

Calories	206
% calories from fat	15
Fat (gm)	3.6
Sat. Fat (gm)	0.4
Cholesterol (mg)	0
Sodium (mg)	296
Protein (gm)	6.7
Carbohydrate (gm)	39.3

EXCHANGES:

Milk	0.0	Bread	2.0
Veg.	1.5	Meat	0.0
Fruit	0.0	Fat	0.5

1½   cups tomatoes, chopped
¼   cup fresh cilantro, chopped

Lightly coat nonstick skillet with oil or cooking spray. Heat 1 tablespoon canola oil. Sprinkle pan with cumin, garlic, and ginger. Toss potatoes with spices, cover, and cook 4 to 6 minutes. Stir occasionally.

Stir in remaining ingredients, except cilantro. Cover and simmer 12 minutes or until potatoes are tender. Stir occasionally.

Spoon vegetables into serving bowl. Sprinkle with chopped cilantro. Serve hot.

Fajita-Style Potatoes

Serves 8

Fajita Marinade

¼   cup canola oil
3   tablespoons fresh lime juice
1   teaspoon ketchup
¼   teaspoon liquid mesquite smoke flavoring (optional)
½   teaspoon garlic powder
¼   teaspoon each ingredient: ground cumin, ground chili powder
2   red bell peppers, cut into thin strips
1   large onion, sliced, separated into rings

Potatoes

4   baking potatoes, 5 to 6 ozs. each, unpeeled and scrubbed
Canola oil, or vegetable cooking spray
1   all-purpose potato, about 6 ozs., peeled, cut into ½-inch strips that resemble a French fry, cooked and drained
4   cloves garlic, minced

Nutritional Data

PER SERVING:

Calories	137
% calories from fat	23
Fat (gm)	3.6
Sat. Fat (gm)	0.3
Cholesterol (mg)	0
Sodium (mg)	11
Protein (gm)	2.4
Carbohydrate (gm)	24.9

EXCHANGES:

Milk	0.0	Bread	1.5
Veg.	0.5	Meat	0.0
Fruit	0.0	Fat	0.5

Fajita Marinade: In bowl, mix oil, lime juice, ketchup, liquid smoke, garlic powder, cumin, and chili powder. Pour marinade into large self-sealing plastic bag. Add bell peppers and onions. Seal bag securely and turn bag several times so vegetables are thoroughly coated. Place bag in flat dish and refrigerate 2 hours. Drain; reserve half of marinade.

Potatoes: Preheat oven to 425 degrees. About 1 hour before serving time, scrub potatoes and stick several times with tip of sharp knife or fork. Set potatoes on nonstick cookie sheet. Bake on center rack of oven 45 minutes to 1 hour or until cooked. Potatoes are done when a knife inserted will test soft, or when squeezed gently will "give" slightly.

Lightly coat large nonstick skillet with oil or cooking spray. Sauté potato strips and garlic, covered, until potatoes begin to brown, stirring often, over medium heat. Add marinated bell peppers and onions, and continue cooking only until vegetables are hot but still crisp. Add 2 to 3 tablespoons marinade as you cook.

Cut hot baked potatoes in half horizontally and gently squeeze open. Place potato halves on serving plate, and spoon vegetables over them. Serve hot.

Potato Ratatouille

Serves 8

3 cups all-purpose potatoes, peeled, partially cooked, drained, and thinly sliced
1 large eggplant, ends cut off, unpeeled, and cubed
   Olive oil, or vegetable cooking spray
1 tablespoon noncholesterol margarine
2 cloves garlic, minced
1 large red or white onion, thinly sliced
2 cups zucchini, thinly sliced
2 large red bell peppers, seeded, thinly sliced
1 28-oz. can crushed tomatoes, undrained
3/4 teaspoon basil
1/2 teaspoon oregano
1/4 teaspoon each ingredient: salt, pepper

Nutritional Data

PER SERVING:

Calories	133
% calories from fat	8
Fat (gm)	1.3
Sat. Fat (gm)	0.2
Cholesterol (mg)	0
Sodium (mg)	253
Protein (gm)	3.7
Carbohydrate (gm)	29.1

EXCHANGES:

Milk	0.0	Bread	1.5
Veg.	1.5	Meat	0.0
Fruit	0.0	Fat	0.0

Partially cook potatoes, covered in water, until just fork-tender. Drain and cool 15 minutes. Sprinkle eggplant with 1 tablespoon salt; let stand 15 minutes, then wash off all salt. Pat dry.

Preheat oven to 350 degrees.

Lightly coat large nonstick skillet or saucepan with oil or cooking spray. Melt margarine. Sauté garlic and onion, partially covered, about 4 minutes over medium heat. Stir occasionally. Remove cover, add potatoes, and cook 2 minutes. Stir occasionally.

Lightly coat 2-quart ovenproof casserole with oil or cooking spray. Spoon onion mixture into casserole. Add remaining vegetables, including eggplant, and stir to combine. Season with basil, oregano, salt, and pepper. Cover and bake on center rack of oven about 1 hour or until vegetables are tender. Remove cover after 30 minutes. Stir vegetables 3 or 4 times during baking.

▣ *Microwave Ratatouille*

Serves 8

1 small eggplant, cubed
1 onion, chopped
6 cloves garlic, peeled and smashed
1 tablespoon olive oil
2 cups tomatoes, cubed (cherry tomatoes, halved, are fine)
1 medium zucchini, or yellow squash, sliced
2 tablespoons chopped fresh basil, or ½ teaspoon dried basil
1 teaspoon dried thyme
1 teaspoon dried oregano
   Salt and pepper, to taste
1 medium red bell pepper, cut into 1-inch squares
1 medium green or yellow bell pepper, cut into 1-inch squares
½-1 teaspoon hot red pepper flakes

Nutritional Data

PER SERVING:

Calories	59
% calories from fat	30
Fat (gm)	2.1
Sat. Fat (gm)	0.3
Cholesterol (mg)	0
Sodium (mg)	8.3
Protein (gm)	1.6
Carbohydrate (gm)	10.1

EXCHANGES:

Milk	0.0	Bread	0.0
Veg.	1.5	Meat	0.0
Fruit	0.0	Fat	0.5

In 2-quart measure or casserole, place eggplant, onion, garlic, and oil. Microwave on High 10 minutes, stirring once or twice. Add tomatoes, zucchini, and spices and microwave on High 10 minutes, stirring once. Add peppers and hot pepper flakes and microwave another 5 minutes on High. Stir to blend. Let rest before serving warm or chilled.

▣ *Spinach Polenta with Herbed Vegetables*

Serves 6

Vegetables

2 teaspoons olive oil
1 medium onion, chopped
1 clove garlic, minced
2 cups cooked garbanzo beans, or 1 15-oz. can garbanzo beans, well drained
2 cups diced zucchini, or yellow squash (or combination of both)
1 large carrot, peeled and diced
1 15-oz. can tomato sauce
1 large bay leaf
1½ teaspoons dried thyme leaves
½ teaspoon dried basil leaves
   Salt, to taste (optional)
⅛ teaspoon black pepper
½ teaspoon granulated sugar (optional)

Nutritional Data

PER SERVING:

Calories	287
% calories from fat	13
Fat (gm)	4.5
Sat. Fat (gm)	0.5
Cholesterol (mg)	0.8
Sodium (mg)	680
Protein (gm)	12.8
Carbohydrate (gm)	53.1

EXCHANGES:

Milk	0.0	Bread	2.5
Veg.	2.0	Meat	0.0
Fruit	0.0	Fat	1.0

Polenta

1	cup yellow cornmeal
1	tablespoon granulated sugar
½	teaspoon salt (scant), or to taste (optional)
2½	cups water
½	cup 1% milk
1	medium onion, diced
1	10-oz. package frozen chopped spinach, thawed and well drained

To Serve

2	teaspoons Parmesan cheese, freshly grated, per serving (optional)

Vegetables: In large saucepan, combine oil, onion, and garlic. Cook over medium heat 5 or 6 minutes or until onion is tender. Add garbanzos, squash, carrot, tomato sauce, bay leaf, thyme, basil, salt, if desired, and pepper. If tomato sauce seems acid, add sugar. Bring to boil. Reduce heat, cover, and simmer, stirring occasionally, 15 to 20 minutes or until flavors are well blended and vegetables are tender. Remove and discard bay leaf.

Polenta: Combine cornmeal, sugar, salt, if desired, water, milk, and onion in 2½-quart microwave-safe casserole. Stir to mix well. Microwave, uncovered, on High (900 w.) 6 to 7 minutes, stopping and stirring with wire whisk after 2 minutes and 4 minutes. After cooking, stir again with wire whisk until mixture is smooth. Stir in spinach. Cover with casserole lid and microwave an additional 3 to 3½ minutes on High. Remove from microwave and let stand an additional 3 to 4 minutes.

To Serve: Serve individual portions of vegetable sauce over Polenta. Garnish with Parmesan cheese, if desired.

Stuffed Pumpkin

Serves 8

1	4-lb. pumpkin, measuring about 8 inches across
	Vegetable cooking spray
5	cups uncooked sweet potatoes, peeled and cut up
½	cup golden raisins
1	teaspoon cinnamon
	Pinch nutmeg
2	Golden Delicious apples, peeled and chopped
3	tablespoons low-calorie pancake syrup

Nutritional Data

PER SERVING:

Calories	200
% calories from fat	2
Fat (gm)	0.4
Sat. Fat (gm)	0.1
Cholesterol (mg)	0
Sodium (mg)	35
Protein (gm)	3.4
Carbohydrate (gm)	49.3

EXCHANGES:

Milk	0.0	Bread	2.0
Veg.	0.0	Meat	0.0
Fruit	1.0	Fat	0.0

Preheat oven to 400 degrees.

Wash and dry pumpkin. Use short, sharp knife to cut out lid about 4 inches from top of pumpkin. Scoop out seeds and stringy flesh and discard. Place pumpkin in baking dish coated with vegetable cooking spray.

Combine sweet potatoes, raisins, cinnamon, nutmeg, and apples in bowl. Mix well. Fill pumpkin with mixture and top with syrup. Fit lid back on pumpkin. Bake about 30 minutes until outside of pumpkin begins to soften. Lower oven temperature to 300 degrees and continue baking 30 minutes more until flesh is tender. If pumpkin is browning, cover it loosely with foil.

To serve, remove lid and scoop filling and pumpkin into serving dish.

Vegetable Lasagna

Serves 8

Vegetable cooking spray
1 small onion, chopped
3 cloves garlic, minced
1 carrot, chopped
1 stalk celery, chopped
2 cups mushrooms, chopped
1 16-oz. can low-sodium chunky tomatoes
1 8-oz. can low-sodium tomato paste mixed
   with 1 cup water
1 teaspoon oregano
1 teaspoon basil
   Salt and black pepper, freshly ground
3 cups small broccoli florets
9 lasagna noodles
1 cup low-fat cottage cheese
2 cups low-fat mozzarella cheese, about
   ³/₄ lb., shredded
¹/₃ cup Parmesan cheese, freshly grated

Nutritional Data

PER SERVING:

Calories	204
% calories from fat	20
Fat (gm)	4.9
Sat. Fat (gm)	2.4
Cholesterol (mg)	12.5
Sodium (mg)	310
Protein (gm)	20
Carbohydrate (gm)	23

EXCHANGES:

Milk	0.0	Bread	0.5
Veg.	3.0	Meat	1.5
Fruit	0.0	Fat	0.0

Coat large saucepan with vegetable cooking spray, add onion, and cook until tender. Stir in garlic, carrot, celery, and mushrooms and cook, stirring often, 5 minutes. Add tomatoes and stir in tomato paste, oregano, basil, salt, and pepper. Simmer, uncovered, 10 minutes or until thickened slightly. Stir in broccoli and continue cooking.

In large pot of boiling water, cook noodles until *al dente;* drain and rinse under cold water.

Preheat oven to 350 degrees. In 13" x 9" baking dish lightly coated with cooking spray, arrange 3 noodles evenly over bottom. Spread with one-half vegetable mixture, then half of cottage cheese. Sprinkle with ¹/₃ mozzarella cheese. Repeat layering procedure once. Arrange remaining noodles over top; sprinkle with remaining mozzarella and Parmesan cheeses.

Bake 35 to 45 minutes or until bubbly.

 # Eggplant Lasagna

Serves 4

1	eggplant (1 lb.)
2	tablespoons water
	Vegetable cooking spray
2	8-oz. cans tomato sauce
1	cup low-fat cottage cheese
	Pepper, freshly ground
½	cup skim mozzarella cheese, shredded
2	tablespoons Parmesan cheese, freshly grated

Nutritional Data

PER SERVING:

Calories	135
% calories from fat	12
Fat (gm)	1.9
Sat. Fat (gm)	1
Cholesterol (mg)	7.5
Sodium (mg)	1077
Protein (gm)	15.1
Carbohydrate (gm)	16.4

EXCHANGES:

Milk	0.0	Bread	0.0
Veg.	3.0	Meat	1.5
Fruit	0.0	Fat	0.0

Peel and dice eggplant in ½-inch cubes. Put into 2-quart casserole with 2 tablespoons water. Cover. Microwave on High 5 to 6 minutes, stirring halfway through cooking. Remove and drain.

Preheat oven to 425 degrees. Coat insides of 4 1½- to 2-cup casseroles with vegetable cooking spray. Divide ½ cup tomato sauce evenly among casseroles. Divide half of eggplant evenly among casseroles. Add pepper to cottage cheese and add to casseroles. Sprinkle with half of mozzarella. Divide 1 cup tomato sauce evenly among casseroles. Place remaining eggplant on top. Cover with remaining tomato sauce, mozzarella, and Parmesan cheese.

Bake 20 to 25 minutes or until lightly browned and eggplant is cooked through.

To Freeze: Place individual portions in separate vacuum-sealed bags; label and freeze up to 2 months.

To Serve: Put bags in boiling water, and bring water to boil again. Boil 10 to 12 minutes. Add garnishes such as parsley or cheese just before serving.

Note: Instead of individual casseroles, lasagna may be made and baked in 8-inch-square baking dish. Increase baking time to 30 minutes.

Vegetable Paella

Serves 6

¾ lb. broccoli, sliced, or 1 10-oz. package frozen chopped broccoli
2 small zucchini, sliced thin
1 medium green bell pepper, chopped
1 medium red bell pepper, chopped
½ cup onion, chopped
2 cloves garlic, minced
¼ cup olive oil
1 16-oz. can chopped tomatoes, undrained
Black pepper, to taste
2¾ cups chicken broth
1½ cups Arborio rice*
1 tablespoon fresh lemon juice
1 cup frozen peas, thawed
⅔ cup Parmesan cheese, freshly grated

Nutritional Data

PER SERVING:

Calories	395
% calories from fat	31
Fat (gm)	13.8
Sat. Fat (gm)	3.7
Cholesterol (mg)	9.2
Sodium (mg)	727
Protein (gm)	14.8
Carbohydrate (gm)	54.2

EXCHANGES:

Milk	0.0	Bread	3.0
Veg.	2.0	Meat	0.5
Fruit	0.0	Fat	2.0

Cook fresh broccoli in small amount of boiling water 5 minutes or until crisp-tender. If using frozen broccoli, cook according to package directions. Drain and reserve.

In paella pan or 12-inch ovenproof skillet, cook zucchini, green and red peppers, onion, and garlic in olive oil until onion is tender. Stir in undrained tomatoes and pepper. Stir in chicken broth, uncooked rice, and lemon juice; mix well. Bring to boiling. Reduce heat and simmer until rice is tender, about 20 minutes. Stir in broccoli, peas, and Parmesan cheese.

Bake, covered, in 350-degree oven 10 minutes.

*Note: Arborio is an Italian rice found in specialty stores. It is best for this recipe because it can absorb a lot of liquid without becoming mushy. Regular rice may be used.

Sweet-and-Sour Vegetable Stir-Fry

Serves 6

1 recipe Sweet-and-Sour Sauce (see p. 513)
1 tablespoon vegetable oil
3 carrots, sliced on a diagonal
2 stalks celery, sliced on a diagonal
1 medium onion, quartered and separated
½ head red cabbage, shredded
½ head green cabbage, shredded
2 medium zucchini, sliced

Nutritional Data

PER SERVING:

Calories	114
% calories from fat	16
Fat (gm)	2.9
Sat. Fat (gm)	0.4
Cholesterol (mg)	0.1
Sodium (mg)	267
Protein (gm)	4.2
Carbohydrate (gm)	21

½	cup water chestnuts, sliced	EXCHANGES:			
¼	cup pimiento, chopped	Milk	0.0	Bread	0.0
		Veg.	4.0	Meat	0.0
		Fruit	0.0	Fat	0.5

Make sauce first and keep warm.

Heat wok or skillet to medium to high heat. Add 1 table-spoon vegetable oil. Stir together carrots, celery, and onion. Cook about 2 minutes. Add cabbage, zucchini, and water chestnuts. Cook about 2 more minutes.

If vegetables seem to be sticking, add ¼ cup water and turn heat down to medium. Cover and cook 1 miniute. Uncover and add pimiento. Stir and remove from heat. Place vegetables in bowl and stir in sauce. Serve at once.

Vegetables and Stir-Fried Rice

Serves 6

		Nutritional Data	
2	tablespoons vegetable oil	PER SERVING:	
½	cup onion, chopped	Calories	235
¼	cup celery, chopped	% calories from fat	28
¼	cup red bell pepper, chopped	Fat (gm)	7.5
¼	cup yellow bell pepper, chopped	Sat. Fat (gm)	1
¼	cup green bell pepper, chopped	Cholesterol (mg)	0.4
½	cup water chestnuts, sliced	Sodium (mg)	144
2	zucchini, sliced	Protein (gm)	6.6
1	yellow squash, sliced	Carbohydrate (gm)	36
2	cups pea pods		
3	cups Stir-Fried Rice (recipe follows)	EXCHANGES:			

EXCHANGES:			
Milk	0.0	Bread	2.0
Veg.	1.5	Meat	0.0
Fruit	0.0	Fat	1.5

Heat wok and add vegetable oil. Add onion, celery, and peppers. Stir-fry 1 minute. Add water chestnuts. Cover 45 seconds. Add zucchini, squash, and pea pods. Stir-fry 1 minute. Add Stir-Fried Rice and stir-fry until heated through.

Stir-Fried Rice

Serves 6

		Nutritional Data	
1	tablespoon vegetable oil	PER SERVING:	
	Egg substitute equal to 1 egg	Calories	142
¼	cup onion, chopped	% calories from fat	17
¼	cup celery, chopped	Fat (gm)	2.6
¼	cup bean sprouts	Sat. Fat (gm)	0.4
1	cup mushrooms	Cholesterol (mg)	0.4
2	teaspoons sherry	Sodium (mg)	135
		Protein (gm)	3.9
		Carbohydrate (gm)	25

¼	cup Vegetable Stock (see p. 42)
3	cups cooked rice
2	teaspoons dark soy sauce
	Dash pepper
¼	teaspoon sugar
2	stalks scallions, chopped

(see p. 42)

EXCHANGES:

Milk	0.0	Bread	1.5
Veg.	0.5	Meat	0.0
Fruit	0.0	Fat	0.5

Heat wok and add oil. Scramble egg substitute in wok. Add onion, celery, bean sprouts, and mushrooms. Add sherry and Vegetable Stock, and cover 45 seconds. Uncover and stir thoroughly. Add soy sauce, pepper, and sugar. Stir thoroughly. Add scallions and rice as you turn flame off. Serve immediately.

To Freeze: Place individual portions in vacuum-sealed bags; label and freeze for up to 2 months.

To Serve: To reheat, put bags in boiling water, and bring water to boil again. Boil 10 to 12 minutes. If serving cold, just defrost and use.

Brown Rice and Thin Noodles

Serves 8

Butter-flavored vegetable cooking spray
½ cup onion, minced
1 cup uncooked thin noodles, crumbled
1 cup uncooked brown rice
3 cups fat-free vegetable broth

Coat large nonstick skillet with cooking spray and heat. Sauté onion until soft, over medium heat. Add noodles and sauté until coated, stirring often. Add rice and stir to combine. Add broth. Cover and continue cooking until broth is absorbed and rice is tender, 30 to 35 minutes. Let stand, covered, 5 minutes before serving.

Nutritional Data

PER SERVING:

Calories	116
% calories from fat	10
Fat (gm)	1.3
Sat. Fat (gm)	0.2
Cholesterol (mg)	4.5
Sodium (mg)	129
Protein (gm)	4.4
Carbohydrate (gm)	22.6

EXCHANGES:

Milk	0.0	Bread	1.5
Veg.	0.0	Meat	0.0
Fruit	0.0	Fat	0.0

Couscous with Steamed Vegetables

Serves 8

2 cups frozen peas
2 cups fresh carrots, thinly sliced
2 cups broccoli florets
2 cups corn, frozen or fresh
3 cups Vegetable Stock (see p. 42)
2 cups couscous
¼ cup scallions, sliced
1 cup fresh parsley, chopped
2 tablespoons Parmesan cheese, freshly grated

(see p. 42)

Nutritional Data

PER SERVING:

Calories	287
% calories from fat	4
Fat (gm)	1.4
Sat. Fat (gm)	0.5
Cholesterol (mg)	3.7
Sodium (mg)	101
Protein (gm)	12.1
Carbohydrate (gm)	55

EXCHANGES:

Milk	0.0	Bread	3.0
Veg.	3.0	Meat	0.0
Fruit	0.0	Fat	0.0

Steam peas, carrots, broccoli, and corn in steamer basket until tender. Set aside.

Bring Vegetable Stock to boil in stockpot. Slowly stir couscous into stock, then remove pan from heat. Cover tightly and let stand 5 minutes. Stir in scallions and parsley. Pile in center of serving plate and surround with steamed vegetables. Sprinkle on cheese.

To Freeze: Place individual portions of couscous and vegetables in separate vacuum-sealed bags; label and freeze for up to 2 months.

To Serve: Put bags in boiling water, and bring water to boil again. Boil 10 to 12 minutes.

Vegetables à la Grecque

Serves 6

1 cup dry white wine
1 recipe Italian Dressing (recipe follows)
1 large celery stalk with leaves, washed and peeled
2 stalks fresh fennel, or ½ teaspoon fennel seeds
2 sprigs fresh thyme, or ½ teaspoon dried thyme
10 peppercorns, cracked
12 coriander seeds, cracked
2 lbs. vegetables (string beans or assortment)

Nutritional Data

PER SERVING:

Calories	95
% calories from fat	15
Fat (gm)	1.6
Sat. Fat (gm)	0.3
Cholesterol (mg)	0
Sodium (mg)	16.8
Protein (gm)	3.6
Carbohydrate (gm)	9.2

EXCHANGES:

Milk	0.0	Bread	0.0
Veg.	4.0	Meat	0.0
Fruit	0.0	Fat	0.0

Combine all ingredients except 2 lbs. vegetables in 4-quart pot and bring to boil. Cover pot, reduce heat, and simmer 1 hour. Strain cooked marinade through cheesecloth or fine sieve into bowl and press down to extract every last bit of taste before discarding vegetables and spices.

Pour clear marinade back into pot. Wash and trim vegetables and simmer in marinade until tender. Lift out with slotted spoon and arrange artfully on platter.

Boil marinade down to 1 cup. Pour marinade over vegetables and allow to cool. Cover and refrigerate 6 to 12 hours.

Italian Dressing

¼ cup fresh lemon juice
¼ cup red wine vinegar
¼ cup white wine
1 teaspoon oregano
1 teaspoon basil
½ teaspoon dry mustard
½ teaspoon onion powder
1 clove garlic, minced
1 tablespoon fresh chives, chopped
1 teaspoon thyme
½ teaspoon rosemary

Combine all ingredients. Chill 1 or 2 hours to allow herbs to blend. Makes ³/₄ cup.

Italian Vegetable Pita with Fresh Basil

Serves 6

2 medium tomatoes, seeded and diced
6 green onions, sliced thin
1 green bell pepper, diced
1 yellow squash, diced
2 small zucchini, diced
6 spinach leaves, chopped
1 cup basil leaves, chopped
2½ teaspoons tarragon vinegar
2 tablespoons olive oil
2 teaspoons Dijon mustard
1 teaspoon sugar
½ teaspoon black pepper, freshly ground
3 pita breads, cut in half

Nutritional Data

PER SERVING:

Calories	154
% calories from fat	31
Fat (gm)	5.8
Sat. Fat (gm)	0.8
Cholesterol (mg)	0
Sodium (mg)	200
Protein (gm)	4.7
Carbohydrate (gm)	23.9

EXCHANGES:

Milk	0.0	Bread	1.0
Veg.	1.5	Meat	0.0
Fruit	0.0	Fat	1.0

Combine all ingredients except bread in bowl. Toss to mix well. Drain off excess liquid, and spoon vegetables into each pita half.

To Freeze: Vacuum seal individual portions of filling; label and freeze for up to 2 months.

To Serve: Thaw in refrigerator, toss well, and spoon filling into pita halves.

Macaroni Salad

Serves 6

3 cups cooked macaroni, drained
1 cup green bell pepper, chopped
1/4 tablespoon fresh cilantro, minced
2 tablespoons fresh chives, minced
3 hard-boiled egg whites, chopped
1/4 teaspoon pepper, coarsely ground
French Dressing (recipe follows)

Mix all ingredients, except French Dressing, together in large bowl while macaroni is hot. Cover and chill in refrigerator several hours. Toss with dressing at serving time.

French Dressing

2 tablespoons balsamic vinegar
1 tablespoon extra-virgin olive oil
1/4 cup fat-free vegetable broth
1/2 teaspoon Dijon mustard
1/2 teaspoon salt
1/4 teaspoon pepper
1½ teaspoons fresh tarragon, minced, or 3/4 teaspoon dry tarragon

Whisk together all ingredients.

Nutritional Data

PER SERVING:

Calories	137
% calories from fat	19
Fat (gm)	2.9
Sat. Fat (gm)	0.4
Cholesterol (mg)	0
Sodium (mg)	227
Protein (gm)	5.5
Carbohydrate (gm)	22.6

EXCHANGES:

Milk	0.0	Bread	1.5
Veg.	0.0	Meat	0.0
Fruit	0.0	Fat	0.5

Fresh Vegetable Quiche

Serves 6

2 cups cooked long-grain white rice
Egg substitute equal to 1 egg, lightly beaten
3/4 cup (3 ozs.) Lorraine cheese, shredded and divided
1/4 teaspoon salt
Vegetable cooking spray
1 cup fresh broccoli, chopped
1 cup fresh cauliflower, chopped

Nutritional Data

PER SERVING:

Calories	165
% calories from fat	18
Fat (gm)	3.4
Sat. Fat (gm)	2.1
Cholesterol (mg)	11
Sodium (mg)	325
Protein (gm)	10.6
Carbohydrate (gm)	23.2

½ cup carrot, finely shredded
½ cup onion, finely shredded
¼ teaspoon salt
Egg substitute equal to 2 eggs, slightly beaten
¾ cup evaporated skim milk
¼ cup water
1 tablespoon fresh chives, minced
1 tablespoon fresh oregano
Pepper, to taste

EXCHANGES:			
Milk	0.0	Bread	1.0
Veg.	1.5	Meat	0.5
Fruit	0.0	Fat	0.5

Preheat oven to 350 degrees. Combine rice, egg substitute, ¼ cup cheese, and salt in small bowl; stir well. Press mixture into 9-inch pie plate coated with cooking spray. Bake 5 minutes. Set aside.

Place chopped broccoli and cauliflower in vegetable steamer over boiling water; cover and steam 5 minutes or until crisp-tender. Drain. Arrange broccoli, cauliflower, carrot, and onion in rice pie shell. Sprinkle with remaining ½ cup cheese.

Combine salt, egg substitute, and last 5 ingredients in small bowl, stir well; pour over cheese. Raise oven to 375 degrees and bake 40 minutes or until set. Let stand 5 minutes. Serve warm.

Vegetable Stew

Serves 6
Vegetable cooking spray
4 cloves garlic, minced
2 onions, sliced
4 carrots, peeled and cut into 1-inch pieces
2 celery stalks, cut into ½-inch pieces
4 medium zucchini, sliced
2 large potatoes, peeled and cut into 1½-inch pieces
2 cups fresh peas
1 18-oz. can salt-free stewed tomatoes
1 28-oz. can salt-free crushed tomatoes
Pepper, to taste
1 teaspoon oregano
10 leaves fresh basil, coarsely chopped
10 mushrooms, sliced

Nutritional Data

PER SERVING:

Calories	189
% calories from fat	5
Fat (gm)	1.1
Sat. Fat (gm)	0.2
Cholesterol (mg)	0
Sodium (mg)	65
Protein (gm)	8.2
Carbohydrate (gm)	40.4

EXCHANGES:			
Milk	0.0	Bread	1.0
Veg.	4.0	Meat	0.0
Fruit	0.0	Fat	0.0

Coat large pan with vegetable cooking spray and add garlic and onions. Sauté a few minutes, then add carrots, celery, zucchini, potatoes, and peas. Add both kinds of tomatoes, pepper, oregano, and basil; simmer 40 minutes until carrots are just tender. Add mushrooms and allow stew to cook 2 to 3 minutes more.

Vegetable Melange

Serves 4

1 cup broccoli florets
1 cup cauliflower florets
½ cup carrots, sliced into thin rounds
½ cup red bell pepper, sliced
1 cup snow peas, trimmed
½ cup fresh bean sprouts
2 tablespoons fresh lemon juice
1 tablespoon fresh chives, chopped
   Pepper
3 cups cooked brown rice

Nutritional Data

PER SERVING:

Calories	216
% calories from fat	7
Fat (gm)	1.7
Sat. Fat (gm)	0.3
Cholesterol (mg)	0
Sodium (mg)	28
Protein (gm)	7.3
Carbohydrate (gm)	44.9

EXCHANGES:

Milk	0.0	Bread	2.5
Veg.	2.0	Meat	0.0
Fruit	0.0	Fat	0.0

Arrange vegetables in 10-inch baking dish or serving platter. Place broccoli and cauliflower in circle on outside, with ring of carrots and red peppers inside of circle. Mound bean sprouts in center and surround with snow peas.

Sprinkle vegetables with lemon juice and cover with wax paper. Microwave on High 3 to 5 minutes, until vegetables are crisp-tender. Let stand covered 3 minutes; then remove paper. Sprinkle with chives and pepper. Serve with rice.

Any combination of vegetables may be substituted, according to availability or choice. Use zucchini or summer squash slices, asparagus, turnips, wax or green beans. Always place softer vegetables in center of arrangement.

Tossed Vegetable Salad

Serves 6

4 cups mixed salad greens, washed and drained
2 medium tomatoes, cut into wedges
2 cups broccoli florets
3 hard-boiled egg whites, chopped
2 carrots, sliced
1 cup cooked beets, diced
1 yellow bell pepper, sliced
½ cup red onion, sliced
½ teaspoon garlic powder
¼ cup diet Italian dressing

Nutritional Data

PER SERVING:

Calories	76
% calories from fat	16
Fat (gm)	1.4
Sat. Fat (gm)	0.2
Cholesterol (mg)	0.7
Sodium (mg)	159
Protein (gm)	4.6
Carbohydrate (gm)	12.9

EXCHANGES:

Milk	0.0	Bread	0.0
Veg.	3.0	Meat	0.0
Fruit	0.0	Fat	0.0

Combine all ingredients, except Italian dressing, in large, deep bowl. Toss salad with Italian dressing at serving time.

Vegetable Tacos

Serves 2

Vegetable cooking spray
1 tablespoon canola oil
4 corn tortillas
1 cup onion, minced
4 teaspoons reduced-fat Monterey Jack cheese, crumbled
½ cup lettuce, shredded
2 cups tomatoes, chopped
4 tablespoons nonfat sour cream
½ recipe Refried Beans (see p. 386)
Taco sauce (optional)

Nutritional Data

PER SERVING:

Calories	522
% calories from fat	17
Fat (gm)	10.5
Sat. Fat (gm)	1.2
Cholesterol (mg)	1.9
Sodium (mg)	419
Protein (gm)	24.6
Carbohydrate (gm)	88.5

EXCHANGES:

Milk	0.0	Bread	4.0
Veg.	4.0	Meat	1.0
Fruit	0.0	Fat	2.0

Coat nonstick skillet with cooking spray and heat oil. Fry tortillas a few seconds on each side. Lay out remaining ingredients for "assembly line" use. Fill each tortilla with onion, cheese, lettuce, tomatoes, sour cream, beans and Taco sauce if used.

Burritos with Refried Beans

Serves 4

⅛ cup reduced-fat Monterey Jack cheese, shredded
3 cups Refried Beans (see p. 386)
2 tablespoons canned chili peppers, drained
½ teaspoon ground cumin
8 6-inch flour tortillas
1 cup onion, minced

Nutritional Data

PER SERVING:

Calories	501
% calories from fat	12
Fat (gm)	6.8
Sat. Fat (gm)	1.3
Cholesterol (mg)	2.5
Sodium (mg)	689
Protein (gm)	23.8
Carbohydrate (gm)	87.9

EXCHANGES:

Milk	0.0	Bread	5.0
Veg.	2.5	Meat	1.0
Fruit	0.0	Fat	0.5

Preheat oven to 350 degrees. Combine cheese and beans in bowl. Add peppers and cumin. Divide filling among tortillas; spread evenly. Fold tortillas and arrange seam side down on baking sheet coated with cooking spray. Bake 10 minutes or until burritos are heated through. Place 2 burritos on each plate. Top with minced onions.

Bean Enchiladas

Serves 8 (2 enchiladas each)

Filling

4 cups Refried Beans (see p. 386)
1 cup onion, minced
½ cup plain nonfat yogurt

Combine all ingredients in mixing bowl. Set aside.

Sauce

3 cloves garlic, minced
4 large tomatoes, peeled, seeded, and minced
2 teaspoons fresh crushed oregano, or 1 teaspoon dried oregano
½ teaspoon each ingredient: sugar, black pepper, ground cumin
1 cup nonfat sour cream

Combine garlic, tomatoes, spices, and sour cream. Place in covered container and refrigerate until ready to use.

Tortillas

Canola oil, or vegetable cooking spray
16 corn tortillas

Heat oil. Using tongs to turn tortillas, fry each about 10 seconds on each side. Drain on paper towels.

To assemble, put Filling on each Tortilla, and roll up. Arrange seam side down in shallow 9" x 13" x 1¾" baking dish coated with cooking spray. Cover with Sauce. Bake, uncovered, at 350 degrees 20 minutes. Garnish with sour cream.

Nutritional Data

PER SERVING:

Calories	303
% calories from fat	6
Fat (gm)	2.1
Sat. Fat (gm)	0.3
Cholesterol (mg)	0.3
Sodium (mg)	327
Protein (gm)	16.4
Carbohydrate (gm)	58.1

EXCHANGES:

Milk	0.5	Bread	3.0
Veg.	1.0	Meat	0.5
Fruit	0.0	Fat	0.0

Zucchini and Cheese Latkes

Serves 6 (5 latkes each)

2 lbs. small zucchini
1 medium potato, peeled
1 tablespoon fresh lemon juice
1 cup green onions, sliced
¼ cup pimiento, chopped
½ cup Lorraine cheese, grated
2 cloves garlic, minced
Egg substitute equal to 1 egg, beaten
1 cup flour
1 tablespoon sugar
½ teaspoon each ingredient: salt, pepper

Nutritional Data

PER SERVING:

Calories	167
% calories from fat	11
Fat (gm)	2.5
Sat. Fat (gm)	1.4
Cholesterol (mg)	6.7
Sodium (mg)	246
Protein (gm)	8.2
Carbohydrate (gm)	29.2

EXCHANGES:

Milk	0.0	Bread	1.5
Veg.	1.0	Meat	0.5
Fruit	0.0	Fat	0.0

Vegetable oil for frying
Mock Sour Cream (see p. 497), or applesauce, if desired

Grate zucchini and potato; remove as much water as possible by squeezing mixture with towel. Put vegetables in large
bowl and toss with lemon juice, green onions, pimiento,
cheese, garlic, and egg substitute. Sift together flour, sugar,
salt, and pepper. Blend into vegetable mixture.

Heat 1/4-inch oil in large skillet until hot. Drop mixture by
heaping tablespoons into hot oil and flatten with back of
spoon. Fry until golden on both sides. Remove from skillet
and place on paper towels to drain. Serve with Mock Sour
Cream or applesauce. Makes about 30 latkes.

Zucchini Pancakes

Serves 6	**Nutritional Data**	
3 cups zucchini, grated	PER SERVING:	
1 cup onion, minced	Calories	72
1 small carrot, grated	% calories from fat	3
1/2 cup all-purpose flour	Fat (gm)	0.3
3/4 teaspoon baking powder	Sat. Fat (gm)	0
1/2 cup egg substitute	Cholesterol (mg)	0
1/2 teaspoon salt	Sodium (mg)	253
1/2 teaspoon white pepper	Protein (gm)	4
1/2 teaspoon dried oregano, or 1 teaspoon	Carbohydrate (gm)	14
fresh oregano		
Butter-flavored vegetable cooking spray	EXCHANGES:	
	Milk 0.0 Bread 1.0	
	Veg. 0.0 Meat 0.0	
	Fruit 0.0 Fat 0.0	

Combine all ingredients, except cooking spray, in large
mixing bowl; blend together. Heat nonstick skillet coated with
cooking spray.

Shape zucchini mixture into pancakes with tablespoon.
Fry until golden brown on each side, turning with spatula.
Serve hot.

Stuffed Zucchini

Serves 6	**Nutritional Data**	
3 medium zucchini	PER SERVING:	
Vegetable cooking spray	Calories	95
1 clove garlic, minced	% calories from fat	28
1/2 cup onion, chopped	Fat (gm)	3.5
1/4 cup parsley, chopped	Sat. Fat (gm)	1.7
1 cup mushrooms, chopped	Cholesterol (mg)	9.9
2 tablespoons all-purpose flour	Sodium (mg)	116
1/4 teaspoon dried oregano, crushed	Protein (gm)	10
	Carbohydrate (gm)	7

		EXCHANGES:			
1	cup (4 oz.) low-fat Monterey Jack cheese, shredded	Milk	0.0	Bread	0.0
2	tablespoons pimiento, chopped	Veg.	1.0	Meat	1.5
1/4	cup Parmesan cheese, freshly grated	Fruit	0.0	Fat	0.0

Cook whole zucchini in boiling, salted water about 10 minutes or until tender. Drain. Cut in half lengthwise. Scoop out centers leaving 1/4-inch shell; chop scooped-out vegetable and set aside.

In large skillet coated with vegetable cooking spray, sauté garlic, onion, and parsley. Add mushrooms and continue cooking about 3 minutes or until tender. Stir in flour and oregano; remove from heat. Stir in Monterey Jack cheese and pimiento; stir in reserved chopped zucchini. Heat mixture through.

Preheat broiler. Fill zucchini shells, using approximately 1/4 cup filling for each. Sprinkle with Parmesan cheese. Broil several inches from source of heat 3 to 5 minutes or until hot and bubbly.

Note: Stuffed zucchini may be assembled in advance, covered, and refrigerated up to 4 hours. Broil 5 to 7 minutes instead of 3 to 5.

Greek Stuffed Zucchini

Serves 6

		Nutritional Data	
12	6-inch zucchini	PER SERVING:	
1/2	cup cooked long-grain rice	Calories	72
1½	cups onion, finely chopped	% calories from fat	6
2	cups celery, finely chopped	Fat (gm)	0.6
1	teaspoon Spike (see "About This Cookbook")	Sat. Fat (gm)	0.1
		Cholesterol (mg)	0
	Pepper, freshly ground	Sodium (mg)	49
1	teaspoon basil	Protein (gm)	3.3
1	teaspoon oregano	Carbohydrate (gm)	15.7
1	cup parsley, chopped		
1	cup tomato, chopped	EXCHANGES:	
3	tablespoons fresh lemon juice		

EXCHANGES:			
Milk	0.0	Bread	0.0
Veg.	3.0	Meat	0.0
Fruit	0.0	Fat	0.0

Slice zucchini in half lengthwise, and scoop out insides to make boats; set aside. In bowl, add rice and remaining ingredients. Add zucchini pulp, chopped. Stuff mixture into zucchini boats. Place boats in microwave-safe dish and cook on High 10 minutes.

To Freeze: Place in microwave-safe container; label and freeze for up to 2 months.

To Serve: Thaw. Cover with microwave-safe plastic wrap, and cook on High 3 to 5 minutes.

Zucchini Stuffed with Mushrooms and Cheese

Serves 6 (2 halves each)

6 medium zucchini (6 oz. each)
Vegetable cooking spray
8 shallots, chopped
1 teaspoon thyme
12 large mushrooms, chopped
3 cloves garlic, minced
½ cup parsley, chopped
½ cup pitted black olives, sliced (optional)
1 tablespoon pimientos, chopped
¼ cup Parmesan cheese, freshly grated

Nutritional Data

PER SERVING:

Calories	60
% calories from fat	20
Fat (gm)	1.6
Sat. Fat (gm)	0.9
Cholesterol (mg)	3.3
Sodium (mg)	88
Protein (gm)	4.5
Carbohydrate (gm)	8.8

EXCHANGES:

Milk	0.0	Bread	0.0
Veg.	2.0	Meat	0.0
Fruit	0.0	Fat	0.0

Preheat oven to 300 degrees. Scrub and trim zucchini; do not peel. Cut lengthwise into halves, and carefully scoop out pulp without damaging shells. Coarsely chop pulp.

In large sauté pan coated with vegetable cooking spray, sauté shallots, thyme, mushrooms, garlic, and zucchini pulp about 5 minutes. Add parsley, olives, pimientos, and Parmesan cheese. Toss to mix well.

Fill zucchini shells with mixture and place them on baking sheet. Bake until zucchini are tender, about 20 minutes. Serve immediately.

Vegetarian Chili

Serves 5

1 cup dry kidney beans
1 cup dry garbanzo beans
Vegetable cooking spray
1 onion, diced
1 large carrot, diced
1 large stalk celery, diced
1 cup mushrooms, sliced
½ green bell pepper, diced
2 cloves garlic, minced
¾ cup tomato puree
2 large tomatoes, peeled and seeded
1 teaspoon (or to taste) cumin, ground
1½ teaspoons (or to taste) chili powder
½ teaspoon pepper

Nutritional Data

PER SERVING:

Calories	342
% calories from fat	8
Fat (gm)	3.1
Sat. Fat (gm)	0.1
Cholesterol (mg)	0
Sodium (mg)	189
Protein (gm)	19.9
Carbohydrate (gm)	62.8

EXCHANGES:

Milk	0.0	Bread	3.5
Veg.	2.0	Meat	0.0
Fruit	0.0	Fat	0.5

Place all beans in saucepan and cover with water. Bring to boil. Boil 2 minutes and remove from heat. Cover and let stand 1 hour. Drain and place in large heavy saucepan. Add 4 cups water and cook until almost done. Drain and reserve.

Sauté onion, carrot, celery, mushrooms, and green pepper in large, sprayed saucepan. Add garlic, and sauté a few seconds. Add tomato puree, tomatoes, cumin, chili powder, pepper, and all beans. Simmer, covered, 40 minutes, adding water as needed to keep moist.

Egg White Omelet

Serves 4

- 4 egg whites
- 1 cup egg substitute
- Butter-flavored vegetable cooking spray
- 1/2 cup onion, chopped
- 1/8 cup pimiento, chopped
- 2 cups white or brown mushrooms, sliced

Nutritional Data

PER SERVING:

Calories	81
% calories from fat	4
Fat (gm)	0.4
Sat. Fat (gm)	0
Cholesterol (mg)	0
Sodium (mg)	150
Protein (gm)	10.6
Carbohydrate (gm)	9.8

EXCHANGES:

Milk	0.0	Bread	0.0
Veg.	1.0	Meat	1.0
Fruit	0.0	Fat	0.0

Beat egg whites stiff, fold in egg substitute, set aside.

Heat nonstick skillet coated with cooking spray. Sauté onion, pimiento, and mushrooms about 5 minutes or until tender. Partially cover if necessary. Fold vegetables into egg mixture.

Coat clean nonstick skillet with cooking spray and heat. Cook omelet as you might cook scrambled eggs, but with less stirring. Turn eggs with spatula until they are cooked. They should remain fluffy and turn golden brown when turned. Serve hot.

Chapter Eight

VEGETABLES

Artichoke Delight

Serves 4

1	10-oz. package frozen artichokes
	Vegetable cooking spray
2	tablespoons shallots, finely chopped
2	tablespoons onions, finely chopped
1	teaspoon Spike (see "About This Cookbook")
1/4	teaspoon black pepper, freshly ground
2	tablespoons white wine vinegar
1/4	cup white wine
1/2	cup boiling water
1	clove garlic, minced
1/2	bay leaf, crushed

Nutritional Data

PER SERVING:

Calories	51
% calories from fat	2
Fat (gm)	0.1
Sat. Fat (gm)	0
Cholesterol (mg)	0
Sodium (mg)	65
Protein (gm)	2.6
Carbohydrate (gm)	9.6

EXCHANGES:

Milk	0.0	Bread	0.0
Veg.	2.0	Meat	0.0
Fruit	0.0	Fat	0.0

Coat large skillet with vegetable cooking spray and add artichokes, shallots, and onions. Cook over medium heat, turning frequently, for 5 minutes or until artichokes are separated and onions are softened but not browned.

Add Spike, pepper, vinegar, and wine. Bring to boil and cook on high for 10 minutes or until liquid is reduced to about 2 tablespoons. Remove artichokes to heated serving dish and keep warm. Add to skillet, boiling water, garlic, and bay leaf. Heat through and pour sauce over artichokes.

Artichokes, Forester's Style

Serves 6

8	artichokes (about 2 lbs.)
	Juice of 1 lemon
3	cloves garlic, minced
1/2	cup Basic Tomato-Basil Sauce (see p. 501), or 1 cup canned Italian plum tomatoes, drained
1/2	lb. mushrooms, cleaned and sliced
1/3	cup water
1/3	cup dry white wine
	Pinch oregano
	Pepper, freshly ground, to taste
2	tablespoons fresh basil, chopped
2	tablespoons fresh parsley, chopped
	Vegetable cooking spray

Nutritional Data

PER SERVING:

Calories	102
% calories from fat	5
Fat (gm)	0.7
Sat. Fat (gm)	0.1
Cholesterol (mg)	0
Sodium (mg)	192
Protein (gm)	6.2
Carbohydrate (gm)	20.2

EXCHANGES:

Milk	0.0	Bread	1.0
Veg.	1.0	Meat	0.0
Fruit	0.0	Fat	0.0

Trim, clean, and quarter artichokes, and remove chokes. Place them in water with juice of 1 lemon until ready to use.

Heat saucepan coated with vegetable cooking spray, add garlic, and sauté 1 minute.

Drain artichokes, add to garlic, and sauté 3 to 4 minutes. Add tomato sauce or tomatoes, mushrooms, water, wine, oregano, and pepper.

Combine thoroughly and simmer, partly covered, stirring occasionally, for 20 to 25 minutes, until artichokes are cooked but still firm. Add basil and parsley and adjust for seasoning.

Asparagus with Mustard Sauce

Serves 8

Asparagus

2½   lbs. asparagus, trimmed

Mustard Sauce

2   tablespoons margarine
3   tablespoons all-purpose flour
1   cup chicken broth, made from
    1 chicken bouillon cube
1   cup skim milk
¼   cup Dijon mustard
1   teaspoon fresh lemon juice
    Dash white pepper

Nutritional Data

PER SERVING:

Calories	68
% calories from fat	17
Fat (gm)	1.4
Sat. Fat (gm)	0.3
Cholesterol (mg)	2.5
Sodium (mg)	267
Protein (gm)	5.5
Carbohydrate (gm)	10.7

EXCHANGES:

Milk	0.0	Bread	0.0
Veg.	2.0	Meat	0.0
Fruit	0.0	Fat	0.5

Mustard Sauce (make first): Melt margarine in medium-size saucepan. Stir in flour and cook 1 minute. Add chicken broth and skim milk, stirring constantly with whisk. Bring to boil. Lower heat and simmer 5 minutes, stirring occasionally.

Remove from heat and whisk in mustard, lemon juice, and white pepper. Keep warm while cooking asparagus; do not let boil.

Asparagus: Bring to boil 2 quarts water in large skillet or Dutch oven. Add asparagus. Cook 3 to 5 minutes or until crisp-tender. Drain in colander. Arrange on serving platter. Pour Mustard Sauce over asparagus and serve.

Pimiento Asparagus

Serves 4

1¼ lbs. asparagus
2 tablespoons fresh lemon juice
2 tablespoons pimientos, chopped
1 tablespoon toasted pine nuts

Snap ends off asparagus and rinse. Arrange on platter in single layer. Drizzle on lemon juice, and sprinkle pimiento pieces on top. Cover with wax paper.

Microwave on High 5 to 6 minutes, turning dish once during cycle. Cook another 1 minute or so if softer spears are desired. Toss pine nuts over asparagus and serve.

Nutritional Data

PER SERVING:

Calories	48
% calories from fat	21
Fat (gm)	1.8
Sat. Fat (gm)	0.1
Cholesterol (mg)	0
Sodium (mg)	5.9
Protein (gm)	4
Carbohydrate (gm)	6.8

EXCHANGES:

Milk	0.0	Bread	0.0
Veg.	1.0	Meat	0.0
Fruit	0.0	Fat	0.5

Pine Nut Green Beans

Serves 4

1 lb. green beans, trimmed and washed
½ cup Italian plum tomatoes, drained and crushed
2 tablespoons toasted pine nuts
Dash pepper

Place green beans and tomatoes in 8-inch baking dish or casserole and stir to mix. Cover with lid or wax paper. Microwave on High 7 to 9 minutes or until tender, stirring twice. Drain off any excess liquid, toss with pine nuts, and season with pepper.

Nutritional Data

PER SERVING:

Calories	60
% calories from fat	35
Fat (gm)	2.8
Sat. Fat (gm)	0
Cholesterol (mg)	0
Sodium (mg)	17
Protein (gm)	2.9
Carbohydrate (gm)	8.8

EXCHANGES:

Milk	0.0	Bread	0.0
Veg.	1.5	Meat	0.0
Fruit	0.0	Fat	0.5

Swedish Green Beans in Mustard Sauce

Serves 6

1½ lbs. whole green beans

Sauce

2 tablespoons diet margarine
2 tablespoons flour
1 teaspon dry mustard
1 tablespoon chopped fresh dill, or 1 teaspoon dried dill

Nutritional Data

PER SERVING:

Calories	81
% calories from fat	29
Fat (gm)	2.8
Sat. Fat (gm)	0.5
Cholesterol (mg)	0.5
Sodium (mg)	352
Protein (gm)	3.4
Carbohydrate (gm)	12.3

½   teaspoon salt
     Pinch pepper
¾   cup skim milk
3   tablespoons mustard
2   teaspoons cider vinegar
2   teaspoons sugar

EXCHANGES:
Milk	0.0	Bread	0.0
Veg.	2.0	Meat	0.0
Fruit	0.0	Fat	0.5

Cook beans; drain and place in saucepan.

Sauce: Melt margarine in small saucepan over moderate heat. Blend in flour, dry mustard, dill, salt, and pepper; cook 1 minute. Add milk, stirring until thickened and smooth, 2 or 3 minutes. Blend in prepared mustard, vinegar, and sugar.

Add beans and cook until heated through, about 3 minutes.

Italian Green Beans

Serves 6

1   lb. green beans, cut into 2-inch pieces
2   teaspoons olive oil
¼   cup seasoned bread crumbs
¼   cup Parmesan, or Romano cheese, freshly grated
     Pepper
6   fresh basil leaves, coarsely chopped
½   cup sun-dried tomatoes

Nutritional Data

PER SERVING:
Calories	83
% calories from fat	32
Fat (gm)	3.1
Sat. Fat (gm)	1.1
Cholesterol (mg)	3.3
Sodium (mg)	314
Protein (gm)	4.1
Carbohydrate (gm)	10.8

EXCHANGES:
Milk	0.0	Bread	0.0
Veg.	2.0	Meat	0.0
Fruit	0.0	Fat	0.5

Steam beans 5 minutes and drain. Heat oil in pan and sauté beans 3 minutes. Add bread crumbs, cheese, and pepper. Toss together thoroughly. Garnish with fresh basil and sun-dried tomatoes.

Hot Spiced Beets

Serves 4

2 cups fresh or canned dietetic beets, sliced
½ cup water
2 cloves
1 bay leaf
1 tablespoon red wine vinegar
1 packet Equal® (see "About This Cookbook")

Nutritional Data

PER SERVING:

Calories	31
% calories from fat	4
Fat (gm)	0.1
Sat. Fat (gm)	0
Cholesterol (mg)	0
Sodium (mg)	53
Protein (gm)	1.1
Carbohydrate (gm)	7.1

EXCHANGES:

Milk	0.0	Bread	0.0
Veg.	1.5	Meat	0.0
Fruit	0.0	Fat	0.0

Drain juice from beets, if using canned. Add ½ cup water to saucepan and bring to boil with cloves and bay leaf. Add vinegar (and beets, if using fresh). Heat 10 minutes. Remove cloves and bay leaf. If using canned beets, add beets to hot liquid and heat through about 1 minute. Remove from heat and stir in Equal®. Serve hot.

Bok Choy

Serves 4

1 lb. bok choy (Chinese celery), about 6 cups
1 teaspoon reduced-sodium soy sauce
1 clove garlic, minced
1 tablespoon frozen apple juice concentrate
½ teaspoon sesame oil
   Dash ground ginger
1 tablespoon roasted pumpkin seeds

Nutritional Data

PER SERVING:

Calories	37
% calories from fat	24
Fat (gm)	1
Sat. Fat (gm)	0.1
Cholesterol (mg)	0
Sodium (mg)	65
Protein (gm)	2.5
Carbohydrate (gm)	4.5

EXCHANGES:

Milk	0.0	Bread	0.0
Veg.	1.0	Meat	0.0
Fruit	0.0	Fat	0.0

Chop bok choy into 1-inch slices and shred tops. Combine with remaining ingredients, except pumpkin seeds, and place in 2-quart glass measure or baking dish. Cover with vented plastic wrap, and microwave on High 3 to 4 minutes, stirring once. Drain, toss with pumpkin seeds, and serve.

Marinated Broccoli

Serves 6

3 bunches broccoli, without stems
1 tablespoon safflower oil
3 tablespoons fat-free beef bouillon
1 tablespoon dried dill weed
1 tablespoon red wine vinegar
2 tablespoons red wine
1 teaspoon garlic powder
1 teaspoon Spike (see "About This Cookbook")
1 tablespoon low-sodium soy sauce
Fresh dill or nasturtium blossoms for garnish

Nutritional Data

PER SERVING:

Calories	31
% calories from fat	27
Fat (gm)	1.2
Sat. Fat (gm)	0.1
Cholesterol (mg)	0
Sodium (mg)	73
Protein (gm)	3.7
Carbohydrate (gm)	3

EXCHANGES:

Milk	0.0	Bread	0.0
Veg.	0.5	Meat	0.0
Fruit	0.0	Fat	0.5

Separate broccoli into florets. Combine remaining ingredients in blender. Blend until mixed well. Pour over broccoli and marinate 4 to 24 hours. Before serving, pour off marinade and garnish with dill or nasturtiums.

Brussels Sprouts Almondine

Serves 4

1 lb. Brussels sprouts, cut in half
¼ cup Chicken Stock (see p. 40)
1 clove garlic, minced
1 teaspoon whole-grain Dijon mustard
1 tablespoon fresh lemon juice
Dash pepper
3 tablespoons blanched almonds, slivered

Nutritional Data

PER SERVING:

Calories	85
% calories from fat	32
Fat (gm)	3.6
Sat. Fat (gm)	0.4
Cholesterol (mg)	0.6
Sodium (mg)	44.2
Protein (gm)	4.6
Carbohydrate (gm)	12.5

EXCHANGES:

Milk	0.0	Bread	0.0
Veg.	2.0	Meat	0.0
Fruit	0.0	Fat	1.0

Discard any discolored outer leaves, and rinse Brussels sprouts. Place in 1-quart casserole or serving dish with Chicken Stock. Cover with wax paper and microwave on High 3 to 4 minutes, stir, and microwave on High another 3 to 4 minutes. Remove from oven and let rest 1 or 2 minutes.

Meantime, combine remaining ingredients, and microwave on High 40 seconds. Drain sprouts and toss with warmed sauce.

Braised Cabbage in Wine

Serves 8

1 large onion, sliced thinly
1 tablespoon fresh rosemary, or 1
   teaspoon dried rosemary
1 medium head cabbage, coarsely
   shredded
1 tablespoon Classic Spaghetti Sauce
   (see p. 500), or canned spaghetti sauce
1 cup dry white wine
   Spike, to taste (see "About This
   Cookbook")
   Pepper, freshly ground, to taste
   Vegetable cooking spray

Nutritional Data

PER SERVING:

Calories	46
% calories from fat	4
Fat (gm)	0.2
Sat. Fat (gm)	0
Cholesterol (mg)	0.3
Sodium (mg)	21
Protein (gm)	1.2
Carbohydrate (gm)	5.9

EXCHANGES:

Milk	0.0	Bread	0.0
Veg.	1.5	Meat	0.0
Fruit	0.0	Fat	0.0

In large saucepan coated with vegetable cooking spray, add onion and rosemary, and sauté over medium heat until onion becomes translucent. Add cabbage, and cook, stirring, 5 minutes until cabbage begins to wilt. Add sauce, white wine, and Spike and pepper to taste. Cover, and cook slowly over low heat for about 20 minutes until cabbage is tender. Serve hot.

 # Caraway Cabbage

Serves 4

1 head green cabbage, about 1- to 1¼ lbs.
2 tablespoons frozen apple juice
   concentrate
2 tablespoons whole-grain Dijon mustard
4 drops sesame oil
1½ tablespoons caraway seeds

Nutritional Data

PER SERVING:

Calories	54
% calories from fat	19
Fat (gm)	1.3
Sat. Fat (gm)	0.1
Cholesterol (mg)	0
Sodium (mg)	124
Protein (gm)	2
Carbohydrate (gm)	10.4

EXCHANGES:

Milk	0.0	Bread	0.0
Veg.	2.0	Meat	0.0
Fruit	0.0	Fat	0.0

Trim stems off cabbage and cut into 8 wedges. Mix together remaining ingredients. Arrange cabbage wedges on their sides on a 12-inch glass baking dish, and coat with mustard mixture. Cover with vented plastic wrap, and microwave on High 5 to 6 minutes. Rotate dish and microwave on High another 5 to 6 minutes, until crisp-tender.

Ruby Red Cabbage

Serves 6

1 medium onion, chopped
4 cloves garlic, minced
2 teaspoons canola oil
¾ lb. red cabbage, shredded (about 4 cups)
¼ cup balsamic vinegar
2 tablespoons frozen orange juice concentrate
1 cup Chicken Stock (see p. 40)
3 tablespoons raisins
1 tablespoon ginger root, peeled and chopped fine
½ teaspoon cloves, powdered
1 bay leaf
Juice of 1 lemon

Nutritional Data

PER SERVING:

Calories	79
% calories from fat	20
Fat (gm)	1.9
Sat. Fat (gm)	0.2
Cholesterol (mg)	1.7
Sodium (mg)	11
Protein (gm)	1.9
Carbohydrate (gm)	14.5

EXCHANGES:

Milk	0.0	Bread	0.0
Veg.	2.0	Meat	0.0
Fruit	0.5	Fat	0.0

Place onion, garlic, and oil in 2-quart casserole or measuring cup, and microwave on High 3 minutes. Mix with shredded cabbage and remaining ingredients, cover with wax paper, and microwave on High 4 minutes. Stir, and microwave on High another 4 minutes. When cabbage is tender, discard bay leaf.

 # *Baby Carrots à l'Orange*

Serves 4

1½ cups unsalted chicken broth
20 baby carrots, or 2 large carrots, peeled and sliced
1 medium onion, chopped
1 small orange, peeled and diced
1½ packets Equal® (see "About This Cookbook")

Nutritional Data

PER SERVING:

Calories	48
% calories from fat	5
Fat (gm)	0.3
Sat. Fat (gm)	0
Cholesterol (mg)	0
Sodium (mg)	26
Protein (gm)	1.5
Carbohydrate (gm)	10.8

EXCHANGES:

Milk	0.0	Bread	0.0
Veg.	2.0	Meat	0.0
Fruit	0.0	Fat	0.0

In heavy saucepan, heat chicken broth to boiling. Add carrots and onion; cover and cook until nearly tender, approximately 7 to 8 minutes. Add orange and cook 4 to 5 minutes more. Remove from heat and stir in Equal®. Drain and serve hot.

Steamed Carrots and Pea Pods

Serves 6

6 medium carrots (3 cups), sliced
6 ozs. pea pods
   Pepper, freshly ground
1 tablespoon unsalted diet margarine

Nutritional Data

PER SERVING:

Calories	44
% calories from fat	22
Fat (gm)	1.1
Sat. Fat (gm)	0.2
Cholesterol (mg)	0
Sodium (mg)	20
Protein (gm)	1.4
Carbohydrate (gm)	7.8

EXCHANGES:

Milk	0.0	Bread	0.0
Veg.	1.5	Meat	0.0
Fruit	0.0	Fat	0.0

Pour boiling water into wok to about ½ inch below steamer rack. Arrange carrots on steamer rack in wok. Cover and steam 15 minutes. Add pea pods and steam additional 3 to 5 minutes. Remove vegetables to serving plate, and season with freshly ground pepper and margarine.

To Freeze: Vacuum seal individual portions; label and freeze for up to 2 months.

To Serve: Put bags in boiling water, and bring to boil again. Boil 10 to 12 minutes.

Carrots Vichy

Serves 4

1 lb. carrots, peeled and cut into slices ½-inch thick
2½ cups water, divided
1 teaspoon granulated sugar
1 teaspoon Spike (see "About This Cookbook")
   Vegetable cooking spray
2 large onions, chopped
1 envelope Butter Buds
2 tablespoons parsley, chopped

Nutritional Data

PER SERVING:

Calories	96
% calories from fat	3
Fat (gm)	0.4
Sat. Fat (gm)	0.1
Cholesterol (mg)	0
Sodium (mg)	398
Protein (gm)	2.2
Carbohydrate (gm)	20.6

EXCHANGES:

Milk	0.0	Bread	0.0
Veg.	3.5	Meat	0.0
Fruit	0.0	Fat	0.0

In heavy saucepan, combine carrots, water, sugar, and Spike. Cover and bring to boil. Lower flame and simmer 10 minutes or until tender. Remove from heat and set aside.

In small skillet coated with vegetable cooking spray, add onions and cook until soft. Add carrots and Butter Buds with ½ cup water. Simmer about 3 minutes. Remove from heat and place carrots in bowl. Top with parsley.

Colorful Cauliflower

Serves 4

1	medium head cauliflower, about 1 lb., trimmed and cut into florets
1¼	cups green bell pepper, chopped
1	medium carrot, diced fine
1	teaspoon caraway seeds
¼	cup water
	Pepper

Nutritional Data

PER SERVING:

Calories	54
% calories from fat	6
Fat (gm)	0.4
Sat. Fat (gm)	0.1
Cholesterol (mg)	0
Sodium (mg)	14
Protein (gm)	2.9
Carbohydrate (gm)	11.5

EXCHANGES:

Milk	0.0	Bread	0.0
Veg.	2.0	Meat	0.0
Fruit	0.0	Fat	0.0

Place cauliflower in 1-quart casserole and sprinkle with green peppers, carrots, and caraway seeds. Add water, cover, and microwave on High 5 to 7 minutes, stirring once. Dust with pepper to taste, and let stand 2 minutes before serving.

Cauliflower Sicilian Style

Serves 6

½	cup leeks (white parts only) or onions, thinly sliced
3	cloves garlic, minced
1	medium cauliflower, washed, trimmed, and cut into small florets
1	medium tomato, thinly sliced
1	green bell pepper, seeded and thinly sliced
½	cup dry white wine
	Pepper, freshly ground, to taste
½	teaspoon ground oregano
2	tablespoons fresh parsley, chopped
2	tablespoons fresh basil, chopped
2	tablespoons capers
2	tablespoons pitted Italian black olives, chopped
1	lemon, cut into 6 wedges
	Vegetable cooking spray

Nutritional Data

PER SERVING:

Calories	68
% calories from fat	17
Fat (gm)	1.6
Sat. Fat (gm)	0.1
Cholesterol (mg)	0
Sodium (mg)	146
Protein (gm)	4.3
Carbohydrate (gm)	9.7

EXCHANGES:

Milk	0.0	Bread	0.0
Veg.	2.5	Meat	0.0
Fruit	0.0	Fat	0.0

In large skillet coated with vegetable cooking spray, sauté leeks or onions until they begin to color, about 5 minutes. Add garlic, and sauté another minute. Stir in cauliflower, and cook over medium heat, stirring constantly, 3 minutes to combine ingredients. Reduce heat, and cook covered 5 minutes.

Remove cover, add tomato, bell pepper, white wine, and pepper. Combine and simmer covered another 5 minutes. Blend in oregano, parsley, basil, and 1 tablespoon each of capers and olives. Heat through, and place cauliflower in heated serving bowl. Sprinkle remaining capers and olives on top, surround with lemon wedges, and serve.

Corn and Peppers

Serves 4

½	cup green bell pepper, diced
½	cup red bell pepper, diced
1	teaspoon canola oil
2	cups corn niblets (canned or frozen and thawed)
¼	teaspoon ground cumin
¼	teaspoon chili powder
	Dash powdered ginger
⅛	teaspoon pepper

Nutritional Data

PER SERVING:

Calories	93
% calories from fat	11
Fat (gm)	1.4
Sat. Fat (gm)	0.1
Cholesterol (mg)	0
Sodium (mg)	7
Protein (gm)	3
Carbohydrate (gm)	20.7

EXCHANGES:

Milk	0.0	Bread	1.0
Veg.	1.0	Meat	0.0
Fruit	0.0	Fat	0.0

Place green and red peppers in 1-quart casserole with oil. Microwave on High 3 minutes. Add remaining ingredients and cover with wax paper. Microwave on High 4 minutes, stirring once midcycle.

Fennel with Tomato Sauce

Serves 6

1	leek, green leaves included, washed well and sliced into thin rounds
3	cloves garlic, minced
4	fennel bulbs (about 4 ozs.), trimmed and cut into wedges 1-inch thick
3	tablespoons Classic Spaghetti Sauce (see p. 500), or canned tomato sauce
¾	cup water
½	teaspoon salt
	Pepper, freshly ground, to taste
1	tablespoon parsley, finely chopped
	Vegetable cooking spray

Nutritional Data

PER SERVING:

Calories	25
% calories from fat	13
Fat (gm)	0.4
Sat. Fat (gm)	0.1
Cholesterol (mg)	1.1
Sodium (mg)	227
Protein (gm)	1.2
Carbohydrate (gm)	4.7

EXCHANGES:

Milk	0.0	Bread	0.0
Veg.	1.0	Meat	0.0
Fruit	0.0	Fat	0.0

Coat large saucepan with vegetable cooking spray, add leek, and sauté over medium heat, stirring frequently, until lightly browned, about 3 minutes. Add garlic, cook 1 minute more, then add fennel wedges, and sauté 2 minutes, turning to coat.

Combine sauce with ¾ cup water, and pour mixture over fennel. Add salt and pepper, cover, reduce heat to low, and simmer, stirring occasionally, 10 to 12 minutes, until fennel is cooked through but still firm. Transfer to heated serving platter, sprinkle with parsley, and serve hot.

Hot Peppered Greens

Serves 4

- 1 lb. kale, collard greens, beet tops, or mustard greens
- 1 tablespoon red pepper flakes
- 3 cloves garlic, mashed
- 1 cup water
- Juice of 1 lemon
- Pinch salt
- 1 tablespoon sunflower seeds

Nutritional Data

PER SERVING:

Calories	58
% calories from fat	25
Fat (gm)	1.9
Sat. Fat (gm)	0.2
Cholesterol (mg)	0
Sodium (mg)	18
Protein (gm)	4.1
Carbohydrate (gm)	8.9

EXCHANGES:

Milk	0.0	Bread	0.0
Veg.	2.0	Meat	0.0
Fruit	0.0	Fat	0.0

Chop greens and mix all ingredients together, except sunflower seeds, in 2-quart measure. Cover with wax paper. Microwave on High 3 to 5 minutes, stirring once during cycle. Serve with sprinkling of sunflower seeds.

Hot Kale

Serves 4

- 1 lb. kale, or turnip greens
- 1 cup Chicken Stock (see p. 40)
- 1 cup water
- ½ teaspoon olive oil
- ¾ cup onion, chopped
- 3 cloves garlic, minced
- 1 tablespoon ginger root, peeled and grated
- 3-4 leaves fresh basil, or ½ teaspoon dried
- ½ teaspoon hot red pepper flakes
- 4 dashes sesame oil
- Juice of 1 lemon
- 1 teaspoon toasted pine nuts

Nutritional Data

PER SERVING:

Calories	73
% calories from fat	22
Fat (gm)	2.1
Sat. Fat (gm)	0.3
Cholesterol (mg)	2.5
Sodium (mg)	22
Protein (gm)	4.9
Carbohydrate (gm)	11

EXCHANGES:

Milk	0.0	Bread	0.0
Veg.	2.0	Meat	0.0
Fruit	0.0	Fat	0.5

Wash greens well in tepid water, and slice into thin strips. Place in 2-quart measure with broth, add water, cover with vented plastic wrap, and microwave on High 7 to 10 minutes, stirring once.

In 2-cup measure, place oil, onion, garlic, ginger, basil, and pepper flakes, and microwave on High 2 minutes. Drain greens, stir in onion mixture, and complete seasoning with sesame oil and lemon juice. Garnish with pine nuts.

Okra Provençal

Serves 6

1	lb. small okra pods, trimmed
1	12-oz. can stewed tomatoes, drained and crushed
4	scallions, chopped
2	cloves garlic, minced
½	cup green bell pepper, chopped
8	small pimiento-stuffed olives
¼	cup parsley, chopped
	Pinch each ingredient: dried thyme, marjoram
2	teaspoons dried basil
	Salt and pepper, to taste

Nutritional Data

PER SERVING:

Calories	54
% calories from fat	13
Fat (gm)	1
Sat. Fat (gm)	0.1
Cholesterol (mg)	0
Sodium (mg)	258
Protein (gm)	2.5
Carbohydrate (gm)	11.4

EXCHANGES:

Milk	0.0	Bread	0.0
Veg.	2.0	Meat	0.0
Fruit	0.0	Fat	0.0

Place okra pods on paper towels in 8" x 12" baking dish. Microwave on High 2 to 3 minutes, until tender, turning once.

Place remaining ingredients in 1-quart measure and cover with wax paper. Microwave on High 5 to 6 minutes. Stir, and add okra pods. Microwave together 1 minute on High to heat through. Stir and serve.

Onions Stuffed with Mushrooms

Serves 6

5	medium red onions
1½	cups mushrooms, finely chopped
2	cloves garlic
4	tablespoons bread crumbs
3	tablespoons Parmesan cheese, freshly grated
2	tablespoons fresh parsley, chopped
2	tablespoons fresh oregano, chopped
1	teaspoon Spike (see "About This Cookbook")
½	teaspoon pepper, freshly ground
	Vegetable cooking spray

Nutritional Data

PER SERVING:

Calories	84
% calories from fat	15
Fat (gm)	1.5
Sat. Fat (gm)	0.7
Cholesterol (mg)	2.5
Sodium (mg)	94
Protein (gm)	3.8
Carbohydrate (gm)	15.2

EXCHANGES:

Milk	0.0	Bread	0.0
Veg.	3.0	Meat	0.0
Fruit	0.0	Fat	0.0

Remove skin and 1 or 2 outer layers of onions. Steam onions until half cooked, about 20 to 30 minutes, depending on size. Test by inserting fork or knife point. It should enter but meet resistance. Drain onions and let cool until they can be handled.

Meanwhile, prepare stuffing by combining remaining ingredients in small mixing bowl.

Cut onions in half across grain. Scoop out pulp in center, leaving solid shell of 3 or 4 layers of onion and bottom intact. Chop ½ cup of pulp fine, and add it to stuffing mixture.

Preheat oven to 350 degrees. Fill onion halves with stuffing. Place snugly side by side in baking dish coated with vegetable cooking spray. Bake 30 minutes. Serve warm or at room temperature.

Creamed Onions and Mushrooms

Serves 8

- 4 tablespoons diet margarine
- 2 tablespoons arrowroot
- 1¾ cups skim milk
- 1 teaspoon Spike (see "About This Cookbook")
- 2 lbs. small white onions (12 per lb.), peeled
- 1 cup mushrooms, sliced
  Black pepper, freshly ground

Nutritional Data

PER SERVING:

Calories	96
% calories from fat	28
Fat (gm)	3.2
Sat. Fat (gm)	0.6
Cholesterol (mg)	0.9
Sodium (mg)	96
Protein (gm)	3.3
Carbohydrate (gm)	14.6

EXCHANGES:

Milk	0.0	Bread	0.0
Veg.	3.0	Meat	0.0
Fruit	0.0	Fat	0.5

Heat 2 tablespoons of margarine in 10-inch casserole, uncovered, and cook on High 1 minute. Whisk in arrowroot and cook uncovered on High 2 minutes more.

Remove from microwave. Whisk in milk and Spike, stirring well. Add onions and stir to coat. Cover tightly with plastic wrap. Cook on High 10 minutes.

Remove from microwave. Uncover and stir in remaining margarine and pepper.

To Freeze: Vacuum seal individual portions; label and freeze for up to 2 months.

To Serve: Put bags in boiling water, and bring to boil again. Boil 10 to 12 minutes.

Green Peas Valencia Style

Serves 4

Vegetable cooking spray
1   medium onion, finely chopped
2   cloves garlic, minced
1   small yellow bell pepper, minced
½   lb. shelled green peas, defrosted
    if frozen
¼   cup white wine
¼   cup water
2   tablespoons fresh parsley, chopped
1   tablespoon fresh thyme, chopped
1   bay leaf, crushed
    Pepper, freshly ground
⅛   teaspoon saffron threads
    Pimiento strips for garnish

Nutritional Data

PER SERVING:

Calories	77
% calories from fat	4
Fat (gm)	0.4
Sat. Fat (gm)	0.1
Cholesterol (mg)	0
Sodium (mg)	6
Protein (gm)	3.8
Carbohydrate (gm)	13.1

EXCHANGES:

Milk	0.0	Bread	0.5
Veg.	1.0	Meat	0.0
Fruit	0.0	Fat	0.0

Coat skillet with vegetable cooking spray and sauté onions and garlic about 3 minutes. Stir in bell pepper, peas, wine, and water. Add herbs and pepper and bring to simmer; cover and cook over low heat until peas are tender, 15 to 20 minutes, or a shorter time if peas are frozen. Stir in saffron threads and cook a few minutes longer. Serve garnished with pimiento.

Tricolored Bell Pepper Stir-Fry

Serves 4

Vegetable cooking spray
3   tablespoons white wine
1   green bell pepper, cut into julienne strips
1   red bell pepper, cut into julienne strips
1   yellow bell pepper, cut into julienne strips
1   medium onion, sliced
¼   cup green onions, sliced
1   tablespoon fresh basil, minced
¼   teaspoon fresh thyme
1   teaspoon garlic powder
2   tablespoons fresh parsley

Nutritional Data

PER SERVING:

Calories	39
% calories from fat	4
Fat (gm)	0.2
Sat. Fat (gm)	0
Cholesterol (mg)	0
Sodium (mg)	4
Protein (gm)	1.1
Carbohydrate (gm)	7.2

EXCHANGES:

Milk	0.0	Bread	0.0
Veg.	1.5	Meat	0.0
Fruit	0.0	Fat	0.0

Coat wok with vegetable cooking spray; place over high heat until hot. Add wine, peppers, onion slices, green onions, basil, thyme, and garlic powder. Stir-fry 3 to 3½ minutes or until vegetables are crisp-tender. If serving as vegetable, place peppers in bowl and garnish with parsley.

To Freeze: Vacuum seal, label, and freeze for up to 2 months.

To Serve: Place bags in boiling water, and bring water to boil again. Boil 10 to 12 minutes.

Baked Potatoes on the Grill

Serves 8

4 baking potatoes, 5 to 6 ozs. each, unpeeled and scrubbed
8 large cloves garlic, unpeeled
Heavy-duty aluminum foil
4 tablespoons cholesterol-free, nonfat sour cream, or plain nonfat yogurt
½ cup fresh chives, chopped

Nutritional Data	
PER SERVING:	
Calories	84
% calories from fat	1
Fat (gm)	0.1
Sat. Fat (gm)	0
Cholesterol (mg)	0
Sodium (mg)	11
Protein (gm)	2.3
Carbohydrate (gm)	19.2

EXCHANGES:			
Milk	0.0	Bread	1.0
Veg.	0.0	Meat	0.0
Fruit	0.0	Fat	0.0

Scrub potatoes under cold running water. Separately wrap potatoes and garlic cloves in heavy-duty aluminum foil. Remove grill rack and set potatoes directly on hot coals, around perimeter of barbecue grill. If you are grilling other food, replace grill rack and cook as directed. Potatoes should be turned every 10 minutes until done. Potatoes are cooked when easily pierced with tip of knife, 35 to 40 minutes, depending on size of potato, heat, and outdoor temperature.

Ten minutes before estimated finish time of potatoes, wrap garlic in aluminum foil and place on grill rack. Turn garlic every few minutes until it can easily be pierced with tip of knife.

Carefully remove potatoes and garlic from grill to serving plate, using pot holders and/or long-handled spoon. Remove foil and cut potatoes in half horizontally. Remove garlic from foil. Squeeze a garlic clove over each baked potato half. Serve hot with dollop of sour cream sprinkled with chives.

Spanakopita Baked Potatoes

Serves 8

4 baking potatoes, 5 to 6 ozs. each,
   unpeeled and scrubbed
   Vegetable cooking spray
4 cloves garlic, minced
1 cup onions, chopped
3 cups fresh spinach, washed well
   and chopped
½ cup nonfat ricotta cheese
¼ teaspoon each ingredient: oregano,
   pepper, basil, ground nutmeg

Nutritional Data

PER SERVING:

Calories	103
% calories from fat	2
Fat (gm)	0.2
Sat. Fat (gm)	0.1
Cholesterol (mg)	1.5
Sodium (mg)	31
Protein (gm)	4.6
Carbohydrate (gm)	22

EXCHANGES:

Milk	0.0	Bread	1.0
Veg.	1.0	Meat	0.0
Fruit	0.0	Fat	0.0

Preheat oven to 425 degrees. Scrub potatoes and pierce them several times with tip of sharp knife or fork. Set potatoes on nonstick cookie sheet. Bake on center rack of oven 45 minutes to 1 hour or until cooked. Potatoes are done when a knife inserted will test soft, or when squeezed gently will "give" slightly.

While potatoes are baking, prepare spinach topping. Lightly coat nonstick skillet with cooking spray. Sauté garlic and onions, covered, until onions are soft, stirring occasionally. Stir in spinach, cover, and continue cooking, stirring occasionally, until spinach is limp. Stir in cheese, oregano, pepper, basil, and nutmeg. Remove from heat.

Cut hot baked potatoes in half horizontally and gently squeeze open. Place potatoes on individual plates and spoon spinach filling over tops. Serve hot.

Shrimp and Asparagus Over Baked Potatoes

Serves 8

4 baking potatoes, 5 to 6 ozs. each,
   unpeeled and scrubbed
   Vegetable cooking spray
½ teaspoon ginger root, peeled and grated
3 cups thin asparagus, cut into 2-inch
   pieces, blanched
2 cups bok choy, sliced thinly
½ cup dried Oriental shiitake mushrooms,
   reconstituted* and drained

Nutritional Data

PER SERVING:

Calories	113
% calories from fat	4
Fat (gm)	0.5
Sat. Fat (gm)	0.1
Cholesterol (mg)	9
Sodium (mg)	20
Protein (gm)	4.9
Carbohydrate (gm)	23

1	cup low-salt Chicken Stock (see p. 40)		EXCHANGES:			
1	tablespoon cornstarch		Milk	0.0	Bread	1.0
½	teaspoon sugar		Veg.	1.5	Meat	0.0
1	tablespoon dry white wine		Fruit	0.0	Fat	0.0
¼	cup shrimp, peeled and chopped					

Preheat oven to 425 degrees. Scrub potatoes and stick with tip of sharp knife or fork several times. Set potatoes on non-stick cookie sheet. Bake on center rack of oven 45 minutes to 1 hour or until cooked. Potatoes are done when knife inserted will test soft, or when squeezed gently will "give" slightly.

While potatoes are baking, prepare vegetables and sauce. Lightly coat nonstick wok or skillet with cooking spray. Cook ginger, asparagus, bok choy, and mushrooms over medium-high heat, covered. Stir often until vegetables are just heated, not soggy.

Whisk together Chicken Stock and cornstarch. Stir in stock mixture, sugar, wine, and shrimp. Reduce heat to simmer and continue cooking until hot, about 1 minute.

To serve, cut hot baked potatoes in half horizontally and gently squeeze open. Spoon vegetables over potatoes and serve hot.

Note: To reconstitute Oriental or other dried mushrooms, cover them with boiling water, let stand 30 minutes, and drain. Squeeze out excess water.

Avocado-Topped Potatoes

Serves 8		**Nutritional Data**	
4	large baking potatoes	PER SERVING:	
	Vegetable oil	Calories	156
1	8-oz. container plain low-fat yogurt	% calories from fat	28
1	ripe avocado, mashed	Fat (gm)	5.1
2	tablespoons skim milk	Sat. Fat (gm)	1
1	tablespoon fresh lemon juice	Cholesterol (mg)	1.8
1	tablespoon onion, grated	Sodium (mg)	115
¼	teaspoon Spike (see "About This	Protein (gm)	4.9
	Cookbook")	Carbohydrate (gm)	24.1
¼	cup imitation bacon bits		
2	tomatoes, cut into wedges	EXCHANGES:	

EXCHANGES:			
Milk	0.0	Bread	1.5
Veg.	0.0	Meat	0.0
Fruit	0.0	Fat	1.0

Rub potatoes with oil. Bake in microwave on High 9 minutes.

Meanwhile, prepare avocado topping. Mix well all ingredients except bacon bits and tomatoes in bowl. Split tops of potatoes lengthwise, and fluff pulp with fork. Spoon avocado topping over potatoes. Sprinkle with bacon bits and garnish with tomato wedges.

To Freeze: Prepare avocado topping and place in vacuum-sealed bags; label and freeze for up to 2 months.

To Serve: Thaw avocado topping in refrigerator, bake potatoes, fill with topping, and garnish with bacon bits and tomato wedges.

Garden-Topped Potatoes

Serves 8		
4	large baking potatoes	
	Vegetable oil	
3	tablespoons diet margarine	
1	large green bell pepper, chopped	
1	cup green onions, sliced	
1	clove garlic, crushed	
½	cup mushrooms, sliced	
1	cup zucchini, sliced	
2	tomatoes, unpeeled and chopped	
¾	cup evaporated skim milk	
¼	cup Parmesan cheese, freshly grated	
¼	teaspoon Spike (see "About This Cookbook")	
	Dash pepper	
2	tablespoons parsley, chopped	

Nutritional Data

PER SERVING:

Calories	145
% calories from fat	20
Fat (gm)	3.4
Sat. Fat (gm)	1
Cholesterol (mg)	3.2
Sodium (mg)	145
Protein (gm)	5.6
Carbohydrate (gm)	24.2

EXCHANGES:

Milk	0.0	Bread	1.5
Veg.	0.5	Meat	0.0
Fruit	0.0	Fat	0.5

Rub potatoes with oil and bake in microwave on High 10 minutes.

Melt margarine in stockpot; add green bell pepper, onions, and garlic and sauté 2 to 3 minutes. Stir in mushrooms and zucchini and sauté 1 to 2 minutes. Add tomatoes and cook 2 minutes. Stir in next 4 ingredients and cook until thoroughly heated.

Split tops of potatoes lengthwise, and fluff pulp with fork. Spoon topping over potatoes and garnish with parsley.

To Freeze: Place individual portions of topping in microwave-safe container; label and freeze for up to 2 months.

To Serve: Thaw, cover with microwave-safe plastic wrap, and microwave on High 4 to 7 minutes. Garnish, if desired.

Mexican-Topped Potatoes

Serves 12

6 large baking potatoes
Vegetable oil
½ lb. bulk turkey sausage
1 lb. fat-free mozzarella cheese, cubed
¼ cup skim milk
1 10-oz. can tomatoes and green chilies, undrained and chopped
Shredded lettuce
Chopped tomato

Nutritional Data

PER SERVING:

Calories	177
% calories from fat	14
Fat (gm)	2.8
Sat. Fat (gm)	0.6
Cholesterol (mg)	23.5
Sodium (mg)	519
Protein (gm)	18.1
Carbohydrate (gm)	21

EXCHANGES:

Milk	0.0	Bread	1.0
Veg.	0.0	Meat	2.0
Fruit	0.0	Fat	0.0

Rub potatoes with oil and bake in microwave on High 10 minutes.

Cook sausage in microwave on High about 8 minutes. Drain and set aside.

Place cheese and milk in microwave-safe dish and cook on High about 2 minutes or until cheese melts. Add to meat mixture with tomatoes and chilies, and mix well.

Split tops of potatoes lengthwise, and fluff pulp with fork. Spoon topping over potatoes. Sprinkle with lettuce and tomato.

To Freeze: Place in microwave-safe containers; label and freeze for up to 2 months.

To Serve: Place in microwave on High 7 to 9 minutes.

Lyonnaise Potatoes

Serves 4

2 Idaho potatoes, about 8 ozs. each, sliced thin, about ⅛-inch thick
2 medium onions, sliced thin
1 tablespoon olive oil
3 cloves garlic, minced
¼ teaspoon salt
⅛ teaspoon pepper
⅛ teaspoon paprika
1 tablespoon parsley, chopped, for garnish

Nutritional Data

PER SERVING:

Calories	180
% calories from fat	18
Fat (gm)	3.6
Sat. Fat (gm)	0.5
Cholesterol (mg)	0
Sodium (mg)	145
Protein (gm)	3.5
Carbohydrate (gm)	34.7

EXCHANGES:

Milk	0.0	Bread	2.0
Veg.	0.5	Meat	0.0
Fruit	0.0	Fat	0.5

Place all ingredients, except parsley, in microwave-safe 3-quart casserole. Cover loosely with plastic wrap and microwave on High 12 to 14 minutes, until tender, stirring gently a few times. Garnish with parsley and let stand a few minutes before serving.

Rosemary-Scented Potatoes Gratin

Serves 12

10	Idaho baking potatoes, scrubbed and peeled
	Vegetable cooking spray
4	cloves garlic, minced
4	shallots, minced
1	handful fresh parsley, chopped
1	tablespoon fresh rosemary, minced
4	tablespoons Parmesan cheese, freshly grated
	Black pepper, freshly ground, to taste
2	cups Chicken Stock (see p. 40)

Nutritional Data

PER SERVING:

Calories	130
% calories from fat	6
Fat (gm)	0.9
Sat. Fat (gm)	0.5
Cholesterol (mg)	3.3
Sodium (mg)	48
Protein (gm)	3.9
Carbohydrate (gm)	26.7

EXCHANGES:

Milk	0.0	Bread	1.5
Veg.	0.5	Meat	0.0
Fruit	0.0	Fat	0.0

Preheat oven to 350 degrees. Slice potatoes into 1/8-inch or thinner circles. Coat 12-inch ovenproof gratin dish with vegetable cooking spray. Slightly overlap potato slices in spiral fashion to cover bottom of pan.

In small mixing bowl, combine garlic, shallots, parsley, rosemary, and Parmesan cheese and season with pepper. Sprinkle about 1/3 of mixture over potatoes. Continue to layer potatoes and cheese mixture until pan is three-fourths filled.

Cover with Chicken Stock, and bake 45 minutes or until potatoes are cooked. Remove from oven and let cool 5 minutes before serving.

Steamed Potatoes in Black Bean Sauce

Serves 8

16	new potatoes, scrubbed and peeled
1/4	lb. large shrimp, shelled, deveined, and cut in half lengthwise
3	ozs. very lean pork, such as tenderloin, ground
3	cloves garlic, minced
1/2	teaspoon powdered ginger
4	green onions, chopped

Nutritional Data

PER SERVING:

Calories	100
% calories from fat	6
Fat (gm)	0.6
Sat. Fat (gm)	0.2
Cholesterol (mg)	29.3
Sodium (mg)	78
Protein (gm)	6.8
Carbohydrate (gm)	16.8

1 cup snow peas, trimmed
1 tablespoon Oriental fermented black
   beans,* soaked 5 minutes to remove salt,
   rinsed and mashed
¼ teaspoon sugar
2 teaspoons each ingredient: light soy
   sauce, cornstarch, dry white wine

EXCHANGES:			
Milk	0.0	Bread	1.0
Veg.	0.0	Meat	0.5
Fruit	0.0	Fat	0.0

Slice potatoes and set aside. Wash shrimp and pat dry with paper towels.

Toss all ingredients, including potatoes and shrimp but excluding cornstarch and wine, in bowl. Whisk together cornstarch and wine. Add to bowl and toss all ingredients again. Place ingredients in heatproof steaming dish such as pie plate.

Over high heat, bring water to boil in steamer. Set heatproof dish on center of steamer rack above water level. Reduce heat to medium-low. Cover pot tightly and continue steaming until potatoes, shrimp, and pork are cooked. Potatoes are done when they can easily be pierced with tip of knife. Cooking will take 15 to 20 minutes.

Serve hot. Good with noodles and/or vegetables.

*Note: Oriental fermented black beans are available at large supermarkets or at Oriental food stores.

Stir-Fry Potatoes and Asian Vegetables

Serves 8

4 boiled potatoes, 5 to 6 ozs. each, peeled
   and cut into ½-inch cubes
   Vegetable cooking spray
4 cloves garlic, minced
½ teaspoon ginger root, peeled and grated
1 cup green onions, chopped
1 tablespoon cornstarch, mixed with 2
   tablespoons water
½ cup low-salt Chicken Stock (see p. 40)
3 cups bok choy, sliced
8 shiitake mushrooms, reconstituted in hot
   water for 20 minutes, drained and sliced
2 cups bean sprouts, rinsed under hot
   running water
2 tablespoons light soy sauce
½ teaspoon curry powder
½ teaspoon black pepper, freshly ground

Nutritional Data

PER SERVING:

Calories	108
% calories from fat	3
Fat (gm)	0.3
Sat. Fat (gm)	0.1
Cholesterol (mg)	0.6
Sodium (mg)	141
Protein (gm)	4.4
Carbohydrate (gm)	23.8

EXCHANGES:			
Milk	0.0	Bread	1.0
Veg.	1.0	Meat	0.0
Fruit	0.0	Fat	0.0

Cube potatoes. If not using potatoes immediately, set them in bowl of cold water. When ready to use, place in saucepan

and cover with water. Bring to boil over medium-high heat.
Reduce heat to medium and continue cooking about 8 minutes or until potatoes are just fork-tender. Drain.

Lightly coat nonstick wok, regular wok, or skillet with cooking spray. Stir-fry garlic, ginger, and green onions, covered, about 3 minutes or until vegetables are tender. Stir occasionally.

Add potatoes and stir-fry, covered, over high heat until just cooked and beginning to brown. Add cornstarch mixture and stock. Stir occasionally to prevent potatoes from sticking to bottom of pan.

Stir in remaining vegetables, one at a time. Sprinkle with soy sauce, curry powder, and pepper. Stir-fry until vegetables are hot and only just cooked. Do not overcook vegetables; they should be crunchy.

Spoon stir-fry into serving bowl, and bring to table hot.

Spinach-Stuffed Mushrooms

Serves 7 (2 mushrooms each)

1	10-oz. package frozen chopped spinach, or 1 bunch fresh spinach
14	large mushrooms
1	tablespoon margarine
1	clove garlic, crushed
1	teaspoon Worcestershire sauce
1/2	cup bread crumbs
1	teaspoon mustard
1/8	teaspoon pepper
2	tablespoons fat-free mayonnaise
1/8	cup Parmesan cheese, freshly grated

Nutritional Data

PER SERVING:

Calories	67
% calories from fat	34
Fat (gm)	2.7
Sat. Fat (gm)	0.8
Cholesterol (mg)	1.4
Sodium (mg)	200
Protein (gm)	2.9
Carbohydrate (gm)	8.6

EXCHANGES:

Milk	0.0	Bread	0.0
Veg.	1.5	Meat	0.0
Fruit	0.0	Fat	0.5

Preheat oven to 350 degrees.

Cook frozen spinach according to package directions. If using fresh spinach, place spinach and small amount of water in medium saucepan. Cook over medium heat 2 to 5 minutes. Drain cooked spinach and press out excess water with back of wooden spoon; set aside.

Remove stems from mushrooms and chop well. In medium skillet, melt margarine. Add chopped mushroom stems and garlic. Sauté until stems are soft; remove from heat. Add Worcestershire sauce, bread crumbs, mustard, pepper, mayonnaise, and cheese. Stir in drained cooked spinach.

Spoon some spinach mixture into each mushroom cap. Place mushrooms, stuffed side up, in 11" x 7" baking pan. Pour ³/₄ cup of water in bottom of pan, being careful not to pour water on mushrooms. Bake 20 minutes or until mushrooms are hot. Remove baked mushrooms from pan and discard any remaining liquid.

Sesame Spinach

Serves 4

1	teaspoon sesame oil
2	cloves garlic, minced
½	onion, chopped
1½	lbs. fresh spinach
1	teaspoon reduced-sodium soy sauce
⅛	teaspoon ginger root, peeled and minced
2	tablespoons sliced water chestnuts, rinsed and drained
2	teaspoons toasted sesame seeds

Nutritional Data

PER SERVING:

Calories	68
% calories from fat	28
Fat (gm)	2.5
Sat. Fat (gm)	0.4
Cholesterol (mg)	0
Sodium (mg)	180
Protein (gm)	5.7
Carbohydrate (gm)	9

EXCHANGES:

Milk	0.0	Bread	0.0
Veg.	1.5	Meat	0.0
Fruit	0.0	Fat	0.5

Place oil in measuring cup with garlic and onion, and microwave on High 1 minute, until tender. Wash spinach well and cut off tough stems; place in 4-quart casserole with just water left on leaves. Cover with vented plastic wrap, and microwave on High 4 to 6 minutes, stirring once, until wilted.

Drain spinach, mix with onion and garlic mixture, add soy sauce, ginger root, and water chestnuts, and microwave on High 1 more minute. Toss with sesame seeds and serve. This is also nice as a salad if served chilled.

Baked Acorn or Hubbard Squash

Serves 4

2	small acorn or hubbard squash
1	cup orange juice
1	teaspoon cinnamon and 1 teaspoon nutmeg mixed together
2	packets Equal® (see "About This Cookbook")

Nutritional Data

PER SERVING:

Calories	120
% calories from fat	4
Fat (gm)	0.6
Sat. Fat (gm)	0.2
Cholesterol (mg)	0
Sodium (mg)	6
Protein (gm)	2.1
Carbohydrate (gm)	29.1

Cut squash into fourths and remove seeds. Braise squash covered in shallow pan until somewhat softened, about 10 to 15 minutes. Sprinkle with orange juice and cinnamon and nutmeg mixture.

EXCHANGES:
Milk	0.0	Bread	1.0
Veg.	0.0	Meat	0.0
Fruit	1.0	Fat	0.0

Bake squash uncovered at 350 degrees about 20 to 25 minutes or until fork can pierce squash easily. Remove from oven and sprinkle with Equal®. Stir center with spoon and serve immediately.

Acorn Squash with Cranberry Topping

Serves 4

1 large acorn squash (about 2 lbs.)
½ cup cranberries
3 tablespoons orange juice concentrate, divided
1 tablespoon water
1 tablespoon dark raisins
4 teaspoons sugar

Nutritional Data

PER SERVING:

Calories	178
% calories from fat	2
Fat (gm)	0.4
Sat. Fat (gm)	0.1
Cholesterol (mg)	0
Sodium (mg)	11
Protein (gm)	3
Carbohydrate (gm)	45.9

EXCHANGES:

Milk	0.0	Bread	2.0
Veg.	0.0	Meat	0.0
Fruit	0.5	Fat	0.0

Cut squash in half and place, cut side down, in glass pie plate; add 1 tablespoon water. Cover loosely with wax paper. Microwave on High 8 to 10 minutes, until tender, rotating plate half-turn halfway through. Set aside.

Combine cranberries, 2 tablespoons orange juice concentrate, 1 tablespoon water, raisins, and sugar in 4-cup glass measure. Microwave 4 to 5 minutes, stirring once halfway through, until slightly thickened.

Drain squash and cut each half lengthwise in half. Return each quarter, cut side up, to pie plate; brush with remaining 1 tablespoon orange juice concentrate. Top evenly with cranberry mixture. Microwave 30 seconds to 1 minute.

To Freeze: Place in microwave-safe container; label and freeze for up to 2 months.

To Serve: Thaw. Cover with microwave-safe plastic wrap, and cook on High 3 to 5 minutes.

🍲 Fruit-Filled Squash

Serves 4

- 2 small acorn squash (about 1 lb. each)
- 1 small baking apple, cored and thinly sliced
- 1 medium Bartlett pear, cored and thinly sliced
- ½ cup packed brown sugar
  Ground cinnamon, or allspice
  Fresh lemon juice
- ¼ cup raisins
- ½ cup Butter Buds
- ¼ cup water

Nutritional Data

PER SERVING:

Calories	313
% calories from fat	2
Fat (gm)	0.6
Sat. Fat (gm)	0.1
Cholesterol (mg)	0
Sodium (mg)	377
Protein (gm)	3
Carbohydrate (gm)	79

EXCHANGES:

Milk	0.0	Bread	3.0
Veg.	0.0	Meat	0.0
Fruit	1.5	Fat	0.0

Cut squash in half lengthwise; remove seeds. Arrange one-fourth of fruit on top of each squash half. Sprinkle each half with 2 tablespoons brown sugar, dash of cinnamon or allspice, and a few drops of lemon juice. Top each half with 1 tablespoon raisins and 1 tablespoon Butter Buds. Wrap each squash half in foil.

Pour ¼ cup water into crockpot. Stack squash, cut side up, in pot and cover. Cook on Low 5½ to 6 hours or on High 4 to 4½ hours.

Lift squash halves from pot; remove foil. Drain any syrup in foil into saucepan and serve with squash.

Note: Other fruits such as oranges, peaches, nectarines, or pineapple may be substituted for apples and pears.

Golden Spaghetti Squash

Serves 6

- 1 spaghetti squash (2½ to 3 lbs.)
- 2 tablespoons diet margarine (at room temperature)
- 2 packets Equal® (see "About This Cookbook")
- ¼ teaspoon ground cinnamon
  Dash salt
- 1 orange, peeled and chopped

Nutritional Data

PER SERVING:

Calories	59
% calories from fat	33
Fat (gm)	2.4
Sat. Fat (gm)	0.4
Cholesterol (mg)	0
Sodium (mg)	45
Protein (gm)	1.6
Carbohydrate (gm)	9.6

EXCHANGES:

Milk	0.0	Bread	0.0
Veg.	1.5	Meat	0.0
Fruit	0.0	Fat	0.5

Preheat oven to 375 degrees. Cut squash in half lengthwise. Using spoon, scrape out seeds and loose stringy portion. Place squash halves, cut side down, on shallow baking pan. Bake 35 to 45 minutes, or until tender.

While baking squash, combine in bowl margarine, Equal®, cinnamon, and salt. Invert baked squash halves. Using fork, pull spaghetti-like strands up. Add half margarine mixture to each cooked squash half. Lightly toss with fork. Top with orange pieces. Serve warm.

Green & Yellow Squash

Serves 4

1 yellow squash, about ¾ lb.
1 zucchini, about ¾ lb.
2 ozs. pimientos, drained and chopped
½ teaspoon dried oregano
1 bay leaf
2 cloves garlic, smashed
2 tablespoons fresh lemon juice
1 teaspoon olive oil
1 tablespoon water
  Pepper, to taste
  Chives, chopped

Nutritional Data

PER SERVING:

Calories	44
% calories from fat	14
Fat (gm)	1.5
Sat. Fat (gm)	0.2
Cholesterol (mg)	0
Sodium (mg)	5.5
Protein (gm)	1.4
Carbohydrate (gm)	7.8

EXCHANGES:

Milk	0.0	Bread	0.0
Veg.	1.5	Meat	0.0
Fruit	0.0	Fat	0.0

Rinse vegetables and trim. Cut squash and zucchini into thin slices. Combine all ingredients, except pepper and chives, in 2-quart casserole. Stir to mix.

Cover with vented plastic wrap and microwave on High 2 to 3 minutes. Stir, and microwave on High another 2 to 3 minutes, until crisp-tender. Let stand covered 2 minutes more. Remove bay leaf, sprinkle with pepper, and garnish with chopped chives.

Sweet Potatoes with Peppers and Tomatoes

Serves 8	**Nutritional Data**	
4 short double-pronged skewers, or regular skewers	PER SERVING:	
2 sweet potatoes, 5 to 7 ozs. each, peeled	Calories	54
	% calories from fat	19
8 banana peppers, or 2 bell peppers, cut in half horizontally, seeded	Fat (gm)	1.2
	Sat. Fat (gm)	0.2
16 cherry tomatoes, washed, stems removed	Cholesterol (mg)	0
	Sodium (mg)	20
Brushing Sauce	Protein (gm)	1.2
	Carbohydrate (gm)	10.6
2 teaspoons noncholesterol margarine, melted		
	EXCHANGES:	
¼ teaspoon each ingredient: ground cumin, ground cinnamon	Milk 0.0 Bread 0.5	
	Veg. 0.5 Meat 0.0	
¼ cup fresh cilantro, or chives, minced	Fruit 0.0 Fat 0.0	
Vegetable cooking spray		

Cut potatoes into 1½-inch chunks and parboil until just fork-tender; drain.

Thread skewers, alternating sweet potatoes, peppers, and cherry tomatoes.

Brushing Sauce: Mix melted margarine with ground cumin, cinnamon, and cilantro. Lightly brush kabobs with Brushing Sauce.

Preheat outdoor grill or use a stove-top grill; make sure that you follow manufacturer's directions. Coat grill rack with cooking spray. Position kabobs over hot, glowing coals about 6 inches from heat. Cook, turning kabobs as vegetables begin to char. Kabobs are done when vegetables are hot and browned.

To serve, place skewers on individual plates and serve hot.

Stuffed Tomatoes

Serves 4	**Nutritional Data**	
4 large tomatoes	PER SERVING:	
3 tablespoons vegetable oil	Calories	329
2 medium onions, chopped	% calories from fat	30
1 cup uncooked long-grain rice	Fat (gm)	11.2
2 cups liquid (tomato pulp and water)	Sat. Fat (gm)	1.5
	Cholesterol (mg)	0
½ cup scallions, sliced	Sodium (mg)	149
⅓ cup mushrooms, chopped	Protein (gm)	6
2 tablespoons bread crumbs	Carbohydrate (gm)	52.3
½ cup tomato juice		
	EXCHANGES:	
	Milk 0.0 Bread 2.5	
	Veg. 2.0 Meat 0.0	
	Fruit 0.0 Fat 2.0	

Slice off top of each tomato, 3/4 to 1 inch from top. Scoop
out and reserve pulp and tomato tops.

In glass measure, microwave oil and onions on High 3½ to
4 minutes or until soft.

Place onions in casserole dish; add rice and tomato pulp
and water (combined to make 2 cups). Add scallions and
mushrooms, and stir. Microwave, covered with wax paper, on
High 5 minutes; reduce to 50% power, or Medium, and
microwave 15 minutes. Let stand 5 minutes.

Stuff rice mixture into tomato shells and replace tops.
Sprinkle with bread crumbs and add tomato juice.

Microwave, uncovered, on High 4 to 5 minutes or until
tomatoes are soft.

To Freeze: Place in microwave-safe container; label and
freeze for up to 2 months.

To Serve: Thaw. Cover with microwave-safe plastic wrap
and cook on High 3 to 5 minutes.

Tomatoes Stuffed with Mushrooms and Cheese

Serves 4	Nutritional Data
	PER SERVING:

4	large tomatoes	
	Vegetable cooking spray	
1	lb. mushrooms, diced	
1	medium onion, chopped	
1	green bell pepper, chopped	
3	cloves garlic, crushed	
½	teaspoon oregano	
½	cup parsley, chopped	
¼	teaspoon cayenne pepper	
¼	cup Parmesan cheese, freshly grated	

Nutritional Data

PER SERVING:

Calories	106
% calories from fat	22
Fat (gm)	3
Sat. Fat (gm)	1.3
Cholesterol (mg)	4.9
Sodium (mg)	138
Protein (gm)	6.9
Carbohydrate (gm)	16.4

EXCHANGES:

Milk	0.0	Bread	0.0
Veg.	3.0	Meat	0.0
Fruit	0.0	Fat	0.5

Preheat oven to 350 degrees. Scoop out center of tomatoes and put aside in small dish. In large, sprayed skillet, over
medium heat, sauté mushrooms, onion, pepper, and garlic
10 minutes. Add tomato pulp, oregano, parsley, and cayenne
pepper; stir and cook together 5 minutes.

Place tomato shells in oiled baking dish, and fill each shell
with sautéed mixture. Sprinkle each with Parmesan cheese
and bake 10 minutes.

Tomato Relish

Serves 4 (¼-cup servings)

2	medium tomatoes, finely chopped
½	onion, minced
½	cup green bell pepper, minced
¼	cup cider vinegar
2	tablespoons chopped fresh basil leaves, or 2 teaspoons dried crushed basil leaves
1	packet Equal® (see "About This Cookbook")
	Salt and pepper, to taste (optional)

Nutritional Data

PER SERVING:

Calories	29
% calories from fat	7
Fat (gm)	0.3
Sat. Fat (gm)	0
Cholesterol (mg)	0
Sodium (mg)	7
Protein (gm)	1
Carbohydrate (gm)	7.7

EXCHANGES:

Milk	0.0	Bread	0.0
Veg.	1.0	Meat	0.0
Fruit	0.0	Fat	0.0

In medium bowl, combine all ingredients. Relish may be used at once or stored in sealed refrigerator container up to 1 week.

Turnip Yam Treat

Serves 4

2	medium turnips, peeled and cubed
2	medium yams, peeled and cubed
¼	cup water
¼	cup nonfat dry milk
¼	teaspoon nutmeg
	Dash dried thyme
1	tablespoon frozen apple juice concentrate
	Salt and pepper, to taste

Nutritional Data

PER SERVING:

Calories	131
% calories from fat	2
Fat (gm)	0.3
Sat. Fat (gm)	0.1
Cholesterol (mg)	0.8
Sodium (mg)	58
Protein (gm)	3.2
Carbohydrate (gm)	30

EXCHANGES:

Milk	0.0	Bread	2.0
Veg.	0.0	Meat	0.0
Fruit	0.0	Fat	0.0

Place cubed turnips and yams in 2-quart glass measure or casserole with water. Cover with paper towel, and microwave on High 10 to 12 minutes, stirring twice, until tender.

Turn into blender or food processor, add remaining ingredients, and puree. Return to microwave to warm 1 minute if necessary. Season with salt and pepper.

This is especially attractive if served in center of ring of broccoli.

Zucchini with Garlic and Tomato

Serves 6

Vegetable cooking spray
1½ lbs. zucchini, washed, trimmed, and sliced into ½-inch rounds
4 cloves garlic, minced
2 large tomatoes, peeled, seeded, and chopped, or 1 cup canned Italian plum tomatoes, drained and chopped
1 teaspoon Spike (see "About This Cookbook")
1 tablespoon fresh basil, chopped
1 tablespoon fresh oregano, chopped
2 tablespoons fresh parsley, chopped
Pepper, freshly ground, to taste

Nutritional Data

PER SERVING:

Calories	28
% calories from fat	6
Fat (gm)	0.2
Sat. Fat (gm)	0
Cholesterol (mg)	0
Sodium (mg)	7
Protein (gm)	1.2
Carbohydrate (gm)	6.6

EXCHANGES:

Milk	0.0	Bread	0.0
Veg.	1.0	Meat	0.0
Fruit	0.0	Fat	0.0

Coat large skillet with vegetable cooking spray. Add zucchini and garlic, and sauté over medium heat, stirring and turning zucchini so that they color on both sides, 4 to 5 minutes. Add tomatoes, Spike, basil, oregano, and pepper, and cook 5 more minutes, stirring occasionally. Turn off heat, and add parsley. Zucchini should still be quite firm and almost crunchy. Serve warm.

Gratin of Zucchini with Tomato

Serves 4

2 large zucchini
1 14½-oz. can chunky tomatoes
½ cup fresh basil, chopped
¼ cup fresh parsley, chopped
2 tablespoons fresh cilantro
½ cup seasoned bread crumbs
¼ cup Parmesan cheese, freshly grated
1 tablespoon diet margarine

Nutritional Data

PER SERVING:

Calories	129
% calories from fat	27
Fat (gm)	4.1
Sat. Fat (gm)	1.6
Cholesterol (mg)	4.9
Sodium (mg)	718
Protein (gm)	6.7
Carbohydrate (gm)	17.6

EXCHANGES:

Milk	0.0	Bread	0.5
Veg.	2.0	Meat	0.0
Fruit	0.0	Fat	1.0

Wash and trim zucchini. Cut lengthwise into ¼-inch slices. Dry zucchini with paper towels. Preheat oven to 375 degrees.

In saucepan, heat chunky tomatoes, then add basil, parsley, and cilantro and simmer 3 minutes. Pour half of tomato mixture into shallow 8" x 12" baking dish. Arrange zucchini slices on top, and cover with remaining tomato mixture. Combine bread crumbs and Parmesan cheese and sprinkle over casserole. Dot with margarine.

Bake 30 to 40 minutes until zucchini is tender and crust golden. Serve piping hot or freeze.

To Freeze: Place in microwave-safe container; label and freeze for up to 2 months.

To Serve: Thaw. Cover with microwave-safe plastic wrap, and cook on High 3 to 5 minutes.

Chapter Nine

RICE, GRAINS & BEANS

Rice with Autumn Vegetables

Serves 4

1	recipe Lemon Risotto (see p. 377)
1	tablespoon olive oil
1/4	cup onion, minced
2	tablespoons garlic, minced
1	large eggplant (about 1 lb.), peeled and cut into 1/2-inch dice
1/2	teaspoon hot red pepper flakes
1/2	cup celery, minced
1	cup cooked garbanzo or kidney beans (rinsed and drained, if canned)
1	cup mushrooms, sliced
1	teaspoon fresh rosemary, minced
1/4	cup parsley, minced
	Spike (see "About This Cookbook"), to taste
	Black pepper, freshly ground, to taste
2	tablespoons Parmesan cheese, freshly grated
	Vegetable cooking spray

Nutritional Data

PER SERVING:

Calories	563
% calories from fat	29
Fat (gm)	18.3
Sat. Fat (gm)	5.2
Cholesterol (mg)	13.5
Sodium (mg)	1187
Protein (gm)	21.4
Carbohydrate (gm)	78.2

EXCHANGES:

Milk	0.0	Bread	5.0
Veg.	0.5	Meat	1.5
Fruit	0.0	Fat	2.5

Make Lemon Risotto and set aside.

Heat oil in large skillet over moderate heat. Add onion and garlic, and sauté until slightly softened, about 3 minutes. Add eggplant, and brown on all sides. Add hot pepper flakes and celery, and cook additional 3 minutes. Remove from heat.

Preheat oven to 375 degrees. Stir beans, mushrooms, rosemary, and half of parsley into eggplant mixture. Combine vegetables and risotto. Season to taste with Spike and pepper.

Transfer to 2-quart casserole, coated with vegetable cooking spray, cover, and bake until heated through, about 20 minutes. Serve from casserole, topped with remaining parsley and Parmesan.

Braised Rice

Serves 6

	Vegetable cooking spray
1/3	cup onion, finely minced
1	cup uncooked long-grain white rice, unwashed
1/4	cup dry white French vermouth
2	cups Chicken Stock (see p. 40), heated in small saucepan
	Pepper, freshly ground

Nutritional Data

PER SERVING:

Calories	138
% calories from fat	4
Fat (gm)	0.5
Sat. Fat (gm)	0.1
Cholesterol (mg)	3.4
Sodium (mg)	6
Protein (gm)	3.5
Carbohydrate (gm)	25.9

1 medium bay leaf
1 Bouquet garni*

EXCHANGES:			
Milk	0.0	Bread	2.0
Veg.	0.0	Meat	0.0
Fruit	0.0	Fat	0.0

Coat skillet with cooking spray and add onion. Sauté onion slowly several minutes until soft. Stir in rice, and sauté, slowly stirring several minutes more until grains, which first become translucent, turn milky white. This step prevents grains from sticking.

Stir in vermouth and let it boil down. Blend in Chicken Stock, correct seasoning, and add bay leaf and Bouquet garni. Bring to simmer, stir to keep from sticking, and let rice cook, covered, about 20 minutes. Remove from heat; remove bay leaf and Bouquet garni; and serve. Makes 3 cups.

*Note: Bouquet garni consists of a few sprigs of parsley, thyme, and basil or tarragon with bay leaf, all in cheesecloth bag.

Dirty Rice

Serves 8

2 teaspoons red pepper (preferably cayenne), ground
1½ teaspoons black pepper
1¼ teaspoons sweet paprika
1 teaspoon dry mustard
1 teaspoon cumin, ground
½ teaspoon ground thyme
½ teaspoon oregano leaves
   Vegetable cooking spray
¼ lb. chicken breast, ground
2 bay leaves
½ cup onion, finely chopped
½ cup celery, finely chopped
½ cup green bell pepper, finely chopped
2 teaspoons garlic, minced
2 tablespoons margarine
2 cups Chicken Stock (see p. 40)
¾ cup uncooked rice (preferably converted)

Nutritional Data

PER SERVING:

Calories	130
% calories from fat	28
Fat (gm)	4
Sat. Fat (gm)	0.8
Cholesterol (mg)	10
Sodium (mg)	52
Protein (gm)	5.5
Carbohydrate (gm)	17.5

EXCHANGES:			
Milk	0.0	Bread	1.0
Veg.	0.0	Meat	0.5
Fruit	0.0	Fat	0.5

Combine first 7 seasoning ingredients in small bowl and set aside. Place ground chicken and bay leaves in large skillet coated with vegetable spray. Cook over high heat until meat is thoroughly browned, about 8 minutes, stirring occasionally.

Stir in seasoning mix, then add onion, celery, peppers, and garlic; stir thoroughly, scraping pan bottom well. Add margarine and stir until melted. Reduce heat to medium and cook about 10 minutes, stirring constantly and scraping pan bottom well.

Add Chicken Stock and stir until any mixture sticking to pan bottom comes loose. Heat to boiling. Add rice and stir thoroughly; cover pan and turn heat to very low; cook until rice is tender, about 25 minutes. Remove bay leaves and serve immediately.

Rice Malgache

Serves 6

Vegetable cooking spray
2 tablespoons shallots, chopped
1 green bell pepper, chopped
1 cup uncooked long-grain rice
1 teaspoon Spike (see "About This Cookbook")
Pinch saffron
1 cup consommé
1½ cups boiling water

Nutritional Data

PER SERVING:

Calories	123
% calories from fat	2
Fat (gm)	0.2
Sat. Fat (gm)	0.1
Cholesterol (mg)	0
Sodium (mg)	108
Protein (gm)	3.3
Carbohydrate (gm)	26.3

EXCHANGES:

Milk	0.0	Bread	1.5
Veg.	0.5	Meat	0.0
Fruit	0.0	Fat	0.0

Coat large heavy saucepan with vegetable cooking spray; add shallots and pepper. Cook until browned. Add rice and cook, stirring constantly, until rice is well coated. Add Spike, saffron, consommé, and water. Bring to boil. Cover and simmer 25 minutes or until rice has absorbed all liquid. Serve hot or cold.

Fried Rice

Serves 8

Vegetable cooking spray
½ cup egg substitute
5 green onions, chopped
3 cups cooked, salted rice
2 tablespoons light, low-salt soy sauce
1 cup cooked lean pork, cubed or shredded
1 small carrot, grated
½ cup water chestnuts, sliced
1 cup cooked green peas

Nutritional Data

PER SERVING:

Calories	147
% calories from fat	10
Fat (gm)	1.6
Sat. Fat (gm)	0.5
Cholesterol (mg)	12.6
Sodium (mg)	371
Protein (gm)	10
Carbohydrate (gm)	22.6

EXCHANGES:

Milk	0.0	Bread	1.5
Veg.	0.0	Meat	1.0
Fruit	0.0	Fat	0.0

Heat skillet coated with cooking spray over medium heat. Cook egg substitute into an omelet, cut into strips, and reserve. Coat skillet again with cooking spray and stir-fry, cooking quickly in stirring motion, the green onions until tender. Mix in rice, soy sauce, pork, carrot, and water chestnuts, stirring well after each addition. Add egg, toss lightly, and transfer fried rice to serving dish. Sprinkle peas over and serve hot.

Mexican Rice

Serves 6

Vegetable cooking spray
1½ cups long-grain rice, washed and drained
3 cloves garlic, minced
1 cup onion, minced
1 large tomato, peeled and chopped
3 cups fat-free chicken broth
1 teaspoon chili powder
½ teaspoon cumin seeds
¼ teaspoon salt
¼ teaspoon pepper

Nutritional Data

PER SERVING:

Calories	199
% calories from fat	5
Fat (gm)	1.1
Sat. Fat (gm)	0.1
Cholesterol (mg)	0
Sodium (mg)	266
Protein (gm)	6.3
Carbohydrate (gm)	41.7

EXCHANGES:

Milk	0.0	Bread	3.0
Veg.	0.0	Meat	0.0
Fruit	0.0	Fat	0.0

Coat nonstick skillet with cooking spray and heat. Add rice and cook until rice begins to brown, stirring occasionally. Add garlic, onion, and tomato; mix well. Sauté 1 minute. Stir in broth and remaining ingredients. Cover tightly and simmer 15 to 20 minutes or until rice is done. Serve hot.

Rice with Shrimp

Serves 4

2 tablespoons olive oil, divided
2 tablespoons red onion, diced
1¼ cups uncooked arborio or long-grain white rice
⅓ cup white wine
4 cups unsalted chicken broth, kept hot over low heat
12 oz. shrimp, shelled and deveined
1 cup peas
1 teaspoon lemon rind, cut into julienne strips
3 tablespoons pimiento, chopped
1 tablespoon fresh lemon juice
½ teaspoon Spike (see "About This Cookbook")
Pepper, freshly ground, to taste
3 tablespoons fresh basil, finely chopped

Nutritional Data

PER SERVING:

Calories	431
% calories from fat	21
Fat (gm)	9.9
Sat. Fat (gm)	1.6
Cholesterol (mg)	132.9
Sodium (mg)	189
Protein (gm)	25.2
Carbohydrate (gm)	55.4

EXCHANGES:

Milk	0.0	Bread	3.5
Veg.	1.0	Meat	2.0
Fruit	0.0	Fat	1.0

Heat 1 tablespoon olive oil in large saucepan over low heat. Add onion. Cook, stirring until tender, 5 minutes. Stir in rice, and coat with oil. Add wine, heat to boiling; stir over high heat until almost evaporated.

Stir in 1 cup of chicken broth. Continue adding broth, about ½ cup at a time, stirring constantly. Each portion should be absorbed before adding the next. With last ½ cup broth, add shrimp, peas, and lemon.

Cook uncovered, stirring constantly, until broth is absorbed and rice is tender to the bite, the dish is moist and creamy, and shrimp are cooked through, 5 to 8 minutes. Add remaining 1 tablespoon olive oil, pimiento, and lemon juice. Stir in Spike and black pepper to taste.

Arrange on platter and sprinkle with basil.

Rice with Raw Vegetable Sauce

Serves 6

2½	cups uncooked arborio rice
4	tomatoes, peeled and seeded
1	cup celery, finely chopped
1	cup carrots, finely chopped
½	cup red or yellow onion, sliced
1	clove garlic, finely chopped
⅓	cup parsley, finely chopped
⅓	cup fresh basil, finely chopped
2	tablespoons olive oil
	Spike (see "About This Cookbook"), to taste
	Black pepper, freshly ground, to taste
	Tabasco sauce, few drops

Nutritional Data

PER SERVING:

Calories	360
% calories from fat	14
Fat (gm)	5.4
Sat. Fat (gm)	0.8
Cholesterol (mg)	0
Sodium (mg)	37
Protein (gm)	7
Carbohydrate (gm)	70.4

EXCHANGES:

Milk	0.0	Bread	4.0
Veg.	1.0	Meat	0.0
Fruit	0.0	Fat	1.0

Cook rice *al dente* in 5 cups boiling water, and drain.

Prepare sauce by combining all remaining ingredients in bowl. If using food processor, whirl small amount of vegetables at a time to ensure that they remain finely chopped, not pureed. They should be crunchy to contrast with softness of rice.

When rice is cooked, place it in glass serving bowl, and pour raw vegetable sauce over it.

Mix well, and serve. You can also put half of sauce over rice and pass other half in sauce bowl to be added by each diner.

Rice in Yogurt Sauce

Serves 4

2 cups plain low-fat yogurt, strained 30 minutes in double thickness of cheesecloth
Egg substitute equal to 1 egg
3 teaspoons fresh mint, chopped, or 1 teaspoon dried mint
1 garlic clove, minced
Spike (see "About This Cookbook"), to taste
Pepper, freshly ground, to taste
¼ cup pimiento, chopped
2 cups cooked long-grain rice

Nutritional Data

PER SERVING:

Calories	190
% calories from fat	3
Fat (gm)	0.7
Sat. Fat (gm)	0.2
Cholesterol (mg)	1.3
Sodium (mg)	96
Protein (gm)	9.5
Carbohydrate (gm)	37.2

EXCHANGES:

Milk	0.5	Bread	2.0
Veg.	0.0	Meat	0.0
Fruit	0.0	Fat	0.0

In medium bowl, stir together all ingredients except rice. Pour yogurt mixture over rice.

Wild Rice

Serves 4

1 teaspoon canola oil
¼ cup shallots, chopped
½ cup celery, chopped
¾ cup uncooked wild rice
2½ cups Chicken Stock (see p. 40)
2 tablespoons pine nuts

Nutritional Data

PER SERVING:

Calories	174
% calories from fat	23
Fat (gm)	4.6
Sat. Fat (gm)	0.3
Cholesterol (mg)	6.3
Sodium (mg)	24
Protein (gm)	8.1
Carbohydrate (gm)	25.9

EXCHANGES:

Milk	0.0	Bread	1.5
Veg.	1.0	Meat	0.0
Fruit	0.0	Fat	1.0

Combine oil with shallots and celery in 2-cup measure, and microwave on High 2 minutes or until tender. Rinse rice well, discarding any debris that floats to surface. Drain.

Place wild rice and Chicken Stock in 2-quart glass measure. Microwave on High 5 minutes, then stir. Microwave on Medium (60%) 30 minutes longer. Let stand 10 minutes, and drain off any excess liquid. When rice is ready to serve, stir in vegetables and pine nuts.

Variations:

1. Add cooked mushrooms and chopped parsley.
2. Substitute walnuts for pine nuts.
3. Add currants and shredded part-skim mozzarella cheese.
4. Use half brown rice, half wild rice.

Wild Rice and Orzo Casserole with Asparagus

Serves 5

²⁄₃ cup uncooked wild rice, rinsed
and drained
3 cups water
2 chicken bouillon cubes
1 medium onion, chopped
1 clove garlic, minced
1 teaspoon dried thyme leaves
1 teaspoon dried marjoram leaves
¼ teaspoon black pepper
½ cup uncooked orzo
10 medium asparagus spears, trimmed
and cut into 1-inch lengths
¾ cup nonfat ricotta cheese
2 ozs. (½ cup) Parmesan cheese,
freshly grated, divided
Chopped red bell pepper, or additional
asparagus tips for garnish (optional)

Nutritional Data

PER SERVING:

Calories	205
% calories from fat	16
Fat (gm)	3.8
Sat. Fat (gm)	2
Cholesterol (mg)	11.6
Sodium (mg)	581
Protein (gm)	15
Carbohydrate (gm)	30.5

EXCHANGES:

Milk	0.0	Bread	2.0
Veg.	0.0	Meat	1.0
Fruit	0.0	Fat	0.0

In large saucepan or small pot, combine rice, water, bouillon cubes, onion, garlic, thyme, marjoram, and pepper. Bring to full boil. Cover, reduce heat, and cook 1 hour (or according to package directions), reducing heat slightly as rice absorbs water.

Twenty minutes before rice is done, in separate pot cook orzo according to package directions, adding asparagus to pot during last 3 minutes of cooking time. Transfer orzo, asparagus, and rice to colander and drain.

Preheat oven to 350 degrees. Transfer rice, asparagus, and orzo mixture to 2½-quart casserole. Stir in ricotta. Stir in all but 2 tablespoons of Parmesan cheese.

At this point, casserole can be refrigerated up to 24 hours.

Sprinkle casserole top with remaining Parmesan cheese. Bake, covered, 25 to 30 minutes or until heated through. Cooking time will be longer if casserole has been refrigerated. Garnish with chopped red bell pepper, or additional asparagus tips, if desired.

Saffron Rice

Serves 8

3	cups fat-free chicken broth
1	cup dry white wine
1	cup onion, minced
2	teaspoons parsley, minced
½	teaspoon saffron
½	teaspoon dried coriander
½	teaspoon fennel seeds
¼	teaspoon ground mace, or nutmeg
2	cups uncooked long-grain rice

Nutritional Data

PER SERVING:

Calories	206
% calories from fat	4
Fat (gm)	0.8
Sat. Fat (gm)	0.1
Cholesterol (mg)	0
Sodium (mg)	131
Protein (gm)	5.3
Carbohydrate (gm)	39.6

EXCHANGES:

Milk	0.0	Bread	3.0
Veg.	0.0	Meat	0.0
Fruit	0.0	Fat	0.0

Combine all ingredients, except rice, in medium saucepan with tight-fitting cover. Bring mixture to boil over medium heat. Add rice, cover, do not stir, and reduce heat to simmer. Cook 20 to 30 minutes or until rice is done.

Rice Mélange

Serves 12

3	cups uncooked rice
1	tablespoon fresh lemon juice
2	large tomatoes, peeled and chopped
¾	lb. green beans, cut up
1½	teaspoons mint, chopped
1	tablespoon parsley, minced
1½	teaspoons fresh oregano, or ½ teaspoon dried oregano
½	teaspoon salt
1	tablespoon dried thyme

French Dressing

2	tablespoons wine vinegar
1	tablespoon olive oil
¼	cup fat-free chicken broth
¾	teaspoon paprika
¼	teaspoon honey mustard
½	teaspoon salt
½	teaspoon black pepper, freshly ground
1	teaspoon fresh thyme, or ½ teaspoon dried thyme

Nutritional Data

PER SERVING:

Calories	196
% calories from fat	8
Fat (gm)	1.7
Sat. Fat (gm)	0.3
Cholesterol (mg)	0
Sodium (mg)	192
Protein (gm)	4.2
Carbohydrate (gm)	40.9

EXCHANGES:

Milk	0.0	Bread	2.5
Veg.	0.5	Meat	0.0
Fruit	0.0	Fat	0.0

Boil rice according to package directions. When cooked, add lemon juice and fluff. Add tomatoes. Cool or chill. Cook green beans until just done. Drain and refresh under cold running water. Toss beans with rice mixture. Add seasonings, using forks to toss all ingredients together.

Make French Dressing by whisking all ingredients together. Pour over Rice Mélange and toss to mix thoroughly.

Mushroom Risotto

Serves 6

		Nutritional Data	
2	tablespoons diet margarine	**PER SERVING:**	
2	tablespoons olive oil	Calories	219
½	cup onion, minced	% calories from fat	35
1	cup uncooked arborio rice	Fat (gm)	8.4
½	cup mushrooms, sliced	Sat. Fat (gm)	1.9
3	cups Chicken Stock (see p. 40)	Cholesterol (mg)	8.3
1	teaspoon Spike (see "About This	Sodium (mg)	128
	Cookbook")	Protein (gm)	5.8
	Pepper, freshly ground	Carbohydrate (gm)	28.3
¼	cup Parmesan cheese, freshly grated		

EXCHANGES:

Milk	0.0	Bread	2.0
Veg.	0.0	Meat	0.0
Fruit	0.0	Fat	1.5

Heat margarine and olive oil in microwave-safe pie plate on High 2 minutes. Add onions and stir to coat. Cook, uncovered, on High 4 minutes. Add rice and mushrooms. Stir to coat. Cook, uncovered, on High 9 minutes more. Remove from microwave.

Let stand, uncovered, 5 minutes to let rice absorb remaining liquid, stirring several times. Stir in Spike, pepper, and Parmesan cheese.

Green Pea Risotto

Serves 6

		Nutritional Data	
1¾	cups Chicken Stock (see p. 40)	**PER SERVING:**	
1	tablespoon olive oil	Calories	164
1	tablespoon whipped butter	% calories from fat	25
1	onion, chopped fine	Fat (gm)	4.6
¾	cup uncooked arborio rice	Sat. Fat (gm)	1.6
2	tablespoons dry white wine	Cholesterol (mg)	7.9
½	cup frozen peas, thawed	Sodium (mg)	67
2	tablespoons Parmesan or Romano	Protein (gm)	4.5
	cheese, freshly grated	Carbohydrate (gm)	24.3
	Salt and pepper, to taste		

EXCHANGES:

Milk	0.0	Bread	1.5
Veg.	0.0	Meat	0.0
Fruit	0.0	Fat	1.0

Place Chicken Stock in 4-cup measure, and microwave on High 3 to 4 minutes, until it simmers. Place oil, butter, and onion in 1-quart measure, and microwave on High 2 minutes, until onions are soft. Add rice and stir to coat.

Pour in hot Chicken Stock and wine. Cover with vented plastic wrap. Microwave on High 4 to 5 minutes, until boiling. Microwave on Medium (50%) 7 to 9 minutes more until rice is tender. Rotate dish, stir in peas, and let stand covered 5 minutes. Stir in cheese and season with salt and pepper.

Spinach Risotto

Serves 6

1	10-oz. package frozen chopped spinach
2	tablespoons olive oil
1	medium onion, chopped
1	clove garlic, minced
2	cups uncooked rice
4	cups Chicken Stock (see p. 40), or canned low sodium
1	teaspoon Spike (see "About This Cookbook")
¼	cup Parmesan cheese, freshly grated

Nutritional Data

PER SERVING:

Calories	324
% calories from fat	19
Fat (gm)	6.9
Sat. Fat (gm)	1.7
Cholesterol (mg)	10
Sodium (mg)	116
Protein (gm)	9.6
Carbohydrate (gm)	53.6

EXCHANGES:

Milk	0.0	Bread	3.0
Veg.	1.0	Meat	0.5
Fruit	0.0	Fat	1.0

Drain spinach well. Combine spinach, olive oil, onion, and garlic in heavy saucepan. Cook over medium heat, stirring constantly, about 5 minutes.

Process mixture until smooth in blender; return to pan. Add rice, Stock, and Spike; cover.

Cook over low heat until liquid is absorbed and rice is tender, about 20 minutes. Stir occasionally. If rice is not tender, add a little water; cook until rice is soft. Serve immediately, topped with grated cheese.

Lemon Risotto

Serves 4

2	tablespoons olive oil
¼	cup onion, minced
1	lemon rind, grated
1½	cups uncooked arborio rice
4½	cups chicken broth
¼	cup plus 2 teaspoons fresh lemon juice
½	cup Parmesan cheese, freshly grated
	Spike (see "About This Cookbook"), to taste
	Pepper, to taste

Nutritional Data

PER SERVING:

Calories	423
% calories from fat	27
Fat (gm)	12.5
Sat. Fat (gm)	3.9
Cholesterol (mg)	11
Sodium (mg)	1109
Protein (gm)	15.9
Carbohydrate (gm)	59.7

EXCHANGES:

Milk	0.0	Bread	4.0
Veg.	0.0	Meat	1.5
Fruit	0.0	Fat	1.5

In heavy saucepan over moderately low heat, add olive oil, onion, and lemon rind; sauté slowly 5 minutes. Add rice; stir to coat with oil. Raise heat to high; toast rice, stirring 30 seconds.

Immediately add ½ cup broth; reduce heat to medium-low, and stir until broth is absorbed. Add ½ cup at a time, stirring constantly, and adding more only when previous portion has been absorbed.

When all stock is absorbed (about 20 to 25 minutes), stir in 1/4 cup lemon juice. Rice should be tender. If not, add warm water slowly until rice is tender yet firm.

Stir in Parmesan cheese, and cook briefly to blend and melt cheese. Season to taste with Spike and pepper. Add remaining lemon juice; serve immediately in warm bowls.

Risotto alla Milanese

Serves 8

2	tablespoons olive oil
1	medium onion, finely minced
3	cups uncooked arborio rice
1/2	cup dry white wine
	Generous pinch saffron
8	cups hot Vegetable Stock (see p. 42)
1/2	cup Parmesan cheese, freshly grated
	Pinch Spike (see "About This Cookbook")
	Truffles (optional)
	Parsley

Nutritional Data

PER SERVING:

Calories	419
% calories from fat	17
Fat (gm)	8.1
Sat. Fat (gm)	2.1
Cholesterol (mg)	4.9
Sodium (mg)	142
Protein (gm)	10.7
Carbohydrate (gm)	73.2

EXCHANGES:

Milk	0.0	Bread	4.0
Veg.	1.5	Meat	0.5
Fruit	0.0	Fat	1.0

Heat oil in large heavy saucepan, add onion, and sauté until transparent. Add rice, and sauté, stirring constantly, 2 to 3 minutes. Add wine, and cook, stirring until it evaporates. Add saffron and combine well. Add hot Vegetable Stock, 1/2 cup at a time, and continue cooking, stirring constantly, until risotto is creamy, smooth, moist, and cooked *al dente*.

Remove from heat, add Parmesan, and combine. Correct for seasoning. Slice truffles over top if you like, and serve immediately on heated serving platter decorated with parsley.

Seafood Risotto with Tomatoes

Serves 6

5	cups Chicken Stock (see p. 40), or canned low sodium
3	tablespoons olive oil
1¾	lbs. crabmeat, picked over for cartilage and broken into large pieces, or bay or sea scallops, or medium shrimp, shelled and deveined
	Spike (see "About This Cookbook")
	Pepper, freshly ground

Nutritional Data

PER SERVING:

Calories	425
% calories from fat	19
Fat (gm)	9
Sat. Fat (gm)	1.3
Cholesterol (mg)	26.3
Sodium (mg)	467
Protein (gm)	16.6
Carbohydrate (gm)	66.9

		EXCHANGES:			
1	envelope Butter Buds mixed in ½ cup skim milk, warmed	Milk	0.0	Bread	3.5
1½	cups onion, diced	Veg.	2.0	Meat	1.0
2	cups uncooked arborio rice	Fruit	0.0	Fat	1.5
3	cups Italian plum tomatoes, drained and diced, juices added to Chicken Stock				
6	artichoke hearts, canned				
2	tablespoons garlic, finely minced				
3	tablespoons lemon zest				
2	tablespoons fresh lemon juice				
8	fresh basil leaves, chopped				
¼	cup parsley, chopped, plus additional for garnish				

Heat Chicken Stock to boiling in saucepan; reduce heat and hold at simmer.

Heat olive oil in large sauté pan over medium heat. Sprinkle shellfish with Spike and pepper. Add shellfish to pan and sauté quickly.

Put Butter Buds and milk in heavy saucepan over low heat. Add onions and cook about 5 minutes. Add rice and cook, stirring to coat with Butter Buds mixture. Add ½ cup hot Stock and cook, stirring constantly, until Stock is absorbed. Continue adding Stock ½ cup at a time, and stirring until rice is almost completely cooked. Add tomatoes, artichoke hearts, garlic, lemon zest, lemon juice, basil, and parsley. Continue to cook.

A minute or two before rice is cooked, add shellfish. Season with Spike and pepper and sprinkle with more parsley.

Golden Barley

Serves 4

		Nutritional Data	
2	cups water	PER SERVING:	
½	cup pearl barley	Calories	121
1	tablespoon golden raisins	% calories from fat	17
1	tablespoon almonds	Fat (gm)	2.4
1	tablespoon peanuts	Sat. Fat (gm)	0.3
¼	cup celery, chopped	Cholesterol (mg)	0
	Pinch ground cardamom	Sodium (mg)	9
	Salt and pepper, to taste	Protein (gm)	3.5
		Carbohydrate (gm)	22.6

EXCHANGES:			
Milk	0.0	Bread	1.5
Veg.	0.0	Meat	0.0
Fruit	0.0	Fat	0.5

Bring water to boil in 1-quart microwave measure and add barley. Cook on High 30 minutes, stirring a few times. When barley is tender, drain and stir in remaining ingredients. Serve warm or chilled as a salad. Dressing may be added as desired.

▣ *Bulgur Pilaf à l'Orange*

Serves 6

¼   cup currants
2   tablespoons sunflower seeds, or slivered almonds
    Rind and juice of 1 orange
¾   cup bulgur, or cracked wheat (3 cups cooked)
1   teaspoon sesame oil
1   small onion, chopped
1½ cups water

Nutritional Data	
PER SERVING:	
Calories	99
% calories from fat	22
Fat (gm)	2.5
Sat. Fat (gm)	0.3
Cholesterol (mg)	0
Sodium (mg)	3
Protein (gm)	3.2
Carbohydrate (gm)	17.4

EXCHANGES:			
Milk	0.0	Bread	1.0
Veg.	0.0	Meat	0.0
Fruit	0.0	Fat	0.5

In blender, process currants, sunflower seeds, orange rind, and juice. Set aside. Place bulgur, sesame oil, and onion in 8-cup measure, and microwave on High 2 minutes. Stir.

In another cup, bring water to boil on High 5 to 6 minutes; then add water to bulgur and microwave on High 5 minutes. Combine with orange mixture, reduce power to Medium (50%), and microwave 12 to 14 minutes. Let stand until liquid is absorbed. Makes 4 cups.

Savory Bulgur Wheat

Serves 6

    Butter-flavored vegetable cooking spray
½   cup onion, chopped
½   cup celery, chopped
1   cup bulgur wheat
2   cups fat-free chicken broth
¼   teaspoon pepper
1   teaspoon fresh tarragon, or ½ teaspoon dried tarragon
½   cup raisins
¾   teaspoon ground cinnamon
½   teaspoon salt

Nutritional Data	
PER SERVING:	
Calories	132
% calories from fat	5
Fat (gm)	0.8
Sat. Fat (gm)	0.1
Cholesterol (mg)	0
Sodium (mg)	304
Protein (gm)	5.1
Carbohydrate (gm)	29.5

EXCHANGES:			
Milk	0.0	Bread	1.5
Veg.	0.0	Meat	0.0
Fruit	0.5	Fat	0.0

Coat nonstick 2-quart pot with cooking spray; sauté onion and celery until tender, stirring often. Stir in bulgur and continue cooking until grain is coated and turns golden brown. Blend in broth, pepper, and tarragon. Add raisins, cinnamon, and salt and mix well. Cover and continue cooking 15 minutes or until all liquid has been absorbed. Serve hot.

Couscous Niçoise

Serves 6

1¼	cups Chicken Stock (see p. 40), or canned low sodium
2	cloves garlic, minced
1½	teaspoons olive oil
1½	cups medium-grain instant couscous
8	cherry tomatoes, cut in half
¼	cup pitted Greek olives, sliced
8	fresh basil leaves, cut julienne
1	tablespoon parsley, minced
1	tablespoon red wine vinegar
1	tablespoon chives, minced
	Black pepper, freshly ground

Nutritional Data

PER SERVING:

Calories	217
% calories from fat	16
Fat (gm)	3.7
Sat. Fat (gm)	0.5
Cholesterol (mg)	2.1
Sodium (mg)	194
Protein (gm)	7
Carbohydrate (gm)	37.7

EXCHANGES:

Milk	0.0	Bread	2.5
Veg.	1.0	Meat	0.0
Fruit	0.0	Fat	0.5

Combine Chicken Stock, garlic, and oil in medium saucepan with tight-fitting lid and bring to boil. Stir in couscous and remove from heat. Cover and let stand 5 minutes. Uncover and fluff with fork until grains are separated.

Add tomatoes, olives, basil, parsley, vinegar, and chives. Toss until completely mixed. Season with freshly ground black pepper. Serve warm or at room temperature.

 # Fluffy Kasha

Serves 4

1¾	cups water
2	teaspoons sesame oil
½	cup kasha (buckwheat groats)
1	egg white
2	cloves garlic, smashed
1	teaspoon reduced-sodium soy sauce
2	teaspoons sesame seeds
	Pepper, to taste

Nutritional Data

PER SERVING:

Calories	106
% calories from fat	29
Fat (gm)	3.6
Sat. Fat (gm)	0.5
Cholesterol (mg)	0
Sodium (mg)	61
Protein (gm)	3.9
Carbohydrate (gm)	16.2

EXCHANGES:

Milk	0.0	Bread	1.0
Veg.	0.0	Meat	0.0
Fruit	0.0	Fat	0.5

Bring water to boil, microwaving on High 5 to 6 minutes. In another 2-quart measure, mix sesame oil and kasha. Microwave on High 1 to 2 minutes until toasted. Stir in egg white and microwave on High another 30 seconds.

Add boiling water and simmer on High 2 minutes. Add garlic and soy sauce and microwave on High another 30 seconds. Let stand 5 minutes. Add sesame seeds, season with pepper, and fluff with fork.

Variation: Microwave ½ cup each mushrooms, onions, and celery with teaspoon of sesame oil on High 2 minutes until tender, and fluff in when kasha is cooked. Peas, zucchini, and spinach may also be combined with kasha.

Millet Primavera

Serves 6

			Nutritional Data	
¾	cup millet (available in health food stores)		**PER SERVING:**	
2	tablespoons olive oil		Calories	172
1	medium onion, chopped		% calories from fat	32
2	stalks celery, diced		Fat (gm)	6.1
1	green or red bell pepper, diced		Sat. Fat (gm)	0.9
1	carrot, diced		Cholesterol (mg)	4.2
1	small zucchini, diced (about ½ cup)		Sodium (mg)	23
2	cloves garlic, minced		Protein (gm)	5
1	teaspoon fresh ginger root, peeled and diced		Carbohydrate (gm)	23.7

EXCHANGES:

Milk	0.0	Bread	1.5
Veg.	1.0	Meat	0.0
Fruit	0.0	Fat	1.0

2½ cups Chicken Stock (see p. 40)
1 teaspoon curry powder (or more if desired)
½ teaspoon dried dill weed
   Salt and black pepper, to taste

Spread millet on 9-inch pie plate, and toast in microwave on High 1 minute. In 2-quart casserole or measure combine next 8 ingredients, and microwave on High 3 to 4 minutes.

Add toasted millet and Chicken Stock, along with curry and dill weed. Cover with vented plastic wrap and microwave on High 20 minutes, stirring a few times. When grain is tender, season with salt and pepper. Makes 3½ cups.

Inca Pilaf

Serves 4

			Nutritional Data	
¼	cup red bell pepper, diced		**PER SERVING:**	
2	cloves garlic, minced		Calories	173
1	small onion, chopped		% calories from fat	18
1	teaspoon sesame oil		Fat (gm)	3.5
¾	cup quinoa (once eaten by the Incas, it is now available in health food stores and some supermarkets; pronounced "keen-wa")		Sat. Fat (gm)	0.5
			Cholesterol (mg)	3.8
			Sodium (mg)	13
			Protein (gm)	7
			Carbohydrate (gm)	28.5

1½ cups Chicken Stock (see p. 40)
½ cup green peas

EXCHANGES:

Milk	0.0	Bread	1.5
Veg.	1.0	Meat	0.0
Fruit	0.0	Fat	1.0

Place pepper, garlic, onion, and sesame oil in 4-quart glass measure. Microwave uncovered on High 2 minutes, and stir.

Add quinoa and Chicken Stock and microwave on High 5 minutes, stirring once. Microwave on Medium (50%) 15 minutes.

Add peas; stir to mix. Microwave on High another 2 minutes or until liquid is absorbed. Grains should be pearly, with white outline visible. Fluff with fork.

Basic Polenta

Serves 6

- 2½ quarts cold water
- ½ lb. yellow cornmeal, coarse or stone-ground
- ½ lb. yellow cornmeal (regular type), finely ground
- Dash black pepper

Nutritional Data	
PER SERVING:	
Calories	274
% calories from fat	9
Fat (gm)	2.7
Sat. Fat (gm)	0.4
Cholesterol (mg)	0
Sodium (mg)	27
Protein (gm)	6.1
Carbohydrate (gm)	58.1

EXCHANGES:			
Milk	0.0	Bread	4.0
Veg.	0.0	Meat	0.0
Fruit	0.0	Fat	0.0

Bring cold water to boil in large pot. Add 2 types of cornmeal to boiling water in very slow stream; stir with wooden spoon to keep mixture smooth or it will become lumpy. Stir slowly about 30 minutes. If lumps form, push them to side of pot and smash with spoon. Add pepper to taste. Serve immediately.

Pimiento Polenta

Serves 4

- 2 cups Chicken Stock (see p. 40)
- ½ cup yellow cornmeal
- ½ cup corn niblets (fresh, canned, or frozen), drained
- 1 tablespoon olive oil
- Pinch salt
- ¼ teaspoon cayenne pepper
- ½ teaspoon dried thyme
- ½ teaspoon dried oregano
- 2 tablespoons Parmesan cheese, freshly grated
- Dash black pepper
- ¼ cup pimientos, sliced, for garnish

Nutritional Data	
PER SERVING:	
Calories	173
% calories from fat	28
Fat (gm)	5.8
Sat. Fat (gm)	1.3
Cholesterol (mg)	7.5
Sodium (mg)	87
Protein (gm)	6.6
Carbohydrate (gm)	25.4

EXCHANGES:			
Milk	0.0	Bread	2.0
Veg.	0.0	Meat	0.0
Fruit	0.0	Fat	1.0

Place Chicken Stock in 2-quart microwave-safe bowl, and cook on High 4 to 6 minutes to heat. To broth, add cornmeal, niblets, olive oil, and next 4 seasonings.

Microwave uncovered on High 12 to 15 minutes, stirring every 5 minutes. When polenta is tender and liquid is absorbed, stir in Parmesan cheese and pepper. Spoon into serving dish and top with pimientos.

Variations:

1. Slice and serve with topping of salsa or tomato sauce.
2. Add microwaved onions, red or green bell peppers, and sliced mushrooms.
3. Mix with a little blue cheese, Gorgonzola, or goat's cheese.
4. Top with part-skim ricotta and a few cooked green peas or chopped broccoli.

Polenta with 3 Cheeses

Serves 6

8 cups water
1 teaspoon salt
1¾ cups polenta or yellow cornmeal
¼ cup low-fat Lorraine cheese, finely diced
¼ cup skim mozzarella cheese, finely diced
½ cup Parmesan cheese, freshly grated

Nutritional Data

PER SERVING:

Calories	194
% calories from fat	25
Fat (gm)	5.5
Sat. Fat (gm)	2.9
Cholesterol (mg)	12.6
Sodium (mg)	568
Protein (gm)	8.8
Carbohydrate (gm)	28

EXCHANGES:

Milk	0.0	Bread	2.0
Veg.	0.0	Meat	0.5
Fruit	0.0	Fat	0.5

Bring water and salt to full rolling boil in heavy 4-quart saucepan. Gradually sprinkle in polenta in thin steady stream, stirring constantly with wooden spoon to prevent lumping. Cook over low heat, stirring constantly, 4 to 5 minutes. Continue cooking over low heat, without cover, 15 minutes.

Stir in Lorraine and mozzarella cheeses, mixing well. Continue cooking another 15 minutes, stirring frequently.

Turn polenta out on heated serving dish. Sprinkle with Parmesan cheese.

▨ Matzoh Meal Polenta

Serves 6

2 cups Chicken Stock (see p. 40)
Generous pinch turmeric
⅔ cup matzoh meal
½ teaspoon hot red pepper flakes
Salt and black pepper, to taste
1 cup mushrooms, sliced
½ cup onion, sliced
1 teaspoon olive oil
1 teaspoon Romano cheese, freshly grated
Tomato sauce (optional)

Nutritional Data

PER SERVING:

Calories	87
% calories from fat	16
Fat (gm)	1.5
Sat. Fat (gm)	0.4
Cholesterol (mg)	4.2
Sodium (mg)	14
Protein (gm)	3.2
Carbohydrate (gm)	14.2

EXCHANGES:

Milk	0.0	Bread	1.0
Veg.	0.0	Meat	0.0
Fruit	0.0	Fat	0.5

In 2-quart measure, microwave Chicken Stock on High 3 minutes, until it boils. Add turmeric and stir. Add matzoh meal, red pepper flakes, salt, and pepper, and microwave on High 2 to 4 minutes, stirring once, until all liquid is absorbed. Turn into serving dish.

Place mushrooms and onion in 2-cup bowl with olive oil, and microwave on High 1 to 2 minutes, until tender. Top polenta with vegetables and dusting of cheese. Tomato sauce may also be used as topping if desired. May be served chilled.

Beans with Vegetables and Herbs

Serves 6

1 cup dried white beans, or 2 cups canned Italian white beans
1 tablespoon flour
2 tablespoons olive oil
1 medium onion, chopped
1 medium carrot, chopped
1 stalk celery, finely chopped
1 hot pepper, fresh or dried, seeded and chopped
1 teaspoon dried sage, crushed
2 teaspoons chives, chopped
2 tablespoons parsley, chopped
1 large red or green bell pepper, seeded and diced
Black pepper, freshly ground, to taste

Nutritional Data

PER SERVING:

Calories	149
% calories from fat	29
Fat (gm)	5
Sat. Fat (gm)	0.8
Cholesterol (mg)	0
Sodium (mg)	19
Protein (gm)	6.1
Carbohydrate (gm)	20.9

EXCHANGES:

Milk	0.0	Bread	1.0
Veg.	1.0	Meat	0.0
Fruit	0.0	Fat	1.0

Soak beans 8 hours in 3 cups water with 1 tablespoon flour. Drain, rinse, and cook in 4 cups water until tender, about 1 hour. Drain, and set aside. If canned beans are used, omit soaking with water and flour and simply drain before assembling rest of dish.

Heat olive oil in large saucepan, add onion, carrot, and celery, and sauté over medium heat, stirring, 5 minutes. Stir in hot pepper, sage, chives, parsley, and bell pepper, and continue to sauté another 5 to 7 minutes, until pepper is tender.

Add 2 cups cooked beans and pepper. Combine well, reduce heat to low, and cook, stirring frequently, another 5 minutes. Serve hot.

Black Beans and Rice

Serves 6

1¼ cups black (turtle) beans
2 cups water
2 tablespoons olive oil
1 medium onion, finely chopped
1 clove garlic, minced
½ medium-sweet green bell pepper,
   seeded and chopped
2 large tomatoes, peeled, seeded,
   and chopped
   Spike (see "About This Cookbook")
   Black pepper, freshly ground
1 cup uncooked short-grain rice

Nutritional Data

PER SERVING:

Calories	253
% calories from fat	18
Fat (gm)	5.2
Sat. Fat (gm)	0.8
Cholesterol (mg)	0
Sodium (mg)	5.2
Protein (gm)	7.9
Carbohydrate (gm)	44.1

EXCHANGES:

Milk	0.0	Bread	2.5
Veg.	1.0	Meat	0.0
Fruit	0.0	Fat	1.0

Put beans to soak 1 to 2 hours in covering of cold water. Drain. Return beans to large saucepan with 2 cups cold water. Bring to simmer, and cook, covered, over low heat until beans are tender, 1½ hours. Check to see if beans need more water to keep from drying out, and add a little boiling water if necessary.

While beans are cooking, heat oil in skillet and sauté onion, garlic, and pepper until onion is soft. Add tomatoes and cook until mixture is smooth and well blended. Season with Spike and pepper.

Drain beans and add tomato mixture, stirring to mix. Add rice and water, stir gently, cover, and cook over very low heat until rice is tender and all liquid absorbed.

Refried Beans

Serves 6

4 cups cooked kidney beans, excess liquid
   drained and reserved
   Vegetable cooking spray
1 cup onion, chopped
2 cloves garlic, minced
1 jalapeño pepper, seeded and chopped
   (use caution; wear rubber gloves and
   do not rub your eyes)
½ teaspoon ground cumin
½ teaspoon (or to taste) each ingredient:
   salt, freshly ground black pepper, chili
   powder

Nutritional Data

PER SERVING:

Calories	165
% calories from fat	4
Fat (gm)	0.7
Sat. Fat (gm)	0.1
Cholesterol (mg)	0
Sodium (mg)	253
Protein (gm)	10.7
Carbohydrate (gm)	30

EXCHANGES:

Milk	0.0	Bread	2.0
Veg.	0.0	Meat	0.5
Fruit	0.0	Fat	0.0

Mash beans with about 1 cup of reserved liquid or enough to soften them. Use masher or food processor. Set aside.

Coat nonstick skillet with cooking spray and heat. Sauté onion and garlic until onion is tender. Add pepper, mashed beans, and seasonings, stirring continuously and cooking about 5 minutes until beans are desired consistency and somewhat dry. Add reserved cooking liquid as necessary. Serve refried beans hot or at room temperature.

Pinto Beans

Serves 8

1 lb. dried pinto beans, washed and picked over
3 cloves garlic, minced
1 cup onion, sliced
¾ teaspoon salt

Place beans in large heavy saucepan and cover them with 3 inches of hot water. Stir in garlic and onion. Cover beans, bring to boil, then simmer, stirring occasionally, until tender. Add water as necessary during cooking.

Nutritional Data

PER SERVING:

Calories	192
% calories from fat	3
Fat (gm)	0.7
Sat. Fat (gm)	0.2
Cholesterol (mg)	0
Sodium (mg)	203
Protein (gm)	11.2
Carbohydrate (gm)	36.2

EXCHANGES:

Milk	0.0	Bread	2.0
Veg.	0.0	Meat	1.0
Fruit	0.0	Fat	0.0

Beans are done when they are tender yet firm to the bite, 2 to 3 hours. Add salt 20 minutes before end of cooking time. Cool beans before proceeding with recipes that require more cooking.

Cooked beans can be eaten straight from the pot or in preparing numerous bean-based dishes. Store cooked beans in refrigerator until you are ready to use them. Beans will keep refrigerated 2 to 3 days.

🖳 Green and Red Beans

Serves 4

½ cup celery, chopped
2 large scallions, chopped
2 cloves garlic, minced
¼ cup green bell pepper, chopped
½ teaspoon dried oregano
⅛ teaspoon cayenne pepper
2 cups cooked kidney or pinto beans (if canned, beans should be rinsed and drained)
1 teaspoon chicken-flavored base
1 teaspoon sesame seeds

Nutritional Data

PER SERVING:

Calories	89
% calories from fat	9
Fat (gm)	0.9
Sat. Fat (gm)	0.1
Cholesterol (mg)	0
Sodium (mg)	176
Protein (gm)	5.7
Carbohydrate (gm)	15.4

EXCHANGES:

Milk	0.0	Bread	1.0
Veg.	1.0	Meat	0.0
Fruit	0.0	Fat	0.0

Place celery, scallions, garlic, green pepper, and spices in 2-cup measure. Microwave on High 5 minutes. Add beans and chicken flavoring, and microwave on High 1 minute. Stir to

mix. When warmed through, toss with sesame seeds. Serve
with brown rice, if desired.

White Beans
à la Provençal

Serves 4 (as side dish)

½ lb. dried white beans (Great Northern,
   navy, or small white), washed and
   picked over
2 tablespoons olive oil, divided
1 red onion, chopped
2 cloves garlic, minced and divided
1 quart water
1 bay leaf
   Spike (see "About This Cookbook")
1 14½-oz. can chunky tomatoes, or 3
   fresh, chopped
1 teaspoon fresh thyme, or ¼ teaspoon
   dried thyme
2 tablespoons fresh basil, chopped
   Black pepper, freshly ground
2 tablespoons fresh parsley, chopped

Nutritional Data

PER SERVING:

Calories	257
% calories from fat	25
Fat (gm)	7.5
Sat. Fat (gm)	1.1
Cholesterol (mg)	0
Sodium (mg)	177
Protein (gm)	12.7
Carbohydrate (gm)	37.2

EXCHANGES:

Milk	0.0	Bread	2.0
Veg.	1.0	Meat	1.0
Fruit	0.0	Fat	1.0

If you're using dried beans, soak in 1 quart water several
hours or overnight, and drain. Heat 1 tablespoon oil in large
heavy saucepan and sauté onion and 1 clove garlic until onion
is tender. Add beans along with 1 quart water and bay leaf.
Bring to boil, reduce heat, cover, and simmer 1½ hours or
until beans are tender. Add Spike to taste, remove bay leaf,
drain, and save cooking liquid.

Heat remaining oil in skillet and sauté remaining garlic
over medium heat 1 minute. Add tomatoes, thyme, and basil
and simmer 10 minutes. Add beans, ½ cup cooking liquid,
and cover. Simmer 10 more minutes. Remove from heat and
stir in pepper to taste and parsley.

Greek Country Beans

Serves 6

1 lb. dried beans (navy, white, broad,
   or lima)
   Vegetable cooking spray
2 large onions, chopped
2 cloves garlic, minced
½ cup Light Tomato Sauce (recipe follows)
2 carrots, diced
2 stalks celery, diced

Nutritional Data

PER SERVING:

Calories	318
% calories from fat	7
Fat (gm)	2.7
Sat. Fat (gm)	0.5
Cholesterol (mg)	0
Sodium (mg)	38
Protein (gm)	17.2
Carbohydrate (gm)	59.4

<table>
<tr><td>1½</td><td>teaspoons Spike (see "About This Cookbook")</td></tr>
</table>

1½   teaspoons Spike (see "About This Cookbook")
½   teaspoon black pepper, freshly ground
1   teaspoon sugar
½   cup parsley, chopped
1   teaspoon oregano

EXCHANGES:			
Milk	0.0	Bread	3.0
Veg.	3.0	Meat	0.0
Fruit	0.0	Fat	0.5

Soak beans overnight in water to cover. (Or cover beans with 2½ cups cold water, bring to boil, boil 2 minutes, and let stand 1 hour.) Drain.

Coat 3-quart saucepan with vegetable cooking spray and sauté onions and garlic 10 minutes over medium heat until golden. Add remaining ingredients and sauté another 10 minutes.

Add beans and enough boiling water to barely cover beans (about 1½ cups). Stir once to mix, cover, and simmer until vegetables and beans are very tender, about 1¼ hours.

Light Tomato Sauce

½   tablespoon olive oil
1   tablespoon garlic, minced
¼   cup onion, chopped
¼   cup mushrooms, sliced
¼   cup celery, chopped
1   lb. Italian tomatoes, undrained
3   basil leaves, chopped
1   tablespoon fresh oregano, chopped
1   teaspoon Spike (see "About This Cookbook")
   Black pepper, freshly ground

Heat oil in heavy 1½ quart saucepan over moderate heat. Add garlic, onions, mushrooms, and celery. Sauté 5 minutes, stirring well. Add tomatoes, basil, and oregano and bring mixture to simmer. Lower heat, cover, and simmer sauce 1 hour. Season to taste with Spike and pepper.

Mid-Eastern Kidney Beans

Serves 4

1   medium onion, chopped
1   clove garlic, minced
1   teaspoon olive oil
1   16-oz. can kidney or pinto beans, rinsed and drained
   Juice of 1 lemon and ½ teaspoon lemon rind
1   teaspoon dried oregano, crushed

Nutritional Data

PER SERVING:	
Calories	118
% calories from fat	11
Fat (gm)	1.6
Sat. Fat (gm)	0.2
Cholesterol (mg)	0
Sodium (mg)	395
Protein (gm)	6.4
Carbohydrate (gm)	21

Black pepper, to taste
Few sprigs parsley for garnish
Lemon wedges for garnish

EXCHANGES:			
Milk	0.0	Bread	1.0
Veg.	1.0	Meat	0.0
Fruit	0.0	Fat	0.5

Place onion, garlic, and oil in 4-cup measure, and microwave on High 2 minutes. Add kidney or pinto beans, and microwave on High 5 minutes. Mix lemon juice, lemon rind, oregano, and pepper to taste.

Stir this mixture into beans and mash lightly with fork. Garnish with parsley sprigs and lemon wedges. Serve as appetizer on bed of greens or as side dish.

Chickpeas, Roman Style

Serves 6

1½ cups dried chickpeas, or 2½ cups canned chickpeas
1 tablespoon flour if dried chickpeas are used
1 teaspoon salt for cooking dried chickpeas
2 tablespoons olive oil
2 teaspoons fresh rosemary, or 1 teaspoon dried rosemary
3 cloves garlic, minced
½ hot pepper, seeded and chopped
2 tablespoons parsley, chopped
3 medium tomatoes, peeled, seeded, and chopped, or 1 cup canned Italian plum tomatoes, drained and chopped
1 teaspoon Spike (see "About This Cookbook")
1 teaspoon oregano
2 tablespoons chives, minced

Nutritional Data

PER SERVING:

Calories	269
% calories from fat	25
Fat (gm)	7.7
Sat. Fat (gm)	2.2
Cholesterol (mg)	3.9
Sodium (mg)	369
Protein (gm)	12.4
Carbohydrate (gm)	38.6

EXCHANGES:

Milk	0.0	Bread	2.5
Veg.	0.5	Meat	0.0
Fruit	0.0	Fat	1.5

Soak dried chickpeas 8 hours in 4 cups water with 1 tablespoon flour. Rinse, place chickpeas in large saucepan with 6 cups water and 1 teaspoon salt, and cook until tender, about 1½ hours. When cooked, drain, and set aside. Cooking liquid can be reserved and used for soup.

While chickpeas are cooking, prepare sauce. Heat olive oil in saucepan, add rosemary, garlic, and hot pepper, and sauté 1 to 2 minutes over medium heat, until garlic begins to color. Add parsley, tomatoes, Spike, and oregano, and simmer over low heat 15 to 20 minutes, until you have a fairly thick tomato sauce.

Add chickpeas and cook 10 minutes, stirring occasionally to blend flavors. Sprinkle with chives, and serve.

Spanish Chickpeas

Serves 6

1	medium onion, chopped fine
2	cloves garlic, minced
2	teaspoons olive oil
1	16-oz. can chickpeas, rinsed and drained
1	medium tomato, chopped
2	tablespoons parsley, chopped
3	leaves fresh basil, or ½ teaspoon dried basil
	Black pepper, freshly ground, to taste

Nutritional Data

PER SERVING:

Calories	102
% calories from fat	26
Fat (gm)	3
Sat. Fat (gm)	0.4
Cholesterol (mg)	0
Sodium (mg)	304
Protein (gm)	4
Carbohydrate (gm)	15.6

EXCHANGES:

Milk	0.0	Bread	1.0
Veg.	0.0	Meat	0.0
Fruit	0.0	Fat	0.5

Mix onion, garlic, and oil in 2-quart measure, and microwave on High 2 minutes, uncovered. Add remaining ingredients and microwave on High 4 minutes, stirring once. Serve warm or chilled. May be used as appetizer, salad, or side dish.

Curried Lentils

Serves 10 (½-cup servings)

1	tablespoon olive oil
3	shallots, minced (about ⅓ cup)
1	carrot, chopped fine
2	cloves garlic, minced
¾	cup brown (or orange) lentils
3	cups Chicken Stock (see p. 40), as needed
½	teaspoon fresh ginger root, peeled and minced
1	teaspoon curry powder
2	stalks celery, chopped small
	Few dashes reduced-sodium soy sauce
	Few dashes sesame oil
2	tablespoons nonfat plain yogurt (optional)

Nutritional Data

PER SERVING:

Calories	50
% calories from fat	31
Fat (gm)	1.8
Sat. Fat (gm)	0.3
Cholesterol (mg)	3
Sodium (mg)	14
Protein (gm)	2.7
Carbohydrate (gm)	5.5

EXCHANGES:

Milk	0.0	Bread	0.5
Veg.	0.0	Meat	0.0
Fruit	0.0	Fat	0.5

In 2-quart measure or casserole, combine olive oil, shallots, carrot, and garlic. Microwave on High 3 minutes, stirring once, until tender. Add lentils, Chicken Stock, and ginger and cover with vented plastic wrap.

Microwave on High 30 to 35 minutes, stirring a few times. Lentils should be tender but crunchy. Drain off any excess liquid. Stir in curry powder, celery, soy sauce, and sesame oil. Add yogurt to moisten, if desired. Makes 5 cups.

Lentil and Rice Pilaf

Serves 6

1 cup dried lentils, washed
4½ cups water
1 bay leaf
1 small chili pepper, minced
1 clove garlic, minced
1 cup plum tomatoes, peeled and chopped
2 tablespoons olive oil
1 onion, chopped
¾ cup uncooked long-grain rice

Nutritional Data

PER SERVING:

Calories	188
% calories from fat	24
Fat (gm)	5
Sat. Fat (gm)	0.7
Cholesterol (mg)	0
Sodium (mg)	6
Protein (gm)	5.8
Carbohydrate (gm)	30.5

EXCHANGES:

Milk	0.0	Bread	2.0
Veg.	0.0	Meat	0.0
Fruit	0.0	Fat	1.0

In medium saucepan, bring lentils and water to rolling boil over high heat. Add bay leaf, chili pepper, garlic, and tomatoes. Simmer, covered, about 35 minutes. Stir occasionally with wooden spoon, until lentils are softened.

While lentils simmer, heat 2 tablespoons oil in large skillet, and sauté onion until translucent. When lentils are softened, add rice and onions to pot and simmer 20 minutes longer, until rice is cooked. Add more water if necessary, and stir occasionally to keep mixture from sticking to bottom of pan. Remove from heat. Discard bay leaf and mix well. Serve warm.

Pesole
(Hominy)

Serves 8

1 20-oz. can pesole (white hominy), drained
1 medium onion, chopped
1 tablespoon chili powder
3 cloves garlic, minced
2 tablespoons ground cumin
1 tablespoon ground oregano
2 cups fresh tomatoes, peeled and chopped, or 1 16-oz. can peeled tomatoes, chopped
½ teaspoon salt
¼ teaspoon black pepper, freshly ground

Nutritional Data

PER SERVING:

Calories	81
% calories from fat	15
Fat (gm)	1.4
Sat. Fat (gm)	0.1
Cholesterol (mg)	0
Sodium (mg)	300
Protein (gm)	2.2
Carbohydrate (gm)	16

EXCHANGES:

Milk	0.0	Bread	0.5
Veg.	1.5	Meat	0.0
Fruit	0.0	Fat	0.0

Place all ingredients in large heavy saucepan. Cover with water and bring mixture to boil; reduce heat to simmer and continue cooking. Cook, covered, 15 minutes, then uncovered 5 to 10 minutes. Add water to cover as needed.

Southern Grits

Serves 6

3   cups water
½   teaspoon salt
4   cloves garlic, minced
¼   teaspoon black pepper
¾   cup quick-cooking white hominy grits

Bring water to rolling boil; add salt, garlic, and pepper. Stir grits into boiling water in slow, steady stream. Cook, stirring or whisking constantly, 3 minutes. Turn off heat and let stand, covered, 5 minutes.

Nutritional Data

PER SERVING:

Calories	75
% calories from fat	3
Fat (gm)	0.2
Sat. Fat (gm)	0
Cholesterol (mg)	0
Sodium (mg)	178
Protein (gm)	1.9
Carbohydrate (gm)	16.1

EXCHANGES:

Milk	0.0	Bread	1.0
Veg.	0.0	Meat	0.0
Fruit	0.0	Fat	0.0

Chapter Ten
PASTA ENTREES

Homemade Pasta

Serves 4 (entree servings)

1½ cups all-purpose flour
2   large eggs

Nutritional Data	
PER SERVING:	
Calories	208
% calories from fat	13
Fat (gm)	3
Sat. Fat (gm)	0.8
Cholesterol (mg)	106.5
Sodium (mg)	32
Protein (gm)	8
Carbohydrate (gm)	36.1

EXCHANGES:			
Milk	0.0	Bread	2.5
Veg.	0.0	Meat	0.0
Fruit	0.0	Fat	0.5

1. Mound flour on cutting board, making well in center. Drop eggs into center of well.

2. Break egg yolks and mix eggs with fork. While mixing eggs, gradually start to incorporate flour into eggs. As flour is incorporated, it will be necessary to move mound of flour toward center, using your hands. Continue mixing until all or almost all flour has been incorporated, forming soft, but not sticky, ball of dough.

Machine Kneading and Cutting

3. *To knead dough using pasta machine,* set machine rollers on widest setting. Cut dough into 2 equal pieces. Lightly flour outside of 1 piece, and pass it through machine. Fold piece of dough into thirds; pass it through machine again, inserting open edges (not the fold) of dough first. Repeat folding and rolling 8 to 12 times or until dough feels smooth and satiny; *lightly flour dough only if it begins to feel sticky.*

Move machine rollers to next widest setting. Pass dough (do not fold dough any longer) through rollers, beginning to roll out and stretch dough. Move machine rollers to next widest setting; pass dough through rollers. Continue process until pasta is as thin as desired. (Often narrowest setting on machine makes pasta too thin; 1 or 2 settings from end is usually best.) *Lightly flour dough if it begins to feel even slightly sticky at any time.*

To cut dough using a pasta machine, set cutting rollers for width of pasta desired; pass dough through cutters. Arrange cut pasta in single layer on lightly floured surface.

Repeat above procedures with second piece of dough.

Hand Kneading and Cutting

4. *To knead dough by hand,* knead on lightly floured surface until dough is smooth and satiny, about 10 minutes. Cover dough lightly with damp towel and let rest 10 minutes.

Place dough on lightly floured surface. Starting in center of dough, roll with rolling pin from center to edge. Continue rolling, always from center to edge (to keep dough as round as possible) until dough is about 1/16-inch thick. *Lightly flour dough if it begins to feel even slightly sticky at any time.*

To cut dough by hand, flour top of dough lightly and roll up. Cut into desired width with sharp knife. Immediately unroll cut pasta to keep noodles from sticking together, and arrange in single layer on lightly floured surface.

5. Pasta can be cooked fresh, or it can be frozen or dried to be cooked later. To freeze pasta, place in heavy plastic freezer bag and freeze. To dry pasta, let stand on floured surface (or hang over rack) until completely dried. (Be sure pasta is completely dried or it will turn moldy in storage.) Store at room temperature in airtight container.

6. To cook fresh, frozen, or dried pasta, heat 4 to 5 quarts lightly salted (optional) water to boiling. Add pasta and begin testing for doneness as soon as water returns to boil. Cooking time will vary from 1 to 2 minutes once water has returned to boil.

Fettuccine Alfredo

Serves 6

1 cup 2% milk
2 tablespoons all-purpose flour
2 tablespoons margarine
½ teaspoon salt
3 cloves garlic, minced
¼ cup Parmesan cheese, freshly grated
1 lb. fettuccine, cooked

Mix all ingredients except fettuccine in ½-quart microwave-safe bowl. Cook uncovered 2 minutes on High. Stir, and cook 1 to 2 minutes longer on High, stirring after 1 minute until thick. Stir in pasta and microwave 1 to 2 minutes until hot.

Nutritional Data

PER SERVING:

Calories	344
% calories from fat	20
Fat (gm)	7.3
Sat. Fat (gm)	2.3
Cholesterol (mg)	6.3
Sodium (mg)	326
Protein (gm)	13.8
Carbohydrate (gm)	54

EXCHANGES:

Milk	0.0	Bread	3.5
Veg.	0.0	Meat	0.5
Fruit	0.0	Fat	1.5

Fettuccine with Chicken Piccata

Serves 6

6 chicken breast halves, boneless and skinless (about 3 ozs. each)
   Flour
   Vegetable cooking spray
1 tablespoon margarine
2 tablespoons flour
1 14½-oz. can low-salt chicken broth
½ cup dry white wine, or low-salt chicken broth

Nutritional Data

PER SERVING:

Calories	301
% calories from fat	18
Fat (gm)	6
Sat. Fat (gm)	0.9
Cholesterol (mg)	43.4
Sodium (mg)	175
Protein (gm)	24.3
Carbohydrate (gm)	35

2	tablespoons fresh lemon juice	EXCHANGES:			
1	tablespoon parsley, finely chopped	Milk	0.0	Bread	2.5
2	teaspoons capers (optional), drained	Veg.	0.0	Meat	2.0
12	ozs. cooked, warm fettuccine	Fruit	0.0	Fat	0.0

Pound chicken with flat side of meat mallet to scant
1/4-inch thickness; dredge lightly with flour. Coat large skillet
with cooking spray; heat over medium heat until hot. Cook
chicken over medium to medium-high heat until browned and
no longer pink in center, 3 to 5 minutes. Remove chicken
from skillet.

Melt margarine in skillet; stir in 2 tablespoons flour and
cook over medium heat 1 to 2 minutes. Stir in chicken broth,
wine, and lemon juice; heat to boiling. Boil, stirring constantly
until slightly thickened, 1 to 2 minutes. Reduce heat and simmer, uncovered, until thickened to medium sauce consistency, about 15 minutes more. Stir in parsley and capers.

Return chicken to sauce; cook over medium-low heat until
chicken is hot through, 2 to 3 minutes. Serve chicken and
sauce over pasta.

Fettuccine with Pork, Greens, and Caramelized Onions

Serves 4	**Nutritional Data**	
4 medium onions, sliced	PER SERVING:	
1 tablespoon olive oil	Calories	389
1 teaspoon sugar	% calories from fat	22
2 14½-oz. cans low-salt chicken broth	Fat (gm)	9.6
2 cups kale, or mustard greens, or	Sat. Fat (gm)	1.6
Swiss chard, thinly sliced	Cholesterol (mg)	60.5
2 cups curly endive, or spinach,	Sodium (mg)	345
thinly sliced	Protein (gm)	30.5
¼ teaspoon salt	Carbohydrate (gm)	46.9
¼ teaspoon black pepper		
Olive-oil-flavored vegetable spray	EXCHANGES:	
12 ozs. lean pork tenderloin, fat	Milk 0.0	Bread 2.5
trimmed, cut into ¼-inch slices	Veg. 3.0	Meat 2.0
8 ozs. cooked, warm fettuccine	Fruit 0.0	Fat 0.5

Cook onions in oil over medium heat in large skillet 5 minutes; reduce heat to low and stir in sugar. Cook until onions
are golden in color and very soft, about 20 minutes.

Stir chicken broth into onions; heat to boiling. Reduce
heat and simmer, uncovered, until broth is reduced by one-
third, about 10 minutes. Add greens; simmer, covered, until

greens are wilted, 5 to 7 minutes. Simmer, uncovered, until broth is almost absorbed by greens, about 5 minutes. Stir in salt and pepper.

Coat large skillet with cooking spray; heat over medium heat until hot. Cook pork slices over medium to medium-high heat until browned and no longer pink in center, about 5 minutes.

Spoon onion mixture over pasta and toss; add pork and toss.

Fettuccine with Asparagus and Shrimp in Parmesan Sauce

Serves 6

1 tablespoon plus 1 teaspoon diet margarine
1 cup mushrooms, sliced
2 cloves garlic, minced
1 cup steamed asparagus spears, diagonally sliced
1 egg white
¼ cup low-fat yogurt
½ cup skim milk
4 ozs. (½ cup) Parmesan cheese, freshly grated
    Dash pepper, freshly ground
18 large shrimp, cooked or canned
1 lb. uncooked fettuccine
2 tablespoons parsley, minced

Nutritional Data

PER SERVING:

Calories	326
% calories from fat	19
Fat (gm)	7.2
Sat. Fat (gm)	2
Cholesterol (mg)	39.9
Sodium (mg)	371
Protein (gm)	20.6
Carbohydrate (gm)	47

EXCHANGES:

Milk	0.0	Bread	3.0
Veg.	0.0	Meat	2.0
Fruit	0.0	Fat	0.0

In stockpot, bring 8 cups water to boil.

Meanwhile, in saucepan, heat margarine until hot; add mushrooms and garlic, and sauté briefly, about 2 minutes. Stir in asparagus and set aside.

In small bowl, combine egg white and yogurt and mix until smooth. Add milk and Parmesan cheese and stir to mix well. Add pepper and shrimp to sauce and heat through. (Be sure to heat on low flame or setting because yogurt will curdle if too high heat is used.)

Cook fettuccine according to package directions. Pour sauce over fettuccine and toss to combine. Sprinkle with parsley.

To Freeze: Place individual portions of pasta and sauce in separate vacuum-sealed bags; label and freeze up to 2 months.

To Serve: Put bags in boiling water, and bring water to boil again. Boil 10 to 12 minutes. Add garnishes such as parsley or cheese just before serving.

Fettuccine à la Grecque

Serves 4

Vegetable cooking spray
2 teaspoons garlic, minced
2 teaspoons dried oregano
1½ cups low-sodium tomato sauce
1 teaspoon basil
Black pepper, freshly ground
12 ozs. uncooked fresh fettuccine
¾ lb. medium shrimp, shelled and deveined
3 ozs. feta cheese, cut into 1-inch chunks
Parsley for garnish

Nutritional Data

PER SERVING:

Calories	415
% calories from fat	18
Fat (gm)	8.4
Sat. Fat (gm)	3.4
Cholesterol (mg)	149.3
Sodium (mg)	553
Protein (gm)	29.9
Carbohydrate (gm)	56.5

EXCHANGES:

Milk	0.0	Bread	3.5
Veg.	2.0	Meat	2.0
Fruit	0.0	Fat	0.0

To make Grecque Sauce, coat skillet with vegetable cooking spray and add garlic and oregano. Cook about 2 minutes. Stir in tomato sauce and basil and simmer 5 minutes more. Season to taste with pepper.

Put pasta in boiling water and cook until *al dente.*

Meanwhile, coat another skillet with cooking spray and add shrimp. Sear about 1 minute on each side. Remove shrimp with slotted spoon. Add Grecque Sauce to pan and simmer 1 to 2 minutes. Stir shrimp into sauce and season to taste with pepper. Drop in chunks of feta and basil.

Drain pasta and transfer to pasta bowl. Add shrimp in Grecque Sauce and toss to combine. Sprinkle with parsley. Serve hot.

Fettuccine with Goat's Cheese

Serves 4

2 cups nonfat plain yogurt
2 tablespoons plain goat's cheese
½ teaspoon garlic powder
¼ teaspoon salt
1 lb. uncooked fettuccine
¼ teaspoon black pepper, freshly ground
¼ cup each ingredient: fresh parsley, fresh basil, both minced

Nutritional Data

PER SERVING:

Calories	421
% calories from fat	11
Fat (gm)	5.2
Sat. Fat (gm)	0.7
Cholesterol (mg)	3.6
Sodium (mg)	430
Protein (gm)	22.8
Carbohydrate (gm)	74.2

EXCHANGES:

Milk	0.5	Bread	4.5
Veg.	0.0	Meat	0.0
Fruit	0.0	Fat	1.0

In medium bowl, mix together yogurt, goat's cheese, and garlic powder. Add salt. Meanwhile, bring large pot of lightly salted water to boil. Cook pasta according to package directions.

Drain well and toss pasta with cheese sauce. Place sauced pasta on 4 dinner plates and season each serving with freshly ground black pepper; sprinkle with parsley and basil. Serve immediately.

Fettuccine with Scallops

Serves 8

- 1 cup water
- 1 cup dry white wine
- 1 tablespoon fresh lemon juice
- 1½ lbs. bay scallops
- 1 medium onion, minced
- 2 large cloves garlic, minced
- 3 tablespoons olive oil
- 2 cups pea pods
- 1 cup radishes, sliced
- 3 cups asparagus, cut in 1-inch pieces
- 2 cups mushrooms, sliced
- 1 cup artichoke hearts
- ½ cup Chicken Stock (see p. 40)
- 2 tablespoons fresh basil, chopped
- 1 cup evaporated skim milk
- 1 lb. fettuccine, cooked and drained
- 1 cup Parmesan cheese, freshly grated

Nutritional Data

PER SERVING:

Calories	453
% calories from fat	24
Fat (gm)	12.5
Sat. Fat (gm)	3.2
Cholesterol (mg)	47.7
Sodium (mg)	575
Protein (gm)	35.5
Carbohydrate (gm)	49

EXCHANGES:

Milk	0.5	Bread	2.5
Veg.	2.0	Meat	3.0
Fruit	0.0	Fat	0.5

In large saucepan, combine water, wine, and lemon juice. Bring to boil. Remove from heat, add scallops, and let steep 30 minutes. Drain.

In large skillet or wok, sauté onion and garlic in olive oil until onion is soft, about 2 minutes. Add pea pods, radishes, asparagus, and mushrooms. Stir-fry 2 minutes. Add artichoke hearts. Stir-fry 2 minutes more. Stir in Chicken Stock and basil. Simmer 3 minutes. Add scallops and milk. Simmer 1 minute.

Combine pasta with scallop mixture, tossing until well mixed. Pour into large serving bowl. Add cheese and toss again. Serve immediately.

Vegetable Lasagna

Serves 8

- 1 lb. uncooked lasagna noodles, or spinach lasagna noodles
- 1 cup green onions, diced
- 3 cloves garlic, crushed
- 2 cups mushrooms, sliced
- 2 tablespoons olive oil
- 2 lbs. spinach leaves, without stems
- 1 teaspoon oregano

Nutritional Data

PER SERVING:

Calories	331
% calories from fat	25
Fat (gm)	10
Sat. Fat (gm)	2.6
Cholesterol (mg)	10.2
Sodium (mg)	404
Protein (gm)	19.4
Carbohydrate (gm)	47.2

¼   teaspoon cayenne pepper
1   cup low-fat cottage cheese
½   cup Parmesan cheese, freshly grated
1   cup pimientos, minced
1   cup Italian parsley, chopped
½   cup part-skim mozzarella cheese,
     shredded

EXCHANGES:

Milk	0.0	Bread	3.0
Veg.	1.0	Meat	1.0
Fruit	0.0	Fat	1.0

Preheat oven to 350 degrees. Boil water to cook pasta in large pot.

In large skillet, sauté green onions, garlic, and mushrooms in oil 3 minutes. Add spinach leaves, oregano, and cayenne pepper and continue cooking, covered, 5 minutes. Remove from heat.

Put cottage cheese, Parmesan cheese, and pimientos in large bowl and blend thoroughly with parsley until well mixed. Drain lasagna noodles and rinse in cold water. Line noodles on flat surface.

Layer noodles in 2-quart baking dish. Spoon layer of spinach mixture over noodles, then a layer of about ¼ cup cottage cheese mixture and 2 tablespoons Parmesan cheese. Make 3 layers of lasagna noodles, spinach mixture, and cottage cheese mixture with Parmesan cheese. After layering lasagna noodles and mixtures, top with shredded mozzarella and pimiento bits. Bake 8 to 10 minutes.

Let lasagna set and cool 10 minutes before serving.

Spinach Lasagna Rolls

Serves 6

Vegetable cooking spray
1   10-oz. package frozen leaf spinach,
     thawed, drained, and chopped
1   15-oz. container nonfat ricotta cheese
½   cup Parmesan cheese, freshly grated
1   egg, beaten to blend
1   tablespoon Italian parsley, chopped
     Spike (see "About This Cookbook"),
     to taste
     Black pepper, to taste
2   cups Classic Spaghetti Sauce (see p. 500),
     or purchased sauce
8   lasagna noodles, freshly cooked
½   cup skim mozzarella cheese, grated

Nutritional Data

PER SERVING:

Calories	321
% calories from fat	27
Fat (gm)	10.9
Sat. Fat (gm)	4.8
Cholesterol (mg)	72.4
Sodium (mg)	625
Protein (gm)	29.3
Carbohydrate (gm)	35.8

EXCHANGES:

Milk	0.0	Bread	1.5
Veg.	2.0	Meat	3.0
Fruit	0.0	Fat	0.0

Preheat oven to 350 degrees. Heat heavy medium skillet coated with vegetable cooking spray over medium-high heat. Add spinach, and cook until tender, about 4 minutes. Cool.

Combine spinach, ricotta, Parmesan cheese, egg, and parsley in large bowl. Season with Spike and pepper. Spread 1 cup spaghetti sauce over bottom of 8-inch-square baking dish.

Pat 1 lasagna noodle dry with paper towel. Set on wax paper sheet. Spread about ⅓ cup ricotta mixture over noodle. Carefully roll up noodle, starting at short end, to enclose filling. Arrange seam side down in prepared dish. Repeat with remaining noodles. Top with remaining 1 cup sauce. Sprinkle with mozzarella. Bake until cheese melts, about 45 minutes.

Salmon Lasagna in White Wine Sauce

Serves 8

Pasta

5   lasagna noodles
1   tablespoon oil

Salmon Mousse

1   lb. fresh salmon, boneless, skinless, and cut into chunks (canned salmon may also be used)
2   egg whites
1   teaspoon Spike (see "About This Cookbook")
½   teaspoon white pepper, freshly ground
1   cup evaporated skim milk

Sauce

Vegetable cooking spray
2   medium carrots, finely chopped
3   medium stalks celery, finely chopped
1   medium onion, minced
1   bell pepper, finely chopped
1   cup dry white wine
1   teaspoon Spike (see "About This Cookbook")
½   teaspoon white pepper, freshly ground
½   cup evaporated skim milk
½   cup low-sodium chicken broth

Nutritional Data

PER SERVING:

Calories	187
% calories from fat	22
Fat (gm)	4.5
Sat. Fat (gm)	0.7
Cholesterol (mg)	11.7
Sodium (mg)	149
Protein (gm)	14.7
Carbohydrate (gm)	17.2

EXCHANGES:

Milk	0.5	Bread	0.5
Veg.	1.0	Meat	1.5
Fruit	0.0	Fat	0.0

Pasta: Cook in boiling water with oil, according to package directions. Drain and immediately plunge into cold water. Remove from water and place on clean towels to drain. Using piece of wax paper as pattern to fit bottom of terrine, cut pasta sheets to size.

Salmon Mousse: In food processor or blender, puree salmon with egg whites, Spike, and pepper until smooth. With motor running, pour in evaporated skim milk. Stop motor and scrape down sides of bowl. Whirl again. Remove to bowl.

Prepare the Terrine: Preheat oven to 350 degrees. Coat terrine (baking dish) with cooking spray. Place piece of pasta on bottom. Spread one-quarter of salmon mousse on top (if you are using 5 or more pasta skins, use less mousse per layer). Continue, alternating layers of pasta and mousse, ending with pasta on top. Cover terrine with lid or foil. Place terrine inside larger pan filled with boiling water halfway up terrine. Bake 30 minutes. To unmold, run knife around lasagna and turn out onto board. Cover to keep warm.

Sauce: Coat skillet with vegetable cooking spray and add carrots, celery, onion, and pepper. Cook slowly 20 minutes. Pour in white wine; cook another 10 minutes. Add Spike and white pepper. Transfer to blender or food processor; puree with evaporated skim milk and chicken broth. Strain through fine-mesh strainer into saucepan. Taste for seasoning and heat through.

Assemble the Dish: Cut lasagna into 8 serving pieces. Pour some sauce over, and pass remainder in sauce bowl.

Sausage Lasagna

Serves 8

2	cups fat-free ricotta cheese
1/4	cup Parmesan cheese, freshly grated
3	cups (12 ozs.) reduced-fat mozzarella cheese, shredded
	Tomato Sauce with Italian Sausage (recipe follows)
12	lasagna noodles (10 ozs.), cooked and kept at room temperature

Nutritional Data

PER SERVING:

Calories	375
% calories from fat	30
Fat (gm)	12.9
Sat. Fat (gm)	6
Cholesterol (mg)	47.3
Sodium (mg)	679
Protein (gm)	31.3
Carbohydrate (gm)	33.9

EXCHANGES:

Milk	0.0	Bread	1.5
Veg.	2.5	Meat	3.5
Fruit	0.0	Fat	0.5

Preheat oven to 350 degrees. Combine cheeses in bowl. Spread 1 cup Tomato Sauce on bottom of 13" x 9" baking pan; top with 4 lasagna noodles, overlapping slightly. Spoon one-third of cheese mixture over noodles, spreading lightly with rubber spatula. Top with 1 cup Tomato Sauce. Repeat layers 2 times, ending with layer of noodles, cheese, and remaining Tomato Sauce.

Bake lasagna, loosely covered with aluminum foil, until sauce is bubbly, about 1 hour.

Tomato Sauce with Italian Sausage (makes about 4½ cups)

	Olive-oil-flavored vegetable cooking spray
2	cups onion, chopped
3	cloves garlic, minced
1	teaspoon dried basil leaves
1	teaspoon dried tarragon leaves
1	teaspoon dried thyme leaves
2	16-oz. cans low-sodium whole tomatoes, undrained, coarsely chopped

2   8-oz. cans low-sodium tomato sauce
1   cup water
1   teaspoon sugar
8   ozs. turkey Italian sausage, cooked
    and well drained
1/4 teaspoon salt
1/4 teaspoon black pepper

Coat large saucepan with cooking spray; heat over medium heat until hot. Sauté onion and garlic until tender, about 5 minutes; stir in herbs and cook 1 to 2 minutes more.

Add tomatoes, tomato sauce, and water; heat to boiling. Reduce heat and simmer, uncovered, until sauce is reduced to about 4 1/2 cups, 15 to 20 minutes. Stir in sugar; stir in sausage, salt, and pepper.

Linguine with Sun-Dried Tomatoes

Serves 4

1   tablespoon olive oil
2   large shallots, chopped
1/2 cup evaporated skim milk
1/2 pint Sun-Dried Tomatoes (see p. 20),
    sliced and drained
1/2 lb. uncooked linguine
1   oz. Romano or Parmesan cheese,
    freshly grated
    Spike (see "About This Cookbook"),
    to taste
    Black pepper, freshly ground, to taste
2   tablespoons pine nuts, toasted
    Italian parsley, minced
    Additional Romano or Parmesan cheese,
    freshly grated

Nutritional Data

PER SERVING:

Calories	318
% calories from fat	29
Fat (gm)	10.9
Sat. Fat (gm)	1.8
Cholesterol (mg)	8.2
Sodium (mg)	232
Protein (gm)	14.8
Carbohydrate (gm)	44.8

EXCHANGES:

Milk	0.0	Bread	2.5
Veg.	1.5	Meat	0.5
Fruit	0.0	Fat	1.5

Heat oil in large skillet over medium heat. Add shallots, and stir 1 minute. Add milk, and bring to boil. Turn off heat, and add Sun-Dried Tomatoes.

Meanwhile, boil linguine in large pot until just tender but still firm to bite, stirring occasionally. Drain well. Return linguine to pot. Add sauce and cheese, and stir to coat. Season with Spike and pepper.

Divide between plates. Sprinkle with pine nuts and parsley. Serve, passing additional cheese.

Linguine with Clam Sauce

Serves 4

- 8 ozs. uncooked linguine
- 1 teaspoon olive oil
- 2 onions, finely chopped
- 3 cloves garlic, minced
- ¼ teaspoon dried oregano, crushed
- ¼ cup sliced water chestnuts, rinsed and drained
- 1 6½-oz. can whole baby clams, drained
- ½ cup parsley, chopped
- 2 tablespoons white wine, or vodka
  Black pepper, to taste

Nutritional Data

PER SERVING:

Calories	350
% calories from fat	9
Fat (gm)	3.3
Sat. Fat (gm)	0.4
Cholesterol (mg)	30.8
Sodium (mg)	61
Protein (gm)	20.8
Carbohydrate (gm)	57.1

EXCHANGES:

Milk	0.0	Bread	3.0
Veg.	2.0	Meat	1.5
Fruit	0.0	Fat	0.0

Cook linguine according to package directions on conventional range top until *al dente*. Drain in colander.

While pasta is cooking, place oil, onions, and garlic in 4-cup measure, and microwave on High 3 to 4 minutes, stirring once. Add oregano and water chestnuts, and microwave on High 1 minute more.

Stir in clams, parsley, and wine or vodka, and microwave on High 1 to 2 minutes, until warmed through. When pasta is cooked and drained, toss with sauce. Season with pepper, to taste.

Italian Macaroni and Beans

Serves 6

- 2 cloves garlic, minced
- 2 tablespoons olive oil
- 2 cups Marinara Sauce (see p. 501)
- 1 teaspoon oregano
- 1 teaspoon garlic powder
- 1 16-oz. can cannellini beans
- ½ lb. uncooked elbow macaroni
  Salt, black pepper, to taste
  Parsley, chopped
  Parmesan cheese, freshly grated
  Italian bread, optional

Nutritional Data

PER SERVING:

Calories	306
% calories from fat	27
Fat (gm)	9.9
Sat. Fat (gm)	2
Cholesterol (mg)	3.8
Sodium (mg)	365
Protein (gm)	13.5
Carbohydrate (gm)	47.2

EXCHANGES:

Milk	0.0	Bread	3.0
Veg.	1.0	Meat	0.5
Fruit	0.0	Fat	1.0

In saucepan, sauté garlic gently in oil until golden brown. Add Marinara Sauce and cook 10 minutes. Stir in spices. Add beans; stir gently and continue to simmer.

Cook macaroni in boiling water until *al dente*. Drain, salt and pepper, to taste, and add to bean mixture. Stir gently. If mixture gets too thick, add a little water. Add parsley and stir well.

Place macaroni and beans in large bowl and sprinkle with Parmesan cheese. Serve immediately or pasta will absorb all liquid. Use Italian bread for dunking.

Macaroni and Cheese

Serves 6 (side-dish servings, about ⅔ cup each)

- ¼ cup onion, finely chopped
- 2 tablespoons margarine
- 3 tablespoons flour
- 1 bay leaf
- 2½ cups skim milk
- ¾ cup (3 ozs.) reduced-fat American cheese, shredded
- ¾ cup (3 ozs.) reduced-fat Cheddar cheese, shredded
- 1 teaspoon Dijon mustard
- ¼ teaspoon black pepper
- 10 ozs. fusilli, or rotini (corkscrews), cooked and kept at room temperature
- 2 tablespoons Parmesan cheese, freshly grated, or dry unseasoned bread crumbs

Nutritional Data

PER SERVING:

Calories	330
% calories from fat	28
Fat (gm)	10
Sat. Fat (gm)	4
Cholesterol (mg)	18.5
Sodium (mg)	559
Protein (gm)	17.4
Carbohydrate (gm)	42

EXCHANGES:

Milk	0.5	Bread	2.5
Veg.	0.0	Meat	1.0
Fruit	0.0	Fat	1.0

Preheat oven to 350 degrees. Sauté onion in margarine until tender, 2 to 3 minutes. Stir in flour and bay leaf and cook 1 to 2 minutes, stirring frequently. Stir in milk; heat to boiling. Boil until thickened, stirring constantly (sauce will be thin). Remove from heat; stir in American and Cheddar cheeses, mustard, and pepper.

Pour sauce over pasta in 1-quart casserole; stir to combine, and sprinkle with Parmesan cheese. Bake, uncovered, until hot through and lightly browned on top, about 30 minutes.

Macaroni and Four Cheeses

Serves 6

1	cup uncooked macaroni
½	cup Parmesan cheese, freshly grated
½	cup Romano cheese, freshly grated
1½	cups skim milk
1	cup low-fat cottage cheese
2	tablespoons all-purpose flour
4	thin onion slices
½	teaspoon dry mustard
½	cup skim mozzarella cheese, shredded
½	cup cracker crumbs, or bread crumbs
1	tablespoon margarine, melted

Nutritional Data

PER SERVING:

Calories	277
% calories from fat	32
Fat (gm)	9.8
Sat. Fat (gm)	5
Cholesterol (mg)	24.2
Sodium (mg)	598
Protein (gm)	19.3
Carbohydrate (gm)	26.8

EXCHANGES:

Milk	0.0	Bread	2.0
Veg.	0.0	Meat	2.0
Fruit	0.0	Fat	0.5

Cook macaroni; drain. In 2-quart baking dish, layer half macaroni, and Parmesan and Romano cheeses. Add remaining macaroni and Parmesan and Romano cheeses.

Preheat oven to 350 degrees. In blender, process milk, cottage cheese, flour, onion, and mustard until smooth. Pour over layered macaroni. Sprinkle mozzarella cheese over top. Combine crumbs and melted margarine; sprinkle on top. Bake 40 minutes.

Macaroni with Olive and Tomato Sauce

Serves 6

2	tablespoons olive oil
1	medium red onion, finely chopped
2	cups fresh tomato, chopped and peeled
4	thin curls of orange rind, grated
1	clove garlic, minced
1-2	cups water
½	cup dry red wine
1	cup Kalamata olives, rinsed, pitted, and sliced
2	scant tablespoons capers, rinsed
3	tablespoons parsley, chopped
1	teaspoon dried thyme
	Black pepper, freshly ground, to taste
1	lb. uncooked macaroni

Nutritional Data

PER SERVING:

Calories	454
% calories from fat	28
Fat (gm)	14.3
Sat. Fat (gm)	1.7
Cholesterol (mg)	0
Sodium (mg)	818
Protein (gm)	11.4
Carbohydrate (gm)	68.5

EXCHANGES:

Milk	0.0	Bread	4.0
Veg.	1.0	Meat	0.0
Fruit	0.0	Fat	3.0

In heavy saucepan, heat olive oil. Add onion and sauté until translucent, stirring with wooden spoon. Add tomatoes, orange rind, and garlic. Stir well. Add about 1 cup water, lower heat, and simmer, covered, until sauce thickens, adding more water if necessary. Add wine, uncover pot slightly, and continue simmering about 30 minutes. Add olives and capers and cook for 5 more minutes. Stir in herbs and pepper and cook 10 minutes more.

While sauce is cooking, cook pasta according to package directions. When pasta is cooked, drain well and top with sauce. Serve hot.

Chicken-Vegetable Manicotti with Spinach Sauce

Serves 4 (3 manicotti each)

Olive-oil-flavored vegetable cooking spray
½ cup onion, chopped
3 cloves garlic, minced
2 cups spinach leaves, chopped
½ cup zucchini, chopped
½ cup yellow summer squash, chopped
1 teaspoon dried basil leaves
1 teaspoon dried oregano leaves
8 ozs. cooked chicken, boneless, skinless, and finely shredded
½ cup reduced-fat ricotta cheese
¼ teaspoon salt
¼ teaspoon black pepper
1 8-oz. package manicotti, cooked and kept at room temperature
Spinach Sauce (recipe follows)

Nutritional Data

PER SERVING:

Calories	510
% calories from fat	24
Fat (gm)	13.7
Sat. Fat (gm)	4
Cholesterol (mg)	46.6
Sodium (mg)	640
Protein (gm)	34.5
Carbohydrate (gm)	65.2

EXCHANGES:

Milk	0.5	Bread	3.0
Veg.	3.0	Meat	1.5
Fruit	0.0	Fat	2.0

Coat large skillet with cooking spray; heat over medium heat until hot. Sauté onion and garlic until tender, about 3 minutes. Add remaining vegetables; sauté until tender, 5 to 8 minutes. Stir in herbs and cook 2 minutes more. Stir in chicken, cheese, salt, and pepper.

Preheat oven to 350 degrees. Spoon about 3 tablespoons chicken-vegetable mixture into each manicotti; arrange in baking pan. Spoon Spinach Sauce over manicotti. Bake loosely covered with aluminum foil until manicotti are hot through and sauce is bubbly, 35 to 40 minutes.

Spinach Sauce

Serves 4

2   cloves garlic, minced
1   tablespoon margarine
1/4 cup all-purpose flour
2   cups 2% milk
1   lb. fresh spinach, washed and chopped
2   teaspoons dried basil leaves
1/8 teaspoon ground nutmeg
4   dashes red pepper sauce
1/4 teaspoon salt

Nutritional Data

PER SERVING:

Calories	141
% calories from fat	40
(17 with 2 oz. pasta)	
Fat (gm)	6.6
Sat. Fat (gm)	2.8
Cholesterol (mg)	9
Sodium (mg)	284
Protein (gm)	8
Carbohydrate (gm)	14.4

EXCHANGES:

Milk	0.5	Bread	0.0
Veg.	2.0	Meat	0.0
Fruit	0.0	Fat	1.0

Sauté garlic in margarine in large saucepan 1 to 2 minutes. Stir in flour and cook over medium heat 1 to 2 minutes more. Stir in milk; heat to boiling. Boil, stirring constantly, until thickened, 1 to 2 minutes.

Stir spinach and remaining ingredients into sauce. Cook, uncovered, over medium heat until spinach is cooked, 5 to 7 minutes.

Spinach and Zucchini Mostaccioli Casserole

Serves 8

10 ozs. uncooked mostaccioli (tubular pasta)
1   10-oz. package frozen chopped spinach, thawed
    Vegetable cooking spray
2   teaspoons vegetable oil
1   cup onion, chopped
2   cloves garlic, minced
1   lb. zucchini, cut into 1-inch pieces
2   14½-oz. cans chunky tomatoes, undrained
3   tablespoons tomato paste
1½ teaspoons basil
3/4 teaspoon oregano
1/4 teaspoon Spike (see "About This Cookbook")
1/4 teaspoon red pepper, crushed
1/2 cup Parmesan cheese, freshly grated and divided

Nutritional Data

PER SERVING:

Calories	210
% calories from fat	18
Fat (gm)	4.4
Sat. Fat (gm)	1.5
Cholesterol (mg)	4.9
Sodium (mg)	361
Protein (gm)	9.9
Carbohydrate (gm)	34.2

EXCHANGES:

Milk	0.0	Bread	2.0
Veg.	2.0	Meat	0.0
Fruit	0.0	Fat	0.5

Cook mostaccioli according to package directions, omitting salt; drain.

Place spinach on paper towels; squeeze until barely moist.

Coat large nonstick skillet with cooking spray; add oil and place over medium-high heat until hot. Add onion and garlic;

sauté until tender. Add zucchini; cook until zucchini is just limp, about 4 minutes. Stir in tomatoes and next 5 ingredients; bring to boil. Reduce heat; simmer, uncovered, 5 minutes, stirring occasionally.

Preheat oven to 350 degrees. Combine pasta, spinach, zucchini mixture, and 1/4 cup Parmesan cheese in bowl; stir well. Spoon into 13" x 9" x 2" baking dish coated with cooking spray. Sprinkle with remaining 1/4 cup cheese. Bake 20 minutes.

To Freeze: Place individual portions of pasta and sauce in separate vacuum-sealed bags; label and freeze up to 2 months.

To Serve: Put bags in boiling water, and bring water to boil again. Boil 10 to 12 minutes. Add garnishes such as parsley or cheese just before serving.

Pignoli and Tomato Orzo

Serves 4

- 1 teaspoon olive oil
- 1 tablespoon pine nuts
- 1/4 cup sun-dried tomatoes
- Salt and black pepper, to taste
- 2 cups Chicken Stock (see p. 40)
- 2 cups water
- 3/4 cup orzo (small quill-shaped pasta)
- 1 tablespoon Romano or Parmesan cheese, freshly grated

Nutritional Data

PER SERVING:

Calories	202
% calories from fat	20
Fat (gm)	4.6
Sat. Fat (gm)	0.8
Cholesterol (mg)	6.9
Sodium (mg)	105
Protein (gm)	9
Carbohydrate (gm)	30.4

EXCHANGES:

Milk	0.0	Bread	2.0
Veg.	0.0	Meat	0.0
Fruit	0.0	Fat	1.0

Soak tomatoes in boiling water until soft; drain and dice. Place pine nuts and tomatoes in measuring cup with oil. Microwave on High 2 minutes, and season with salt and pepper. Let stand.

Bring Chicken Stock and water to boil by microwaving on High about 5 minutes. Add orzo and microwave on High 6 to 8 minutes, until tender. Drain and mix with pine nuts and tomatoes. Stir in grated cheese.

Pasta Primavera

Serves 6

1 lb. uncooked fettucine
1/4 cup olive oil
2 cloves garlic, chopped
1/2 teaspoon oregano
1/2 teaspoon basil
1 cup broccoli florets
1 cup cauliflower florets
1 cup artichoke hearts
1 cup asparagus spears, cut into
　1-inch pieces
1 cup green bell peppers, chopped
1 cup cherry tomatoes, halved
1/2 cup Parmesan cheese, freshly grated

Nutritional Data

PER SERVING:

Calories	393
% calories from fat	32
Fat (gm)	14.7
Sat. Fat (gm)	2.9
Cholesterol (mg)	6.6
Sodium (mg)	322
Protein (gm)	16.7
Carbohydrate (gm)	53.6

EXCHANGES:

Milk	0.0	Bread	3.0
Veg.	2.0	Meat	0.5
Fruit	0.0	Fat	2.0

Cook fettucine in boiling salted water until *al dente*. As pasta cooks, heat olive oil in large skillet and sauté garlic 2 to 3 minutes. Add herbs and vegetables and sauté quickly over high heat until vegetables are crisp-tender. Toss drained pasta with vegetables. Sprinkle with Parmesan cheese.

Pasta Santa Fe

Serves 4

1 medium onion, sliced
3 cloves garlic, minced
2 tablespoons vegetable oil
2 medium zucchini, sliced
2 medium tomatoes, cut into wedges
2 poblano peppers, sliced
1 cup whole kernel corn, fresh or
　frozen, thawed
2 tablespoons chili powder
1 teaspoon dried oregano leaves
1/2 teaspoon ground cumin
2 tablespoons cilantro, or parsley, minced
1/2 teaspoon salt
1/4 teaspoon black pepper
8 ozs. trio maliano (combination of
　corkscrews, shells, and rigatoni), cooked
　and kept warm

Nutritional Data

PER SERVING:

Calories	350
% calories from fat	24
Fat (gm)	9.6
Sat. Fat (gm)	1.2
Cholesterol (mg)	0
Sodium (mg)	327
Protein (gm)	11.6
Carbohydrate (gm)	58

EXCHANGES:

Milk	0.0	Bread	3.0
Veg.	2.0	Meat	0.0
Fruit	0.0	Fat	2.0

Sauté onion and garlic in oil in large skillet until tender, about 5 minutes. Add remaining vegetables, chili powder, oregano, and cumin. Cook, uncovered, over medium to medium-low heat until vegetables are crisp-tender, 12 to 15 minutes. Stir in cilantro, salt, and pepper.

Spoon vegetable mixture over pasta and toss.

Pasta Pomadoro

Serves 4

8 ozs. uncooked spaghetti, or ziti
6 ozs. tomato sauce
¼ cup nonfat dry milk
3 scallions, chopped
½ cup green peas
¼ teaspoon dried basil
Black pepper, to taste

Cook pasta *al dente* according to package directions on conventional range top. In bowl, mix together remaining ingredients. Cover with wax paper, and microwave on High 2 to 3 minutes, until heated through. Stir to combine. Mix with spaghetti and serve.

Nutritional Data

PER SERVING:

Calories	271
% calories from fat	4
Fat (gm)	1.2
Sat. Fat (gm)	0.2
Cholesterol (mg)	0.8
Sodium (mg)	283
Protein (gm)	10.8
Carbohydrate (gm)	54

EXCHANGES:

Milk	0.0	Bread	3.0
Veg.	2.0	Meat	0.0
Fruit	0.0	Fat	0.0

Pasta with Garlic Sauce

Serves 6

2 cups low-fat cottage cheese
4 tablespoons evaporated skim milk
Dash white pepper
8 cloves garlic, minced
2 teaspoons Tamari soy sauce
3 tablespoons chives, minced
1 lb. uncooked thin spaghetti
3 tablespoons Italian parsley, chopped
½ cup Parmesan cheese, freshly grated

Nutritional Data

PER SERVING:

Calories	409
% calories from fat	11
Fat (gm)	4.8
Sat. Fat (gm)	2.3
Cholesterol (mg)	10.3
Sodium (mg)	589
Protein (gm)	24.3
Carbohydrate (gm)	65.6

EXCHANGES:

Milk	0.0	Bread	4.0
Veg.	0.0	Meat	2.0
Fruit	0.0	Fat	0.0

Place first 6 ingredients in blender or food processor. Mix until completely smooth.

Place in double boiler on medium heat. Heat until bubbly around edges. Cook spaghetti, pour on sauce, and toss gently. Garnish with parsley. Sprinkle with Parmesan cheese. Serve immediately.

Pasta with Mushroom Sauce

Serves 6

- ½ cup dried porcini mushrooms (other dried mushrooms may be used)
- 1 medium onion, chopped
- 2 large cloves garlic, minced
- 2 tablespoons diet margarine
- 2 tablespoons olive oil
- 1 cup evaporated skim milk
- 1 6-oz. can tomato paste
- 1 teaspoon instant chicken bouillon granules
- 1 teaspoon dried marjoram, crushed
  Black pepper, to taste
- 1 lb. uncooked fettuccine

Nutritional Data

PER SERVING:

Calories	363
% calories from fat	23
Fat (gm)	9.7
Sat. Fat (gm)	1
Cholesterol (mg)	1.3
Sodium (mg)	600
Protein (gm)	15.3
Carbohydrate (gm)	57.6

EXCHANGES:

Milk	0.5	Bread	2.5
Veg.	2.0	Meat	0.0
Fruit	0.0	Fat	2.0

Rehydrate mushrooms according to package directions; drain liquid. Cut up any large mushrooms.

Cook mushrooms, onion, and garlic in margarine and olive oil until tender. Stir in milk, tomato paste, bouillon, marjoram, and pepper if desired. Heat through.

Meanwhile, cook fettuccine in boiling water until just tender. Drain. Serve warm pasta topped with mushroom sauce.

To Freeze: Place individual portions of pasta and sauce in separate vacuum-sealed bags; label and freeze up to 2 months.

To Serve: Put bags in boiling water, and bring water to boil again. Boil 10 to 12 minutes. Add garnishes such as parsley or cheese just before serving.

Pasta with Tomato, Eggplant, and Bell Pepper Sauce

Serves 6

- 2 tablespoons olive oil
- 10 medium tomatoes (about 2 lbs.), peeled, cored, seeded, and coarsely chopped
- 1 large eggplant, unpeeled and cut into bite-size cubes
- 4 large red bell peppers, cored, seeded, and cut into bite-size pieces
- ½ teaspoon hot pepper flakes

Nutritional Data

PER SERVING:

Calories	370
% calories from fat	18
Fat (gm)	7.4
Sat. Fat (gm)	1
Cholesterol (mg)	0
Sodium (mg)	29
Protein (gm)	12.7
Carbohydrate (gm)	65.7

1   tablespoon *herbes de Provence*
1   lb. uncooked rotini, or tubular pasta

EXCHANGES:			
Milk	0.0	Bread	3.5
Veg.	2.0	Meat	0.0
Fruit	0.0	Fat	1.5

Heat olive oil in large, deep-sided skillet over medium-high heat. Add tomatoes and eggplant. Sauté about 10 minutes, stirring from time to time. Add bell peppers and season with pepper flakes and *herbes de Provence*. Cover and simmer gently about 1 hour.

Just before serving, bring large pot of water to rolling boil. Add pasta and cook just until tender. Drain.

To serve, divide pasta evenly among dinner plates. Spoon sauce over pasta, allowing each diner to toss pasta when served.

Pasta with Creamy Pesto

Serves 4

2   cups fresh basil leaves, loosely packed
1   cup evaporated skim milk
1   lb. uncooked tagliatelle, or fettuccine
½   cup Parmesan cheese, freshly grated

Nutritional Data
PER SERVING:

Calories	500
% calories from fat	13
Fat (gm)	7.1
Sat. Fat (gm)	2.9
Cholesterol (mg)	11.9
Sodium (mg)	325
Protein (gm)	25.8
Carbohydrate (gm)	82.6

In food processor or blender, chop basil. Add milk and whisk to smooth consistency. Place creamy pesto sauce in large bowl in which pasta will be served.

Bring large pot of water to rolling boil. Add pasta and cook just until tender. Drain.

EXCHANGES:			
Milk	0.5	Bread	5.0
Veg.	0.0	Meat	1.0
Fruit	0.0	Fat	1.0

Just before serving, stir Parmesan cheese into sauce and blend thoroughly. Add pasta to bowl, toss, and serve.

Red and Yellow Pepper Pasta

Serves 4

6   ozs. uncooked pasta (shells, rotelles, or angel hair)
1   lb. red and yellow bell peppers, seeded and chopped (4 cups)
2   cloves garlic, minced
1   small red onion, quartered and sliced
1   teaspoon olive oil
2   tablespoons tomato paste diluted with ½ cup water

Nutritional Data
PER SERVING:

Calories	211
% calories from fat	11
Fat (gm)	2.6
Sat. Fat (gm)	0.4
Cholesterol (mg)	0
Sodium (mg)	75.7
Protein (gm)	7.4
Carbohydrate (gm)	40.6

2	tablespoons chopped fresh basil, or 2 teaspoons dried basil	EXCHANGES:			
2	tablespoons balsamic vinegar	Milk	0.0	Bread	2.0
	Dash salt and black pepper	Veg.	2.0	Meat	0.0
		Fruit	0.0	Fat	0.5

Cook pasta according to package directions until *al dente* on conventional range top, drain, and keep warm.

Meanwhile, place peppers, garlic, onion, and olive oil in 1-quart measure or casserole and microwave on High 2 to 3 minutes, until tender. Stir.

Add tomato paste, basil, and enough water to make sauce, and vinegar. Microwave another 1 minute on High to warm. Combine with pasta and season with salt and pepper, to taste.

▣ *Creamy Spinach Pasta*

Serves 4

		Nutritional Data	
6	ozs. uncooked spinach pasta	PER SERVING:	
2	tablespoons Parmesan or Romano cheese, freshly grated	Calories	211
		% calories from fat	28
½	cup part-skim ricotta cheese	Fat (gm)	6.5
¼	cup nonfat plain yogurt	Sat. Fat (gm)	2.5
1	tablespoon chives, chopped	Cholesterol (mg)	43.2
2	tablespoons walnuts, chopped	Sodium (mg)	119
		Protein (gm)	11.4
		Carbohydrate (gm)	26.9

Cook pasta according to package directions on conventional range top until *al dente*. Drain and keep warm.

EXCHANGES:			
Milk	0.0	Bread	2.0
Veg.	0.0	Meat	1.0
Fruit	0.0	Fat	0.5

Meanwhile, place remaining ingredients, except walnuts, in blender and process until creamy. Turn into 2-cup measure and cover with paper towel. Microwave on High 1 to 2 minutes, stirring, just until warm. Stir into pasta and top with walnuts.

Straw and Hay Noodles

Serves 8

		Nutritional Data	
½	lb. uncooked green spinach noodles	PER SERVING:	
½	lb. uncooked no-yolk noodles	Calories	212
1	cup plain nonfat yogurt	% calories from fat	10
2	tablespoons Parmesan cheese, freshly grated	Fat (gm)	2.4
		Sat. Fat (gm)	0.7
	Salt and ground nutmeg, to taste	Cholesterol (mg)	24.5
½	cup chives, chopped	Sodium (mg)	64
		Protein (gm)	9.7
		Carbohydrate (gm)	37.6

Cook pasta in large pot of boiling lightly salted water until *al dente*, or just tender. Toss pasta with yogurt, cheese, salt, nutmeg, and chives. Transfer mixture to warm serving dish and serve immediately.

EXCHANGES:			
Milk	0.0	Bread	2.5
Veg.	0.0	Meat	0.0
Fruit	0.0	Fat	0.5

Pasta with Lemon, Mussels, and Black Olives

Serves 6

¼ cup fresh lemon juice
¼ cup wine vinegar
¼ cup unsweetened apple juice
2 shallots, cut into rings
½ cup pitted oil-cured black olives
2 teaspoons fresh thyme, minced
Zest of 2 lemons, grated
Black pepper, coarsely ground
1 lb. uncooked thin pasta, such as angel hair or capellini
2 lbs. fresh mussels

Nutritional Data

PER SERVING:

Calories	407
% calories from fat	19
Fat (gm)	8.7
Sat. Fat (gm)	1.2
Cholesterol (mg)	32
Sodium (mg)	592
Protein (gm)	24.1
Carbohydrate (gm)	57.8

EXCHANGES:			
Milk	0.0	Bread	4.0
Veg.	0.0	Meat	2.0
Fruit	0.0	Fat	0.5

Pour lemon juice, vinegar, apple juice, and shallots into small bowl. Set sauce aside.

In large shallow serving bowl, combine olives, thyme, and lemon zest. Season with pepper and toss to blend.

Bring large pot of water to rolling boil. Add pasta and cook just until tender. Drain. Add pasta to ingredients in serving bowl.

Meanwhile, thoroughly scrub mussels and rinse. Beard mussels (do not do this in advance or they will die and spoil). Place mussels in large shallow skillet and cover. Cook over high heat, covered, just until mussels open, 2 to 3 minutes; do not overcook. Remove from heat, discarding any mussels that didn't open.

Remove mussels from shells and add to pasta. Add sauce; toss.

Pasta Niçoise

Serves 4

Salad

3 cups cooked pasta, shells or twists
16 pitted black olives, sliced
2 cups green beans, lightly steamed
¼ cup scallions, sliced
1 tomato, diced
1 can water-packed white albacore tuna, drained

Dressing

½ cup parsley, chopped
¼ cup tarragon vinegar
¼ cup water
2 teaspoons canola or safflower oil
1 large clove garlic, crushed
½ teaspoon Dijon mustard
1 teaspoon ground oregano
Black pepper, freshly ground, to taste

Nutritional Data

PER SERVING:

Calories	251
% calories from fat	22
Fat (gm)	6.2
Sat. Fat (gm)	0.9
Cholesterol (mg)	19
Sodium (mg)	351
Protein (gm)	18.1
Carbohydrate (gm)	31.9

EXCHANGES:

Milk	0.0	Bread	2.0
Veg.	1.0	Meat	1.5
Fruit	0.0	Fat	0.0

Toss pasta with other ingredients and tuna. Put dressing ingredients in blender, and mix until smooth. Pour over pasta, toss, and serve.

To Freeze: Place individual portions of pasta and dressing in separate vacuum-sealed bags; label and freeze up to 2 months.

To Serve: Put bags in boiling water, and bring water to boil again. Boil 10 to 12 minutes. Add garnishes such as parsley or cheese just before serving.

Pasta Puttanesca

Serves 6

2 tablespoons olive oil
½ cup onion, minced
2 tablespoons garlic, minced
2½ cups tomatoes, peeled, seeded, and chopped
1 teaspoon hot red pepper flakes
1 tablespoon capers
1 cup unpitted Kalamata olives
1 lb. uncooked spaghetti
2 tablespoons parsley, minced

Nutritional Data

PER SERVING:

Calories	399
% calories from fat	21
Fat (gm)	9.4
Sat. Fat (gm)	1.3
Cholesterol (mg)	0
Sodium (mg)	627
Protein (gm)	11.6
Carbohydrate (gm)	67.6

EXCHANGES:

Milk	0.0	Bread	4.0
Veg.	1.0	Meat	0.0
Fruit	0.0	Fat	2.0

Heat olive oil in large skillet over low heat. Add onion and garlic; sauté slowly until very soft, about 10 minutes. Add

tomatoes; simmer 10 minutes. Add pepper flakes; cook
1 minute. Stir in capers and olives.

Bring large pot of salted water to boil. Add spaghetti, and
cook until pasta is just tender. Drain thoroughly, and add to
sauce in skillet. Toss together well, and serve immediately,
garnished with minced parsley.

Pasta with Fresh Seafood Sauce

Serves 6

- 1 lb. uncooked linguine
- 1 medium onion, chopped
- 2 cloves garlic, minced
- 2 tablespoons olive oil
- ½ cup dry white wine
- 2 cups tomatoes, peeled, seeded, and diced
- 1 teaspoon oregano, minced
- 1 tablespoon basil, minced
- 1 teaspoon thyme, minced
- 1 cup Italian parsley, chopped
- 3 cups fresh seafood (calamari, mussels, clams, shrimp, crabmeat, lobster, cod, bass, or swordfish), chopped

Nutritional Data

PER SERVING:

Calories	374
% calories from fat	22
Fat (gm)	9.3
Sat. Fat (gm)	1
Cholesterol (mg)	21
Sodium (mg)	351
Protein (gm)	20.2
Carbohydrate (gm)	51.1

EXCHANGES:

Milk	0.0	Bread	3.0
Veg.	1.0	Meat	1.5
Fruit	0.0	Fat	1.0

In large pot, boil water to cook pasta.

In large skillet, sauté onion and garlic in olive oil 2 minutes; add white wine and continue cooking. After 5 minutes
more, add tomatoes and herbs with parsley; cook another 5
minutes. Add chopped seafood and cook 3 to 4 minutes more.
(Do not overcook seafood.) Remove from heat.

Cook pasta and drain. Place pasta in large bowl; mix in
seafood sauce. Serve immediately.

Penne with Sausage, Peas, Goat's Cheese, and Tomato Confit

Serves 4

¾ lb. Italian turkey sausage
1 lb. uncooked penne
2 cups petite peas, cooked or thawed if
   frozen
   Tomato Confit (recipe follows)
4 tablespoons goat's cheese

Nutritional Data	
PER SERVING:	
Calories	741
% calories from fat	29
Fat (gm)	23.9
Sat. Fat (gm)	5.7
Cholesterol (mg)	82.3
Sodium (mg)	658
Protein (gm)	35.9
Carbohydrate (gm)	94.4

EXCHANGES:			
Milk	0.0	Bread	6.0
Veg.	1.0	Meat	2.0
Fruit	0.0	Fat	4.0

Crumble sausage, and sauté in nonstick pan about 20 minutes. Set aside. Cook penne according to package directions. Drain, and place in large pasta bowl. Add peas and Tomato Confit. Top each portion with goat's cheese.

Tomato Confit

4 ripe red tomatoes
1 tablespoon shallots, or scallions, finely
   minced
½ teaspoon red wine vinegar
1 tablespoon olive oil
   Spike, to taste
   Black pepper, freshly ground, to taste
8 fresh basil leaves, chopped
2 tablespoons parsley, minced

Peel, seed, and juice tomatoes, then fold them gently in bowl with shallots or scallions, vinegar, oil, and Spike and pepper, to taste. Fold in basil leaves. Let steep 10 minutes to blend flavors. Turn into sieve to drain. Return to bowl, correct seasoning, and fold in parsley.

Chicken and Sweet Potato Ravioli with Curry Sauce

Serves 4 (4 ravioli each)

8 ozs. baked chicken breast, boneless, skinless, and shredded
1 cup mashed sweet potatoes
2 small cloves garlic, minced
½ teaspoon ground ginger
¼ teaspoon salt
¼ teaspoon ground white pepper
32 wonton wrappers
Water
Curry Sauce (recipe follows)

Nutritional Data

PER SERVING:

Calories	383
% calories from fat	13
Fat (gm)	5.5
Sat. Fat (gm)	1.1
Cholesterol (mg)	37.2
Sodium (mg)	587
Protein (gm)	19.8
Carbohydrate (gm)	62.4

EXCHANGES:

Milk	0.0	Bread	4.0
Veg.	0.5	Meat	1.5
Fruit	0.0	Fat	0.0

Mix chicken, sweet potatoes, garlic, ginger, salt, and pepper. Spoon about 2 teaspoons chicken mixture onto wonton wrapper; brush edges of wrapper with water. Top with second wonton wrapper and press edges together to seal. Repeat with remaining wonton wrappers and chicken mixture.

Heat about 2 quarts water to boiling in large saucepan; add 4 to 6 ravioli. Reduce heat and simmer, uncovered, until ravioli float to surface and are *al dente*, 3 to 4 minutes. Remove ravioli with slotted spoon; repeat cooking procedure with remaining ravioli. Serve with Curry Sauce.

Curry Sauce (makes about 1 cup)

2 tablespoons onion, finely chopped
2 cloves garlic, minced
1 tablespoon margarine
1 tablespoon flour
2 teaspoons curry powder
⅛ teaspoon cayenne pepper
1 cup canned low-salt chicken broth
2-4 tablespoons dry white wine (optional)

Sauté onion and garlic in margarine in small saucepan 2 to 3 minutes; stir in flour, curry powder, and pepper. Cook 1 minute more, stirring constantly.

Stir chicken broth and wine into saucepan; heat to boiling. Boil until sauce is thickened (sauce will be thin), stirring constantly.

Shrimp and Artichoke Ravioli with Tarragon Sauce

Serves 4 (4 ravioli each)

Olive-oil-flavored vegetable cooking spray

8   ozs. shrimp, peeled, deveined, and finely chopped
1   1/4-oz. can (or jar) artichoke hearts, drained, rinsed, and finely chopped
1   clove garlic, minced
1/4 teaspoon ground nutmeg
3   tablespoons dry white wine, or water
32   wonton wrappers
     Water
     Tarragon Sauce (recipe follows)

Nutritional Data

PER SERVING:

Calories	331
% calories from fat	5
Fat (gm)	1.9
Sat. Fat (gm)	0.4
Cholesterol (mg)	95.1
Sodium (mg)	719
Protein (gm)	20.4
Carbohydrate (gm)	53

EXCHANGES:

Milk	0.0	Bread	3.0
Veg.	2.0	Meat	1.0
Fruit	0.0	Fat	0.0

Coat large skillet with cooking spray; heat over medium heat until hot. Add shrimp, artichoke hearts, garlic, nutmeg, and wine. Cook over medium heat until shrimp are cooked and liquid is gone, about 5 minutes. Cool.

Place about 2 teaspoons shrimp mixture on wonton wrapper; brush edges of wrapper with water. Top with second wonton wrapper and press edges together to seal. Repeat with remaining wonton wrappers and shrimp mixture.

Heat about 2 quarts water to boiling in large saucepan; add 4 to 6 ravioli. Reduce heat and simmer, uncovered, until ravioli float to surface and are *al dente*, 3 to 4 minutes. Remove ravioli with slotted spoon; repeat cooking procedure with remaining ravioli. Serve with Tarragon Sauce.

Tarragon Sauce (makes about 1 cup)

2   medium shallots, finely chopped
1   tablespoon finely chopped fresh tarragon leaves, or 1/2 teaspoon dried tarragon
1/2 cup dry white wine, or canned low-salt chicken broth
1   cup canned low-salt chicken broth, divided
1   tablespoon flour
1/4 teaspoon salt
1/8 teaspoon ground white pepper

Heat shallots, tarragon, and wine to boiling in small saucepan; reduce heat and simmer, uncovered, until mixture is reduced to 1/4 cup.

Add ½ cup chicken broth; heat to boiling. Mix flour and remaining ½ cup chicken broth; stir into boiling mixture. Boil until thickened (sauce will be thin), stirring constantly. Stir in salt and pepper.

Rigatoni with Vegetables

Serves 8

- 2 tablespoons olive oil
- 1 tablespoon parsley, chopped
- 1 clove garlic, minced
- ½ cup onion, chopped
- 3 carrots, minced
- ¼ head cabbage, shredded
- 1 zucchini, cubed
- 3 large tomatoes, peeled and cubed
- ½ cup Chicken Stock (see p. 40)
- 1 tablespoon basil, minced
- ½ tablespoon chervil, minced
- Black pepper, to taste
- 1 tablespoon Spike (see "About This Cookbook")
- 1 tablespoon oregano, minced
- 1 lb. uncooked rigatoni
- ¾ cup Romano cheese, freshly grated
- ¾ cup Parmesan cheese, freshly grated

Nutritional Data

PER SERVING:

Calories	349
% calories from fat	28
Fat (gm)	11.1
Sat. Fat (gm)	4.3
Cholesterol (mg)	18.9
Sodium (mg)	333
Protein (gm)	16.9
Carbohydrate (gm)	46.3

EXCHANGES:

Milk	0.0	Bread	2.5
Veg.	1.5	Meat	1.0
Fruit	0.0	Fat	1.5

Place oil in large saucepan, heat and add parsley, garlic, onion, and carrots and cook until soft. Add cabbage, zucchini, tomatoes, Chicken Stock, and seasonings. Cover and cook slowly 45 minutes, stirring occasionally.

Cook rigatoni until *al dente*, drain, and place in bowl. Mix well; stir in vegetable sauce, both cheeses, and toss. Serve in large individual bowls that have been warmed.

Rigatoni with Escarole and Sausage

Serves 4

¾	lb. Italian turkey sausage
1	head escarole, leaves cut into 1-inch-long strips
2	cloves garlic, minced
1	lb. uncooked rigatoni
1	oz. Romano cheese, freshly grated
	Spike (see "About This Cookbook"), to taste
1½	cups fresh bread crumbs
	Vegetable cooking spray

Nutritional Data

PER SERVING:

Calories	628
% calories from fat	26
Fat (gm)	17.8
Sat. Fat (gm)	3.7
Cholesterol (mg)	62.2
Sodium (mg)	669
Protein (gm)	30.5
Carbohydrate (gm)	85.8

EXCHANGES:

Milk	0.0	Bread	5.5
Veg.	1.0	Meat	2.0
Fruit	0.0	Fat	2.0

Cook sausage in heavy large skillet over medium heat until brown and cooked through, about 10 minutes. Cool sausage slightly. Cut into ¼-inch slices. Set aside.

Cook escarole in large pot of boiling water until just tender, about 5 minutes. Drain well.

Heat heavy large skillet coated with vegetable cooking spray over high heat. Add sausage, escarole, and garlic, and sauté mixture 3 minutes.

Meanwhile, boil rigatoni in large pot until just tender but still firm to bite. Drain well. Transfer to large broiler-proof dish. Turn on broiler.

Add sausage mixture and Romano to rigatoni, and toss. Season with Spike. Sprinkle with bread crumbs. Broil until bread crumbs are golden brown, about 1 minute.

Rigatoni with Italian Sausage and Fennel Pesto

Serves 6

1	lb. smoked Italian turkey sausage (bulk or links)
1½	cups fennel bulb, or celery, thinly sliced
1	cup onion, chopped
2	cloves garlic, minced
1	8-oz. can low-sodium whole tomatoes, drained and chopped
	Fennel Pesto (recipe follows)

Nutritional Data

PER SERVING:

Calories	406
% calories from fat	29
Fat (gm)	13
Sat. Fat (gm)	2.9
Cholesterol (mg)	48.2
Sodium (mg)	711
Protein (gm)	24.6
Carbohydrate (gm)	48.3

12   ozs. rigatoni, or other tube pasta, cooked
      and kept warm

EXCHANGES:			
Milk	0.0	Bread	2.5
Veg.	1.0	Meat	2.0
Fruit	0.0	Fat	2.0

Cook sausage in large skillet over medium heat until browned, 8 to 10 minutes. Remove sausage from skillet and drain on paper towels; drain excess fat from skillet. If using sausage links, slice into 1/2-inch pieces.

Add fennel, onion, and garlic to skillet; sauté until onion is transparent. Stir in tomatoes and sausage; stir in Fennel Pesto. Heat to boiling; reduce heat and simmer, covered, about 15 minutes.

Spoon sauce mixture over pasta and toss.

Fennel Pesto (makes about 1 1/3 cups)

1   tablespoon fennel seeds
     Hot water
1   cup fennel bulb, or celery, chopped
1/2 cup parsley, loosely packed
2   cloves garlic
14   walnut halves (about 1 oz.)
3   tablespoons water
1   tablespoon olive oil
1/4 cup Parmesan cheese, freshly grated

Place fennel seeds in small bowl; pour hot water over to cover. Let stand 10 minutes; drain.

Mix fennel, fennel seeds, parsley, and garlic in food processor or blender until finely chopped. Add walnuts, 3 tablespoons water, and oil; mix until walnuts are finely chopped. Stir in Parmesan cheese.

Spinach-Mushroom Rotolo with Marinara Sauce

Serves 6

     Olive-oil-flavored vegetable cooking spray
2   cups mushrooms, sliced
1   10-oz. package fresh spinach, washed
     and chopped
2   cloves garlic, minced
1   teaspoon dried basil leaves
1   teaspoon dried tarragon leaves
1/2 8-oz. package reduced-fat cream cheese,
     room temperature
1/2 cup fat-free ricotta cheese

Nutritional Data

PER SERVING:	
Calories	286
% calories from fat	30
Fat (gm)	10.3
Sat. Fat (gm)	2.7
Cholesterol (mg)	8.7
Sodium (mg)	686
Protein (gm)	12.5
Carbohydrate (gm)	38

¼	teaspoon salt
¼	teaspoon black pepper
12	lasagna noodles, cooked and kept at room temperature
	Marinara Sauce (see p. 501)

Marinara Sauce (see p. 501)

EXCHANGES:

Milk	0.0	Bread	1.5
Veg.	3.0	Meat	0.0
Fruit	0.0	Fat	2.0

Preheat oven to 350 degrees.

Coat large skillet with cooking spray; heat over medium heat until hot. Cook mushrooms, covered, until they release juices, 3 to 5 minutes. Add spinach, garlic, and herbs to skillet; cook, covered, until spinach is wilted, 2 to 3 minutes. Cook, uncovered, over medium to medium-high heat until liquid is gone, about 10 minutes; cool.

Combine cheeses, salt, and pepper in bowl; stir in mushroom mixture. Spread 3 to 4 tablespoons cheese mixture on each noodle; roll up and place in baking dish.

Spoon Marinara Sauce over rotolo. Bake, loosely covered with aluminum foil, until rotolo are hot through and sauce is bubbly, 20 to 30 minutes.

Vegetable-Sauced Rotelles

Serves 6

10	ozs. uncooked rotelles (spirals), tomato and spinach flavored
½	red onion, chopped
1	medium green bell pepper, chopped
2	cloves garlic, minced
4	mushrooms, sliced
1	teaspoon olive oil
¼	teaspoon oregano
¼-½	teaspoon red pepper flakes
10	ozs. tomato sauce
2	tablespoons part-skim mozzarella cheese, shredded

Nutritional Data

PER SERVING:

Calories	200
% calories from fat	12
Fat (gm)	2.6
Sat. Fat (gm)	0.5
Cholesterol (mg)	1.3
Sodium (mg)	305
Protein (gm)	8
Carbohydrate (gm)	36.8

EXCHANGES:

Milk	0.0	Bread	2.0
Veg.	1.0	Meat	0.0
Fruit	0.0	Fat	0.5

Cook pasta according to package directions until *al dente*. Drain and set aside.

Mix next 4 ingredients with olive oil in 2-quart casserole, and microwave on High 3 minutes. Add remaining ingredients, except cheese, cover with vented plastic wrap, and microwave on High another 1 minute, until warm.

Mix in pasta and sprinkle with cheese. Microwave, uncovered, about 40 seconds to 1 minute, until cheese is melted.

Ricotta-Stuffed Shells with Spinach Pesto

Serves 4 (3 shells each)
Vegetable cooking spray
¼ cup onion, finely chopped
2 cloves garlic, minced
½ teaspoon dried basil leaves
½ cup fresh spinach, chopped
¾ cup low-fat ricotta cheese
¼ teaspoon ground nutmeg
¼ teaspoon salt
¼ teaspoon black pepper
12 cooked conchiglie (jumbo pasta shells), about 4 ozs.
Spinach Pesto (recipe follows)
2 tablespoons red or green bell peppers, roasted or raw, chopped
Basil sprigs

Nutritional Data

PER SERVING:

Calories	178
% calories from fat	24
Fat (gm)	4.7
Sat. Fat (gm)	0.8
Cholesterol (mg)	7.2
Sodium (mg)	216
Protein (gm)	9.5
Carbohydrate (gm)	24.6

EXCHANGES:

Milk	0.0	Bread	1.5
Veg.	1.0	Meat	0.5
Fruit	0.0	Fat	0.5

Coat medium skillet with cooking spray; sauté onion, garlic, and dried basil until onion is tender, 3 to 4 minutes. Add spinach; cook over medium heat until spinach is wilted, about 5 minutes.

Preheat oven to 350 degrees. Blend spinach mixture into cheese; stir in nutmeg, salt, and pepper. Stuff mixture into shells; place in baking pan. Bake, covered, until hot through, about 20 minutes.

Arrange shells on small serving plates; spoon Spinach Pesto over shells or serve on the side. Sprinkle with bell peppers; garnish with basil sprigs.

Spinach Pesto (makes 8 tablespoons)

1 cup fresh spinach, loosely packed
3 tablespoons finely chopped fresh basil leaves, or 1 tablespoon dried basil
1 clove garlic, minced
1 tablespoon Parmesan cheese, freshly grated
2 teaspoons olive oil
1 teaspoon fresh lemon juice

Mix all ingredients, except lemon juice, in food processor or blender until smooth. Season with lemon juice.

Let stand 2 to 3 hours for flavors to blend, or refrigerate until serving time. Serve at room temperature.

Shells à la Forienza

Serves 8

- 4 large red bell peppers, seeded and sliced
- ¼ cup vodka
- 1 lb. cooked no-egg pasta shells
- ½ teaspoon salt
- ½ teaspoon black pepper
- 1 16-oz. can tomatoes, undrained and pureed
- 6 stalks celery, sliced
- 1 tablespoon Parmesan cheese, freshly grated
- 1 cup plain nonfat yogurt

Nutritional Data

PER SERVING:

Calories	256
% calories from fat	7
Fat (gm)	2.1
Sat. Fat (gm)	0.4
Cholesterol (mg)	1.1
Sodium (mg)	298
Protein (gm)	10.7
Carbohydrate (gm)	45.2

EXCHANGES:

Milk	0.0	Bread	2.5
Veg.	2.0	Meat	0.0
Fruit	0.0	Fat	0.5

Place peppers in deep bowl; mix in vodka and toss. Allow mixture to marinate 3 hours. Arrange hot shells in large serving bowl. Sprinkle with salt and pepper. Add tomato puree and celery.

Combine Parmesan cheese and yogurt in small bowl; drizzle over pasta and toss. Remove peppers from marinade and add to pasta dish. Toss and serve warm.

Shells with Fresh Tomato Sauce

Serves 6

- 1 medium onion, diced
- 3 cloves garlic, minced
- 2 teaspoons olive oil
- 5 tomatoes, chopped
- ¾ cup white wine
  Leaves from ½ bunch fresh basil, finely chopped
- 1 cup mushrooms, sliced
- 1 tablespoon fresh marjoram, or ½ teaspoon dried marjoram
  Salt and black pepper, freshly ground
- ¾ lb. uncooked no-egg pasta shells
- 1 tablespoon Parmesan cheese, freshly grated

Nutritional Data

PER SERVING:

Calories	267
% calories from fat	13
Fat (gm)	3.8
Sat. Fat (gm)	0.7
Cholesterol (mg)	0.8
Sodium (mg)	40
Protein (gm)	9.6
Carbohydrate (gm)	44.9

EXCHANGES:

Milk	0.0	Bread	3.0
Veg.	1.5	Meat	0.0
Fruit	0.0	Fat	0.5

Sauté onion and garlic with olive oil until soft. Add tomatoes, wine, and basil. Cook over medium heat 5 minutes, then add mushrooms, marjoram, salt, and pepper and cook 5 minutes more.

Cook pasta in boiling salted water until just cooked. Drain and divide among heated pasta bowls. Spoon sauce over and sprinkle with Parmesan cheese.

Light Stuffed Shells

Serves 6

8	ozs. uncooked giant no-egg pasta shells
1	tablespoon canola oil
	Vegetable cooking spray
1	10-oz. package frozen chopped spinach, drained well
1	cup 1% cottage cheese, mixed smooth
	Salt and ground nutmeg, to taste
½	cup egg substitute

Nutritional Data

PER SERVING:

Calories	195
% calories from fat	17
Fat (gm)	3.8
Sat. Fat (gm)	0.6
Cholesterol (mg)	1.7
Sodium (mg)	214
Protein (gm)	12.5
Carbohydrate (gm)	27.7

EXCHANGES:

Milk	0.0	Bread	1.5
Veg.	1.0	Meat	1.0
Fruit	0.0	Fat	0.0

Cook giant shells in boiling salted water until *al dente* and drain on paper towels; reserve.

Preheat oven to 400 degrees.

To prepare filling, heat oil in medium saucepan coated with cooking spray over medium heat; stir in spinach. Heat until dry. Mix in cheese, salt, and nutmeg. Mix in egg substitute and stir until well blended. Fill shells and place filled side up in ovenproof casserole coated with cooking spray. Bake 15 minutes or until hot. Serve immediately.

Stuffed Shells

Serves 6

¾	quart Marinara Sauce (see p. 501)
3	egg whites
1	lb. low-fat cottage cheese
1	cup skim mozzarella cheese, shredded
4	tablespoons parsley, chopped
10	fresh basil leaves
	Dash black pepper
24	uncooked giant ziti shells
	Parmesan cheese, freshly grated, to garnish

Nutritional Data

PER SERVING:

Calories	412
% calories from fat	26
Fat (gm)	11.8
Sat. Fat (gm)	4.6
Cholesterol (mg)	19.6
Sodium (mg)	752
Protein (gm)	28.2
Carbohydrate (gm)	48.3

EXCHANGES:

Milk	0.0	Bread	3.0
Veg.	2.0	Meat	2.5
Fruit	0.0	Fat	0.5

Prepare Marinara Sauce and put aside.

In large bowl, combine egg whites, cottage cheese, mozzarella cheese, parsley, basil, and pepper.

Cook giant shells in boiling water until *al dente*. Don't overcook because if ziti are too limp, it's hard to fill them.

Drain and stuff each shell with a few tablespoons of cheese mixture.

Preheat oven to 350 degrees. Cover bottom of large baking dish with about ½ inch of Marinara Sauce. Arrange stuffed shells side by side in sauce. Drizzle remaining sauce over top and down center of shells. Sprinkle with Parmesan cheese and bake, covered, until bubbly.

Spaghetti and Meatballs

Serves 8

Sauce

1   recipe Marinara Sauce (see p. 501)

Meatballs

1   lb. turkey, ground
½   lb. beef, ground
1   small onion, minced
1   clove garlic, minced
½   teaspoon oregano, minced
½   teaspoon fresh basil, minced
½   teaspoon black pepper
¼   cup bread crumbs
3   tablespoons olive oil

Spaghetti

1   lb. uncooked thin spaghetti
   Parsley, chopped

Nutritional Data

PER SERVING:

Calories	502
% calories from fat	35
Fat (gm)	19.6
Sat. Fat (gm)	5.1
Cholesterol (mg)	43.7
Sodium (mg)	345
Protein (gm)	25.1
Carbohydrate (gm)	56.1

EXCHANGES:

Milk	0.0	Bread	3.0
Veg.	1.5	Meat	3.0
Fruit	0.0	Fat	2.0

Sauce: Prepare sauce and set aside.

Meatballs: Mix all meatball ingredients (except olive oil) in medium bowl. Form into 1½-inch-round meatballs. Arrange in single layer in nonstick skillet. Sauté in olive oil over medium heat, turning often until golden on all sides, about 15 minutes. Transfer to paper towels.

Add meatballs to Marinara Sauce and simmer 15 minutes more.

Spaghetti: Cook spaghetti in boiling water until *al dente*. Drain; toss with about ½ cup sauce for each serving. Serve with meatballs. Sprinkle parsley on top.

Spaghetti with Turkey Sauce

Serves 8

Olive-oil-flavored vegetable cooking spray
- 1 tablespoon olive oil
- 3 cloves garlic
- 1 cup onion, sliced
- 1 lb. turkey breast, skin removed and ground
- 2 16-oz. cans tomatoes, drained (reserve juice), and pureed
- 1 6-oz. can tomato paste
- 2 cups water
- ½ teaspoon sugar
- 1 teaspoon fresh oregano, chopped, or ½ teaspoon dried oregano
- ½ teaspoon salt
- ½ teaspoon black pepper
- 1 teaspoon fresh basil, chopped, or ½ teaspoon dried basil
- 1 lb. uncooked thin spaghetti

Nutritional Data

PER SERVING:

Calories	348
% calories from fat	11
Fat (gm)	4.3
Sat. Fat (gm)	0.8
Cholesterol (mg)	24.8
Sodium (mg)	402
Protein (gm)	20.4
Carbohydrate (gm)	56.5

EXCHANGES:

Milk	0.0	Bread	3.0
Veg.	2.0	Meat	1.5
Fruit	0.0	Fat	0.0

Coat nonstick pot with cooking spray. Heat oil. Sauté garlic and onion over medium heat until tender, stirring occasionally. Add turkey and sauté until lightly browned, stirring occasionally. Stir in remaining ingredients, except spaghetti. Simmer, uncovered, 20 minutes, stirring occasionally. Adjust seasonings. Cook spaghetti according to package directions, drain, divide onto 8 heated plates, and spoon sauce over.

Turkey Tetrazzini

Serves 8

- 8 ozs. mushrooms, sliced
- 2 tablespoons margarine
- 2 tablespoons flour
- 1 14½-oz. can low-salt chicken broth
- 1 cup skim milk
- ½ cup dry white wine, or skim milk
- 16 ozs. cooked spaghettini (thin spaghetti)
- 12 ozs. cooked turkey, or chicken breast, boneless, skinless, and cubed
- ¼ cup Parmesan cheese, freshly grated
- ¼ teaspoon ground nutmeg
- ¼ teaspoon salt
- ¼ teaspoon black pepper

Nutritional Data

PER SERVING:

Calories	370
% calories from fat	16
Fat (gm)	6.5
Sat. Fat (gm)	1.7
Cholesterol (mg)	35.7
Sodium (mg)	218
Protein (gm)	23.6
Carbohydrate (gm)	50.3

EXCHANGES:

Milk	0.0	Bread	3.0
Veg.	1.0	Meat	2.0
Fruit	0.0	Fat	0.5

Preheat oven to 350 degrees.

Sauté mushrooms in margarine in large saucepan until tender, about 5 minutes. Stir in flour; cook over medium heat 1 to 2 minutes more. Stir in chicken broth, milk, and wine and heat to boiling. Boil, stirring constantly, until thickened, 1 to 2 minutes (sauce will be very thin). Stir in pasta, turkey, Parmesan cheese, nutmeg, salt, and pepper.

Spoon pasta mixture into 2-quart casserole or baking dish. Bake, uncovered, until lightly browned on top and bubbly, about 45 minutes.

Spaghetti with Anchovies

Serves 2

2	tablespoons olive oil
4	large cloves garlic, minced
3/4	ozs. canned anchovy fillets, drained and chopped
8	ozs. uncooked spaghetti
1	teaspoon fresh lemon juice
	Black pepper, freshly ground, to taste
	Italian parsley, chopped
	Parmesan cheese, freshly grated

Nutritional Data

PER SERVING:

Calories	602
% calories from fat	25
Fat (gm)	16.7
Sat. Fat (gm)	2.3
Cholesterol (mg)	9
Sodium (mg)	395
Protein (gm)	18.7
Carbohydrate (gm)	92.9

EXCHANGES:

Milk	0.0	Bread	6.0
Veg.	0.5	Meat	0.5
Fruit	0.0	Fat	3.0

Heat oil in heavy small skillet over low heat. Add garlic, and cook 2 minutes. Add anchovies and cook until garlic just begins to color, 3 minutes.

Meanwhile, boil spaghetti in large pot until just tender but still firm to bite, stirring occasionally. Drain well. Return spaghetti to pot.

Add oil mixture and lemon juice, and toss to coat. Season with pepper.

Divide between plates. Sprinkle generously with parsley. Serve, passing Parmesan.

Spaghettini Arrabbiata

Serves 6

Spaghettini

1	lb. uncooked thin spaghetti
	Olive-oil-flavored vegetable cooking spray
4	cloves garlic, minced
1	red bell pepper, cut into thin strips
1	yellow bell pepper, cut into thin strips

Nutritional Data

PER SERVING:

Calories	452
% calories from fat	30
Fat (gm)	15.5
Sat. Fat (gm)	3.3
Cholesterol (mg)	6.6
Sodium (mg)	206
Protein (gm)	15.4
Carbohydrate (gm)	64.3

1 green bell pepper, cut into thin strips
½ yellow squash, thinly sliced
2 cups broccoli, florets only
1 cup mushrooms, sliced
½ cup Parmesan cheese, freshly grated
Fresh basil leaves

Dressing

5 tablespoons olive oil
¼ cup raspberry or tarragon vinegar
2 cloves garlic, minced
1 tablespoon fresh lemon juice
Dash Worcestershire sauce
1 teaspoon fresh parsley, chopped
1 teaspoon fresh basil, chopped
¼ teaspoon fresh tarragon, chopped
¼ teaspoon fresh thyme, chopped
½ teaspoon white pepper
1 teaspoon Dijon mustard

EXCHANGES:			
Milk	0.0	Bread	4.0
Veg.	1.0	Meat	0.5
Fruit	0.0	Fat	2.5

Spaghettini: Put large pot of water on stove to boil for spaghettini. Cook according to package directions.

Meanwhile, sauté garlic, peppers, and squash in large, sprayed skillet 5 minutes. Add broccoli and mushrooms and sauté until tender, about 10 minutes.

Dressing: Mix all ingredients in blender until smooth.

Place pasta in large bowl and top with vegetables. Spoon on Dressing and toss well. Sprinkle on Parmesan cheese, garnish with basil leaves, and serve immediately.

French Spaghetti

Serves 6

Vegetable cooking spray
1¼ cups green bell peppers, chopped
1 onion, chopped
3 shallots, chopped
1 lb. tomatoes, chopped and undrained
1 tablespoon fresh basil, chopped
1 teaspoon fresh tarragon, chopped
1 teaspoon fresh thyme, chopped
½ cup mushrooms, sliced
¼ cup unpitted black olives, sliced
1 tablespoon diet margarine
4 teaspoons all-purpose flour
¾ cup evaporated skim milk
¾ cup skim milk
1 lb. cooked spaghetti
¼ cup Parmesan cheese, freshly grated

Nutritional Data

PER SERVING:

Calories	433
% calories from fat	13
Fat (gm)	6.2
Sat. Fat (gm)	1.5
Cholesterol (mg)	4.8
Sodium (mg)	349
Protein (gm)	17.3
Carbohydrate (gm)	77.6

EXCHANGES:			
Milk	0.5	Bread	4.0
Veg.	2.5	Meat	0.0
Fruit	0.0	Fat	1.0

Coat 10-inch skillet with vegetable cooking spray and add peppers, onion, and shallots. Sauté until tender. Stir in undrained tomatoes and bring to boil. Reduce heat and simmer, uncovered, for 2 hours. Add herbs and simmer another 10 minutes. Stir in mushrooms and olives.

To make white sauce, melt margarine in saucepan and stir in flour. Add evaporated skim milk and skim milk all at once. Cook and stir until thickened and bubbly. Remove from heat.

Preheat oven to 350 degrees.

To assemble, arrange spaghetti in 8" x 8" x 2" baking dish. Top with white sauce, then tomato-mushroom sauce. Sprinkle with Parmesan cheese. Bake, uncovered, about 25 minutes or until heated through.

Basque Spaghetti

Serves 6

1 lb. uncooked thin spaghetti
2 tablespoons olive oil
3 large cloves garlic, chopped
20 medium shrimp, peeled and deveined
Black pepper, to taste
3 tablespoons parsley, minced (divided)
½ cup Parmesan cheese, freshly grated

Nutritional Data

PER SERVING:

Calories	406
% calories from fat	20
Fat (gm)	8.9
Sat. Fat (gm)	2.5
Cholesterol (mg)	42.6
Sodium (mg)	194
Protein (gm)	18.5
Carbohydrate (gm)	61.6

EXCHANGES:

Milk	0.0	Bread	4.0
Veg.	0.0	Meat	1.0
Fruit	0.0	Fat	1.0

In large saucepan, bring 3 quarts of water to boil. Add spaghetti and cook until tender, but still firm, 8 to 10 minutes.

Meanwhile, heat olive oil over medium heat in large skillet. Add garlic, cooking until golden; discard garlic pieces. Add shrimp, pepper, and 2 tablespoons parsley to skillet. Cook 1 to 3 minutes until shrimp turns pink. Remove skillet from heat.

Drain spaghetti and add to skillet. Add Parmesan cheese. Mix and transfer to warmed serving bowl. Sprinkle with parsley; serve.

Chicken Tortelloni with Tomato-Mushroom Sauce

Serves 6

Vegetable cooking spray
- ¼ cup onion, chopped
- 1 small leek (white part only), very thinly sliced
- 3 tablespoons shallots, chopped
- 4 large mushrooms, chopped
- ¼ cup dry sherry, or low-salt chicken broth
- ¼ teaspoon salt
- ¼ teaspoon black pepper
- 1 cup low-salt chicken broth
- 1 medium tomato, chopped
- 1½ teaspoons dried thyme leaves
- 2 bay leaves
- 1 9-oz. package cooked chicken tortelloni, kept warm
- 2 tablespoons capers, drained (optional)

Nutritional Data

PER SERVING:

Calories	167
% calories from fat	16
Fat (gm)	3.1
Sat. Fat (gm)	1.5
Cholesterol (mg)	20.2
Sodium (mg)	219
Protein (gm)	8.7
Carbohydrate (gm)	25.8

EXCHANGES:

Milk	0.0	Bread	1.5
Veg.	1.0	Meat	0.0
Fruit	0.0	Fat	0.5

Coat medium saucepan with cooking spray; heat over medium heat until hot. Sauté onion, leek, shallots, and mushrooms until very soft, 7 to 10 minutes. Add sherry; cook over high heat until liquid is almost absorbed, 2 to 3 minutes. Stir in salt and pepper.

Add chicken broth, tomato, thyme, and bay leaves to saucepan; heat to boiling. Reduce heat and simmer, uncovered, until tomato is very soft, about 15 minutes; discard bay leaves. Whirl mixture in food processor or blender until smooth. Return to saucepan; cook over medium heat until hot.

Spoon sauce over tortelloni; sprinkle with capers.

 # Tortelloni with Tuna

Serves 8

- ¾ lb. uncooked tortelloni (cheese or meat)
- 1 cup fresh or frozen peas, thawed
- ½ green bell pepper, chopped
- ½ cup scallions, chopped
- 1 6½-oz. can water-packed tuna, drained
- 1 14-oz. can artichoke hearts, drained and quartered
- ½ cup fresh parsley, chopped
- ¼ cup fresh basil, chopped

Dressing

- 2 tomatoes, diced
- 2 tablespoons white wine vinegar

Nutritional Data

PER SERVING:

Calories	261
% calories from fat	27
Fat (gm)	8
Sat. Fat (gm)	2.7
Cholesterol (mg)	27
Sodium (mg)	328
Protein (gm)	17.2
Carbohydrate (gm)	32.1

EXCHANGES:

Milk	0.0	Bread	2.0
Veg.	1.0	Meat	1.0
Fruit	0.0	Fat	1.0

2   tablespoons olive oil
2   teaspoons Dijon mustard
1   clove garlic, minced
3   tablespoons scallions, chopped
1   teaspoon fresh oregano, minced
1   teaspoon fresh basil, minced
1/4 cup Parmesan cheese, freshly grated

In stockpot, cook tortelloni until *al dente;* drain and rinse under cold water. Drain thoroughly.

In salad bowl, combine pasta, peas, bell pepper, scallions, tuna, artichokes, parsley, and basil.

Mix Dressing ingredients in blender until smooth. Pour over pasta and toss well. Serve warm or refrigerate and serve cold.

To Freeze: Place individual portions of pasta and Dressing in separate vacuum-sealed bags; label and freeze up to 2 months.

To Serve: Put bags in boiling water, and bring water to boil again. Boil 10 to 12 minutes. Add garnishes such as parsley or cheese just before serving.

Turkey Ziti

Serves 6
Vegetable cooking spray
1   lb. lean turkey, ground
1/2 cup onion, finely chopped
1/4 cup plain dry bread crumbs
2   teaspoons parsley, finely chopped
1   teaspoon oregano
1   teaspoon garlic, minced
3/4 teaspoon Worcestershire sauce
1   teaspoon Spike (see "About This Cookbook")
1/2 teaspoon black pepper, freshly ground
1   teaspoon dried thyme leaves
1   teaspoon dried basil leaves
1/8 teaspoon crushed red pepper
1   28-oz. can crushed tomatoes in puree
1   8-oz. can tomato sauce
1/2 cup water
8   ozs. ziti, freshly cooked, drained, and returned to pot
4   ozs. skim mozzarella cheese, shredded
2   tablespoons Parmesan cheese, freshly grated

Nutritional Data

PER SERVING:

Calories	349
% calories from fat	28
Fat (gm)	10.6
Sat. Fat (gm)	4.1
Cholesterol (mg)	40.4
Sodium (mg)	866
Protein (gm)	23.2
Carbohydrate (gm)	39.7

EXCHANGES:

Milk	0.0	Bread	2.0
Veg.	2.0	Meat	2.0
Fruit	0.0	Fat	1.0

Mix first 12 ingredients in medium bowl until well blended.

Preheat oven to 400 degrees. Coat 13" x 9" x 2" baking pan with vegetable cooking spray.

Heat large skillet coated with vegetable cooking spray and place over high heat. When skillet is hot, crumble in meat mixture. Cook 5 minutes or until it loses its pink color, stirring often to break up meat.

Add crushed tomatoes, tomato sauce, and water; bring to boil. Reduce heat to low, cover, and simmer 15 minutes, stirring several times. Add to drained ziti in pot, and stir to mix.

Scrape all into baking pan; sprinkle cheese over top. Cover with foil, and bake, 10 minutes. Remove foil and bake, uncovered, 5 minutes or until lightly browned.

Chapter Eleven

PIZZA

Basic Pizza Crust

Serves 24
Makes 2 (12-inch) round crusts;
or 2 (9- by 12-inch) rectangular crusts;
or 12 (6 to 7-inch) round crusts

½	teaspoon honey
1	cup (scant) warm water (110 degrees, or warm to touch)
1	package active dry yeast
2¾	cups all-purpose flour, or bread flour, or combination
½	teaspoon salt
1	tablespoon good quality olive oil

Nutritional Data

PER SERVING:

Calories	58
% calories from fat	11
Fat (gm)	0.7
Sat. Fat (gm)	0.1
Cholesterol (mg)	0
Sodium (mg)	44.7
Protein (gm)	1.6
Carbohydrate (gm)	11.2

EXCHANGES:

Milk	0.0	Bread	1.0
Veg.	0.0	Meat	0.0
Fruit	0.0	Fat	0.0

To proof yeast, stir honey into water in measuring cup or small bowl. Sprinkle yeast over water and stir until yeast dissolves. Let mixture stand in draft-free area about 5 minutes or until yeast begins to bubble.

Meanwhile, mix flour with salt and oil in food processor fitted with steel blade, or in electric mixer with dough hook. (To mix dough by hand, use bowl and wooden spoon.)

Pour in yeast mixture and process until soft, almost sticky dough is formed, about 5 to 10 seconds. If using electric mixer, mix 3 minutes or until smooth dough is formed. If mixing dough by hand, mix ingredients until smooth, slightly sticky dough is formed, about 3 minutes.

Knead dough by hand on lightly floured surface or pastry cloth until smooth. If dough is too sticky, add flour by the tablespoon until it reaches desired consistency. Put dough in bowl and cover lightly with oiled plastic wrap and aluminum foil or kitchen towel.

Let dough rise until it doubles in bulk, about 45 minutes to 1 hour. Punch dough down and let stand 5 minutes. Knead a few minutes more on lightly floured board or pastry cloth. Dough is now ready to use with your favorite sauce and toppings (not included in Nutritional Data above).

Yellow or White Cornmeal
❊ Basic Pizza Crust

Serves 24
Makes 2 (12-inch) round crusts;
or 2 (9- by 12-inch) rectangular crusts;
or 12 (6 to 7-inch) round crusts

½ teaspoon honey
1 cup (scant) warm water (110 degrees, or warm to touch)
1 package active dry yeast
2 cups all-purpose flour
¾ cup yellow or white cornmeal (both taste alike)
½ teaspoon salt
2 tablespoons good quality olive oil

Nutritional Data	
PER SERVING:	
Calories	63
% calories from fat	20
Fat (gm)	1.4
Sat. Fat (gm)	0.2
Cholesterol (mg)	0
Sodium (mg)	46
Protein (gm)	1.5
Carbohydrate (gm)	11.1

EXCHANGES:			
Milk	0.0	Bread	1.0
Veg.	0.0	Meat	0.0
Fruit	0.0	Fat	0.0

Proof yeast by stirring honey into warm water in measuring cup or small bowl. Sprinkle yeast over water and stir until yeast dissolves. Let mixture stand in draft-free area about 5 minutes or until yeast begins to bubble.

Meanwhile, mix flour and cornmeal with salt and oil in food processor fitted with steel blade, or in electric mixer with dough hook. (To mix dough by hand, use bowl and wooden spoon.)

Pour in yeast mixture and process until soft, almost sticky dough is formed, about 5 to 10 seconds. If using electric mixer, mix 3 minutes or until smooth dough is formed. If mixing dough by hand, mix ingredients until smooth, slightly sticky dough is formed, about 3 to 5 minutes.

Knead dough by hand on lightly floured surface or pastry cloth until smooth. If dough is too sticky, add flour by the tablespoon until it reaches desired consistency. Put dough in bowl and cover lightly with oiled plastic wrap and aluminum foil or kitchen towel.

Let dough rise until it doubles in bulk, about 45 minutes to 1 hour. Punch dough down and let stand 5 minutes. Knead a few minutes more on lightly floured board or pastry cloth. Dough is now ready to use with your favorite sauce and toppings (not included in Nutritional Data above).

Whole Wheat

Basic Pizza Crust

Serves 24
Makes 2 (12-inch) round crusts;
or 2 (9- by 12-inch) rectangular crusts;
or 12 (6 to 7-inch) round crusts

½	teaspoon honey	
1	cup (scant) warm water (110 degrees, or warm to touch)	
1	package active dry yeast	
¾	cup whole wheat flour	
2	cups all-purpose flour	
½	teaspoon salt	
1	tablespoon good quality olive oil	

Nutritional Data

PER SERVING:

Calories	57
% calories from fat	12
Fat (gm)	0.7
Sat. Fat (gm)	0.1
Cholesterol (mg)	0
Sodium (mg)	44.8
Protein (gm)	1.7
Carbohydrate (gm)	10.9

EXCHANGES:

Milk	0.0	Bread	1.0
Veg.	0.0	Meat	0.0
Fruit	0.0	Fat	0.0

Proof yeast by stirring honey into warm water in measuring cup or small bowl. Sprinkle yeast over water and stir until yeast dissolves. Let mixture stand in draft-free area about 5 minutes or until yeast begins to bubble.

Meanwhile, mix flour with salt and oil in food processor fitted with steel blade, or in electric mixer with dough hook. (To mix dough by hand, use bowl and wooden spoon.)

Pour in yeast mixture and process until soft, almost sticky dough is formed, about 5 to 10 seconds. If using electric mixer, mix 3 minutes or until smooth dough is formed. If mixing dough by hand, mix ingredients until smooth, slightly sticky dough is formed, about 3 to 5 minutes.

Knead dough by hand on lightly floured surface or pastry cloth until smooth. If dough is too sticky, add flour by the tablespoon until it reaches desired consistency. Put dough in bowl and cover lightly with oiled plastic wrap and aluminum foil or kitchen towel.

Let dough rise until it doubles in bulk, about 45 minutes to 1 hour. Punch dough down and let stand 5 minutes. Knead a few minutes more on lightly floured board or pastry cloth. Dough is now ready to use with your favorite sauce and toppings (not included in Nutritional Data above).

❄ *Big Batch Pizza Crust*

Serves 32 (makes 4, 12-inch crusts)

- 1 envelope (2 teaspoons) active dry yeast
- 1 teaspoon granulated sugar
- 1¼ cups warm water (105-115 degrees)
- 5 cups all-purpose or bread flour
- 2 large eggs
- 2 teaspoons salt
  Vegetable cooking spray

Nutritional Data	
PER SERVING:	
Calories	77
% calories from fat	6
Fat (gm)	0.5
Sat. Fat (gm)	0.1
Cholesterol (mg)	13.3
Sodium (mg)	137
Protein (gm)	2.5
Carbohydrate (gm)	15.2

EXCHANGES:			
Milk	0.0	Bread	1.0
Veg.	0.0	Meat	0.0
Fruit	0.0	Fat	0.0

Stir yeast and sugar into water. Let stand about 10 minutes until foamy.

In food processor, put flour, eggs, and salt in work bowl fitted with metal blade. Turn processor on, and pour yeast mixture through feed tube in steady stream. Process until dough cleans sides of bowl, then process 45 seconds longer (this replaces much kneading) or until dough is smooth and elastic.

By hand or with electric mixer, mix yeast mixture and eggs in large bowl. Add flour, and stir or beat until dough pulls away from sides of bowl. Turn dough out on lightly floured surface, and knead 5 minutes or until smooth and elastic.

Put dough into large bowl coated with vegetable cooking spray. Turn dough to coat. Cover bowl with plastic wrap. Let dough rise in warm, draft-free place 1 hour or until doubled.

Punch down dough, and divide into 4 equal pieces. **Shape** pieces into smooth balls. (Dough can be made ahead up to this point and refrigerated or frozen.) Let rest 30 minutes so dough will be easier to handle. Dough will rise but not double in volume.

For each pizza, coat 12-inch-round pizza pan, or large inverted cookie sheet with cooking spray.

Preheat oven to 500 degrees.

Place dough on lightly floured surface. With floured hands, pat into 6-inch round. Stretch or roll out dough with rolling pin into 11-inch circle. Lift onto prepared pan, and press dough with knuckles or fingers out to edges of pizza pan or into 12-inch circle on inverted cookie sheet.

Add sauce and toppings (not included in Nutritional Data above) and bake on lowest rack 10 to 12 minutes or until edges of crust are browned and crisp. Cut in wedges with pizza wheel or knife.

❋ *Rapid Rise Pizza Crust*

Serves 8 (makes 1, 14-inch crust)

3   cups all-purpose flour
1   package rapid-rising dry yeast
¾   teaspoon salt
1   cup very warm water (125-130 degrees)
2   tablespoons olive oil
    Cornmeal

Nutritional Data

PER SERVING:

Calories	203
% calories from fat	17
Fat (gm)	3.8
Sat. Fat (gm)	0.6
Cholesterol (mg)	0
Sodium (mg)	201
Protein (gm)	5.2
Carbohydrate (gm)	36.2

EXCHANGES:

Milk	0.0	Bread	2.5
Veg.	0.0	Meat	0.0
Fruit	0.0	Fat	0.5

In large bowl, combine 2 cups flour, undissolved yeast, and salt. Stir very warm water and oil into dry ingredients. Stir in enough remaining flour to make soft dough.

Knead dough on lightly floured surface until smooth and elastic, about 4 to 6 minutes. Cover, let rest on floured surface 10 minutes.

Lightly oil 1 14-inch or 2 12-inch-round pizza pans. Sprinkle with cornmeal.

Preheat oven to 400 degrees.

Form dough into smooth ball. Roll dough to fit pan or pans.

Add your favorite sauce and toppings. Slice raw vegetables thinly to prevent soggy pizza.

Bake 20 to 30 minutes or until done. Time depends on size and thickness of crust and selected toppings.

Note: Sauce and toppings are not included in Nutritional Data above.

Rapid Rise Pizza Crust Variations

Nutritional Data below is based on 14-inch crust (see preceding recipe) cut into 8 servings

Garlic and Herb Crust

Add 2 teaspoons basil, oregano, or rosemary leaves and 1 clove finely minced garlic along with dry ingredients.

Nutritional Data

PER SERVING:

Calories	204
% calories from fat	17
Fat (gm)	3.8
Sat. Fat (gm)	0.6
Cholesterol (mg)	0
Sodium (mg)	201
Protein (gm)	5.3
Carbohydrate (gm)	36.5

EXCHANGES:

Milk	0.0	Bread	2.5
Veg.	0.0	Meat	0.0
Fruit	0.0	Fat	0.5

Cornmeal Crust

Replace ½ cup of all-purpose flour with ½ cup cornmeal as you combine dry ingredients.

Nutritional Data

PER SERVING:

Calories	142
% calories from fat	13
Fat (gm)	2.1
Sat. Fat (gm)	0.3
Cholesterol (mg)	0
Sodium (mg)	134
Protein (gm)	3.5
Carbohydrate (gm)	27.1

EXCHANGES:

Milk	0.0	Bread	1.5
Veg.	0.0	Meat	0.0
Fruit	0.0	Fat	0.5

Cheese Crust

Add ½ cup freshly grated Parmesan cheese along with other dry ingredients.

Nutritional Data

PER SERVINC:

Calories	153
% calories from fat	17
Fat (gm)	2.9
Sat. Fat (gm)	0.8
Cholesterol (mg)	2.5
Sodium (mg)	192
Protein (gm)	4.9
Carbohydrate (gm)	26.5

EXCHANGES:

Milk	0.0	Bread	1.5
Veg.	0.0	Meat	0.5
Fruit	0.0	Fat	0.5

Whole Wheat Crust

Replace 1 cup of all-purpose flour with 1 cup whole wheat flour as you combine dry ingredients.

Nutritional Data

PER SERVING:

Calories	133
% calories from fat	14
Fat (gm)	2.1
Sat. Fat (gm)	0.3
Cholesterol (mg)	0
Sodium (mg)	134
Protein (gm)	4
Carbohydrate (gm)	25.3

EXCHANGES:

Milk	0.0	Bread	1.5
Veg.	0.0	Meat	0.0
Fruit	0.0	Fat	0.5

Chunky Tomato Sauce

Serves 24 (makes 3-3½ cups)

¼	cup Chicken Stock, or Vegetable Stock (see pp. 40, 42)
3	cloves garlic, minced
1½	cups onion, minced
1	28-oz. can crushed tomatoes
1	6-oz. can tomato paste
1½	teaspoons each ingredient: basil, oregano
2	bay leaves
½	teaspoon fennel seeds
1	teaspoon honey
½	teaspoon salt
¼	teaspoon black pepper

Nutritional Data

PER SERVING:

Calories	19
% calories from fat	8
Fat (gm)	0.2
Sat. Fat (gm)	0
Cholesterol (mg)	0.1
Sodium (mg)	155
Protein (gm)	0.8
Carbohydrate (gm)	4.2

EXCHANGES:

Milk	0.0	Bread	0.0
Veg.	1.0	Meat	0.0
Fruit	0.0	Fat	0.0

Heat stock in saucepan over medium heat. Add garlic and onion and sauté a few minutes until onion is soft. Mix in tomatoes, tomato paste, basil, oregano, bay leaves, fennel seeds, honey, salt, and pepper.

Bring sauce to boil. Reduce heat to simmer, and continue cooking, uncovered, 35 minutes or until sauce thickens. Stir occasionally.

Discard bay leaves. Cool. If you are not going to use sauce immediately, put it in covered container and refrigerate until needed. Stir before using.

Bell Pepper Sauce

Serves 12 (makes about 3¼ cups)

	Canola oil, or vegetable cooking spray
5	large bell peppers, seeded and chopped
½	cup red onion, minced
½	teaspoon each ingredient: garlic powder, ground cumin
¼	teaspoon each ingredient: salt, red pepper flakes, chili powder
1½	cups low-fat ricotta cheese

Nutritional Data

PER SERVING:

Calories	35
% calories from fat	22
Fat (gm)	0.9
Sat. Fat (gm)	0
Cholesterol (mg)	4
Sodium (mg)	241
Protein (gm)	3
Carbohydrate (gm)	4.3

EXCHANGES:

Milk	0.0	Bread	0.0
Veg.	1.0	Meat	0.0
Fruit	0.0	Fat	0.0

Coat saucepan with canola oil or cooking spray; sauté peppers and onion until soft. Cover; stir occasionally. Stir in garlic powder, cumin, salt, red pepper flakes, and chili powder. Cool.

Pour mixture into blender or food processor. Add cheese and puree.

Place sauce in covered container and refrigerate until ready to use.

Barbecue Sauce

Serves 12 (makes about 3 cups)	Nutritional Data	
2 tablespoons canola oil	PER SERVING:	
2 tablespoons garlic, minced	Calories	64
½ cup onion, minced	% calories from fat	33
½ cup ketchup	Fat (gm)	2.5
2 cups tomatoes, peeled, chopped,	Sat. Fat (gm)	0.2
and seeded	Cholesterol (mg)	0
½ cup chili sauce	Sodium (mg)	324
2 tablespoons dark brown sugar	Protein (gm)	0.9
2 teaspoons chili powder	Carbohydrate (gm)	10.5
½ teaspoon Worcestershire sauce	EXCHANGES:	
¼ teaspoon each ingredient: salt, black	Milk 0.0 Bread	0.0
pepper	Veg. 1.5 Meat	0.0
	Fruit 0.0 Fat	0.5

Heat oil in saucepan. Sauté garlic and onion in pan until tender, about 4 to 5 minutes, over medium heat, stirring occasionally.

Mix in remaining ingredients. Bring sauce to boil; reduce heat to simmer. Continue cooking 15 minutes, stirring occasionally. Cool.

Pour sauce into container, cover, and refrigerate until ready to serve. Stir before serving.

Cheese and Tomato Pizza

Serves 12	Nutritional Data	
1 Basic 12-inch Pizza Crust (see first	PER SERVING:	
3 recipes in chapter)	Calories	107
2 tablespoons oregano	% calories from fat	13
Canola oil, or vegetable cooking spray	Fat (gm)	1.6
1 28-oz. can crushed tomatoes	Sat. Fat (gm)	0.5
2 tablespoons tomato paste	Cholesterol (mg)	4.2
¾ teaspoon oregano	Sodium (mg)	314
½ teaspoon basil	Protein (gm)	7.8
¼ teaspoon black pepper	Carbohydrate (gm)	15.8
6 ozs. nonfat mozzarella cheese, shredded	EXCHANGES:	
4 tablespoons Parmesan cheese,	Milk 0.0 Bread	1.0
freshly grated	Veg. 0.0 Meat	0.5
	Fruit 0.0 Fat	0.0

Prepare dough on lightly floured pastry cloth. When kneading dough, mix in 2 tablespoons oregano. Shape and stretch dough into oiled 12-inch circular or rectangular pan.

Drain tomatoes and mix with tomato paste. Mix in ³/₄ tea-spoon oregano, basil, and pepper. Spread tomatoes over crust.

Sprinkle pizza with mozzarella and Parmesan cheeses.

Preheat oven to 425 degrees.

Place pizza on lowest rack in oven and bake 20 minutes or until done. Pizza is done when rim is just beginning to color. Serve hot.

Tomato, Basil, and Cheese Pizza

Serves 6

- 1 Basic 12-inch Pizza Crust (see first 3 recipes in chapter)
- 2 teaspoons olive oil
- ½ cup Parmesan cheese, freshly grated (divided)
- 3 large tomatoes, unpeeled and cut into ¼-inch slices (about 1½ lbs.)
- 4 cloves garlic, minced
- 1 teaspoon Spike (see "About This Cookbook")
- 1 teaspoon thyme
- 1 teaspoon tarragon
- ¼ teaspoon black pepper, freshly ground
- ½ cup fresh basil, chopped

Nutritional Data

PER SERVING:

Calories	197
% calories from fat	26
Fat (gm)	5.8
Sat. Fat (gm)	2
Cholesterol (mg)	6.6
Sodium (mg)	256
Protein (gm)	7.9
Carbohydrate (gm)	29.1

EXCHANGES:

Milk	0.0	Bread	1.5
Veg.	0.5	Meat	0.5
Fruit	0.0	Fat	1.0

Preheat oven to 500 degrees.

Shape and stretch dough into oiled 12-inch circular or rectangular pan. Brush crust with olive oil. Sprinkle with ¼ cup cheese, leaving ½-inch border. Arrange tomatoes over cheese, overlapping. Top with garlic, remaining ¼ cup cheese, Spike, thyme, tarragon, pepper, and basil. Bake 12 minutes on bottom rack of oven. Remove pizza to cutting board. Let stand 5 minutes.

Southwest Chili Pizza

Serves 12

- 1 Basic 12-inch Pizza Crust (see first 3 recipes in chapter)
- ²/₃ lb. lean beef, fine or coarse-ground
- 1 clove garlic, minced
- ½ cup onion, chopped
- 2 teaspoons chili powder
- 1 teaspoon ground cumin
- ¼ teaspoon oregano

Nutritional Data

PER SERVING:

Calories	133
% calories from fat	27
Fat (gm)	3.9
Sat. Fat (gm)	1.3
Cholesterol (mg)	15.7
Sodium (mg)	94
Protein (gm)	8
Carbohydrate (gm)	16.3

⅛ teaspoon red pepper flakes
1 cup cooked red beans, mashed
1 8-oz. can tomatoes, chopped and drained

EXCHANGES:			
Milk	0.0	Bread	1.0
Veg.	0.0	Meat	1.0
Fruit	0.0	Fat	0.0

Sauté meat, garlic, and onion over medium heat in saucepan until meat loses its color. Stir meat occasionally. As you stir, mix in chili powder, cumin, oregano, and pepper flakes.

Mix in beans and tomatoes. Bring mixture to boil. Reduce heat to simmer and continue cooking 30 minutes. Taste to adjust seasonings. Chili should be slightly thick. Cool and drain.

Preheat oven to 425 degrees.

Prepare dough. Shape and stretch dough into 12-inch oiled rectangular pan.

Spread 2 cups drained chili on pizza. Bake pizza 20 minutes until crust begins to color and pizza is hot. Serve immediately.

Sausage Pizza

Serves 12

Homemade Sausage

½ lb. lean pork, ground
½ teaspoon each ingredient: garlic powder, sage, orange rind
¼ teaspoon each ingredient: ground pepper, cumin seeds

Pizza

1 Whole Wheat Basic 12-inch Pizza Crust (see p. 442)
2 tablespoons orange rind
1 tablespoon margarine
1½ cups Chunky Tomato Sauce (see p. 446)
¼ cup low-fat cheese, freshly grated
½ cup green onions, chopped

Nutritional Data

PER SERVING:

Calories	111
% calories from fat	25
Fat (gm)	3.1
Sat. Fat (gm)	0.7
Cholesterol (mg)	9
Sodium (mg)	215
Protein (gm)	6
Carbohydrate (gm)	15.3

EXCHANGES:			
Milk	0.0	Bread	1.0
Veg.	0.5	Meat	0.5
Fruit	0.0	Fat	0.0

Sausage: To make sausage, mix pork with garlic, sage, ½ teaspoon orange rind, pepper, and cumin. Refrigerate in covered container until ready to prepare pizza.

Pizza: Knead dough together with 2 tablespoons orange rind. Shape and stretch dough onto oiled pizza pan. Set aside.

Preheat oven to 425 degrees.

Heat margarine in small nonstick skillet. Add Sausage and cook until pork loses its color. Mix in sauce.

Sprinkle sausage mixture over Pizza and top with cheese and onions.

Set Pizza on lowest rack in oven, if possible on preheated pizza tile or stone. Bake 20 minutes. Crust will be cooked when rim is golden brown.

Chicken and Blue Cheese Pizza

Serves 12 (6 individual pizzas)

1 Basic Pizza Crust (see first 3 recipes in chapter)
2 tablespoons margarine
2 cups mushrooms, sliced
2 cups chicken breast, chopped
½ teaspoon sage
¼ teaspoon each ingredient: salt, black pepper
⅓ cup blue cheese, crumbled
2 tablespoons walnuts, chopped

Nutritional Data

PER SERVING:

Calories	128
% calories from fat	32
Fat (gm)	4.4
Sat. Fat (gm)	1.3
Cholesterol (mg)	20.7
Sodium (mg)	179
Protein (gm)	9.7
Carbohydrate (gm)	12

EXCHANGES:

Milk	0.0	Bread	1.0
Veg.	0.0	Meat	1.0
Fruit	0.0	Fat	0.0

Stretch and shape crust into 6 individual 7-inch pizzas. Sprinkle paddle lightly with cornmeal; set aside.

Heat margarine in nonstick skillet over medium heat. Sauté mushrooms and chopped chicken until just cooked. Stir occasionally. Season with sage, salt, and pepper.

Spread mushroom-chicken mixture over pizzas. Top with blue cheese and walnuts.

Preheat oven with pizza tile to 425 degrees.

Slide pizzas onto paddle, and with long-handled spatula, move them onto tile.

Cook 20 minutes or until pizzas are done. Crust will be brown and toppings hot. Cut pizzas in half. Serve hot.

Fajita Pizza

Serves 12

Pizza

1 Basic 12-inch Pizza Crust (see first 3 recipes in chapter)
  Canola oil, or nonstick cooking spray

Southwest Marinade

1½ cups light beer
2 tablespoons mustard
5 tablespoons red wine vinegar
5 tablespoons dark brown sugar
½ teaspoon garlic powder

Fajitas

2 chicken breasts, boneless and skinless
1 cup green bell pepper, sliced

Nutritional Data

PER SERVING:

Calories	150
% calories from fat	12
Fat (gm)	2
Sat. Fat (gm)	0.4
Cholesterol (mg)	24.3
Sodium (mg)	104
Protein (gm)	11.2
Carbohydrate (gm)	20.2

EXCHANGES:

Milk	0.0	Bread	1.0
Veg.	1.0	Meat	1.0
Fruit	0.0	Fat	0.0

1   cup onion, sliced in rounds, separated
    into rings
5   green onions, minced
1/2 cup cilantro, minced

Pizza: Stretch and shape dough by hand or use rolling pin on lightly floured board. Shape dough into 12-inch circle.

Marinade: Combine all marinade ingredients in saucepan. Simmer 4 minutes, stirring occasionally. Remove from heat; cool.

Fajitas: Cut chicken breasts into 1/2-inch strips. Marinate chicken in glass dish 45 minutes. Drain and reserve marinade.

Preheat barbecue grill. Coat grill screen with oil or cooking spray. Grill chicken strips, peppers, and onion rings over hot coals. Vegetables will cook in about 4 minutes; turn once. Brush vegetables with reserved marinade as they grill. Chicken cooks in about 6 minutes, turning once or twice.

Remove food from grill and arrange it on pizza crust, which may be placed on pizza screen, coated lightly with oil or cooking spray, or on paddle sprinkled lightly with cornmeal. Sprinkle pizza with green onions and cilantro.

While coals are hot, set pizza on tile. Cover and cook until pizza is done, about 5 to 6 minutes; crust will color slightly when pizza is finished. Using long-handled spatula, remove pizza onto paddle and place on serving dish. Bring to table hot.

Creole Pizza

Serves 15

1   16-oz. can crushed tomatoes, undrained
3/4 cup celery, finely chopped
3/4 cup red bell pepper, finely chopped
1/2 cup onion, finely chopped
3   tablespoons sweet pickle relish
1   lb. large shrimp, peeled and deveined
1/4 teaspoon each ingredient: salt, black
    pepper, marjoram
1   package pizza dough, in dairy case of
    supermarket

Nutritional Data

PER SERVING:

Calories	87
% calories from fat	10
Fat (gm)	0.9
Sat. Fat (gm)	0.1
Cholesterol (mg)	46.4
Sodium (mg)	259
Protein (gm)	7.1
Carbohydrate (gm)	12.3

EXCHANGES:

Milk	0.0	Bread	0.5
Veg.	1.0	Meat	0.5
Fruit	0.0	Fat	0.0

Pour crushed tomatoes into saucepan. Stir in celery, bell pepper, onion, and relish. Bring sauce to boil. Reduce heat to simmer, and cook, uncovered, 15 minutes, stirring occasionally.

Mix in shrimp, salt, pepper, marjoram. Continue cooking 5 minutes. Cool.

Preheat oven to 500 degrees.

Unroll dough. Stretch and press dough into lightly oiled or nonstick cookie sheet, or 15" x 10" rectangular pan.

Spoon cooled Creole sauce over pizza.

Bake pizza on lowest rack of oven 10 to 15 minutes or until crust begins to color.

Cut into squares. Serve hot.

Clam Pizza with Thyme

Serves 8

1	Basic 12-inch Pizza Crust (see first 3 recipes in chapter)
36	littleneck clams, scrubbed
2	tablespoons olive oil
6	cloves garlic, minced
1/4	cup Parmesan cheese, freshly grated
1 1/3	teaspoon ground thyme
	Black pepper, freshly ground, to taste
	Crushed red pepper (optional)

Nutritional Data

PER SERVING:

Calories	167
% calories from fat	32
Fat (gm)	5.8
Sat. Fat (gm)	1.2
Cholesterol (mg)	16.7
Sodium (mg)	150
Protein (gm)	9.3
Carbohydrate (gm)	18.9

EXCHANGES:

Milk	0.0	Bread	1.0
Veg.	0.0	Meat	1.0
Fruit	0.0	Fat	1.0

Prepare Basic Pizza Crust.

Preheat oven to 500 degrees, and place pizza stone, if using, on bottom of oven.

Shuck clams over bowl in sink, allowing clams and their juice to fall into bowl. When all clams have been shucked, swish each in juice to rinse off any sand and shell bits. Coarsely chop any clams that are not very small, and put all in clean bowl.

Let clam juice sit 5 minutes so that sand and grit settle to bottom. Pour clear liquor into cup, leaving grit behind. Stir 1/4 cup of liquor into shucked clams along with olive oil and garlic. Generously sprinkle cornmeal over large flat cookie sheet.

On cookie sheet, shape dough into 14-inch round. Pinch edges to form rim. Prick surface of dough with fork. Spoon clam mixture evenly over dough to within 1/2 inch of rim. Sprinkle pizza with Parmesan cheese. Shake pan to see if pizza is sticking; if it is, carefully lift dough where trouble spot is and add cornmeal underneath.

With quick jerk, slide pizza off sheet and onto hot stone; if not using stone, simply set cookie sheet on bottom rack of oven.

Bake pizza about 5 minutes, until crusty brown on bottom. Remove from oven, season with thyme, black pepper, and crushed red pepper. Serve immediately.

Seafood and Artichoke Pizza

Serves 6

1 Basic 12-inch Pizza Crust (see first 3 recipes in chapter)
½ lb. small fresh shrimp, unpeeled
6 green onions
1 tablespoon plus 1 teaspoon cornstarch
¾ cup evaporated skim milk
½ cup part-skim mozzarella cheese, shredded
¼ cup dry white wine
½ teaspoon garlic powder
½ teaspoon black pepper, freshly ground
½ lb. fresh bay scallops
1 14-oz. can artichoke hearts, drained and coarsely chopped
6 fresh basil leaves
2 tablespoons Parmesan cheese, freshly grated

Nutritional Data

PER SERVING:

Calories	288
% calories from fat	14
Fat (gm)	4.6
Sat. Fat (gm)	1.7
Cholesterol (mg)	82.1
Sodium (mg)	420
Protein (gm)	24.5
Carbohydrate (gm)	36.7

EXCHANGES:

Milk	0.0	Bread	2.0
Veg.	1.0	Meat	2.0
Fruit	0.0	Fat	0.0

Prepare Basic Pizza Crust.

Peel and devein shrimp. Cut each shrimp crosswise into 3 pieces; set aside.

Diagonally slice green onions; set aside.

Combine cornstarch and milk in medium saucepan; stir well. Bring to boil over medium heat, and cook 3 minutes or until thickened, stirring constantly. Remove from heat; stir in mozzarella cheese and next 3 ingredients.

Preheat oven to 500 degrees.

Spread sauce evenly over prepared pizza crust, leaving ½-inch border. Arrange shrimp, onions, scallops, artichokes, and basil leaves over sauce. Bake 12 minutes on bottom rack of oven. Sprinkle Parmesan cheese over pizza. Bake additional 7 minutes or until cheese melts. Remove pizza to cutting board and let stand 5 minutes.

Shrimp and Feta Pizza

Serves 8

½ recipe Whole Wheat variation of Rapid Rise Pizza Crust (see p. 445)
Vegetable cooking spray
Olive-oil-flavored vegetable cooking spray
½ teaspoon dried basil
½ teaspoon dried oregano
36 medium shrimp, shelled and deveined

Nutritional Data

PER SERVING:

Calories	162
% calories from fat	28
Fat (gm)	5.1
Sat. Fat (gm)	2.7
Cholesterol (mg)	62.6
Sodium (mg)	294
Protein (gm)	11.9
Carbohydrate (gm)	17.2

		EXCHANGES:		
2	cups snow peas, thinly sliced	Milk	0.0	Bread	1.0
1	cup scallions, chopped	Veg.	0.5	Meat	1.0
2	cloves garlic, minced	Fruit	0.0	Fat	0.5
4½	ozs. feta cheese, crumbled				

Prepare ½ recipe Whole Wheat Rapid Rise Pizza Crust. Set aside to rise.

Preheat oven to 475 degrees.

Coat 14-inch pizza pan with nonstick cooking spray. Roll dough on prepared pan; pinch edges to form rim. Prick surface of dough with fork; coat with olive-oil-flavored vegetable cooking spray. Sprinkle with ½ of basil and oregano.

Bake dough 10 to 12 minutes, until golden.

Meanwhile, in large, nonstick skillet coated with cooking spray, sauté shrimp, peas, scallions, and garlic. Sprinkle with remaining basil and oregano, and cook, stirring frequently, 5 to 6 minutes.

Spread shrimp mixture evenly over prebaked crust. Sprinkle with feta cheese. Bake 5 to 8 minutes more or until cheese softens.

Smoked Salmon and Chive Pizza

Serves 12

- 1 White Cornmeal Basic 12-inch Pizza Crust (see p. 441)
  Vegetable cooking spray
- 2 cups Vidalia onion, or other mild onion, thinly sliced
- ¼ cup low-fat cheese, freshly grated
- ½ cup chives, chopped
- ¼ lb. smoked salmon, shredded

Nutritional Data

PER SERVING:

Calories	87
% calories from fat	19
Fat (gm)	1.8
Sat. Fat (gm)	0.3
Cholesterol (mg)	2.6
Sodium (mg)	138
Protein (gm)	4.4
Carbohydrate (gm)	13.6

EXCHANGES:

Milk	0.0	Bread	1.0
Veg.	0.0	Meat	0.5
Fruit	0.0	Fat	0.0

Shape and stretch dough by hand or with rolling pin on lightly floured pastry board and fit into 9" x 12" pan coated with cooking spray.

Preheat oven, with pizza tile on lowest rack, to 425 degrees.

Sauté onions in skillet coated with cooking spray until soft and just beginning to color; stir occasionally. Cool.

Spread onion over pizza. Sprinkle cheese, chives, and salmon over onion.

Place pizza on tile and bake 20 minutes or until pizza crust is light golden brown and topping is hot. Serve immediately.

Pesto Pizza

Serves 8 (1, 6-inch pizza each)

1½ cups fresh basil leaves, firmly packed
1½ tablespoons Parmesan cheese (¼ oz.), freshly grated
1½ tablespoons olive oil
1 clove garlic, minced
3 tablespoons nonfat yogurt
2 large tomatoes, sliced (optional)
   Lemon pepper
1 Basic Pizza Crust (see first 3 recipes in chapter)

Nutritional Data

PER SERVING:

Calories	127
% calories from fat	29
Fat (gm)	4.1
Sat. Fat (gm)	0.7
Cholesterol (mg)	1
Sodium (mg)	96
Protein (gm)	3.7
Carbohydrate (gm)	19.2

EXCHANGES:

Milk	0.0	Bread	1.0
Veg.	1.0	Meat	0.0
Fruit	0.0	Fat	0.5

In food processor or blender, combine basil, cheese, olive oil, and garlic. Mix until well blended. Add yogurt, and whirl until smooth. Season with lemon pepper. (Pesto topping can be prepared ahead and stored, covered, in refrigerator up to 2 days.)

Preheat oven to 500 degrees. Place pizza stone, baking tiles, or inverted baking sheet on lowest rack of oven.

Divide pizza dough into 8 pieces. Using your fists, stretch one piece into 6-inch round. Alternatively, with rolling pin, roll out on lightly floured surface. (Keep remaining dough covered with towel or plastic wrap as you work.)

Place round on cornmeal-dusted pizza peel or inverted baking sheet, using enough cornmeal so dough slides easily. Stretch or roll second round of dough and place beside first. Spread 1 tablespoon pesto on each round of dough. If desired, arrange ½ cup sliced tomatoes (not included in Nutritional Data) over top of each one. Season lightly with lemon pepper.

Carefully slide pizzas from peel or baking sheet onto heated pizza stone, baking tiles, or baking sheet. Bake 10 to 14 minutes, or until bottoms are crisp and browned. Working with 2 pizzas at once, repeat with remaining dough and toppings.

Pizza Primavera

Serves 8

1 Basic 12-inch Pizza Crust (see first 3 recipes in chapter)
2 cups broccoli florets
1 cup julienne-cut carrots, 1½ inches long
½ cup snow peas, halved crosswise
½ cup julienne-cut zucchini, 1½ inches long
2 tablespoons cornstarch
1 cup evaporated skim milk
¼ cup Parmesan cheese, freshly grated

Nutritional Data

PER SERVING:

Calories	183
% calories from fat	18
Fat (gm)	3.7
Sat. Fat (gm)	1.6
Cholesterol (mg)	7.5
Sodium (mg)	237
Protein (gm)	9.3
Carbohydrate (gm)	27.3

		EXCHANGES:			
¼	cup dry white wine	Milk	0.0	Bread	1.5
1	teaspoon Spike (see "About This Cookbook")	Veg.	1.0	Meat	0.5
½	teaspoon garlic powder	Fruit	0.0	Fat	0.5
¼	teaspoon black pepper, freshly ground				
⅓	cup green onions, sliced				
3	tablespoons fresh basil, chopped				
½	cup part-skim mozzarella cheese, shredded				
6	cherry tomatoes, cut in half				
6	pitted black olives, sliced				

Prepare Basic Pizza Crust.

Cook broccoli and carrots in boiling water 2 minutes. Add snow peas and zucchini; cook 1 minute. Drain and rinse under cold running water; set aside.

Combine cornstarch and milk in large saucepan; stir well. Bring to boil and cook 2 minutes or until thickened, stirring constantly. Remove from heat; stir in ¼ cup Parmesan cheese and next 4 ingredients. Add broccoli mixture, onions, and basil, tossing gently; set aside.

Preheat oven to 500 degrees.

Sprinkle mozzarella cheese over prepared crust, leaving ½-inch border. Spoon vegetable mixture on top of cheese. Decorate with tomatoes and olives. Bake 12 minutes on bottom rack of oven. Remove pizza to cutting board; let stand 5 minutes.

French Onion Pizza

Serves 8 (1, 6-inch pizza each)

		Nutritional Data	
2	cups onion (2 medium), sliced	PER SERVING:	
1	Basic Pizza Crust (see first 3 recipes in chapter)	Calories	139
		% calories from fat	22
	Cornmeal	Fat (gm)	3.4
	Vegetable cooking spray	Sat. Fat (gm)	1.6
½	cup pitted Kalamata, or Baeta olives, chopped (optional)	Cholesterol (mg)	8
		Sodium (mg)	134
1	tablespoon fresh rosemary, or 1 teaspoon dried rosemary, crumbled	Protein (gm)	6.3
		Carbohydrate (gm)	20.7
4	ozs. skim mozzarella cheese, grated		
	Black pepper, freshly ground, to taste	EXCHANGES:	

Milk	0.0	Bread	1.0
Veg.	1.0	Meat	0.5
Fruit	0.0	Fat	0.5

Heat nonstick skillet coated with cooking spray over medium heat. Add onions, and sauté about 10 minutes, or until lightly browned and very tender. Let cool.

Preheat oven to 500 degrees. Place pizza stone, baking tiles, or inverted baking sheet on lowest rack of oven.

Add olives and rosemary to pizza dough, and knead on lightly floured surface until well mixed. Divide dough into 8 pieces. Working with 2 pieces at once, form dough into rounds, and place on cornmeal-dusted pizza peel or inverted baking sheet.

Sprinkle 1/8 of cheese over each pizza round, and arrange 2 slices of onions over top. Season with pepper.

Carefully slide pizzas onto heated pizza stone, baking tiles, or baking sheet, and bake 10 to 14 minutes, or until bottoms are crisp and browned. Repeat with remaining dough and toppings.

Provençal Onion Pizza

Serves 6

1	Basic 12-inch Pizza Crust (see first 3 recipes in chapter)
1	tablespoon olive oil
4	lbs. (8 large or 12 medium) onions, very thinly sliced
1/4	cup red wine
1	teaspoon *herbes de Provence*
	Black pepper, freshly ground
6	unpitted black olives

Nutritional Data

PER SERVING:

Calories	264
% calories from fat	16
Fat (gm)	4.8
Sat. Fat (gm)	0.6
Cholesterol (mg)	0
Sodium (mg)	124
Protein (gm)	6.8
Carbohydrate (gm)	48.8

EXCHANGES:

Milk	0.0	Bread	2.0
Veg.	3.0	Meat	0.0
Fruit	0.0	Fat	1.0

Heat olive oil in skillet and add onions. Cook, stirring often, until onions are translucent. Add wine and herbs, and cook gently, stirring occasionally, about 15 minutes, until onions are golden brown and beginning to carmelize. Add freshly ground pepper to taste. Onions should not brown or stick to pan. Add water if necessary.

Preheat oven to 500 degrees. Roll out dough, line pizza pan with it, and top with onions. Cut olives in half and make designs over onions. Bake 20 minutes or until crust is browned and crisp. Remove from oven and serve hot, or let cool and serve at room temperature.

Pizza Rustica

Serves 8

1	Whole Wheat Basic 12-inch Pizza Crust (see p. 442)
1	clove garlic, minced
1	tablespoon olive oil
1	10-oz. package frozen spinach, chopped, thawed, and well drained
2	medium tomatoes, peeled, seeded, and chopped

Nutritional Data

PER SERVING:

Calories	152
% calories from fat	30
Fat (gm)	5.2
Sat. Fat (gm)	1.8
Cholesterol (mg)	8
Sodium (mg)	163
Protein (gm)	7.5
Carbohydrate (gm)	19.7

¼ cup snipped fresh basil, or 1 tablespoon dried, crushed basil

Vegetable cooking spray

1 cup part-skim mozzarella cheese, shredded

1 egg white

EXCHANGES:			
Milk	0.0	Bread	1.0
Veg.	1.0	Meat	0.5
Fruit	0.0	Fat	0.5

In medium skillet, cook garlic in hot oil 30 seconds. Add spinach. Cook and stir 1 minute only until spinach is wilted and removed from heat. Set aside.

Stir together tomatoes and basil; set aside.

Pat half of dough into bottom of 12-inch pizza pan coated with cooking spray. Layer in following order, leaving 1-inch border: ½ cup mozzarella cheese, spinach mixture, tomato-basil mixture, and remaining mozzarella.

On floured surface, roll remaining dough to 12-inch circle. Place over filling and seal to bottom crust, pressing filling down lightly and crimping crusts together in decorative manner. Cover and let rise in warm place 1 hour.

Preheat oven to 375 degrees. Brush pizza with mixture of egg white and 1 tablespoon water. Bake 40 minutes or until done, covering with foil last 10 minutes, if necessary, to prevent overbrowning.

Salad Pizza

Serves 8

1 Basic 12-inch Pizza Crust (see first 3 recipes in chapter)

Vegetable cooking spray

1 cup radicchio, thinly sliced

1 cup arugula, thinly sliced

1½ cups red onion, thinly sliced and separated into rings

2 large plum tomatoes, coarsely chopped

1 tablespoon balsamic vinegar

1 teaspoon Spike (see "About This Cookbook")

¼ teaspoon black pepper

3 ozs. skim mozzarella cheese, shredded

Nutritional Data

PER SERVING:

Calories	92
% calories from fat	23
Fat (gm)	2.4
Sat. Fat (gm)	1.2
Cholesterol (mg)	6
Sodium (mg)	89
Protein (gm)	4.5
Carbohydrate (gm)	13.5

EXCHANGES:			
Milk	0.0	Bread	0.5
Veg.	1.0	Meat	0.0
Fruit	0.0	Fat	0.5

Prepare Basic Pizza Crust. Set aside.

Preheat oven to 475 degrees. Coat 12-inch pizza pan with nonstick cooking spray. Press dough into pan; pinch edges to form rim. Prick surface of dough with fork; bake 10 to 15 minutes, until golden. Remove from oven.

Meanwhile, in large bowl, combine radicchio, arugula, onion, and tomatoes. Add vinegar, Spike, and pepper; toss to mix well. Set aside 15 minutes.

With slotted spoon, place radicchio mixture onto baked dough; spread to within 1 inch of edge. Sprinkle with cheese. Bake 5 to 10 minutes longer, until cheese melts.

Wild Mushroom Pizza

Serves 8

1	Basic 12-inch Pizza Crust (see first 3 recipes in chapter)
1	oz. dried porcini, or other dried wild mushrooms, chopped
1¼	cups boiling water
2	teaspoons olive oil
2	ozs. oyster mushrooms, hard stem ends removed
1	medium onion, chopped
1	clove garlic, minced
2	tablespoons red wine (Marsala preferred)
3	ozs. shiitake mushrooms, stems discarded and caps thinly sliced
⅓	cup evaporated skim milk
1	large tomato, seeded and chopped
½	cup frozen green peas, thawed
	Spike (see "About This Cookbook"), to taste
⅛	teaspoon black pepper, freshly ground

Nutritional Data

PER SERVING:

Calories	171
% calories from fat	13
Fat (gm)	2.5
Sat. Fat (gm)	0.4
Cholesterol (mg)	0.3
Sodium (mg)	93
Protein (gm)	5.8
Carbohydrate (gm)	31.8

EXCHANGES:

Milk	0.0	Bread	1.5
Veg.	2.0	Meat	0.0
Fruit	0.0	Fat	0.5

Prepare Basic Pizza Crust. Set aside. Meanwhile, soak dried mushrooms in boiling water.

In large skillet, heat oil. Sauté oyster mushrooms 1 minute or until lightly browned. Remove oyster mushrooms to small bowl, and set aside.

Add to skillet, onion and garlic; cook until onion is lightly browned. Add wine, dried mushrooms, 1 cup soaking water, shiitake mushrooms, and milk. Cook until mixture thickens to sauce. Remove from heat, and stir in tomato, peas, Spike, and pepper.

Preheat oven to 475 degrees. Divide pizza dough in half. Lightly grease 2 9-inch-round pizza pans or large baking sheet. Shape dough halves into 9-inch rounds, and place in pizza pans or baking sheet. Pinch edge to form rim. Prick surface of dough with fork.

Fill pizza rounds with mushroom mixture. Bake on lower oven rack 8 minutes. Top pizzas with reserved oyster mushrooms and bake 2 to 4 minutes longer or until crust is golden brown. Serve hot.

Potato-Crusted Pizza

Serves 6

Crust

1 lb. potatoes, peeled and cut for cooking
1 oz. part-skim mozzarella cheese, shredded
½ tablespoon skim milk
3 egg whites
1 cup all-purpose flour
   Vegetable cooking spray

Topping

   Vegetable cooking spray
3 large cloves garlic, minced
1 teaspoon tarragon
1 teaspoon thyme
6 fresh basil leaves, snipped
1 cup mushrooms, sliced
½ cup Italian parsley, chopped
6 plum tomatoes, peeled and diced
3 tablespoons Romano cheese, freshly grated

Nutritional Data

PER SERVING:

Calories	210
% calories from fat	11
Fat (gm)	2.5
Sat. Fat (gm)	1.2
Cholesterol (mg)	6.3
Sodium (mg)	112
Protein (gm)	9.2
Carbohydrate (gm)	38.8

EXCHANGES:

Milk	0.0	Bread	2.0
Veg.	2.0	Meat	0.5
Fruit	0.0	Fat	0.0

Crust: Preheat oven to 400 degrees. Boil potatoes until soft; drain potatoes and mash smooth, free of lumps, adding cheese. Add milk and egg whites, and stir them into potato mixture. Add flour. Spread mixture onto 12-inch metal pizza pan well coated with vegetable cooking spray, and bake until crust is lightly browned and fork inserted in center comes out clean. Perforate entire surface of crust with fork.

Topping: Coat skillet with vegetable cooking spray and add garlic, tarragon, thyme, basil, and mushrooms. Cook about 2 minutes over medium heat. Remove from heat, and stir in tomatoes and Italian parsley. Place Topping on crust. Sprinkle on Romano cheese. Place under broiler about 6 inches from flame. Cook until cheese is bubbly and crust edges are brown. Decorate with dash of chopped parsley, cut into 6 portions, and serve.

Pizza Maria

Serves 8

Crust

½ cup whole wheat flour
1 teaspoon dried basil
1 teaspoon dried thyme
3 cloves garlic, minced
8 egg whites
   Dash white pepper

Nutritional Data

PER SERVING:

Calories	92
% calories from fat	31
Fat (gm)	3.3
Sat. Fat (gm)	1.1
Cholesterol (mg)	3.3
Sodium (mg)	138
Protein (gm)	7
Carbohydrate (gm)	9.3

1 tablespoon olive oil
Vegetable cooking spray

Filling

2 cups tomatoes, diced
½ cup fresh basil, minced, or parsley, chopped
¼ cup mushrooms, chopped
⅓ cup Parmesan cheese, freshly grated

EXCHANGES:			
Milk	0.0	Bread	0.5
Veg.	0.5	Meat	0.5
Fruit	0.0	Fat	0.5

Crust: Preheat oven to 350 degrees. Combine all ingredients for pizza crust, except olive oil, in mixing bowl. Blend and pour into 12-inch pizza pan coated with cooking spray. Bake 15 minutes. Remove from oven and brush olive oil over surface of pizza crust.

Filling: Add diced tomatoes, basil, mushrooms, and Parmesan cheese. Bake another 5 to 10 minutes.

Cheesecake Pizza

Serves 20

Graham Cracker Crust (12-inch)

1½ cups graham cracker crumbs
1 teaspoon ground cinnamon
⅓ cup diet margarine, melted

Filling

3 cups nonfat ricotta cheese
1 cup golden raisins
3 tablespoons dark rum
1 tablespoon each ingredient: grated lemon rind, fresh lemon juice, honey
½ teaspoon ground cinnamon
1 egg plus 2 egg whites, beaten
¾ cup fine bread crumbs
½ cup pine nuts

Nutritional Data

PER SERVING:

Calories	151
% calories from fat	28
Fat (gm)	5.1
Sat. Fat (gm)	0.4
Cholesterol (mg)	14.3
Sodium (mg)	138
Protein (gm)	7.9
Carbohydrate (gm)	20.2

EXCHANGES:			
Milk	0.0	Bread	1.0
Veg.	0.0	Meat	0.5
Fruit	0.5	Fat	0.5

Graham Cracker Crust: Mix crumbs, cinnamon, and melted margarine together. Pat crust into 12-inch pizza pan. Preheat oven to 375 degrees.

Filling: Spoon cheese into deep bowl. Soak raisins in rum 10 minutes. Mix in raisins, lemon rind, lemon juice, honey, and cinnamon. Blend in beaten eggs and bread crumbs. Spoon filling over crust. Sprinkle with nuts.

Bake pizza 30 minutes. Crust will be golden and cheese cooked. Cool and serve.

Cut into 20, 2-inch pieces.

✳ Vegetarian Tortilla Pizza

Serves 2

Vegetable cooking spray
- 3 tablespoons Bermuda onion, chopped
- 1 clove garlic, minced
- ½ cup mushrooms, sliced
- ½ cup sun-dried tomatoes
- ⅓ cup carrot, coarsely shredded
- ¼ cup red, green, or yellow bell peppers, chopped
- 1 tablespoon fresh cilantro, minced
- 2 (6-inch) flour tortillas
- ¾ cup (3 ozs.) part-skim mozzarella cheese, shredded (divided)
- ½ cup canned kidney beans, drained

Nutritional Data

PER SERVING:

Calories	337
% calories from fat	26
Fat (gm)	10.1
Sat. Fat (gm)	4.8
Cholesterol (mg)	24
Sodium (mg)	878
Protein (gm)	19.7
Carbohydrate (gm)	44

EXCHANGES:

Milk	0.0	Bread	2.0
Veg.	2.0	Meat	1.5
Fruit	0.0	Fat	1.0

Coat nonstick skillet with cooking spray and preheat. Add onion and garlic; sauté 1 minute. Add mushrooms, tomatoes, and carrot; sauté 2 minutes. Add peppers and sauté 2 minutes more. Stir in cilantro; set aside.

Place tortillas on baking sheet and broil 6 inches from heat 2 minutes. Turn tortillas over; broil 1 minute or until crisp. Remove from oven. Top each tortilla with ¼ cup plus 1 tablespoon cheese, ¼ cup beans, half of vegetable mixture, and 1 tablespoon remaining cheese. Broil 6 inches from heat 1 minute or until cheese melts.

To Freeze: Place in microwave-safe container; label and freeze up to 2 months.

To Serve: Thaw. Cover with microwave-safe plastic wrap, and cook on High 3 to 5 minutes.

▦ French Bread Pizza

Serves 8

- ¼ lb. chuck, ground
- ¼ lb. turkey, ground
- ¼ cup green bell pepper, chopped
- ¼ cup onion, chopped
- 1 tablespoon garlic powder
- 1 cup marinara sauce
- 2 cups mushrooms, sliced
- 1 teaspoon dried oregano
- 1 (1 lb.) loaf French bread
- ¼ cup (2 ozs.) skim mozzarella cheese, shredded

Nutritional Data

PER SERVING:

Calories	252
% calories from fat	24
Fat (gm)	6.9
Sat. Fat (gm)	2.2
Cholesterol (mg)	18.1
Sodium (mg)	589
Protein (gm)	12.4
Carbohydrate (gm)	35.5

EXCHANGES:

Milk	0.0	Bread	2.0
Veg.	1.0	Meat	1.0
Fruit	0.0	Fat	0.5

Break up ground beef and turkey in very small chunks in 2-quart casserole. Add green pepper, onion, and garlic powder. Microwave 5 to 7 minutes, stirring about every 2 minutes. Add marinara sauce, mushrooms, and oregano and microwave another 4 minutes.

Slice bread in half lengthwise; place cut sides up on baking sheet. Spread meat mixture evenly over bread. Top with mozzarella cheese. Microwave 2 minutes or until cheese melts.

To Freeze: Place in microwave-safe container; label and freeze up to 2 months.

To Serve: Thaw. Cover with microwave-safe plastic wrap, and cook on High 3 to 5 minutes.

English Muffin Pizza

Serves 8

1½	teaspoons Barbecue Sauce (see p. 514) for each muffin half
	Canola oil, or vegetable cooking spray
4	English muffins, split into halves
2	red bell peppers, seeded and sliced
¼	teaspoon black pepper
½	cup low-fat Cheddar cheese, shredded

Nutritional Data

PER SERVING:

Calories	97
% calories from fat	17
Fat (gm)	1.9
Sat. Fat (gm)	0.6
Cholesterol (mg)	3.8
Sodium (mg)	316
Protein (gm)	4
Carbohydrate (gm)	15.9

EXCHANGES:

Milk	0.0	Bread	1.0
Veg.	0.0	Meat	0.5
Fruit	0.0	Fat	0.0

Brush muffins with Barbecue Sauce.

Coat nonstick skillet with oil or cooking spray. Sauté peppers 2 minutes. Season with pepper.

Preheat oven to 375 degrees. Sprinkle muffins with bell peppers and cheese. Place on nonstick cookie sheet.

Bake muffins on lowest rack of oven 10 minutes or until cheese is bubbly.

Chapter Twelve

Breads, Muffins, Breakfast & Brunch

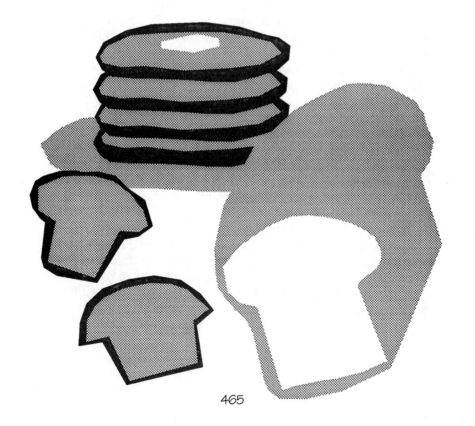

Banana Bread

Serves 12 (1 slice each)
Vegetable cooking spray
1½ cups all-purpose unbleached flour
¼ cup rye flour
1½ teaspoons baking powder
½ teaspoon baking soda
¼ teaspoon salt
½ teaspoon powdered ginger
1 cup ripe banana, mashed (about 2 medium bananas)
1 tablespoon fresh lemon juice
3 tablespoons frozen orange juice concentrate
⅓ cup diet margarine
2 eggs (1 yolk only)
⅓ cup evaporated skim milk
½ cup pecans or walnuts, chopped (optional)
6 teaspoons currants, divided
Few dashes cinnamon

Nutritional Data

PER SERVING:

Calories	126
% calories from fat	23
Fat (gm)	3.3
Sat. Fat (gm)	0.7
Cholesterol (mg)	18
Sodium (mg)	214
Protein (gm)	3.5
Carbohydrate (gm)	21

EXCHANGES:

Milk	0.0	Bread	1.0
Veg.	0.0	Meat	0.0
Fruit	0.5	Fat	0.5

Coat bottom of 9" x 5" glass loaf pan with nonstick vegetable cooking spray. In bowl, mix together flours, baking powder, baking soda, salt, and ginger. In another small bowl, mash bananas, mix with lemon juice, and set aside.

In large bowl, combine orange juice, margarine, eggs and milk. Stir in chopped nuts and 5 teaspoons currants. Fold in mashed bananas and add dry ingredients, mixing well. Turn into microwave-safe pan, and top with 1 teaspoon currants and few dashes of cinnamon.

Place in microwave on inverted saucer. Microwave on Medium-High (70%) 3½ to 4 minutes. Turn pan and continue microwaving at 70% another 3½ to 4 minutes. Microwave on High 4 to 5 minutes, until knife inserted into center of bread comes out clean.

If browned top is desired, place under conventional oven broiler 30 seconds. Let cool 10 minutes. Remove from pan. If bottom is still damp, return to microwave, bottom up, and microwave on High 1 to 2 minutes, until no longer wet.

This bread gets better after refrigeration for a day (if it's not all eaten!).

Cocoa Banana Bread

Serves 12 (1 slice each)

Butter-flavored vegetable cooking spray
- ¼ cup diet margarine
- ¾ cup fructose (fruit sugar, see "About This Cookbook")
- 2 medium-ripe bananas, mashed
- 2 egg whites
- 1¾ cups all-purpose flour
- 3 tablespoons unsweetened Dutch cocoa
- ¼ teaspoon salt
- 1 teaspoon each ingredient: baking soda, baking powder
- ½ cup nonfat vanilla yogurt
- 1 teaspoon vanilla

Nutritional Data

PER SERVING:

Calories	168
% calories from fat	22
Fat (gm)	4
Sat. Fat (gm)	0.8
Cholesterol (mg)	0.2
Sodium (mg)	200
Protein (gm)	3
Carbohydrate (gm)	30

EXCHANGES:

Milk	0.0	Bread	1.0
Veg.	0.0	Meat	0.0
Fruit	1.0	Fat	1.0

Preheat oven to 350 degrees. Coat loaf pan with cooking spray and dust lightly with flour. Set aside.

In large bowl of electric mixer, beat margarine and fructose. Mix in mashed bananas and egg whites. Add flour, cocoa, salt, baking soda, and baking powder. Add yogurt and vanilla. Batter should be smooth.

Pour batter into prepared pan. Bake in center of oven 50 to 60 minutes. Cake will test done when tester or bamboo skewer inserted in cake comes out dry.

Let stand 5 minutes. Unmold and cool on wire rack. Slice and serve.

Buttermilk Soda Bread

Serves 16 (1 slice each)

- 1 cup rye flour
- 1 cup unbleached all-purpose flour
- ¼ cup wheat germ
- 1 teaspoon baking soda
- 2 teaspoons double-acting baking powder
- ½ teaspoon salt
- 2 cups buttermilk
- 2 tablespoons canola oil
- 2 tablespoons sunflower seeds
- 2 tablespoons currants

Vegetable cooking spray
Poppy seeds

Nutritional Data

PER SERVING:

Calories	93
% calories from fat	28
Fat (gm)	2.9
Sat. Fat (gm)	0.4
Cholesterol (mg)	1.1
Sodium (mg)	219
Protein (gm)	3
Carbohydrate (gm)	13.9

EXCHANGES:

Milk	0.0	Bread	1.0
Veg.	0.0	Meat	0.0
Fruit	0.0	Fat	0.5

In large bowl, mix together first 6 ingredients. In another bowl, combine buttermilk and canola oil, and then stir into flour mixture and blend. Add sunflower seeds and currants, and turn into 8" x 10" baking dish coated with nonstick cooking spray. Top with a few dashes of poppy seeds, and place dish on inverted saucer in oven.

Microwave on High 5 minutes. Rotate dish and microwave on High another 7 to 8 minutes. Bread is done when toothpick inserted comes out clean or top springs back when touched. Remove and let cool.

Mixed Grain Bread

Serves 40 (1 slice each)	**Nutritional Data**

Ingredients		Nutritional Data

Serves 40 (1 slice each)

2½	cups lukewarm water
2	tablespoons corn or barley malt
2	tablespoons active dry yeast
2	tablespoons Dijon mustard
1	cup rye flakes
1	cup wheat flakes
1	cup oat bran
¼	cup cornmeal
2½	cups unbleached flour
2	cups whole wheat flour
	Vegetable cooking spray

Nutritional Data

PER SERVING:

Calories	69
% calories from fat	6
Fat (gm)	0.5
Sat. Fat (gm)	0.1
Cholesterol (mg)	0
Sodium (mg)	27
Protein (gm)	2.6
Carbohydrate (gm)	14.7

EXCHANGES:

Milk	0.0	Bread	1.0
Veg.	0.0	Meat	0.0
Fruit	0.0	Fat	0.0

Mix water and malt in large bowl. Add yeast and stir to dissolve. Add mustard and mix well. Add rye flakes, wheat flakes, oat bran, and cornmeal, and stir until well blended. Gradually add unbleached and whole wheat flours ½ cup at a time, until mixture can be kneaded (it'll be sticky).

On well-floured surface, knead 10 minutes or until dough is elastic. Coat large bowl with nonstick cooking spray and place dough in it, turning once to bring coated side up. Cover with plastic wrap and let rise in warm place 45 to 60 minutes or until doubled in volume.

Punch down dough, cut in half, and fit into 2 9" x 5" loaf pans coated with nonstick cooking spray. Let rise again until doubled in volume, about 30 minutes. Spray each loaf with water from a plant mister.

Preheat oven to 375 degrees.

Bake about 45 minutes or until loaves sound hollow when tapped, spraying with water again midway through baking. Remove from pans and cool on wire racks. Make 2 loaves (20 slices per loaf).

Florentine Bread

Serves 24

1 package active dry yeast
1 teaspoon salt
3 cups unbleached flour
1 cup warm (105 degrees) water
3 tablespoons olive oil plus oil for
   brushing crust
1 tablespoon garlic, minced
   Cornmeal
   Coarse salt
1 teaspoon fresh rosemary, minced
1 teaspoon fresh oregano, minced

Nutritional Data

PER SERVING:

Calories	78
% calories from fat	23
Fat (gm)	2
Sat. Fat (gm)	0.3
Cholesterol (mg)	0
Sodium (mg)	89
Protein (gm)	2.2
Carbohydrate (gm)	12.7

EXCHANGES:

Milk	0.0	Bread	1.0
Veg.	0.0	Meat	0.0
Fruit	0.0	Fat	0.0

Combine yeast, salt, and flour in large bowl. Combine water and oil in small bowl. Add liquid to dry ingredients, and mix until they form rough mass.

Knead mixture in bowl with hands until it holds together, then turn it out onto lightly floured surface and knead in garlic. Continue kneading until dough is smooth and elastic, about 8 minutes. Form into ball, and let rest on lightly floured surface, covered, 1 hour.

Preheat oven to 375 degrees.

Roll dough into 12" x 14" rectangle, and transfer to baking sheets sprinkled with cornmeal. Use fingertips to make indentations in dough at 2-inch intervals. Sprinkle dough lightly with coarse salt, and drizzle olive oil over top. Sprinkle with rosemary and oregano.

Bake until golden, about 15 minutes. Remove from oven and brush with olive oil. Cool slightly on rack; serve warm. Makes 1 12" x 14" rectangle.

Polenta Bread

Serves 8

2   tablespoons garlic, minced
1   cup polenta (coarse yellow cornmeal)
1½   teaspoons salt
1   cup red bell peppers, chopped
3   eggs, separated
2   cups skim milk
½   cup evaporated skim milk
1   tablespoon fresh basil, minced
½   teaspoon red pepper flakes
¼   cup liquid Butter Buds
     Vegetable cooking spray

Nutritional Data

PER SERVING:

Calories	144
% calories from fat	15
Fat (gm)	2.4
Sat. Fat (gm)	0.7
Cholesterol (mg)	81.5
Sodium (mg)	564
Protein (gm)	7.8
Carbohydrate (gm)	22.3

EXCHANGES:

Milk	0.5	Bread	1.0
Veg.	0.5	Meat	0.0
Fruit	0.0	Fat	0.5

In small skillet coated with vegetable cooking spray, over moderately low heat, sauté garlic until fragrant. Remove from heat. Combine polenta, salt, and bell pepper in bowl, and set aside.

Put egg yolks, skim milk, and evaporated milk in saucepan, and whisk well. Bring to boil, whisking constantly. Add cornmeal mixture gradually, then add garlic, basil, and red pepper flakes. Cook 2 minutes, stirring constantly with wooden spoon. Add Butter Buds, and cook additional 2 minutes.

Preheat oven to 375 degrees. Coat 8-cup soufflé dish or casserole with vegetable cooking spray. Place dish in oven 5 minutes to warm it.

Beat egg whites with pinch of salt until stiff peaks form. Gently fold whites into thickened cornmeal. Pour mixture into hot soufflé dish. Bake until puffed and golden, about 30 minutes. Serve immediately.

Eggless Challah Bread

Serves 6

1½ packages dry yeast
1 tablespoon sugar
½ cup lukewarm water
4 cups all-purpose flour
1 cup lukewarm water
1 tablespoon sugar
1½ teaspoons salt
2 tablespoons homogenized shortening

Nutritional Data

PER SERVING:

Calories	362
% calories from fat	13
Fat (gm)	5.1
Sat. Fat (gm)	1.4
Cholesterol (mg)	0
Sodium (mg)	535
Protein (gm)	9.4
Carbohydrate (gm)	68.5

EXCHANGES:

Milk	0.0	Bread	4.5
Veg.	0.0	Meat	0.0
Fruit	0.0	Fat	1.0

Place yeast and 1 tablespoon sugar in bowl. Add ½ cup lukewarm water, mixing well. Yeast should dissolve and start to bubble. Measure flour into large bowl. Pour bubbling yeast into well made in center of flour.

Add remaining ingredients and knead dough. Stand mixing bowl in damp cloth to anchor it. Knead dough with heel of your hand. Be sure to get all dough away from sides and bottom of bowl. Keep kneading until dough begins to blister and comes off your hands. Lightly coat surface of dough with shortening. Cover bowl with clean linen towel, and set it in warm place to rise, about 40 minutes.

After rising, test dough by plunging your finger into center of mound of dough. If your indentation remains, dough has risen sufficiently.

Divide dough into 4 parts. Pat and roll 3 parts into long cylinders; braid the 3 cylinders together. Divide remaining part again into 3 small parts, form into cylinders, and braid. Place small braid on top of large braid.

Place dough on greased baking sheet. Cover again with towel. Let rise in warm place until dough is almost doubled, 30 to 40 minutes.

Preheat oven to 400 degrees. Place challah in oven and immediately reduce temperature to 375 degrees; bake 50 minutes. Bread should be well browned and crusty. Cool on rack.

Note: Brush surface of loaf with egg white and sprinkle with poppy seeds just before baking for special crust.

 # *Gingerbread*

Serves 8

- 1½ cups all-purpose flour
- ½ teaspoon baking soda
- 1 teaspoon cinnamon
- 1 teaspoon ginger
- ½ teaspoon cloves
- ⅛ teaspoon nutmeg
- ¼ cup diet margarine
- ½ cup sugar
- 2 egg whites
- ½ cup light molasses
- 2 tablespoons hot water
- ½ cup buttermilk

Nutritional Data	
PER SERVING:	
Calories	221
% calories from fat	13
Fat (gm)	3.3
Sat. Fat (gm)	0.6
Cholesterol (mg)	0.6
Sodium (mg)	177
Protein (gm)	3.8
Carbohydrate (gm)	44.7

EXCHANGES:			
Milk	0.0	Bread	3.0
Veg.	0.0	Meat	0.0
Fruit	0.0	Fat	0.5

Mix flour with baking soda and spices; set aside.

Cream margarine with sugar. Add egg whites and beat well. Combine molasses and hot water; add gradually to creamed mixture, blending well. Alternately, add dry ingredients in thirds and buttermilk in halves to creamed mixture, beating until smooth after each addition.

Turn into well-greased and floured 2-lb. coffee can. Cover and place in crockpot. Cook on High 2 to 3 hours.

To Freeze: Vacuum seal individual portions; label and freeze up to 2 months.

To Serve: Put bags in boiling water, and bring to boil again. Boil 10 to 12 minutes.

Note: Low-calorie whipped topping tastes good on top of gingerbread (not included in Nutritional Data).

Bagels

Serves 12 (1 bagel each)

4	tablespoons oil
2	tablespoons sugar
½	teaspoon salt
1	cup hot water
2	packages dry yeast
1	egg
3¾	cups flour, sifted

Nutritional Data

PER SERVING:

Calories	200
% calories from fat	24
Fat (gm)	5.3
Sat. Fat (gm)	0.8
Cholesterol (mg)	17.8
Sodium (mg)	95
Protein (gm)	5.1
Carbohydrate (gm)	32.5

EXCHANGES:

Milk	0.0	Bread	2.0
Veg.	0.0	Meat	0.0
Fruit	0.0	Fat	1.0

Preheat oven to 400 degrees.

Mix oil, sugar, and salt with hot water. When it cools to lukewarm, add yeast to dissolve.

Beat egg until frothy. Add it to liquid, then mix in flour. Knead dough and shape it into large ball; place in bowl and cover. When dough has risen, knead it again and place it in bowl, covered, to rise again. After dough has risen second time, shape it into 12 donuts.

Place on baking sheets and bake 15 minutes at 400 degrees. Lower temperature to 350 degrees and continue baking 15 minutes more. Makes 12 bagels.

 # Blueberry Cobbler

Serves 8

2	cups fresh blueberries
⅓	cup whole wheat flour
⅓	cup unbleached all-purpose flour
1	teaspoon baking soda
3	tablespoons frozen orange juice concentrate
1	cup nonfat plain yogurt
1	teaspoon poppy seeds

Nutritional Data

PER SERVING:

Calories	85
% calories from fat	5
Fat (gm)	0.5
Sat. Fat (gm)	0.1
Cholesterol (mg)	0.5
Sodium (mg)	182
Protein (gm)	3.3
Carbohydrate (gm)	17.5

EXCHANGES:

Milk	0.0	Bread	0.5
Veg.	0.0	Meat	0.0
Fruit	1.0	Fat	0.0

Wash blueberries and pick over, discarding any debris. Turn into 8-inch-square baking dish.

Mix together flours and baking soda. Stir in orange juice and yogurt and when blended, pour over berries. Sprinkle poppy seeds over dough and place in oven on inverted saucer.

Microwave on High 4 to 5 minutes. Rotate dish and microwave on High another 4 to 5 minutes. Cobbler is done when it springs back when touched lightly. Top with sugar to taste, or blend of cottage cheese and part-skim ricotta, if desired (not included in Nutritional Data).

Apple Muffins

Serves 12 (1 muffin each)

2	cups whole wheat flour
1/4	cup toasted wheat germ
1	tablespoon baking powder
1	teaspoon cinnamon
1/2	teaspoon allspice
1/2	teaspoon nutmeg
1 1/4	cups apples, coarsely chopped
1	cup raisins
1	egg white, beaten
3/4	cup skim milk
1/4	cup apple juice
	Vegetable cooking spray

Glaze

1/4	teaspoon cinnamon
12	packets Equal® (see "About This Cookbook")
3	tablespoons boiling water

Nutritional Data

PER SERVING:

Calories	131
% calories from fat	5
Fat (gm)	0.8
Sat. Fat (gm)	0.2
Cholesterol (mg)	0.3
Sodium (mg)	98
Protein (gm)	4.5
Carbohydrate (gm)	28.9

EXCHANGES:

Milk	0.0	Bread	1.0
Veg.	0.0	Meat	0.0
Fruit	1.0	Fat	0.0

Preheat oven to 400 degrees. Combine all dry ingredients. Add apples and raisins. Combine all liquid ingredients. Add to dry mixture. Blend well.

Coat muffin tin with vegetable cooking spray. Fill each form two-thirds full. Bake 20 to 25 minutes or until golden brown on top. Using fork, prick holes in top of each muffin.

Glaze: Blend ingredients together and drizzle over each muffin. Makes 12 muffins.

Cocoa Bran Muffins

Serves 12 (1 muffin each)

1 1/2	cups bran cereal
1 1/4	cups skim milk
2	egg whites, slightly beaten
2	tablespoons diet margarine, melted and cooled
1 1/4	cups all-purpose flour
3	tablespoons cocoa
1/3	cup fructose (fruit sugar, see "About This Cookbook")
1/4	teaspoon salt
1	tablespoon each ingredient: baking soda, grated orange peel

Nutritional Data

PER SERVING:

Calories	109
% calories from fat	13
Fat (gm)	2
Sat. Fat (gm)	0.3
Cholesterol (mg)	0.4
Sodium (mg)	352
Protein (gm)	4
Carbohydrate (gm)	22

EXCHANGES:

Milk	0.0	Bread	1.0
Veg.	0.0	Meat	0.0
Fruit	0.5	Fat	0.0

Preheat oven to 400 degrees. Set paper liners in cupcake pan. Using mixing bowl, blend cereal with milk. Stir in beaten egg whites and margarine. Blend in flour, cocoa, fructose, salt, baking soda, and grated orange peel.

Spoon batter into prepared pan. Bake 17 to 20 minutes or until muffins are golden brown and cake tester or bamboo skewer comes out dry.

Cool out of pan. Serve warm or cold.

Oat Bran Muffins

Serves 12 (1 muffin each)

			Nutritional Data	
2½	cups oat bran		**PER SERVING:**	
2	tablespoons raisins		Calories	115
1	teaspoon baking powder		% calories from fat	34
½	teaspoon orange peel, grated		Fat (gm)	5.5
	Few dashes ground ginger		Sat. Fat (gm)	0.8
			Cholesterol (mg)	18.3
¼	teaspoon ground cinnamon		Sodium (mg)	77
⅛	teaspoon salt		Protein (gm)	5.5
¼	cup almonds (or walnuts), halved		Carbohydrate (gm)	19
¾	cup buttermilk			
¼	cup plus 2 tablespoons frozen orange juice concentrate		**EXCHANGES:**	
2	eggs (1 yolk only)		Milk 0.0	Bread 1.0
2	tablespoons canola oil		Veg. 0.0	Meat 0.0
			Fruit 0.0	Fat 1.0

Mix dry ingredients, except almonds or walnuts, together in large bowl, and mix remaining ingredients in another bowl. Combine both mixtures well and turn into microwave-safe muffin tin lined with double paper liners (or use paper hot cups cut off to about 1½ inches).

Top each with a nut, and microwave 6 muffins at a time on High 5 to 6 minutes, rotating once. Muffins are done when springy to touch or inserted toothpick comes out clean. Makes 12 muffins.

Banana Bran Muffins

Serves 24 (1 muffin each)

			Nutritional Data	
1½	cups whole wheat flour		**PER SERVING:**	
1½	cups unprocessed bran		Calories	65
2	teaspoons baking soda		% calories from fat	5
2	teaspoons ground cinnamon		Fat (gm)	0.4
1	teaspoon ground nutmeg		Sat. Fat (gm)	0.1
3	egg whites		Cholesterol (mg)	0.2
½	cup honey		Sodium (mg)	118
½	cup buttermilk		Protein (gm)	2.3
½	cup water		Carbohydrate (gm)	15.2
1	small ripe banana, mashed			
1	teaspoon vanilla extract		**EXCHANGES:**	
	Rind of 1 orange, grated		Milk 0.0	Bread 1.0
	Vegetable cooking spray		Veg. 0.0	Meat 0.0
			Fruit 0.0	Fat 0.0

Preheat oven to 400 degrees. Coat muffin tins with vegetable cooking spray.

In medium bowl, combine flour, bran, baking soda, cinnamon, and nutmeg.

In small bowl, mix egg whites, honey, buttermilk, water, banana, and vanilla. Add to flour mixture, stirring just until moistened. Add·orange rind and mix well.

Pour batter into muffin tins, filling half full. Bake 15 minutes or until wooden toothpick inserted in center comes out clean. Cool muffins in tins on wire rack. Makes 24 muffins.

 # Blueberry Bran Muffins

Serves 12 (1 muffin each)

1¼	cups whole wheat flour
¾	cup toasted wheat germ
1½	cups bran flakes
2	teaspoons baking powder
1	teaspoon baking soda
¼	teaspoon ground ginger
2	cups fresh blueberries
⅓	cup orange juice concentrate
1	egg
1½	cups buttermilk

Glaze

¼	teaspoon cinnamon
12	packets Equal® (see "About This Cookbook")
3	tablespoons boiling water

Nutritional Data

PER SERVING:

Calories	137
% calories from fat	12
Fat (gm)	1.9
Sat. Fat (gm)	0.5
Cholesterol (mg)	18.9
Sodium (mg)	237
Protein (gm)	5.9
Carbohydrate (gm)	26.6

EXCHANGES:

Milk	0.0	Bread	1.5
Veg.	0.0	Meat	0.0
Fruit	0.5	Fat	0.0

Preheat oven to 350 degrees. Mix first 6 ingredients. Add blueberries, juice, egg, and buttermilk and blend well.

Coat muffin tin with vegetable cooking spray. Fill each form two-thirds full. Bake 30 to 35 minutes or until golden brown on top. Using fork, prick holes in top of each muffin.

Glaze: Blend ingredients together and drizzle over each muffin. Makes 12 muffins.

 # Blueberry Muffins

Serves 12 (1 muffin each)

1½	cups all-purpose flour
2	teaspoons baking powder
½	teaspoon salt
½	teaspoon vanilla
2	eggs
½	cup skim milk
2	tablespoons oil
1	cup frozen blueberries, thawed and juice reserved

Nutritional Data

PER SERVING:

Calories	106
% calories from fat	29
Fat (gm)	3.4
Sat. Fat (gm)	0.6
Cholesterol (mg)	35.7
Sodium (mg)	162
Protein (gm)	3.2
Carbohydrate (gm)	15.3

		EXCHANGES:			
3	tablespoons hot skim milk	Milk	0.0	Bread	1.0
10	packets Equal® (see "About This Cookbook")	Veg.	0.0	Meat	0.0
		Fruit	0.0	Fat	0.5

Place flour, baking powder, and salt in bowl. Blend eggs, 1/2 cup milk, oil, vanilla, and 1/2 cup reserved blueberry juice and blend until smooth. Stir into flour mixture along with blueberries until flour is thoroughly mixed.

Preheat oven to 400 degrees. Fill paper-lined muffin cups two-thirds full with batter. Bake 20 to 25 minutes. Remove from oven and prick muffin tops in center with fork. Using pastry brush, glaze tops of muffins with hot milk. Roll muffin tops in bowl of Equal®.

Oatmeal Muffins

Serves 12 (1 muffin each)

- 1 cup all-purpose flour
- 1 cup whole wheat flour
- 1 cup uncooked, quick-cooking oatmeal
- 1/2 teaspoon cinnamon
- 1/4 teaspoon nutmeg
- 3 teaspoons baking powder
- 1 cup apple juice
- 2 egg whites mixed with 1 yolk
- 1/4 cup corn oil
- Vegetable cooking spray

Nutritional Data

PER SERVING:

Calories	156
% calories from fat	32
Fat (gm)	5.7
Sat. Fat (gm)	0.8
Cholesterol (mg)	17.8
Sodium (mg)	93.5
Protein (gm)	4.4
Carbohydrate (gm)	22.4

EXCHANGES:

Milk	0.0	Bread	1.5
Veg.	0.0	Meat	0.0
Fruit	0.0	Fat	1.0

Preheat oven to 400 degrees.

In bowl, mix flours, oatmeal, spices, and baking powder. Add apple juice, eggs, and oil; stir only until everything is moistened. Coat muffin pans with vegetable cooking spray and fill them about three-quarters full. Bake 15 to 20 minutes or until puffed and golden brown. Serve warm. Makes 12 muffins.

Orange Raisin Muffins

Serves 12 (1 muffin each)

2 cups whole wheat pastry flour
1½ teaspoons baking powder
1 egg, beaten
¾ cup orange juice
¼ cup canola oil
⅓ cup honey
½ teaspoon vanilla extract
¼ cup golden raisins
1 tablespoon orange rind, grated
Vegetable cooking spray

Nutritional Data

PER SERVING:

Calories	162
% calories from fat	29
Fat (gm)	5.4
Sat. Fat (gm)	0.5
Cholesterol (mg)	17.8
Sodium (mg)	48
Protein (gm)	3.5
Carbohydrate (gm)	26.8

EXCHANGES:

Milk	0.0	Bread	1.0
Veg.	0.0	Meat	0.0
Fruit	0.5	Fat	1.0

Preheat oven to 350 degrees.

In large bowl, combine flour and baking powder. In small bowl, combine egg, orange juice, oil, honey, and vanilla extract. Add to dry ingredients, with raisins and orange rind, and stir just until combined.

Pour batter into muffin pan coated with nonstick cooking spray. Bake 20 minutes, until muffins are golden brown. Makes 12 muffins.

Golden Carrot Muffins

Serves 12 (1 muffin each)

1 cup all bran (sugar free)
¾ cup skim milk
4 carrots, shredded (about 2 cups)
1 cup whole wheat flour
2 tablespoons frozen orange juice concentrate
2 tablespoons canola oil
1 tablespoon fresh lemon juice
1 tablespoon sunflower seeds
1 teaspoon baking powder
1 teaspoon baking soda
1 teaspoon ground cinnamon
½ teaspoon ground ginger
⅛ teaspoon salt
1 egg, beaten
1 tablespoon unsweetened coconut, shredded

Nutritional Data

PER SERVING:

Calories	102
% calories from fat	29
Fat (gm)	3.6
Sat. Fat (gm)	0.5
Cholesterol (mg)	18
Sodium (mg)	227
Protein (gm)	3.6
Carbohydrate (gm)	16.5

EXCHANGES:

Milk	0.0	Bread	1.0
Veg.	0.5	Meat	0.0
Fruit	0.0	Fat	0.5

In 2-quart bowl, combine bran with milk and shredded carrots (shred carrots in food processor to save time). Let stand 5 minutes while mixing all remaining ingredients, except coconut.

Line microwave-safe muffin tin with 2 paper liners (or use cut-off paper hot cups instead), and fill each cup one-half full. Top each muffin with sprinkle of coconut.

Microwave on High 5 to 5½ minutes, until muffins are springy when touched. Makes 12 muffins. It is best to microwave 6 muffins at a time.

Cocoa Zucchini Muffins

Serves 12 (1 muffin each)

1¾	cups all-purpose flour
¼	cup cocoa
1	teaspoon each ingredient: baking powder, baking soda
¼	teaspoon salt
½	cup real egg substitute
½	cup fructose (fruit sugar, see "About This Cookbook")
2	tablespoons diet margarine, room temperature
¾	cup zucchini, unpeeled and grated
⅓	cup plain nonfat yogurt

Nutritional Data

PER SERVING:

Calories	112
% calories from fat	10
Fat (gm)	1
Sat. Fat (gm)	0.2
Cholesterol (mg)	0.1
Sodium (mg)	182
Protein (gm)	4
Carbohydrate (gm)	22

EXCHANGES:

Milk	0.0	Bread	1.0
Veg.	0.0	Meat	0.0
Fruit	0.5	Fat	0.0

Preheat oven to 400 degrees. Set paper liners in cupcake pan.

In deep mixing bowl, blend flour, cocoa, baking powder, baking soda, and salt.

Stir in egg substitute, fructose, margarine, and zucchini. Do not over mix. Blend in yogurt.

Spoon muffin batter into paper liners.

Bake muffins in center of oven 20 to 25 minutes. Muffins are done when cake tester inserted in center comes out dry. Cool on wire rack. Serve warm.

Corn Muffins

Serves 12 (1 muffin each)

¾	cup skim milk
¼	cup low-fat yogurt
3	tablespoons sugarless maple syrup
2	eggs
1	cup whole wheat pastry flour
¾	cup cornmeal
½	teaspoon baking soda
¼	cup pimiento, well drained and chopped Vegetable cooking spray

Nutritional Data

PER SERVING:

Calories	89
% calories from fat	14
Fat (gm)	1.4
Sat. Fat (gm)	0.4
Cholesterol (mg)	36
Sodium (mg)	86
Protein (gm)	3.8
Carbohydrate (gm)	16.1

EXCHANGES:

Milk	0.0	Bread	1.0
Veg.	0.0	Meat	0.0
Fruit	0.0	Fat	0.0

Preheat oven to 375 degrees.

In medium bowl, combine milk, yogurt, maple syrup, and eggs. Blend well.

In another bowl, mix together flour, cornmeal, and baking soda; add to liquid ingredients. Add pimiento and mix well.

Spoon batter into muffin pan lightly coated with nonstick cooking spray. Bake 15 to 20 minutes. Cool on wire rack. Makes 12 muffins.

Gourmet Cheese Muffins

Serves 12 (1 muffin each)

- 1 cup buttermilk
- 1 egg
- 1½ tablespoons canola oil
- 1 cup all-purpose unbleached flour
- ¼ cup whole wheat flour
- 1 teaspoon baking powder
- ½ teaspoon baking soda
- ¼ teaspoon salt
- 6 tablespoons Parmesan cheese, freshly grated
- ½ teaspoon dried rosemary, crushed
  Vegetable cooking spray

Nutritional Data

PER SERVING:

Calories	91
% calories from fat	34
Fat (gm)	3.4
Sat. Fat (gm)	1
Cholesterol (mg)	21
Sodium (mg)	210
Protein (gm)	3.9
Carbohydrate (gm)	11

EXCHANGES:

Milk	0.0	Bread	1.0
Veg.	0.0	Meat	0.0
Fruit	0.0	Fat	0.5

Beat together buttermilk, egg, and oil. In another large bowl, sift together flours, baking powder, baking soda, and salt.

Combine grated cheese and rosemary in separate dish and mix. Add 5 tablespoons of it to flour mixture and blend. Pour buttermilk mixture into flour and combine.

Coat microwave-safe muffin dish with vegetable cooking spray. Turn batter into cups (filling each about two-thirds full), and top each one with some of the Parmesan-rosemary blend. Place on inverted saucer and microwave on High 4 to 5 minutes (rotating once), until either toothpick inserted in center comes out clean or muffins spring back when touched.

Muffin tin probably has room for only 6 muffins, so repeat when first batch is finished. If microwave-safe muffin pan is hard to find, use cut-off paper hot cups instead. Makes 12 muffins.

✳ *Fruit-Filled Muffins*

Serves 8 (1 muffin each)

- 2 cups all-purpose flour
- ¼ cup granulated sugar
- 1 tablespoon baking powder
- ¼ teaspoon salt
- 1 large egg
- 1 cup plain yogurt, or buttermilk
- ¼ cup (½ stick) diet margarine, melted
- 1 teaspoon vanilla extract
- ¼ cup fruit-only preserves (orange, marmalade, strawberry, raspberry, and blueberry are especially good, but be inventive)

Nutritional Data

PER SERVING:

Calories	221
% calories from fat	17
Fat (gm)	4.2
Sat. Fat (gm)	1
Cholesterol (mg)	28.4
Sodium (mg)	284
Protein (gm)	5.5
Carbohydrate (gm)	39.7

EXCHANGES:

Milk	0.0	Bread	2.5
Veg.	0.0	Meat	0.0
Fruit	0.0	Fat	1.0

Preheat oven to 375 degrees. Grease 8 regular muffin cups or use foil baking cups.

Thoroughly mix flour, sugar, baking powder, and salt in large bowl. In smaller bowl, whisk egg with yogurt, margarine, and vanilla until smooth. Pour over flour mixture, folding in just until dry ingredients are moistened.

Spoon 1 heaping tablespoon of batter into each muffin cup. Make small well in center of each, and fill with about 1 teaspoon of preserves. Top with about 2 more tablespoons batter to cover preserves.

Bake 25 to 30 minutes or until golden brown. Let cool about 5 minutes before removing from pans.

To Freeze: Vacuum seal individual muffins; label and freeze up to 1 month.

To Serve: Thaw on counter or in refrigerator. Warm in microwave, if desired.

Popovers

Serves 12 (1 popover each)

- 2 eggs
- 2 egg whites
- 1 cup skim milk
- 1 tablespoon diet margarine, melted
- 1 cup whole wheat pastry flour
  Vegetable cooking spray

Nutritional Data

PER SERVING:

Calories	61
% calories from fat	22
Fat (gm)	1.5
Sat. Fat (gm)	0.4
Cholesterol (mg)	35.8
Sodium (mg)	42
Protein (gm)	3.7
Carbohydrate (gm)	8.4

EXCHANGES:

Milk	0.0	Bread	0.5
Veg.	0.0	Meat	0.5
Fruit	0.0	Fat	0.0

Preheat oven to 400 degrees.

In medium bowl, beat eggs and egg whites with electric mixer at high speed until foamy. Continue beating as you add milk, margarine, and flour.

When mixture is smooth and all ingredients well combined, divide batter among 12 muffin cups lightly coated with nonstick cooking spray. Fill cups two-thirds full.

Bake 15 minutes. Reduce heat to 350 degrees and bake additional 10 to 15 minutes or until golden brown. Do not open oven door until baking time has been completed or popovers will not rise properly. Makes 12 popovers.

Currant Scones

Serves 8 (1 scone each)

½   cup all-purpose unbleached flour
¼   cup whole wheat flour
¼   cup yellow cornmeal
1½ teaspoons baking powder
¼   teaspoon salt
1   tablespoon whipped butter
1   tablespoon canola oil
¼   cup part-skim mozzarella cheese, or other low-fat cheese, shredded
½   teaspoon maple extract
2   egg whites
⅓   cup skim milk
2   teaspoons caraway seeds
2   tablespoons currants
     Paprika
     Vegetable cooking spray

Nutritional Data

PER SERVING:

Calories	99
% calories from fat	32
Fat (gm)	3.6
Sat. Fat (gm)	1.1
Cholesterol (mg)	4.6
Sodium (mg)	175
Protein (gm)	3.9
Carbohydrate (gm)	13.1

EXCHANGES:

Milk	0.0	Bread	1.0
Veg.	0.0	Meat	0.0
Fruit	0.0	Fat	0.5

In large bowl, combine flour, cornmeal, baking powder, and salt. Stir in butter, oil, and cheese, until mixture is crumbly. Beat egg whites and milk with maple extract and stir into flour mixture. Add caraway seeds and currants and blend.

Dust board with flour and knead dough into ball. Roll into 7-inch circle and cut into 8 even wedges. Dust tops of each wedge with a little paprika.

Coat 9-inch pie plate with nonstick cooking spray and arrange wedges on plate. Place pie plate on inverted saucer and microwave on Medium (50%) 6 minutes, until puffy, rotating pie plate every 2 minutes. Turn scones over and microwave on bottom side 1 minute more at 50% power.

Let cool. Serve with dollop of part-skim ricotta cheese or a little sugar-free fruit preserves, if desired. Makes 8 scones.

Yogurt-Poppy Seed Scones

Serves 12 (1 scone each)

		Nutritional Data	
2⅔	cups all-purpose flour	PER SERVING:	
3	tablespoons sugar	Calories	196
1	teaspoon baking powder	% calories from fat	34
6	tablespoons (¾ stick) chilled margarine, cut into small pieces	Fat (gm)	7.3
		Sat. Fat (gm)	1.5
		Cholesterol (mg)	18.9
2	egg whites	Sodium (mg)	122
1	egg, separated	Protein (gm)	5.6
1	cup plain yogurt	Carbohydrate (gm)	26.8
3	tablespoons poppy seeds		
1	tablespoon water	EXCHANGES:	
	Vegetable cooking spray	Milk 0.0 Bread 1.5	
		Veg. 0.0 Meat 0.5	
		Fruit 0.0 Fat 1.5	

Preheat oven to 400 degrees. Coat cookie sheet with non-stick vegetable cooking spray.

Combine first 3 ingredients in large bowl. Using pastry blender or 2 knives, cut in margarine until mixture resembles coarse meal. Mix egg whites and yolk of separated egg. Stir into batter. Blend in yogurt and poppy seeds. Mix well.

Turn mixture out onto lightly floured surface. Knead briefly until dough comes together. Roll out to thickness of 1 inch. Cut into circles with 2-inch biscuit cutter or glass beaker. Gather scraps; reroll and cut additional scones. Place on prepared cookie sheet.

Mix remaining egg white with water. Brush tops of scones to glaze. Bake until golden brown, about 20 minutes. Serve immediately.

To Freeze: Freezer-bag individual scones; label and freeze up to 1 month.

To Serve: Thaw on counter or in refrigerator. Warm in microwave, if desired.

Granola

Serves 26

		Nutritional Data	
3	cups rolled oats	PER SERVING:	
1	cup wheat germ	Calories	86
½	cup raw sunflower seeds	% calories from fat	34
¼	cup sesame seeds	Fat (gm)	3.4
2½	tablespoons honey	Sat. Fat (gm)	0.5
2	teaspoons vegetable oil	Cholesterol (mg)	0
2	tablespoons raisins	Sodium (mg)	2
		Protein (gm)	3.5
		Carbohydrate (gm)	11.4

Preheat oven to 300 degrees.

Put all ingredients, except raisins, in large bowl. After mixing well, bake in roasting pan 15 minutes. Every 5 minutes, open oven and stir granola thoroughly so all parts get brown and crisp. Cool; add scattering of raisins. Store in large jar or canister.

This will make a good breakfast-in-a-hurry with skim milk. Or stir 2 tablespoons of granola into container of plain low-fat yogurt. You can even take granola with you to work and nibble on it dry.

To Freeze: Vacuum seal individual portions; label and freeze up to 2 months.

To Serve: Defrost on counter.

EXCHANGES:			
Milk	0.0	Bread	1.0
Veg.	0.0	Meat	0.0
Fruit	0.0	Fat	0.5

Buckwheat Cereal with Raisins

Serves 4

- 2½ cups water
- ¼ teaspoon salt
- ½ cup roasted buckwheat kernels
- 1 tablespoon nonfat margarine
- 2 cups skim milk
- ¼ cup raisins

Bring water and salt to rapid boil in medium saucepan. Stir in buckwheat and margarine. Cook, uncovered, stirring occasionally, 10 minutes or until done. Serve with skim milk and sprinkle with raisins. Serve hot.

Nutritional Data

PER SERVING:

Calories	142
% calories from fat	5
Fat (gm)	0.8
Sat. Fat (gm)	0.3
Cholesterol (mg)	2
Sodium (mg)	222
Protein (gm)	6.9
Carbohydrate (gm)	28.5

EXCHANGES:			
Milk	0.5	Bread	1.0
Veg.	0.0	Meat	0.0
Fruit	0.5	Fat	0.0

Swedish Pancakes

Serves 9 (2 pancakes each)

- 3 egg whites
- 1¾ cups skim milk, divided
- 4 tablespoons diet margarine, melted
- 1 cup cake flour
- ¼ teaspoon ground cinnamon
- All-fruit preserves
- Vegetable cooking spray

Whisk egg whites in large bowl. Add ¾ cup of milk to margarine and mix well. Add flour and cinnamon, and stir with wooden spoon until smooth. Stir

Nutritional Data

PER SERVING:

Calories	89
% calories from fat	28
Fat (gm)	2.7
Sat. Fat (gm)	0.5
Cholesterol (mg)	0.8
Sodium (mg)	101
Protein (gm)	3.8
Carbohydrate (gm)	11.9

EXCHANGES:			
Milk	0.0	Bread	1.0
Veg.	0.0	Meat	0.0
Fruit	0.0	Fat	0.5

in remaining 1 cup of milk. Batter can be made in blender or food processor, if desired. Stir well and thin with milk as necessary. Result should be consistency of light cream.

Coat large griddle with vegetable cooking spray and heat until very hot. Water droplets should dance on griddle when it is ready.

Pour batter, using 1 tablespoon for each pancake. Cook, turning once, until golden on both sides. It usually isn't necessary to add more cooking spray to griddle with subsequent batches, but do so if it seems necessary. Pancakes are usually served right away, but can be kept warm in 200-degree oven if you are making a large batch. Serve hot with preserves. Makes 18 pancakes.

❄ Whole Wheat Pancakes

Serves 4 (4 pancakes each)

½ cup all-purpose flour
½ cup whole wheat flour
1 teaspoon baking powder
¾ cup skim milk
2 tablespoons frozen apple juice concentrate, thawed and undiluted
1½ tablespoons vegetable oil
1 tablespoon brown sugar
2 egg whites, beaten
Vegetable cooking spray

Nutritional Data

PER SERVING:

Calories	199
% calories from fat	25
Fat (gm)	5.6
Sat. Fat (gm)	0.8
Cholesterol (mg)	0.8
Sodium (mg)	138
Protein (gm)	6.5
Carbohydrate (gm)	31.1

EXCHANGES:

Milk	0.0	Bread	2.0
Veg.	0.0	Meat	0.0
Fruit	0.0	Fat	1.0

Combine all-purpose flour, whole wheat flour, and baking powder in large bowl and stir well. Combine skim milk, thawed apple juice concentrate, vegetable oil, brown sugar, and egg whites. Add to flour mixture and stir well.

Spoon 2 tablespoons batter per pancake onto hot, nonstick griddle coated with cooking spray. Turn pancakes when tops are covered with bubbles and edges look coated. Makes 16, 3-inch pancakes.

To Freeze: Place in microwave-safe container; label and freeze up to 2 months.

To Serve: Thaw. Cover with microwave-safe plastic wrap, and cook on High 3 to 5 minutes.

Cinnamon Whole Wheat Crepes

Serves 6 (2 crepes each)

1	cup whole wheat pastry flour
1½	cups skim milk
2	eggs
½	teaspoon cinnamon
	Vegetable cooking spray

Nutritional Data

PER SERVING:

Calories	115
% calories from fat	16
Fat (gm)	2.2
Sat. Fat (gm)	0.7
Cholesterol (mg)	72
Sodium (mg)	54
Protein (gm)	6.9
Carbohydrate (gm)	17.9

EXCHANGES:

Milk	0.5	Bread	1.0
Veg.	0.0	Meat	0.0
Fruit	0.0	Fat	0.0

Place all ingredients in blender. Process on medium speed until smooth, stopping and scraping down sides with spatula as necessary. Place blender container with batter in refrigerator 30 minutes.

Process again briefly on medium speed.

Pour 2 to 3 tablespoons of batter in heated crepe pan, lightly coated with cooking spray. Rotate pan gently to spread thin layer of batter across bottom. Cook crepe about 1 minute over medium heat or until surface of crepe appears dry and bottom is golden. Invert pan over cooling rack covered with tea towel. Repeat with remaining batter, blending batter briefly before making each crepe.

Makes 12 crepes.

Note: A special treat is to fill these crepes with sautéed apple wedges with raisins (not included in Nutritional Data). Wonderful for breakfast or dessert.

Strawberry and Cream Cheese Crepes

NO SUGAR ADDED

Serves 6 (2 crepes each)

Batter

2	eggs
¼	cup skim milk
2	tablespoons water
4	tablespoons all-purpose flour
⅛	teaspoon salt
	Vegetable cooking spray

Filling

3	ozs. fat-free cream cheese
6	tablespoons dry curd cottage cheese
1	egg

Nutritional Data

PER SERVING:

Calories	108
% calories from fat	24
Fat (gm)	2.9
Sat. Fat (gm)	0.9
Cholesterol (mg)	108.8
Sodium (mg)	240
Protein (gm)	8.6
Carbohydrate (gm)	11.6

EXCHANGES:

Milk	0.0	Bread	0.5
Veg.	0.0	Meat	1.0
Fruit	0.0	Fat	0.0

4   packets Equal® (see "About This
Cookbook")
Strawberry Sauce
2   cups fresh strawberries
1   tablespoon fresh lemon juice
6   packets Equal® (see "About This
Cookbook")

Batter: Place eggs, milk, and water in bowl. Beat well,
and add flour and salt. Beat again until smooth. Coat crepe
pan with vegetable cooking spray and heat pan over medium
heat. When pan is hot, spoon 2 tablespoons of batter into
pan and rotate pan to spread evenly. Crepe is ready when
edges are browned. Turn crepe onto plate and fill.

Filling: Place all ingredients in blender and process until smooth. Spread Filling on crepe and roll up jelly-roll style.
Dust with Equal® and top with Strawberry Sauce.

Sauce: Process all ingredients in blender and spoon
over crepes.

Strawberry and Cottage Cheese Crepes

Serves 6 (4 crepes each)

Crepes

1   cup strawberries, hulled
2   tablespoons sugar, divided
1¾   cups cake flour
¾   cup low-fat cottage cheese
3   egg whites and 1 yolk, lightly beaten
1   teaspoon baking powder
1½   teaspoons vanilla
⅛   teaspoon baking soda
Pinch salt
Vegetable cooking spray

Strawberry Sauce

1½   cups strawberries, hulled and divided
⅔   cup honey, or 8 packets Equal® (see
"About This Cookbook")

Nutritional Data

PER SERVING:

Calories	309
% calories from fat	5
Fat (gm)	1.6
Sat. Fat (gm)	0.5
Cholesterol (mg)	36.8
Sodium (mg)	228
Protein (gm)	8.7
Carbohydrate (gm)	65.1

EXCHANGES:

Milk	0.0	Bread	2.5
Veg.	0.0	Meat	0.0
Fruit	2.0	Fat	0.0

Crepes: Slice strawberries, toss with 1 tablespoon sugar,
and set aside. Combine remaining ingredients, except vegetable cooking spray, and mix until just moistened. Mix in
strawberries.

Coat crepe pan with vegetable cooking spray, heat pan,
and drop batter into pan by tablespoon, rotating pan to
spread batter evenly. Cook until bubbles appear on top; turn

once. Crepes can be kept warm in low oven while you finish cooking them and make sauce.

Sauce: To make sauce, place 1 cup strawberries in blender with honey or Equal®. Process until berries are crushed, about 1 minute. Pour sauce over crepe and garnish with remaining strawberries.

Makes 24, 2½-inch crepes.

Note: Not only is this a great brunch and breakfast recipe but it is also a terrific dessert, very elegant.

Mount Crepe

Serves 8

1½	cups cake flour
¼	cup cocoa
1	cup skim milk
¼	cup real egg substitute
1	egg white
2	teaspoons fructose (fruit sugar, see "About This Cookbook")
2	tablespoons diet margarine, melted
	Butter-flavored vegetable cooking spray
	Filling (recipe follows)

Nutritional Data

PER SERVING:

Calories	181
% calories from fat	14
Fat (gm)	3
Sat. Fat (gm)	0.7
Cholesterol (mg)	8
Sodium (mg)	112
Protein (gm)	15
Carbohydrate (gm)	32

EXCHANGES:

Milk	0.0	Bread	1.0
Veg.	0.0	Meat	1.5
Fruit	0.5	Fat	0.0

In large deep bowl or food processor, blend together flour, cocoa, milk, egg substitute, egg white, fructose, and melted margarine. Let stand 20 minutes.

Coat 10-inch nonstick skillet with cooking spray. With ladle, pour about 5 tablespoons batter into hot pan. Swirl batter evenly in pan. Pour off excess batter after pan bottom is covered with batter.

Cook crepe over medium heat until bottom is cooked. Turn crepe over and continue cooking until done. Invert crepe on clean kitchen towel. Continue until all crepes are done. While crepes are cooling, prepare Filling.

Filling

1¼	lbs. nonfat ricotta cheese, or skim cottage cheese
⅓	cup nonfat vanilla yogurt
1	8-oz. can thin peach slices, drained, reserve 2 tablespoons juice
1	teaspoon aspartame, or 2 tablespoons sugar

In large bowl, mix cheese, yogurt, and peaches (reserve 3 slices for top of "mount"). Mash peaches as you mix filling, adding aspartame and enough juice from peaches to make smooth Filling.

To Assemble: Set first crepe in center of serving dish. Spread lightly with filling. Continue until all crepes have been stacked. Top with final layer of peach-cheese filling, and place remaining peach slices on top. You can arrange top slices in flower shape for elegance.

Slice crepe "mount" carefully with sharp or serrated knife into 8 servings.

Chocolate Potato Waffles

Serves 4 (1 waffle each)

- ¾ cup all-purpose flour
- 3 tablespoons cocoa
- 2 teaspoons fructose (fruit sugar, see "About This Cookbook")
- 1½ teaspoons baking powder
- ½ teaspoon baking soda
- ¼ teaspoon salt
- 2 egg whites
- 4 teaspoons diet margarine, melted and cooled
- 1 cup buttermilk
- 1 cup cooked mashed potatoes
  Butter-flavored nonstick cooking spray
- 1 cup vanilla nonfat yogurt
- 1 tablespoon candied ginger

Nutritional Data

PER SERVING:

Calories	203
% calories from fat	14
Fat (gm)	3
Sat. Fat (gm)	1
Cholesterol (mg)	4
Sodium (mg)	798
Protein (gm)	9
Carbohydrate (gm)	37

EXCHANGES:

Milk	0.0	Bread	2.5
Veg.	0.0	Meat	0.0
Fruit	0.0	Fat	0.5

Sift flour, cocoa, fructose, baking powder, baking soda, and salt into large bowl.

In electric mixer bowl, lightly beat egg whites. Beat in cooled margarine and buttermilk. Add flour/cocoa mixture and potatoes.

Heat waffle iron coated with cooking spray. Pour ¼ cup waffle mixture into center of waffle iron. Cook until brown, according to manufacturer's directions.

In small bowl, combine yogurt and ginger for topping.

Place waffles on individual plates and top each with tablespoon of ginger-yogurt. Serve hot.

 # French Toast

Serves 6 (1 slice each)

- 1 tablespoon diet margarine
- 1 egg, slightly beaten
- ¼ cup skim milk
- ½ teaspoon vanilla
  Dash salt
- 6 slices diet bread
  *Cinnamon-Equal® mixture, to taste

Nutritional Data

PER SERVING:

Calories	72
% calories from fat	27
Fat (gm)	2.3
Sat. Fat (gm)	0.5
Cholesterol (mg)	35.7
Sodium (mg)	154
Protein (gm)	3.5
Carbohydrate (gm)	10.7

Heat margarine in heavy skillet. Place egg, milk, vanilla, and salt into bowl; blend with fork. Dip bread into egg mixture and sauté in margarine on both sides to golden brown. Sprinkle each side with cinnamon-Equal® mixture.

Note: Equal® combines beautifully with cinnamon in a proportion of 2 teaspoons cinnamon to 6 packets Equal®.

EXCHANGES:

Milk	0.0	Bread	1.0
Veg.	0.0	Meat	0.0
Fruit	0.0	Fat	0.0

French Toast à l'Orange

Serves 4 (1 slice each)
Egg substitute equal to 4 eggs
4 tablespoons skim milk
½ cup orange juice
   Rind of 1 orange, freshly grated
¼ teaspoon cinnamon
2 tablespoons diet margarine
4 slices whole wheat bread
   Maple syrup, light

Nutritional Data

PER SERVING:

Calories	145
% calories from fat	25
Fat (gm)	4.2
Sat. Fat (gm)	0.8
Cholesterol (mg)	0.3
Sodium (mg)	305
Protein (gm)	8.7
Carbohydrate (gm)	19.3

EXCHANGES:

Milk	0.0	Bread	1.0
Veg.	0.0	Meat	1.0
Fruit	0.0	Fat	0.5

In wide bowl, whip egg substitute, milk, orange juice, rind, and cinnamon. Heat skillet over medium-high heat and add margarine. Dip bread in egg mixture to coat both sides and place in skillet.

Cook until toast looks lightly browned on bottom when you lift it with spatula, about 2 minutes. Turn toast over and brown other side. Serve with syrup (not included in Nutritional Data). Makes 4 slices.

Neapolitan French Toast

Serves 6 (2 slices each)
1 teaspoon garlic, minced
1 tablespoon fennel seed, lightly crushed
   in a mortar
1 tablespoon black pepper, freshly ground
1 teaspoon salt
   Egg substitute equal to 5 eggs
3 tablespoons olive oil
1 loaf Italian bread, cut into ¾-inch slices
2 tablespoons Parmesan cheese,
   freshly grated

Nutritional Data

PER SERVING:

Calories	254
% calories from fat	29
Fat (gm)	8.3
Sat. Fat (gm)	1.5
Cholesterol (mg)	1.6
Sodium (mg)	465
Protein (gm)	10.7
Carbohydrate (gm)	33.8

EXCHANGES:

Milk	0.0	Bread	2.0
Veg.	0.0	Meat	1.0
Fruit	0.0	Fat	1.0

Preheat oven to 350 degrees.

Combine garlic, fennel, pepper, and salt in small bowl, and set aside.

Whisk together egg substitute and 3 tablespoons olive oil. Dip bread slice in egg mixture one at a time and let soak briefly to absorb some egg. Arrange bread slices on large, lightly oiled baking sheet. If bread is slightly stale, you may need additional egg substitute. Dust bread slices with half of fennel mixture.

Bake 10 minutes. Turn slices, brush with remaining fennel mixture, and bake 10 minutes more. Sprinkle with Parmesan, and bake additional 5 minutes or until bread is golden. Serve hot with soup.

Makes 12 slices.

Omelet Flan

Serves 8

12 egg whites, or 2 cartons egg substitute
2   tablespoons flour
¼   cup skim milk
½   teaspoon Spike (see "About This Cookbook")
    Black pepper, freshly ground, to taste
2   tablespoons parsley, chopped
2   tablespoons basil, chopped
2   tablespoons chives, chopped
1   oz. Gruyère or fontina cheese, grated
¼   cup Parmesan cheese, freshly grated
1½ cups Basic Tomato-Basil Sauce (see p. 501), or purchased
1   tomato, sliced
8   fresh basil leaves
    Vegetable cooking spray

Nutritional Data

PER SERVING:

Calories	117
% calories from fat	30
Fat (gm)	4
Sat. Fat (gm)	1.9
Cholesterol (mg)	13.3
Sodium (mg)	322
Protein (gm)	11.9
Carbohydrate (gm)	8.7

EXCHANGES:

Milk	0.0	Bread	0.0
Veg.	1.5	Meat	1.5
Fruit	0.0	Fat	0.0

Beat eggs, flour, milk, Spike, and pepper together in mixing bowl until eggs are light and frothy. Add chopped herbs, mix well, and set aside.

Coat 8- or 9-inch omelet pan with vegetable cooking spray. Add ¼ cup of egg batter, tip pan to distribute, and cook over low heat until browned on bottom. Then turn omelet and brown other side. Transfer omelet to plate, and continue until all omelets are prepared, adding butter to pan as necessary.

Preheat oven to 350 degrees.

To assemble stack, coat baking dish slightly larger in diameter than diameter of omelets with vegetable cooking spray. Combine Gruyère or fontina and Parmesan in mixing bowl. Place omelet in bottom of dish; cover with 2 tablespoons of tomato sauce and 2 tablespoons of cheese mixture. Repeat until all ingredients are used. Cover top omelet with remaining tomato sauce and cheeses, allowing sauce to spill over sides.

Bake 15 minutes, until cheese is melted and begins to brown. Remove from oven, and transfer to heated serving platter. Garnish with tomato slices and basil. Serve hot, cutting stack in wedges like a cake.

Cocoa Skillet Soufflé

Serves 2

- 3 tablespoons unsweetened Dutch cocoa
- 7 tablespoons evaporated skim milk, divided
- 4 tablespoons fructose (fruit sugar, see "About This Cookbook"), divided
- ¼ cup real egg substitute
- 2 large egg whites
- ¼ teaspoon cream of tartar
  Vegetable cooking spray

Nutritional Data

PER SERVING:

Calories	161
% calories from fat	5
Fat (gm)	0.9
Sat. Fat (gm)	0.3
Cholesterol (mg)	2
Sodium (mg)	165
Protein (gm)	12
Carbohydrate (gm)	30

EXCHANGES:

Milk	0.5	Bread	0.0
Veg.	0.0	Meat	1.0
Fruit	1.0	Fat	0.0

Place cocoa in small bowl and add 4 tablespoons milk. Whisk until smooth. Add remaining 3 tablespoons milk and 2 tablespoons fructose and mix well. You will have ⅔ cup mixture.

Measure out ⅓ cup mixture, pour into small saucepan, and reserve; this will be heated later for sauce.

Combine remaining ⅓ cup cocoa mixture with egg substitute, mixing well.

Beat egg whites until they hold soft peaks; add cream of tartar and continue beating until stiff. With beaters running, add remaining 2 tablespoons fructose in steady stream; turn off beaters as soon as sugar is incorporated. Fold meringue into cocoa/egg mixture.

Meanwhile, heat 10-inch-diameter skillet (measured, to rim) coated with cooking spray. Spoon mixture into pan and cook 10 minutes over low heat.

Note: Since chocolate burns easily, watch carefully to see that bottom of soufflé does not burn.

As soon as bottom is set (top will still be fluffy-soft), ease omelet onto serving platter. Heat reserved sauce and pour around sides of omelet. Cut in half to serve.

Artichoke Frittata

Serves 6

8	medium artichoke hearts
1	tablespoon fresh lemon juice
4	tablespoons flour
12	egg whites, or 2 cartons egg substitute
1	teaspoon Spike (see "About This Cookbook")
1	tablespoon Italian seasoning
	Black pepper, freshly ground
	Vegetable cooking spray

Nutritional Data

PER SERVING:

Calories	74
% calories from fat	2
Fat (gm)	0.2
Sat. Fat (gm)	0
Cholesterol (mg)	0
Sodium (mg)	146
Protein (gm)	9
Carbohydrate (gm)	9.5

EXCHANGES:

Milk	0.0	Bread	0.0
Veg.	1.0	Meat	1.0
Fruit	0.0	Fat	0.0

Place artichoke hearts in bowl of water with lemon juice. Drain artichokes well, and pat them dry. Dredge artichoke hearts in flour. Coat 10-inch skillet with vegetable cooking spray, and sauté artichokes, a few at a time, until crisp and golden. Drain on paper towels. Continue until all artichokes are sautéed.

Beat eggs in mixing bowl until light and frothy, and season with Spike, Italian seasoning, and pepper. Using same skillet, spread artichokes evenly on bottom of pan, and add eggs. Reduce heat to low, and continue to cook until bottom of omelet begins to brown.

Place pan under broiler a couple of minutes to brown top and set eggs. Serve hot or at room temperature.

Frittata Profumata

Serves 6

10	sprigs Italian parsley, leaves only, minced
15	fresh basil leaves, torn into thirds
15	whole mint leaves, minced
	Egg substitute equal to 12 eggs
	Spike (see "About This Cookbook"), to taste
	Black pepper, freshly ground, to taste
	Vegetable cooking spray

Nutritional Data

PER SERVING:

Calories	59
% calories from fat	2
Fat (gm)	0.1
Sat. Fat (gm)	0
Cholesterol (mg)	0
Sodium (mg)	169
Protein (gm)	10.9
Carbohydrate (gm)	3

EXCHANGES:

Milk	0.0	Bread	0.0
Veg.	0.0	Meat	1.0
Fruit	0.0	Fat	0.0

Wash parsley, basil, and mint, and dry on paper towels. Finely chop parsley on board. Begin to make frittata, following directions below. Then add chopped parsley, basil, mint, Spike, and a little pepper to beaten egg substitute. Mix lightly with fork.

Finish making frittata and sprinkle with a little more black pepper before serving. Frittata may be served hot or at room temperature.

How to Prepare a Frittata

Break eggs into large crockery bowl. Number of eggs or egg substitute varies. See individual recipes. If omelet pan is new, be sure to season it first.

1. With a fork, break yolks and beat them lightly so no air bubbles or foam begins to form.

2. Place 10-inch omelet pan over medium heat. Coat pan with vegetable spray. When pan is hot, add beaten eggs or egg substitute. Keep puncturing bottom with fork as eggs set to allow liquid on top to move to bottom. This helps eggs set uniformly.

3. When eggs are well set and frittata is well detached from bottom of pan, put upside-down plate over pan.

4. Hold plate firmly.

5. Reverse pan.

6. Turn frittata out onto plate.

7. Return pan to heat and carefully slide frittata into pan and cook other side. When eggs are well set on second side (about 1 minute), reverse frittata onto a serving plate.

Zucchini-Parmesan Frittata

Serves 6

Egg substitute equal to 12 eggs
1 tablespoon water
½ teaspoon black pepper, freshly ground
½ teaspoon nutmeg
Vegetable cooking spray
1 medium zucchini, thinly sliced
1 small red bell pepper, seeded and cut into ½-inch squares
¼ cup Parmesan cheese, freshly grated

Nutritional Data

PER SERVING:

Calories	78
% calories from fat	16
Fat (gm)	1.4
Sat. Fat (gm)	0.9
Cholesterol (mg)	3.3
Sodium (mg)	244
Protein (gm)	12.4
Carbohydrate (gm)	3.8

EXCHANGES:

Milk	0.0	Bread	0.0
Veg.	1.0	Meat	1.0
Fruit	0.0	Fat	0.0

In bowl, beat egg substitute with water to blend, then beat in pepper and nutmeg. Set aside.

Coat vegetable cooking spray on 10-inch omelet pan with ovenproof handle, and place over medium heat. Add zucchini and bell pepper; cook, stirring until softened (about 8 minutes).

Spread vegetables evenly in pan. Pour in egg substitute mixture. Cook, puncturing mixture with fork to let uncooked portion flow underneath, until it begins to set on top but is still moist (about 5 minutes).

Remove frittata from heat; sprinkle with cheese, then broil about 6 inches below heat until puffy and lightly browned (about 2 minutes). Slide onto plate and cut into wedges to serve.

Chapter Thirteen

DINNER SAUCES

Light Béarnaise Sauce

Serves 10 (¼-cup servings)

¼ cup Chicken Stock or Vegetable Stock
   (see pp. 40 and 42)
1 shallot, minced
¼ cup flour, or 2 tablespoons arrowroot
2 cups skim milk
½ cup nonfat dry milk
1 bay leaf
½ teaspoon white pepper

Nutritional Data

PER SERVING:

Calories	43
% calories from fat	4
Fat (gm)	0.2
Sat. Fat (gm)	0.1
Cholesterol (mg)	1.7
Sodium (mg)	44
Protein (gm)	3.3
Carbohydrate (gm)	6.9

EXCHANGES:

Milk	0.5	Bread	0.0
Veg.	0.0	Meat	0.0
Fruit	0.0	Fat	0.0

Heat Chicken or Vegetable Stock and shallot over moderate heat in saucepan. Gradually add flour or arrowroot, and blend with wire whisk. Simmer and stir until heated through but not browned.

Remove from heat and add remaining ingredients. Return to heat and cook, stirring occasionally, until thickened. This sauce is excellent over steak, or it can be used for vegetables.

Makes 2½ cups.

Dijonaise Sauce

Serves 8 (2-tablespoon servings)

1 cup fat-free mayonnaise
3 tablespoons Dijon mustard
1 teaspoon fresh lemon juice

Nutritional Data

PER SERVING:

Calories	29
% calories from fat	11
Fat (gm)	0.4
Sat. Fat (gm)	0.1
Cholesterol (mg)	0
Sodium (mg)	455
Protein (gm)	0.3
Carbohydrate (gm)	6.4

EXCHANGES:

Milk	0.0	Bread	0.5
Veg.	0.0	Meat	0.0
Fruit	0.0	Fat	0.0

Combine all ingredients, and mix well. Refrigerate before serving. Use on salmon, sandwiches, or chicken. It also works well in potato or tuna salad.

Makes 1 cup.

Honey Dijon Sauce

Serves 10 (¹/₄-cup servings)

1½	cups defatted Chicken Stock (see p. 40)
½	cup Dijon mustard
½	cup honey
2	tablespoons shallots, minced
1½	teaspoons paprika
1½	teaspoons cornstarch dissolved in 2 tablespoons white wine

Bring first 5 ingredients to boil and simmer 15 minutes. Thicken with cornstarch and wine mixture, and simmer another 5 minutes. Makes 2½ cups.

Nutritional Data

PER SERVING:

Calories	74
% calories from fat	11
Fat (gm)	1
Sat. Fat (gm)	0.2
Cholesterol (mg)	1.5
Sodium (mg)	164
Protein (gm)	1.3
Carbohydrate (gm)	15.3

EXCHANGES:

Milk	0.0	Bread	1.0
Veg.	0.0	Meat	0.0
Fruit	0.0	Fat	0.0

Mock Hollandaise Sauce

Serves 8 (1-tablespoon servings)

¼	cup Mock Sour Cream (see next recipe)
¼	cup plain nonfat yogurt
1	teaspoon fresh lemon juice
½	teaspoon mustard

In small saucepan, combine all ingredients. Cook and stir over very low heat until heated through; do not boil. Serve over poultry and vegetables. Makes ½ cup.

Nutritional Data

PER SERVING:

Calories	9
% calories from fat	6
Fat (gm)	0.1
Sat. Fat (gm)	0
Cholesterol (mg)	0.3
Sodium (mg)	21
Protein (gm)	1
Carbohydrate (gm)	1.1

EXCHANGES:

Milk	0.0	Bread	0.0
Veg.	0.0	Meat	0.0
Fruit	0.0	Fat	0.0

Mock Sour Cream

Serves 8 (2-tablespoon servings)

¾	cup plain nonfat yogurt
¼	cup cottage cheese
1	tablespoon fresh lemon juice

Place all ingredients in blender and process until smooth. Makes 1 cup.

Nutritional Data

PER SERVING:

Calories	18
% calories from fat	6
Fat (gm)	0.1
Sat. Fat (gm)	0.1
Cholesterol (mg)	0.7
Sodium (mg)	45
Protein (gm)	2.1
Carbohydrate (gm)	2

EXCHANGES:

Milk	0.1	Bread	0.0
Veg.	0.0	Meat	0.1
Fruit	0.0	Fat	0.0

Mock Crème Fraîche

Serves 6

1½   cups low-fat cottage cheese
½   cup plain low-fat yogurt
¼   cup low-fat ricotta cheese

Put all ingredients into food processor and run until everything is perfectly blended and smooth, no more than 7 to 8 seconds. Transfer mixture to bowl and, using wire whisk, beat well to add as much air as possible, until mixture is fluffy and light. It should expand to about 2½ cups in 3 to 4 minutes.

Pour mixture into jars and set in warm place or on hot plate of yogurt maker to stay at a steady 75 degrees and begin to ferment. This should take about 2 hours. Mixture will thicken and take on a subtle acid flavor.

Makes about 2½ cups, which can be stored in refrigerator up to 2 weeks for use in many recipes.

Nutritional Data

PER SERVING:

Calories	61
% calories from fat	17
Fat (gm)	1.1
Sat. Fat (gm)	0.6
Cholesterol (mg)	5
Sodium (mg)	250
Protein (gm)	8.9
Carbohydrate (gm)	3.4

EXCHANGES:

Milk	0.0	Bread	0.0
Veg.	0.0	Meat	1.0
Fruit	0.0	Fat	0.0

White Sauce

Serves 24 (2-tablespoon servings)

3   tablespoons diet margarine
6   tablespoons whole wheat flour
3   cups skim milk

In saucepan, melt margarine and stir until golden brown. Stir in flour until crumbly. Whisk in milk. Stir over medium heat, beating with whisk until thickened. Use as directed in recipe. Makes 3 cups.

Nutritional Data

PER SERVING:

Calories	23
% calories from fat	30
Fat (gm)	0.8
Sat. Fat (gm)	0.2
Cholesterol (mg)	0.5
Sodium (mg)	32
Protein (gm)	1.3
Carbohydrate (gm)	2.8

EXCHANGES:

Milk	0.0	Bread	0.0
Veg.	0.0	Meat	0.0
Fruit	0.0	Fat	0.5

Basic Brown Sauce

Serves 8 (¹/₄-cup servings)	*Nutritional Data*	
2 tablespoons Butter Buds	PER SERVING:	
2 medium carrots, diced	Calories	50
1 medium onion, chopped	% calories from fat	5
2 sprigs parsley	Fat (gm)	0.1
Pinch thyme	Sat. Fat (gm)	0
1 small bay leaf	Cholesterol (mg)	0
2 tablespoons flour	Sodium (mg)	189
1 cup dry white wine	Protein (gm)	1.7
1½ cups consommé (canned may be used)	Carbohydrate (gm)	5.8
1 tablespoon tomato paste	EXCHANGES:	
½ teaspoon Spike (see "About This Cookbook")	Milk 0.0 Bread 0.0	
	Veg. 1.0 Meat 0.0	
¼ teaspoon black pepper, freshly ground	Fruit 0.0 Fat 0.0	

Mix 1 envelope Butter Buds with ¹/₂ cup warm water. Place 2 tablespoons in small saucepan and add carrots, onions, parsley, thyme, and bay leaf. Cook over low heat, stirring constantly, until vegetables are golden brown.

Stir in flour and cook until slightly brown. Stir in wine and consommé. Add tomato paste, Spike, and pepper. Bring to boil. Cover and simmer 30 minutes. Strain.

Makes 2 cups.

 # Dill Sauce

Serves 16 (¹/₈-cup servings)	*Nutritional Data*	
2 cups plain low-fat yogurt	PER SERVING:	
4 teaspoons dried dill weed	Calories	19
½ teaspoon Spike (see "About This Cookbook")	% calories from fat	22
	Fat (gm)	0.5
	Sat. Fat (gm)	0.3
Fresh dill sprigs	Cholesterol (mg)	1.8
	Sodium (mg)	20
	Protein (gm)	1.5
	Carbohydrate (gm)	2.1
	EXCHANGES:	
	Milk 0.0 Bread 0.0	
	Veg. 0.0 Meat 0.0	
	Fruit 0.0 Fat 0.0	

Combine all ingredients, except dill, and mix well. Cover tightly and store in refrigerator. Garnish with dill sprigs before serving. Makes 2 cups.

To Freeze: Place in microwave-safe container; label and freeze up to 2 months.

To Serve: Thaw and serve cold, or reheat in microwave on High 2 to 3 minutes.

Balsamic Vinegar Sauce

Serves 6 (1/2-cup servings)

- 2 cups defatted Chicken Stock (see p. 40)
- 1/4 cup shallots, minced
- 1 tablespoon cornstarch dissolved in 1/4 cup water
- 2 tablespoons balsamic vinegar
- 2 tablespoons sugar
  Salt and black pepper, to taste

Nutritional Data

PER SERVING:

Calories	43
% calories from fat	7
Fat (gm)	0.3
Sat. Fat (gm)	0.1
Cholesterol (mg)	3.4
Sodium (mg)	5.6
Protein (gm)	1.3
Carbohydrate (gm)	8

EXCHANGES:

Milk	0.0	Bread	0.5
Veg.	0.0	Meat	0.0
Fruit	0.0	Fat	0.0

Bring stock and shallots to boil. Reduce heat and simmer 5 minutes. Thicken with cornstarch and water mixture. Add vinegar and sugar, and simmer 5 minutes to combine flavors. Season with salt and pepper. Makes 3 cups.

Classic Spaghetti Sauce

Serves 8 (1/2-cup servings)

- 3/4 lb. lean turkey, ground
- 1 cup onion, chopped
- 1/2 cup green bell pepper, chopped
- 1/4 cup celery, chopped
- 2 cloves garlic, minced
- 2 16-oz. cans tomatoes, undrained and cut up
- 1 6-oz. can tomato paste
- 1/3 cup water
- 2 tablespoons fresh parsley, chopped
- 1 teaspoon sugar
- 1 tablespoon fresh basil, chopped
- 1 teaspoon fresh oregano, chopped
- 1/2 teaspoon fresh marjoram, crushed
- 1/4 teaspoon black pepper, freshly ground

Nutritional Data

PER SERVING:

Calories	109
% calories from fat	29
(15 with 2 ozs. pasta)	
Fat (gm)	3.7
Sat. Fat (gm)	0.9
Cholesterol (mg)	15.8
Sodium (mg)	376
Protein (gm)	8
Carbohydrate (gm)	12.7

EXCHANGES:

Milk	0.0	Bread	0.0
Veg.	2.5	Meat	1.0
Fruit	0.0	Fat	0.0

In large saucepan or Dutch oven, cook ground turkey, onion, green pepper, celery, and garlic until meat is brown. Drain fat. Carefully stir in undrained tomatoes, tomato paste, water, parsley, sugar, basil, oregano, marjoram, and pepper.

Bring to boil; reduce heat. Cover, and simmer 30 minutes. Uncover, and simmer 10 to 15 minutes more or to desired consistency, stirring occasionally.

Makes about 4 cups.

Marinara Sauce

Serves 8 (¹/₂-cup servings)

2 medium onions, chopped
6 cloves garlic, minced
2 tablespoons olive oil
2 16-oz. cans plum tomatoes, drained
  and chopped
¹/₂ cup dry white wine, or tomato juice
¹/₄ cup tomato paste
2 tablespoons fresh lemon juice
¹/₂ teaspoon salt
¹/₄ teaspoon black pepper

Nutritional Data

PER SERVING:

Calories	85
% calories from fat	37
(11 with 2 ozs. pasta)	
Fat (gm)	3.8
Sat. Fat (gm)	0.5
Cholesterol (mg)	0
Sodium (mg)	325
Protein (gm)	1.9
Carbohydrate (gm)	10.2

EXCHANGES:

Milk	0.0	Bread	0.0
Veg.	2.0	Meat	0.0
Fruit	0.0	Fat	0.5

Sauté onions and garlic in oil in large saucepan until tender, about 5 minutes. Stir in tomatoes, wine, and tomato paste; heat to boiling. Reduce heat and simmer, uncovered, until mixture is medium sauce consistency, about 20 minutes. Stir in lemon juice, salt, and pepper. Makes 4 cups.

Basic Tomato-Basil Sauce

Serves 8 (¹/₂-cup servings)

2 teaspoons olive oil
1 cup onion, finely chopped
3 cloves garlic, minced
10 fresh tomatoes, chopped, or 2 28-oz. cans
   plum tomatoes, undrained and chopped
¹/₄ cup fresh basil, chopped
3 teaspoons fresh oregano, minced
¹/₄ teaspoon black pepper, freshly ground

Nutritional Data

PER SERVING:

Calories	60
% calories from fat	22
(11 with 2 ozs. pasta)	
Fat (gm)	1.6
Sat. Fat (gm)	0.2
Cholesterol (mg)	0
Sodium (mg)	325
Protein (gm)	2.2
Carbohydrate (gm)	10.9

EXCHANGES:

Milk	0.0	Bread	0.0
Veg.	2.0	Meat	0.0
Fruit	0.0	Fat	0.0

Heat oil in large skillet over medium heat until hot. Add onion and garlic, and sauté until tender. Stir in tomatoes, and bring to boil. Add remaining ingredients; stir well.

Reduce heat to low, and cook, uncovered, 1 hour and 20 minutes or until thickened, stirring frequently. Serve over cooked pasta, in casseroles, or any time you need a good tomato sauce.

Makes 4 cups.

Cilantro Tomato Sauce

Serves 6 (½-cup servings)	Nutritional Data	
2 lbs. plum tomatoes, or regular tomatoes	PER SERVING:	
6 sprigs fresh cilantro	Calories	52
4 shallots, or green onions	% calories from fat	9
4 cloves garlic, minced	(8 with 2 ozs. pasta)	
3 tablespoons orange rind, grated	Fat (gm)	0.6
4 teaspoons cornstarch	Sat. Fat (gm)	0.1
2 teaspoons oregano	Cholesterol (mg)	0
1 teaspoon Spike (see "About This	Sodium (mg)	16
Cookbook")	Protein (gm)	1.8
½ teaspoon black pepper, freshly ground	Carbohydrate (gm)	11.6

EXCHANGES:

Milk	0.0	Bread	0.0
Veg.	2.0	Meat	0.0
Fruit	0.0	Fat	0.0

In blender or food processor, combine ingredients; cover, and mix until smooth. Place sieve over saucepan; pour tomato mixture into sieve, pressing with back of spoon. Discard seeds, skin, and anything left in sieve.

In saucepan, cook and stir tomato mixture until thickened and bubbly. Cook and stir 5 minutes more. Season to taste with Spike and black pepper.

Makes about 3 cups.

Romesco Sauce

Serves 8 (2-tablespoon servings)	Nutritional Data	
1 tomato, peeled, seeded, and chopped	PER SERVING:	
1 small, dried hot chili pepper, minced	Calories	26
3 cloves garlic, minced	% calories from fat	2
¾ cup white wine	(7 with 2 ozs. pasta)	
2 tablespoons wine vinegar	Fat (gm)	0.1
2 tablespoons sherry	Sat. Fat (gm)	0
1 teaspoon Spike (see "About This	Cholesterol (mg)	0
Cookbook")	Sodium (mg)	3
Black pepper, freshly ground	Protein (gm)	0.3
	Carbohydrate (gm)	1.8

EXCHANGES:

Milk	0.0	Bread	0.0
Veg.	0.0	Meat	0.0
Fruit	0.0	Fat	0.5

Pound tomato, chili pepper, and garlic to smooth paste with mortar and pestle. Combine wine, vinegar, and sherry. Add liquid mixture, drop by drop, into paste, stirring constantly in same direction. Season with Spike and pepper, to taste.

Makes about 1 cup sauce.

Puttanesca Sauce

Serves 4

Olive-oil-flavored vegetable
cooking spray

2 cloves garlic, minced

2 lbs. Italian plum tomatoes, drained and put through food mill or coarse sieve

8 pitted black olives, sliced

1 teaspoon capers

1 teaspoon basil

2 tablespoons parsley, chopped

¼ teaspoon hot pepper flakes

Nutritional Data

PER SERVING:

Calories	65
% calories from fat	21
(11 with 2 ozs. pasta)	
Fat (gm)	1.8
Sat. Fat (gm)	0.2
Cholesterol (mg)	0
Sodium (mg)	112
Protein (gm)	2.3
Carbohydrate (gm)	12.7

EXCHANGES:

Milk	0.0	Bread	0.0
Veg.	2.0	Meat	0.0
Fruit	0.0	Fat	0.0

Coat large skillet with vegetable cooking spray, and sauté garlic until soft but not brown. Add tomatoes, stir, and simmer about 10 minutes. Stir in olives, capers, basil, parsley, and pepper flakes.

Pesto Sauce

Serves 4 (¼-cup servings)

8 cloves garlic

3 cups fresh basil leaves, tightly packed

1 cup parsley, chopped

⅔ cup Parmesan cheese, freshly grated

¾ cup water

¼ cup white wine vinegar

3 teaspoons capers

2 teaspoons Dijon mustard

Nutritional Data

PER SERVING:

Calories	105
% calories from fat	44
(21 with 2 ozs. pasta)	
Fat (gm)	5.5
Sat. Fat (gm)	3.3
Cholesterol (mg)	13.2
Sodium (mg)	395
Protein (gm)	8.7
Carbohydrate (gm)	7.1

EXCHANGES:

Milk	0.0	Bread	0.0
Veg.	1.0	Meat	1.0
Fruit	0.0	Fat	0.5

Position knife blade in food processor (see Note). Drop in garlic and process 5 seconds or until minced. Add basil and parsley; process 10 seconds or until minced. Add cheese; process until blended. Slowly add remaining ingredients through food chute, with processor running, blending until smooth. Makes about 1 cup.

Note: A blender can also be used, but add ¼ cup of water along with basil and parsley. Add remaining water slowly at end of blending.

Alfredo Sauce

Serves 6 (¹/₂-cup servings)

3	tablespoons margarine
¹/₄	cup all-purpose flour
2¹/₂	cups skim milk
¹/₄	cup Parmesan cheese, freshly grated
¹/₈	teaspoon ground nutmeg
¹/₂	teaspoon salt
¹/₄	teaspoon black pepper

Nutritional Data

PER SERVING:

Calories	125
% calories from fat	52
(25 with 2 ozs. pasta)	
Fat (gm)	7.2
Sat. Fat (gm)	2
Cholesterol (mg)	5
Sodium (mg)	374
Protein (gm)	5.8
Carbohydrate (gm)	9.2

EXCHANGES:

Milk	0.5	Bread	0.5
Veg.	0.0	Meat	0.0
Fruit	0.0	Fat	1.5

Melt margarine in medium saucepan; stir in flour. Cook over medium heat 1 minute, stirring constantly. Stir in milk; heat to boiling. Boil, stirring constantly, until thickened, 1 to 2 minutes.

Reduce heat to low and stir in cheese, nutmeg, salt, and pepper; cook 1 to 2 minutes. Makes about 3 cups.

White Clam Sauce

Serves 8

¹/₈	cup olive oil
4	cloves garlic, minced
1	8-oz. bottle clam juice
	Juice of ¹/₂ lemon
¹/₂	cup dry white wine
¹/₂	tablespoon oregano
2	tablespoons parsley, minced
¹/₂	cup mushrooms, sliced
2	basil leaves, coarsely chopped
3	6-oz. cans minced clams

Nutritional Data

PER SERVING:

Calories	140
% calories from fat	31
(18 with 2 ozs. pasta)	
Fat (gm)	4.7
Sat. Fat (gm)	0.6
Cholesterol (mg)	42.7
Sodium (mg)	110
Protein (gm)	16.9
Carbohydrate (gm)	4.4

EXCHANGES:

Milk	0.0	Bread	0.5
Veg.	0.0	Meat	2.0
Fruit	0.0	Fat	0.0

Heat oil and sauté garlic to golden brown. Add clam juice, lemon juice, wine, oregano, and parsley; heat thoroughly about 20 minutes. Add mushrooms and simmer about 5 minutes. Add basil and clams to hot clam juice mixture just before draining pasta.

Garlic and Peppers Sauce

Serves 4 (½-cup servings)
Olive-oil-flavored vegetable
   cooking spray
3 cloves garlic, minced
½ cup white wine
2 red bell peppers, coarsely chopped
2 yellow bell peppers, coarsely chopped
1 green bell pepper, coarsely chopped
1 cup mushrooms, sliced
2 tablespoons parsley, chopped
6 basil leaves, coarsely torn
   Black pepper, freshly ground
   Parmesan cheese, freshly grated

Nutritional Data

PER SERVING:

Calories	55
% calories from fat	5
(7 with 2 ozs. pasta)	
Fat (gm)	0.3
Sat. Fat (gm)	0
Cholesterol (mg)	0
Sodium (mg)	5.5
Protein (gm)	1.5
Carbohydrate (gm)	8

EXCHANGES:

Milk	0.0	Bread	0.0
Veg.	2.0	Meat	0.0
Fruit	0.0	Fat	0.0

Coat small saucepan with vegetable cooking spray and place over low heat. Sauté garlic until soft. Add wine and peppers and cook until peppers are tender, about 8 minutes. Add mushrooms and continue to cook 5 minutes more. Add parsley, basil, and black pepper and cook 5 minutes more. Pour sauce over 1 lb. cooked pasta and sprinkle with cheese. Makes about 2 cups.

Thick and Hearty Mushroom Sauce

Serves 6 (½-cup servings)
1 cup white wine
1½ tablespoons cornstarch
1 lb. mushrooms, thinly sliced
¼ cup onion, diced
1 clove garlic, minced
2 cups defatted Chicken Stock (see p. 40)
1 tablespoon Italian seasoning
   Salt and black pepper, to taste

Nutritional Data

PER SERVING:

Calories	71
% calories from fat	8
Fat (gm)	0.7
Sat. Fat (gm)	0.1
Cholesterol (mg)	3.4
Sodium (mg)	9
Protein (gm)	2.9
Carbohydrate (gm)	7.1

EXCHANGES:

Milk	0.0	Bread	0.0
Veg.	1.0	Meat	0.0
Fruit	0.0	Fat	1.0

Dissolve cornstarch in wine. Combine remaining ingredients, except salt and pepper, and bring to boil. Reduce heat and simmer 3 to 4 minutes. Thicken with cornstarch and wine mixture, stirring constantly. Simmer gently another 3 to 5 minutes. Season with salt and pepper. Makes 3 cups.

Provençal Sauce

Serves 6 (¹/₄-cup servings)

6　medium tomatoes
　Olive-oil-flavored vegetable
　cooking spray
1　clove garlic, minced
1　tablespoon parsley, chopped
½　teaspoon Spike (see "About This
　Cookbook")
⅛　teaspoon black pepper, freshly ground
3　fresh basil leaves, chopped

Nutritional Data

PER SERVING:

Calories	27
% calories from fat	12
Fat (gm)	0.4
Sat. Fat (gm)	0.1
Cholesterol (mg)	0
Sodium (mg)	11.6
Protein (gm)	1.1
Carbohydrate (gm)	6

EXCHANGES:

Milk	0.0	Bread	0.0
Veg.	1.0	Meat	0.0
Fruit	0.0	Fat	0.0

Place tomatoes in boiling water 1 minute. Peel, remove seeds, and chop.

In saucepan coated with vegetable cooking spray, add garlic, tomatoes, parsley, Spike, and pepper. Cook gently 30 minutes. Add basil and cook 10 minutes more. Serve hot over chicken, veal, or on a rice side dish.

Makes about 1½ cups.

Lisbon Sauce

Serves 6 (¹/₄-cup servings)

　Olive-oil-flavored vegetable cooking
　spray
1　small onion, finely chopped
½　cup mushrooms, chopped
½　cup white wine
3　tablespoons flour
1　cup beef broth
1　tablespoon tomato puree
1　tablespoon parsley, chopped
½　teaspoon Spike (see "About This
　Cookbook")
　Black pepper, freshly ground

Nutritional Data

PER SERVING:

Calories	38
% calories from fat	4
Fat (gm)	0.2
Sat. Fat (gm)	0.1
Cholesterol (mg)	0
Sodium (mg)	143
Protein (gm)	1.2
Carbohydrate (gm)	4.9

EXCHANGES:

Milk	0.0	Bread	0.0
Veg.	1.5	Meat	0.0
Fruit	0.0	Fat	0.0

Coat saucepan with vegetable cooking spray. Add onion and mushrooms, and cook over moderate heat 3 minutes. Add wine and simmer 10 minutes until wine has reduced slightly. Stir in flour and add beef broth gradually. Stir with whisk to form smooth sauce. Stir in tomato puree and parsley. Season with Spike and pepper. Serve this sauce with fish and meat dishes. Makes 1½ cups.

Tomato Coulis

Serves 16 (½-cup servings)	Nutritional Data	
6 lbs. tomatoes (about 12 average)	**PER SERVING:**	
2 tablespoons white wine	Calories	46
2 cups yellow onion, finely chopped	% calories from fat	11
Spike (see "About This Cookbook") and	Fat (gm)	0.6
black pepper, freshly ground, to taste	Sat. Fat (gm)	0.1
8 fresh basil leaves, minced, or 1 table-	Cholesterol (mg)	0
spoon dried basil	Sodium (mg)	18
1 cup parsley, chopped	Protein (gm)	1.8
	Carbohydrate (gm)	9.9

EXCHANGES:

Milk	0.0	Bread	0.0
Veg.	2.0	Meat	0.0
Fruit	0.0	Fat	0.0

Bring large saucepan of water to boil. Drop tomatoes into boiling water one at a time 10 to 15 seconds. Remove with slotted spoon and drop into bowl of cold water. Continue until all tomatoes have been scalded, then drain them.

Peel tomatoes and cut horizontally into halves. Use melon baller to scoop out seeds and liquid inside tomatoes. Coarsely chop tomatoes and reserve.

Heat wine in large kettle. Add onion, cover, and cook over low heat until onion is tender, about 20 minutes. Stir in chopped tomatoes and bring to boil. Season with Spike and freshly ground black pepper. Reduce heat and simmer, uncovered, about 40 minutes or until coulis is somewhat reduced and thickened.

Transfer coulis to food processor fitted with steel blade or blender, and puree. Return coulis to kettle and add basil and parsley. Simmer 5 minutes more, or longer if you would like thicker puree. Makes about 2 quarts.

 # Spinach Sauce

Serves 12 (2-tablespoon servings)	Nutritional Data	
½ lb. fresh spinach, trimmed of tough stems	**PER SERVING:**	
and well washed	Calories	13
1 teaspoon olive oil	% calories from fat	29
Black pepper, to taste	Fat (gm)	0.5
⅛ teaspoon ground nutmeg	Sat. Fat (gm)	0.1
¼ teaspoon ground cardamom	Cholesterol (mg)	0.2
1 tablespoon fresh lemon juice	Sodium (mg)	22
½ cup nonfat plain yogurt at room	Protein (gm)	1.1
temperature	Carbohydrate (gm)	1.5

EXCHANGES:

Milk	0.0	Bread	0.0
Veg.	0.0	Meat	0.0
Fruit	0.0	Fat	0.0

Place wet spinach in 2-quart casserole or measure, and microwave on High 1 to 2 minutes, until wilted. Puree in food processor or blender with all remaining ingredients except yogurt.

Return to casserole and microwave on High another 1 minute, stirring. Blend in yogurt and adjust seasoning. Serve over fish, poultry, pasta, or rice or use as appetizer dip.

Lemon Herb Sauce

Serves 4

Olive-oil-flavored vegetable
    cooking spray
1   teaspoon Italian herb seasoning
    Juice of 2 lemons
½   cup plus 2 tablespoons white wine
2   cloves garlic, minced
½   cup parsley, chopped
    Black pepper, freshly ground

Nutritional Data

PER SERVING:

Calories	32
% calories from fat	2
Fat (gm)	0.1
Sat. Fat (gm)	0
Cholesterol (mg)	0
Sodium (mg)	6
Protein (gm)	0.5
Carbohydrate (gm)	3.4

EXCHANGES:

Milk	0.0	Bread	0.0
Veg.	1.5	Meat	0.0
Fruit	0.0	Fat	0.0

Coat small saucepan with vegetable cooking spray. Add all ingredients, and cook over medium heat until all are heated through, about 5 minutes. This sauce is wonderful on veal, chicken, pasta, or with vegetables.

Lemon Wine Sauce for Fish

Serves 10

1   tablespoon cornstarch
1   cup Rhine or other dry white wine
1½ tablespoons diet margarine
2   tablespoons fresh lemon juice
1   lemon, sliced

Nutritional Data

PER SERVING:

Calories	30
% calories from fat	24
Fat (gm)	0.9
Sat. Fat (gm)	0.2
Cholesterol (mg)	0
Sodium (mg)	21
Protein (gm)	0.2
Carbohydrate (gm)	2.3

EXCHANGES:

Milk	0.0	Bread	0.0
Veg.	0.0	Meat	0.0
Fruit	0.5	Fat	0.0

Make smooth paste of cornstarch and wine. Melt margarine in small saucepan. Add wine paste and cook, stirring constantly, until sauce is clear and slightly thickened. Add lemon juice and slices. Heat a few minutes longer and pour over baked, broiled, or poached fish. Makes 1¼ cups sauce.

To Freeze: Place in microwave-safe container; label and freeze up to 2 months.

To Serve: Thaw and serve cold, or reheat in microwave on High 2 to 3 minutes.

Greek Lemon Sauce

Serves 4 (½-cup servings)

2 cups defatted Chicken Stock (see p. 40)
1 clove garlic, minced
½ teaspoon dried oregano
2 tablespoons shallots, minced
Juice and zest of 1 lemon
Salt and black pepper, to taste

Combine first 4 ingredients. Bring to boil, then reduce heat and simmer 5 minutes. Add lemon juice and zest. Season with salt and pepper. Makes about 2 cups.

Nutritional Data

PER SERVING:

Calories	22
% calories from fat	19
Fat (gm)	0.6
Sat. Fat (gm)	0
Cholesterol (mg)	0
Sodium (mg)	169
Protein (gm)	2.6
Carbohydrate (gm)	3.3

EXCHANGES:

Milk	0.0	Bread	0.0
Veg.	1.0	Meat	0.0
Fruit	0.0	Fat	0.0

Avgolemono Sauce

Serves 6 (¼-cup servings)

Egg substitute equal to 3 eggs
Juice of 1 lemon
1 cup hot chicken broth

Beat egg substitute until frothy. Slowly add lemon juice, beating constantly. Add hot broth, drop by drop, and then a little more at a time, beating constantly. Makes about 1½ cups.

Nutritional Data

PER SERVING:

Calories	22
% calories from fat	10
Fat (gm)	0.2
Sat. Fat (gm)	0.1
Cholesterol (mg)	0.2
Sodium (mg)	171
Protein (gm)	3.4
Carbohydrate (gm)	1.3

EXCHANGES:

Milk	0.0	Bread	0.0
Veg.	0.0	Meat	0.5
Fruit	0.0	Fat	0.0

Aioli

Serves 8 (2-tablespoon servings)

1 cup nonfat mayonnaise
5 cloves garlic, minced
1 teaspoon Spike (see "About This Cookbook")
2 tablespoons fresh lemon juice
½ teaspoon dry mustard
White pepper, freshly ground

Place all ingredients in blender and process until smooth. Serve with fish or vegetables. Makes about 1 cup.

Nutritional Data

PER SERVING:

Calories	29
% calories from fat	2
Fat (gm)	0.1
Sat. Fat (gm)	0
Cholesterol (mg)	0
Sodium (mg)	380
Protein (gm)	0.2
Carbohydrate (gm)	7

EXCHANGES:

Milk	0.0	Bread	0.0
Veg.	1.0	Meat	0.0
Fruit	0.0	Fat	0.0

Caper Sauce

Serves 4 (2-tablespoon servings)

½	cup nonfat plain yogurt
2	tablespoons capers, rinsed and drained
2	teaspoons Dijon mustard
3	teaspoons parsley, chopped
¼	teaspoon paprika
¼	teaspoon black pepper

Combine all ingredients in 1-cup measure, and microwave on High 30 seconds to 1 minute, just until warm. Spoon over poached fish, such as salmon, or poultry. Makes about ½ cup.

Nutritional Data

PER SERVING:

Calories	29
% calories from fat	8
Fat (gm)	0.3
Sat. Fat (gm)	0.1
Cholesterol (mg)	0.5
Sodium (mg)	138
Protein (gm)	1.9
Carbohydrate (gm)	5.1

EXCHANGES:

Milk	0.0	Bread	0.0
Veg.	1.0	Meat	0.0
Fruit	0.0	Fat	0.0

Olive Salsa

Serves 6

6	medium tomatoes
4	pitted black olives, sliced
2	teaspoons parsley, chopped
2	tablespoons red onion, chopped
¼	cup fresh lemon juice
¼	cup balsamic vinegar
¼	cup white wine
1	teaspoon oregano
2	tablespoons fresh basil, coarsely chopped
	Spike (see "About This Cookbook")
	Black pepper, freshly ground

Nutritional Data

PER SERVING:

Calories	51
% calories from fat	12
Fat (gm)	0.8
Sat. Fat (gm)	0.1
Cholesterol (mg)	0
Sodium (mg)	39
Protein (gm)	1.2
Carbohydrate (gm)	9.7

EXCHANGES:

Milk	0.0	Bread	0.0
Veg.	2.0	Meat	0.0
Fruit	0.0	Fat	0.0

Chop tomatoes into ½-inch chunks. Combine with remaining ingredients except lemon juice, vinegar, and wine. Let stand 30 minutes. Pour off any liquid that has accumulated from the salsa; add lemon juice, vinegar, and wine. Adjust seasonings with Spike and pepper. This sauce can be used over shellfish, fish, chicken, or veal.

Veggie Salsa

Serves 12 (1/2-cup servings)

1 zucchini, diced
1 yellow squash, diced
1 large red onion, diced
1 red bell pepper, diced
1 green bell pepper, diced
1 large carrot, diced
3 large tomatoes, chopped
3 tablespoons red wine vinegar
1 bunch green onions, thinly sliced
1 cup low-sodium tomato juice
1 tablespoon olive oil
  Salt and black pepper, to taste

Nutritional Data

PER SERVING:

Calories	37
% calories from fat	29
Fat (gm)	1.4
Sat. Fat (gm)	0.2
Cholesterol (mg)	0
Sodium (mg)	8.3
Protein (gm)	1.1
Carbohydrate (gm)	6.3

EXCHANGES:

Milk	0.0	Bread	0.0
Veg.	1.0	Meat	0.0
Fruit	0.0	Fat	0.5

Mix ingredients and let stand at least 1 hour. Makes about 6 cups.

Harissa

Serves 10 (2 1/2-tablespoon servings)

2 cups dried hot red chili peppers, soaked and drained
6 cloves garlic, peeled
1 teaspoon coarse salt (divided)
6 tablespoons coriander seeds
4 tablespoons cumin seeds
1 tablespoon olive oil
10 tablespoons white wine (divided)

Nutritional Data

PER SERVING:

Calories	91
% calories from fat	25
Fat (gm)	2.5
Sat. Fat (gm)	0.2
Cholesterol (mg)	0
Sodium (mg)	412
Protein (gm)	1
Carbohydrate (gm)	13.2

EXCHANGES:

Milk	0.0	Bread	0.0
Veg.	3.0	Meat	0.0
Fruit	0.0	Fat	0.5

Pound garlic cloves in mortar with half of salt until smooth. Remove from mortar and reserve.

Add drained chili peppers to mortar and pound to smooth paste with remaining coarse salt. Remove and add to pounded garlic.

Combine coriander and cumin seeds in mortar and pound until powdered. Return pounded garlic and chili peppers to mortar and add olive oil and 4 tablespoons wine. Pound until smooth. Continue this process, adding in remaining wine, until sauce is smooth and well blended. It will keep indefinitely in sealed jar in refrigerator.

Use with saffron-flavored fish, soups, stews, and couscous. A good harissa should be thick, with consistency of light mayonnaise. Serve it in little side dish with very small spoon. Makes about 1 1/2 cups.

Jamaican Jerk Sauce

Serves 8 (¼-cup servings)

1 large onion
1 whole garlic bulb, peeled and blanched in boiling water
¼ cup pimiento
¼ cup pickled jalapeño
¼ cup honey
1 tablespoon Worcestershire sauce
1 teaspoon fresh thyme
1 teaspoon cinnamon
½ teaspoon nutmeg
½ teaspoon black pepper
¼ teaspoon cayenne pepper
1 teaspoon chili sauce, or Tabasco sauce
2 tablespoons olive oil

Nutritional Data

PER SERVING:

Calories	101
% calories from fat	31
Fat (gm)	3.7
Sat. Fat (gm)	0.5
Cholesterol (mg)	0
Sodium (mg)	100
Protein (gm)	1.5
Carbohydrate (gm)	17.1

EXCHANGES:

Milk	0.0	Bread	1.0
Veg.	0.0	Meat	0.0
Fruit	0.0	Fat	0.5

Puree all ingredients in food processor or blender. Makes 2 cups.

Island Rum-Lime Sauce

Serves 6 (½-cup servings)

2 cups defatted Chicken Stock (see p. 40)
¼ cup shallots, minced
2 large cloves garlic, minced
1 tablespoon cornstarch dissolved in ¼ cup water
2 tablespoons light rum
Juice of 1 lime
¼ cup parsley, minced
Salt and black pepper, to taste

Nutritional Data

PER SERVING:

Calories	37
% calories from fat	9
Fat (gm)	0.4
Sat. Fat (gm)	0.1
Cholesterol (mg)	3.4
Sodium (mg)	6.3
Protein (gm)	1.5
Carbohydrate (gm)	3.8

EXCHANGES:

Milk	0.0	Bread	0.5
Veg.	0.0	Meat	0.0
Fruit	0.0	Fat	0.0

Bring Chicken Stock, shallots, and garlic to boil. Reduce heat and simmer 5 minutes. Thicken with cornstarch and water mixture. Add rum and boil 1 minute. Add lime juice and remove from heat. Season with parsley, salt, and pepper. Makes 3 cups.

Light Thai Peanut Sauce

Serves 8 (¼-cup servings)

1 cup defatted Chicken Stock (see p. 40)
3 tablespoons chunky-style, low-fat, low-sodium peanut butter
1 clove garlic
1 cup carrot, shredded
2 tablespoons rice wine vinegar, or other white vinegar
2 tablespoons sugar
1 tablespoon hot pepper flakes

Nutritional Data

PER SERVING:

Calories	61
% calories from fat	35
Fat (gm)	2.5
Sat. Fat (gm)	0.5
Cholesterol (mg)	1.3
Sodium (mg)	10
Protein (gm)	2.4
Carbohydrate (gm)	7.8

EXCHANGES:

Milk	0.0	Bread	0.5
Veg.	0.0	Meat	0.0
Fruit	0.0	Fat	0.5

Combine all ingredients and heat thoroughly, stirring to completely incorporate peanut butter. Do not boil. Makes 2 cups.

Sweet-and-Sour Sauce

Serves 8 (2-tablespoon servings)

1 tablespoon cornstarch
⅓ cup chicken broth
⅓ cup red wine vinegar
2 tablespoons frozen concentrated pineapple juice
2 tablespoons pimiento, chopped
1 tablespoon soy sauce
¼ teaspoon garlic powder
¼ teaspoon ground ginger
2 packets Equal® (see "About This Cookbook")

Nutritional Data

PER SERVING:

Calories	27
% calories from fat	5
Fat (gm)	0.2
Sat. Fat (gm)	0
Cholesterol (mg)	0
Sodium (mg)	166
Protein (gm)	0.8
Carbohydrate (gm)	6.1

EXCHANGES:

Milk	0.0	Bread	0.5
Veg.	0.0	Meat	0.0
Fruit	0.0	Fat	0.0

Combine cornstarch and chicken broth in small saucepan. Stir in all remaining ingredients except Equal®. Cook over medium heat, stirring, until thickened and bubbly. Remove from heat and stir in Equal®. Serve warm. Makes 1 cup.

Spicy Barbecue Sauce

Serves 18 (2-tablespoon servings)

1½	tablespoons diet margarine
¾	cup onion, chopped
1½	cups dietetic ketchup
1	cup plus 2 tablespoons vinegar
¾	cup diet pancake syrup
¾	cup water
3	beef bouillon cubes
1½	tablespoons Worcestershire sauce
2¼	teaspoons salt
¼	teaspoon black pepper
3	drops Tabasco sauce
1	packet Equal® (see "About This Cookbook")

Nutritional Data

PER SERVING:

Calories	37
% calories from fat	13
Fat (gm)	0.6
Sat. Fat (gm)	0.1
Cholesterol (mg)	0
Sodium (mg)	611
Protein (gm)	0.5
Carbohydrate (gm)	8.6

EXCHANGES:

Milk	0.0	Bread	0.0
Veg.	1.5	Meat	0.0
Fruit	0.0	Fat	0.0

Melt margarine in saucepan. Add onion and sauté until lightly browned. Then add remaining ingredients except Equal®. Boil slowly 15 minutes, or until sauce is glossy and thick. Remove from heat and stir in Equal®. Makes 2¼ cups.

❋ Zesty Cocktail Sauce

Serves 8 (2-tablespoon servings)

¾	cup low-sodium dietetic ketchup
2	tablespoons horseradish, to taste
2	tablespoons fresh lemon juice
¼	cup celery, finely chopped
1	tablespoon fresh basil, minced, or 2 teaspoons dried and crumbled
1	tablespoon parsley, minced
1	teaspoon Worcestershire sauce
	Dash Tabasco

Nutritional Data

PER SERVING:

Calories	5
% calories from fat	2
Fat (gm)	0
Sat. Fat (gm)	0
Cholesterol (mg)	0
Sodium (mg)	61
Protein (gm)	0.1
Carbohydrate (gm)	1.2

EXCHANGES:

Milk	0.0	Bread	0.0
Veg.	0.0	Meat	0.0
Fruit	0.0	Fat	0.0

Combine all ingredients in medium bowl. Mix well. Makes about 1 cup.

To Freeze: Place in microwave-safe container; label and freeze up to 2 months.

To Serve: Thaw and serve cold, or reheat in microwave oven on High 2 to 3 minutes.

Light Tartar Sauce

Serves 12 (¹/₄-cup servings)

2 cups nonfat mayonnaise
¹/₄ cup onion, diced
¹/₄ cup capers, chopped
¹/₄ cup low-salt pickle, chopped
2 tablespoons parsley, minced
1 tablespoon fresh lemon juice
1 teaspoon sugar
   Dash chili sauce, or Tabasco

Combine ingredients and let refrigerate at least 1 hour before using. Makes 3 cups.

Nutritional Data

PER SERVING:

Calories	42
% calories from fat	1
Fat (gm)	0
Sat. Fat (gm)	0
Cholesterol (mg)	0
Sodium (mg)	562
Protein (gm)	0.1
Carbohydrate (gm)	10.6

EXCHANGES:

Milk	0.0	Bread	0.5
Veg.	0.0	Meat	0.0
Fruit	0.0	Fat	0.0

Cranberry Sauce for Fowl

Serves 8 (2-tablespoon servings)

1 16-oz. package cranberries
3 ripe pears, peeled
1 cup sugar
2 splashes white wine
¹/₂ cup cranberry juice

Combine all ingredients in blender and mix until smooth. Sauce should be gravy texture. Serve with all your holiday turkeys and poultry. Makes 1 cup.

Nutritional Data

PER SERVING:

Calories	173
% calories from fat	2
Fat (gm)	0.4
Sat. Fat (gm)	0
Cholesterol (mg)	0
Sodium (mg)	2
Protein (gm)	0.5
Carbohydrate (gm)	43.9

EXCHANGES:

Milk	0.0	Bread	0.0
Veg.	0.0	Meat	0.0
Fruit	3.0	Fat	0.0

Cranberry and Orange Sauce

Serves 16 (2-tablespoon servings)

1 12-oz. package fresh cranberries
¹/₄ cup frozen orange juice concentrate
1 orange
2 tablespoons walnuts, chopped

Wash cranberries and discard any debris. Combine in 1-quart casserole or measure with orange juice. Cover with vented plastic wrap, and microwave on High 5 minutes, until soft. Cut orange into quarters, then eighths.

Nutritional Data

PER SERVING:

Calories	27
% calories from fat	19
Fat (gm)	0.6
Sat. Fat (gm)	0
Cholesterol (mg)	0
Sodium (mg)	0
Protein (gm)	0.5
Carbohydrate (gm)	5.5

EXCHANGES:

Milk	0.0	Bread	0.0
Veg.	0.0	Meat	0.0
Fruit	0.5	Fat	0.0

Let cranberries cool a bit before turning half of them into food processor with half of orange sections. Puree, and pour into serving bowl. Process remaining cranberries and oranges and add to serving bowl. Chill before serving, and garnish with chopped walnuts. Makes 2 cups.

Chapter Fourteen

DESSERT SAUCES

Raspberry Sauce

Serves 8 (¼-cup servings)

1   12-oz. package frozen raspberries
½   cup sugar
    Sugar Twin brown sugar substitute equal
    to ½ cup brown sugar
    Juice and zest of 1 lemon
2   tablespoons fruit-flavored brandy

Puree raspberries and strain out seeds through fine strainer or cheesecloth. Add sugar, sugar substitute, lemon juice, zest, and brandy. Refrigerate at least 1 hour before serving. Makes 2 cups.

Nutritional Data

PER SERVING:

Calories	89
% calories from fat	2
Fat (gm)	0.2
Sat. Fat (gm)	0
Cholesterol (mg)	0
Sodium (mg)	3.6
Protein (gm)	0.4
Carbohydrate (gm)	20.7

EXCHANGES:

Milk	0.0	Bread	0.0
Veg.	0.0	Meat	0.0
Fruit	1.5	Fat	0.0

Summer Raspberry Coulis

Serves 8 (2-tablespoon servings)

1   pint fresh or frozen, thawed, raspberries
¼   cup sugar
1   teaspoon fresh lemon juice

In blender or food processor, combine raspberries, sugar, and lemon juice. Puree until smooth. Strain puree; discard seeds. Makes 1 cup.

Nutritional Data

PER SERVING:

Calories	39
% calories from fat	4
Fat (gm)	0.2
Sat. Fat (gm)	0
Cholesterol (mg)	0
Sodium (mg)	0.1
Protein (gm)	0.3
Carbohydrate (gm)	9.9

EXCHANGES:

Milk	0.0	Bread	0.0
Veg.	0.0	Meat	0.0
Fruit	0.5	Fat	0.0

Apricot Sauce

Serves 8 (¼-cup servings)

1½   cups fruit-only apricot jam
½   cup water
2   tablespoons sugar (optional)
1   tablespoon apricot brandy

In saucepan, heat apricot jam and gradually stir in water and sugar. Heat to boiling point, then cook over low heat 5 to 10 minutes, stirring constantly. Strain. Stir in brandy. Serve hot or cold; excellent over puddings. Makes 2 cups.

Nutritional Data

PER SERVING:

Calories	169
% calories from fat	0
Fat (gm)	0.1
Sat. Fat (gm)	0
Cholesterol (mg)	0
Sodium (mg)	7.4
Protein (gm)	0.4
Carbohydrate (gm)	42.5

EXCHANGES:

Milk	0.0	Bread	0.0
Veg.	0.0	Meat	0.0
Fruit	3.0	Fat	0.0

Store in covered jar in cold place. Before covering, if desired, top with 1 or 2 tablespoons apricot brandy.

Pear Sauce

Serves 10 (¼-cup servings)

4	cups pears (about 1½ lbs.), peeled and cubed
2	tablespoons water
3	tablespoons brown sugar
⅛	teaspoon ground crystallized ginger

Combine pears and water in medium saucepan; cook, covered, over low heat 15 minutes or until tender. Stir in brown sugar and ginger; partially mash until chunky. Cook over low heat 5 minutes, stirring frequently. Serve warm or chilled.

Nutritional Data

PER SERVING:

Calories	56
% calories from fat	4
Fat (gm)	0.3
Sat. Fat (gm)	0
Cholesterol (mg)	0
Sodium (mg)	2
Protein (gm)	0.3
Carbohydrate (gm)	14.5

EXCHANGES:

Milk	0.0	Bread	0.0
Veg.	0.0	Meat	0.0
Fruit	1.0	Fat	0.0

You can store pear sauce in refrigerator in an airtight container up to 1 week. Makes 2½ cups.

Brown Sugar Banana Sauce

Serves 4 (½-cup servings)

½	cup brown sugar
	Sugar Twin brown sugar substitute equal to ½ cup brown sugar
½	cup water
2	large bananas, sliced
1	tablespoon cinnamon
¼	cup rum

Combine brown sugar, sugar substitute, and water. Bring to boil to make thick syrup. Add bananas, cinnamon, and rum. Bring to boil again. Serve warm. Makes 2 cups.

Nutritional Data

PER SERVING:

Calories	205
% calories from fat	1
Fat (gm)	0.3
Sat. Fat (gm)	0.1
Cholesterol (mg)	0
Sodium (mg)	18
Protein (gm)	0.7
Carbohydrate (gm)	44.5

EXCHANGES:

Milk	0.0	Bread	0.0
Veg.	0.0	Meat	0.0
Fruit	3.5	Fat	0.0

Brandied Cherry Sauce

Serves 8 (2-tablespoon servings)

2	tablespoons sugar	
1	teaspoon cornstarch	
1/8	teaspoon ground allspice	
1	cup fresh or frozen, thawed, pitted dark sweet cherries	
1/2	cup water	
1	tablespoon brandy, or 1/4 to 1/2 teaspoon brandy extract	
1	tablespoon fresh lemon juice	

Nutritional Data

PER SERVING:

Calories	28
% calories from fat	2
Fat (gm)	0.1
Sat. Fat (gm)	0
Cholesterol (mg)	0
Sodium (mg)	1
Protein (gm)	0.2
Carbohydrate (gm)	6

EXCHANGES:

Milk	0.0	Bread	0.0
Veg.	0.0	Meat	0.0
Fruit	0.5	Fat	0.0

Mix sugar, cornstarch, and allspice in medium skillet or chafing dish. Stir in cherries, water, brandy, and lemon juice. Cook over medium heat until mixture boils and thickens, stirring constantly; boil 1 minute, stirring constantly. Serve warm. Makes about 1 cup.

Orange Sauce

Serves 16 (2-tablespoon servings)

3	tablespoons cornstarch	
	Dash salt	
1 1/3	cups hot water	
3	packets Equal® (see "About This Cookbook")	
4	teaspoons diet margarine	
1/2	cup quick-frozen concentrated orange juice	

Nutritional Data

PER SERVING:

Calories	25
% calories from fat	18
Fat (gm)	0.5
Sat. Fat (gm)	0.1
Cholesterol (mg)	0
Sodium (mg)	13
Protein (gm)	0
Carbohydrate (gm)	5.2

EXCHANGES:

Milk	0.0	Bread	0.0
Veg.	0.0	Meat	0.0
Fruit	0.5	Fat	0.0

Combine cornstarch and salt in saucepan. Add hot water gradually, stirring constantly. Cook and stir over medium heat until thick and somewhat clear, about 5 minutes. Remove from heat and stir in Equal® and margarine. Mix in concentrated orange juice. Blend until smooth. Makes about 2 cups.

Orange Yogurt Sauce

Serves 6

1 cup plain yogurt
1 teaspoon orange rind, grated
2 tablespoons brown sugar, or 2 packets Equal® (see "About This Cookbook")
½ teaspoon orange extract

Mix all ingredients together. This is wonderful over fresh fruit. Makes about 1 cup.

Nutritional Data

PER SERVING:

Calories	43
% calories from fat	12
Fat (gm)	0.6
Sat. Fat (gm)	0.4
Cholesterol (mg)	2.3
Sodium (mg)	28
Protein (gm)	2
Carbohydrate (gm)	7.3

EXCHANGES:

Milk	0.5	Bread	0.0
Veg.	0.0	Meat	0.0
Fruit	0.0	Fat	0.0

Strawberry Sauce

Serves 10 (2-tablespoon servings)

2 cups fresh strawberries (frozen can be used, but thaw first)
2 teaspoons cornstarch
4 packets Equal® (see "About This Cookbook")

Place strawberries in blender and mix until berries are mashed. Place mashed berries in small saucepan and add cornstarch. Cook over medium heat until mixture boils, stirring constantly. Remove from heat and stir in Equal®. Refrigerate sauce until well chilled. Makes 1¼ cups.

Nutritional Data

PER SERVING:

Calories	13
% calories from fat	7
Fat (gm)	0.1
Sat. Fat (gm)	0
Cholesterol (mg)	0
Sodium (mg)	0
Protein (gm)	0.2
Carbohydrate (gm)	3

EXCHANGES:

Milk	0.0	Bread	0.0
Veg.	0.0	Meat	0.0
Fruit	0.0	Fat	0.0

Note: Substitute peaches, pineapple, cherries, blueberries, or raspberries, for strawberries, if you wish.

Strawberry-Pineapple Sauce

Serves 10 (3-tablespoon servings)

1 8-oz. jar fruit-only strawberry jam
1 8-oz. jar fruit-only pineapple jam
¼ cup sweet wine or brandy

Combine jams and thin to sauce consistency with wine or brandy. This sauce is especially good over frozen

Nutritional Data

PER SERVING:

Calories	128
% calories from fat	0
Fat (gm)	0
Sat. Fat (gm)	0
Cholesterol (mg)	0
Sodium (mg)	6
Protein (gm)	0.3
Carbohydrate (gm)	31.8

vanilla or strawberry yogurt or over pineapple sherbet. Makes about 2 cups.

EXCHANGES:

Milk	0.0	Bread	0.0
Veg.	0.0	Meat	0.0
Fruit	2.0	Fat	0.0

Strawberry Topping

Serves 10 (2-tablespoon servings)

3 cups unsweetened strawberries, fresh or frozen

½ envelope (1½ teaspoons) unflavored gelatin

1½ teaspoons fresh lemon juice

4 packets Equal® (see "About This Cookbook")

Nutritional Data

PER SERVING:

Calories	17
% calories from fat	8
Fat (gm)	0.2
Sat. Fat (gm)	0
Cholesterol (mg)	0
Sodium (mg)	1
Protein (gm)	0.7
Carbohydrate (gm)	3.6

EXCHANGES:

Milk	0.0	Bread	0.0
Veg.	0.0	Meat	0.0
Fruit	0.0	Fat	0.0

Put strawberries in saucepan. Cook, covered, over low heat without water about 10 minutes. Remove lid and bring fruit to boiling point. Boil 1 minute and remove from heat.

Soften gelatin in lemon juice. Pour some of hot juice from strawberries into gelatin. Stir until gelatin is completely dissolved. Add Equal® and dissolved gelatin to strawberries. Cool, then refrigerate.

You can adapt this recipe for any fresh fruit topping, especially berries. Leftovers are great on crepes and puddings. Makes 1¼ cups.

Kiwi Topping

Serves 4 (¼-cup servings)

½ cup unsweetened apple juice

2 tablespoons melon-flavored liqueur

1 teaspoon cornstarch

⅔ cup peeled, sliced kiwi fruit

2 packets Equal® (see "About This Cookbook")

Nutritional Data

PER SERVING:

Calories	67
% calories from fat	3
Fat (gm)	0.2
Sat. Fat (gm)	0
Cholesterol (mg)	0
Sodium (mg)	3
Protein (gm)	0.4
Carbohydrate (gm)	13.3

EXCHANGES:

Milk	0.0	Bread	0.0
Veg.	0.0	Meat	0.0
Fruit	1.0	Fat	0.0

Combine first 3 ingredients in small, nonaluminum saucepan; stir well. Bring to boil over medium heat, stirring constantly; cook 1 minute, stirring constantly.

Remove from heat; stir in kiwi fruit. Stir in Equal®. Cool completely. Serve over frozen, low-fat yogurt or angel food cake. Makes 1 cup.

Sangria Sundae Sauce

Serves 8 (4-tablespoon servings)

1 8¼-oz. can pineapple chunks; or fresh pineapple
1 tablespoon cornstarch
½ cup dry red wine
2 tablespoons frozen lemonade concentrate
2 oranges, peeled and sectioned
2 fresh peaches, peeled and sliced

Nutritional Data

PER SERVING:

Calories	55
% calories from fat	1
Fat (gm)	0.1
Sat. Fat (gm)	0
Cholesterol (mg)	0
Sodium (mg)	10
Protein (gm)	0.6
Carbohydrate (gm)	11.7

EXCHANGES:

Milk	0.0	Bread	0.0
Veg.	0.0	Meat	0.0
Fruit	1.0	Fat	0.0

Drain pineapple, reserving syrup. In small saucepan, stir reserved syrup into cornstarch. Add wine and lemonade concentrate. Cook and stir over medium heat until mixture thickens and bubbles. Stir in pineapple chunks, orange sections, and peach slices. Serve warm or cold over angel food cake, frozen yogurt, or ice milk. Makes 2 cups.

Butter Pecan Sauce

Serves 14 (2-tablespoon servings)

1 cup diet pancake syrup
1 teaspoon butter-flavor extract
Dash salt
½ cup skim milk
¼ cup chopped pecans

Nutritional Data

PER SERVING:

Calories	43
% calories from fat	26
Fat (gm)	1.3
Sat. Fat (gm)	0.1
Cholesterol (mg)	0.1
Sodium (mg)	37
Protein (gm)	0.4
Carbohydrate (gm)	8

EXCHANGES:

Milk	0.0	Bread	0.0
Veg.	0.0	Meat	0.0
Fruit	0.5	Fat	0.5

Boil syrup until small amount forms soft ball in cold water (or to temperature of 236 degrees). Remove from heat and add butter extract and salt. Stir well and cool. Add milk and pecans. Makes 1¾ cups.

Vanilla Sauce

Serves 6 (¼-cup servings)

1 egg
3 tablespoons flour
¼ teaspoon salt
1¼ cups skim milk
10 packets Equal® (see "About This Cookbook")
1 teaspoon vanilla extract

Nutritional Data

PER SERVING:

Calories	48
% calories from fat	19
Fat (gm)	1
Sat. Fat (gm)	0.3
Cholesterol (mg)	36
Sodium (mg)	126
Protein (gm)	3.2
Carbohydrate (gm)	6

Beat egg lightly and set aside. Combine flour and salt in small saucepan. Gradually add milk, stirring well. Cook and stir over medium heat until mixture boils. Boil 1 minute.

Blend small amount of hot mixture into beaten egg; then add egg mixture to saucepan. Stir constantly.

Remove from heat; stir in Equal® and vanilla. Cool and refrigerate. Makes 1½ cups.

EXCHANGES:			
Milk	0.5	Bread	0.0
Veg.	0.0	Meat	0.0
Fruit	0.0	Fat	0.0

Vanilla "Cream"

Serves 20 (¼-cup servings)

- 4 tablespoons cornstarch
- 4 cups skim milk
- ½ cup sugar
- 1 vanilla bean
  Egg substitute equal to 4 eggs

Nutritional Data

PER SERVING:

Calories	48
% calories from fat	2
Fat (gm)	0.1
Sat. Fat (gm)	0.1
Cholesterol (mg)	0.8
Sodium (mg)	42
Protein (gm)	2.7
Carbohydrate (gm)	9

EXCHANGES:			
Milk	0.0	Bread	0.5
Veg.	0.0	Meat	0.0
Fruit	0.0	Fat	0.0

Place cornstarch in 1-quart saucepan. Whisk in a little milk to dissolve cornstarch. Whisk in remaining milk and sugar. Add vanilla bean. Cook over medium heat, stirring constantly, 5 to 10 minutes or until mixture boils and thickens.

Remove from heat, and whisk in egg substitute. Return to heat, and cook, stirring constantly, 5 minutes. When custard is thick enough to coat spoon, strain it through fine sieve into large bowl. Let cool before serving.

This thick sauce is suitable for baked or steamed pudding and for baked or poached fruit. Makes about 5 cups.

 # Chocolate Sauce I

Serves 4 (2-tablespoon servings)

- 2 tablespoons sugar
- 2 tablespoons unsweetened cocoa
- 1 teaspoon cornstarch
- ½ cup water
- ½ teaspoon vanilla extract

Nutritional Data

PER SERVING:

Calories	34
% calories from fat	6
Fat (gm)	0.3
Sat. Fat (gm)	0.1
Cholesterol (mg)	0
Sodium (mg)	2
Protein (gm)	0.5
Carbohydrate (gm)	8.6

EXCHANGES:			
Milk	0.0	Bread	0.5
Veg.	0.0	Meat	0.0
Fruit	0.0	Fat	0.0

Combine all ingredients in small saucepan; bring to boil over medium heat, stirring constantly. Boil mixture 1 minute, stirring constantly. Remove from heat and let sauce cool. Makes ½ cup sauce.

To Freeze: Place in microwave-safe container; label and freeze up to 2 months.

To Serve: Thaw and serve cold, or reheat in microwave on High 2 to 3 minutes.

 # Chocolate Sauce II

Serves 4 (2-tablespoon servings)	Nutritional Data	
1 teaspoon cornstarch	**PER SERVING:**	
½ cup water	Calories	58
2 tablespoons unsweetened cocoa	% calories from fat	4
3 tablespoons honey	Fat (gm)	0.3
½ teaspoon vanilla extract	Sat. Fat (gm)	0.1
	Cholesterol (mg)	0
Combine cornstarch and water in	Sodium (mg)	2
small saucepan; add remaining ingredi-	Protein (gm)	0.5
ents, stirring until smooth. Cook mix-	Carbohydrate (gm)	15.1

Combine cornstarch and water in small saucepan; add remaining ingredients, stirring until smooth. Cook mixture over medium heat, until it begins to boil, about 1 minute, stirring constantly. Cover and chill. Makes ½ cup sauce.

EXCHANGES:

Milk	0.0	Bread	0.0
Veg.	0.0	Meat	0.0
Fruit	1.0	Fat	0.0

To Freeze: Place in microwave-safe container; label and freeze up to 2 months.

To Serve: Thaw and serve cold, or reheat in microwave on High 2 to 3 minutes.

Chocolate Sauce III

Serves 6 (2-tablespoon servings)	Nutritional Data	
⅓ cup Dutch process cocoa	**PER SERVING:**	
¼ cup firmly packed brown sugar	Calories	59
½ cup nonfat buttermilk	% calories from fat	8
2 teaspoons crème de cacao	Fat (gm)	0.6
	Sat. Fat (gm)	0.2
	Cholesterol (mg)	0
	Sodium (mg)	28
	Protein (gm)	1.6
	Carbohydrate (gm)	13.4

Combine cocoa and sugar in small saucepan. Gradually add buttermilk, stirring well. Place over medium heat and cook until sugar dissolves. Stir in liqueur; remove from heat. Makes ¾ cup sauce.

EXCHANGES:

Milk	0.0	Bread	1.0
Veg.	0.0	Meat	0.0
Fruit	0.0	Fat	0.0

To Freeze: Place in microwave-safe container; label and freeze up to 2 months.

To Serve: Thaw and serve cold, or reheat in microwave on High 2 to 3 minutes.

Hot Fudge Sauce

Serves 8 (2-tablespoon servings)

- ¾ cup sugar
- ½ cup Dutch cocoa
- 1 5-oz. can evaporated skim milk
- ⅓ cup light corn syrup
- ⅓ cup margarine
- 1 teaspoon vanilla extract

Combine sugar and cocoa in small saucepan; blend in evaporated skim milk and corn syrup. Cook over medium heat, stirring constantly, until mixture boils; boil and stir 1 minute. Remove from heat; stir in margarine and vanilla. Serve warm. Makes 1 cup.

Nutritional Data

PER SERVING:

Calories	208
% calories from fat	33
Fat (gm)	8.1
Sat. Fat (gm)	1.6
Cholesterol (mg)	1
Sodium (mg)	124
Protein (gm)	2.6
Carbohydrate (gm)	34.3

EXCHANGES:

Milk	0.0	Bread	2.0
Veg.	0.0	Meat	0.0
Fruit	0.0	Fat	1.5

Coffee Sauce

Serves 6 (4-tablespoon servings)

Egg substitute equal to 2 eggs
- ½ cup strong boiling coffee
- ¼ cup sugar
- ½ cup evaporated skim milk

Beat egg substitute. Slowly beat in coffee and add sugar. Cook over but not in boiling water, and stir sauce in top of double boiler with spoon. Chill. Shortly before serving, fold in evaporated skim milk. Makes about 1½ cups.

Nutritional Data

PER SERVING:

Calories	58
% calories from fat	1
Fat (gm)	0
Sat. Fat (gm)	0
Cholesterol (mg)	0
Sodium (mg)	53
Protein (gm)	3.3
Carbohydrate (gm)	11.2

EXCHANGES:

Milk	0.0	Bread	1.0
Veg.	0.0	Meat	0.0
Fruit	0.0	Fat	0.0

Bourbon Sauce

Serves 6 (4-tablespoon servings)

- 1 teaspoon cornstarch
- 1 cup milk
- ½ teaspoon vanilla extract
- 3 ozs. egg substitute
- 2 tablespoons bourbon whiskey
- 3 packets Equal® (see "About This Cookbook")

Dissolve cornstarch in 2 tablespoons milk. Scald remaining milk and vanilla in heavy, small saucepan. Whisk cornstarch mixture into milk. Place egg

Nutritional Data

PER SERVING:

Calories	42
% calories from fat	17
Fat (gm)	0.8
Sat. Fat (gm)	0.5
Cholesterol (mg)	3
Sodium (mg)	41
Protein (gm)	2.6
Carbohydrate (gm)	3.2

EXCHANGES:

Milk	0.0	Bread	0.0
Veg.	0.0	Meat	0.5
Fruit	0.0	Fat	0.0

substitute in bowl and whisk in milk mixture. Whisk everything back into saucepan, and stir over medium heat until sauce thickens enough to coat back of spoon. *Do not boil.*

Remove from heat. Stir in bourbon and Equal®. Makes about 1½ cups.

Custard Sauce

Serves 12 (¼-cup servings)

3 eggs
8 packets Equal® (see "About This Cookbook")
2½ cups skim milk
1 teaspoon vanilla extract

Nutritional Data	
PER SERVING:	
Calories	41
% calories from fat	31
Fat (gm)	1.3
Sat. Fat (gm)	0.4
Cholesterol (mg)	54
Sodium (mg)	42
Protein (gm)	3.3
Carbohydrate (gm)	3.4

EXCHANGES:			
Milk	0.5	Bread	0.0
Veg.	0.0	Meat	0.0
Fruit	0.0	Fat	0.0

Beat eggs briefly. Put eggs in top of double boiler. Put hot water in bottom of double boiler, but do not let top pan touch water. Add milk slowly, stirring constantly, and cook over medium heat until mixture coats metal spoon. Water in double boiler should not boil.

Remove top of double boiler from heat, and stir in vanilla and Equal® into custard. Place top of double boiler in cold water until custard cools. Cover and chill several hours. Makes 3 cups.

Custard sauce is excellent over miniature cream puffs or sponge cake.

Eggnog Sauce

Serves 8 (4-tablespoon servings)

1 tablespoon flour
Dash salt
1 egg, separated
1¼ cups skim milk
2 packets Equal® (see "About This Cookbook")
⅛ teaspoon nutmeg
1 cap full rum extract
1 packet Equal®

Nutritional Data	
PER SERVING:	
Calories	30
% calories from fat	23
Fat (gm)	0.7
Sat. Fat (gm)	0.2
Cholesterol (mg)	27
Sodium (mg)	28
Protein (gm)	2.2
Carbohydrate (gm)	3.2

EXCHANGES:			
Milk	0.5	Bread	0.0
Veg.	0.0	Meat	0.0
Fruit	0.0	Fat	0.0

Combine flour and salt in top of double boiler. Add egg yolk and beat well. Gradually add milk, stirring constantly. Cook over rapidly boiling water 5 minutes, stirring occasionally.

Remove from heat and add 2 packets Equal® and nutmeg. Blend, then add rum extract. Blend again. Cool.

Beat egg white until foamy. Add remaining packet of Equal® to egg white, beating constantly until mixture will stand in soft peaks. Fold in egg yolk mixture. Makes 2 cups.

Classic Light Fruit Sauce

Serves 8 (2-tablespoon servings)

3   cups fresh berries; or 1¼-1½ lbs. other fruit such as peaches and pears

7   packets Equal® (see "About This Cookbook")

1   teaspoon fresh lemon or orange juice; or 1 to 2 teaspoons flavored brandy or liqueur

Nutritional Data	
PER SERVING:	
Calories	36
% calories from fat	5
Fat (gm)	0.2
Sat. Fat (gm)	0
Cholesterol (mg)	0
Sodium (mg)	3.3
Protein (gm)	0.4
Carbohydrate (gm)	8.8

EXCHANGES:			
Milk	0.0	Bread	0.0
Veg.	0.0	Meat	0.0
Fruit	0.5	Fat	0.0

Puree fruit in processor or blender. Strain sauce through fine sieve, pressing to extract as much liquid as possible. Whisk in 7 packets of Equal®. Cover and refrigerate at least 30 minutes. (Can be prepared 1 day ahead.) Stir in juice, brandy, or liqueur to taste, just before serving, if desired. Makes about 1 cup.

Lemon Rum Sauce

Serves 4 (2-tablespoon servings)

1   tablespoon lemon rind

2   tablespoons fresh lemon juice

2   tablespoons granulated sugar

3   tablespoons fruit-only orange marmalade

¼   cup water

2   tablespoons rum, or 2 teaspoons rum extract

    Orange peel strips for garnish

Nutritional Data	
PER SERVING:	
Calories	82
% calories from fat	0
Fat (gm)	0
Sat. Fat (gm)	0
Cholesterol (mg)	0
Sodium (mg)	2
Protein (gm)	0.1
Carbohydrate (gm)	17.7

EXCHANGES:			
Milk	0.0	Bread	0.0
Veg.	0.0	Meat	0.0
Fruit	1.5	Fat	0.0

In saucepan, mix together lemon rind, lemon juice, sugar, marmalade, and water and bring mixture to boil. Boil 1 minute. Remove from heat, add rum, and transfer to serving dish. Garnish with orange peel. Makes about ½ cup.

❄ *Rum Raisin Sauce*

Serves 5 (2-tablespoon servings)

3/4 cup evaporated skim milk
1 tablespoon sugar
1/2 teaspoon cornstarch
1/4 cup raisins
1/2 teaspoon vanilla extract
1/2 teaspoon rum extract

Combine first 3 ingredients in small saucepan and place over medium heat; cook 10 minutes or until thickened, stirring frequently. Cook 1 minute more, then stir in raisins and vanilla. Remove from heat and stir in rum extract. Serve warm. Makes 1/2 cup plus 2 tablespoons.

To Freeze: Place in microwave-safe container; label and freeze up to 2 months.

To Serve: Thaw and serve cold, or reheat in microwave on High 2 to 3 minutes.

Nutritional Data

PER SERVING:

Calories	65
% calories from fat	1
Fat (gm)	0.1
Sat. Fat (gm)	0.1
Cholesterol (mg)	1
Sodium (mg)	45
Protein (gm)	3.1
Carbohydrate (gm)	13.1

EXCHANGES:

Milk	0.5	Bread	0.0
Veg.	0.0	Meat	0.0
Fruit	0.5	Fat	0.0

Yogurt Sour Cream

Serves 16 (1-tablespoon servings)

2 cups nonfat plain yogurt
Flavors as desired (see below; not included in Nutritional Data)

Place yogurt in cheesecloth or coffee-filter-lined sieve, and let drip over bowl in refrigerator 4 to 6 hours or overnight, until yogurt has consistency of thick sour cream. Makes 1 cup.

Flavored Yogurt Sour Cream: For a sweet flavor, add cinnamon, vanilla extract, or frozen orange juice concentrate. For savory tastes, add herbs such as dill, tarragon, parsley, oregano, or caraway before placing yogurt in sieve.

Nutritional Data

PER SERVING:

Calories	16
% calories from fat	3
Fat (gm)	0.1
Sat. Fat (gm)	0
Cholesterol (mg)	0
Sodium (mg)	22
Protein (gm)	1.6
Carbohydrate (gm)	2.2

EXCHANGES:

Milk	0.0	Bread	0.0
Veg.	0.0	Meat	0.0
Fruit	0.0	Fat	0.0

Chapter Fifteen

CAKES & COOKIES

Chocolate Cake

Serves 12

2   cups Basic Chocolate Baking Mix
    (recipe follows)
    Egg substitute equal to 2 eggs
½   cup light mayonnaise
½   cup skim milk

Preheat oven to 350 degrees. Mix all ingredients in bowl. Pour into greased 9-inch-round cake pan. Bake 25 minutes.

Frost with Mocha Minute Frosting (recipe follows)

Nutritional Data

PER SERVING:

Calories	208
% calories from fat	21
Fat (gm)	5.2
Sat. Fat (gm)	0.8
Cholesterol (mg)	3.7
Sodium (mg)	90
Protein (gm)	3
Carbohydrate (gm)	40.8

EXCHANGES:

Milk	0.0	Bread	2.5
Veg.	0.0	Meat	0.0
Fruit	0.0	Fat	0.5

Mocha Minute Frosting

3   tablespoons cocoa
1   cup granulated sugar
⅓   cup evaporated skim milk
¼   cup diet margarine
1   teaspoon instant coffee granules
1   teaspoon mocha extract

Mix all ingredients except mocha extract. Bring to boil and simmer 1 minute. Remove from heat, add mocha extract, and beat until thick enough to spread.

Basic Chocolate Baking Mix

3   cups sugar
2   cups unsifted all-purpose flour
2   cups unsweetened cocoa powder
1½   teaspoons baking powder

Combine all ingredients in zip-close bag. Shake thoroughly to mix. Store in bag or canister with tight-fitting lid. Makes 7 cups.

To Store: Place in air-tight container, and store up to 1 year.

Nutritional Data

PER CUP:

Calories	511
% calories from fat	4
Fat (gm)	2.7
Sat. Fat (gm)	0.6
Cholesterol (mg)	0
Sodium (mg)	89
Protein (gm)	8.4
Carbohydrate (gm)	127.1

EXCHANGES:

Milk	0.0	Bread	7.0
Veg.	0.0	Meat	0.0
Fruit	0.0	Fat	0.0

Chocolate Cupcakes

Serves 6

1 cup Basic Chocolate Baking Mix (see preceding recipe)
2 egg whites
¼ cup light mayonnaise
¼ cup skim milk

Preheat oven to 350 degrees. Mix all ingredients in bowl. Bake 18 to 20 minutes in paper-lined, 6-muffin pan.

Nutritional Data

PER SERVING:

Calories	121
% calories from fat	22
Fat (gm)	3.1
Sat. Fat (gm)	0.4
Cholesterol (mg)	3.5
Sodium (mg)	48
Protein (gm)	2.9
Carbohydrate (gm)	22.5

EXCHANGES:

Milk	0.0	Bread	1.5
Veg.	0.0	Meat	0.0
Fruit	0.0	Fat	0.5

Chocolate Sponge Cake

Serves 10

5 egg whites
⅛ teaspoon salt
⅛ teaspoon cream of tartar
½ cup granulated sugar
½ cup sifted cake flour
½ cup cocoa
2 teaspoons strong coffee
½ teaspoon vanilla extract
¼ teaspoon chocolate extract
3 tablespoons confectioners' sugar

Nutritional Data

PER SERVING:

Calories	84
% calories from fat	5
Fat (gm)	0.5
Sat. Fat (gm)	0.1
Cholesterol (mg)	0
Sodium (mg)	57
Protein (gm)	3
Carbohydrate (gm)	18.9

EXCHANGES:

Milk	0.0	Bread	1.0
Veg.	0.0	Meat	0.0
Fruit	0.0	Fat	0.0

Preheat oven to 300 degrees. Line 15" x 10" jelly-roll pan with greased wax paper.

In large bowl, beat egg whites, salt, and cream of tartar until mixture just mounds on spoon (not quite to soft peak stage). Using spatula, fold in granulated sugar, large spoonful at a time. Sift half of flour over egg white mixture and fold gently; repeat with remaining flour. Add cocoa and mix well. Fold in coffee, vanilla, and chocolate extract.

Spread in prepared pan and bake 25 minutes or until firm to touch. Sift half confectioners' sugar over cake; cover with tea towel and invert baking pan. Carefully remove wax paper, using sharp knife. Trim any crusty edges.

For Jelly Roll

While cake is hot, roll up in towel, jelly-roll fashion; let cool. Make filling (see Fresh Strawberry Mousse or Filling,

p. 614) if using cake as jelly roll. Cake and filling can be prepared to this point, covered, and refrigerated up to 1 day.

Unroll cake and spread evenly with filling. Roll up, using
towel to help roll. Sift remaining confectioners' sugar over top.
Place seam-side-down on serving platter.

For Torte

Gently transfer unrolled Chocolate Sponge Cake to wire rack;
cover and cool completely. Cut into 3 (10" x 5") rectangles.

Spread Strawberry Mousse (see p. 614) filling evenly over
each rectangle and stack rectangles, filling-side-up, on platter;
cover and chill 1 hour. Cut stack in half lengthwise; place cake
halves side by side on serving platter, cut-side-down. Cover
and chill 30 minutes. Spoon sauce on top.

Chocolate Hearts
❋ with Assorted Berries

Serves 14

1 Chocolate Sponge Cake (see preceding recipe)
1 cup confectioners' sugar
½ cup strawberries, sliced
½ cup raspberries
½ cup blackberries
2 teaspoons sugar
1 recipe Chocolate Sauce II (see p. 525)

Nutritional Data

PER SERVING:

Calories	106
% calories from fat	4
Fat (gm)	0.5
Sat. Fat (gm)	0.1
Cholesterol (mg)	0
Sodium (mg)	41
Protein (gm)	2.4
Carbohydrate (gm)	25.2

EXCHANGES:

Milk	0.0	Bread	1.0
Veg.	0.0	Meat	0.0
Fruit	0.5	Fat	0.0

Cut cake into 28 hearts, using 2½-inch heart-shaped cookie cutter; discard remaining cake. Sprinkle cake hearts with
confectioners' sugar; set aside.

Combine berries with sugar and mix well.

To serve, spoon about 1 tablespoon Chocolate Sauce onto
plate; top with cake heart, 2 tablespoons berries, and another
cake heart. Repeat procedure with remaining ingredients.

To Freeze: Freeze chocolate hearts by wrapping them
in aluminum foil; label and freeze up to 2 months. Freeze
berries by placing them in vacuum-sealed bag and freeze up
to 2 months.

To Serve: Thaw and serve.

Chocolate Mocha Crème Cake

Serves 12

Cake

4	eggs, separated
¼	cup water
2	tablespoons strong coffee
⅓	cup cocoa
¾	cup all-purpose flour
2	teaspoons baking powder
6	packets Equal® (see "About This Cookbook")

Frosting

1	envelope diet dessert topping mix (makes 2 cups)
½	cup cold water
1	teaspoon vanilla extract
¼	cup unsweetened cocoa
2	teaspoons instant coffee crystals
8	packets Equal®

Nutritional Data

PER SERVING:

Calories	81
% calories from fat	23
Fat (gm)	2.2
Sat. Fat (gm)	0.6
Cholesterol (mg)	71
Sodium (mg)	83
Protein (gm)	3.7
Carbohydrate (gm)	12.1

EXCHANGES:

Milk	0.0	Bread	1.0
Veg.	0.0	Meat	0.0
Fruit	0.0	Fat	0.5

Cake: Beat egg yolks only with water and coffee until thick and lemon-colored. Fold in cocoa, flour, and baking powder. Beat egg whites only until stiff, but not dry, and peaks form. Fold into chocolate mixture.

Preheat oven to 375 degrees. Spread batter into 2 greased and wax-paper-lined 8-inch-round pans. Bake 20 to 25 minutes or until cake tester inserted near center comes out clean. Cool slightly in pans. Remove from pans and remove wax paper. Sprinkle 3 packets Equal® on each cake layer.

Frosting: Combine topping mix and cold water in mixing bowl. Beat at high speed until topping is thick and fluffy. Add vanilla, cocoa, coffee, and 8 packets Equal®. Continue beating until well blended. Spread frosting between layers and on top of cake.

Mocha Angel Cake

Serves 12

1½	cups egg whites, about 10 to 12, room temperature
1	teaspoon cream of tartar
1	cup sugar, divided
¼	teaspoon salt
1¼	teaspoons vanilla extract
¾	cup cake flour, sifted

Nutritional Data

PER SERVING:

Calories	105
% calories from fat	2
Fat (gm)	0.2
Sat. Fat (gm)	0.1
Cholesterol (mg)	0
Sodium (mg)	92
Protein (gm)	4
Carbohydrate (gm)	23

¼	cup Dutch-processed cocoa	EXCHANGES:			
2	teaspoons instant coffee	Milk	0.0	Bread	1.5
½	teaspoon ground cinnamon	Veg.	0.0	Meat	0.0
		Fruit	0.0	Fat	0.0

Preheat oven to 350 degrees. Cut sheet of wax paper to fit bottom of 10-inch tube cake pan.

Beat egg whites in large bowl of electric mixer until light. Blend in cream of tartar and 3 tablespoons sugar. Continue beating and adding sugar until all but 1 tablespoon of sugar has been incorporated and egg whites are firm. Mix in salt and vanilla.

Onto sheet of wax paper or paper plate, sift flour again with remaining sugar and cocoa, coffee, and cinnamon.

Sprinkle flour mixture, in thirds, over egg whites. Using rubber spatula, with deep strokes and twisting spatula as you stir, incorporate flour mixture into egg whites. Do not over mix, as you do not want to deflate egg whites. Spoon batter into prepared pan.

Bake cake in center of oven 50 to 55 minutes or until cake is lightly browned on top and springs back when gently touched; or use cake tester.

Cake must cool inverted; tube pan has "legs" to provide for this. Remove cake from pan when cooled completely. Cut with serrated knife.

Angel cake does not freeze well. Wrapped tightly, it will store 3 or 4 days.

Cocoa Gingerbread Cake

Serves 12

Butter-flavored vegetable cooking spray
- ⅓ cup diet margarine
- ⅓ cup fructose (fruit sugar, see "About This Cookbook")
- ½ cup real egg substitute
- ½ cup molasses
- 1¾ cups all-purpose flour
- ⅓ cup cocoa
- 2 teaspoons baking powder
- ½ teaspoon baking soda
- 1¾ teaspoons ginger, peeled, grated
- ¾ teaspoon ground cinnamon
- ⅛ teaspoon ground nutmeg
- ¼ teaspoon salt
- ¾ cup buttermilk

Nutritional Data

PER SERVING:

Calories	149
% calories from fat	18
Fat (gm)	3
Sat. Fat (gm)	0.6
Cholesterol (mg)	0.6
Sodium (mg)	229
Protein (gm)	3
Carbohydrate (gm)	28

EXCHANGES:

Milk	0.0	Bread	1.0
Veg.	0.0	Meat	0.0
Fruit	1.0	Fat	0.5

Preheat oven to 350 degrees. Coat 9" x 9" nonstick baking pan with cooking spray.

Using electric mixer, combine margarine and fructose. Blend in egg substitute and molasses.

Sift flour, cocoa, baking powder, baking soda, ginger, cinnamon, nutmeg, and salt. Add dry ingredients to batter alternately with buttermilk. Batter should be smooth.

Pour batter into prepared pan. Bake in center of oven 35 to 45 minutes or until tester inserted in cake comes out clean.

Cool cake 5 minutes in pan. Turn cake out by inverting onto wire rack; cool. Cut cake and serve. Good with scoop of noncholesterol vanilla ice cream.

Cocoa Tea Cake

Serves 10

Butter-flavored vegetable cooking spray

2	scant cup all-purpose flour
2/3	cup fructose (fruit sugar, see "About This Cookbook")
1/4	cup unsweetened Dutch cocoa
1	teaspoon baking powder
1	teaspoon baking soda
1/4	teaspoon salt
1/2	cup skim milk
1/2	cup plain nonfat yogurt
1/4	cup real egg substitute
1/4	cup canola blend (corn oil and canola oil packaged blend)
1	teaspoon vanilla extract
1/2	teaspoon chocolate extract
1/4	cup raisins (optional)

Nutritional Data

PER SERVING:

Calories	198
% calories from fat	27
Fat (gm)	6
Sat. Fat (gm)	0.7
Cholesterol (mg)	0.4
Sodium (mg)	111
Protein (gm)	5
Carbohydrate (gm)	32

EXCHANGES:

Milk	0.0	Bread	1.5
Veg.	0.0	Meat	0.0
Fruit	0.5	Fat	1.0

Preheat oven to 350 degrees. Coat 4½" x 8½" x 2½" pan with cooking spray. Set aside.

In large bowl of electric mixer, combine flour, fructose, cocoa, baking powder, baking soda, and salt. Blend in milk, yogurt, egg substitute, oil, vanilla, chocolate extract, and raisins (optional).

Pour batter into prepared pan. Bake in center of oven 55 to 60 minutes or until done. Cake will spring back when lightly touched or test dry with cake tester or bamboo skewer.

Cool cake on rack. Slice thin and serve with sliced fruit or dollop of chocolate light ice cream.

Black Forest Cake Roll

Serves 10

Filling

1 8-oz. can dietetic red sour pitted cherries
1 teaspoon cornstarch
2 packets Equal® (see "About This Cookbook")
1/8 teaspoon almond extract
   Few drops red food coloring (optional)

Cake

3/4 cup all-purpose flour, sifted
1 teaspoon baking powder
5 egg whites
   Egg substitute equal to 5 eggs
1/8 teaspoon salt
1/2 cup brewed coffee
1/3 cup cocoa
10 packets Equal®
   Vegetable cooking spray

Topping

1 envelope diet whipped topping mix
   (makes 2 cups)

Nutritional Data

PER SERVING:

Calories	90
% calories from fat	4
Fat (gm)	0.4
Sat. Fat (gm)	0.1
Cholesterol (mg)	0
Sodium (mg)	137
Protein (gm)	6
Carbohydrate (gm)	15.5

EXCHANGES:

Milk	0.0	Bread	1.0
Veg.	0.0	Meat	0.5
Fruit	0.0	Fat	0.0

Filling: Make filling first so that it is firm enough to spread.
Drain cherries, reserving liquid and a few cherries for garnish. In small saucepan combine cornstarch and reserved liquid; stir until smooth. Cook over medium heat, stirring constantly, until mixture comes to boil. Reduce heat and cook 1 minute longer. Remove from heat and stir in cherries. Let cool to lukewarm, then stir in Equal®, almond extract, and food coloring. Refrigerate while you are making cake.

Cake: Preheat oven to 400 degrees. Coat 15½" x 10½" x 1" jelly-roll pan with vegetable spray. Line only bottom of pan with wax paper and coat with vegetable spray.

Sift together flour and baking powder onto clean piece of wax paper. Reserve.

Beat together egg whites and salt in large bowl until soft peaks form. Beat egg substitute with coffee until light and fluffy. Add cocoa and beat again. Beat in reserved flour mixture. Gently fold in beaten egg whites until no streaks of white remain.

Turn batter into prepared jelly-roll pan, spreading evenly. Bake 5 to 7 minutes, or until top springs back when lightly pressed with fingertip. Loosen cake around edges with knife. Invert onto clean towel. Very carefully peel off paper using knife to help peel paper, if necessary. Sprinkle cake with 10 packets Equal®. Starting at short end, roll up cake and towel together. Place seam-side-down on rack to cool.

Topping: Meanwhile, prepare whipped topping mix according to package directions; reserve ¼ cup. Unroll cake and spread remaining topping mix evenly, leaving 1-inch border around edge of cake. Spoon cherry Filling on top of whipped topping, being careful to spread evenly. Do not fill cake too much or filling will seep out when you reroll cake.

Reroll cake without towel. Place seam-side-down on serving plate and top with reserved whipped topping. Garnish with cherries, if desired.

Dutch Cocoa Roll

Serves 12

Vegetable cooking spray
7 tablespoons real egg substitute
⅔ cup fructose (fruit sugar, see "About This Cookbook"), divided
7 tablespoons unsweetened Dutch cocoa
1 teaspoon vanilla extract
5 egg whites
½ teaspoon cream of tartar
Ricotta Cheese Filling (recipe follows)
Confectioners' sugar

Nutritional Data

PER SERVING:

Calories	94
% calories from fat	12
Fat (gm)	1
Sat. Fat (gm)	0.1
Cholesterol (mg)	5
Sodium (mg)	73
Protein (gm)	7
Carbohydrate (gm)	7

EXCHANGES:

Milk	0.0	Bread	0.0
Veg.	0.0	Meat	0.5
Fruit	1.0	Fat	0.0

Adjust oven rack to center of oven and preheat oven to 325 degrees.

Line 10" x 15" jelly-roll pan with cooking parchment and coat parchment and pan sides with nonstick cooking spray.

Combine egg substitute, ⅓ cup fructose, cocoa, and vanilla in bowl of electric mixer and beat until well mixed.

In separate bowl, beat egg whites until they hold soft peaks. Add cream of tartar, and continue beating until they hold stiff peaks. With beaters running, add remaining ⅓ cup fructose in thin stream. As soon as sugar has been added, turn off beaters.

Fold meringue into cocoa batter. Spread batter in prepared pan and bake 20 to 25 minutes or until cake pulls away from sides of pan.

Remove from oven and let cool 5 minutes in pan. If necessary, use sharp knife to loosen cake from sides of pan.

Turn out onto large, damp muslin towel. Carefully and slowly, peel off paper. Fold towel over cake on all sides.

Roll cake (long-side-up) slowly in towel. Carefully place cake in refrigerator. When cold, unroll cake carefully on serving platter.

Spread Ricotta Cheese Filling over cake and carefully reroll. Cover with plastic wrap and refrigerate until chilled, about 2 hours.

At serving time, cut cake into quarters. Cut each quarter into 3 slices. Sprinkle slices with confectioners' sugar.

Ricotta Cheese Filling

1   15-oz. container low-fat ricotta cheese
1/3   cup low-sugar strawberry jam (or any flavor desired)
1   tablespoon aspartame, or sugar to taste

Place ricotta, jam, and aspartame in food processor and pulse until soft.

Baked Chocolate Alaska

Serves 10

3/4   cup egg whites, about 5 to 6, room temperature
1/4   teaspoon cream of tartar
1/2   cup sugar
1/4   teaspoon salt
1/2   teaspoon vanilla extract
1/2   teaspoon chocolate extract
3/4   cup cake flour, sifted
3   tablespoons unsweetened Dutch cocoa
1   quart noncholesterol chocolate ice cream
   Meringue (recipe follows)

Nutritional Data

PER SERVING:

Calories	186
% calories from fat	5
Fat (gm)	1
Sat. Fat (gm)	trace
Cholesterol (mg)	0
Sodium (mg)	110
Protein (gm)	7
Carbohydrate (gm)	37

EXCHANGES:

Milk	0.0	Bread	2.5
Veg.	0.0	Meat	0.0
Fruit	0.0	Fat	0.0

Preheat oven to 350 degrees. Cut sheet of wax paper to fit bottom of loaf pan. This is not necessary if pan is coated with cooking spray.

Beat egg whites in large bowl of electric mixer until light. Sprinkle cream of tartar and 3 tablespoons sugar over egg whites; beat to incorporate. Continue adding sugar until all has been incorporated and egg whites are firm. Mix in salt, vanilla, and chocolate extract.

Onto sheet of wax paper or paper plate, sift flour again with cocoa.

Sprinkle flour mixture, in thirds, over egg whites. Using rubber spatula and deep, twisting motion, incorporate flour mixture into egg whites. Do not over mix as you do not want to deflate egg whites. Spoon batter into prepared pan.

Bake cake in center of oven about 30 minutes or until cake springs back when gently touched; or use cake tester.

Cake must cool inverted. Arrange 4 cups to support inverted pan. Remove cake from pan when cool.

Using serrated knife, slice cake in half. Serve ½ at another meal. Place remaining half of cake on nonstick cookie sheet. Top with ice cream, leaving ½-inch border. Freeze cake and ice cream.

Meringue

5 egg whites
½ teaspoon cream of tartar
¼ cup fructose (fruit sugar, see "About This Cookbook")
1 teaspoon vanilla extract

When ready to serve Baked Alaska, preheat oven to 450 degrees.

Beat egg whites until soft peaks form. Sprinkle cream of tartar and fructose over whites. Continue beating until fructose is absorbed. Sprinkle vanilla over whites and continue beating until firm peaks form.

Working quickly, take cake from freezer and cover with meringue, sealing edges completely. Place cake in oven and bake 4 minutes or until Meringue is golden brown. Slide Baked Alaska onto serving plate, slice, and serve immediately.

Angel Food Cake
(with Orange Sauce)

Serves 8

1 6.95-oz. package angel food loaf cake mix
½ cup water
½ cup hazelnuts or almonds, coarsely chopped, toasted
1 cup orange juice
2 tablespoons orange-flavor liqueur
2 medium oranges, peeled and sectioned

Preheat oven to 375 degrees.

Combine cake mix and water in large bowl. Mix at low speed until moistened. Beat 2 minutes at high speed. Fold in nuts and pour into ungreased 9" x 5" loaf pan. Bake 25 to 30 minutes or until cracks on top appear dry. Cool completely in pan, tipped on side on wire rack.

Combine orange juice and liqueur in small saucepan. Heat to boiling, reduce heat, and simmer 10 minutes. Add oranges and simmer until heated through; spoon over cake slices.

Nutritional Data

PER SERVING:

Calories	190
% calories from fat	28
Fat (gm)	6.2
Sat. Fat (gm)	0.5
Cholesterol (mg)	0
Sodium (mg)	252
Protein (gm)	3.6
Carbohydrate (gm)	30.7

EXCHANGES:

Milk	0.0	Bread	1.5
Veg.	0.0	Meat	0.0
Fruit	0.5	Fat	1.0

Peaches 'n' Cream Angel Cake

Serves 10

1	6.95-oz. package angel food loaf cake mix
1/2	cup water
1	3-oz. package cream cheese, softened
7	ozs. sweetened condensed milk (not evaporated milk)
1/3	cup fresh lemon juice
1	teaspoon almond extract
2-3	drops yellow food coloring (optional)
1	envelope diet dessert topping mix, whipped with 2 packets Equal® (see "About This Cookbook")
1	cup fresh peaches, peeled and chopped
2	packets Equal®
	Additional fresh peach slices for garnish

Nutritional Data

PER SERVING:

Calories	194
% calories from fat	22
Fat (gm)	4.8
Sat. Fat (gm)	3
Cholesterol (mg)	16.2
Sodium (mg)	201
Protein (gm)	4.1
Carbohydrate (gm)	33.3

EXCHANGES:

Milk	0.5	Bread	1.0
Veg.	0.0	Meat	0.0
Fruit	0.0	Fat	1.0

Preheat oven to 375 degrees.

Combine cake mix and water in large bowl. Mix at low speed until moistened. Beat 2 minutes at high speed. Pour into ungreased 9" x 5" loaf pan. Bake 25 to 30 minutes or until cracks on top appear dry. Cool completely in pan, tipped on side on wire rack.

Cut 1-inch slice crosswise from top of cake; set aside. With sharp knife, cut around cake 1 inch from center hole and 1 inch from outer edge, leaving bottom 1 inch of cake intact to serve as base. Remove center portion of cake and tear it into bite-size pieces; reserve.

In larger mixer bowl, beat cheese until fluffy. Gradually beat in sweetened condensed milk until smooth. Stir in lemon juice, almond extract, and, if desired, food coloring. Fold in 1/3 of topping mix; reserve 2/3 for topping. Refrigerate.

Place cut peaches in bowl and sprinkle with Equal®. Fold peaches and reserved, torn cake pieces into remaining cream mixture; fill cake cavity. Replace top slice of cake; frost with reserved topping mix. Chill 3 hours or until set. Garnish with additional peaches, if desired. Store in refrigerator. Makes one 10-inch cake.

❆ *Grand Marnier Cake*

Serves 12

1	6.95-oz. package angel food loaf cake mix
½	cup water
1	6-oz. can frozen orange juice, melted
1	8-oz. jar fruit-only orange marmalade
1	jigger Grand Marnier
1	envelope diet dessert topping mix
1	teaspoon Grand Marnier
	Toasted, slivered almonds

Nutritional Data

PER SERVING:

Calories	155
% calories from fat	1
Fat (gm)	0.1
Sat. Fat (gm)	0
Cholesterol (mg)	0
Sodium (mg)	128
Protein (gm)	1.9
Carbohydrate (gm)	35.9

EXCHANGES:

Milk	0.0	Bread	1.5
Veg.	0.0	Meat	0.0
Fruit	1.0	Fat	0.0

Preheat oven to 375 degrees.

Combine cake mix and water in large bowl. Mix at low speed until moistened. Beat 2 minutes at high speed. Pour into ungreased 9" x 5" loaf pan. Bake 25 to 30 minutes or until cracks on top appear dry. Cool completely in pan, tipped on side on wire rack.

Cool orange juice and combine with orange marmalade mixture. Poke holes in cake from top to bottom, using cake tester or fork. Do not break side walls. Drizzle orange mixture slowly into holes until all is used. Refrigerate 24 hours or freeze at this time.

A few hours before serving, sprinkle 1 jigger of Grand Marnier over cake. Then ice with topping mix, with 1 teaspoon Grand Marnier added.

Sprinkle toasted, slivered almonds on top.

Angel Cupcakes

Serves 18 (1 cupcake each)

¾	cup egg whites, about 5 to 6, room temperature
½	teaspoon cream of tartar
½	cup sugar, divided
¼	teaspoon salt
¾	teaspoon vanilla extract
½	cup, scant, cake flour, sifted
2½	tablespoons unsweetened Dutch cocoa
¼	teaspoon ground nutmeg
⅛	teaspoon ground allspice

Nutritional Data

PER SERVING:

Calories	38
% calories from fat	3
Fat (gm)	0.1
Sat. Fat (gm)	trace
Cholesterol (mg)	0
Sodium (mg)	45
Protein (gm)	1
Carbohydrate (gm)	8

EXCHANGES:

Milk	0.0	Bread	0.5
Veg.	0.0	Meat	0.0
Fruit	0.0	Fat	0.0

Preheat oven to 350 degrees. Do not use cupcake liners because cupcakes must cool inverted and will fall out of pan if in liners.

Beat egg whites in large bowl of electric mixer until light. Sprinkle cream of tartar and 3 tablespoons sugar over egg whites; beat to incorporate. Continue adding sugar until all has been incorporated and egg whites are firm. Mix in salt and vanilla.

Onto sheet of wax paper or paper plate, sift flour again with cocoa, nutmeg, and allspice.

Using rubber spatula, sprinkle flour mixture, in thirds, over egg whites. Using deep, twisting motion with spatula, incorporate flour mixture lightly into egg whites. Do not over mix, as you do not want to deflate egg whites.

Bake cupcakes in center of oven 15 to 20 minutes or until cakes spring back when gently touched; or use cake tester.

Cupcakes must cool inverted. Arrange 4 cups or glasses to support corners of inverted pan. Remove cakes from pan when cooled completely.

Lemon Crème Cake

Serves 10

Filling

Egg substitute equal to 5 eggs
1 14-oz. can sweetened condensed milk (*not* evaporated milk)
½ cup fresh lemon juice
   Few drops yellow food coloring (optional)
5 packets Equal® (see "About This Cookbook")

Cake

¾ cup all-purpose flour, sifted
1 teaspoon baking powder
5 egg whites
   Egg substitute equal to 5 eggs
⅛ teaspoon salt
¼ cup fresh lemon juice
⅛ teaspoon lemon rind, grated
5 packets Equal®
   Vegetable cooking spray

Nutritional Data

PER SERVING:

Calories	205
% calories from fat	15
Fat (gm)	3.5
Sat. Fat (gm)	2.2
Cholesterol (mg)	13.5
Sodium (mg)	220
Protein (gm)	11.1
Carbohydrate (gm)	32.6

EXCHANGES:

Milk	1.0	Bread	1.5
Veg.	0.0	Meat	0.0
Fruit	0.0	Fat	0.5

Filling: Make filling first so that it has had time to set before you begin cake. In medium bowl, add egg substitute; stir in milk, lemon juice, and food coloring. Add 5 packets Equal® and beat again. Refrigerate until cake is cooled and ready to fill.

Cake: Preheat oven to 400 degrees. Coat 15½" x 10½" x 1" jelly-roll pan with vegetable cooking spray. Line only bottom with wax paper; do not let paper come up sides of pan. Generously coat paper with cooking spray. Sift together flour and baking powder onto clean piece of wax paper. Reserve.

Beat together egg whites and salt in large bowl until soft peaks form. Beat egg substitute with lemon juice and lemon rind in large bowl until light and fluffy. Beat reserved flour mixture into egg mixture. Gently fold in beaten egg whites until no streaks of white remain. Turn batter into prepared jelly-roll pan, spreading evenly.

Bake 5 to 7 minutes or until top springs back when lightly pressed with fingertip. Cake should not be brown. Loosen cake around edges with tip of knife. Invert onto clean towel. Very carefully peel off paper. (Use knife to help peel off wax paper.)

Starting at short end, roll up cake and towel together. Place roll seam-side-down, on rack. Cool completely. When jelly roll is cool, unroll carefully. Sprinkle with 5 packets Equal®.

Spread roll evenly with Filling; reroll without towel. Place roll, seam-side-down, on serving plate. Refrigerate, covered, until ready to serve. Garnish with remaining lemon crème, if desired.

Marble Cake

Serves 10

Butter-flavored vegetable cooking spray

⅓ cup diet margarine, room temperature
¾ cup fructose (fruit sugar, see "About This Cookbook")
1 teaspoon vanilla extract
1¾ cups cake flour, sifted
2 teaspoons baking soda
¼ teaspoon salt
¾ cup skim milk
3 egg whites, beaten stiff
¼ cup unsweetened Dutch cocoa
2 tablespoons hot water
¼ teaspoon baking soda
1 tablespoon fructose (fruit sugar, see "About This Cookbook")

Nutritional Data

PER SERVING:

Calories	160
% calories from fat	19
Fat (gm)	3
Sat. Fat (gm)	0.6
Cholesterol (mg)	0.3
Sodium (mg)	335
Protein (gm)	4
Carbohydrate (gm)	29

EXCHANGES:

Milk	0.0	Bread	1.0
Veg.	0.0	Meat	0.0
Fruit	1.0	Fat	0.5

Preheat oven to 350 degrees. Coat loaf pan with cooking spray.

Using electric mixer, beat margarine, fructose, and vanilla.

Sift flour again with baking soda and salt. You can use a strainer and sift onto sheet of wax paper or paper plate.

Add flour mixture alternately with milk to margarine/vanilla mixture. Fold in beaten egg whites.

In small bowl, blend cocoa, water, baking soda, and fructose.

Divide batter in half. Stir cocoa mixture into ½ of batter. Pour other ½ of batter into pan. Drop cocoa batter by tablespoons in dollops over vanilla batter. With knife, swirl cocoa batter through vanilla batter.

Bake in center of oven 55 to 60 minutes. Cake is done when tester or bamboo skewer inserted in center comes out dry. Cool cake on wire rack. Slice and serve. Always good with sliced fruit.

 # Light Pound Cake
(or *Lemon Pound Cake)

Serves 16	Nutritional Data	
2¼ cups unbleached all-purpose flour	PER SERVING:	
¾ teaspoon baking powder	Calories	173
¼ teaspoon baking soda	% calories from fat	31
¼ teaspoon salt	Fat (gm)	6.1
½ cup (1 stick) corn-oil margarine, softened	Sat. Fat (gm)	1
1 cup sugar	Cholesterol (mg)	0.4
3 egg whites	Sodium (mg)	159
1½ teaspoons vanilla extract*	Protein (gm)	2.9
¾ cup buttermilk	Carbohydrate (gm)	26.8
Vegetable cooking spray		

EXCHANGES:

Milk	0.0	Bread	2.0
Veg.	0.0	Meat	0.0
Fruit	0.0	Fat	1.0

Preheat oven to 350 degrees. Put flour, baking powder, baking soda, and salt into medium bowl. Mix well and set aside.

Cream margarine and sugar in large bowl until smooth. Beat in egg whites and vanilla until smooth. Alternately add flour mixture and buttermilk in 2 batches each, blending well after each addition.

Spoon batter into 7" x 4½" loaf pan that has been coated with vegetable cooking spray. Bake until golden and cake has pulled away from sides of pan, about 1 hour. Cool on wire rack.

*Lemon Pound Cake

Substitute 2 teaspoons fresh lemon juice for vanilla extract, and add grated zest of 1 lemon.

To Freeze: Wrap cake in aluminum foil; label and freeze up to 2 months.

To Serve: Thaw and slice to serve.

Apple Cake

Serves 16
Vegetable cooking spray
⅔ cup sugar
½ cup packed brown sugar
¼ cup vegetable oil
3 egg whites
⅔ cup cake flour (all-purpose flour may be used, if preferred)
⅔ cup whole wheat flour
½ cup bran cereal
1½ teaspoons baking soda
1 teaspoon ground cinnamon
¼ teaspoon ground allspice
3 cups apples, unpeeled and shredded
½ cup low-fat yogurt
Confectioners' sugar (optional)

Nutritional Data

PER SERVING:

Calories	149
% calories from fat	22
Fat (gm)	3.8
Sat. Fat (gm)	0.5
Cholesterol (mg)	0.4
Sodium (mg)	153
Protein (gm)	2.5
Carbohydrate (gm)	28.1

EXCHANGES:

Milk	0.0	Bread	1.5
Veg.	0.0	Meat	0.0
Fruit	0.5	Fat	0.5

Preheat oven to 350 degrees. Coat 13" x 9" x 2" baking pan with nonstick vegetable spray.

In large bowl, combine sugars, oil, and egg whites. Beat with wooden spoon until well blended. Add flours, cereal, baking soda, cinnamon, and allspice; stir just until moistened. Stir in yogurt and shredded apples. Pour batter into prepared pan.

Bake 25 to 30 minutes. Cool. Sift confectioners' sugar onto cake.

To Freeze: Wrap cake in aluminum foil; label and freeze up to 2 months.

To Serve: Thaw and slice to serve.

Apple Tart

Serves 10
Vegetable cooking spray
4 medium apples, peeled and cut into ¼-inch slices
2 eggs
½ cup low-fat yogurt
¼ cup honey
¼ cup flour
¼ teaspoon vanilla extract
1 tablespoon apple jelly
2 tablespoons apple juice

Nutritional Data

PER SERVING:

Calories	96
% calories from fat	12
Fat (gm)	1.4
Sat. Fat (gm)	0.5
Cholesterol (mg)	43.3
Sodium (mg)	21
Protein (gm)	2.2
Carbohydrate (gm)	19.4

EXCHANGES:

Milk	0.0	Bread	0.5
Veg.	0.0	Meat	0.0
Fruit	1.0	Fat	0.0

Preheat oven to 375 degrees. Coat 9-inch tart pan with removable bottom with nonstick cooking spray. Arrange apple slices in 2 concentric circles, slightly overlapping each other in pan.

In medium bowl, combine eggs, yogurt, honey, flour, and vanilla. Spoon over apple slices until all are covered. Bake 30 minutes.

In small saucepan, combine jelly and juice over low heat. Brush evenly over tart, and bake 10 minutes more or until browned.

Tarte Tatin

Serves 8

1	cup cake flour
2	tablespoons sugar
3	tablespoons cold margarine
2-3	tablespoons ice water
5	cups Granny Smith apples (about 2½ lbs.), peeled, cored, and cut into scant ½-inch slices
½	cup sugar
¼	teaspoon ground nutmeg
1	tablespoon fresh lemon juice
¼	cup sugar
2	tablespoons margarine

Nutritional Data

PER SERVING:

Calories	239
% calories from fat	27
Fat (gm)	7.4
Sat. Fat (gm)	1.5
Cholesterol (mg)	0
Sodium (mg)	83.1
Protein (gm)	1.3
Carbohydrate (gm)	43.3

EXCHANGES:

Milk	0.0	Bread	2.0
Veg.	0.0	Meat	0.0
Fruit	0.5	Fat	1.5

Combine cake flour and sugar in medium bowl. With pastry blender or 2 knives, cut in margarine until mixture resembles coarse crumbs. Sprinkle in water, 1 tablespoon at a time, mixing lightly with fork after each addition until pastry just holds together. Cover dough and refrigerate 15 minutes. On lightly floured surface, roll pastry into 11-inch circle; cover loosely with plastic wrap and set aside.

Preheat oven to 425 degrees.

Toss apples with combined ½ cup sugar and nutmeg; sprinkle with lemon juice. Set aside. Place ¼ cup sugar in 10-inch skillet with ovenproof handle. *Cook over medium heat until sugar melts and is golden brown, about 5 minutes, stirring occasionally. Add apple mixture and margarine; cook 5 minutes or until apples are just tender, stirring occasionally. Remove from heat.

Arrange apples in skillet so they are slightly mounded in center. Place pastry on top of apples; tuck in edges. Cut slits in pastry to allow steam to escape. Bake 20 to 25 minutes or until lightly browned. Invert onto serving platter. Serve warm or at room temperature.

*Note: Watch carefully—sugar can burn easily!

Apple Crisp

Serves 8

Vegetable cooking spray
6   medium tart apples, thinly sliced
1   teaspoon fresh lemon juice
½   teaspoon cinnamon
¼   teaspoon lemon rind, finely grated
    Dash ground cloves
1   cup frozen cranberries*
1   cup rolled oats
½   cup whole wheat flour
    Dash nutmeg
2   tablespoons sunflower oil
2   tablespoons sugar-free maple syrup

Nutritional Data

PER SERVING:

Calories	162
% calories from fat	24
Fat (gm)	4.5
Sat. Fat (gm)	0.5
Cholesterol (mg)	0
Sodium (mg)	8
Protein (gm)	2.9
Carbohydrate (gm)	30

EXCHANGES:

Milk	0.0	Bread	1.0
Veg.	0.0	Meat	0.0
Fruit	1.0	Fat	1.0

Preheat oven to 350 degrees.

Place apples in 8" x 8" baking dish coated with nonstick vegetable cooking spray. Sprinkle with lemon juice, cinnamon, lemon rind, and cloves. Toss until slices are coated. Sprinkle cranberries over top.

In medium bowl, combine oats, flour, and nutmeg. Pour oil and maple syrup over oats mixture and stir with spoon until mixture is well combined and crumbly. Sprinkle topping over apples.

Bake 45 minutes. Serve warm. Vanilla frozen yogurt goes well with this.

Note: Raisins can be substituted for cranberries.

Streusel-Topped Carrot Cake

Serves 12

Carrot Cake

1   cup packed light brown sugar
4   tablespoons margarine, softened
2   eggs
2   egg whites
3   cups carrots, shredded
½   cup dark raisins
2   cups all-purpose flour
1   teaspoon baking powder
1   teaspoon baking soda
1   teaspoon ground cinnamon
½   teaspoon ground nutmeg

Nutritional Data

PER SERVING:

Calories	254
% calories from fat	21
Fat (gm)	5.9
Sat. Fat (gm)	1.3
Cholesterol (mg)	35.5
Sodium (mg)	226
Protein (gm)	4.5
Carbohydrate (gm)	46.7

EXCHANGES:

Milk	0.0	Bread	2.5
Veg.	0.0	Meat	0.0
Fruit	0.5	Fat	1.0

Streusel Topping

3   tablespoons brown sugar
3   tablespoons all-purpose flour
1   tablespoon margarine

Carrot Cake: Preheat oven to 350 degrees. Grease 9-inch springform pan lightly and sprinkle with flour.

Combine brown sugar and margarine in large bowl; beat until light and fluffy. Add eggs and egg whites, one at a time, beating well after each addition. Mix in carrots and raisins.

Combine flour, baking powder, baking soda, cinnamon, and nutmeg in medium bowl; add to batter. Mix well. Spoon batter into prepared pan.

Streusel Topping: Mix sugar and flour; cut in margarine until mixture resembles coarse crumbs. Sprinkle topping over batter.

Bake 30 to 35 minutes or until cake springs back when lightly touched in center. Cool in pan on wire rack 15 minutes; remove side from pan. Serve warm or at room temperature.

*Strawberry Almond Shortcake

Serves 8

3   cups fresh strawberries, sliced
4   packets Equal® (see "About This Cookbook"), or 2 tablespoons sugar
1²⁄₃ cups all-purpose flour
1   tablespoon sugar
2   teaspoons baking soda
1   teaspoon baking powder
3   tablespoons diet margarine
1   egg, beaten
1   teaspoon almond extract
½   cup buttermilk, or skim milk
      Vegetable cooking spray
1   envelope diet whipped topping mix

Nutritional Data

PER SERVING:

Calories	174
% calories from fat	18
Fat (gm)	3.4
Sat. Fat (gm)	0.7
Cholesterol (mg)	27.2
Sodium (mg)	436
Protein (gm)	4.3
Carbohydrate (gm)	30

EXCHANGES:

Milk	0.0	Bread	1.5
Veg.	0.0	Meat	0.0
Fruit	0.5	Fat	0.5

Combine strawberries and Equal® or sugar; refrigerate at least 1 hour.

In medium bowl, stir together flour, 1 tablespoon sugar, baking soda, and baking powder; cut in margarine until mixture resembles coarse crumbs.

Combine egg, almond extract, and buttermilk; add to flour mixture all at once, stirring until mixed.

Preheat oven to 450 degrees. Coat 8-inch-round baking pan with nonstick vegetable cooking spray. With lightly floured hands, spread dough into pan. Bake about 10 minutes or until golden. Cool.

Split cake in half; place bottom portion on serving plate. Top with some of the berries. Place top portion over berries. Spread diet whipped topping over cake and spoon on remaining berries. Place several dollops of topping over berries.

Note: This dessert can also be made with peaches, blueberries, raspberries, or blackberries.

Berry Shortcake

Serves 4

		Nutritional Data
1	cup all-purpose flour	PER SERVING:
2	teaspoons baking powder	
½	teaspoon salt	Calories 330
2½	tablespoons vegetable shortening	% calories from fat 24
⅓	cup skim milk	Fat (gm) 8.8
1	cup strawberries, washed, drained, and cut in halves	Sat. Fat (gm) 2.6
		Cholesterol (mg) 2.8
		Sodium (mg) 515
1	cup blueberries, washed and drained	Protein (gm) 10.2
1	cup raspberries, washed and drained	Carbohydrate (gm) 54.1
2	cups nonfat vanilla yogurt	

EXCHANGES:

Milk	1.5	Bread	1.5
Veg.	0.0	Meat	0.0
Fruit	1.0	Fat	1.0

Preheat oven to 350 degrees.

In deep bowl, combine flour, baking powder, and salt. Cut in vegetable shortening with pastry fork or food processor. Stir in milk. Dough will form ball.

Roll dough out on lightly floured pastry cloth to ¼-inch thickness. Cut out biscuits with 3-inch cookie cutter. Place biscuits on nonstick cookie sheet. Bake in center of oven 10 to 12 minutes. Biscuits will be firm and golden brown.

To serve, split open each biscuit. Scatter berries on top and spoon yogurt over berries.

Strawberry Roly-Poly

Serves 8

		Nutritional Data
2¼	cups unbleached all-purpose flour	PER SERVING:
1	teaspoon baking soda	
¼	teaspoon salt	Calories 276
3	tablespoons granulated sugar	% calories from fat 24
¼	cup vegetable shortening	Fat (gm) 7.3
⅔	cup 2% milk	Sat. Fat (gm) 2.3
2½	cups strawberries, hulled and mashed	Cholesterol (mg) 1.5
2	tablespoons nonfat margarine, crumbled	Sodium (mg) 258
½	cup granulated sugar	Protein (gm) 4.6
	Vegetable cooking spray	Carbohydrate (gm) 48.3

EXCHANGES:

Milk	0.0	Bread	2.0
Veg.	0.0	Meat	0.0
Fruit	1.0	Fat	1.5

Preheat oven to 350 degrees.

Mix together flour, baking soda, salt, and sugar. Cut in shortening, using pastry knife or food processor fitted with steel blade. Blend in milk. Turn dough onto lightly floured board; roll dough 1/4-inch thick.

Spread dough with strawberries and sprinkle with margarine and sugar. Roll dough jelly-roll style. Place on cookie sheet lightly coated with cooking spray.

Bake 35 minutes or until cake tests done. Cool 5 minutes. Transfer roly-poly to serving dish. Slice and serve.

New York-Style Cheesecake

Serves 12

Graham Cracker Crumb Crust
(see p. 574)

2	12-oz. containers nonfat cream cheese, softened
3/4	cup sugar
2	eggs
2	tablespoons cornstarch
1	teaspoon vanilla extract
1	cup reduced-fat sour cream

Nutritional Data

PER SERVING:

Calories	237
% calories from fat	25
Fat (gm)	6.4
Sat. Fat (gm)	0.8
Cholesterol (mg)	47.9
Sodium (mg)	527
Protein (gm)	12.7
Carbohydrate (gm)	30.7

EXCHANGES:

Milk	0.0	Bread	2.0
Veg.	0.0	Meat	1.0
Fruit	0.0	Fat	1.0

Preheat oven to 350 degrees. Make crumb crust, patting mixture on bottom and 1/2 inch up side of 9-inch springform pan. Increase oven temperature to 400 degrees.

Beat cream cheese and sugar in large bowl until light and fluffy; beat in eggs, cornstarch, and vanilla. Add sour cream, mixing until well blended. Pour mixture into prepared crust.

Bake until cheesecake is set but still slightly soft in center, 45 to 50 minutes. Turn oven off; let cheesecake cool in oven with door ajar 3 hours. Refrigerate 8 hours or overnight.

Skinny Cheesecake

Serves 8

Butter-flavored vegetable cooking spray
½   cup graham cracker crumbs
1½ tablespoons margarine, melted and cooled
1   package unflavored gelatin
½   cup cold water
⅓   cup boiling water
½   teaspoon lemon rind, grated
½   cup fresh lemon juice
¼   cup granulated sugar
2   tablespoons water
2   cups 1% cream-style cottage cheese
½   teaspoon lemon extract

Nutritional Data

PER SERVING:

Calories	125
% calories from fat	26
Fat (gm)	3.7
Sat. Fat (gm)	0.8
Cholesterol (mg)	2.5
Sodium (mg)	295
Protein (gm)	8.3
Carbohydrate (gm)	14.9

EXCHANGES:

Milk	0.0	Bread	1.0
Veg.	0.0	Meat	1.0
Fruit	0.0	Fat	0.0

Coat 8" x 8" cake pan with butter-flavored nonstick cooking spray. Mix crumbs with melted margarine and line pan bottom. Set aside.

Soak gelatin in cold water. Combine boiling water and lemon rind and add to gelatin; add lemon juice and sugar, stirring until completely dissolved. Chill until consistency of unbeaten egg whites.

Put 2 tablespoons water, cottage cheese, and lemon extract into blender or food processor; mix at high speed 10 to 15 seconds. Add partially set gelatin mixture. Continuing at high speed, process 15 seconds or until well blended. Pour filling into prepared pan and chill. When set, 3 to 4 hours, cut into 8 servings.

Della Robbia No-Bake Cheesecake

Serves 10

Graham Cracker Crust (recipe follows)

Filling

1   tablespoon plus 1 teaspoon unflavored gelatin
1   tablespoon plus 1 teaspoon fresh lemon juice
1   tablespoon water
2   eggs separated, room temperature
½   cup skim milk
2   packets Equal® (see "About This Cookbook")
    Pinch salt

Nutritional Data

PER SERVING:

Calories	183
% calories from fat	33
Fat (gm)	6.6
Sat. Fat (gm)	1.1
Cholesterol (mg)	44.8
Sodium (mg)	370
Protein (gm)	9.5
Carbohydrate (gm)	20.3

EXCHANGES:

Milk	0.0	Bread	1.0
Veg.	0.0	Meat	1.0
Fruit	0.0	Fat	1.0

    2   cups 1% low-fat, large-curd
        cottage cheese
1¼   teaspoons vanilla extract
 ³/₄   teaspoon lemon peel, grated
 ²/₃   cup diet whipped topping mix
    6   packets Equal®
    2   tablespoons apple jelly
    2   teaspoons water
        Assorted fresh fruit such as raspberries,
        sliced strawberries, seedless grapes, and
        orange segments

Prepare Graham Cracker Crust and set aside.

Sprinkle gelatin over lemon juice and 1 tablespoon water in medium bowl. Whisk yolks to blend in small bowl. Bring milk and salt to boil in heavy, small saucepan. Whisk milk into yolks, a little at a time. Return mixture to saucepan and stir over medium-low heat until custard thickens and coats back of metal spoon, about 6 or 7 minutes. Do not boil. Pour into medium bowl. Stir in 2 packets Equal®. Stir until gelatin dissolves.

Puree cottage cheese in food processor or blender with half of custard. Transfer to large bowl. Blend in remaining custard, vanilla, and lemon peel. Using electric mixer, beat whites in medium bowl until stiff peaks form. Gently fold into cheese mixture.

Prepare whipped topping mix, and fold into cheese mixture. Sprinkle 6 packets Equal® over mixture and mix well. Pour filling over crust. Cover and refrigerate overnight.

Stir apple jelly and 2 teaspoons water in heavy, small saucepan until slightly thickened.

Pat fruit dry and arrange in decorative pattern over cake. Brush jelly glaze over fruit. Refrigerate.

Graham Cracker Crust

1½   cups graham cracker crumbs
 ¹/₃   cup diet margarine, melted

Preheat oven to 350 degrees. Combine crumbs with melted diet margarine in bowl. Press firmly on bottom and sides of 10-inch pie pan. Bake 8 to 10 minutes. Cool.

Espresso Parfait Cheesecake

Serves 10

Crust

1	cup finely crushed zwieback
2	tablespoons diet margarine, melted
1	tablespoon honey

Filling

1	envelope unflavored gelatin
¼	cup water
2	egg yolks, beaten
½	cup skim milk
⅓	cup ricotta cheese
2	teaspoons instant espresso coffee (regular instant can also be used)
1	teaspoon vanilla extract
⅓	cup water
2	packets Equal® (see "About This Cookbook")

Topping

1	envelope diet whipped topping mix
½	cup skim milk
4	egg whites
2	packets Equal®
	Vegetable cooking spray

Nutritional Data

PER SERVING:

Calories	118
% calories from fat	30
Fat (gm)	3.7
Sat. Fat (gm)	1.2
Cholesterol (mg)	46.4
Sodium (mg)	103
Protein (gm)	5.4
Carbohydrate (gm)	14

EXCHANGES:

Milk	0.0	Bread	1.0
Veg.	0.0	Meat	0.5
Fruit	0.0	Fat	0.5

Crust: Combine zwieback, margarine, and honey. Reserve 2 tablespoons of mixture for topping. Press remaining mixture onto bottom of 7" or 8" springform pan coated with vegetable cooking spray. Chill.

Filling: Soften gelatin in ¼ cup water. In saucepan, combine egg yolks, ½ cup milk, ricotta cheese, coffee crystals, vanilla, and ⅓ cup water. Stir in gelatin mixture.

Cook and stir over medium heat 20 minutes or until mixture coats spoon; do not boil. Remove from heat and stir in 2 packets Equal®. Chill until partially set, stirring occasionally.

Topping: Prepare topping mix according to package directions, using ½ cup skim milk. Fold into gelatin mixture. Beat egg whites, and 2 packets Equal® until they form stiff peaks. Add to gelatin mixture by folding in gently. Turn into prepared pan; cover and chill until firm, about 6 hours. To serve, remove sides of pan and sprinkle with reserved cracker crumbs.

Spicy Cheesecake

Serves 8

Vegetable cooking spray
1 16-oz. container low-fat cottage cheese
2 eggs
4 tablespoons instant nonfat dry milk powder
1 teaspoon vanilla extract
½ teaspoon lemon rind, grated
2 egg whites
¼ teaspoon cream of tartar
4 teaspoons cinnamon
12 packets Equal® (see "About This Cookbook")

Nutritional Data

PER SERVING:

Calories	83
% calories from fat	21
Fat (gm)	1.9
Sat. Fat (gm)	0.8
Cholesterol (mg)	56.2
Sodium (mg)	272
Protein (gm)	10.3
Carbohydrate (gm)	5.6

EXCHANGES:

Milk	0.0	Bread	0.0
Veg.	0.0	Meat	1.5
Fruit	0.0	Fat	0.0

Preheat oven to 350 degrees. Coat bottom and side of 8-inch springform pan with vegetable cooking spray.

Combine cottage cheese, eggs, 2 tablespoons of milk powder, vanilla, and lemon rind in blender; cover. Whirl until smooth, scraping down sides as necessary.

Beat egg whites with cream of tartar in medium bowl until foamy. Gradually beat in remaining 2 tablespoons of milk powder. Continue beating until soft peaks form. Fold egg whites into cheese mixture until no streaks of white remain.

Pour mixture into prepared pan. Bake 35 minutes or until top is browned and wooden toothpick comes out clean when inserted into center.

Combine cinnamon and Equal® and sprinkle over cake like a blanket.

Yogurt Cheesecake

Serves 8

2 cups unflavored Yogurt Cheese (recipe follows)
Vegetable cooking spray
½ cup graham cracker crumbs
¼ cup sugar
1 tablespoon cornstarch
6 egg whites
1 tablespoon vanilla extract

Nutritional Data

PER SERVING:

Calories	160
% calories from fat	7
Fat (gm)	1.1
Sat. Fat (gm)	0.2
Cholesterol (mg)	2.7
Sodium (mg)	197
Protein (gm)	11.8
Carbohydrate (gm)	24.8

EXCHANGES:

Milk	1.0	Bread	1.0
Veg.	0.0	Meat	0.0
Fruit	0.0	Fat	0.0

Make Yogurt Cheese recipe, and drain 24 hours. Preheat oven to 325 degrees.

For crust, coat 7-inch springform pan with nonstick vegetable cooking spray. Sprinkle with graham cracker crumbs. Refrigerate crust while making filling.

Beat Yogurt Cheese, sugar, and cornstarch in medium mixer bowl until creamy. Beat in egg whites and vanilla. Pour into prepared pan. Bake until set, 45 to 55 minutes. Turn off oven and let cake remain in oven 1 hour. Remove cake from oven and refrigerate.

Note: You can serve with sauce, such as chocolate or raspberry, or with plain fresh fruit to taste. Another idea is to sprinkle mixture of sugar or Equal® with cinnamon over top. It is not recommended that you freeze this cake.

Yogurt Cheese

16   ozs. plain nonfat yogurt

Line strainer with double layer of cheesecloth or large coffee filter. Pour in yogurt. Place yogurt-filled strainer over bowl, at least 1 inch above its bottom; refrigerate overnight. Scoop thickened yogurt into another bowl; discard cheesecloth. Use also in desserts that call for cream cheese or as base for dips.

Brownies

Serves 12 (1 brownie each)	*Nutritional Data*	
Butter-flavored vegetable cooking spray	PER SERVING:	
¼ cup real egg substitute		
¼ cup diet margarine, melted and cooled	Calories	168
¾ cup fructose (fruit sugar, see "About This Cookbook")	% calories from fat	17
	Fat (gm)	3
	Sat. Fat (gm)	0.6
2 tablespoons water	Cholesterol (mg)	0
3 tablespoons cocoa	Sodium (mg)	278
2¾ cups fine, plain bread crumbs	Protein (gm)	4
¼ teaspoon salt	Carbohydrate (gm)	32
½ teaspoon baking powder		
½ cup golden raisins	EXCHANGES:	

Milk	0.0	Bread	1.0
Veg.	0.0	Meat	0.0
Fruit	1.0	Fat	0.5

Preheat oven to 350 degrees. Coat 9" x 8" square baking pan.

In bowl of electric mixer, mix egg substitute, cooled margarine, and fructose.

In separate bowl, mix water and cocoa together; it will be stiff. Add to batter. Blend in crumbs, salt, baking powder, and raisins.

Pour batter into prepared pan. Bake in center of oven 25 to 30 minutes. When done, cake tester will come out dry, and top of brownies will be firm to touch.

Cool. Cut into 12 squares.

Chewy Cocoa Brownies

Serves 25 (1 brownie each)

1 cup all-purpose flour
1 cup sugar
¼ cup unsweetened cocoa
5 tablespoons margarine, melted
¼ cup skim milk
1 egg
2 egg whites
¼ cup honey
1 teaspoon vanilla extract

Nutritional Data

PER SERVING:

Calories	77
% calories from fat	29
Fat (gm)	2.6
Sat. Fat (gm)	0.5
Cholesterol (mg)	8.6
Sodium (mg)	35
Protein (gm)	1.3
Carbohydrate (gm)	12.7

EXCHANGES:

Milk	0.0	Bread	1.0
Veg.	0.0	Meat	0.0
Fruit	0.0	Fat	0.5

Preheat oven to 350 degrees.

Mix flour, sugar, and cocoa in medium bowl. Stir in margarine, milk, egg, egg whites, honey, and vanilla until smooth. Pour mixture into greased and floured 8" x 8" baking pan.

Bake until brownies spring back when touched and begin to pull away from sides of pan, about 30 minutes. Cool completely on wire rack; cut into 25 squares.

Heavenly Fudge

Serves 2

½ cup canned crushed pineapple, no sugar added
⅓ cup nonfat dry milk powder
2 teaspoons unsweetened cocoa
2 packets Equal® (see "About This Cookbook")

In medium bowl, combine all ingredients until no traces of milk powder or cocoa remain. Turn mixture into individual loaf pan or 10-ounce custard cup and place in freezer until firm.

Nutritional Data

PER SERVING:

Calories	86
% calories from fat	3
Fat (gm)	0.3
Sat. Fat (gm)	0.1
Cholesterol (mg)	2.1
Sodium (mg)	64
Protein (gm)	4.6
Carbohydrate (gm)	17.7

EXCHANGES:

Milk	0.5	Bread	0.0
Veg.	0.0	Meat	0.0
Fruit	0.5	Fat	0.0

Choco Ball Cookies

Serves 12 (2 cookies each)

- ¼ cup unsweetened cocoa
- ½ cup skim milk
- 6 tablespoons diet margarine
- 3 cups quick-cooking oats
- 2 teaspoons vanilla extract
- ¼ cup unsweetened, shredded coconut
- 10 packets Equal® (see "About This Cookbook")

Bring cocoa, milk, and margarine to boil. Cook 1 minute, stirring constantly. Remove from heat. Stir in remaining ingredients. Form into balls and place on cookie sheet. Chill until firm. Keep refrigerated. Makes 24.

Nutritional Data

PER SERVING:

Calories	121
% calories from fat	35
Fat (gm)	4.9
Sat. Fat (gm)	1.3
Cholesterol (mg)	0.2
Sodium (mg)	72
Protein (gm)	4
Carbohydrate (gm)	16.4

EXCHANGES:

Milk	0.0	Bread	1.0
Veg.	0.0	Meat	0.0
Fruit	0.0	Fat	1.0

Chocolate Rum Balls

Serves 24 (2 each)

- 3½ cups (about 12 ozs.) vanilla wafer crumbs
- 1 cup confectioners' sugar, divided
- ¼ cup unsweetened cocoa
- ⅓ cup dark or light rum
- ⅓ cup light or dark corn syrup

Combine ingredients, using only ½ cup confectioners' sugar, in bowl and mix well. Shape into 1-inch balls. Roll in reserved ½ cup confectioners' sugar. Store in tightly covered container. Makes 48 balls.

Chocolate Bourbon Balls: Follow basic recipe above but substitute ⅓ cup bourbon for rum.

Nutritional Data

PER SERVING:

Calories	104
% calories from fat	19
Fat (gm)	2.2
Sat. Fat (gm)	0.4
Cholesterol (mg)	8.6
Sodium (mg)	39
Protein (gm)	0.9
Carbohydrate (gm)	18.6

EXCHANGES:

Milk	0.0	Bread	1.0
Veg.	0.0	Meat	0.0
Fruit	0.0	Fat	0.5

Chocolate Coconut Bonbons

Serves 10 (2 bonbons each)

- 4 zwieback rounds
- 1 teaspoon cocoa powder
- 2 tablespoons water
- 4 packets Equal® (see "About This Cookbook")
- 1 tablespoon unsweetened coconut, finely chopped

Nutritional Data

PER SERVING:

Calories	16
% calories from fat	26
Fat (gm)	0.5
Sat. Fat (gm)	0.3
Cholesterol (mg)	0.6
Sodium (mg)	7
Protein (gm)	0.3
Carbohydrate (gm)	2.7

Crush zwieback until very fine. Mix cocoa and water, then add zwieback and remaining ingredients. Divide mixture into 2 parts. Divide each part into 10 pieces (approximately ½ teaspoon each). Roll each piece into ball.

EXCHANGES:

Milk	0.0	Bread	0.0
Veg.	0.0	Meat	0.0
Fruit	0.0	Fat	0.0

Serve these chewy, chocolate cookies with hot cup of cocoa. Makes 20 bonbons.

Chocolate Madeleines

Serves 15 (2 each)

3	ozs. unsweetened chocolate
2	ozs. semisweet chocolate
3	tablespoons skim milk
1	cup whole wheat flour
1	cup unbleached flour
2	teaspoons baking soda
1½	cups espresso
¼	cup apple juice
2	tablespoons unsalted butter
½	cup sugar
1	whole egg plus 2 whites
	Vegetable cooking spray

Nutritional Data

PER SERVING:

Calories	162
% calories from fat	33
Fat (gm)	6.4
Sat. Fat (gm)	3.1
Cholesterol (mg)	18.7
Sodium (mg)	190
Protein (gm)	4.2
Carbohydrate (gm)	25.2

EXCHANGES:

Milk	0.0	Bread	1.5
Veg.	0.0	Meat	0.0
Fruit	0.0	Fat	1.0

Preheat oven to 350 degrees.

Put both chocolates and milk in double boiler and cook over low heat until chocolate is melted, about 5 minutes. Remove from heat and set aside to cool slightly.

Blend flour and baking soda together and set aside. Combine espresso and apple juice in separate bowl.

Cream butter and sugar together in mixer. Add eggs and mix well. Add melted chocolate. Alternately add flour and espresso mixtures. Mix until all ingredients are blended.

Coat madeleine pan with vegetable cooking spray and fill each scallop ¾ full. Bake 10 to 15 minutes. Leave madeleines in pan until completely cooled, then transfer to airtight containers for storing. Makes 30 madeleines.

Marriage Cookies

Serves 48 (1 cookie each)	Nutritional Data	
Cookies	**PER SERVING:**	
1³/4 cups unbleached all-purpose flour, sifted	Calories	72
	% calories from fat	28
8 tablespoons (1 stick) butter or shortening	Fat (gm)	2.3
³/4 cup sugar	Sat. Fat (gm)	1.3
¹/2 teaspoon allspice	Cholesterol (mg)	5.4
¹/2 teaspoon baking powder	Sodium (mg)	39
³/4 teaspoon baking soda	Protein (gm)	0.9
¹/4 cup Dutch-process cocoa	Carbohydrate (gm)	12.6
¹/4 cup walnuts, coarsely ground	**EXCHANGES:**	
1 cup raisins, coarsely chopped		
¹/2 cup skim milk	Milk 0.0 Bread 0.0	
Vegetable cooking spray	Veg. 0.0 Meat 0.0	
	Fruit 0.5 Fat 0.5	

Frosting

1¹/2 cups confectioners' sugar, sifted
2¹/2 tablespoons evaporated skim milk
1 teaspoon butter or margarine, softened
1 teaspoon rum extract
Pastel-colored sugar sprinkles (optional)

Cookies: Beat flour and butter or shortening in bowl until well blended. Beat in sugar, allspice, baking powder, baking soda, cocoa, nuts, and raisins. Stir in milk, and mix well to make soft dough.

Preheat oven to 350 degrees.

Drop teaspoonfuls of dough about 1 inch apart onto 2 cookie sheets coated with vegetable cooking spray. Bake 10 minutes or until firm. Transfer to wire racks to cool.

Frosting: Combine all frosting ingredients into bowl, and beat until smooth. Dip top of each cookie into frosting. Place cookies on racks, and top with colored sprinkles (not included in Nutritional Data). Let frosting dry before storing. These will keep in airtight containers up to 2 weeks, or they can be frozen 3 to 4 months. Makes 48.

Date Bars

Serves 12 (2 bars each)	Nutritional Data	
³/4 cup dates, chopped	**PER SERVING:**	
2 tablespoons diet margarine	Calories	80
1 egg	% calories from fat	22
1 tablespoon skim milk	Fat (gm)	2
1 teaspoon vanilla extract	Sat. Fat (gm)	0.8
4 packets Equal® (see "About This Cookbook")	Cholesterol (mg)	17.8
	Sodium (mg)	102
	Protein (gm)	1.4
3 cups toasted rice cereal	Carbohydrate (gm)	15

¼ cup unsweetened coconut, chopped Vegetable cooking spray	EXCHANGES:			
	Milk	0.0	Bread	0.5
	Veg.	0.0	Meat	0.0
	Fruit	0.5	Fat	0.5

Mix chopped dates, margarine, egg, milk, and vanilla in medium saucepan. Cook over medium heat about 5 minutes until mixture is thick. Cool, then stir in Equal® and cereal. For bars, press mixture into 8-inch-square pan, coated with vegetable cooking spray. Sprinkle with coconut and refrigerate until firm. Cut into 24 bars.

 # Apricot and Date Bars

Serves 24

2 cups dried apricots, chopped
2 cups dates, chopped
1 cup unsweetened, crushed pineapple
¾ cup water
1 tablespoon vanilla extract
2 cups whole wheat flour
⅔ cup oat flakes (may be chopped in blender)
1 cup diet margarine
½ cup unsweetened coconut (optional)
½ cup nuts, finely chopped (optional)
4 packets Equal® (see "About This Cookbook")

Nutritional Data

PER SERVING:

Calories	150
% calories from fat	24
Fat (gm)	4.3
Sat. Fat (gm)	0.7
Cholesterol (mg)	0
Sodium (mg)	89
Protein (gm)	2.5
Carbohydrate (gm)	28.2

EXCHANGES:

Milk	0.0	Bread	0.5
Veg.	0.0	Meat	0.0
Fruit	1.5	Fat	0.5

Preheat oven to 350 degrees.

Combine apricots, dates, pineapple, and water; cook until thick and smooth. Add vanilla. Set fruit mixture aside. Combine remaining ingredients to form crumb mixture. Pour ½ of mixture into greased 9" x 12" pan. Firmly press to make crust.

Add fruit mixture, then remaining topping. Pat down well. Bake 30 minutes or until light brown. Let cool and then sprinkle with 4 packets Equal®. Cut into 24 squares.

Peppermint Clouds

Serves 24 (1 per serving)

3 egg whites
⅛ teaspoon cream of tartar
¼ teaspoon salt
¾ cup sugar
⅓ cup (2 ozs.) peppermint candies, crushed

Preheat oven to 300 degrees.

In medium-size bowl, beat egg whites until foamy. Add cream of tartar and salt; beat to soft peaks. Beat in sugar gradually, beating until mixture forms stiff, shiny peaks. Reserve 2 tablespoons crushed candy; fold remaining candy into egg white mixture.

Drop mixture by tablespoons onto aluminum foil-lined cookie sheets. Sprinkle tops of cookies with reserved candy. Bake until cookies begin to brown and feel crisp when touched, 20 to 25 minutes. Cool in pans on wire racks.

Nutritional Data

PER SERVING:

Calories	35
% calories from fat	0
Fat (gm)	0
Sat. Fat (gm)	0
Cholesterol (mg)	0
Sodium (mg)	30
Protein (gm)	0.4
Carbohydrate (gm)	8.6

EXCHANGES:

Milk	0.0	Bread	0.5
Veg.	0.0	Meat	0.0
Fruit	0.0	Fat	0.0

Hazelnut Macaroons

Serves 15 (2 macaroons each)

4 egg whites
⅛ teaspoon cream of tartar
¼ teaspoon salt
1 cup sugar
1 cup canned sweetened coconut
¼ cup hazelnuts or pecans, finely chopped

Preheat oven to 300 degrees.

In medium bowl, beat egg whites until foamy. Add cream of tartar and salt; beat to soft peaks. Beat in sugar gradually, beating until mixture forms stiff, shiny peaks. Fold in coconut; fold in hazelnuts.

Drop mixture by tablespoons onto aluminum foil-lined cookie sheets. Bake until cookies begin to brown and feel crisp when touched, 20 to 25 minutes. Cool in pans on wire racks. Makes 30.

Nutritional Data

PER SERVING:

Calories	95
% calories from fat	29
Fat (gm)	3.2
Sat. Fat (gm)	1.6
Cholesterol (mg)	0
Sodium (mg)	70
Protein (gm)	1.4
Carbohydrate (gm)	16

EXCHANGES:

Milk	0.0	Bread	1.0
Veg.	0.0	Meat	0.0
Fruit	0.0	Fat	0.5

Lemon Drops

Serves 14 (2 cookies each)

36 vanilla cookies
3 tablespoons fresh lemon juice
1/4 teaspoon lemon extract
4 packets Equal® (see "About This Cookbook")

Crush cookies until very fine. Mix cookie crumbs with lemon juice, lemon extract, and Equal®. Divide mixture into 2 parts. Divide each part into 14 pieces. Roll each piece into ball. Makes 28.

Nutritional Data

PER SERVING:

Calories	50
% calories from fat	28
Fat (gm)	1.5
Sat. Fat (gm)	0.3
Cholesterol (mg)	6.4
Sodium (mg)	26
Protein (gm)	0.5
Carbohydrate (gm)	8.3

EXCHANGES:

Milk	0.0	Bread	0.5
Veg.	0.0	Meat	0.0
Fruit	0.0	Fat	0.0

Orange Drops

Serves 10 (2 cookies each)

36 vanilla cookies
2 tablespoons orange juice concentrate
3 packets Equal® (see "About This Cookbook")
3 tablespoons unsweetened coconut, finely chopped

Crush cookies until fine. Mix cookie crumbs with orange juice concentrate, Equal®, and coconut. Divide mixture into 2 parts. Divide each part into 10 pieces and roll into balls. Makes 20.

Nutritional Data

PER SERVING:

Calories	79
% calories from fat	31
Fat (gm)	2.7
Sat. Fat (gm)	0.8
Cholesterol (mg)	9
Sodium (mg)	36
Protein (gm)	0.9
Carbohydrate (gm)	12.7

EXCHANGES:

Milk	0.0	Bread	1.0
Veg.	0.0	Meat	0.0
Fruit	0.0	Fat	0.5

Cinnamon Oatmeal Cookies

Serves 42 (1 cookie each)

5 tablespoons margarine, softened
1/4 cup low-fat plain yogurt
2 egg whites
1 teaspoon vanilla extract
1 cup packed light brown sugar
1 cup all-purpose flour
1 1/4 cups quick-cooking oats
1/2 teaspoon baking soda
1/4 teaspoon baking powder
1 teaspoon ground cinnamon
1/4 teaspoon salt

Nutritional Data

PER SERVING:

Calories	54
% calories from fat	26
Fat (gm)	1.5
Sat. Fat (gm)	0.3
Cholesterol (mg)	0.1
Sodium (mg)	51
Protein (gm)	1
Carbohydrate (gm)	9.2

EXCHANGES:

Milk	0.0	Bread	0.5
Veg.	0.0	Meat	0.0
Fruit	0.0	Fat	0.5

Preheat oven to 375 degrees.

In large bowl, beat margarine, yogurt, egg whites, and vanilla until smooth. Mix in brown sugar. Mix in combined flour, oats, baking soda, baking powder, cinnamon, and salt.

Drop mixture by tablespoons onto greased cookie sheets. Bake until cookies are lightly browned, 10 to 12 minutes. Cool on wire racks. Makes 42.

Cardamom Crisps

Serves 60 (1 per serving)

Crisps

1¾	cups all-purpose flour
½	cup sugar
1½	teaspoons ground cardamom
¼	teaspoon salt
7	tablespoons margarine, softened
1	egg
1	teaspoon vanilla
1	egg white, beaten

Vanilla Glaze

1	cup powdered sugar
1	tablespoon margarine, melted
1	teaspoon vanilla
2	tablespoons skim milk

Nutritional Data

PER SERVING:

Calories	43
% calories from fat	34
Fat (gm)	1.6
Sat. Fat (gm)	0.3
Cholesterol (mg)	3.6
Sodium (mg)	29
Protein (gm)	0.6
Carbohydrate (gm)	6.6

EXCHANGES:

Milk	0.0	Bread	0.5
Veg.	0.0	Meat	0.0
Fruit	0.0	Fat	0.5

Crisps: Preheat oven to 350 degrees.

Combine flour, sugar, cardamom, and salt in medium-size bowl; cut in margarine with pastry blender or 2 knives until mixture resembles coarse crumbs. Mix in whole egg and vanilla, stirring just enough to form a soft dough.

Place dough in bottom of greased jelly roll pan, 15 x 10 inches. Pat and spread dough, using fingers and small spatula or knife, until bottom of pan is evenly covered. Brush dough with beaten egg white.

Bake until edges of cookies are lightly browned, 20 to 25 minutes. Cool in pan several minutes.

Vanilla Glaze: Mix powdered sugar and margarine with vanilla and enough milk to make glaze consistency. Drizzle glaze over warm cookies and cut into 60 squares.

Favorite Sugar Cookies

Serves 36 (1 per serving)

4	tablespoons margarine, softened
⅔	cup sugar
1	egg
1½	tablespoons lemon juice
1½	cups all-purpose flour
½	teaspoon baking soda
½	teaspoon ground nutmeg
	Granulated sugar

Nutritional Data

PER SERVING:

Calories	47
% calories from fat	28
Fat (gm)	1.5
Sat. Fat (gm)	0.3
Cholesterol (mg)	5.9
Sodium (mg)	34
Protein (gm)	0.7
Carbohydrate (gm)	7.8

EXCHANGES:

Milk	0.0	Bread	0.5
Veg.	0.0	Meat	0.0
Fruit	0.0	Fat	0.5

Preheat oven to 375 degrees. In a medium-size bowl, beat margarine until fluffy. Beat in ⅔ cup sugar, egg, and lemon juice. Mix in combined flour, baking soda, and nutmeg.

Roll dough into ¾-inch balls; roll balls in granulated sugar and place on ungreased cookie sheets. Flatten to 2 inch diameter with bottom of glass. Bake until beginning to brown, about 10 minutes. Cool on wire racks. Makes 36.

Almond Crescents

Serves 12 (3 crescents each)

¼	cup plus 1 tablespoon diet margarine, room temperature
1½	tablespoons light honey
2	tablespoons blanched almonds, ground
1	cup whole wheat pastry flour, sifted
⅓	cup sugar
1	teaspoon almond extract
1	teaspoon sugar
1	teaspoon cinnamon

Nutritional Data

PER SERVING:

Calories	95
% calories from fat	30
Fat (gm)	3.3
Sat. Fat (gm)	0.5
Cholesterol (mg)	0
Sodium (mg)	55
Protein (gm)	1.6
Carbohydrate (gm)	15.8

EXCHANGES:

Milk	0.0	Bread	1.0
Veg.	0.0	Meat	0.0
Fruit	0.0	Fat	0.5

Preheat oven to 300 degrees. Beat margarine in large bowl of electric mixer until light and creamy. Add honey and mix well. Add almonds and beat again. Stir in flour, ⅓ cup sugar, and almond extract with wooden spoon. Lightly flour baking sheet.

Roll small handful of dough between palms to form short cylinder. Transfer to work surface, and use palm to roll into longer cylinder about ⅜-inch thick. Cut into 2 separate pieces. Transfer to prepared baking sheet. Bend ends of pieces to form crescents, or half-moons. Repeat with remaining dough. Bake 20 to 25 minutes. Cool on wire rack.

Put 1 teaspoon sugar and cinnamon in small bowl. Mix well. Dredge each cookie in mixture and set aside. Store in container. Makes about 3 dozen cookies.

Cream Cheese Pinwheels

Serves 30 (2 pinwheels each)

1	cup diet margarine*, room temperature
1	8-oz. package fat-free cream cheese, room temperature
2	cups all-purpose flour
1/4	cup fruit-only apricot preserves
1/4	cup fruit-only strawberry preserves
1/4	cup powdered sugar

Nutritional Data

PER SERVING:

Calories	83
% calories from fat	34
Fat (gm)	3.1
Sat. Fat (gm)	0.5
Cholesterol (mg)	0.8
Sodium (mg)	124
Protein (gm)	2.2
Carbohydrate (gm)	11.6

EXCHANGES:

Milk	0.0	Bread	1.0
Veg.	0.0	Meat	0.0
Fruit	0.0	Fat	0.5

Beat margarine and cream cheese in large bowl with electric mixer until well blended and smooth. With electric mixer on low speed, add flour; beat until blended. Divide dough into fourths. Shape each into rectangle and flatten to 1-inch thickness. Wrap and refrigerate overnight or until firm enough to roll.

Preheat oven to 350 degrees. Have cookie sheets ready. Work with one portion of dough at a time. On lightly floured surface with floured rolling pin, roll dough out to 10" x 7½" rectangle; trim edges. With sharp knife, cut into 2¼-inch squares. Place squares 1 inch apart on ungreased cookie sheets.

For pinwheels, drop ½ teaspoon of preserves in center of each square. Starting from tips, slit corner of each square 1 inch toward center. Fold every other half corner to center like a pinwheel, overlapping tips. Pinch firmly in center.

Bake 13 to 15 minutes until tips are lightly browned. Remove from oven and place on racks to cool. Sprinkle with powdered sugar. Makes 15.

*Note: Do not use margarine with liquid oil listed on package as first ingredient.

Chocolate Biscotti

Serves 36 (1 biscotti each)

2½	cups unbleached all-purpose flour
1	cup sugar
1	teaspoon baking soda
½	teaspoon salt
1	teaspoon allspice
2	tablespoons unsweetened cocoa powder (preferably Dutch process)
½	teaspoon chocolate extract
3	eggs
1¼	cups blanched whole almonds, lightly toasted and coarsely chopped
	Vegetable cooking spray

Nutritional Data

PER SERVING:

Calories	84
% calories from fat	27
Fat (gm)	2.6
Sat. Fat (gm)	0.3
Cholesterol (mg)	17.7
Sodium (mg)	71
Protein (gm)	2.3
Carbohydrate (gm)	13.3

EXCHANGES:

Milk	0.0	Bread	1.0
Veg.	0.0	Meat	0.0
Fruit	0.0	Fat	0.5

Preheat oven to 350 degrees.

In large bowl, combine flour, sugar, baking soda, salt, allspice, and cocoa powder. Mix well.

In small bowl, whisk together chocolate extract and eggs; add mixture to flour mixture, beating until dough is formed. Stir in almonds.

Turn dough out onto lightly floured surface, knead it several times, and divide it into thirds. With floured hands, form each piece of dough into log 10 inches long by 2½ inches wide, and arrange logs at least 4 inches apart on baking sheet lined with foil and lightly coated with vegetable cooking spray.

Bake logs in middle of oven 25 minutes, and let them cool on baking sheet on rack 10 minutes.

On cutting board, cut logs diagonally crosswise into ¾-inch-thick slices. Arrange biscotti, cut-side-down, on baking sheet, and bake 5 minutes on each side.

Transfer biscotti to racks to cool, and store in airtight containers. Makes 36.

Cappuccino Biscotti

Serves 32 (1 biscotti each)

2	cups unbleached all-purpose flour
1	cup sugar
½	teaspoon baking soda
½	teaspoon double-acting baking powder
½	teaspoon salt
2	teaspoons instant coffee crystals
¼	cup plus 1 tablespoon strong-brewed espresso, cooled
1	tablespoon skim milk
1	large egg yolk
1	teaspoon mocha extract

Nutritional Data

PER SERVING:

Calories	92
% calories from fat	30
Fat (gm)	3.2
Sat. Fat (gm)	0.2
Cholesterol (mg)	6.7
Sodium (mg)	81
Protein (gm)	1.4
Carbohydrate (gm)	15.2

EXCHANGES:

Milk	0.0	Bread	1.0
Veg.	0.0	Meat	0.0
Fruit	0.0	Fat	0.5

3/4 cup hazelnuts, toasted, skinned, and coarsely chopped
1/2 cup semisweet chocolate chips
   Vegetable cooking spray

Preheat oven to 300 degrees.

In bowl, combine flour, sugar, baking soda, baking powder, salt, and instant coffee; mix well.

In small bowl, whisk together espresso, milk, egg yolk, and mocha extract; add mixture to flour mixture, beating until dough is formed. Stir in hazelnuts and chocolate chips.

Turn dough out onto floured surface, knead it several times, and halve it. With floured hands, form each piece of dough into log 12 inches long and 2 inches wide, and arrange logs at least 4 inches apart on baking sheet lined with foil and lightly coated with vegetable cooking spray. Bake logs in middle of oven 35 minutes, and let them cool on baking sheet on rack 10 minutes.

On cutting board, cut logs diagonally crosswise into 3/4-inch-thick slices. Arrange biscotti, cut-side-down, on baking sheet, and bake at 300 degrees 5 to 6 minutes on each side, or until they are pale golden.

Transfer biscotti to racks to cool, and store them in airtight containers. Makes 32.

Anise Biscotti

Serves 48 (1 biscotti each)

2 cups unbleached all-purpose flour
1 cup sugar
1 tablespoon anise seeds, crushed
1 teaspoon baking powder
1/2 teaspoon baking soda
1/4 teaspoon salt
2 large eggs
2 large egg whites
2 tablespoons lemon zest, grated
1 tablespoon fresh lemon juice
   Vegetable cooking spray

Nutritional Data

PER SERVING:

Calories	39
% calories from fat	6
Fat (gm)	0.3
Sat. Fat (gm)	0.1
Cholesterol (mg)	8.9
Sodium (mg)	32
Protein (gm)	1
Carbohydrate (gm)	8.2

EXCHANGES:

Milk	0.0	Bread	0.5
Veg.	0.0	Meat	0.0
Fruit	0.0	Fat	0.0

Preheat oven to 325 degrees.

Combine flour, sugar, anise seeds, baking powder, baking soda, and salt. Whisk together eggs, egg whites, lemon zest, and lemon juice, and add to dry ingredients. Mix well.

Working on floured surface with damp hands, shape dough into 2 logs, each about 14 inches long and 1 1/2 inches thick. Set logs on baking sheet lined with foil and lightly coated with vegetable cooking spray, and bake 20 to 25 minutes or until firm to touch. Transfer logs to rack to cool.

Cut logs diagonally into ½-inch-thick slices. Stand slices upright on baking sheet, and bake at 300 degrees 40 minutes. Let cool before storing. Makes 48.

Chapter Sixteen

PIES & PASTRIES

Banana Cream Pie

Serves 8

Zwieback Crust (recipe follows)

Filling

3	egg yolks, beaten
1/4	teaspoon salt
2 1/2	tablespoons cornstarch
2	cups skim milk
1	tablespoon diet margarine
1	teaspoon vanilla extract
5	packets Equal® (see "About This Cookbook")
2	ripe bananas, peeled and thinly sliced

Nutritional Data

PER SERVING:

Calories	164
% calories from fat	²9
Fat (gm)	5.4
Sat. Fat (gm)	1.4
Cholesterol (mg)	82
Sodium (mg)	181
Protein (gm)	4.8
Carbohydrate (gm)	24.4

EXCHANGES:

Milk	0.0	Bread	1.0
Veg.	0.0	Meat	0.0
Fruit	0.5	Fat	1.0

Prepare Zwieback Crust and set aside.

Filling: Combine egg yolks, salt, and cornstarch. In double boiler, scald milk. Pour milk slowly over egg mixture, stirring constantly. Return custard to top of double boiler and cook over hot water, stirring until it thickens. Remove from heat. Stir in margarine, vanilla, and Equal®. Place sliced bananas in bottom of Zwieback Crust. Pour custard on top. Chill before serving.

Zwieback Crust

1	cup zwieback, finely crushed
2	tablespoons diet margarine, melted
1	tablespoon honey
1	packet Equal® (see "About This Cookbook")
	Vegetable cooking spray

Combine zwieback, margarine, honey, and Equal®. Reserve 2 tablespoons of mixture for topping. Press remaining mixture onto bottom of 7- or 8-inch springform pan coated with vegetable cooking spray. Chill.

No-Bake Yogurt Banana Pie

Serves 8

Vanilla Cookie Pie Crust (recipe follows)

2	bananas
1/4	cup firmly packed light brown sugar
2	cups 1% cottage cheese
2	cups nonfat vanilla yogurt
1	teaspoon vanilla extract
1/4	teaspoon ground nutmeg

Nutritional Data

PER SERVING:

Calories	172
% calories from fat	14
Fat (gm)	2.6
Sat. Fat (gm)	0.9
Cholesterol (mg)	3.7
Sodium (mg)	319
Protein (gm)	10.7
Carbohydrate (gm)	26.3

Prepare Vanilla Cookie Pie Crust and set aside.

Slice bananas and toss them with sugar. Spread bananas evenly over bottom of pie crust.

EXCHANGES:

Milk	0.5	Bread	0.5
Veg.	0.0	Meat	1.0
Fruit	0.5	Fat	0.0

In large bowl of electric mixer, beat cottage cheese, yogurt, vanilla, and nutmeg until smooth, about 6 minutes. Spoon yogurt filling into pie crust.

Cover pie lightly with foil. Freeze pie 2 hours before serving. Allow pie to soften slightly at room temperature before serving.

Vanilla Cookie Pie Crust

	Butter-flavored vegetable cooking spray
25	vanilla wafers (1¾ inches wide)
1½	tablespoons nonfat margarine, melted and cooled
½	teaspoon ground cinnamon

Coat 9-inch nonstick pie pan with butter-flavored cooking spray.

Crush wafers, using rolling pin or food processor fitted with steel blade. Put crumbs in bowl. Mix in melted margarine and cinnamon. Sprinkle crumbs over bottom of pan, and with back of soup spoon, press some crumbs up sides of pan and firmly onto bottom of pan.

Chill crust 30 minutes before using.

Banana-Strawberry Cream Pie

Serves 8

Graham Cracker Crumb Crust
(recipe follows)

¼	cup graham cracker crumbs
1	tablespoon margarine
⅓	cup sugar
¼	cup cornstarch
2	tablespoons flour
⅛	teaspoon salt
2½	cups skim milk
3	egg yolks
1	teaspoon vanilla extract
¼	teaspoon ground cinnamon
⅛	teaspoon ground nutmeg
1	cup strawberries, sliced
2	medium bananas

Nutritional Data

PER SERVING:

Calories	315
% calories from fat	33
Fat (gm)	9.7
Sat. Fat (gm)	2.1
Cholesterol (mg)	88.4
Sodium (mg)	356
Protein (gm)	8.4
Carbohydrate (gm)	49.5

EXCHANGES:

Milk	0.0	Bread	2.0
Veg.	0.0	Meat	0.0
Fruit	1.5	Fat	2.0

Make pie crust, adding ¼ cup graham crumbs and 1 tablespoon margarine to recipe and using 9-inch pie pan.

Mix sugar, cornstarch, flour, and salt in medium saucepan; stir in milk. Cook over medium heat until mixture boils and thickens; boil 1 minute, stirring constantly.

Stir about ½ cup of mixture into egg yolks; stir egg mixture back into saucepan. Cook over low heat, stirring constantly, until thickened.

Remove from heat; stir in vanilla, cinnamon, and nutmeg. Cool to room temperature, stirring frequently. Refrigerate until chilled, 1 to 2 hours.

Set aside 4 to 6 strawberry slices. Slice 1 to 1½ bananas and arrange in crust with remaining strawberries. Spoon custard into crust; refrigerate until set, 4 to 6 hours. Slice remaining banana and garnish pie with banana and strawberry slices.

Graham Cracker Crumb Crust

1¼   cups graham cracker crumbs
2   tablespoons sugar
3   tablespoons margarine, melted

Preheat oven to 350 degrees. Combine graham crumbs, sugar, and margarine in 8- or 9-inch pie pan; pat mixture evenly on bottom and side of pan. Bake 8 to 10 minutes or until edge is lightly browned. Cool on wire rack.

Chocolate Sour Cream Pie

Serves 8

Crust

3   tablespoons margarine, melted
1¼   cups graham cracker crumbs

Filling

2   tablespoons unsweetened Dutch cocoa
1½   teaspoons cornstarch
¾   teaspoon cinnamon
     Large pinch allspice
     Large pinch nutmeg
3   tablespoons skim milk
⅓   cup real egg substitute
¼   cup fructose (fruit sugar, see "About This Cookbook")
1   cup no-fat sour cream
¼   teaspoon vanilla extract

Meringue

2   large egg whites
¼   teaspoon cream of tartar
¼   cup confectioners' sugar

Nutritional Data

PER SERVING:

Calories	185
% calories from fat	31
Fat (gm)	6.6
Sat. Fat (gm)	0.9
Cholesterol (mg)	0.1
Sodium (mg)	198
Protein (gm)	5.4
Carbohydrate (gm)	27.2

EXCHANGES:

Milk	0.0	Bread	1.5
Veg.	0.0	Meat	0.5
Fruit	0.0	Fat	1.0

Adjust oven rack to center of oven and preheat oven to 350 degrees.

Crust: Melt margarine and add graham cracker crumbs, mixing well. Pat onto bottom of 9-inch pie pan. Bake 5 minutes. Remove pan, and lower heat to 300 degrees.

Filling: Combine cocoa, cornstarch, cinnamon, allspice, and nutmeg with skim milk, stirring with wire whisk until smooth.

Place egg substitute and fructose in top of double boiler and mix well with wire whisk. Add cocoa mixture and mix again until well combined. Stir in sour cream and vanilla.

Cook over simmering water, stirring constantly, until thickened. Spoon into prepared pie shell.

Return pie to oven at 300 degrees and bake 15 minutes. Remove from oven and cool to just warm. Keep oven at 300 degrees.

Meringue: Beat egg whites until they hold soft peaks. Add cream of tartar and beat until they hold stiff peaks. With beaters running, add confectioners' sugar by spoonfuls. As soon as sugar is incorporated, turn beaters off.

Use spatula to swirl Meringue attractively over top of pie. Return to oven and bake 15 minutes or until delicately browned on top.

Remove from oven. Serve immediately or chill. At serving time, cut pie into quarters. Cut each quarter into 2 pieces.

Chocolate Cheese Pie

Serves 10

Crust

3   tablespoons diet margarine
2/3 cup graham cracker crumbs

Filling

1½ cups 1% cottage cheese, room temperature
1/3 cup unsweetened Dutch cocoa
1   cup nonfat cream cheese, room temperature
    Skim milk:
    1/3 cup skim milk, room temperature
    1/2 cup cold skim milk, for whipped topping
1   tablespoon asparatame sweetener
1   teaspoon vanilla extract
1/2 cup water
1   envelope plus 1½ teaspoons unflavored gelatin
1   envelope diet whipped topping mix

Nutritional Data

PER SERVING:

Calories	133
% calories from fat	22
Fat (gm)	3
Sat. Fat (gm)	0.8
Cholesterol (mg)	4
Sodium (mg)	413
Protein (gm)	12
Carbohydrate (gm)	13

EXCHANGES:

Milk	0.0	Bread	1.0
Veg.	0.0	Meat	1.0
Fruit	0.0	Fat	0.0

Crust: Preheat oven to 375 degrees. Melt margarine and mix with graham crumbs. Press crumbs firmly against bottom and about ½ inch up sides of 10-inch pie pan. Bake 5 minutes; remove and allow to cool.

Filling: Place cottage cheese and cocoa in food processor or blender and mix a few seconds until smooth. Add cream cheese, ⅓ cup skim milk, asparatame, and vanilla and pulse until well mixed. If necessary, stop processor and scrape down sides of bowl.

Place ½ cup water in top of double boiler and sprinkle gelatin over water to soften. Place double boiler over simmering water until gelatin is melted. Use rubber spatula to scrape gelatin into cheese/cocoa batter, mixing well.

Cover batter and refrigerate until gelatin is consistency of very thick egg whites. Transfer batter to electric mixer bowl and beat for a moment. Transfer batter back to first bowl.

Place whipped topping mix in electric mixer bowl. Add remaining ½ cup milk and stir well with wire whisk. Beat topping according to package directions until stiff. Add cheese/cocoa batter to mixer bowl. Beat a few seconds until well combined.

Spoon batter into pie pan. Lay piece of wax paper over filling and refrigerate, covered, until set, about 4 hours. To serve, cut pie in half, then cut each half into 5 wedges.

Chocolate Pudding Pie

Serves 8

3   egg whites
¼   teaspoon cream of tartar
½   teaspoon vanilla extract
½   cup granulated sugar
    Butter-flavored vegetable cooking spray
1   package sugar-free instant chocolate pudding

Nutritional Data	
PER SERVING:	
Calories	95
% calories from fat	6
Fat (gm)	0.6
Sat. Fat (gm)	0.1
Cholesterol (mg)	1
Sodium (mg)	194
Protein (gm)	3.9
Carbohydrate (gm)	19.2

EXCHANGES:			
Milk	0.0	Bread	1.5
Veg.	0.0	Meat	0.0
Fruit	0.0	Fat	0.0

Preheat oven to 250 degrees.

Beat egg whites, cream of tartar, and vanilla until soft peaks form. Sprinkle half of sugar over egg whites and beat to incorporate. Repeat process with remaining sugar. Beat until stiff peaks form.

Transfer meringue into pie pan coated with cooking spray. Using back of spoon, spread meringue evenly over bottom of pie pan, pushing meringue 2 to 3 inches above sides of plate to form crust.

Bake crust 1 hour. Remove from heat and allow crust to dry 1½ hours or until firm.

Prepare pudding according to package directions, using

skim milk. Cool. Spoon pudding into meringue shell, and chill completely before serving.

Cherry Cheese Pie

Serves 6

Graham Cracker Crust

1	cup graham cracker crumbs
2	tablespoons diet margarine, melted
2	packets Equal® (see "About This Cookbook")

Cherry Glaze

1	16-oz. can dietetic red sour pitted cherries
2	teaspoons cornstarch
3	packets Equal®
1/8	teaspoon almond extract
8	drops red food coloring (optional)

Cheese Filling

1	teaspoon unflavored gelatin
1	tablespoon cold water
1¼	cups low-fat cottage cheese
½	teaspoon vanilla extract
3	packets Equal®

Nutritional Data

PER SERVING:

Calories	184
% calories from fat	23
Fat (gm)	4.8
Sat. Fat (gm)	0.7
Cholesterol (mg)	2.1
Sodium (mg)	341
Protein (gm)	8.2
Carbohydrate (gm)	27.5

EXCHANGES:

Milk	0.0	Bread	1.0
Veg.	0.0	Meat	0.5
Fruit	1.0	Fat	0.5

Graham Cracker Crust: Combine crumbs with diet margarine and 2 packets Equal® by cutting in melted margarine until mixture resembles coarse crumbs. Press firmly in bottom and sides of 8- or 9-inch pie pan. Refrigerate until ready to use.

Cherry Glaze: Drain cherries, reserving liquid. In small saucepan, combine cornstarch and reserved cherry liquid; stir until smooth. Cook over medium heat, stirring constantly, until mixture comes to boil. Reduce heat and cook 1 minute longer. Remove from heat; stir in cherries. Let cool to lukewarm, then stir in 3 packets Equal®, almond extract, and coloring.

Cheese Filling: Combine gelatin and cold water in small bowl; let stand 1 minute. Set bowl in ½ inch boiling water. Heat just until gelatin is dissolved. Remove from water; let cool slightly. In blender, combine cottage cheese and vanilla. Blend until smooth. With motor running, gradually add dissolved gelatin. Transfer to bowl and add 3 packets Equal®. Chill, stirring occasionally, just until slightly thickened, about 20 minutes.

Fill pie crust with Cheese Filling. Wait until pie is firm, about 3 hours, and spread Cherry Glaze on top. Refrigerate until ready to serve.

Mocha Chiffon Pie

Serves 8

Crust

3	tablespoons diet margarine
⅔	cup graham cracker crumbs

Filling

2	tablespoons unsweetened Dutch cocoa
1	cup strong black coffee, warm
½	cup fructose (fruit sugar, see "About This Cookbook"), or aspartame*
6	tablespoons real egg substitute
¼	cup water
1	envelope plus ¼ teaspoon un-flavored gelatin
1	envelope diet whipped topping mix
½	cup skim milk, cold

Nutritional Data

PER SERVING:

Calories	122
% calories from fat	22
Fat (gm)	3
Sat. Fat (gm)	0.5
Cholesterol (mg)	0.3
Sodium (mg)	120
Protein (gm)	3
Carbohydrate (gm)	20

EXCHANGES:

Milk	0.0	Bread	1.0
Veg.	0.0	Meat	0.0
Fruit	0.5	Fat	0.5

Adjust oven rack to center of oven and preheat oven to 350 degrees.

Crust: Melt margarine and add crumbs. Stir until well combined. Pat crumbs onto bottom of 9-inch pie pan. Bake 5 minutes. Remove from oven and allow to cool.

Filling: Place cocoa in heavy-bottomed pan and add 2 tablespoons coffee. Stir until smooth; then add remaining coffee and fructose. Stir in egg substitute. Cook over low heat, stirring constantly, until mixture thickens enough to lightly coat spoon.

Place ¼ cup water in top of double boiler, and sprinkle gelatin over water to soften. Melt gelatin over simmering water. When completely melted, stir gelatin into cocoa/coffee mixture. Allow to cool.

Place whipped topping in electric mixer bowl. Add skim milk and stir well with wire whisk to combine. Beat according to package directions until topping is thick. Fold into cocoa/coffee mixture.

Spoon Filling into baked pie shell. Refrigerate 4 hours or until firm. Cut pie into quarters; cut each quarter in half.

Note: If using aspartame, stir 3½ teaspoons into cocoa/coffee mixture before folding in whipped topping mixture. Then fold whipped topping into mixture.

🅽🆂🅰 Cranberry Chiffon Pie

Serves 8

Graham Cracker Crust (see p. 577)

Filling

2	tablespoons cornstarch
2	cups cranberry juice
1	envelope (1 tablespoon) un-flavored gelatin
¼	teaspoon salt
3	packets Equal® (see "About This Cookbook")
3	egg whites
1	cup diet whipped topping
	Orange rind, grated

Nutritional Data

PER SERVING:

Calories	150
% calories from fat	26
Fat (gm)	4.3
Sat. Fat (gm)	0.3
Cholesterol (mg)	0.2
Sodium (mg)	208
Protein (gm)	3.1
Carbohydrate (gm)	24.7

EXCHANGES:

Milk	0.0	Bread	1.0
Veg.	0.0	Meat	0.0
Fruit	0.5	Fat	1.0

Prepare Graham Cracker Crust and set aside.

Filling: Put cornstarch in small saucepan and dissolve it in small amount of cranberry juice. Add remaining juice, gelatin, and salt. Cook and stir over medium heat until mixture thickens and bubbles. Remove from heat and stir in Equal®.

Pour cranberry mixture into bowl. Chill, stirring frequently, until mixture mounds slightly when dropped from spoon. Beat egg whites until stiff peaks form. Fold in cranberry mixture, then whipped topping. Pour into prepared crust. Refrigerate until firm.

Garnish this pie with whipped topping and grated orange rind.

Yogurt Blueberry Pie

Serves 9

Vanilla Cookie Pie Crust (see p. 573)

2	3-oz. packages diet raspberry Jell-O
2	cups boiling water
½	cup cold water
2	cups nonfat vanilla yogurt
1	cup fresh blueberries, or frozen, thawed and drained

Nutritional Data

PER SERVING:

Calories	162
% calories from fat	10
Fat (gm)	1.7
Sat. Fat (gm)	0.4
Cholesterol (mg)	1.1
Sodium (mg)	111
Protein (gm)	18.6
Carbohydrate (gm)	18.2

EXCHANGES:

Milk	0.5	Bread	1.0
Veg.	0.0	Meat	0.0
Fruit	1.0	Fat	0.0

Prepare Vanilla Cookie Pie Crust in 9-inch pie pan and chill 20 minutes. Set aside.

Pour dry Jell-O into mixing bowl. Stir in boiling water and mix until smooth. Blend in cold water and set aside, letting gelatin mixture cool to room temperature. Stir in yogurt.

Place filling in refrigerator and chill until almost set, about 1 hour. Mix in blueberries. Mound filling into pie crust.

Refrigerate 2 to 3 hours, or until pie is firm, before serving.

Chilled Peach Yogurt Pie

Serves 8

Gingersnap Pie Crust (see p. 585)
- 1 cup peaches, chopped
- 2 tablespoons fresh orange juice
- 2 tablespoons light brown sugar
- 3 cups vanilla nonfat yogurt
- 1/4 teaspoon ground nutmeg
- 1/2 cup diet whipped topping mix

Nutritional Data

PER SERVING:

Calories	224
% calories from fat	23
Fat (gm)	5.9
Sat. Fat (gm)	1.1
Cholesterol (mg)	1.9
Sodium (mg)	208
Protein (gm)	5.2
Carbohydrate (gm)	38.6

EXCHANGES:

Milk	1.0	Bread	1.0
Veg.	0.0	Meat	0.0
Fruit	0.5	Fat	1.0

Prepare Gingersnap Pie Crust in 9-inch pie pan. Refrigerate crust 20 minutes or longer.

Toss peaches with orange juice and sugar in deep bowl. Stir in yogurt. Blend in nutmeg and whipped topping.

Mound yogurt filling on crust. Cover lightly with foil. Refrigerate pie 2 hours or until firm.

Apple and Blueberry Custard Pie

Serves 8

Vegetable cooking spray
- 3 cups Rome apples (4 medium-large), peeled and sliced
- 1 cup blueberries
- 1½ cups skim milk
- 1½ cups egg substitute
- 2 egg whites
- 1/2 cup all-purpose flour, sifted
- 1/4 cup granulated sugar
- 1½ teaspoons vanilla
- 3/4 teaspoon ground cinnamon

Nutritional Data

PER SERVING:

Calories	130
% calories from fat	3
Fat (gm)	0.4
Sat. Fat (gm)	0.1
Cholesterol (mg)	0.8
Sodium (mg)	101
Protein (gm)	7.3
Carbohydrate (gm)	24.6

EXCHANGES:

Milk	0.0	Bread	1.0
Veg.	0.0	Meat	0.0
Fruit	1.0	Fat	0.0

Preheat oven to 350 degrees. Coat deep 10-inch nonstick pie pan with vegetable cooking spray. Toss apple slices and blueberries evenly in pan.

Combine milk, egg substitute, and slightly beaten egg whites. Add remaining ingredients and blend with whisk. Spread batter over apples and blueberries. Bake 1 hour or until custard forms and cake tests done (when inserted, a toothpick will come out clean). Serve warm.

Key Lime Pie

Serves 8

Basic Pie Crust (recipe follows)
- ¾ cup sugar, or aspartame* equivalent
- 1 envelope unflavored gelatin
- 1¼ cups skim milk
- 6 ozs. reduced-fat cream cheese, softened
- ⅓ cup fresh lime juice
- Lime slices
- Fresh mint

Nutritional Data

PER SERVING:

Calories	258
% calories from fat	28
Fat (gm)	8.3
Sat. Fat (gm)	3.2
Cholesterol (mg)	8.1
Sodium (mg)	257
Protein (gm)	6.4
Carbohydrate (gm)	41.1

EXCHANGES:

Milk	0.0	Bread	2.5
Veg.	0.0	Meat	0.0
Fruit	0.0	Fat	1.5

Preheat oven to 350 degrees. Prepare pie crust, using 8-inch pie pan. Line pastry with weights (see Note on p. 582) and bake until golden brown, 15 to 20 minutes. Cool on wire rack.

Mix sugar* and gelatin in small saucepan; stir in milk. Cook over low heat until sugar and gelatin are dissolved, stirring constantly; remove from heat.

Beat cream cheese in small bowl until fluffy; beat in lime juice until smooth. Gradually add milk mixture, blending until smooth.

Pour into cooled pie crust. Refrigerate until set, about 2 to 4 hours. Garnish with lime slices and mint.

*Note: If using aspartame sweetener, stir equivalent amount to sugar into filling after it has been cooked and cooled slightly.

Basic Pie Crust

- 1¼ cups all-purpose flour
- 2 tablespoons sugar
- ¼ teaspoon salt
- 3 tablespoons margarine, cold
- 4-5 tablespoons ice water

Nutritional Data

PER SERVING:

Calories	121
% calories from fat	33
Fat (gm)	4.4
Sat. Fat (gm)	0.9
Cholesterol (mg)	0
Sodium (mg)	117
Protein (gm)	2.1
Carbohydrate (gm)	18.1

EXCHANGES:

Milk	0.0	Bread	1.0
Veg.	0.0	Meat	0.0
Fruit	0.0	Fat	1.0

Combine flour, sugar, and salt in medium bowl. With pastry blender or 2 knives, cut in margarine until mixture resembles coarse crumbs. Sprinkle with water, 1 tablespoon at a time, mixing lightly with fork after each addition until pastry just holds together.

On lightly floured surface, roll dough into circle 2 inches larger in diameter than pie pan. Wrap pastry around rolling pin and unroll into 8- or 9-inch pie or tart pan, easing it into bottom and side of pan. Trim edges, fold under, and flute. Bake as pie recipe directs.

Makes 1 8- or 9-inch pie crust.

Note: When pie crust is baked before it is filled, recipe might indicate baking with weights so that bottom of crust remains flat. Line bottom of pastry with aluminum foil and fill with single layer of pie weights or dried beans. Remove weights and foil 5 minutes before end of baking time indicated in recipe. If not using weights or dried beans, piercing bottom of pastry with tines of fork will help crust remain flat.

Slim Lemon Pie

Serves 8
Graham Cracker Crust (see p. 577)

Filling

1	envelope unflavored gelatin
½	cup water
1½	cups (12 ozs.) light lemon yogurt
6	packets Equal® (see "About This Cookbook")
1	teaspoon lemon peel, grated
	Yellow food coloring (optional)
⅓	cup nonfat dry milk
⅓	cup ice water
1	tablespoon fresh lemon juice
	Lemon and lime slices

Nutritional Data

PER SERVING:

Calories	114
% calories from fat	25
Fat (gm)	3.2
Sat. Fat (gm)	0.3
Cholesterol (mg)	1.8
Sodium (mg)	148
Protein (gm)	4.5
Carbohydrate (gm)	16.9

EXCHANGES:

Milk	0.0	Bread	1.0
Veg.	0.0	Meat	0.0
Fruit	0.5	Fat	0.5

Prepare Graham Cracker Crust and set aside.

Filling: In small saucepan, sprinkle gelatin over water; cook over low heat until gelatin dissolves. Cool slightly . In medium bowl, combine yogurt, Equal®, lemon peel, and food coloring; stir in gelatin mixture. Chill until mixture mounds when dropped from spoon, about 30 minutes.

In small bowl, combine nonfat dry milk, ice water, and lemon juice; beat on high speed until stiff peaks form, about 5 minutes. Fold into gelatin-yogurt mixture.

Spoon Filling into Graham Cracker Crust. Refrigerate until set, about 3 hours or overnight. Garnish with lemon and lime slices.

Pumpkin Pie

Serves 8

2 cups pumpkin pie filling
½ cup skim milk
2 eggs, beaten
2 tablespoons sugar-free maple syrup
1 teaspoon ground cinnamon
¼ teaspoon ground allspice
Dash ground nutmeg
Dash ground cloves
1 9-inch pie shell, unbaked

Nutritional Data

PER SERVING:

Calories	190
% calories from fat	34
Fat (gm)	7.3
Sat. Fat (gm)	0.5
Cholesterol (mg)	53.5
Sodium (mg)	279
Protein (gm)	3.9
Carbohydrate (gm)	28.3

EXCHANGES:

Milk	0.0	Bread	2.0
Veg.	0.0	Meat	0.0
Fruit	0.0	Fat	1.0

Preheat oven to 375 degrees.

In medium bowl, combine pumpkin, milk, eggs, maple syrup, cinnamon, allspice, nutmeg, and cloves. Pour pumpkin filling into pie shell. Bake 1 hour or until knife inserted in center of filling comes out clean. Let cool before serving.

Low-Cholesterol Pumpkin Pie

Serves 8

1 9-inch pie shell, unbaked
¾ cup egg substitute
1 12-oz. can pumpkin
½ cup plus 2 tablespoons sugar
¼ teaspoon salt
¼ teaspoon ginger, peeled and grated
¼ teaspoon ground cloves
¼ teaspoon ground cinnamon
1 cup evaporated skim milk

Nutritional Data

PER SERVING:

Calories	203
% calories from fat	26
Fat (gm)	6
Sat. Fat (gm)	1.5
Cholesterol (mg)	1
Sodium (mg)	300
Protein (gm)	6.1
Carbohydrate (gm)	32

EXCHANGES:

Milk	0.0	Bread	2.0
Veg.	0.0	Meat	0.0
Fruit	0.0	Fat	1.0

Preheat oven to 400 degrees.

Blend egg substitute and pumpkin together. Mix in sugar and remaining ingredients. Pour pumpkin filling into crust.

Cover edges of pie shell with aluminum foil strips to prevent scorching. Bake pie in center of oven 10 minutes. Reduce heat to 325 degrees and continue baking 40 minutes or until pie tests done. Remove foil after 20 minutes of baking. Cool pie on rack and serve chilled.

Pumpkin Chiffon Pie

Serves 8

1 cup canned pumpkin
½ cup evaporated skim milk
1¼ teaspoons ground cinnamon
¼ teaspoon ground mace
¼ teaspoon ground allspice
1½ teaspoons vanilla extract
1 envelope unflavored gelatin
½ cup cold water
¼ cup frozen apple juice concentrate
3 egg whites
4 graham crackers, ground
Vegetable cooking spray

Nutritional Data

PER SERVING:

Calories	66
% calories from fat	7
Fat (gm)	0.5
Sat. Fat (gm)	0.2
Cholesterol (mg)	0.5
Sodium (mg)	65
Protein (gm)	3.9
Carbohydrate (gm)	11.3

EXCHANGES:

Milk	0.0	Bread	1.0
Veg.	0.0	Meat	0.0
Fruit	0.0	Fat	0.0

In large bowl, combine pumpkin, milk, cinnamon, mace, allspice, and vanilla. Set aside.

Stir gelatin and water together in small pan. Place over low heat and stir until gelatin is dissolved. Remove from heat and stir in apple juice concentrate.

Stir gelatin mixture into pumpkin mixture and chill 20 to 30 minutes, or until slightly thickened. Beat egg whites until stiff peaks form. Fold into pumpkin mixture. Spoon filling into 9-inch pie pan that has been coated with vegetable cooking spray and ground graham crackers. Chill until firm.

Sweet Potato Pie

Serves 8

Vegetable cooking spray
½ cup graham cracker crumbs
1½ cups cooked mashed sweet potatoes or yams
¼ cup egg substitute
2 egg whites, lightly beaten
¼ cup dark brown sugar
1 tablespoon candied ginger, chopped (optional)
1 teaspoon ground cinnamon
½ teaspoon ground ginger
¼ teaspoon each ingredient: ground cloves, ground nutmeg, salt
1 cup buttermilk

Nutritional Data

PER SERVING:

Calories	147
% calories from fat	8
Fat (gm)	1.4
Sat. Fat (gm)	0.2
Cholesterol (mg)	1.1
Sodium (mg)	173
Protein (gm)	4.1
Carbohydrate (gm)	29.9

EXCHANGES:

Milk	0.0	Bread	2.0
Veg.	0.0	Meat	0.0
Fruit	0.0	Fat	0.0

Adjust rack to center of oven. Preheat oven to 375 degrees. Sprinkle graham cracker crumbs over bottom of lightly sprayed 9-inch pie pan.

Using large bowl, combine sweet potatoes, eggs, brown sugar, candied ginger, spices, and buttermilk. Beat together all ingredients in large bowl of electric mixer until combined. Pour mixture into prepared pie pan.

Bake 50 to 55 minutes or until pie is done. Pie tests done when bamboo skewer or other pie tester is inserted and comes out clean. Cool pie before serving. You can garnish pie with dollop of nonfat dairy whip, if desired

Butternut Maple Pie

Serves 8

Gingersnap Pie Crust (recipe follows)
3/4 cup egg substitute
1/4 teaspoon salt
2 tablespoons cornstarch
2½ cups cooked butternut squash, mashed and cooled
1/4 cup maple syrup
1½ cups warm skim milk
3/4 teaspoon ground cinnamon
1/4 teaspoon ground nutmeg
1/4 teaspoon ground ginger

Nutritional Data

PER SERVING:

Calories	211
% calories from fat	25
Fat (gm)	6
Sat. Fat (gm)	1.2
Cholesterol (mg)	0.8
Sodium (mg)	277
Protein (gm)	5
Carbohydrate (gm)	36

EXCHANGES:

Milk	0.0	Bread	2.5
Veg.	0.0	Meat	0.0
Fruit	0.0	Fat	1.0

Make crust and set aside.

Preheat oven to 450 degrees.

Mix egg substitute with salt and cornstarch. Blend in squash and maple syrup. In slow, steady stream, mix milk into egg substitute mixture. Stir in cinnamon, nutmeg, and ginger.

Pour filling into pie crust. Bake pie in center of oven 10 minutes. Lower heat to 325 degrees and continue baking 30 minutes or until pie tests done: a knife inserted in center of pie will come out clean.

Cool pie on rack. Serve cold or at room temperature.

Gingersnap Pie Crust

1¼ cups gingersnaps, ground
1/4 cup sugar
3 tablespoons margarine, or butter, melted
Butter-flavored vegetable cooking spray

Preheat oven to 375 degrees. Combine all ingredients and press into a 9-inch pie pan coated with cooking spray. Press crumbs on bottom and up sides of pan. Bake crust 5 minutes. Cool or chill 20 minutes before using.

Fresh Strawberry Rhubarb Pie

Serves 8

Basic Pie Crust, doubled to make 2 crusts (see p. 581)

Filling

1 pint strawberries, washed and hulled
3 cups fresh rhubarb,* chopped
3 tablespoons honey
¼ cup cornstarch

Nutritional Data	
PER SERVING:	
Calories	182
% calories from fat	23
Fat (gm)	4.7
Sat. Fat (gm)	0.9
Cholesterol (mg)	0
Sodium (mg)	120
Protein (gm)	2.7
Carbohydrate (gm)	32.8

EXCHANGES:			
Milk	0.0	Bread	1.5
Veg.	0.0	Meat	0.0
Fruit	0.5	Fat	1.0

Prepare two pie crusts for 9-inch pans. Preheat oven to 400 degrees.

Filling: Combine all filling ingredients; mix lightly. Spoon into pie crust. Place second crust on top, seal, and cut slits in several places. Bake at 400 degrees for 10 minutes. Lower temperature to 325 degrees and bake 35 minutes more or until golden.

*Note: A 16-oz. package of defrosted frozen rhubarb may be substituted for fresh rhubarb.

Strawberry-Rhubarb Pie with Graham Cracker Crust

Serves 8

¼ cup graham cracker crumbs
1 tablespoon diet margarine, melted
4 cups rhubarb, sliced ½ inch, leaves discarded
¾ cup sugar
3 tablespoons quick-cooking tapioca
½ teaspoon ground cinnamon
2 tablespoons fresh orange juice
1 cup fresh strawberries, hulled and crushed, or frozen strawberries, defrosted
1 tablespoon nonfat margarine
¼ cup graham cracker crumbs

Nutritional Data	
PER SERVING:	
Calories	145
% calories from fat	11
Fat (gm)	1.8
Sat. Fat (gm)	0.2
Cholesterol (mg)	0
Sodium (mg)	70
Protein (gm)	1.2
Carbohydrate (gm)	32.3

EXCHANGES:			
Milk	0.0	Bread	1.0
Veg.	0.0	Meat	0.0
Fruit	1.0	Fat	0.0

Preheat oven to 425 degrees.

Sprinkle ¼ cup graham cracker crumbs combined with margarine on bottom of 9-inch pie pan. Set aside.

Place cut rhubarb in large bowl. Mix sugar, tapioca, and cinnamon in separate small bowl. Toss sugar mixture with rhubarb.

Stir orange juice with strawberries. Add strawberries to rhubarb mixture and blend in margarine.

Spread filling in pie pan, mounding fruit somewhat higher in center. Sprinkle pie with remaining crumbs.

Bake pie in center of oven 50 to 60 minutes or until pie is done and fruit is tender. Cool pie on rack. Serve at room temperature.

Baked Alaska Pie

Serves 8

Vanilla Cookie Pie Crust (see p. 573)
- 3 cups nonfat vanilla frozen yogurt
- 2 tablespoons candy canes, crushed
- 4 egg whites, room temperature
- ½ tablespoon cream of tartar
- ⅓ cup sugar

Prepare Vanilla Cookie Pie Crust and chill 20 minutes. Set aside.

Preheat oven to 500 degrees.

Stir yogurt to soften. Mix in crushed candy canes. Spread yogurt mixture in cooled pie crust. Cover with foil and freeze until solid.

When ready to serve, beat egg whites with cream of tartar until soft peaks form. Sprinkle sugar over egg whites. Continue beating until stiff. Mound meringue over yogurt and spread to edges, completely sealing.

Place pie on cookie sheet. Bake 2½ to 3 minutes or until tips of meringue are golden brown. Serve immediately.

Nutritional Data

PER SERVING:

Calories	201
% calories from fat	9
Fat (gm)	1.9
Sat. Fat (gm)	0.4
Cholesterol (mg)	0
Sodium (mg)	125
Protein (gm)	4.6
Carbohydrate (gm)	40.8

EXCHANGES:

Milk	0.0	Bread	3.0
Veg.	0.0	Meat	0.0
Fruit	0.0	Fat	0.0

Apple Pandowdy

Serves 8

Pastry Dough

- 1⅛ cups unbleached all-purpose flour
- ½ teaspoon salt
- ¼ cup vegetable shortening
- 3-4 tablespoons ice water

Filling

- 2¼ lbs. cooking apples, such as Granny Smith
- ¾ cup granulated sugar
- ¾ teaspoon ground cinnamon
- ¼ teaspoon salt
- 3 tablespoons all-purpose flour

Nutritional Data

PER SERVING:

Calories	280
% calories from fat	22
Fat (gm)	7.1
Sat. Fat (gm)	2.1
Cholesterol (mg)	0
Sodium (mg)	205
Protein (gm)	2.4
Carbohydrate (gm)	54.1

EXCHANGES:

Milk	0.0	Bread	2.0
Veg.	0.0	Meat	0.0
Fruit	1.5	Fat	1.0

¼   teaspoon ground mace
1   teaspoon nonfat margarine
    Vegetable cooking spray

Pastry Dough: Combine flour and salt. Cut vegetable short-ening into flour; mixture will resemble coarse meal. Sprinkle water, a tablespoon at a time, over dough. Mix in enough water so that dough is cohesive. Shape into dough ball, wrap in plastic, and refrigerate 1 hour. (Dough can be prepared a day before using.) Roll out dough to fit over 1-quart casserole.

Preheat oven to 425 degrees.

Filling: Peel, core, and slice apples. In bowl, mix together sugar, cinnamon, salt, flour, and mace. Crumble in margarine. Toss apples with sugar/flour mixture.

Arrange apples in casserole, coated with cooking spray. Carefully set pastry dough over apples. Allow dough to slightly overhang edge of dish, yet press crust firmly to dish. Flute edges and make ½-inch steam vent in center.

Bake 30 minutes. Reduce heat to 350 degrees. Break up crust with back of spoon, turning it and apples over. Continue baking 8 to 10 minutes. Serve Apple Pandowdy hot or warm. Good with chilled nonfat vanilla yogurt (optional).

Peach Crumble

Serves 8	**Nutritional Data**	
4 cups peaches, peeled and sliced	PER SERVING:	
⅓ cup firmly packed light brown sugar	Calories	252
2 tablespoons fresh orange juice	% calories from fat	11
Butter-flavored vegetable cooking spray	Fat (gm)	3.2
	Sat. Fat (gm)	0.6
2 tablespoons cornstarch	Cholesterol (mg)	0
⅓ cup unbleached all-purpose flour	Sodium (mg)	37
2 tablespoons margarine, or butter, cut into	Protein (gm)	3.9
½-inch pieces	Carbohydrate (gm)	52.9
⅓ cup granulated sugar		
1 teaspoon orange peel, grated	EXCHANGES:	

Milk	0.0	Bread	3.0
Veg.	0.0	Meat	0.0
Fruit	1.0	Fat	0.5

Preheat oven to 350 degrees.

Toss sliced peaches with brown sugar and orange juice. Arrange peach slices in 9" x 9" baking pan coated with cooking spray.

Combine cornstarch and flour and cut in butter. Mix in granulated sugar and orange peel. Sprinkle mixture over peaches.

Bake 35 minutes or until fruit is tender. Spoon crumble into sauce dishes and serve with vanilla yogurt, if desired (not included in Nutritional Data).

Pear Grunt

Serves 8

2	cups biscuit flour
½	cup skim milk
2	tablespoons orange peel, grated and divided
6	cups peaches, peeled, pitted, and cut into bite-size pieces
⅓	cup granulated sugar
½	teaspoon ground cinnamon
1	cup water
3	tablespoons cornstarch

Nutritional Data

PER SERVING:

Calories	229
% calories from fat	3
Fat (gm)	0.7
Sat. Fat (gm)	0.1
Cholesterol (mg)	0.3
Sodium (mg)	9
Protein (gm)	5.6
Carbohydrate (gm)	51.3

EXCHANGES:

Milk	0.0	Bread	2.5
Veg.	0.0	Meat	0.0
Fruit	1.0	Fat	0.0

Mix biscuit flour, milk, and 1 tablespoon orange peel; set aside.

In nonstick skillet, mix peach pieces, remaining orange peel, sugar, cinnamon, water, and cornstarch. Bring mixture to boil, reduce heat to simmer, and cook 5 minutes. Stir occasionally.

Increase heat to medium, and spoon biscuit dough onto peaches. Cover and cook 10 minutes. Spoon grunt into sauce dishes and serve hot.

Berry Grunt

Serves 8

3	cups fresh blueberries or raspberries, or frozen, defrosted and drained
1	cup water
½	cup plus 2 tablespoons granulated sugar
1½	cups all-purpose flour
1½	teaspoons baking powder
¼	teaspoon ground nutmeg
¼	teaspoon salt
⅔	cup buttermilk

Nutritional Data

PER SERVING:

Calories	178
% calories from fat	3
Fat (gm)	0.7
Sat. Fat (gm)	0.2
Cholesterol (mg)	0.7
Sodium (mg)	150
Protein (gm)	3.5
Carbohydrate (gm)	40

EXCHANGES:

Milk	0.0	Bread	1.5
Veg.	0.0	Meat	0.0
Fruit	1.0	Fat	0.0

Stir berries, water, and sugar together in saucepan. Simmer 5 minutes, stirring often.

Meanwhile, combine flour, baking powder, nutmeg, and salt. Blend in buttermilk; do not overmix. Drop batter over berries, making 8 dumplings. Cover and simmer 8 to 10 minutes.

Serve berries hot in small dish with dumpling.

Blueberry Buckle

Serves 8

2½	cups fresh blueberries, or frozen, defrosted and drained	
2	tablespoons all-purpose flour	
2	tablespoons vegetable shortening	
¾	cup granulated sugar	
¼	cup egg substitute	
½	cup skim milk	
2	cups all-purpose flour	
1¾	teaspoons baking powder	
¼	teaspoon salt	
¼	cup granulated sugar	
1	teaspoon ground cinnamon	
1	teaspoon ground nutmeg	
	Vegetable cooking spray	

Nutritional Data

PER SERVING:

Calories	283
% calories from fat	12
Fat (gm)	3.8
Sat. Fat (gm)	1.1
Cholesterol (mg)	0.3
Sodium (mg)	161
Protein (gm)	4.9
Carbohydrate (gm)	58.2

EXCHANGES:

Milk	0.0	Bread	3.0
Veg.	0.0	Meat	0.0
Fruit	1.0	Fat	0.5

Preheat oven to 375 degrees.

Toss blueberries with 2 tablespoons flour. Place in bottom of 8-inch baking pan or pie pan coated with cooking spray.

Cream vegetable shortening and ¾ cup sugar until light. Mix in egg substitute and milk. Blend in flour, baking powder, and salt. Spoon batter over top of berries.

Combine ¼ cup sugar, cinnamon, and nutmeg. Sprinkle over top of batter.

Bake 40 to 45 minutes or until cake tester comes out clean. Serve warm with nonfat frozen yogurt (not included in Nutritional Data).

Cranberry-Pear Cobbler

Serves 8

¾	cup granulated sugar	
¾	cup water	
½	cup fresh orange juice, divided	
1½	cups fresh cranberries, washed and picked over	
3	cups pears, cored and chopped	
1½	cups unbleached all-purpose flour, sifted	
1½	teaspoons baking powder	
⅛	teaspoon salt	
¼	cup vegetable shortening	
½	cup 2% milk	
	Butter-flavored vegetable cooking spray	

Nutritional Data

PER SERVING:

Calories	297
% calories from fat	22
Fat (gm)	7.4
Sat. Fat (gm)	2.2
Cholesterol (mg)	1.1
Sodium (mg)	104
Protein (gm)	3.5
Carbohydrate (gm)	56.6

EXCHANGES:

Milk	0.0	Bread	2.0
Veg.	0.0	Meat	0.0
Fruit	1.5	Fat	1.5

Preheat oven to 375 degrees.

Blend sugar with water and ¼ cup orange juice in saucepan. Cook mixture over medium heat until it comes to boil. Stir in cranberries. Again bring mixture to boil. Reduce heat to medium and continue cooking 10 minutes, stirring occasionally. Cool stewed cranberries.

Combine cranberries and pears with remaining orange juice. Spoon fruit evenly into 6 ramekins or custard cups coated with cooking spray.

Mix flour, baking powder, and salt in bowl. Cut in vegetable shortening. Stir in enough milk to make soft dough. Using tablespoon, shape dumpling on each ramekin.

Bake 30 minutes or until biscuits are golden brown. Remove cobbler from oven and serve warm.

Apricot Cobbler

Serves 8

- 6 cups apricots, pitted and sliced
- ½ cup granulated sugar
- 2 tablespoons cornstarch
  Butter-flavored vegetable cooking spray
- 1½ cups all-purpose flour, sifted
- 1½ teaspoons baking powder
- ⅛ teaspoon salt
- ¼ cup vegetable shortening
- ½ cup skim milk

Nutritional Data

PER SERVING:

Calories	253
% calories from fat	24
Fat (gm)	7
Sat. Fat (gm)	2
Cholesterol (mg)	0.2
Sodium (mg)	109
Protein (gm)	4.2
Carbohydrate (gm)	44.8

EXCHANGES:

Milk	0.0	Bread	2.0
Veg.	0.0	Meat	0.0
Fruit	1.0	Fat	1.0

Preheat oven to 375 degrees.

Toss apricots with sugar and cornstarch. Spoon fruit into 1-quart baking dish coated with cooking spray.

Mix flour, baking powder, and salt in bowl. Cut in vegetable shortening. Stir in enough milk to make soft dough. Using tablespoon, shape dumplings over fruit.

Bake 35 to 40 minutes or until dumplings are golden brown. Remove cobbler from oven and serve warm.

Pear Betty

Serves 8

Graham Cracker Crust
(recipe follows)
- 4½ cups soft pears, peeled and sliced
- 2 teaspoons fresh lemon juice
- ½ cup firmly packed light brown sugar
- ¼ cup all-purpose flour
- ¾ teaspoon ground cinnamon
- ¼ teaspoon ground mace

Nutritional Data

PER SERVING:

Calories	226
% calories from fat	10
Fat (gm)	2.7
Sat. Fat (gm)	0
Cholesterol (mg)	0
Sodium (mg)	150
Protein (gm)	2.1
Carbohydrate (gm)	50

2	tablespoons nonfat margarine, melted and cooled	EXCHANGES:			
¼	cup graham crackers, crumbled	Milk	0.0	Bread	2.0
		Veg.	0.0	Meat	0.0
		Fruit	1.0	Fat	0.5

Make crust and set aside to chill. Preheat oven to 375 degrees.

Toss pear slices with lemon juice, brown sugar, flour, cinnamon, mace, and margarine. Fill pie crust with pear mixture and sprinkle with remaining crumbs.

Bake 25 minutes or until pears are fork-tender. Pear Betty is best served warm. It is especially good with nonfat vanilla yogurt (not in Nutritional Data).

Graham Cracker Crust

1 cup graham crackers, crumbled
2 tablespoons granulated sugar
¾ teaspoon ground cinnamon
2 tablespoons nonfat margarine, melted and cooled

Toss graham cracker crumbs with granulated sugar, cinnamon, and melted margarine in deep bowl. Pat crumbs into 9-inch pie pan. Chill 20 minutes.

Cherry Crisp

Serves 8

1 cup quick-cooking rolled oats
½ cup firmly packed light brown sugar
½ cup all-purpose flour
1 teaspoon ground cinnamon
¼ tablespoon ground cardamom seeds
2 tablespoons vegetable shortening
4 cups fresh cherries, or frozen, defrosted and drained
Vegetable cooking spray

Nutritional Data

PER SERVING:

Calories	185
% calories from fat	20
Fat (gm)	4.2
Sat. Fat (gm)	1.2
Cholesterol (mg)	0
Sodium (mg)	8.4
Protein (gm)	3.2
Carbohydrate (gm)	35.4

EXCHANGES:

Milk	0.0	Bread	1.0
Veg.	0.0	Meat	0.0
Fruit	1.0	Fat	1.0

Preheat oven to 375 degrees.

Toss oats, sugar, flour, cinnamon, and cardamom. Cut in shortening. Arrange cherries in 8-inch-square pan coated with cooking spray. Sprinkle rolled oats mixture over cherries.

Bake 30 minutes or until topping is golden color. Serve warm with ice cream or yogurt (not included in Nutritional Data).

Cherry Slump

Serves 8

5 cups sour cherries, washed, drained, and pitted
½ cup granulated sugar
1 tablespoon lemon peel, grated
1 tablespoon fresh lemon juice
3 tablespoons cornstarch
1 cup water
Butter-flavored vegetable cooking spray
1 cup all-purpose flour
1½ teaspoons baking powder
½ cup skim milk
1 tablespoon lemon peel, grated

Nutritional Data

PER SERVING:

Calories	172
% calories from fat	2
Fat (gm)	0.5
Sat. Fat (gm)	0.1
Cholesterol (mg)	0.3
Sodium (mg)	73
Protein (gm)	3.1
Carbohydrate (gm)	40.3

EXCHANGES:

Milk	0.0	Bread	1.5
Veg.	0.0	Meat	0.0
Fruit	1.0	Fat	0.0

Preheat oven to 350 degrees.

In saucepan, toss cherries with sugar, lemon peel, lemon juice, and cornstarch mixed with water. Bring mixture to boil over medium heat, stirring often. Pour cherries into 9" x 9" nonstick baking dish coated with cooking spray. Bake 15 minutes.

Mix flour and baking powder in bowl. Stir in milk and lemon peel. Using tablespoon, shape 8 individual biscuits and spoon over fruit. Cover and bake 15 minutes. Remove cover and bake 5 minutes more.

To serve, spoon biscuit onto each dessert dish; slice open and spoon fruit over. Serve hot

Strawberry Slump

Serves 8

6 cups strawberries, hulled and cut into halves
½ cup sugar, or ⅓ cup fructose (fruit sugar, see "About This Cookbook")
3 tablespoons cornstarch
1 cup water
Butter-flavored vegetable cooking spray
1 cup all-purpose flour
1½ teaspoons baking powder
½ cup skim milk

Nutritional Data

PER SERVING:

Calories	156
% calories from fat	3
Fat (gm)	0.6
Sat. Fat (gm)	0.1
Cholesterol (mg)	0.2
Sodium (mg)	71
Protein (gm)	2.8
Carbohydrate (gm)	36

EXCHANGES:

Milk	0.0	Bread	1.5
Veg.	0.0	Meat	0.0
Fruit	1.0	Fat	0.0

Preheat oven to 350 degrees.

In saucepan, toss strawberries with sugar, cornstarch, and water. Bring mixture to boil. Reduce to simmer and cook 5 minutes, stirring often. Spoon mixture into 9" x 9" nonstick baking pan coated with cooking spray. Bake 5 minutes.

Meanwhile, mix flour, baking powder, and milk in bowl. Using pot holders, remove fruit mixture from oven and drop biscuit dough, by heaping tablespoon, directly onto fruit. Cover and return to oven to bake 15 minutes more. Remove cover and bake 5 minutes more.

To serve, spoon a biscuit onto each dessert dish; slice open and spoon fruit over. Serve hot.

Chapter Seventeen

DESSERTS

Pineapple-Lemon Trifle

Serves 12

1 18.25-oz. package reduced-fat white
   cake mix
1⅓ cups water
3 egg whites
1½ cups pineapple chunks, drained
   Lemon Custard (recipe follows)
1 pint strawberries, sliced
2 medium bananas, sliced
¾ cup frozen diet whipped topping, thawed

Nutritional Data

PER SERVING:

Calories	276
% calories from fat	15
Fat (gm)	4.7
Sat. Fat (gm)	1.3
Cholesterol (mg)	35.9
Sodium (mg)	359
Protein (gm)	4.3
Carbohydrate (gm)	54.9

EXCHANGES:

Milk	0.0	Bread	3.0
Veg.	0.0	Meat	0.0
Fruit	0.5	Fat	1.0

Preheat oven to 350 degrees.

Prepare cake mix according to package directions, using 1⅓ cups water and 3 egg whites. Bake in lightly greased and floured 13" x 9" baking pan 28 to 30 minutes or until top springs back when touched. Cool on wire rack. Cut half cake into 1-inch cubes. (Reserve or freeze remaining cake for another use.)

Whirl pineapple chunks in blender or food processor until smooth. Layer ⅓ cake cubes in bottom of 2-quart glass serving bowl. Spoon ⅓ Lemon Custard and ⅓ pineapple puree over cake cubes; top with ⅓ of strawberries and bananas. Repeat layers twice. Refrigerate until chilled, about 1 hour. Garnish with whipped topping.

Lemon Custard

¼ cup sugar
2 tablespoons cornstarch
2 tablespoons flour
1 cup skim milk
⅓ cup fresh lemon juice
2 eggs, slightly beaten
¼ teaspoon ground nutmeg

Mix sugar, cornstarch, and flour in medium saucepan; stir in milk and lemon juice. Cook over medium heat until mixture boils and thickens; boil 1 minute, stirring constantly.

Stir about ½ cup of mixture into eggs; stir egg mixture back into saucepan. Cook over low heat, stirring constantly, until thickened. Remove from heat; stir in nutmeg. Refrigerate until chilled, 1 to 2 hours.

Fresh Fruit Trifle

Serves 12 (¾-cup servings)

- 1½ cups skim milk
- ½ cup 1% low-fat cottage cheese
- 2½ tablespoons cornstarch
- 2 tablespoons instant nonfat dry milk
- 2 teaspoons vanilla extract
  Grated rind of 1 orange
- 3 packets Equal® (see "About This Cookbook")
- ½ cup fruit-only strawberry jam
- ¼ cup orange-flavored liqueur
- 1 4-oz. loaf commercial angel food cake
- 2½ cups fresh strawberries, hulled and cut into halves
- 2½ cups fresh blueberries
- 4 kiwi fruits, peeled and thinly sliced
- 4 medium oranges, peeled and sectioned

Nutritional Data

PER SERVING:

Calories	170
% calories from fat	3
Fat (gm)	0.6
Sat. Fat (gm)	0.1
Cholesterol (mg)	1
Sodium (mg)	134
Protein (gm)	4.2
Carbohydrate (gm)	36.6

EXCHANGES:

Milk	0.0	Bread	1.5
Veg.	0.0	Meat	0.0
Fruit	1.0	Fat	0.0

Combine first 4 ingredients in electric blender and process until smooth. Pour mixture into top of double boiler; bring water to boil. Reduce heat to low; cook, stirring constantly, 10 minutes or until mixture thickens. Remove from heat; stir in vanilla, orange rind, and 3 packets Equal®.

Combine strawberry jam and orange liqueur in small saucepan; bring to boil, stirring constantly. Remove mixture from heat and let it cool completely.

Trim crusts from cake, and cut into ½-inch slices. Line bottom of 3-quart glass bowl with half of cake slices; brush with half of strawberry mixture Arrange half of strawberries, blueberries, kiwi fruit, and oranges around bottom edge of bowl on top of cake slices. Spoon half of cooled custard mixture over fruit. Repeat this procedure with remaining ingredients. Cover and chill about 8 hours.

Cassata Siciliana

Serves 10

- 1 6.95-oz. package angel food loaf cake mix
- ½ cup water
- 1 cup low-fat ricotta cheese
- ¼ cup sugar
- 2 tablespoons mixed candied fruit, finely chopped
- 1 oz. semisweet chocolate, finely chopped
- 1 teaspoon lemon rind, grated

Nutritional Data

PER SERVING:

Calories	206
% calories from fat	11
Fat (gm)	2.5
Sat. Fat (gm)	0.8
Cholesterol (mg)	0.5
Sodium (mg)	268
Protein (gm)	5
Carbohydrate (gm)	39.1

¼ cup dark rum	**EXCHANGES:**
Chocolate Sauce (recipe follows)	Milk 0.0 Bread 2.5
	Veg. 0.0 Meat 0.0
	Fruit 0.0 Fat 0.5

Preheat oven to 375 degrees.

Combine cake mix and water in large bowl. Mix at low speed until moistened. Beat 2 minutes at high speed. Pour into ungreased 9" x 5" loaf pan. Bake 25 to 30 minutes or until cracks on top appear dry. Cool completely in pan tipped on side on wire rack.

With serrated knife, slice cake horizontally into 3 equal layers.

Combine ricotta cheese, sugar, candied fruit, chocolate, and lemon rind in small bowl.

Place 1 cake layer, crust side down, in 9" x 5" loaf pan lined with plastic wrap. Brush cake with 1 tablespoon rum; spread with half of ricotta mixture. Top with second cake layer, brush with 1 tablespoon rum, and spread with remaining ricotta mixture. Top with remaining cake layer, and brush with remaining rum. Cover with plastic wrap, pressing firmly to compact layers.

Refrigerate, weighted with 16-ounce can, overnight. Slice cake and arrange on serving plate; drizzle with Chocolate Sauce.

Chocolate Sauce

¼   cup unsweetened cocoa
2   tablespoons sugar
1   tablespoon cornstarch
⅓   cup dark corn syrup
¼   cup 2% milk
1   teaspoon margarine
2   teaspoons vanilla extract

Combine cocoa, sugar, and cornstarch in small saucepan. Stir in corn syrup and milk until smooth. Cook over medium heat until mixture boils and thickens, stirring constantly. Remove from heat; stir in margarine and vanilla. Cool.

 # Fancy Fruit Soup

Serves 4	***Nutritional Data***
½ cup dried apricots	PER SERVING:
½ cup canned orange-pineapple-banana	Calories 126
juice (or orange juice)	% calories from fat 10
½ cup prunes, pitted	Fat (gm) 1.5
1 cinnamon stick	Sat. Fat (gm) 0.2
4 whole cloves	Cholesterol (mg) 0.1
2 slices lemon	Sodium (mg) 8
2 tablespoons nonfat plain yogurt	Protein (gm) 2
	Carbohydrate (gm) 29.6

1 tablespoon pecans, chopped
1 teaspoon unsweetened coconut

EXCHANGES:

Milk	0.0	Bread	0.0
Veg.	0.0	Meat	0.0
Fruit	2.0	Fat	0.0

Place apricots in medium bowl with ½ cup juice and cover with vented plastic wrap. Microwave on High 1 minute. Add prunes, cinnamon stick, cloves, and lemon and microwave on High another 2 minutes, until fruit is soft. Remove cloves and cinnamon stick, mix in yogurt, and serve with sprinkling of pecans and coconut, if desired. This is even better after chilling overnight.

Fresh Fruit Hawaiian

Serves 4

1 cup fresh pineapple, cut into chunks
1 papaya, peeled, seeded, and cubed
½ cup fresh strawberries, sliced
1 kiwi fruit, peeled and sliced
1 teaspoon fresh lime juice
2 packets Equal® (see "About This Cookbook")

Combine pineapple, papaya, strawberries, kiwi fruit, and lime juice. Sprinkle with Equal® and lime juice. Chill thoroughly.

Nutritional Data

PER SERVING:

Calories	100
% calories from fat	4
Fat (gm)	0.5
Sat. Fat (gm)	0
Cholesterol (mg)	0
Sodium (mg)	9
Protein (gm)	0.9
Carbohydrate (gm)	24.2

EXCHANGES:

Milk	0.0	Bread	0.0
Veg.	0.0	Meat	0.0
Fruit	1.5	Fat	0.0

✳ Autumn Fruit Compote

Serves 10

2 8-oz. packages mixed dried fruits
1 cup raisins
2½ cups apple cider
½ cup sugar
2 lemon slices
10 whole cloves
1 6-inch stick cinnamon
½ cup brandy
Nonfat whipped topping (optional)

Nutritional Data

PER SERVING:

Calories	257
% calories from fat	1
Fat (gm)	0.4
Sat. Fat (gm)	0
Cholesterol (mg)	0
Sodium (mg)	16
Protein (gm)	1.5
Carbohydrate (gm)	61

EXCHANGES:

Milk	0.0	Bread	0.0
Veg.	0.0	Meat	0.0
Fruit	4.0	Fat	0.0

Cut dried fruits into large pieces. In wok, place mixed dried fruits and raisins. Stir in apple cider and sugar. Bring to boil. Stud lemon slices with cloves; add to wok. Add stick cinnamon. Reduce heat; cover and simmer about 20 minutes or until fruit is tender.

Discard lemon slices and stick cinnamon. Add brandy. Cool slightly. Spoon into serving dishes; top with nonfat whipped topping, if desired.

To Freeze: Vacuum seal each portion; label and freeze up to 2 months.

To Serve: Put bags in boiling water, and bring water to boil again. Boil 10 to 12 minutes.

Fresh Fruit Salad with Grand Marnier

Serves 8

- Juice of 1 lemon
- 1/4 cup sugar
- 3 tablespoons Grand Marnier
- 2 tablespoons honey
- 1 cup orange sections, seedless
- 1 cup green grapes, seedless
- 1 cup strawberries, hulled
- 1 cup blueberries
- 1 cup cantaloupe balls
- 1 cup raspberries

Nutritional Data

PER SERVING:	
Calories	115
% calories from fat	3
Fat (gm)	0.4
Sat. Fat (gm)	0.1
Cholesterol (mg)	0
Sodium (mg)	4
Protein (gm)	0.9
Carbohydrate (gm)	26.7

EXCHANGES:			
Milk	0.0	Bread	0.0
Veg.	0.0	Meat	0.0
Fruit	2.0	Fat	0.0

Combine lemon juice, sugar, Grand Marnier, and honey. Add fruit and blend well. Chill until ready to serve.

To Freeze: Vacuum seal each portion; label and freeze up to 2 months.

To Serve: Thaw in refrigerator or in bowl of water. Serve chilled.

Mixed Fruit Tortoni

Serves 12

- 1 1/2 cups fresh raspberries, or frozen, thawed
- 3 envelopes (1.3 ozs. each) diet whipped topping mix
- 1 1/2 cups 2% milk
- 1/2 cup sweet cherries, pitted, cut into halves, and divided
- 1/3 cup apricots, peeled, pitted, and cubed
- 1/3 cup pineapple, peeled, cored, and cubed

Nutritional Data

PER SERVING:	
Calories	94
% calories from fat	8
Fat (gm)	0.8
Sat. Fat (gm)	0.4
Cholesterol (mg)	2.3
Sodium (mg)	31
Protein (gm)	1.3
Carbohydrate (gm)	17.3

4 tablespoons sugar
¼ cup pistachio nuts, or slivered almonds, chopped and divided

EXCHANGES:			
Milk	0.0	Bread	0.0
Veg.	0.0	Meat	0.0
Fruit	1.0	Fat	0.0

Whirl raspberries in food processor or blender until smooth; strain and discard seeds.

Blend whipped topping and milk in large bowl; beat at high speed until topping forms soft peaks, about 4 minutes. Fold raspberry puree into whipped topping.

Reserve 12 cherry halves. Combine remaining cherries, apricots, and pineapple in small bowl; sprinkle with sugar and stir. Fold fruit into whipped topping mixture.

Reserve 2 tablespoons nuts. Fold remaining nuts into whipped topping mixture.

Spoon about ½ cup mixture into 12 cupcake liners; garnish tops of each with reserved cherry halves and nuts. Place cupcake liners in muffin or baking pan; freeze until firm, 6 hours or overnight.

Sweet Potato Fruit Bake

Serves 4

1 sweet potato, or yam, peeled and sliced (about 2 cups)
2 tablespoons unsweetened pineapple juice
1 cup apple,* peeled and diced
¾ cup unsweetened pineapple* tidbits
2 tablespoons apricot preserves, no sugar added
6 whole cloves
   Few dashes cinnamon
1 tablespoon blanched almonds, slivered
1 tablespoon unsweetened coconut, shredded

Nutritional Data

PER SERVING:

Calories	107
% calories from fat	12
Fat (gm)	1.5
Sat. Fat (gm)	0.5
Cholesterol (mg)	0
Sodium (mg)	5
Protein (gm)	1.2
Carbohydrate (gm)	23.6

EXCHANGES:			
Milk	0.0	Bread	1.0
Veg.	0.0	Meat	0.0
Fruit	0.5	Fat	0.0

Place sweet potato pieces with pineapple juice in 4-cup glass measure or casserole, and cover with vented plastic wrap. Microwave on High 5 minutes, turning and stirring once or until potatoes are tender.

Mix apple, pineapple tidbits, apricot preserves, and cloves. Arrange potatoes on 9-inch glass pie plate and top with fruit mixture. Sprinkle with cinnamon. Cover with wax paper, and microwave on High 3 to 4 minutes. Let cool a few minutes and top with almonds and coconut.

*Note: Other fruits such as oranges, kiwis, or berries may be substituted for pineapple tidbits and apples.

Fruit and Dip

Serves 10

1	8-oz. carton orange low-fat yogurt
½	cup cranberry-orange relish
¼	teaspoon ground nutmeg
¼	teaspoon ground ginger
1	medium apple
1	medium nectarine
1	tablespoon fresh lemon juice
1	cup grapes, seedless
1	cup strawberries
1	cup fresh pineapple, cut into chunks
1	medium banana, cut into chunks
3	packets Equal® (see "About This Cookbook")
	Lettuce leaves

Nutritional Data

PER SERVING:

Calories	70
% calories from fat	7
Fat (gm)	0.6
Sat. Fat (gm)	0.2
Cholesterol (mg)	1
Sodium (mg)	14
Protein (gm)	1.5
Carbohydrate (gm)	16.3

EXCHANGES:

Milk	0.0	Bread	0.0
Veg.	0.0	Meat	0.0
Fruit	1.0	Fat	0.0

Combine yogurt, relish, nutmeg, and ginger. Cover and chill. Just before serving, core apple and remove pit from nectarine. Slice apple and nectarine; brush with lemon juice.

Place all fruit in bowl and sprinkle with Equal®. Arrange lettuce leaves on platter and top with fruit. Serve dip alongside in bowl, with picks for easy handling.

Crème Fraîche

Serves 10 (2-tablespoon servings)

1	cup nonfat ricotta cheese
¼	cup buttermilk

Whip cheese and buttermilk in blender until smooth. Pour into dish and microwave on High 1 to 2 minutes, until just warm. Let stand a few hours before chilling. Use dollop over fruit desserts.

Nutritional Data

PER SERVING:

Calories	19
% calories from fat	2
Fat (gm)	0.1
Sat. Fat (gm)	0
Cholesterol (mg)	2.7
Sodium (mg)	19
Protein (gm)	3.4
Carbohydrate (gm)	1.9

EXCHANGES:

Milk	0.0	Bread	0.0
Veg.	0.0	Meat	0.0
Fruit	0.0	Fat	0.0

Cherries Jubilee

Serves 4

1 1-lb. can Bing cherries
2 tablespoons arrowroot, dissolved in 2
   tablespoons water
1 tablespoon kirsch

Drain cherries. Reserve juice from can. In chafing dish or skillet, heat juice. Bring to boil and cook 10 minutes. Add cherries. Bring again to boil. Add arrowroot and continue boiling a few seconds until liquid thickens. Sprinkle with slightly warmed kirsch and cautiously, with long match, ignite. Serve quickly.

Nutritional Data

PER SERVING:

Calories	103
% calories from fat	1
Fat (gm)	0.2
Sat. Fat (gm)	0
Cholesterol (mg)	0
Sodium (mg)	3
Protein (gm)	0.7
Carbohydrate (gm)	24.6

EXCHANGES:

Milk	0.0	Bread	0.0
Veg.	0.0	Meat	0.0
Fruit	1.5	Fat	0.0

Cherry Clafouti

Serves 8

   Vegetable cooking spray
1 lb. black cherries
¼ cup skim milk
4 tablespoons mild-flavored honey
3 egg whites
1 egg yolk
1 tablespoon vanilla extract
   Pinch salt
½ cup unbleached white flour, sifted

Nutritional Data

PER SERVING:

Calories	113
% calories from fat	6
Fat (gm)	0.7
Sat. Fat (gm)	0.2
Cholesterol (mg)	26.8
Sodium (mg)	28
Protein (gm)	3.3
Carbohydrate (gm)	23.4

EXCHANGES:

Milk	0.0	Bread	1.0
Veg.	0.0	Meat	0.0
Fruit	0.5	Fat	0.0

Preheat oven to 350 degrees. Coat 10-inch baking dish with cooking spray.

Pit cherries and place them in bowl; strain off any juices from pits; retain juice.

In blender or food processor, mix together milk, honey, juice from pitted cherries, eggs, vanilla, and salt. Add flour and continue to blend together 1 minute more, until completely smooth.

Pour batter into bowl containing cherries, mix well, and turn into coated baking dish. Bake 45 minutes to 1 hour, until clafouti is puffed and browned and knife comes out clean when inserted in center. Serve hot or warm. Clafouti will fall a bit upon cooling.

Peach Clafouti

Serves 2

1½ cups peaches, peeled and sliced
⅓ cup milk
⅓ cup half-and-half
1 egg, room temperature
2 tablespoons all-purpose flour
½ teaspoon vanilla extract
5 packets Equal® (see "About This Cookbook")
   Diet whipped topping (optional)
   Vegetable cooking spray

Nutritional Data

PER SERVING:

Calories	207
% calories from fat	35
Fat (gm)	8.1
Sat. Fat (gm)	4.2
Cholesterol (mg)	124
Sodium (mg)	68
Protein (gm)	7.4
Carbohydrate (gm)	27

EXCHANGES:

Milk	0.0	Bread	0.0
Veg.	0.0	Meat	1.0
Fruit	1.5	Fat	1.5

Preheat oven to 375 degrees. Coat 2 8-oz. au gratin dishes or 1 small baking dish with vegetable cooking spray. Arrange peaches in single layer in dish(es). Mix milk, half-and-half, egg, flour, and vanilla until smooth.

Pour batter over peaches. Bake clafouti until puffed and golden, 35 to 40 minutes. Remove from oven and sprinkle with Equal®. Garnish with whipped topping, if desired.

Baked Apples

Serves 4

4 small baking apples
¼ cup unsweetened apple juice
1 cup water
1 teaspoon cinnamon
1 small orange, sliced
2 packets Equal® (see "About This Cookbook")

Nutritional Data

PER SERVING:

Calories	99
% calories from fat	4
Fat (gm)	0.5
Sat. Fat (gm)	0.1
Cholesterol (mg)	0
Sodium (mg)	0.6
Protein (gm)	0.5
Carbohydrate (gm)	25.6

Preheat oven to 350 degrees. Core apples and remove ¼ of top peel. Place apples in shallow baking pan. Combine water, juice, and cinnamon. Pour over apples. Arrange orange slices around apples to help flavor liquid.

EXCHANGES:

Milk	0.0	Bread	0.0
Veg.	0.0	Meat	0.0
Fruit	1.5	Fat	0.0

Cover pan with aluminum foil and bake about 20 to 30 minutes or until fork-tender. Remove from oven and sprinkle with Equal®.

Dessert Burritos with Apple-Fig Filling

Serves 6

3	cups cooking apples, peeled and chopped
½	cup dried figs, chopped
¼	cup granulated sugar
¼	cup light brown sugar
2	tablespoons cornstarch
3	tablespoons dry white wine
2	teaspoons ground cinnamon
¼	teaspoon nutmeg, freshly ground
¼	teaspoon ground allspice
6	flour tortillas

Nutritional Data

PER SERVING:

Calories	264
% calories from fat	7
Fat (gm)	2.1
Sat. Fat (gm)	0.4
Cholesterol (mg)	0
Sodium (mg)	11
Protein (gm)	3.7
Carbohydrate (gm)	59.1

EXCHANGES:

Milk	0.0	Bread	2.0
Veg.	0.0	Meat	0.0
Fruit	2.0	Fat	0.0

Using large pot, simmer apples, figs, sugars, cornstarch, wine, and spices over medium heat. Add water, ¼ cup at a time, as apples cook. Simmer 20 minutes, stirring occasionally. Cool.

Spread cooled apple-fig mixture in center of each tortilla. Roll and serve.

Jane's Red Applesauce

Serves 4

3	Golden Delicious apples, cut into eighths
½	cup fresh cranberries
1	tablespoon frozen orange juice concentrate
1	cinnamon stick
4	pecan halves

Nutritional Data

PER SERVING:

Calories	80
% calories from fat	15
Fat (gm)	1.5
Sat. Fat (gm)	0.1
Cholesterol (mg)	0
Sodium (mg)	0
Protein (gm)	0.4
Carbohydrate (gm)	18

EXCHANGES:

Milk	0.0	Bread	0.0
Veg.	0.0	Meat	0.0
Fruit	1.5	Fat	0.0

Place all ingredients, except pecans, in 1-quart measure and cover with well-vented plastic wrap. Microwave on High 3 minutes. Stir, and microwave on High 2 to 3 minutes more, until apples are soft. Discard cinnamon stick, turn into food mill, and grind over bowl. Chill until ready to serve, and top with a few pecans.

Prune Whip

Serves 6

6 ozs. dietetic canned prunes, undrained
1 teaspoon unflavored gelatin, softened in warm water
1 teaspoon fresh lemon juice
¼ teaspoon vanilla extract
1 packet Equal® (see "About This Cookbook")
2 egg whites, stiffly beaten

Nutritional Data

PER SERVING:

Calories	39
% calories from fat	1
Fat (gm)	0.1
Sat. Fat (gm)	0
Cholesterol (mg)	0
Sodium (mg)	19
Protein (gm)	1.9
Carbohydrate (gm)	8.4

EXCHANGES:

Milk	0.0	Bread	0.0
Veg.	0.0	Meat	0.0
Fruit	0.5	Fat	0.0

In blender, puree prunes with juice they are packed in. Add softened gelatin and blend again. Simmer puree, uncovered, in heavy pan to reduce mixture; cool slightly. Add lemon juice, vanilla, and Equal®.

Gently fold puree into beaten egg whites. Portion prune whip into small individual serving dishes and chill thoroughly.

Apricot Prune Whip

Serves 4

½ cup water
½ cup dried apricots
½ cup prunes, pitted
1 cup soft tofu (bean curd)
2 teaspoons pure vanilla extract
2 tablespoons nonfat dry milk
4 medium strawberries, or raspberries

Nutritional Data

PER SERVING:

Calories	150
% calories from fat	18
Fat (gm)	3.2
Sat. Fat (gm)	0.5
Cholesterol (mg)	0.4
Sodium (mg)	19
Protein (gm)	6.9
Carbohydrate (gm)	26

EXCHANGES:

Milk	0.0	Bread	0.0
Veg.	0.0	Meat	1.0
Fruit	1.5	Fat	0.0

Place water, apricots, and prunes in 2-cup measure, and microwave on High 2 to 3 minutes, until soft. Let cool. Place fruit in food processor with remaining ingredients, except berries, and whip until smooth. Serve warm or chilled, topped with strawberries for garnish.

Bananas Foster

Serves 4

¼ cup packed light brown sugar
1½ teaspoons cornstarch
½ cup water
1 tablespoon rum
1 teaspoon vanilla extract
2 medium bananas, peeled and sliced

Nutritional Data

PER SERVING:

Calories	237
% calories from fat	20
Fat (gm)	5.5
Sat. Fat (gm)	0.5
Cholesterol (mg)	0
Sodium (mg)	6
Protein (gm)	3.4
Carbohydrate (gm)	43.2

¼	cup toasted pecan halves	EXCHANGES:			
1⅓	cups frozen low-fat vanilla yogurt	Milk	0.0	Bread	2.0
		Veg.	0.0	Meat	0.0
		Fruit	1.0	Fat	1.0

Mix brown sugar and cornstarch in small saucepan; stir in water. Cook over medium heat until thickened, stirring constantly. Reduce heat to low; stir in rum and vanilla. Gently stir in bananas and simmer 1 to 2 minutes or until bananas are warm; stir in pecans. Serve warm over frozen yogurt.

 # Spicy Bananas

Serves 4		**Nutritional Data**	
2	small bananas	PER SERVING:	
4	tablespoons frozen apple juice	Calories	88
	concentrate	% calories from fat	7
¼	teaspoon ground cinnamon	Fat (gm)	0.7
¼	teaspoon ground allspice	Sat. Fat (gm)	0.2
	Dash ground nutmeg	Cholesterol (mg)	0
	Dash ground cloves	Sodium (mg)	5
1	teaspoon sunflower seeds	Protein (gm)	0.9
4	strawberries, sliced	Carbohydrate (gm)	21.2

EXCHANGES:

Milk	0.0	Bread	0.0
Veg.	0.0	Meat	0.0
Fruit	1.5	Fat	0.0

Slice bananas into thin rounds and place in bowl with remaining ingredients, except strawberries. Toss gently to coat. Microwave on High 1½ to 2 minutes, until bananas are heated through. Remove to dessert dishes and top with sliced berries.

Peaches Amaretto

Serves 8		**Nutritional Data**	
8	cups fresh peaches (about 3 lbs.), peeled and sliced	PER SERVING:	
		Calories	154
½	cup amaretto	% calories from fat	6
8	small amaretto cookies, crushed, or 8 tablespoons granola	Fat (gm)	1
		Sat. Fat (gm)	0
		Cholesterol (mg)	0
		Sodium (mg)	40
		Protein (gm)	1.7
		Carbohydrate (gm)	30.3

Combine peaches and amaretto in large dish; cover and chill about 2 hours. Spoon into 8 dessert dishes; sprinkle with cookies or granola.

EXCHANGES:

Milk	0.0	Bread	0.5
Veg.	0.0	Meat	0.0
Fruit	2.0	Fat	0.0

To Freeze: Vacuum seal each portion; label and freeze up to 2 months.
To Serve: Thaw in refrigerator or in bowl of water. Serve chilled.

Peaches in Chianti

Serves 8

8   medium to large freestone peaches, ripe but firm
2   tablespoons fresh lemon juice
3   tablespoons sugar
1   cup Chianti wine
8   Anise Biscotti (see p. 569), or biscotti of choice

Nutritional Data	
PER SERVING:	
Calories	116
% calories from fat	3
Fat (gm)	0.4
Sat. Fat (gm)	0.1
Cholesterol (mg)	8.9
Sodium (mg)	38
Protein (gm)	1.6
Carbohydrate (gm)	23.3

EXCHANGES:

Milk	0.0	Bread	1.0
Veg.	0.0	Meat	0.0
Fruit	0.5	Fat	0.0

Peel peaches, and cut into eighths. Place in stainless steel, glass, or ceramic bowl. Add lemon and sugar, and mix gently but well. Let stand 5 minutes. Pour wine over peaches, and cover. Refrigerate 8 hours or overnight.

To serve, arrange peach segments in wine glasses or wide-mouthed dessert glasses, and spoon a little wine into each glass. Serve with biscotti.

Poached Peaches with Ginger

Serves 4

4   fresh peaches, halved
1/2 cup water
2   tablespoons fresh lemon juice
1   slice fresh ginger, 1 x 1/4 inch
1   cinnamon stick, 2 inches long
1   cup grapes, halved
     Dash cinnamon

Nutritional Data	
PER SERVING:	
Calories	54
% calories from fat	2
Fat (gm)	0.2
Sat. Fat (gm)	0
Cholesterol (mg)	0
Sodium (mg)	1
Protein (gm)	0.8
Carbohydrate (gm)	14.4

EXCHANGES:

Milk	0.0	Bread	0.0
Veg.	0.0	Meat	0.0
Fruit	1.0	Fat	0.0

Preheat oven to 350 degrees. Place peaches, skin side up, in baking dish. Combine water, lemon juice, ginger, and cinnamon stick and pour over peaches. Cover and bake 30 minutes. Remove from oven, and place peaches on 4 dessert plates. Add grapes and sprinkle with cinnamon.

Peaches Melba

Serves 6

1 cup sugar, or 12 packets Equal®*
1 cup water
1 teaspoon vanilla extract
3 large, firm peaches
1 pint raspberries
¼ cup sugar
1 quart vanilla frozen yogurt

Nutritional Data

PER SERVING:

Calories	259
% calories from fat	5
Fat (gm)	1.6
Sat. Fat (gm)	0
Cholesterol (mg)	0
Sodium (mg)	0
Protein (gm)	5.3
Carbohydrate (gm)	56.9

EXCHANGES:

Milk	0.0	Bread	3.0
Veg.	0.0	Meat	0.0
Fruit	0.5	Fat	0.0

In saucepan, combine 1 cup sugar* and water. Place over medium heat and stir constantly until mixture boils. Cover and boil 5 minutes. Remove from heat and stir in vanilla extract. Set aside.

Wash, pare, cut into halves, and pit peaches. Put syrup mixture back over medium heat. Add peaches, 2 halves at a time, and simmer 3 minutes. Chill in refrigerator.

Meanwhile, wash and process raspberries in blender. Stir in ¼ cup sugar. Chill in refrigerator.

When ready to serve, spoon yogurt into 6 glass dishes. Place ½ peach on each dish and spoon raspberries into center of each peach half. Serve immediately.

Note: If using Equal®, boil water alone and remove from heat before adding Equal®. Add vanilla extract and set aside. Proceed as above.

Pears with Rum Raisin Sauce

Serves 4

4 Bartlett pears (Bosc or Anjou can also be used)
  Fresh lemon juice
6 tablespoons Grand Marnier
  Rum Raisin Sauce (see p. 529)

Nutritional Data

PER SERVING:

Calories	252
% calories from fat	3
Fat (gm)	0.8
Sat. Fat (gm)	0.1
Cholesterol (mg)	1.5
Sodium (mg)	57
Protein (gm)	4.6
Carbohydrate (gm)	50.1

EXCHANGES:

Milk	0.5	Bread	0.0
Veg.	0.0	Meat	0.0
Fruit	3.5	Fat	0.0

Peel and core pears, rubbing each with lemon juice. Stand pears upright in shallow dish and pour 1½ tablespoons Grand Marnier over each pear. Set dish on rack over boiling water, cover pot, and steam 5 minutes. Baste pears with liquid in dish, and steam 5 minutes more.

Test pears to see if they are done by inserting cake tester into one of them; tester should go in easily, but flesh of pear should remain slightly firm. Baste again and steam 2 minutes more.

Transfer pears to individual serving plates and spoon Rum Raisin Sauce over each. Serve warm.

To Freeze: Vacuum seal each portion; label and freeze up to 2 months.

To Serve: Put bags in boiling water, and bring water to boil again. Boil 10 to 12 minutes.

Pineapple Air

Serves 4

1 8-oz. can crushed pineapple (juice packed)
3 tablespoons nonfat dry milk
2 egg yolks, beaten
1 packet Equal® (see "About This Cookbook")
½ teaspoon vanilla extract
2 egg whites
1 packet Equal®
4 pineapple chunks (optional for garnish)

Nutritional Data

PER SERVING:

Calories	87
% calories from fat	27
Fat (gm)	2.6
Sat. Fat (gm)	0.8
Cholesterol (mg)	107.1
Sodium (mg)	49
Protein (gm)	4.5
Carbohydrate (gm)	11.6

EXCHANGES:

Milk	0.0	Bread	0.0
Veg.	0.0	Meat	0.5
Fruit	1.0	Fat	0.0

Drain pineapple well, reserving juice. Chill pineapple. Add water to reserved juice, if necessary, to make ½ cup. Dissolve dry milk powder in pineapple juice.

In small, heavy saucepan, combine milk mixture and egg yolks. Cook over low heat, stirring constantly until mixture thickens and coats metal spoon. Remove from heat and stir in 1 packet Equal®.

Place saucepan in pan of ice water to cool. Stir in vanilla. When cooled, cover and chill egg mixture 2 to 4 hours.

At serving time, fold pineapple into cooked mixture. Using electric mixer and small mixer bowl, beat egg whites at high speed until soft peaks form. Gradually add 1 packet Equal®, beating until stiff peaks form. Gently fold egg whites into pineapple mixture. Spoon into chilled serving dishes. Garnish with a pineapple chunk.

Russian Rhubarb

Serves 4

1 lb. fresh rhubarb, trimmed and cut into 1-inch pieces (about 2 cups)
1 stick cinnamon
2 tablespoons frozen orange juice concentrate
1 cup strawberries, sliced
1 tablespoon hazelnuts, chopped

Nutritional Data	
PER SERVING:	
Calories	49
% calories from fat	24
Fat (gm)	1.4
Sat. Fat (gm)	0.1
Cholesterol (mg)	0
Sodium (mg)	3
Protein (gm)	1.2
Carbohydrate (gm)	9

EXCHANGES:			
Milk	0.0	Bread	0.0
Veg.	0.0	Meat	0.0
Fruit	0.5	Fat	0.5

Place rhubarb, cinnamon stick, and orange juice in 1-quart glass casserole. Cover with vented plastic wrap, and microwave on High 3 to 4 minutes. Stir, and microwave on High 3 to 4 minutes more, covered.

When rhubarb is tender, add strawberries and let rest 5 minutes. Discard cinnamon stick before serving, warm or chilled. Serve with sprinkling of hazelnuts.

Strawberry Rhubarb Compote

Serves 4

3 cups strawberries, hulled and sliced
1/4 cup sugar
1 tablespoon fresh lemon juice
   Cold water
2 tablespoons cornstarch
1 cup rhubarb, diced
1/2 teaspoon orange peel, grated
   Plain nonfat yogurt
   Orange slices (for garnish)

Nutritional Data	
PER SERVING:	
Calories	105
% calories from fat	4
Fat (gm)	0.5
Sat. Fat (gm)	0
Cholesterol (mg)	0
Sodium (mg)	3
Protein (gm)	1
Carbohydrate (gm)	25.8

EXCHANGES:			
Milk	0.0	Bread	0.0
Veg.	0.0	Meat	0.0
Fruit	1.5	Fat	0.0

Place first 3 ingredients in bowl; mix well.

Dissolve cornstarch in water and add, with rhubarb and orange peel, to small saucepan. Cook over medium heat until mixture boils and thickens and rhubarb is tender, stirring constantly, about 10 minutes. Transfer rhubarb mixture to bowl with strawberries and mix well.

Place entire fruit mixture in saucepan and cook on medium heat for about 10 minutes. Remove from heat and cool.

Spoon into 4 wine goblets and refrigerate until well chilled, about 1 hour. Top compote with dollop of yogurt and an orange slice.

To Freeze: Vacuum seal each portion; label and freeze up to 2 months.

To Serve: Thaw in refrigerator or in bowl of water. Serve chilled.

Strawberries and Figs

Serves 4

1   12-oz. package frozen strawberries, thawed
½   cup refined sugar
12 fresh figs, washed and halved
4   dollops (2 oz.) vanilla yogurt
    Fresh mint sprigs

Place strawberries and sugar in food processor, and puree.

On each of 4 dessert plates, place 6 fig halves (open side up). Pour strawberry puree on top. Add dollop of yogurt. Place sprig of mint on top.

Nutritional Data

PER SERVING:

Calories	246
% calories from fat	3
Fat (gm)	0.8
Sat. Fat (gm)	0.2
Cholesterol (mg)	0.8
Sodium (mg)	15
Protein (gm)	2.6
Carbohydrate (gm)	62.9

EXCHANGES:

Milk	0.0	Bread	0.0
Veg.	0.0	Meat	0.0
Fruit	4.0	Fat	0.0

Strawberries Romanoff

Serves 4

1 pint fresh strawberries, rinsed, hulled, and halved
3 tablespoons brandy
2 tablespoons Grand Marnier, or other orange liqueur
1 teaspoon sunflower oil
1 tablespoon orange zest, grated
   Pinch nutmeg, grated

Arrange strawberries in 4 champagne glasses; refrigerate.

Combine remaining ingredients in small saucepan. Cook over medium heat until mixture starts to simmer, about 1 minute. Remove from heat and carefully ignite with long match. Shake pan well until flames subside, then spoon 1 tablespoon of mixture over each portion of strawberries.

Nutritional Data

PER SERVING:

Calories	84
% calories from fat	15
Fat (gm)	1.4
Sat. Fat (gm)	0.1
Cholesterol (mg)	0
Sodium (mg)	1
Protein (gm)	0.5
Carbohydrate (gm)	8.5

EXCHANGES:

Milk	0.0	Bread	0.0
Veg.	0.0	Meat	0.0
Fruit	1.5	Fat	0.0

Strawberry Tulips

Serves 6

		Nutritional Data	
12	large strawberries	PER SERVING:	
3	ozs. Yogurt Cheese (see p. 27), softened	Calories	43
2	tablespoons confectioners' sugar	% calories from fat	6
1	tablespoon light sour cream	Fat (gm)	0.3
1	tablespoon orange rind, grated	Sat. Fat (gm)	0
	Mint leaves for garnish (optional)	Cholesterol (mg)	1.4
		Sodium (mg)	31
		Protein (gm)	2.6
		Carbohydrate (gm)	7.7

EXCHANGES:

Milk	0.0	Bread	0.0
Veg.	0.0	Meat	0.0
Fruit	0.5	Fat	0.0

Remove stems from berries, forming a flat base. Place berries pointed end up. Using sharp knife, carefully slice berries in half vertically through center to within 1/4 inch of base. Cut each half into 3 wedges, forming 6 petals (do not slice through base). Pull petals apart gently.

In small bowl, beat Yogurt Cheese, confectioners' sugar, sour cream, and orange rind until light and fluffy. Using small spoon, fill berries with yogurt mixture. Garnish with mint in place of stems, if desired. (This is a delightful mini-dessert to serve with coffee after a large meal.)

To Freeze: Place in microwave-safe container; label, and freeze up to 2 months.

To Serve: Thaw in refrigerator and garnish before serving, if desired.

Zabaglione and Strawberries

Serves 4

		Nutritional Data	
1½	baskets fresh strawberries	PER SERVING:	
¼	cup sweet Marsala wine	Calories	67
4	packets Equal® (see "About This Cookbook")	% calories from fat	5
		Fat (gm)	0.4
	Egg substitute equal to 3 eggs	Sat. Fat (gm)	0
		Cholesterol (mg)	0
		Sodium (mg)	72
		Protein (gm)	4.6
		Carbohydrate (gm)	9.9

EXCHANGES:

Milk	0.0	Bread	0.0
Veg.	0.0	Meat	0.5
Fruit	0.5	Fat	0.0

Wash and hull strawberries. If strawberries are very large, cut in half. Arrange berries in 4 wine goblets; set aside. Pour wine over Equal® in large metal bowl that you hold over saucepan of simmering, *not boiling*, water. Bottom should not touch water (you can use double boiler, but don't let bottom of pan touch water or egg substitute will curdle). Add egg substitute.

Cook over simmering water, beating constantly with electric beater at low speed 5 minutes, or just until mixture mounds slightly; remove bowl from pan of water at once. Continue beating at low speed 5 minutes more, or until mixture is almost cold. Pour over strawberries and serve at once. (Cover and chill to serve later, no longer than 3 hours, so sauce holds its airy lightness.)

Strawberry
 # Cheese Pudding

Serves 6		*Nutritional Data*	
1	basket fresh strawberries, sliced	PER SERVING:	
3	tablespoons strawberry liqueur	Calories	131
2	cups cottage cheese	% calories from fat	12
	Egg substitute equal to 5 eggs	Fat (gm)	1.7
		Sat. Fat (gm)	0.6
¼	cup light sour cream	Cholesterol (mg)	6.5
1	teaspoon cinnamon	Sodium (mg)	382
½	teaspoon nutmeg	Protein (gm)	14.3
¼	teaspoon ground cloves	Carbohydrate (gm)	11
4	packets Equal® (see "About This Cookbook")		

EXCHANGES:

Milk	0.0	Bread	0.0
Veg.	0.0	Meat	2.0
Fruit	0.5	Fat	0.0

Preheat oven to 325 degrees. Soak strawberries in liqueur 1 hour. Drain and reserve liquid. In blender, whirl cottage cheese and egg substitute to smooth puree. Pour into greased 2-quart casserole dish. Arrange strawberries on top. Bake 30 minutes.

Meanwhile, stir remaining strawberry marinade into sour cream, cinnamon, nutmeg, cloves, and Equal®. Spoon over strawberries and bake 10 minutes more. Serve hot.

Fresh Strawberry
Mousse or Filling

Serves 6		*Nutritional Data*	
1	envelope unflavored gelatin	PER SERVING:	
¼	cup orange juice	Calories	128
3	cups fresh strawberries, hulled	% calories from fat	2
¼	cup confectioners' sugar	Fat (gm)	0.3
1	envelope diet whipped topping	Sat. Fat (gm)	0
4	egg whites	Cholesterol (mg)	0
¼	cup granulated sugar	Sodium (mg)	50
	Strawberries, hulled (to garnish mousse)	Protein (gm)	3.9
		Carbohydrate (gm)	25.5

In small microwave-safe dish, sprinkle gelatin over orange juice and let stand 5 minutes to soften. Microwave on High 10 seconds until gelatin has dissolved.

EXCHANGES:			
Milk	0.0	Bread	1.0
Veg.	0.0	Meat	0.0
Fruit	1.0	Fat	0.0

Place strawberries in blender; add confectioners' sugar and process until smooth. Transfer to mixing bowl and stir in gelatin mixture. Refrigerate until mixture has consistency of raw egg whites (about 20 minutes).

Prepare diet whipped topping and set aside.

In large bowl, beat egg whites until soft peaks form; gradually add granulated sugar, beating until stiff peaks form. Whisk about ¼ of beaten egg whites into strawberry mixture. Fold strawberry mixture along with whipped topping into remaining egg whites.

Pour into 6-cup serving bowl or individual dessert dishes. You can also use this mousse as filling for Chocolate Sponge Cake (see p. 533).

To Freeze: Place in freezer container, label, and freeze up to 2 months.

To Serve: Thaw, then use as you like.

Strawberry Mousse

Serves 4

- 1 10-oz. package unsweetened frozen strawberries, thawed
- 1½ envelopes unflavored gelatin
- ¼ cup sugar
- 2 egg whites
- 1 cup diet whipped topping

Nutritional Data

PER SERVING:

Calories	142
% calories from fat	1
Fat (gm)	0.1
Sat. Fat (gm)	0
Cholesterol (mg)	0
Sodium (mg)	49
Protein (gm)	4.8
Carbohydrate (gm)	27.6

EXCHANGES:			
Milk	0.0	Bread	1.0
Veg.	0.0	Meat	0.0
Fruit	1.0	Fat	0.0

Puree strawberries in blender. Transfer to saucepan, and sprinkle gelatin over top. Place over low heat; stir to dissolve gelatin. Transfer to large bowl. Place over ice water, stirring often, until mixture begins to thicken. Add sugar and mix thoroughly.

Beat egg whites until stiff peaks form. Fold whipped topping, then egg whites, into strawberry mixture. Spoon mixture into small dessert dishes. Chill.

Chocolate Mousse

Serves 5 (½-cup servings)

¼ cup unsweetened Dutch cocoa
4 teaspoons cornstarch
1½ cups skim milk, divided
1 teaspoon vanilla extract
1½ teaspoons aspartame
1 envelope diet whipped topping mix

Nutritional Data

PER SERVING:

Calories	51
% calories from fat	9
Fat (gm)	0.5
Sat. Fat (gm)	0.2
Cholesterol (mg)	1
Sodium (mg)	42
Protein (gm)	3
Carbohydrate (gm)	9

EXCHANGES:

Milk	0.5	Bread	0.0
Veg.	0.0	Meat	0.0
Fruit	0.0	Fat	0.0

Combine cocoa and cornstarch in heavy-bottomed saucepan. Add ⅓ cup skim milk. Blend with wire whisk until smooth. Add another ⅔ cup milk, whisking well to combine.

Heat to boil, stirring constantly with wire whisk. Remove from heat and allow to cool. When cool, stir in vanilla and aspartame.

Place whipped topping in electric mixer bowl along with remaining ½ cup milk. Mix well with wire whisk. Beat according to package directions until thick. Fold whipped topping into cooled cocoa mixture.

Divide among 5 individual dishes or place in serving bowl. Refrigerate, covered, until serving time.

Cantaloupe Mousse

Serves 4

2 cups cantaloupe, cubed
2 tablespoons orange liqueur
2 envelopes unflavored gelatin
¼ cup water
⅓ cup frozen diet whipped topping, thawed
Melon slices for garnish (optional)

Nutritional Data

PER SERVING:

Calories	77
% calories from fat	11
Fat (gm)	1
Sat. Fat (gm)	0
Cholesterol (mg)	0
Sodium (mg)	15
Protein (gm)	3.7
Carbohydrate (gm)	10.9

EXCHANGES:

Milk	0.0	Bread	0.0
Veg.	0.0	Meat	0.0
Fruit	1.0	Fat	0.0

Place cubed melon and liqueur in blender or food processor. Cover and mix until smooth.

In medium saucepan, stir together gelatin and water. Let stand 5 minutes. Cook and stir over low heat until gelatin is dissolved. Stir in pureed cataloupe mixture.

Chill to consistency of corn syrup, stirring several times. When gelatin is partiallly set (consistency of unbeaten egg whites), fold in whipped topping. Pour into 4 individual ½-cup molds. Chill about 2 hours or until firm.

To serve, unmold onto serving plates. Garnish with fresh melon slices.

Chocolate Pudding with Raspberry Sauce

Serves 8

Margarine
8 tablespoons sugar, divided
8 ozs. semisweet chocolate
2 tablespoons fruit-only apricot jam
8 egg whites, divided
1 tablespoon bread crumbs, finely ground
Pinch salt
¼ cup liqueur, such as amaretto, brandy, rum, etc. (optional)
Raspberry Sauce (see p. 518)
Fresh mint for garnish

Nutritional Data

PER SERVING:

Calories	330
% calories from fat	23
Fat (gm)	9.3
Sat. Fat (gm)	5.6
Cholesterol (mg)	0
Sodium (mg)	68
Protein (gm)	6.1
Carbohydrate (gm)	57.5

EXCHANGES:

Milk	0.0	Bread	2.0
Veg.	0.0	Meat	0.0
Fruit	1.5	Fat	2.0

Use margarine to grease 1-quart pudding mold, including inside of lid. Add about 3 tablespoons sugar, replace lid, and shake vigorously so entire surface is coated. Shake out any excess sugar. Set aside.

Melt chocolate over hot water. Stir. When melted, remove from heat and allow to cool slightly.

Put jam and 2 egg whites in large bowl and beat until well blended. Add 4 tablespoons sugar and beat until well mixed. Add bread crumbs, liqueur, and melted chocolate. Mix well.

Beat remaining 6 egg whites with salt. When soft peaks have formed, add remaining tablespoon of sugar and continue beating until stiff.

Beat 4 tablespoons of egg whites into chocolate mixture and fold remainder in gently. Pour into prepared mold, cover, and steam 1 hour. If pudding is to be served hot, leave mold in steamer, with heat turned off, until serving time. If it is to be served cold, remove from steamer, cool, and refrigerate.

Do not remove pudding from mold until ready to serve. When ready to serve, run knife around edges of pudding and unmold onto platter. Serve with Raspberry Sauce and mint garnish.

Chocolate Pudding

Serves 4

½   cup sugar
⅓   cup unsweetened cocoa
2   tablespoons cornstarch
⅛   teaspoon salt
2   cups 2% milk
2   egg yolks, slightly beaten
2   teaspoons vanilla

Nutritional Data

PER SERVING:

Calories	223
% calories from fat	21
Fat (gm)	5.6
Sat. Fat (gm)	2.4
Cholesterol (mg)	116
Sodium (mg)	136
Protein (gm)	6.8
Carbohydrate (gm)	39.4

EXCHANGES:

Milk	0.5	Bread	2.0
Veg.	0.0	Meat	0.0
Fruit	0.0	Fat	1.0

Mix sugar, cocoa, cornstarch, and salt in medium-size saucepan; stir in milk. Cook over medium heat until mixture boils and thickens, stirring constantly; boil 1 minute, stirring constantly.

Stir about ½ cup milk mixture into egg yolks. Stir egg yolk mixture back into saucepan. Heat to boiling over medium heat, stirring constantly; boil 1 minute (no longer!), stirring constantly. Stir in vanilla.

Spoon into dessert bowls. Refrigerate, covered with plastic wrap, until chilled, 1 to 2 hours.

Whipped Banana Pudding

Serves 8

½   teaspoon unflavored gelatin, softened in water
1   large banana
1   packet Equal® (see "About This Cookbook")
½   teaspoon lemon rind, grated (optional)
8   drops yellow food coloring
2   cups plain low-fat yogurt

Nutritional Data

PER SERVING:

Calories	50
% calories from fat	17
Fat (gm)	0.9
Sat. Fat (gm)	0.6
Cholesterol (mg)	3.5
Sodium (mg)	40
Protein (gm)	3.3
Carbohydrate (gm)	7.5

EXCHANGES:

Milk	0.5	Bread	0.0
Veg.	0.0	Meat	0.0
Fruit	0.0	Fat	0.0

Mix all ingredients except yogurt in blender until smooth. Fold in yogurt. Pour into individual sherbet glasses. Chill well.

Blueberry Bread Pudding

Serves 8

6 slices whole wheat bread
3 tablespoons margarine, softened
1 egg
2 egg whites
½ cup sugar
¼ teaspoon salt
2 cups skim milk
1 teaspoon vanilla extract
1 cup fresh or frozen blueberries

Nutritional Data	
PER SERVING:	
Calories	179
% calories from fat	29
Fat (gm)	5.9
Sat. Fat (gm)	1.2
Cholesterol (mg)	27.6
Sodium (mg)	290
Protein (gm)	5.7
Carbohydrate (gm)	26.9

EXCHANGES:			
Milk	0.0	Bread	1.5
Veg.	0.0	Meat	0.0
Fruit	0.5	Fat	1.0

Preheat oven to 350 degrees. Lightly grease 9-inch baking dish.

Spread margarine on one side of each slice of bread; cut into 2-inch squares and place in prepared dish.

Combine egg, egg whites, sugar, and salt in medium bowl. Meanwhile, heat milk in small saucepan until just boiling; stir milk into egg mixture. Stir in vanilla and blueberries; pour over bread cubes.

Place baking dish in 10" x 15" roasting pan; pour 1 inch hot water into pan. Bake 35 to 40 minutes or until knife inserted near center comes out clean. Serve warm or room temperature.

Bread Pudding with Raisins

Serves 6

1 envelope unflavored gelatin
2 cups milk
2 eggs, slightly beaten
1 teaspoon vanilla extract
6 packets Equal® (see "About This Cookbook")
2½ cups white bread cubes (about 4 slices)
¼ cup raisins
¼ teaspoon nutmeg

Nutritional Data	
PER SERVING:	
Calories	128
% calories from fat	27
Fat (gm)	3.8
Sat. Fat (gm)	1.6
Cholesterol (mg)	77
Sodium (mg)	128
Protein (gm)	7
Carbohydrate (gm)	16.3

EXCHANGES:			
Milk	0.0	Bread	0.0
Veg.	0.0	Meat	1.0
Fruit	1.0	Fat	0.0

Soften gelatin in ¼ cup milk. Scald remaining milk in top of double boiler. Add softened gelatin. Stir until gelatin dissolves completely. Pour hot milk slowly over eggs, stirring constantly. Return to double boiler, and cook over hot water until mixture coats spoon. Remove from heat.

Add vanilla and Equal®. Beat until frothy. Stir in bread cubes and raisins. Pour into 1½-quart mold that has been rinsed in cold water. Cover and refrigerate.

At serving time, unmold and sprinkle with nutmeg. This dish can also be served with a fruit sauce.

Cocoa Bread Pudding

Serves 4

Butter-flavored vegetable cooking spray

3 slices noncholesterol bread
2 tablespoons golden raisins
2 cups skim milk, scalded and cooled
2 tablespoons unsweetened cocoa
½ cup real egg substitute
3 tablespoons fructose (fruit sugar, see "About This Cookbook")
1 teaspoon vanilla extract
¼ teaspoon chocolate extract

Nutritional Data

PER SERVING:

Calories	154
% calories from fat	7
Fat (gm)	1
Sat. Fat (gm)	0.4
Cholesterol (mg)	2
Sodium (mg)	195
Protein (gm)	9
Carbohydrate (gm)	28

EXCHANGES:

Milk	0.5	Bread	1.0
Veg.	0.0	Meat	0.0
Fruit	0.5	Fat	0.0

Preheat oven to 350 degrees. Coat 1½-quart casserole with cooking spray.

Remove crust from bread. Cut into 1-inch squares. Arrange bread and raisins in casserole. Set aside.

In mixing bowl, combine cooled milk with cocoa, egg substitute, fructose, vanilla, and chocolate extract. Pour milk mixture over bread and raisins.

Set casserole in larger, ovenproof pan. Fill larger pan with hot water halfway up sides of casserole. Bake 50 minutes to 1 hour. When done, knife or bamboo skewer inserted in center of pudding will come out clean. Leave pudding in pan to cool. Can be served warm or cold.

Brown Rice and Raisin Pudding

Serves 8

- 2 cups cooked* brown rice, set aside
  Butter-flavored vegetable cooking spray
- 3 cups skim milk
- ¼ cup unsweetened Dutch cocoa
- 1 cup real egg substitute
- ⅛ teaspoon salt
- ¼ cup fructose (fruit sugar, see "About This Cookbook")
- 1 teaspoon ground cinnamon
- 1 teaspoon vanilla extract
- ½ teaspoon chocolate extract
- ⅓ cup golden raisins
- 2 egg whites, beaten

Nutritional Data

PER SERVING:

Calories	134
% calories from fat	6
Fat (gm)	0.9
Sat. Fat (gm)	0.2
Cholesterol (mg)	1
Sodium (mg)	129
Protein (gm)	8
Carbohydrate (gm)	25

EXCHANGES:

Milk	0.0	Bread	1.0
Veg.	0.0	Meat	0.5
Fruit	0.5	Fat	0.0

Preheat oven to 350 degrees. Coat 1½-quart casserole with cooking spray.

Mix together milk, cocoa, egg substitute, salt, fructose, cinnamon, vanilla, chocolate extract, and raisins. Add rice. Fold in beaten egg whites.

Pour into prepared casserole. Place in oven in larger pan, with hot water reaching halfway up sides of casserole. Bake 50 to 60 minutes or until knife inserted in pudding comes out clean. Serve warm.

If top of pudding begins to get too brown, cover with aluminum foil.

*To cook brown rice, bring 1¾ cups water to boil. Add 1 cup brown rice. Cover. Simmer 30 minutes or until rice is tender.

 # Apple Rice Pudding

Serves 4

- 2 cups cooked rice
- 2 cups skim milk
- 1 cup apples, chopped
- 1 teaspoon vanilla extract
- 4 large egg whites
  Pinch salt
- 6 packets Equal® (see "About This Cookbook"), mixed with ½ teaspoon cinnamon
  Plain low-fat yogurt (optional)

Nutritional Data

PER SERVING:

Calories	188
% calories from fat	3
Fat (gm)	0.5
Sat. Fat (gm)	0.2
Cholesterol (mg)	2
Sodium (mg)	119
Protein (gm)	9.9
Carbohydrate (gm)	34.6

EXCHANGES:

Milk	0.5	Bread	1.0
Veg.	0.0	Meat	0.0
Fruit	0.5	Fat	0.0

Preheat oven to 350 degrees. Grease 8-inch ovenproof casserole.

Combine rice, milk, apples, and vanilla in medium bowl. Put egg whites and salt in mixing bowl. Slowly beat with mixer until soft peaks form. Fold into rice mixture. Pour into casserole.

Place casserole in larger pan of water and bake 30 minutes. Remove casserole and stir in Equal® and cinnamon. Serve warm or at room temperature with dollop of plain low-fat yogurt.

▨ Banana Rice Pudding

Serves 6

1	cup cooked brown rice (use ½ cup brown rice and 2 cups water. Microwave on High 20 minutes, stirring)
1	large banana, mashed
½	cup nonfat powdered milk
¾	cup water
1	teaspoon sesame seeds
1½	teaspoons maple extract
1	teaspoon ground cinnamon
	Dash ground nutmeg
¼	cup frozen orange juice concentrate
1	tablespoon raisins
2	egg whites, beaten until stiff
1	tablespoon sunflower seeds

Nutritional Data

PER SERVING:

Calories	119
% calories from fat	11
Fat (gm)	1.5
Sat. Fat (gm)	0.2
Cholesterol (mg)	1
Sodium (mg)	52
Protein (gm)	5
Carbohydrate (gm)	21.7

EXCHANGES:

Milk	0.0	Bread	1.0
Veg.	0.0	Meat	0.0
Fruit	0.5	Fat	0.0

Mix together all ingredients except last two. Fold egg whites into rice mixture, and turn into 4" x 8" loaf pan. Top with sunflower seeds. Place pan on inverted saucer, and microwave on High 5 to 7 minutes, until set. Serve warm or chilled.

▮ No-Egg Rice Pudding

Serves 8

1	cup converted rice
2½	cups skim milk
⅔	cup sugar
½	cup golden raisins
½	teaspoon nutmeg
	Peel of ½ lemon, grated
½	teaspoon vanilla extract
1½	cups diet whipped topping mix

Nutritional Data

PER SERVING:

Calories	246
% calories from fat	1
Fat (gm)	0.4
Sat. Fat (gm)	0.2
Cholesterol (mg)	1.3
Sodium (mg)	54
Protein (gm)	4.6
Carbohydrate (gm)	53.7

EXCHANGES:

Milk	0.5	Bread	2.0
Veg.	0.0	Meat	0.0
Fruit	1.0	Fat	0.0

Place all ingredients except whipped topping in crockpot and mix well. Cover and cook on Low 4 to 6 hours. Serve warm with whipped topping.

To Freeze: Vacuum seal each portion; label and freeze up to 2 months.

To Serve: Put bags in boiling water, and bring water to boil again. Boil 10 to 12 minutes.

Cool Carob Pudding

Serves 4

¼ cup unsweetened carob powder, or cocoa
2 cups evaporated skim milk
1 teaspoon pure vanilla extract
1 teaspoon instant coffee (decaf optional)
1 teaspoon frozen orange juice concentrate
Filberts, chopped

Nutritional Data

PER SERVING:

Calories	117
% calories from fat	2
Fat (gm)	0.3
Sat. Fat (gm)	0.2
Cholesterol (mg)	4
Sodium (mg)	150
Protein (gm)	10
Carbohydrate (gm)	19.5

EXCHANGES:

Milk	1.5	Bread	0.0
Veg.	0.0	Meat	0.0
Fruit	0.0	Fat	0.0

Combine all ingredients, except nuts, in blender and turn into 4-cup measure. Cover tightly with vented plastic wrap, and microwave on High 3 to 4 minutes. Place in freezer about 1 hour before serving. Stir with fork, spoon into dessert dishes, and top with sprinkle of nuts.

Warm Indian Pudding

Serves 6

¼ cup yellow cornmeal
2¾ cups skim milk
¾ cup light molasses
⅓ cup packed light brown sugar
¼ teaspoon salt
3 tablespoons margarine
¼ cup dark raisins
½ teaspoon ground cinnamon
¼ teaspoon ground nutmeg
⅛ teaspoon ground cloves
⅛ teaspoon ground ginger
¼ cup skim milk

Nutritional Data

PER SERVING:

Calories	277
% calories from fat	19
Fat (gm)	6.1
Sat. Fat (gm)	1.3
Cholesterol (mg)	2
Sodium (mg)	231
Protein (gm)	4.9
Carbohydrate (gm)	52.8

EXCHANGES:

Milk	0.5	Bread	1.0
Veg.	0.0	Meat	0.0
Fruit	2.0	Fat	1.0

Preheat oven to 325 degrees. Combine cornmeal and 1 cup milk in small bowl; set aside.

Heat remaining 1¾ cups of milk in medium saucepan until steaming. Stir in cornmeal mixture and cook until thickened, 15 minutes, stirring occasionally. Stir in molasses, sugar, and salt. Cool 2 to 3 minutes to dissolve sugar. Remove from heat; stir in margarine, raisins, cinnamon, nutmeg, cloves, and ginger.

Spoon mixture into greased 1½-quart casserole. Pour ¼ cup milk over mixture; bake, uncovered, 1¼ hours or until knife inserted near center comes out clean. Serve warm.

Indonesian Pudding

Serves 4

1	yam (about ¼ lb.), peeled and cut into small cubes
2	tablespoons frozen orange juice concentrate
1	cinnamon stick
1½	bananas (about 1 cup), peeled and sliced
½	cup skim milk
1	tablespoon oat bran
1	teaspoon pure vanilla extract
	Pinch nutmeg
6	pecan halves
1	teaspoon unsweetened coconut, shredded

Nutritional Data

PER SERVING:

Calories	143
% calories from fat	17
Fat (gm)	2.9
Sat. Fat (gm)	0.5
Cholesterol (mg)	0.5
Sodium (mg)	19
Protein (gm)	2.8
Carbohydrate (gm)	28.5

EXCHANGES:

Milk	0.0	Bread	1.0
Veg.	0.0	Meat	0.0
Fruit	1.0	Fat	0.5

Place yam cubes in 8-cup glass measure with orange juice concentrate and cinnamon stick. Cover with vented plastic wrap, and microwave on High 4 to 6 minutes, until soft, rotating cup and stirring midcycle. Add remaining ingredients, except pecans and coconut, and microwave, covered, on High 2 minutes more.

Turn into blender or food processor and whip until smooth. Serve warm (or chill in freezer 1 hour) in dessert dishes, topped with pecans and sprinkling of coconut.

Noodle Pudding

Serves 10

½	lb. eggless wide noodles
5	egg whites
⅔	cup evaporated skim milk
2	cups raisins
1	16-oz. can crushed pineapple, undrained
8	packets Equal® (see "About This Cookbook"), mixed with 1½ teaspoons cinnamon
	Vegetable cooking spray

Nutritional Data

PER SERVING:

Calories	218
% calories from fat	3
Fat (gm)	0.8
Sat. Fat (gm)	0.2
Cholesterol (mg)	0.5
Sodium (mg)	55
Protein (gm)	7.2
Carbohydrate (gm)	48.1

EXCHANGES:

Milk	0.0	Bread	1.0
Veg.	0.0	Meat	0.5
Fruit	2.0	Fat	0.0

Cook noodles according to package directions and drain. Preheat oven to 375 degrees.

Beat egg whites until stiff. Gradually add skim milk. Add egg mixture, pineapple with juice, and raisins to cooked noodles. Mix.

Coat 9" x 13" baking pan with vegetable cooking spray. Pour mixture into pan. Bake 45 to 60 minutes or until set and top is golden brown. Remove from oven and top with Equal® and cinnamon.

Coffee Sour Cream Mold

Serves 10 (½-cup servings)

- 1 tablespoon plus ½ teaspoon unflavored gelatin
- ¼ cup cold water
- 2 tablespoons unsweetened Dutch cocoa
- 8 tablespoons fructose (fruit sugar, see "About This Cookbook"), divided
- ¼ cup skim milk
- 2 cups nonfat sour cream
- 1 teaspoon vanilla extract
- 2 egg whites
- ¼ teaspoon cream of tartar

Nutritional Data

PER SERVING:

Calories	65
% calories from fat	1
Fat (gm)	0.1
Sat. Fat (gm)	trace
Cholesterol (mg)	0.1
Sodium (mg)	39
Protein (gm)	7
Carbohydrate (gm)	10

EXCHANGES:

Milk	0.0	Bread	0.5
Veg.	0.0	Meat	0.5
Fruit	0.0	Fat	0.0

Place gelatin in top of double boiler and sprinkle with cold water to soften. Melt over simmering water.

Place cocoa and 6 tablespoons fructose in top of double boiler and add skim milk. Stir with wire whisk until smooth. Mix in sour cream and heat over simmering water, stirring constantly, until just warm.

Add gelatin, mixing well; then stir in vanilla. Cover and refrigerate until consistency of unbeaten egg whites.

Beat egg whites until they hold soft peaks. Add cream of tartar and beat until they hold stiff peaks. With beaters running, add remaining 2 tablespoons fructose in thin stream. Shut off beaters when fructose has been incorporated.

Fold meringue into cocoa/sour cream mixture. Spoon into 6-cup mold or glass serving bowl. Cover and refrigerate until serving time. When ready to serve, bring bowl to table. Or if you've put mixture into mold, dip mold in warm water, then invert onto serving platter.

Coffee Custard

Serves 4

Egg substitute equal to 3 eggs
6   packets Equal® (see "About This Cookbook")
1   envelope unflavored gelatin
2   tablespoons diet margarine, melted
1½   teaspoons instant coffee
½   teaspoon vanilla extract
1¼   cups skim milk
    Chocolate curls for garnish (optional)

Nutritional Data

PER SERVING:

Calories	87
% calories from fat	32
Fat (gm)	3
Sat. Fat (gm)	0.6
Cholesterol (mg)	1.3
Sodium (mg)	167
Protein (gm)	8.1
Carbohydrate (gm)	6.4

EXCHANGES:

Milk	0.5	Bread	0.0
Veg.	0.0	Meat	1.0
Fruit	0.0	Fat	0.0

In blender, combine egg substitute, Equal®, gelatin, margarine, instant coffee, and vanilla. Process on low speed about 30 seconds; scrape down sides. Heat milk to boiling. Cover blender, start motor, remove cover, and add hot milk; mix 10 seconds. Pour into custard dishes; chill until set, about 3 hours. Garnish with chocolate curls, if desired.

Coffee Custard in Meringue Shells

Serves 4

Coffee Custard (see preceding recipe)

Meringue Shells

3   egg whites
    Pinch salt
3   teaspoons crème de cacao
1½   packets Equal® (see "About This Cookbook")
    Vegetable cooking spray

Nutritional Data

PER SERVING:

Calories	113
% calories from fat	24
Fat (gm)	3
Sat. Fat (gm)	0.6
Cholesterol (mg)	1.3
Sodium (mg)	210
Protein (gm)	10.7
Carbohydrate (gm)	8.5

EXCHANGES:

Milk	0.5	Bread	0.0
Veg.	0.0	Meat	1.5
Fruit	0.0	Fat	0.0

Make Coffee Custard. Chill in bowl until set.

Preheat oven to 250 degrees.

Place egg whites and salt in bowl. Beat together until frothy. Gradually add crème de cacao. Continue beating until whites are stiff, glossy, and stand in stiff peaks.

Coat 4-muffin tin with vegetable cooking spray. Fill cups with meringue, hollowing out top with back of spoon. Bake 1 hour. Remove from oven and dust with Equal®. Fill with Coffee Custard; refrigerate.

Pumpkin Custard

Serves 6

- 5 egg whites
- 2 cups skim milk
- ½ teaspoon vanilla extract
- ½ cup pureed pumpkin
- ¼ teaspoon mace
- ¼ teaspoon nutmeg
- ¼ teaspoon cinnamon
- ¼ teaspoon ground cloves
- 12 packets Equal® (see "About This Cookbook")
- 4 teaspoons cinnamon

Nutritional Data

PER SERVING:

Calories	64
% calories from fat	5
Fat (gm)	0.3
Sat. Fat (gm)	0.2
Cholesterol (mg)	1.3
Sodium (mg)	90
Protein (gm)	6
Carbohydrate (gm)	9.5

EXCHANGES:

Milk	0.5	Bread	0.0
Veg.	0.0	Meat	0.5
Fruit	0.0	Fat	0.0

Preheat oven to 350 degrees.

Blend egg whites and small amount of milk until just combined; do not overmix. Add remaining milk, vanilla, pumpkin, and spices. Blend just enough to combine ingredients.

Fill 6 warmed custard cups with mixture. Place them in pan of hot water and bake 45 minutes or until set. Remove from oven and sprinkle with combined Equal® and cinnamon.

Peach-Leaf Custard

Serves 16 (¼-cup servings)

- 6 peach leaves
- 3 cups skim milk
- 5 egg yolks
- 1 cup sugar
   Cornstarch

In heavy saucepan, bring milk to boil with peach leaves, then set mixture aside to infuse 15 minutes.

In large bowl, beat egg yolks and sugar together until yolks are pale and light. Stir in pinch of cornstarch. Bring milk to boil again. Stirring constantly, pour it into egg yolks a little at a time.

Nutritional Data

PER SERVING:

Calories	80
% calories from fat	18
Fat (gm)	1.7
Sat. Fat (gm)	0.6
Cholesterol (mg)	67.3
Sodium (mg)	26
Protein (gm)	2.4
Carbohydrate (gm)	14.3

EXCHANGES:

Milk	1.0	Bread	0.0
Veg.	0.0	Meat	0.0
Fruit	0.0	Fat	0.0

Pour custard mixture into saucepan, and place it over low heat. Cook custard about 3 minutes, stirring with wooden spoon. As soon as custard thickens, remove it from heat. Discard peach leaves, and let custard cool. Makes 4 cups.

Flan

Serves 6

¼ cup sugar
1 teaspoon water
1 12-oz. can evaporated skim milk
½ cup skim milk
¾ cup egg substitute
¼ cup sugar
⅛ teaspoon salt
½ teaspoon almond extract
2 cups assorted fresh berries (strawberries, blueberries, raspberries)

Nutritional Data

PER SERVING:

Calories	157
% calories from fat	2
Fat (gm)	0.3
Sat. Fat (gm)	0.1
Cholesterol (mg)	2.3
Sodium (mg)	172
Protein (gm)	8.4
Carbohydrate (gm)	30.7

EXCHANGES:

Milk	0.5	Bread	1.0
Veg.	0.0	Meat	0.0
Fruit	0.5	Fat	0.0

Place ¼ cup sugar and 1 teaspoon water into heavy saucepan; set over medium heat. Cook, stirring constantly, until sugar melts and syrup is golden brown. Pour into 6, 6-oz. custard cups; let cool.

Combine milks in medium saucepan, and heat until bubbles form around edge of pan.

Combine egg substitute, ¼ cup sugar, salt, and almond extract; beat well. Gradually stir about 1 cup hot milk into egg mixture; add remaining milk, stirring constantly.

Preheat oven to 325 degrees. Pour mixture evenly into custard cups; cover with aluminum foil. Place custard cups in shallow pan; add hot water to depth of 1 inch. Bake 25 minutes or until knife inserted near center comes out clean. Remove cups from water and chill at least 4 hours.

To serve, loosen edges of custard with spatula; invert onto plates. Arrange assorted berries around flan.

Chocolate Flan with Chocolate Sauce

Serves 6

Sugar Topping

¼ cup sugar
1 teaspoon water

Flan

1 12-oz. can evaporated skim milk
½ cup skim milk
¾ cup real egg substitute
2 tablespoons cocoa
¼ cup fructose (fruit sugar, see "About This Cookbook")
¾ teaspoon vanilla extract
14 teaspoon chocolate extract
Chocolate Sauce (recipe follows)

Nutritional Data

PER SERVING:

Calories	124
% calories from fat	2
Fat (gm)	0.3
Sat. Fat (gm)	0.1
Cholesterol (mg)	3
Sodium (mg)	118
Protein (gm)	8
Carbohydrate (gm)	23

EXCHANGES:

Milk	0.5	Bread	1.0
Veg.	0.0	Meat	0.0
Fruit	0.0	Fat	0.0

Preheat oven to 325 degrees. Use 1-quart metal ring mold.

Sugar Topping: In small, heavy saucepan, cook sugar with 1 teaspoon water over medium heat until syrup becomes golden color. Stir occasionally, being careful not to burn sugar. Working quickly, pour syrup into metal ring mold. Using pot holders, tip mold from side to side so that sugar is evenly distributed on bottom of mold. Set aside to harden.

Flan: In medium saucepan, combine evaporated skim milk and skim milk. Scald and cool. In separate pan, heat and whisk together egg substitute with cocoa, fructose, vanilla, and chocolate extract. Slowly pour milk into cocoa mixture. Transfer flan to ring mold.

Set ring mold into large pan and pour hot water halfway up side of mold. Bake 65 to 75 minutes or until tester or bamboo skewer inserted in center of flan comes out clean. Remove from oven, cool, and refrigerate 3 hours.

Prepare Chocolate Sauce while flan is refrigerating.

Using knife, loosen edges of flan. Invert it onto serving dish. Spoon 2 tablespoons Chocolate Sauce over each flan serving.

Chocolate Sauce

1 12-oz. can evaporated skim milk
3 tablespoons cocoa
⅓ cup fructose (fruit sugar, see "About This Cookbook")
2 tablespoons cornstarch
1 teaspoon vanilla extract
½ teaspoon chocolate extract
2 tablespoons rum, or chocolate liqueur

In small, heavy saucepan, scald milk. Stir in cocoa and fructose. Simmer until fructose dissolves.

Remove ¼ cup of sauce; whisk in cornstarch. Simmer, stirring cornstarch, until sauce thickens slightly, 1 to 2 minutes. Remove from heat; stir in vanilla, chocolate extract, and liqueur. Place in covered container and refrigerate until needed. Serve hot or cold. Makes 1 cup plus 2 tablespoons.

Coffee Flan

Serves 4

- 2 eggs, 1 yolk only
- 1 cup evaporated skim milk
- 1 teaspoon instant coffee (optional)
- ½ teaspoon pure vanilla extract
  Few drops maple flavoring
- 1 tablespoon frozen orange juice concentrate
- 1 tablespoon orange zest, grated
  Cinnamon
- 1 tablespoon sugar-free strawberry or raspberry preserves (optional)

Nutritional Data

PER SERVING:

Calories	83
% calories from fat	15
Fat (gm)	1.4
Sat. Fat (gm)	0.5
Cholesterol (mg)	55.3
Sodium (mg)	104
Protein (gm)	7.4
Carbohydrate (gm)	9.7

EXCHANGES:

Milk	0.5	Bread	0.0
Veg.	0.0	Meat	1.0
Fruit	0.0	Fat	0.0

Beat eggs well and set aside. Pour milk into 1-quart measuring cup, and microwave on High 2 minutes, until it boils. Add coffee if desired and stir to mix. Mix with eggs and remaining ingredients, except preserves.

Turn into 4 custard cups. Microwave on Medium-High (70%) 3 minutes, rotating cups in oven once or twice. Remove and chill in refrigerator. When ready to serve, invert onto dish and top with dollop of berry preserves.

Oeufs à la Neige
(Floating Island)

Serves 6

- 2½ cups skim milk
- ⅓ cup granulated sugar
- ½ teaspoon lemon rind, grated
- 3 egg whites
- ¼ teaspoon salt
- ¼ cup confectioners' sugar
  Egg substitute equal to 4 eggs
- 1 teaspoon cornstarch
- 8 tablespoons granulated sugar

Nutritional Data

PER SERVING:

Calories	190
% calories from fat	1
Fat (gm)	0.2
Sat. Fat (gm)	0.1
Cholesterol (mg)	1.7
Sodium (mg)	224
Protein (gm)	8.7
Carbohydrate (gm)	39

EXCHANGES:

Milk	0.5	Bread	2.0
Veg.	0.0	Meat	0.0
Fruit	0.0	Fat	0.0

Scald milk in large skillet. Add ⅓ cup sugar and lemon rind. Cover. Take skillet off heat.

In bowl, beat egg whites with salt until foamy, then gradually beat in confectioners' sugar, beating until stiff.

Return skillet to heat and bring milk to boil. Lower heat and keep at gentle simmer. With kitchen spoon, lift spoonfuls of beaten egg whites and drop them into milk. Never do more than 4 spoonfuls at a time. Cool 1½ minutes. Turn egg whites and cook other side 2 minutes. Remove with slotted spoon and drain on dry cloth.

Whisk together egg substitute, cornstarch, and 8 tablespoons sugar in small bowl. Whisk hot milk into mixture, then pour back into skillet. Cook over medium heat, stirring constantly, until thickened, about 5 minutes. Remove from heat, and pour mixture into serving bowl. Chill.

When ready to serve, float cooked egg whites on top of sauce.

Maple Coffee Parfait

Serves 4

1 envelope unflavored gelatin
¼ cup sugar-free maple pancake syrup
2 cups very hot black coffee
Nutmeg, or cinnamon

Sprinkle gelatin slowly into syrup to soften. Add very hot coffee and stir until combined thoroughly with syrup and gelatin. Divide into 4 dessert dishes and chill. Just before serving, top with sprinkle of nutmeg or cinnamon.

Nutritional Data

PER SERVING:

Calories	32
% calories from fat	0
Fat (gm)	0
Sat. Fat (gm)	0
Cholesterol (mg)	0
Sodium (mg)	33
Protein (gm)	1.6
Carbohydrate (gm)	6.7

EXCHANGES:

Milk	0.0	Bread	0.0
Veg.	0.0	Meat	0.0
Fruit	0.5	Fat	0.0

Blueberry Sundae Topping

Serves 8 (2-tablespoon servings)	Nutritional Data	
4 cups fresh blueberries	PER SERVING:	
2 tablespoons fresh lemon juice	Calories	52
1 teaspoon vanilla extract	% calories from fat	4
2 teaspoons cornstarch	Fat (gm)	0.3
2 tablespoons water	Sat. Fat (gm)	0
12 packets Equal® (see "About This	Cholesterol (mg)	0
Cookbook"), or 1½ cups sugar	Sodium (mg)	4
	Protein (gm)	0.5
	Carbohydrate (gm)	12.9

EXCHANGES:

Milk	0.0	Bread	0.0
Veg.	0.0	Meat	0.0
Fruit	1.0	Fat	0.0

Puree blueberries in food processor or blender. In 2-quart saucepan, combine blueberry puree, lemon juice, and vanilla extract. Cook over medium heat 5 minutes or until bubbly.

Combine cornstarch and water. Add to fruit mixture, stirring constantly until thickened, about 3 minutes. Remove from heat; stir in Equal® or sugar.

Using back of spoon, press mixture through wire mesh strainer to remove blueberry skins. Serve over vanilla frozen yogurt.

Lemon Ice

Serves 6	Nutritional Data	
½ cup sugar	PER SERVING:	
½ cup boiling water	Calories	65
1 cup cold water	% calories from fat	0
¼ teaspoon lemon peel, finely grated	Fat (gm)	0
½ cup fresh lemon juice	Sat. Fat (gm)	0
12 mint leaves	Cholesterol (mg)	0
	Sodium (mg)	0.3
	Protein (gm)	0.1
	Carbohydrate (gm)	17.8

EXCHANGES:

Milk	0.0	Bread	0.0
Veg.	0.0	Meat	0.0
Fruit	1.0	Fat	0.0

Dissolve sugar in boiling water. Add cold water, lemon peel, and lemon juice. Pour into 9" x 5" x 3" loaf pan. Freeze about 4 hours or until icy.

Stir lemon mixture, then freeze 1 to 3 hours more or until nearly firm, stirring every 30 minutes.

Or freeze overnight without stirring until nearly firm. Then place lemon ice mixture in blender or food processor. Cover and whirl until fluffy, stopping once or twice to scrape sides.

Spoon lemon ice into small stemmed glasses. Garnish with mint leaves.

Mint Sherbet

Serves 4 (1-cup servings)

- 1 envelope (1 tablespoon) unflavored gelatin
- 2 tablespoons cold water
- 1½ cups skim milk
- 10 packets Equal® (see "About This Cookbook")
- 1/· cup fresh lemon juice
- Pinch salt
- ¼ cup crème de menthe
- 1 egg white
- Fresh mint leaves for garnish (optional)

Nutritional Data

PER SERVING:

Calories	109
% calories from fat	1
Fat (gm)	0.2
Sat. Fat (gm)	0.1
Cholesterol (mg)	1.5
Sodium (mg)	64
Protein (gm)	5.6
Carbohydrate (gm)	15.4

EXCHANGES:

Milk	0.5	Bread	0.0
Veg.	0.0	Meat	0.0
Fruit	1.0	Fat	0.0

Sprinkle gelatin over cold water and wait for it to soften. Heat milk in saucepan until it is steaming but not boiling. Remove from heat, add gelatin, and Equal®, and stir to dissolve. Add lemon juice, salt, and crème de menthe. Do not worry if mixture curdles.

Pour into ice cube tray and freeze 1 hour. Do not let mixture freeze solid. Beat egg white until stiff peaks form. Transfer frozen mixture into mixing bowl, and beat until fluffy but not melted. Fold in egg white, pour into covered container, and freeze.

Chocolate Blintzes

Serves 12 (1 blintz each)

- ¼ cup real egg substitute
- 2 egg whites
- 1 cup, scant, all-purpose flour
- 3 tablespoons unsweetened Dutch cocoa
- ½ cup water
- ½ cup skim milk
- 2 tablespoons diet margarine, melted and cooled
- 2 tablespoons sugar
- Butter-flavored vegetable cooking spray, or 2 teaspoons diet margarine
- 3 tablespoons diet margarine
- Filling (recipe follows)

Nutritional Data

PER SERVING:

Calories	144
% calories from fat	28
Fat (gm)	5
Sat. Fat (gm)	0.5
Cholesterol (mg)	5
Sodium (mg)	138
Protein (gm)	6
Carbohydrate (gm)	21

EXCHANGES:

Milk	0.0	Bread	1.0
Veg.	0.0	Meat	0.5
Fruit	0.0	Fat	1.0

In large, deep bowl or food processor, blend together egg substitute, egg whites, flour, cocoa, water, milk, cooled margarine, and sugar. Let batter stand 20 minutes.

Coat 5- or 6 inch nonstick skillet or crepe pan with cooking spray. With ladle, pour about 3 tablespoons batter onto hot pan. Swish batter evenly in pan, covering bottom. Pour off excess batter after pan bottom is covered.

Cook blintz over medium heat until bottom is cooked. Turn blintz over and continue cooking until done. Invert blintz on clean kitchen towel. Continue until all blintzes are done. While blintzes are cooling, prepare Filling.

Filling

1	lb. light farmer cheese, or skim cottage cheese
1/2	cup nonfat vanilla yogurt
1/4	cup sugar
3	tablespoons fructose (fruit sugar, see "About This Cookbook")
1/4	teaspoon salt

In deep bowl, combine cheese, yogurt, sugar, fructose, and salt.

To Assemble: Spoon about 1½ tablespoons Filling down center of blintz. Fold over both sides and bring up both ends (envelope style). Place blintz seam side down on lightly floured plate until serving time.

To Serve: When ready to serve, melt margarine in nonstick skillet. Cook blintzes until lightly browned on both sides. Serve immediately. You might want to serve with small amount of chocolate sauce or sprinkle of confectioners' sugar.

Chapter Eighteen

BEVERAGES

Cocoa Vanilla Mix

Serves 45 (1 mug each)

Cocoa Mix

1½   cups unsweetened Dutch cocoa
6   tablespoons aspartame sweetener
1   vanilla bean

Hot Cocoa

¾   cup skim milk
2   level teaspoons Cocoa Mix
½   marshmallow

Nutritional Data	
PER SERVING:	
Calories	88
% calories from fat	6
Fat (gm)	0.6
Sat. Fat (gm)	0.3
Cholesterol (mg)	3
Sodium (mg)	98
Protein (gm)	8
Carbohydrate (gm)	13

EXCHANGES:			
Milk	1.0	Bread	0.0
Veg.	0.0	Meat	0.0
Fruit	0.0	Fat	0.0

To Make Mix: Combine cocoa and aspartame in small jar. Cut vanilla bean in thirds and bury in mix. Cover tightly and store on cupboard shelf to use as needed.

To Make 1 Mug Hot Cocoa: Heat ¾ cup skim milk in saucepan. Place 2 level teaspoons Cocoa Mix in bowl. Add 2 tablespoons hot milk to Cocoa Mix and stir with whisk to combine. Stir in remaining milk, mixing well.

Pour into mug. Top with ½ marshmallow. Serve immediately.

Mock Orange Julius

Serves 2

½   6-oz. can frozen orange juice concentrate, undiluted
½   cup each ingredient: skim milk, water
1   tablespoon sugar
½   teaspoon vanilla extract
6-8   medium ice cubes

Nutritional Data	
PER SERVING:	
Calories	117
% calories from fat	2
Fat (gm)	0.2
Sat. Fat (gm)	0.1
Cholesterol (mg)	1
Sodium (mg)	33
Protein (gm)	3.1
Carbohydrate (gm)	25.8

EXCHANGES:			
Milk	0.0	Bread	0.0
Veg.	0.0	Meat	0.0
Fruit	2.0	Fat	0.0

Combine orange juice concentrate, milk, water, sugar, and vanilla in blender. Whirl at high speed. Add ice cubes and blend until cubes are dissolved. Makes about 1¼ cups.

Mock Sour

Serves 4

2 cups orange juice
¼ cup fresh lemon juice
6 packets Equal® (see "About This Cookbook")
¼ cup water
8 ice cubes
1 cap full rum extract

Combine all ingredients except rum extract in blender. Whirl 1 minute. Add rum extract and whirl again. Pour into 4 glasses and serve.

Nutritional Data

PER SERVING:

Calories	69
% calories from fat	3
Fat (gm)	0.3
Sat. Fat (gm)	0
Cholesterol (mg)	0
Sodium (mg)	1
Protein (gm)	0.9
Carbohydrate (gm)	16.1

EXCHANGES:

Milk	0.0	Bread	0.0
Veg.	0.0	Meat	0.0
Fruit	1.0	Fat	0.0

Breakfast Shake

Serves 1

½ large (8 to 10-inch) banana, frozen
½ cup orange juice
½ cup skim milk
2 tablespoons wheat germ
½ teaspoon vanilla extract
1 teaspoon vegetable oil
2 ice cubes

Peel banana, cut in half, and wrap halves separately in aluminum foil or other airtight wrapper to freeze overnight. Next day, combine all ingredients in blender or food processor. Cover and whirl until smooth. Serve immediately.

Nutritional Data

PER SERVING:

Calories	250
% calories from fat	23
Fat (gm)	6.7
Sat. Fat (gm)	1.1
Cholesterol (mg)	2
Sodium (mg)	66
Protein (gm)	9
Carbohydrate (gm)	40.4

EXCHANGES:

Milk	0.5	Bread	1.0
Veg.	0.0	Meat	0.0
Fruit	2.0	Fat	1.0

Banana Shake

Serves 2

1 banana, sliced
2 packets Equal® (see "About This Cookbook")
2 cups skim milk
Dash cinnamon

Put banana, Equal®, and milk in blender and whirl on high setting until banana is liquefied. Pour mixture into tall glasses and top with dash of cinnamon.

Nutritional Data

PER SERVING:

Calories	143
% calories from fat	4
Fat (gm)	0.7
Sat. Fat (gm)	0.4
Cholesterol (mg)	4
Sodium (mg)	127
Protein (gm)	8.9
Carbohydrate (gm)	26.3

EXCHANGES:

Milk	1.0	Bread	0.0
Veg.	0.0	Meat	0.0
Fruit	1.0	Fat	0.0

Grasshopper Shake

Serves 2

1 cup Mint Sherbet (see p. 633)
1 cup skim milk
   Mint leaves (optional)

Mix sherbet and milk together in blender until shake is smooth and thick. Serve immediately. Garnish with fresh mint leaf.

Nutritional Data

PER SERVING:

Calories	97
% calories from fat	3
Fat (gm)	0.3
Sat. Fat (gm)	0.2
Cholesterol (mg)	2.8
Sodium (mg)	95
Protein (gm)	7
Carbohydrate (gm)	13.7

EXCHANGES:

Milk	1.0	Bread	0.0
Veg.	0.0	Meat	0.0
Fruit	0.5	Fat	0.0

Cantaloupe Smoothee

Serves 2

½ ripe cantaloupe
¾ cup skim milk
1 cup plain low-fat yogurt
¾ cup crushed ice
1 packet Equal® (see "About This Cookbook")

Peel cantaloupe and remove seeds. Cut into 1-inch cubes, and put in blender. Add milk, yogurt, crushed ice, and Equal®, and process at highest speed until thick and smooth.

Other fruit such as strawberries, raspberries, or bananas can be used.

Nutritional Data

PER SERVING:

Calories	162
% calories from fat	13
Fat (gm)	2.4
Sat. Fat (gm)	1.2
Cholesterol (mg)	8.5
Sodium (mg)	141
Protein (gm)	10.5
Carbohydrate (gm)	26.4

EXCHANGES:

Milk	1.0	Bread	0.0
Veg.	0.0	Meat	0.0
Fruit	1.0	Fat	0.5

Creamy Mocha Cooler

Serves 1

3 tablespoons Kahlua-flavored fat-free nondairy creamer
⅓ cup cold water
2½ teaspoons unsweetened Dutch cocoa
1 tablespoon sugar
5 ice cubes

Place all ingredients in blender. Whirl at high speed until ice is dissolved.

Nutritional Data

PER SERVING:

Calories	129
% calories from fat	3
Fat (gm)	0.4
Sat. Fat (gm)	0.1
Cholesterol (mg)	0
Sodium (mg)	3
Protein (gm)	0.9
Carbohydrate (gm)	33.1

EXCHANGES:

Milk	0.0	Bread	0.0
Veg.	0.0	Meat	0.0
Fruit	2.0	Fat	0.0

Iced Mocha

Serves 2

4 teaspoons unsweetened Dutch cocoa
2 large pinches cinnamon
1¼ cups double-strength coffee, divided
4 tablespoons fructose (fruit sugar, see "About This Cookbook")
3 tablespoons Kahlua-flavored fat-free nondairy creamer
2 large glasses filled with ice cubes

Place cocoa in small bowl and add cinnamon and 4 teaspoons coffee. Stir with wire whisk until smooth. Add remaining coffee, fructose, and Kahlua-flavored creamer. Stir again. Divide between 2 ice-filled glasses.

Nutritional Data

PER SERVING:

Calories	73
% calories from fat	4
Fat (gm)	0.3
Sat. Fat (gm)	0.5
Cholesterol (mg)	0
Sodium (mg)	8
Protein (gm)	0.9
Carbohydrate (gm)	18

EXCHANGES:

Milk	0.0	Bread	1.0
Veg.	0.0	Meat	0.0
Fruit	0.0	Fat	0.0

Strawberry Kiss

Serves 1

5 strawberries
½ cup crushed ice
1 cup sparkling mineral water, or club soda
1 packet Equal® (see "About This Cookbook")
1 whole strawberry for garnish

Hull and cut up strawberries and place in blender. Add ice, mineral water, and Equal®. Cover and process on high speed until mixture is smooth. Pour into large glass. Garnish with whole strawberry.

Nutritional Data

PER SERVING:

Calories	29
% calories from fat	5
Fat (gm)	0.2
Sat. Fat (gm)	0
Cholesterol (mg)	0
Sodium (mg)	4
Protein (gm)	0.8
Carbohydrate (gm)	6.9

EXCHANGES:

Milk	0.0	Bread	0.0
Veg.	0.0	Meat	0.0
Fruit	0.5	Fat	0.0

Peach Frostee

Serves 2

1 16-oz. can peach slices, undrained
½ cup dry milk powder
1 teaspoon vanilla extract
Dash cinnamon
5 ice cubes

In blender, combine canned sliced peaches, dry milk powder, vanilla, and

Nutritional Data

PER SERVING:

Calories	168
% calories from fat	1
Fat (gm)	0.2
Sat. Fat (gm)	0.1
Cholesterol (mg)	3
Sodium (mg)	103
Protein (gm)	7.4
Carbohydrate (gm)	35.8

cinnamon. Cover and process until smooth. Add 5 ice cubes, one at a time with motor running. Mix until smooth.

EXCHANGES:			
Milk	1.0	Bread	0.0
Veg.	0.0	Meat	0.0
Fruit	1.5	Fat	0.0

Pineapple Punch

Serves 24

1½ cups cold water
1 6-inch cinnamon stick
12 whole cloves
6 packets Equal® (see "About This Cookbook")
1 46-oz. can unsweetened pineapple juice
1½ cups orange juice
½ cup fresh lemon juice
2 16-oz. bottles low-calorie, lemon-lime carbonated beverage, chilled

Nutritional Data

PER SERVING:

Calories	37
% calories from fat	1
Fat (gm)	0
Sat. Fat (gm)	0
Cholesterol (mg)	0
Sodium (mg)	7
Protein (gm)	0.3
Carbohydrate (gm)	9.2

EXCHANGES:

Milk	0.0	Bread	0.0
Veg.	0.0	Meat	0.0
Fruit	0.5	Fat	0.0

In saucepan, combine water, cinnamon, and cloves. Cover and simmer 15 minutes. Remove from heat and strain into large pitcher. Cool. Add Equal® and fruit juices; chill. Just before serving, pour into large punch bowl; slowly pour in lemon-lime carbonated beverage. Serve over ice cubes.

Virgin Mary

Serves 1

6 ozs. salt-free V-8 Juice, or tomato juice
1 tablespoon horseradish
Juice of 1 lemon, or lime
Dash Worcestershire sauce
Dash pepper
1 stalk celery

Place all ingredients except celery into blender and process 1 minute. Pour into chilled glass with ice cubes and garnish with celery.

Nutritional Data

PER SERVING:

Calories	54
% calories from fat	0
Fat (gm)	0
Sat. Fat (gm)	0
Cholesterol (mg)	0
Sodium (mg)	210
Protein (gm)	1.4
Carbohydrate (gm)	13.8

EXCHANGES:

Milk	0.0	Bread	0.0
Veg.	2.0	Meat	0.0
Fruit	0.0	Fat	0.0

Gazpacho Drink

Serves 4

¼ cup green onions and onion tops, cut into pieces
1 medium cucumber, peeled and diced (1 cup)
1 medium bell pepper, cut up (1 cup)
1 clove garlic, minced
2 tablespoons tarragon vinegar
4 dashes hot pepper sauce
½ teaspoon Spike (see "About This Cookbook")
Dash red food coloring
4 celery sticks for garnish

Nutritional Data

PER SERVING:

Calories	22
% calories from fat	5
Fat (gm)	0.2
Sat. Fat (gm)	0
Cholesterol (mg)	0
Sodium (mg)	2
Protein (gm)	0.8
Carbohydrate (gm)	5.3

EXCHANGES:

Milk	0.0	Bread	0.0
Veg.	1.0	Meat	0.0
Fruit	0.0	Fat	0.0

Place all ingredients except celery sticks in blender and process thoroughly. If blender jar is not large enough, mix in small batches, and transfer drink to 1-quart pitcher.

Refrigerate, covered, to chill several hours. Pour into 4, 8-oz. or larger glasses. Use celery sticks for garnish.

Champagne Cocktail

Serves 15

1 orange, peel only
2 lumps sugar
Angostura bitters
¼ cup cognac
3 bottles dry champagne

Wash and peel orange, carefully removing only skin, not pith. Put orange peel into cocktail shaker with sugar (moistened with 3 dashes Angostura bitters), cognac, and champagne. Shake well.

Nutritional Data

PER SERVING:

Calories	114
% calories from fat	0
Fat (gm)	0
Sat. Fat (gm)	0
Cholesterol (mg)	0
Sodium (mg)	0
Protein (gm)	0.3
Carbohydrate (gm)	4.6

EXCHANGES:

Milk	0.0	Bread	0.0
Veg.	0.0	Meat	0.0
Fruit	2.0	Fat	0.0

 # Sangria

Serves 8

1 bottle (750 ml) dry red or rose wine
2 cups carbonated water
2 oranges
2 lemons or limes
½ cup sugar

Chill, separately, wine and carbonated water. Cut 1 orange and 1 lemon

Nutritional Data

PER SERVING:

Calories	141
% calories from fat	0
Fat (gm)	0
Sat. Fat (gm)	0
Cholesterol (mg)	0
Sodium (mg)	63
Protein (gm)	0.4
Carbohydrate (gm)	20.8

into slices. Squeeze juice from remaining fruits into pitcher; stir in sugar. Stir in wine; add carbonated water and fruit slices. Serve in pitcher with wooden paddle for stirring.

To Freeze: Place in quart container, without fruit; label and freeze up to 3 months.

To Serve: Thaw and place in pitcher with fruit and ice.

EXCHANGES:			
Milk	0.0	Bread	0.0
Veg.	0.0	Meat	0.0
Fruit	2.5	Fat	0.0

🍶 Hot Mulled Cider

Serves 16

½   cup brown sugar
2   quarts cider
1   teaspoon whole allspice
1½   teaspoons whole cloves
2   cinnamon sticks
    Orange slices

Put all ingredients in crockpot. If desired, tie whole spices in cheesecloth or put in tea strainer. Cover and cook on Low 2 to 8 hours. Serve from crockpot with ladle. Makes about 8 cups.

Note: If spices are added loose, strain before serving.

To Freeze: Place in quart containers; label and freeze up to 3 months.

To Serve: Thaw and heat on top of stove until steaming.

Nutritional Data

PER SERVING:

Calories	74
% calories from fat	1
Fat (gm)	0.1
Sat. Fat (gm)	0
Cholesterol (mg)	0
Sodium (mg)	3
Protein (gm)	0.1
Carbohydrate (gm)	8.1

EXCHANGES:			
Milk	0.0	Bread	0.0
Veg.	0.0	Meat	0.0
Fruit	1.5	Fat	0.0

🍶 Hot Spiced Wine

Serves 16

½   cup brown sugar
2   bottles (750 ml) wine (sweet sherry, claret, or port)
1   teaspoon whole allspice
1½   teaspoons whole cloves
2   cinnamon sticks
    Orange slices

Put all ingredients in crockpot. Cover and cook on Low 2 to 8 hours. Serve from crockpot with ladle. Makes about 8 cups.

To Freeze: Place in quart containers; label and freeze up to 3 months.

To Serve: Thaw and reheat on top of stove until steaming.

Nutritional Data

PER SERVING:

Calories	151
% calories from fat	0
Fat (gm)	0.1
Sat. Fat (gm)	0
Cholesterol (mg)	0
Sodium (mg)	6
Protein (gm)	0.3
Carbohydrate (gm)	14

EXCHANGES:			
Milk	0.0	Bread	0.0
Veg.	0.0	Meat	0.0
Fruit	2.5	Fat	0.0

Wassail
(With or Without Rum)

Serves 12

- 2 quarts apple juice or cider
- 1 pint low-calorie cranberry juice
- ¾ cup sugar
- 1 teaspoon aromatic bitters
- 2 sticks cinnamon
- 1 teaspoon whole allspice
- 1 small orange, studded with whole cloves
- 1 cup rum (optional)

Put all ingredients in crockpot. Cover and cook on High 1 hour, then on Low 4 to 8 hours. Serve warm from crockpot. Nutritional Data does not include rum. Makes about 12 cups.

To Freeze: Place in quart containers; label and freeze up to 3 months.

To Serve: Thaw and reheat on top of stove until steaming.

Nutritional Data

PER SERVING:

Calories	135
% calories from fat	1
Fat (gm)	0.2
Sat. Fat (gm)	0
Cholesterol (mg)	0
Sodium (mg)	7
Protein (gm)	0.1
Carbohydrate (gm)	34

EXCHANGES:

Milk	0.0	Bread	0.8
Veg.	0.0	Meat	0.0
Fruit	2.0	Fat	0.0

Adam's Tea

Serves 8

- 7 cups water
- 10 dried apple slices
- 1 teaspoon ground cardamom
- 1 teaspoon ground cinnamon
- 4 cinnamon-apple herb tea bags
- 3 Irish breakfast or other black tea bags
- 2 tablespoons sugar

Combine first 4 ingredients in large saucepan; bring to boil. Reduce heat and simmer 15 minutes. Remove from heat. Add tea bags, cover, and let stand 10 minutes. Discard tea bags. Add sugar and let stand to cool. Serve over ice cubes, and top each glass with an apple slice.

Nutritional Data

PER SERVING:

Calories	42
% calories from fat	1
Fat (gm)	0.1
Sat. Fat (gm)	0
Cholesterol (mg)	0
Sodium (mg)	12
Protein (gm)	0.1
Carbohydrate (gm)	11

EXCHANGES:

Milk	0.0	Bread	0.0
Veg.	0.0	Meat	0.0
Fruit	0.5	Fat	0.0

Russian Tea

Serves 24

2 tablespoons whole cloves
8 cups water
10 tea bags
½ cup sugar
2 cups orange juice
2 cups peach juice
Juice of 1 lemon

Boil cloves in water 3 minutes. Add tea bags; let steep 5 minutes. Strain. Add sugar and juices; reheat. Serve hot.

Nutritional Data

PER SERVING:

Calories	37
% calories from fat	4
Fat (gm)	0.2
Sat. Fat (gm)	0
Cholesterol (mg)	0
Sodium (mg)	4
Protein (gm)	0.2
Carbohydrate (gm)	9

EXCHANGES:

Milk	0.0	Bread	0.0
Veg.	0.0	Meat	0.0
Fruit	0.5	Fat	0.0

Greek Mint Tea

Serves 6

6 teaspoons dried mint
6 cups water

Boil dried mint in water. Strain and serve.

Nutritional Data

PER SERVING:

Calories	2
% calories from fat	0
Fat (gm)	0
Sat. Fat (gm)	0
Cholesterol (mg)	0
Sodium (mg)	8
Protein (gm)	0.2
Carbohydrate (gm)	0.2

EXCHANGES:

Milk	0.0	Bread	0.0
Veg.	0.0	Meat	0.0
Fruit	0.0	Fat	0.0

Moroccan Mint Tea

Serves 3

3½ cups boiling water
1½ tablespoons green tea
1 handful fresh mint leaves and stalks
Sugar, or artificial sweetener, to taste (optional)

Rinse out 3-cup teapot with hot water. Add tea. Pour in ½ cup boiling water, swish around in pot quickly, and empty water (leaving tea in pot). This is supposed to remove any bitterness from tea.

Nutritional Data

PER SERVING:

Calories	2
% calories from fat	0
Fat (gm)	0
Sat. Fat (gm)	0
Cholesterol (mg)	0
Sodium (mg)	1
Protein (gm)	0.1
Carbohydrate (gm)	0.3

EXCHANGES:

Milk	0.0	Bread	0.0
Veg.	0.0	Meat	0.0
Fruit	0.0	Fat	0.0

Stuff mint leaves and stalks down into pot and add sugar. Fill pot with boiling water. Let steep 5 to 8 minutes, checking occasionally to be sure mint doesn't rise above water. Stir and taste, adding sugar if necessary. Serve traditionally in small glasses set in silver holders

Fascomiol
(Sage Tea)

Serves 6

6 cups water
12 teaspoons ground sage

Bring water to boil and add sage. Cover and let stand 6 to 7 minutes before serving.

Nutritional Data

PER SERVING:

Calories	4
% calories from fat	29
Fat (gm)	0.2
Sat. Fat (gm)	0.1
Cholesterol (mg)	0
Sodium (mg)	7
Protein (gm)	0.1
Carbohydrate (gm)	0.9

EXCHANGES:

Milk	0.0	Bread	0.0
Veg.	0.0	Meat	0.0
Fruit	0.0	Fat	0.0

❄ Cran-Orange Tea

Serves 12

6 cups water
2 tea bags (any plain tea will do)
2 cups cranberry juice cocktail
2 cups orange juice
¼ cup sugar
2 tablespoons fresh lemon juice
4 whole cloves
1 3-inch cinnamon stick
Crushed ice

Nutritional Data

PER SERVING:

Calories	60
% calories from fat	2
Fat (gm)	0.1
Sat. Fat (gm)	0
Cholesterol (mg)	0
Sodium (mg)	3
Protein (gm)	0.3
Carbohydrate (gm)	15

EXCHANGES:

Milk	0.0	Bread	0.0
Veg.	0.0	Meat	0.0
Fruit	1.0	Fat	0.0

Bring water to boil; pour over tea bags. Cover and let stand 10 minutes. Discard tea bags. Combine tea and all other ingredients except ice in stockpot; simmer 10 minutes. (Do not boil.) Let stand to cool; cover and chill. Serve over crushed ice. Makes 2½ quarts.

To Freeze: Place in quart containers; label and freeze up to 3 months.

To Serve: Thaw and serve with ice.

Café au Lait

Serves 1

½ cup coffee, strong, freshly brewed
½ cup skim milk

Pour equal amounts of hot, freshly brewed strong coffee and warm regular or evaporated skim milk into cup simultaneously.

Nutritional Data

PER SERVING:

Calories	45
% calories from fat	5
Fat (gm)	0.2
Sat. Fat (gm)	0.1
Cholesterol (mg)	2
Sodium (mg)	65
Protein (gm)	4.3
Carbohydrate (gm)	6.4

EXCHANGES:

Milk	0.5	Bread	0.0
Veg.	0.0	Meat	0.0
Fruit	0.0	Fat	0.0

Espresso, Cappuccino, and Americano

Espresso originated in the early 1900s because an impatient gentleman in Naples hated waiting for his coffee to brew and asked an engineer to speed up the process by forcing water through the coffee grounds with pressure. According to espresso experts, body, aroma, and froth are the essences of good espresso. A good cup should have: strong flavor, rich aroma, a pleasing after taste, and thick, long-lasting, creamy froth. The way the beans are roasted and ground, the espresso machine, and the coffee maker's skill are all important factors.

To brew espresso, purchase a finely ground, dark-roast coffee at the supermarket or at a coffee shop. Use an espresso maker, which brews quickly, under pressure, to produce coffee with a foamy head. (If you don't have an espresso maker, you can compromise and brew espresso in a drip coffee maker; or even use instant espresso coffee crystals.) Espresso is usually served in tiny cups with sugar and a twist of lemon peel.

Cappuccino is another popular Italian coffee. It is a blend of one-third espresso and two-thirds steamed milk.

Americano, on the other hand, is simply a traditionally sized espresso expanded in volume to a full cup by the addition of hot water.

Iced Espresso

Serves 5

4 tablespoons cocoa
2 cups espresso coffee, either instant or brewed
3 cups skim milk
  Sugar substitute equal to 4 tablespoons sugar
15-20 ice cubes

Nutritional Data

PER SERVING:

Calories	47
% calories from fat	8
Fat (gm)	0.5
Sat. Fat (gm)	0.2
Cholesterol (mg)	1.7
Sodium (mg)	57
Protein (gm)	4.2
Carbohydrate (gm)	7.7

EXCHANGES:

Milk	0.5	Bread	0.0
Veg.	0.0	Meat	0.0
Fruit	0.0	Fat	0.0

Place cocoa and espresso in 2-quart saucepan and cook until hot, beating to a froth with wire whisk or hand egg-beater. Add skim milk and beat until mixture is frothy. Remove from heat. Add sugar substitute. Refrigerate, covered, to room temperature. Place 3 ice cubes in each of 5, 10-ounce glasses. Pour mixture over ice cubes.

INDEX

D

E

F

G

H

I

J

K

L

M

R

S

W

Z

Y